The Allied Air War and Urban Memory

The cultural legacy of the air war on Germany is explored in this comparative study of two bombed cities from different sides of the subsequently divided nation. Contrary to what is often assumed, allied bombing left a lasting imprint on German society, spawning vibrant memory cultures that can be traced from the 1940s to the present. While the deaths of half a million civilians and the destruction of much of Germany's urban landscape provided 'usable' rallying points in the great political confrontations of the day, the cataclysms were above all remembered on a local level, in the very spaces that had been hit by the bombs and transformed beyond recognition. The author investigates how lived experience in the shadow of Nazism and war was translated into cultural memory by local communities in Kassel and Magdeburg struggling to find ways of coming to terms with catastrophic events unprecedented in living memory.

JÖRG ARNOLD teaches Modern European History at the University of Freiburg. His publications include *Luftkrieg: Erinnerungen in Deutschland und Europa* ('The Air War: Memories in Germany and Europe') (co-edited with Dietmar Süß and Malte Thießen, 2009).

Studies in the Social and Cultural History of Modern Warfare

General Editors

Jay Winter, *Yale University*

Advisory Editors

Omer Bartov, *Brown University*
Carol Gluck, *Columbia University*
David M. Kennedy, *Stanford University*
Paul Kennedy, *Yale University*
Antoine Prost, *Université de Paris-Sorbonne*
Emmanuel Sivan, *Hebrew University of Jerusalem*
Robert Wohl, *University of California, Los Angeles*

In recent years the field of modern history has been enriched by the exploration of two parallel histories. These are the social and cultural history of armed conflict, and the impact of military events on social and cultural history.

Studies in the Social and Cultural History of Modern Warfare presents the fruits of this growing area of research, reflecting both the colonization of military history by cultural historians and the reciprocal interest of military historians in social and cultural history, to the benefit of both. The series offers the latest scholarship in European and non-European events from the 1850s to the present day.

A full list of titles in the series can be found at:
www.cambridge.org/modernwarfare

The Allied Air War and Urban Memory

The Legacy of Strategic Bombing in Germany

Jörg Arnold

CAMBRIDGE
UNIVERSITY PRESS

CAMBRIDGE UNIVERSITY PRESS
Cambridge, New York, Melbourne, Madrid, Cape Town,
Singapore, São Paulo, Delhi, Tokyo, Mexico City

Cambridge University Press
The Edinburgh Building, Cambridge CB2 8RU, UK

Published in the United States of America by Cambridge University Press,
New York

www.cambridge.org
Information on this title: www.cambridge.org/9781107004962

First published 2011

Printed in the United Kingdom at the University Press, Cambridge

A catalogue record for this publication is available from the British Library

Library of Congress Cataloguing in Publication data
Arnold, Jörg, 1973–
The Allied air war and urban memory : the legacy of strategic bombing in
Germany / Jörg Arnold.
    p.   cm. – (Studies in the social and cultural history of modern warfare ; 35)
Includes bibliographical references and index.
ISBN 978-1-107-00496-2
1. Kassel (Germany) – History – Bombardment, 1943.   2. Magdeburg
(Germany) – History – Bombardment, 1945   3. World War, 1939–1945 –
Campaigns – Germany – Kassel.   4. World War, 1939–1945 – Campaigns –
Germany – Magdeburg.   5. Bombing, Aerial – Germany – Kassel – History.
6. Bombing, Aerial – Germany – Magdeburg – History.   7. Collective
memory – Germany – Kassel.   8. Collective memory – Germany –
Magdeburg.   I. Title.   II. Series.
D757.9.K37A76   2011
940.54′213 – dc22   2011012625

ISBN 978-1-107-00496-2 Hardback

In memory
of
Elisabeth Arnold

Contents

Illustrations

N.B. Every effort has been made to contact the copyright-holders of all illustrations and maps reproduced in this book. In the event of any error copyright-holders are requested to contact the publisher so that due accreditation can be sought for any future edition.

Maps

Preface

On 1 June 2010, at 9:30 p.m., a huge blast ripped through the quiet university town of Göttingen. The explosion was caused by an aerial bomb that had lain buried in the ground for sixty-five years. It was discovered the week before during earthworks on a piece of little-used ground. Finds such as this were not unusual in early twenty-first-century Germany. Duds from World War II were still unearthed regularly whenever long-neglected plots of land were subjected to redevelopment measures in any larger town. Discovery was usually accompanied by minor scares among the local public, some reporting in the local press and quick removal by technical experts. But this time, the defusing exercise went horribly wrong, triggering an explosion that could be heard for miles around. Three people were killed and two more seriously injured in the incident.

I learnt of what had happened in Göttingen as I revised my manuscript on the allied air war and urban memory for publication. The tragedy served as a terrible reminder that bombs, whatever else they might do, in the first instance kill and destroy. To think about the long-term impact of strategic bombing is to think about the long-term impact of deadly violence. While it can be argued, of course, that in the case of Nazi Germany this violence was well deserved, necessary and, ultimately, beneficial even to the Germans themselves, this does not alter the fact that for German city-dwellers to address the legacy of the allied air war after 1945 was to address legacies of death, destruction and survival amidst catastrophe. As the incident in Göttingen illustrates, the rationalisations for which city-dwellers reached, the idioms that they used and the rituals that they performed were played out in spaces that were themselves saturated with a past that could surface at any time – not just as discourse and text, but as tangible relics and objects that could be as dangerous as ever.

I became interested in the subject of the air war and urban memory through a combination of personal and academic factors. I remember well from my adolescence the stories that I was told about the bombing of

Kassel. These were stories that did not fit in with self-confident narratives of survival, new beginnings and successful arrival. Indeed, these were stories that did not fit in with anything. They spoke of death, loss and bitterness, and often ended in either uncomfortable silences or bitter arguments, or both. Later, as a history student at Edinburgh, Southampton and Heidelberg, I was increasingly drawn towards the study of Nazism, the war and its aftermath, partly, I suppose, out of a naïve belief that the scholarly scrutiny of the past held definitive answers. So when, after graduation, I was offered the opportunity to read for a doctorate at the University of Southampton, it seemed only natural to explore in greater depth a question that had troubled me for as long as I had been conscious of my own country's horrific past: how did Germans deal with the suffering that had been meted out to them in the context of a war that they themselves had unleashed, prosecuted in a singularly ruthless manner and used as cover for the perpetration of genocide? The present book is the much revised outcome of this enquiry.

During the many years that it took me to complete this study, I incurred numerous debts to a great number of academic institutions and individuals. It is a pleasure to acknowledge their support and to express my sincere gratitude to them.

First of all, I would like to thank my supervisor, Neil Gregor (Southampton), who took an exceptional interest in this project throughout the long period of gestation and beyond. I have benefited enormously from his insightful comments, generous advice and warm support, both with the project and, more generally, with the dream of turning a passion for history into a living. Richard Overy (Exeter) and Joachim Schloer (Southampton) were kind enough to act as examiners for the original thesis and to turn the viva into a memorable experience not altogether unpleasant. For both I am very grateful.

This study could not have been written without the funding that I received from several institutions. Awards from the Arts and Humanities Research Council (AHRC) and the University of Southampton provided for my maintenance during my years as a PhD student. In the early stages of this project, I was also granted a one-month doctoral fellowship by the German Historical Institute in Washington, DC, in order to undertake archival research in the National Archives at College Park, Maryland. Financial security, but also intellectual stimulus, was provided by the institutions for which I have had the privilege to work since I received my doctorate in 2007. The Department of History, Classics and Archaeology at the University of Edinburgh is a wonderful institution in a breathtaking city. I enjoyed greatly my year as a teaching associate in 2007/8, and valued very much the help and suggestions that I received from my colleagues. Equally supportive, and living in an environment no less beautiful, have been the staff members of the Historisches Seminar at the University of Freiburg. I owe special thanks to Ulrich Herbert for his continuing support and, not least of all, his patience with a project the conclusion of which dragged on for much longer than anticipated when I joined the department in 2008. During the latter stages of the revision in particular, the assistance of Jörg Michael Klenk and Sebastian Schöttler has been invaluable.

I would also like to thank the members of staff at the numerous libraries and archives that I consulted during the course of my research. Throughout, I was received kindly and my numerous requests were dealt with swiftly and efficiently. In particular, I should like to mention Roland Klaube (now retired) and his team at the Stadtarchiv Kassel, as well as Maren Ballerstedt and the members of staff at the Stadtarchiv Magdeburg, for their help. In addition, I am grateful to the many individuals in Kassel, Magdeburg and elsewhere who shared their thoughts with me and allowed me to make use of their private collections. Particularly valuable support has been provided by Werner Dettmar, Karin Grünwald, Rudi Hartwig, Maik Hattenhorst, Domprediger Giselher Quast and Manfred Wille. Thanks are also due to the institutions and individuals who have kindly granted permission to reproduce images from their various collections. I should especially like to mention Gerhard Potratz, Petra Hartmetz-Groß, Renate Klein at the picture archive of Verlag Dierichs, Friedhelm Fenner at the Amt für Vermessung & Geoinformation Kassel and Jan Böttger at the Bildarchiv Preußischer Kulturbesitz.

Conference audiences at Southampton, Washington, DC, Magdeburg, Jena, Bochum and Freiburg have given me the opportunity to present aspects of my work. I am grateful for their comments both encouraging and critical. Jan Eike Dunkhase, Dietmar Süß and Malte Thießen have read through the entire manuscript. I appreciate greatly their helpful comments. The same holds true of the two anonymous readers at Cambridge University Press, whose detailed reports made me aware of the differences between a thesis and a monograph. I am grateful to the Syndics of the Press and the general editor of the series, Jay Winter, for accepting my manuscript for publication. I owe a special debt of gratitude to senior commissioning editor Michael Watson, assistant editor Chloe Howell, copy editor Carol Fellingham Webb and production editor Sarah Roberts for all their patience and hard work.

On a different level, I would like to thank those people who have provided invaluable support over the years, in times both good and difficult: Kerstin Bellemann, Philip Bracher, Torsten Meyer, Jürgen Schmidt and

Christian Schneider; my brother, Michael Arnold, and my sister, Sandra Bergmann. I will always be grateful to Meg Ross and her family for the warm hospitality with which they received me when I first came to stay in the UK in 1994, and for the generous support that they have extended ever since. To my parents, Gerda and Helmut Arnold, I owe more than I can say; and also to my grandparents, who were a constant presence during my childhood and adolescence.

Finally, I would like to thank my wife, Ilona Arnold, for her friendship, love and trust. We met during the research for this book in Magdeburg in 2004. Since then, two worlds have become one. In 2009, we were joined by our baby daughter, Emilia Charlotte, who teaches us daily of the beauty of discovery.

Freiburg im Breisgau
March 2011

Abbreviations

AfS	Archiv für Sozialgeschichte
AHR	*American Historical Review*
AKPS	Archiv der Kirchenprovinz Sachsen
APuZ	*Aus Politik und Zeitgeschichte*
BA	Bundesarchiv
BGM Kassel	Brüder Grimm Museum, Kassel
BHE	Bund der Heimatvertriebenen und Entrechteten
CDU	Christlich Demokratische Union Deutschlands
CEH	*Contemporary European History*
DNVP	Deutschnationale Volkspartei
DRZW	*Das Deutsche Reich und der Zweite Weltkrieg*
EKD	Evangelische Kirche in Deutschland
EKG	*Evangelisches Kirchengesangbuch*
FDP	Freie Demokratische Partei
FRG	Federal Republic of Germany
GDR	German Democratic Republic
GG	*Geschichte und Gesellschaft*
GWU	*Geschichte in Wissenschaft und Unterricht*
HA	*Hessische Allgemeine*
HN	*Hessische Nachrichten*
HNA	*Hessische/Niedersächsische Allgemeine*
HZ	*Historische Zeitschrift*
IMS	*Informationen zur modernen Stadtgeschichte*
IWM	Imperial War Museum
JCH	*Journal of Contemporary History*
KHM	Kulturhistorisches Museum, Magdeburg
KLZ	*Kurhessische Landeszeitung*
KNN	*Kasseler Neueste Nachrichten*
KP	*Kasseler Post*
KPD	Kommunistische Partei Deutschlands
KZ	*Kasseler Zeitung*
LA	Landesarchiv

LDP(D)	Liberal-Demokratische Partei (Deutschlands)
LDZ	*Liberal-Demokratische Zeitung*
LHA	Landeshauptarchiv
LKA	Landeskirchliches Archiv
MNN	*Mitteldeutsche Neueste Nachrichten*
NA	National Archives
NATO	North Atlantic Treaty Organisation
NL	*Nachlass*
NSDAP	Nationalsozialistische Deutsche Arbeiterpartei
NSV	Nationalsozialistische Volkswohlfahrt
POW	Prisoner of War
PWG	Partei Freie Wählergemeinschaft
RAF	Royal Air Force
SB	Sekretariat Bischof
SD	Sicherheitsdienst
SED	Sozialistische Einheitspartei Deutschlands
SPD	Sozialdemokratische Partei Deutschlands
StA	Stadtarchiv
StAK	Stadtarchiv Kassel
StAM	Stadtarchiv Magdeburg
StMK	Stadtmuseum Kassel
SVZ	*Sozialistische Volkszeitung*
TRE	*Theologische Real-Enzyklopädie*
USAAF	United States Army Air Force
USSBS	United States Strategic Bombing Survey
VB	*Völkischer Beobachter*
VfZ	*Vierteljahreshefte für Zeitgeschichte*
V & R	Vandenhoeck & Ruprecht
ZfG	*Zeitschrift für Geschichtswissenschaft*

Kassel

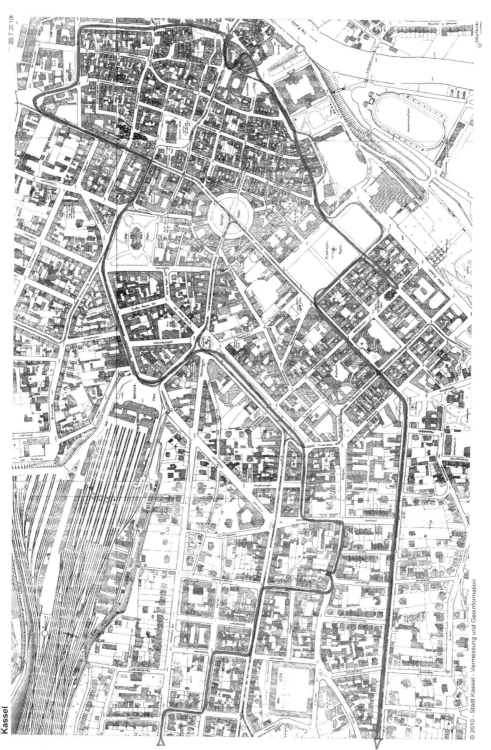

Map 1. The old town of Kassel before World War II showing Gebhard Niemeyer's journey through the devastated city on 23 October 1943.

Map 2. The 'new city on historic ground': the old town of Kassel after
the rebuilding in 1964. Note the new Kurt-Schumacher-Straße cutting
through the historic old town and the virtual disappearance of the Lower
New Town (*Unterneustadt*) on the right bank of the river Fulda.

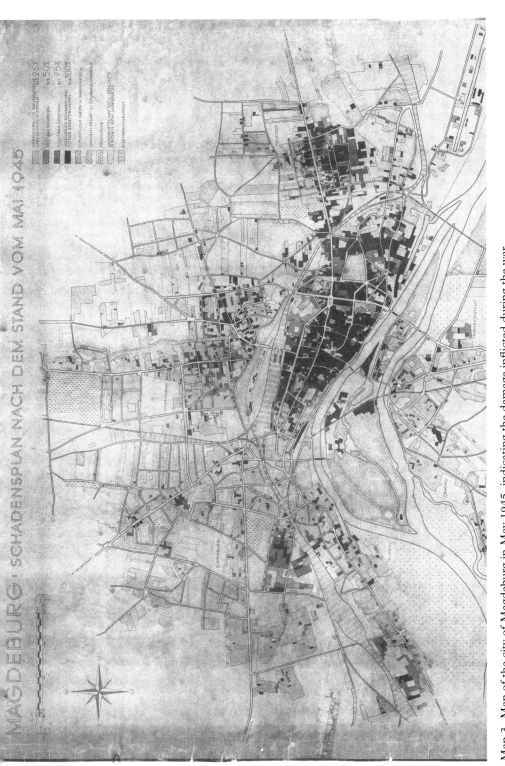

Map 3. Map of the city of Magdeburg in May 1945, indicating the damage inflicted during the war.

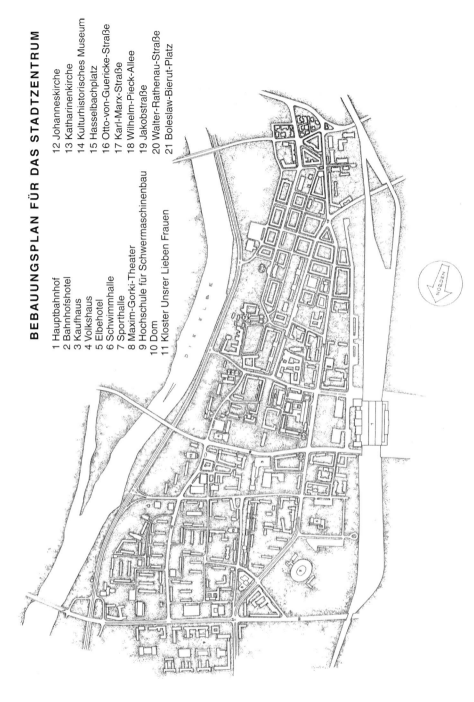

BEBAUUNGSPLAN FÜR DAS STADTZENTRUM

1 Hauptbahnhof
2 Bahnhofshotel
3 Kaufhaus
4 Volkshaus
5 Elbehotel
6 Schwimmhalle
7 Sporthalle
8 Maxim-Gorki-Theater
9 Hochschule für Schwermaschinenbau
10 Dom
11 Kloster Unsrer Lieben Frauen

12 Johanneskirche
13 Katharinenkirche
14 Kulturhistorisches Museum
15 Hasselbachplatz
16 Otto-von-Guericke-Straße
17 Karl-Marx-Straße
18 Wilhelm-Pieck-Allee
19 Jakobstraße
20 Walter-Rathenau-Straße
21 Boleslaw-Bierut-Platz

DIE ELBE

NORDEN

Map 4. The 'Socialist metropolis' under construction. Magdeburg street map, 1959.

Introduction: a poem and an image

The municipal archive of the city of Kassel holds a small file that consists of different versions of a long poem. The piece is alternatively called 'Thus Died My Home Town' (*So starb meine Heimatstadt*), 'Thus Died My Home Town of Kassel', or simply 'Thus Died Kassel'.[1] The various titles refer to a particularly devastating air attack by the Royal Air Force against the North Hessian city in World War II. On 22 October 1943, 1,800 tons of high explosives and incendiaries were dropped on Kassel, producing a catastrophic conflagration that destroyed 60 per cent of the built environment. Somewhere between 6,000 and 8,000 people were killed, while 150,000 residents out of a total population of 220,000 were made homeless.[2] According to a British post-war estimate, the attack also resulted in the production loss for the German war economy of 150 heavy tanks, 400–500 locomotives and 300 heavy guns.[3]

The air raid did not strike the city out of the blue. It occurred four years into a German war of conquest and annihilation in which the (non-Jewish German) residents of Kassel, as citizens of the German Reich, had played an active part from the very beginning.[4] The area bombardment of

---

[1] Stadtarchiv Kassel (StAK), S8 C53, Luftangriff vom 22.10.1943. Literarische Verarbeitung. For the text plus translation see Appendix 1.

[2] Compare Dettmar, 'Kassel im Luftkrieg', pp. 18–20. The official figure of the local chief of police was 5,830. See StAK, S8 C40, 'Erfahrungsbericht', 7 December 1943. In April 1944, the mayor reported to the Nazi district leader a death toll of 6,496 'people's comrades'; 1,500 people were still unaccounted for. See Staatsarchiv Marburg, Best. 165 no. 8818, mayor to NSDAP, 4 April 1944. A report by the United States Strategic Bombing Survey (USSBS) from the summer of 1945 put the death toll at 7,000 (plus 500 missing). In National Archives II (NA II) RG 243 E-6 # 64 (b) k 21 (box 563). A British report from October 1945 mentioned 8,500 fatalities. Copy in StAK, S8 B13. In local memory, the death toll is usually put at around 10,000. On the raid itself see Groehler, *Bombenkrieg*, pp. 140–7; Dettmar, *Zerstörung*.

[3] StAK, S8 B13, 'The Effect of Air Attack on the City and District of Kassel', 21 October 1945, p. 5.

[4] For the importance of the town as an armaments centre in the eyes of British military planners see the entry on Kassel in the 'Bomber's Baedeker', part I (2nd edn, 1944), pp. 381–5, copy in NA II RG 243 E-6 # 39 5 (box 383). For the impact of bombing on production see the case studies by the USSBS: Munitions Division, Motor Vehicles and

1

22 October 1943 formed part of a strategic air offensive against Germany's urban centres that was waged by the Western allies to help bring this war to an end.[5] In a relentless campaign that reached its climax in the years 1943–5, allied air forces dropped roughly 1.3 million tons of bombs over the territory of the Reich, reducing much of Germany's urban landscape to rubble, killing half a million civilians and tying down a substantial part of Germany's war resources.[6] Nor was the raid of 22 October 1943 the only one against a city that, according to British wartime analysis, was 'one of the most important centres of German armament production'.[7] But as the one air attack that 'completely overshadowed' all other aspects of the air war in Kassel in terms of both material destruction and loss of life,[8] '22 October 1943' took pride of place in private as well as public recollections of the bombing war and, indeed, World War II as a whole.

The very existence of the poem 'Thus Died My Home Town' testifies to the hold that this particular air raid commanded over the popular imagination. Although, as a work of art, the text holds limited interest other than as an illustration of the conventions (and limitations) of popular *Heimat* verse, as a cultural artefact, the piece offers a first pathway into the processes by which lived experience was translated into cultural memory within the context of Nazism and war.[9]

Tanks Plant Report no. 7: 'Henschel & Sohn AG' (October 1945), NA II RG 243 E-6 # 85 (box 704); Ordnance Section, Munitions Division, Plant Report no. 3, 'Henschel & Sohn GmbH: plant no. 1: gun shops' (September 1945), ibid., # 104 (box 762); Aircraft Division, Aero Engine Plant Report no. 5, 'Henschel Flugmotorenwerke' (September 1945), ibid., # 19; Aircraft Division, Air Frames Report no. 8, 'Gerhard Fieseler Werke GmbH' (October 1945), ibid., # 13 (box 239).

[5] The literature on the strategic air war is vast. While the importance of the campaign as a whole is not in doubt, the relative contribution of area bombing to the defeat of the German Reich is still a matter of controversy. For concise evaluations see Childers, '"Facilis decensus averni est"'; Overy, *Why the Allies Won*, pp. 101–33; Beaumont, 'Bomber Offensive'. For recent accounts of the campaign as a whole see, in addition to the literature mentioned in footnote 2 above, the contributions by Horst Boog, Klaus A. Maier and Ralf Blank in the official German history of World War II, *Das Deutsche Reich und der Zweite Weltkrieg (DRZW)* ed., Militärgeschichtliches Forschungsamt; Müller, *Bombenkrieg*; Connelly, *Reaching for the Stars*. On the legal and ethical side of bombing see Messerschmidt, 'Strategic Air War and International Law'; Hays Parks, 'Air War and the Laws of War'; Garrett, *Ethics and Airpower*; Grayling, *Among the Dead Cities*; Bloxham, 'Dresden as a War Crime'.

[6] Groehler, *Bombenkrieg*, pp. 446–9.

[7] StAK, S8 C39, 'Area Attack Assessment – Detailed Report Kassel', no date [October 1943], p. 2.

[8] StAK, S8 B13, 'The Effect of Air Attack on the City and District of Kassel', 21 October 1945, p. 2.

[9] This attempt to treat popular fiction as a historical document is indebted to Fritzsche, 'Volkstümliche Erinnerung'.

'Thus Died My Home Town' is an elegy of eighty or so lines that confronts the reality of death in the air war.[10] The term 'death' is used both metaphorically and descriptively, as an illustration of the whole-sale destruction of the urban environment, the 'home town', and as a reminder that bombing violently terminated the lives of thousands of citizens. In focusing on death, the poem points to a central dimension of memory cultures that formed around the experience of indiscriminate bombing. Contrary to what is sometimes assumed in the scholarly litera-ture, mass death haunted the living, and the attempts to impart meaning and to find solace occupied centre stage in local discourses on World War II area bombing.[11]

Structurally, the poem is made up of three parts. The exposition anthropomorphises the city; it depicts a woman who 'harbours in her walls unspeakable pain'. In so doing, the text not only employs a con-ventional trope of *Heimat* poetry, but also invokes a frame of reference that prioritises the local over the national, indigenous – albeit largely invented[12] – traditions over the context of World War II. Both the imag-ination of 'Frau Chasalla' and the emphasis on a 'thousand years' of urban history (l. 5) – a reference to the millennial celebration of 1913 – invoked a set of ideas that associated the city with beauty, harmony and continuity.[13] In the poem, this *longue durée* is contrasted with the catas-trophic rupture of a single night, with 'annihilation' suffered despite the valiant efforts of 'German youths' 'to protect the *Heimat*' (ll. 3–24).

While the exposition sets the elegiac tone, the main body of the text recounts harrowing scenes of agony, crushed hope and death. Remark-ably, individual episodes offer very little solace even when telling stories of successful rescue. On the contrary, the survival of some is inextricably linked to the death of others. Lines 42–8, for example, tell of a man who saves from a burning building a woman and a child whom he wrongly believes to be his family. By the time he finds out that 'a stranger he has carried to life', it is too late. The building has collapsed, burying 'his dearest, his happiness' underneath.

Whereas the main body of the text recounts stories from the epi-centre of the attack, the conclusion expresses collective feelings, draws lessons and passes moral judgement. The poem in its early versions is

---

[10] The version 'So starb meine Heimatstadt Kassel', dated 'Kassel, 23 October 1943', will be used as the textual basis for the following discussion.

[11] J. Assmann, *Das kulturelle Gedächtnis*, p. 61.

[12] The personification of Kassel was a late nineteenth-century invention that had gained wide popularity in the city's millennial celebration in 1913. See Schweizer, *Geschichts-deutung*, pp. 15–20, 239.

[13] Ibid., p. 15.

unequivocal in its moral stance. It blames the disastrous events on Britain, speaking of the 'hatred' and thirst for 'retaliation' that unites a collective 'us':

> The phosphorous flames have destroyed human happiness
> As flames of hatred they will fall back [on England][14]
> The hatred born in this night
> Has finally united us as one community.   (ll. 66–9)

While a close reading of the text can help to identify important themes that were central to local experiences of aerial bombing – death, despair, hatred – the archival record also allows for some first tentative remarks about the ways in which these experiences were rewritten in the decades that followed. In the weeks and months after the air attack, the text appears to have functioned as some kind of counter-memory to National Socialist propaganda. Both the fact that the poet has chosen to remain anonymous and the existence of a great number of textual variations point to informal modes of circulation. The poem was copied out by hand in order to satisfy a demand for stories about the conflagration that did not conform to the line of interpretation adopted by the state-controlled media.[15] Although there were unmistakable echoes in the poem of certain strands of Nazi propaganda, arguably more important were the differences. Dwelling on death, loss and despair, 'Thus Died My Home Town' gave expression to a sense of finality that Nazi propaganda sought to avoid at all costs.

After the war, the poem turned into a 'memory artefact' that was used by different protagonists of an evolving memory culture – journalists, city bureaucrats, ordinary residents – in order to illustrate the catastrophic dimensions of air attack. In the process, the text underwent significant rewritings, as on the tenth anniversary in 1953, when the *Kasseler Zeitung* printed a version from which all references to 'hatred' and 'retaliation' had been deleted. Beginning in the 1960s, dozens of citizens sent their personal copies from the war to the city archive or the local newspaper, often on the occasion of anniversaries of the bombing.[16] Others added new stanzas in which they warned against the catastrophic consequences of another war.[17] In 1983, the text featured prominently in a historical exhibition that was held to commemorate the fortieth anniversary of the

---

[14] 'On England' is added in a version that carries the title 'So starb meine Heimatstadt'.

[15] StAK, S8 C53, Ms. Bernhardine N. to *Kulturamt*, 22 September 1983.

[16] The first such letter dates from 1963. See StAK, S8 C53, Karl K. to city administration, 21 October 1963.

[17] StAK, S8 C 53, Klaus Pottin, 'So starb Kassel . . . 1943', 1972.

Figure 1. 'Magdeburg in Mourning' in the ruins of the Johanniskirche at war's end.

attack.[18] Even then, however, the variant on display was not identical with the text that had circulated during the war.

Whereas in Kassel the impact of aerial warfare on the locality was memorialised through the medium of lyrical poetry, 250 kilometres to the north-east, in the city of Magdeburg, similar functions were fulfilled by a photograph that showed a sculpture in the ruins of a church (Fig. 1). The

---

[18] StAK, S8 E9 [Textvorlagen]. Compare chapter 8 below.

sculpture carried the title 'Magdeburg in Mourning' (*Trauernde Magdeburg*); it personified the city as a woman with a bowed head and a lowered sword. The sculpture formed part of a nineteenth-century Reformation monument, which commemorated the destruction of medieval Magdeburg at the hands of Catholic troops at the height of the Thirty Years War in 1631.[19]

Situated in the German Democratic Republic (GDR) from 1945/9 to 1990, and since unification, in the province of Saxony-Anhalt, Magdeburg offers a fascinating comparison with Kassel. Here too, in public discourse, the experience of dozens of air raids was telescoped into the memory of a single attack. On 16 January 1945, a large fleet of RAF bombers dropped around 1,000 tons of bombs on a city that allied planners considered of vital industrial and commercial importance to the German war effort.[20] The indiscriminate area attack created extensive fires, destroying 77.3 per cent of the built environment in the target area; 190,000 residents were made homeless in the raid while at least 1,930 people were killed.[21] A post-war investigation by the United States Strategic Bombing Survey (USSBS) spoke of the attack as a 'solar plexus blow' that served 'to cut down total factory production indirectly by keeping large numbers of workers away from their work and smashing many essential city services'.[22]

The photograph dates from the immediate post-war period, possibly from 1946.[23] It shows the sculpture of 'Magdeburg in Mourning' amidst the rubble of the Johanniskirche, Magdeburg's oldest parish church. The

---

[19] On the revival in the nineteenth century of public interest in the city's destruction see Cramer, *The Thirty Years' War and German Memory*, pp. 141–77.

[20] NA (Kew), AIR 14/3775, K Reports Magdeburg, 15 April 1945; NA II RG 243 E-6 # 39 4 (box 383), 'City as Target', no date [1945].

[21] This is the official figure by the chief of police. See NA II RG 243 E-6 # 39 9, 'Erfahrungsbericht über den schweren Terrorangriff', 5 March 1945. As in Kassel, the precise number of deaths is heavily contested. The statistical yearbook of 1947 gives a figure of 6,000. Groehler, *Bombenkrieg*, p. 396, puts the death toll at around 4,000, while the SED elites insisted on a figure of 16,000. See *Statistisches Jahrbuch der Stadt Magdeburg*, p. 49. On the air raid see Wille, 'Tod und Zerstörung'. On the importance of Magdeburg for the German war economy in the eyes of British analysts see the entry in the 'Bomber's Baedeker'.

[22] NA II RG 243 E-6 # 39 4 (box 383), 'Physical Damage to Magdeburg as a Whole', 1945, p. 5. The same report considered negligible the effects of the area raid on the output of the city's four major industrial plants, two of which had already been effectively bombed out of operation by US Air Force precision raids. See ibid., # 39 12 (box 384), 'Report on Magdeburg', p. 3. These industrial plants were the Junkers aircraft and aero Engine works (rated 1+ in the 'Bomber's Baedeker'), the Krupp-Gruson engineering and armaments works (rated 1+), the Polte gun manufacturer (rated 1) and the BRABAG synthetic oil works (rated 2). For the effects of various types of bombing on production see NA II RG 243 E-6 # 39 3 (Junkers), # 39 2 (Krupp), # 39 1 (Polte) and # 39 10 (BRABAG).

[23] Stadtarchiv Magdeburg (StAM), Rep. 18/4, Ra 4, 'Niederschrift', 2 January 1946.

undamaged figure is framed by an archway that creates the visual impression of a halo, evoking associations of Christian martyrdom as well as of survival amidst chaos. In the immediate post-war period, the motif was popular with local photographers and the civil authorities alike, who drew on the image in their attempts to rally a dispirited population to the reconstruction effort.[24]

This changed as local self-government was eroded as part of a broader transformation of East German society along the Soviet model from 1948 onwards. By that time, the power holders of the Socialist Unity Party (SED) had lost interest in a motif that harked back to Magdeburg's past as a stronghold of Protestantism and emphasised transcendental endurance over worldly activism.[25] No more visual representations would appear in the print media, while the sculpture itself was removed from the church ruin and deposited in the backyard of a local museum. Yet there were limits to the extent to which the authorities were able to reshape the visual canon. Despite the fact that the dominant agents of public memory marginalised 'Magdeburg in Mourning' for close to forty years, the motif retained a residual hold on the popular imagination, as became apparent in the context of the 'second' Cold War of the 1980s. Against the backdrop of heightened fears over an atomic war, local residents remembered a sculpture that appeared to symbolise the destruction of their home town, and began to demand that 'Magdeburg in Mourning' be returned to its old place in the Johanniskirche.[26] Although the administration harboured serious reservations, fearing the potential of the sculpture to become a symbol of pacifism,[27] the authorities eventually gave in. In the summer of 1989, they agreed to have the sculpture returned to the church, where it has remained to the present day.[28]

Both the poem and the image are cultural artefacts that were spawned by the experience of aerial bombing. The exploration of the broader memory cultures in which these artefacts sat and through which they moved forms the subject matter of this study.

Approach

When the analysts of the USSBS published their 'summary report' on the allied air war in the autumn of 1945, they underlined the decisive

---

[24] See the different versions in StAM, N 754, NG 75, NG 737; E. R. Müller, 'Magdeburg, die Arbeitsstadt am Elbstrom', *Freiheit*, 7 June 1947, p. 4. See also 'Memento: Magdeburg, 16. Januar 1945', *Volksstimme*, 15 January 1948.

[25] On the context see Weber, *Geschichte der DDR*, pp. 163–223; Schmiechen-Ackermann, 'Magdeburg als Stadt des Schwermaschinenbaus', pp. 817–22.

[26] StAM, 80/4696n, 'Betr.: Plastik "Trauernde Magdeburg"', 30 September 1980, p. 1.

[27] StAM, Rep. 41/604, fos. 16f., 'Memorandum', 17 December 1987.

[28] The sculpture was relocated on 12 August 1989.

contribution that air power had made to victory in Europe. They also commented on the psychological impact of strategic bombing on German society. 'Allied air power', they wrote, had 'brought home to the German people the full impact of modern war with all its horror and suffering'. Venturing a gaze into the future, they predicted that 'its imprint on the German nation will be lasting'.[29]

Writing shortly after the end of hostilities, having toured dozens of ruined cities and conducted thousands of interviews with ordinary Germans as well as military and political leaders, the analysts of the survey took as self-evident two insights that historians have begun to appreciate more fully only recently. The first was a frank acknowledgement of the vast scale of the 'horror and suffering' that Germans had brought upon themselves; the second was that the repercussions of the war as a whole and of the air war in particular would linger on long after the dead had been buried, the streets been cleared of rubble and the cities been rebuilt. The experience of 'modern war' would shape the ways in which Germans saw themselves and the world around them for decades to come.

Since the turn of the millennium, a number of studies have appeared that have reconfigured the prisms through which the history of Germany in the second half of the twentieth century can be viewed. Sceptical of an influential current in historical writing that made 'modernisation' and 'arrival' into central analytical categories – at liberal democracy, the West or civil society in the Federal Republic;[30] at modern dictatorship, the East or a 'paralysed' society in the German Democratic Republic[31] – they have turned their attention to the abiding presence of a shared past of violence in the two successor states of the Third Reich.[32] For all their differences in emphasis and approach, these 'histories of the aftermath' share in common the assumption that, in order to understand the trajectory of German society and culture in the second half of the twentieth century[33] – the desperate quest for a return to 'normalcy' and the yearning for security;[34] the social anxieties running just below the surface of economic prosperity and social stability;[35] the tone of arrogant

---

[29] USSBS, *Summary Report*, p. 16.

[30] For a good discussion of the historiography see Nolte, 'Einführung', 175–82.

[31] See the concise discussion in Ihme-Tuchel, *DDR*, pp. 89–95; also Fulbrook, *The People's State*, pp. 10–17.

[32] The pioneering work is Naumann (ed.), *Nachkrieg*. See also Biess, *Homecomings*; Wierling, 'Krieg im Nachkrieg'; Gregor, *Haunted City*; Bessel, *Germany 1945*; Goltermann, *Gesellschaft der Überlebenden*.

[33] Biess, *Homecomings*, p. 10.

[34] Bessel, *Germany 1945*, p. 278; Conze, 'Sicherheit als Kultur'; Conze, *Suche nach Sicherheit*.

[35] Naumann, 'Einleitung', pp. 12f.; Schildt, 'German Angst'. Frank Biess is currently working on a project that explores the experiential foundations of proverbial German angst.

self-righteousness frequently adopted by the very people who claimed
to stand in for a societal liberalisation – one must take seriously the
idea that this was a society that had emerged, in Richard Bessel's memorable phrase, from 'a wave of violence almost without parallel'.[36] On
this view, Germany after 1945, for an indeterminate period the duration of which was progressively pushed forward,[37] was a *post-war* society
in which the many legacies of violence continued to shape the present.
Such a perspective does not deny the importance of the Cold War. It also
fully acknowledges the long shadow that Nazism cast over both post-war
Germanys,[38] but seeks to integrate the post-history of fascism into a
broader context of a post-history of war. It holds that the confrontation
with Nazism and with the singularity of the Holocaust took shape within
a society that struggled to make sense of the multidimensional 'shocks of
violence' that it had experienced in the period 1939–45/6.[39]

This book aims to make a contribution to the perspective of the postwar
(*Nachkrieg*) by examining the long-term 'imprint' that the strategic air
war left on German society in east and west. By way of a comparative case
study, it looks at the cities of Kassel and Magdeburg in the period from
1940 to the early 2000s. Its primary focus is neither the bombing itself
nor the social legacy of the destruction, although both will play an important role in the narrative that follows.[40] Rather, the book is interested in
the ways in which the air war entered the cultural inventories of the two
post-war Germanys. It examines the stories that were told, the meanings
that were imparted and the practices that were performed in memory
of events that had exposed Germans to man-made catastrophe as never
before. The validity of these stories, meanings and practices was made
difficult for post-war Germans by at least two factors. For one, there was
the knowledge, however imperfectly owned up to, that the events had
unfolded in consequence of a war that Germany had itself unleashed.
Moreover, there was the additional burden of discredited narrativisa-
tions. After all, National Socialism, the very force that bore ultimate
responsibility for what had happened, had also played a dominant role in
coining the idioms and shaping the discursive boundaries through which
the experience of aerial bombardment was commonly expressed.

The study works from a number of assumptions that need briefly to be
explicated here. Firstly, it holds that the best way to examine the cultural
ramifications of the bombing is to focus on individual urban communities

---

[36] Bessel, 'War to End All Wars', p. 72.   [37] Naumann, 'Frage nach dem Ende'.
[38] For a recent survey of the post-history of Nazism see Reichel, Schmid and Steinbach
(eds.), *Der Nationalsozialismus*.
[39] Bessel, 'War to End all Wars'; Biess, *Homecomings*, p. 9; Gregor, 'Trauer und städtische
Identitätspolitik'.
[40] On the social history of the bombing see Süß, 'Tod aus der Luft'.

because it was here, on the level of individual cities, that the air war had the most immediate and profound impact.[41] Secondly, the study self-consciously adopts a *longue durée* approach that stretches from the unfolding of events in the early 1940s to the early 2000s. In so doing, it becomes possible to assess the extent to which legacies of the catastrophic events lingered on after the material impact had been overcome and generational change had turned lived experience into cultural memory. Finally, Germany after 1945, of course, was not only a post-war society but also a Cold War society that was divided between the antagonistic power blocs of a bi-polar world. It is in order to make a contribution to a comparative history of the two Germanys that the two cities of Kassel and Magdeburg have been selected for this case study. Although part of central Germany before the war, the two cities found themselves on opposite sides of the inner-German border between 1945/9 and 1990, Kassel in the West and Magdeburg in the East.

A comparative case study as proposed here allows for representations of the air war to be studied within the context of the history of German division between 1949 and 1989.[42] It can make a contribution to our understanding of the asymmetrical relationship, the 'interweaving and delimitation', between the two successor states of the Third Reich. At the same time, in employing a time frame that goes beyond the history of German division, it becomes possible to assess how important the ideological confrontations of the Cold War really were for the trajectories of urban memory. Did different communities experience the bombings in different ways or were there important similarities? Were the local memory cultures propelled on to different trajectories by the emergence of antagonistic political cultures from 1945 onwards? And finally, was there a convergence of memory after unification, or did differences persist? If so, were there perhaps also other factors at work in influencing the shape of memory, such as the abiding power of local traditions or of religious ways of seeing the world?

One way to examine the emergence and trajectory of memory cultures is to focus on the 'realms of memory' where 'memory crystallizes and secretes itself'.[43] Divested of its baggage of 'cultural melancholia',[44] French scholar Pierre Nora's now classic concept of *lieux de mémoire* still offers a helpful tool for unravelling the manifestations and workings of public memory. It provides a pathway of enquiry that draws attention to

---

[41] For a discussion of the benefits and pitfalls of a local approach to the study of memory see Gregor, *Haunted City*, pp. 8–14.

[42] Kleßmann, 'Verflechtung und Abgrenzung'.

[43] Nora, 'Between Memory and History', 7.

[44] Kritzman, 'In Remembrance of Things French', p. ix.

a central structural element of all war memories. In both communities under consideration here, public memories of the strategic air offensive – a protracted campaign lasting several years and involving hundreds of alarms and dozens of raids – tended to 'crystallize' around commemoration days, which in turn referred back to the experience of particularly destructive air attacks.

While air war memories tended to coalesce around moments in time, there was also an important spatial dimension to the phenomenon. After all, the bombs had left indelible 'imprint[s]' on *cities*, and it was within the built, lived and imagined environment of these very cities that the air war was remembered.[45] In his posthumously published fragment, *The Collective Memory*, the sociologist Maurice Halbwachs emphasised the importance of the physical environment for the formation of group memories, and speculated that the majority of residents of any given city 'may well be more sensitive to a certain street being torn up, or a certain building or home being razed, than to the gravest national, political or religious events'.[46] In World War II bombing, not only single streets or apartment blocks disappeared, but entire city districts, leading to radical disjunctions between the actual physical reality and the 'maps' that contemporaries carried in their minds[47] – a phenomenon that struck many outside observers travelling in Germany in the post-war years, most prominently Hannah Arendt, who famously commented on Germans sending each other picture postcards of sights that no longer existed.[48] The example suggests that the spatial dimension of air war memory extended beyond narrow topographies of memorial sites – the concrete spaces in which memorials were erected and rituals performed – to the built-up environments themselves. The bombs had radically altered physical spaces, and in doing so, had also fractured the social and symbolic configurations through which these spaces were defined.

Although different cities could have been selected for a comparative investigation of air war memory – and indeed further comparative work would be highly welcome – a good case can be made for the heuristic value of comparing Kassel and Magdeburg.[49] Because they shared many structural elements in common, the importance for the evolution of

---

[45] This distinction follows Funck, 'Stadt und Krieg im 20. Jahrhundert', 6; for useful reflections on the urban in an age of total war see also Funck and Chickering (eds.), *Endangered Cities*; von Saldern, 'Stand und Perspektiven'.

[46] Halbwachs, *The Collective Memory*, p. 131.

[47] On the concept of 'mental maps' see Conrad (ed.), *Mental Maps*.

[48] Arendt, 'Aftermath of Nazi Rule', 342.

[49] The following according to *Magdeburg. Die Geschichte der Stadt*, *passim*, and Klaube, *Chronik*, *passim*, unless otherwise indicated.

public memory of a number of striking differences can be identified much more clearly. Most important among these was the time-lag between the air raids on the two cities (Kassel was bombed in 1943, Magdeburg in 1945); the existence or otherwise of referential frames that would allow for an integration of bombing into received cultural patterns (Weimar-era Magdeburg was known as a 'modern' city that had experienced catastrophe in the Thirty Years War; Kassel was counted among the loveliest of German towns precisely because the city's architectural heritage had until then largely escaped natural or man-made destruction); and, of course, their integration into the antagonistic states of the Federal Republic and the German Democratic Republic throughout the duration of the Cold War.

Both towns were founded long before the rise of modern nationalism in the nineteenth century, boasting histories that stretched back well into the Middle Ages. At the same time, neither Kassel nor Magdeburg possessed strong traditions of independent self-government, unlike Hamburg or Frankfurt am Main. While Kassel had been the capital of the medium-size principality of the Hessian landgraves until the annexation by Prussia in 1866, Magdeburg was known since the early modern period as Prussia's pre-eminent 'fortress town'. Both communities underwent rapid growth during the second half of the nineteenth century, and by the early twentieth century had developed into administrative and industrial centres of some importance. In the period 1871–1914, population figures rose by a factor of three, to around 150,000 in Kassel and 280,000 in Magdeburg. Their rank among Germany's cities was reflected by the fact that they functioned as regional capitals, Kassel of the Prussian province of Hesse Nassau and Magdeburg of the province of Saxony.

In the first decades of the twentieth century, the political cultures of the two cities were characterised by deep socio-political cleavages between a national-conservative middle-class milieu – after 1918 represented by the Deutschnationale Volkspartei (DNVP) – and an equally strong working-class milieu – represented by the Social Democratic Party (SPD). Magdeburg was the city where both the nationalist war veterans' organisation of the Stahlhelm and the republican war veterans' organisation of the Reichsbanner were founded during the troubled Weimar Republic. These rifts were a reflection of rapid industrial growth alongside the persistence of an older tradition, in which the military and the civil service enjoyed a strong presence.[50] The rise to power of the Nazi party in the two cities followed the national pattern, although with some important

---

[50] Tullner, 'Modernisierung und Scheinblüte'; Tullner, 'Modernisierung und mitteldeutsche Hauptstadtpolitik'; Krause-Vilmar, 'Hitlers Machtergreifung', p. 14.

variations.[51] Whereas, in both, the general elections of September 1930 marked a breakthrough for Nazism, Magdeburg, the 'red city in a red countryside', was the only major town in Germany in which the Social Democrats managed to hold on to power until the spring of 1933.[52] In Kassel, by comparison, the Social Democrats lost their leading role in municipal politics as early as the mid-1920s.

In the Third Reich, Kassel was the seat of a Nazi party district leader (*Gauhauptstadt*), but Magdeburg was not. Apart from that, the trajectories of the two communities showed broadly similar patterns. Here, as elsewhere throughout the Reich, a substantial number of local businesses and individuals profited from the persecution and expropriation of local Jewry, and, during the war, of forced labour.[53] Both benefited from the armaments-driven economic boom and witnessed extensive industrial expansion well into the early 1940s. It is probably not much of an over-statement to count them among the principal 'armouries' of the Third Reich, with particular strengths in the production of tanks, aeroplanes and synthetic fuels.[54] This importance for Germany's war effort also made them into early and prime targets for the Royal Air Force, and later on, also for the United States Army Air Force. By the time the air raids started in deadly earnest in 1942, both communities had reached an all-time high in their population figures, with 220,000 people living in Kassel and almost 350,000 in Magdeburg.

In terms of both loss of life and material destruction, Kassel and Magdeburg suffered exceptionally in the air war.[55] This was despite the fact that they were given official priority in anti-aircraft defence on account of their industrial importance.[56] None the less, Kassel sustained at least 9,202 civilian fatalities in the air raids, which was almost twice the number of soldiers killed in action.[57] This figure translated into a mortality rate of 4.3 per cent of the pre-war population, which put the city above even Hamburg (2.4 per cent).[58] Moreover, Kassel lost 60 per cent

---

[51] See Krause-Vilmar, 'Hitlers Machtergreifung', pp. 22f.; Frenz, 'Organisation'; Hattenhorst, 'Stadt der Mitte'.

[52] *Die rote Stadt im roten Land* (Magdeburg, 1929) was the title of an SPD-sponsored publication about the history of the regional Social Democratic Party. Compare Hattenhorst, 'Städtische Identität'.

[53] Frenz, 'NS-Wirtschaftspolitik'; Krause-Vilmar, 'Ausländische Zwangsarbeiter'; Prinz, 'Judenverfolgung in Kassel'; Tullner, 'Modernisierung und Scheinblüte'; *Unerwünscht – Verfolgt – Ermordet*.

[54] Hattenhorst, 'Stadt der Mitte', p. 796.

[55] See the discussion in Hohn, *Zerstörung*, pp. 271, 286.

[56] Groehler, *Bombenkrieg*, p. 243.

[57] Hauptamt Statistik Kassel to author, 3 September 2004.

[58] Figures according to *Statistischer Bericht der Stadt Kassel* (1952), p. 30. The report also mentions 5,480 Wehrmacht casualties and classifies a further 5,000 as 'missing'. On Hamburg see Brunswig, *Feuersturm*, pp. 448–57.

of its pre-war residential flats as a result of the air war.[59] Magdeburg, likewise, suffered considerably, although not quite to the same extent. At least 5,653 people or 1.7 per cent of the pre-war population died in the air war,[60] while 50 per cent of the residential flats were destroyed.[61]

After 1945, neither of the two cities ever managed to regain the importance that it had enjoyed before the war. Despite a substantial recovery, the population figures in the two cities remained considerably lower than they had been in the early 1940s. Ten years after the war, 180,000 people lived in Kassel; in 1985, there were 185,000. For Magdeburg, the respective figures were 260,000 and 290,000. Stagnation in part resulted from the fact that both cities were severely affected by the division of Germany, which turned them from regional hubs in central Germany into outposts without a hinterland on opposite sides of the inner-German border. As a direct consequence of both the destruction and the geographical location, the two cities lost their functions as state capitals, Kassel to Wiesbaden and Magdeburg to Halle, although both were to some extent compensated by being declared centres of smaller administrative units. Politically, the Social Democrats attained a leading position in municipal politics in Kassel, where they held power from 1945 to 1993.[62] In Magdeburg, meanwhile, an initial post-war revival of Social Democratic influence was broken in 1950 when leading administrators were arrested and replaced by functionaries who toed the line of the ruling Communists.[63]

After German unification in 1990, Magdeburg was declared capital of the reconstituted state of Saxony-Anhalt, but economically and demographically it was severely affected by the unification crisis. The early 1990s saw wide-scale deindustrialisation, structural unemployment and substantial decline in the resident population, from 290,000 in 1985 to around 230,000 in 2005. Politically, the Social Democrats managed to re-establish themselves as the dominant force in municipal politics. Kassel, by comparison, underwent less dramatic change but in 1993, the dominance of Social Democracy came to an end when, for the first time since 1945, a Conservative politician of the Christian Democratic Union (CDU) was elected as mayor. Throughout the period under

---

[59] Hohn, *Zerstörung*, table 42, Kassel (7).
[60] Fatalities according to the findings of the USSBS, which were based on the records of the City Air Raid Police. See NA II RG 243 E-6 # 39 12 (box 384), 'Physical Damage to Magdeburg as a Whole', 1945, p. 7.
[61] Hohn, *Zerstörung*, table 60, Magdeburg (7).
[62] Klaube, *Chronik*, p. 104.
[63] Schmiechen-Ackermann, 'Magdeburg als Stadt des Schwermaschinenbaus', pp. 819–22.

consideration, Protestantism was the dominant religious denomination in both cities.

Historiographical overview

Recent research into the cultural impact of the strategic air war has gone some way in dispelling earlier notions about an alleged absence of the bombing war from the political cultures of the two Germanys.[64] The so-called 'bombing war controversy' of the early 2000s, which followed in the wake of two controversial publications by the late novelist Winfried G. Sebald and the freelance historian Jörg Friedrich, was still largely dominated by ideas of 'amnesia' and 'tabuisation'.[65] Yet the notion that the air war played no role in public memory cultures east and west of the Iron Curtain does not hold up in the face of the empirical evidence, as a number of smaller pieces and an important monograph study have convincingly demonstrated since then. Quite the opposite was the case: 'In truth, no other historical event . . . has left a more abiding tradition,' as Malte Thießen has observed with regard to the persistence of the mnemonic discourses surrounding the fire bombing of Hamburg in July 1943.[66] The same could be said of many other cities, in both East and West Germany.

In the German Democratic Republic, the Communist elites, after some initial restraint during the early years of occupation, went to great lengths in exploiting painful memories of mass death and destruction for the political confrontations of the Cold War. As Gilad Margalit, Matthias Neutzner and Thomas Fache have convincingly demonstrated, above all the bombing of Dresden on 13–14 February 1945 served state-sponsored propagandists as a powerful symbol of both 'imperialist' atrocity and German victimhood.[67] Meanwhile, and contrary to what is sometimes still taken for granted today,[68] the air war also occupied a prominent

---

[64] Süß, 'Review Article'; Thießen, 'Gemeinsame Erinnerungen'; Arnold, Süß, and Thießen (eds.), *Luftkrieg*.

[65] Sebald, *On the Natural History of Destruction*; Friedrich, *The Fire*. Much has been written on the controversy surrounding Friedrich's book. For thoughtful evaluations see Moeller, 'On the History of Man-made Destruction'; Ebbinghaus, 'Deutschland im Bombenkrieg'; as well as the responses collected in Kettenacker (ed.), *Ein Volk von Opfern?*

[66] Thießen, 'Gedenken an "Operation Gomorrha"', 47. Compare also Thießen, *Eingebrannt ins Gedächtnis*.

[67] Margalit, 'Der Luftangriff auf Dresden'; Neutzner, 'Vom Anklagen zum Erinnern'; Fache, 'Gegenwartsbewältigungen'.

[68] Gutschow, 'Stadtzerstörung und Gedenken', p. 272. For similar earlier views, which the authors have modified since then, see Moeller, *War Stories*, p. 5; Naumann, 'Leerstelle Luftkrieg'.

place in the public discourses of the 'old' Federal Republic of Germany, albeit on the communal rather than the state level. In cities such as Hamburg, Pforzheim, Würzburg and many others, annual commemorations were held in memory of the bombing, generally with broad popular participation.[69] Here, public memory was dominated by the local elites of city and Church, who harnessed the air war to the task of physical and spiritual reconstruction while largely avoiding thorny questions of agency and causality.

Much of this scholarship adopts a functionalist approach to the study of memory, working on the premise that the memory of past events serves the needs of the present. On this view, memorial cultures are best explained by looking at the political motivations and social contexts of the present rather than the lived experiences of the historical events themselves.[70] In the memorable phrase of one scholar, memorial cultures are '*Gegenwartsbewältigungen*'.[71] Such an approach has done much to shed light on the politics of memory, demonstrating the bewildering array of contradictory myths to which narratives of World War II bombing have contributed – myths of resilience and sacrifice, overpowering and victimhood, guilt and atonement. It has also considerably broadened our understanding of the 'agents' of public memory and their goals of political mobilisation, social integration and community building.

Yet, for all its merits, the present historiography shows a troubling tendency to prioritise questions of function over 'existential' issues of loss and bereavement.[72] This imbalance is largely a consequence of the two parameters within which most studies operate. The first is the Cold War, the second the history of 'coming to terms with Nazism'. While there are, of course, valid historiographical as well as moral reasons for examining the post-history of the strategic air war through those prisms, there exists a danger of reducing the cultural repercussions of urban catastrophe to mere reflections of either geopolitical struggle or of German society's inability to confront widespread complicity in the crimes of Nazism, or both.[73] All too often, the result is a history of the memory of the bombing with the bombing 'left out'.[74]

This book builds on the recent work on air war memory and, at the same time, attempts to go beyond this work both empirically and

---

[69] See Thießen, 'Die "Katastrophe" als symbolischer Bezugspunkt'.

[70] Thießen, *Eingebrannt ins Gedächtnis*, p. 19.   [71] Fache, 'Gegenwartsbewältigungen'.

[72] Goebel, *The Great War and Medieval Memory*, p. 2. A similar point is made by Gregor, *Haunted City*, p. 10.

[73] The benefits but also the limitations of such an approach are exemplified by the work of Gilad Margalit. See Margalit, 'Dresden and Hamburg' and Margalit, *Guilt, Suffering, and Memory*.

[74] Confino, 'Telling about Germany', p. 194.

conceptually. Empirically, the study aims to verify and, at times, to modify findings that mostly have been suggested in short, exploratory articles rather than on the basis of a close scrutiny of the available evidence. In particular, it adds a comparative dimension, which has largely been missing from the work so far.[75] Conceptually, the book takes lived experience as a starting point for the exploration of post-war memory cultures. While the study remains cognisant of the importance of concerns of the present in the shaping and narrating of the past, it keeps a critical distance from the 'presentism' that is so easily made into a guiding criterion in the exploration of memory.[76] While acknowledging the important role that '*Gegenwartsbewältigung*' played in shaping the idioms of memory, an effort will be made to recapture the deeply disturbing potential that radiated from the events themselves. Indiscriminate fire bombings were both destructive and deadly to an extent that defied the imagination of contemporaries. It is to this dual 'imprint' that this study seeks to do justice by examining legacies of death (and survival) alongside legacies of destruction (and rebuilding).[77]

The methodological viewpoint underlying the approach that is proposed here can best be expressed through a famous early dictum by Karl Marx, who wrote in his *Eighteenth Brumaire* of 1851 that 'men make their own history, but they do not make it as they please; they do not make it under self-selected circumstances, but under circumstances existing already, given and transmitted from the past'.[78] Likewise, one could argue that men (and women) construct their own memories but not as they please, rather from 'circumstances . . . given and transmitted from the past'. Here too, 'the tradition of all the dead generations weighs like a nightmare on the brains of the living'.[79] Put differently, the history of air war memory belongs in the category of 'histories of the aftermath' just as much as in the category of 'histories of arrival'.

Thesis and chapter outline

The book takes seriously contemporary perceptions that framed the experience of aerial warfare in terms of catastrophe. It argues that local communities struggled to come to terms with events that, whatever else they may have been, were unprecedented cataclysms of urban history. In their attempts to make commensurable what had happened,

---

[75] The two notable exceptions are Georg Seiderer's work on Nuremberg and Würzburg and Malte Thießen's work on Hamburg and Lübeck. See Seiderer, 'Der Luftkrieg im öffentlichen Gedenken'; Thießen, 'Lübeck's "Palmarum" and Hamburg's "Gomorrha"'.

[76] J. Assmann, 'Das kollektive Gedächtnis', pp. 72–7.

[77] Ibid., p. 77; Koselleck, 'Erinnerungsschleusen und Erfahrungsschichten', p. 266.

[78] Marx, *The Eighteenth Brumaire*, p. 15.   [79] Ibid.

communities everywhere turned to the traditions available to them, not unlike their predecessors after 1918.

Recent literature on the cultural ramifications of World War I has rightly pointed towards the continuation of traditional modes of expression, alongside the 'birth of the modern age' (Modris Eksteins), in the crucible of that conflict.[80] The same literature has, however, been too rash in positing a sharp cultural rupture for World War II.[81] The past may have been 'shattered' by Nazism, war and genocide, but it was from this fractured past, this study contends, that local communities attempted to retrieve languages that would give meaning to the experience of airborne disaster. These languages were 'traditional' in the sense that they drew on a well-established canon of classical, Christian and romantic motifs and images that dealt with urban catastrophe.[82] As the Egyptologist Jan Assmann has observed, the lament over the loss of cities forms one of the oldest literary genres of all, which can be traced back as far as the Sumerian civilisation of the third millennium BC.[83] At the same time, and this is the second overarching thesis running through the chapters that follow, traditional languages were transmitted to the present via the nationalist discourse of World War I, in which airborne destruction had played a certain limited role; and, more importantly, via the racialist discourse of National Socialism, which had appropriated them for its own pernicious ends. To put this differently: the traditional languages with which urban communities tried to make sense of the cataclysmic events were far from innocent but bore, to a greater or lesser degree, the ideological imprint of Nazism. Wherever the post-war agents of public discourse turned in their articulation of the experience of aerial warfare, they encountered the sites, practices and narratives of their Nazi predecessors.[84]

In order to untangle the complex relationship between tradition and innovation, continuity and rupture, it is helpful to proceed thematically rather than chronologically. This book breaks down the edifice of a 'memorial culture' into three separate discursive fields or 'vectors', each of which not only prioritised one particular aspect of the experience of area bombing but also brought forth typical media in which this experience was conveyed.[85] Each vector was embedded in a distinct cultural tradition that prescribed the discursive boundaries and limited the choices available to the agents who operated in this area.

---

[80] Winter, *Sites of Memory*, p. 5.   [81] Ibid., p. 9.   [82] Ibid., p. 5.
[83] J. Assmann, 'Die Lebenden und die Toten', pp. 31f. I do not agree with Assmann that Germans after 1945 did not mourn the loss of their cities.
[84] Compare also Thießen, 'Lübeck's "Palmarum" and Hamburg's "Gomorrha"', p. 68.
[85] I have borrowed the term from Wood, *Vectors of Memory*, pp. 5f.

This study proposes to structure the analysis of urban memory cultures thematically around the themes of death, destruction and survival. While chapter 1 sketches the emergence of *lieux de mémoire* in both cities, chapters 2 to 8 trace the trajectories of three important vectors of memory from the 1940s to the mid-1990s. Chapters 2, 3 and 4 look at the evolution of the public commemoration of mass death, whereas chapters 5 and 6 examine the ways in which urban communities tried to come to terms with the legacy of destruction. Chapters 7 and 8 analyse the peculiarities of local history writing on the air war. Finally, the conclusion pulls the various threads together, takes the story up to the early 2000s and seeks to integrate the case studies into a broader picture.

As the 'prototype of cultural memory',[86] the confrontation with death stood at the centre of the first discursive field, and, in many ways, of local memory as a whole.[87] Urban memory of the air war was indistinguishable from the memory of violent mass death, and the cultural practices that urban communities developed in order to commemorate the dead formed the backbone of public memory. Chapters 2, 3 and 4 trace the evolution of public commemorations from their inception as Nazi funeral ceremonies in the 1940s to the fiftieth-anniversary commemorations in the 1990s. In paradigmatic fashion, the diachronic study of public commemoration shows up the extent to which the cultural and political concerns of the present interacted with traditional forms of public mourning in order to answer a set of recurring questions. Why so much death and suffering? Who are the dead, and who are 'we', the commemorators? What 'lessons' do the dead hold for the living?

During the war, Nazism identified the dead both as victims of a crime and as sacrificers for the racial community. By comparison, the Church put the notion of affliction at the centre of its attempts to make sense of what had happened. After 1945, the dead were subsumed under the label of victimhood – of the war, a natural disaster, Anglo-American imperialism and, less frequently, of Nazism or the Germans themselves.

While the experience of violent mass death was crucial to local memory cultures, indiscriminate area raids not only killed people in their thousands but also transformed the familiar cityscape beyond recognition. They robbed the residents of their homes as well as their social and symbolic environments. The confrontation with urban destruction formed the second vector of memory, interwoven with the commemoration of the dead, but revolving around a different set of questions such as: what were the reasons for the destruction of the city? Did the

---

[86] Assmann, *Das kulturelle Gedächtnis*, p. 61.
[87] See Reichel, *Politik mit der Erinnerung*, pp. 17–20.

devastation amount to a catastrophe, or did it, on the contrary, present an opportunity to 'heal' what had long been ailing?

As chapters 5 and 6 argue, local communities drew on the idea of *Heimat* in order to conceptualise the material and social impact of the air war on their cities. During the 1950s and 1960s, the rebuilding effort was framed in terms of *Heimat* lost and *Heimat* regained, whereas from the 1970s, a post-modern critique started to denounce the post-war reconstruction as a 'second' destruction and looked to the pre-war city as a place of nostalgic longing.

Finally, there was the theme of survival, the attempt at telling stories that would convey the experience of ordinary residents under the bombs and explain how 'it really was'. The third discursive field was dominated by the efforts of local journalists, lay historians and eyewitnesses to produce authoritative accounts of the historical events. Here too, different actors in various socio-cultural contexts produced alternative answers to a recurrent set of questions. What was the relationship between local catastrophe and wider developments? How did urban communities experience the cataclysmic events? And finally, who was responsible? As chapters 7 and 8 argue, local histories rarely attempted to provide a critical perspective on the events in question, but generally buttressed up popular notions about the air raid, its causes and consequences. Rather than functioning as a corrective to memory, (local) historiography formed an integral part of the culture from which it emerged.[88]

In order to analyse continuity and change in space and time, this study draws on a wide range of sources and makes use of various methodological approaches. The material analysed extends from the speeches held at funeral ceremonies to the rituals enacted at commemorations; from lyrical *Heimat* poetry to the specialist discourse of urban planning; from the anniversary coverage in the local press to public exhibitions that took the air war as their subject matter. In addition, diaries, letters and other personal, or ego-, documents are used in order to tease out similarities and differences between public representations of the bombing and semi-public or private undercurrents.

---

[88] See Jarausch, 'Zeitgeschichte und Erinnerung'; Hockerts, 'Zugänge zur Zeitgeschichte'.

1   From experience to memory: the emergence of *lieux de mémoire*, 1943–1947

Introduction: what makes a memory place?

In Kassel and Magdeburg, memory of the air war is the memory of catastrophe.[1] At the centre of the cultures of remembrance in the two cities stand devastating fire raids,[2] the RAF attack on Kassel of 22 October 1943 and the RAF raid on Magdeburg of 16 January 1945. The two air raids have given rise to commemoration days that can be understood – in Pierre Nora's famous metaphor – as 'places' or *lieux* in which memory has been 'condensed, embodied or crystallised'.[3] Their annual return forces the two urban communities to return to the experience of aerial warfare, to remember the destruction and to commemorate the dead. In newspaper articles, public ceremonies and exhibitions, but also in personal reminiscences and conversations,[4] the past is relived, imparted with meaning and compared with the present.

How did this happen? Why 22 October and 16 January? How were the multiple experiences of six years of war and numerous air raids telescoped into the memory of a single day? Why did certain stories about the bombing become entrenched in public discourse while others played a marginal role only or were not told at all? To ask such questions is to address the continuities and discontinuities between experience and memory, between individual perceptions and collective representations.[5] This chapter argues that the fire bombings turned into collective *lieux de mémoire* in the months following the cataclysmic events. In Kassel, '22 October 1943' attained the status of a memory place between October 1943 and the summer of 1944, whereas in Magdeburg, the period of

---

[1] See Gray and Oliver (eds.), *Memory of Catastrophe*, pp. 1–18.
[2] For the term, see USSBS, *Fire Raids*.
[3] Nora, *Geschichte und Gedächtnis*, p. 7. Hue-Tam Ho Tai makes a similar point in relation to Verdun in 'Review Essay: Remembered Realms', 906–22, here 919f.
[4] Thießen, 'Der "Feuersturm" im kommunikativen Gedächtnis', p. 319.
[5] Compare Confino, 'Telling about Germany', p. 200.

January 1945 to the summer of 1947 was crucial. In this, the three factors of experience, volition and context played a critical role.

Firstly, there was personal experience. The disruptive impact of fire attacks as carried out by the RAF against Kassel and Magdeburg was such that tens of thousands of people were confronted with circumstances, sense-impressions and perceptions that had a potentially traumatic impact.[6] Even when making allowance for the high degree of day-to-day violence in a brutalised society that was engaged in a total war against the enemy within and without,[7] the experience of huge conflagrations, massive loss of life and wide-scale devastation left indelible traces in the minds of many contemporaries.[8] Collective representations of the air war thus emerged within a multi-layered web of personal memories.[9] While the resulting narratives did not remain static, they were also not malleable at will. Oscillating between the poles of death and survival, rupture and continuity, loss and gain, they revolved around a set of themes that changed little over time.

Although primary experience played an important role, this was not, in itself, sufficient for the emergence of calendrical memory places. Despite the impact of the events on the daily lives of a great number of local residents, there was nothing inevitable about the telescoping of six years of war into a single day. 'At first, there must be a will to commit something to memory,' as Pierre Nora observes.[10] In order to stop the process of forgetting, individuals and/or institutions must make efforts to record the events for posterity and to recreate them, be this through the writing down of personal memories or the celebration of commemorative events.

Finally, there were pre-existing interpretive frames.[11] As Reinhart Koselleck has argued, the experience of World War II was not independent of the mental structures with which people tried to make sense of the myriad sense-impressions and perceptions that they encountered.[12] Nor were these impressions and perceptions immune to the nature of the society that engendered them. In one way or another, they bore the imprint of National Socialist propaganda and reflected the racial, social and gender hierarchies of the Nazified *body politic*.[13] In addition, and in particular

---

[6] Förster and Beck, 'Post-Traumatic Stress Disorder', p. 15.

[7] See Echternkamp, 'Im Kampf'.

[8] See Bessel, 'The Shadow of Death'. See also, with a view to the victims of Nazi extermination politics, Koselleck, 'Formen und Traditionen des negativen Gedächtnisses', p. 23.

[9] Nora, *Geschichte und Gedächtnis*, p. 11.   [10] Ibid., p. 32.

[11] On the concept of the 'frame' see Goffmann, 'Frame Analysis'.

[12] Koselleck, 'Erinnerungsschleusen und Erfahrungsschichten'.

[13] For an instructive comparison of German soldiers' perceptions in World War I and World War II see Latzel, *Deutsche Soldaten – nationalsozialistischer Krieg?*

for a local context, historical tradition played an important role. In this respect, a crucial difference existed between the two cities under consideration here. Whereas in Kassel urban destruction was without parallel in local history, Magdeburg residents could draw on the well-established precedent of the town's near-total destruction in the Thirty Years War of the seventeenth century.[14]

This chapter reconstructs the emergence of collective memory places of the air war. As the first section argues, the difference in time between the two raids had important consequences for memory formation. Whereas in Kassel local catastrophe occurred within the context of a national framework that seemed characterised by a degree of stability, in Magdeburg local disaster formed part of the death throes of Nazi Germany, whose pursuit of a lost war was producing a 'vast zone of death and destruction' all across Europe.[15] In Kassel, the air raid of 22 October 1943 was followed by a long respite in which individuals and local institutions found the time to document primary experiences and to rework memories into narratives.[16] As a consequence, '22 October 1943' was firmly established as a collective *lieu de mémoire* before the war was over. In Magdeburg, by comparison, the raid of 16 January 1945 occurred against the backdrop of a broader cataclysm that left little time for the work of memory. In early 1945, the date denoted just one – albeit particularly terrifying – episode in a chain of events that was transforming the familiar environment beyond recognition.

Looking at the two cities separately, the second section focuses on Kassel while the third deals with Magdeburg. The former argues that by the summer of 1944, the fire bombing had turned into a universally recognisable memory place. The meaning of '22 October', however, remained disputed between official propaganda on the one hand and a semi-public undercurrent of popular opinion on the other. While Nazi propagandists stressed the resilience of the racial community in the face of adversity, many residents emphasised rupture and loss. In Magdeburg, by contrast, '16 January 1945' as a collective *lieu de mémoire* was essentially a post-war creation.

Different contexts

The time-lag of more than one year between the heavy raids on Kassel and Magdeburg led to significant differences in the ways in which the

[14] See Cramer, *The Thirty Years' War and German Memory*, pp. 141–77.
[15] Geyer, 'There is a Land', p. 121.
[16] Hausmann, *Handbuch Notfallpsychologie*, stresses the importance of narrative in coping with traumatic experiences.

two events were experienced and remembered. The attack on Kassel occurred at a time when the destructive impact of the combined bomber offensive was among the primary concerns of German popular opinion, and was causing alarm among municipal as well as state and party elites.[17] In 1943, the incineration of entire city districts by single raids was still a recent development, and nobody knew what the consequences would be for municipal life, morale and the war industry. If the Hamburg raids of July 1943 had shown what area bombing was capable of, then the bombing of Kassel in October 1943 proved that such destruction was repeatable despite strengthened air defences.

In Kassel itself, the attack was followed by a period of relative quiet that lasted close to one year. To be sure, there was a heavy daytime raid by the USAAF on 19 April 1944, but strategic bombing against the city did not recommence in force until September 1944.[18] While the lull in the air war allowed for the reconstruction in the city of a semblance of normality out of chaos, it also threw into sharp relief the rupture that the fire bombing had caused. As one well-informed contemporary observer, the managing director at the Henschel industrial plant, noted on 30 October 1944, one year after the attack, 'So far-reaching have been the consequences of 22 October 1943 for Kassel . . . and for the life of each and every one in this city that the envisaged final report [on the air raid] has had to be postponed over and over again.'[19] Equally important, there were no dramatic changes in the overall military and political situation over the course of the first six months following the attack. The German army throughout the period was retreating on all fronts, but was doing so in an organised fashion without suffering any decisive defeats until the summer of 1944.

The combination of the timing of the attack together with the extraordinarily destructive impact made sure that the bombing of Kassel attracted an unusual degree of attention, not just locally but also at the national level. The response by Joseph Goebbels, Reich propaganda minister and chair of the inter-ministerial committee on air raid damage, was a case

[17] Speer, *Inside the Third Reich*, pp. 363–79, here p. 370. On popular opinion see the confidential mood reports compiled by the SD, reprinted in *Meldungen*, ed. Boberach vols. 13–15. See also StA Stuttgart, Bestand Luftschutz no. 222, 'Luftkriegserfahrungen aus anderen Städten', 3 February 1944. I would like to thank Dr Dietmar Süß for making this document available to me.

[18] A British post-war study divides the air war against Kassel into two phases: the Bomber Command raids of October 1943 and the succession of raids by both air forces from September 1944 until the end of the war. See StAK, S8 B13, 'The Effect of Air Attack on the City and District of Kassel', 21 October 1945, p. 2.

[19] StAK, S3 no. 404, R. A. Fleischer, 'Kassel im Kriege. Erlebnisse aus den Jahren 1943–1945', p. 8.

in point. Goebbels grew so alarmed at early reports of the situation in Kassel, and in particular at the disruption of all communication lines, that on 23 October he sent one of his most trusted aides, Ministerialdirektor Alfred-Ingemar Berndt, to the city in order to obtain first-hand information and to supervise emergency relief.[20] Two weeks later, he visited Kassel personally, where he attended a conference of the civil defence task force (*Gaueinsatzstab*) and gave a speech in front of local party officials.[21] This was the first visit to the city by a high functionary of the Nazi leadership since Hitler's appearance at the Greater German Warrior Day in June 1939. The Goebbels diary contains no fewer than fifteen entries on the raid and its aftermath.[22] Other high dignitaries, such as the transport minister and chairman of the railway network, Julius Dorpmüller, also made trips to the city.[23]

Although the air raid received only limited coverage in the national press, the regional *Kurhessische Landeszeitung* reported extensively on the attack for a period of about four weeks. The articles were written by Nazi propagandists who sought to integrate the catastrophic event into the wider Nazi world view. The same journalists who popularised Nazi ideology were, however, also local residents, whose shock over the devastation resonated even in their propaganda pieces. After 1945/9, some of them would continue to play important roles in local journalism and publishing, and perpetuate slightly altered versions of narratives which they had developed in the service of the Nazi regime.[24] The Protestant Church, too, published a statement that was to be read from pulpits all over the bishopric on Christmas Day 1943. It sought to console the survivors and express hope in the promise of Christ. At the same time, the text was resonant with motifs of Nazi rhetoric, speaking of 'terror' and 'murder'.[25]

---

[20] Goebbels, *Tagebücher* II/10, 24 October 1943, p. 156.

[21] On the visit see 'Reichsminister Dr. Goebbels in Kassel', *KLZ*, 5 November 43, p. 1; 'Terror wird uns zu keiner Zeit beugen', *KLZ*, 6 November 1943, p. 1. The speech is reprinted in Goebbels, *Goebbels-Reden*, vol. II, pp. 259–85.

[22] Goebbels, *Tagebücher* II/10, 23 October 1943, 24 October, 25 October, 26 October, 2 November, 3 November, 6–8 November, 20 December, 23 December, 31 December.

[23] StAK, S3 no. 404, Fleischer, 'Kassel im Kriege', p. 7.

[24] See, for example, G. M. Vonau, 'Bomben auf 1000 Jahre. Terror vernichtete das historische Gesicht Kassels', *KLZ*, 12 November 1943, p. 1; Vonau, 'Zusammenrücken', *KLZ*, 1 November 1943, p. 3; Vonau, 'Zehn Jahre danach', in Helm (ed.), *Kassel vor dem Feuersturm*, 2nd edn (1953); Willi Lindner, 'Stilles Heldentum im Kampf mit dem Tode', *KLZ*, 3 November 1943, p. 4; Lindner, 'Gegen die Unken', *KLZ*, 19 November 1943, p. 4; Lindner, 'Kassel, Leben zwischen Ruinen', *Marburger Presse*, 14 February 1947.

[25] 'Das Licht scheint in der Finsternis', *Kirchliches Amtsblatt* 58/10, 15 December 1943, p. 66.

Contemporary coverage of the attack was not restricted to the (local) Nazi press and the Churches. The air raid also spawned numerous internal reports and a host of private correspondence. One observer, writing a week after the attack, commented on the problems that the delivery of 'mountain heaps' of telegrams and enquiries by concerned relations must cause to the postal service.[26] The increase in the production of red tape was not unusual in itself. It was a consequence of official regulations, which required all agencies involved in air raid protection, from the chief of police down to individual air raid wardens, to file reports on their activities. Meanwhile, the desire on the part of ordinary residents to inform friends and relatives about their whereabouts seems only too understandable. What was remarkable, however, was the extraordinary care and attention that often went into the creation of these documents, resulting in a wealth of detailed official accounts, private letters, poetry and photographs. Between 22 October 1943 and the summer of 1944, local party and state functionaries as well as private individuals produced a set of visual and textual representations of the air raid on which 'memory workers' of subsequent years could draw.[27]

The response of Dr Karl Paetow (1904–93) was certainly extraordinary but not altogether untypical. An art historian by trade, Paetow had worked as Kassel's official municipal historian since 1935, in which position he had blended a cultural historical approach with National Socialist racial ideology.[28] In the aftermath of 22 October 1943, Paetow was put in charge of the Enquiry Office for the Missing (*Vermisstensuchstelle*), a newly established agency that collected information about people who had gone missing during the attack and functioned as a first port of call for concerned relatives. In this position, Paetow engaged in what was an early exercise in oral history. He instructed his employees to refer to his desk people who had 'particularly harrowing . . . stories' to tell, and wrote 'everything down as they spoke', as Paetow explained forty years after the event in a letter to a publishing house. In the same letter, he claimed to have acted on his own initiative in order 'to record the terrible events of the bombing night . . . for history'.[29] Whether or not this was a post-war rationalisation that glossed over contemporary instructions by the Nazi city authorities is impossible to say, but Paetow's efforts did

---

[26] StAK, S3 no. 404, Fleischer, 'Kassel im Kriege', p. 7.
[27] See StAK, S8 C40–48 for official situation reports, S8 C51 for private correspondence, S8 C53 for fictional representations; StAK, photo archive and IWM London, Photograph Archive, GSA 387 for photographs.
[28] See StAK, A.4.41 no. 455, Karl Paetow, 'Drei Jahre Stadtforschung', no date [1938]. Compare also StAK, S1 no. 3114, Karl Paetow.
[29] BGM Kassel, NL Paetow, Mappe LXII, fo. 1, Paetow to Lektorat Motorbuch Verlag, no date [1981].

result in the production, in the spring and summer of 1944, of more than one hundred eyewitness accounts that recorded the experiences of ordinary Kasselaner in the air raid. By the time Paetow tried (unsuccessfully) to have the collection published in 1981, they had long functioned as memory artefacts and selectively been drawn upon by journalists and local historians as seemingly authentic 'survivors' reports'.[30]

Ordinary residents, too, engaged in memory work. They carefully kept letters and postcards which they had received from friends and relatives. Some would secretly take photographs of the burning city and the smouldering ruins, while the bereaved erected makeshift crosses on the ruins in order to commemorate the loss of their loved ones.[31] One resident cut out thousands of death notices from the regional daily, the *Kurhessische Landeszeitung*, and put them in a Nazi propaganda book about the years 1918–34. Was this a pragmatic decision, or was the person making an ironic comment on the 'glory' of the Thousand Year Reich?[32] Even more remarkable, perhaps, was the popular success of the anonymous poem 'Thus Died My Home Town', which has been discussed in the introduction above.

When Magdeburg was subjected to an area attack in January 1945 on the scale suffered by Kassel fifteen months earlier, the broader political context was much less conducive to the production of memory artefacts. By January 1945, hundreds of cities had been levelled by RAF Bomber Command, and devastating incendiary attacks were a frequent occurrence. In contrast to Kassel, the raid on Magdeburg was not followed by a lull in the air war that would have allowed people to reflect on their experiences and work them into narratives. On the contrary, the area attack ushered in a period of intense warfare that was characterised by further heavy raids and constant alarms. This in turn was followed, in April 1945, by weeks of ground fighting in the city itself.

The air raid of 16 January 1945 coincided with the launching of a major offensive by the Red Army on the Eastern Front. 'The Eastern Front in Flames', screamed the headline of the *Völkischer Beobachter* on 16 January.[33] For once, this was no exaggeration. The offensive marked the decisive breakthrough for the anti-Hitler coalition; it ushered in the downfall of the Third Reich. As Rüdiger Overmans has shown in a careful

---

[30] This was also the title of the fiftieth-anniversary publication, *Überlebensberichte*. Recently the freelance historian Jörg Friedrich has made use of the accounts in *Brandstätten*, p. 240.

[31] For examples of sites of memory erected on the rubble see StAK, Fotoarchiv, Gedenkstätten auf Trümmern.

[32] StAK, S8 C62, 'Die Nachkriegszeit 1918–1934. Todesanzeigen Terrorangriff 22. Oktober 1943'.

[33] 'Die Ostfront in Flammen', *Völkischer Beobachter*, 16 January 1945 (Berlin edition), p. 1.

study of German military losses, January 1945 was the deadliest month of the entire war, leaving a staggering death toll of no fewer than 450,000 Wehrmacht soldiers.[34] Three months later, the greater part of Magdeburg, which was situated west of the river Elbe, had been occupied by American troops, who were replaced by British occupation forces at the end of May, who in turn made way for the Soviets in July.[35]

Against the backdrop of a dramatically deteriorating military situation, the air raid attracted very limited attention from outside the region. Unlike Dresden a month later, the destruction of Magdeburg in January 1945 was not depicted as a 'symbol of resistance' against the allied onslaught.[36] The Wehrmacht bulletin spoke of a 'terror attack' that had destroyed 'mainly residential areas' but no details were given in the national media.[37] There was no concerted propaganda campaign at the hands of the propaganda ministry. In Goebbels' diary, the raid was mentioned only twice.[38]

While the internal reports on Kassel in October 1943 had been marked by extraordinary attention to detail, Magdeburg in January 1945 elicited no more than routine responses. The summary 'experience report' by the Kassel chief of police had consisted of fifty-one pages; the 'final report' by his Magdeburg counterpart numbered only two.[39] The regional Nazi press, too, showed none of the interest that it had taken in Kassel fifteen months earlier, and would take again in Dresden the following month. While there was the obligatory stock-in-trade of National Socialist propaganda – the denunciation of the air raid as a crime, public praise for the 'proud bearing' of the population and promises of party assistance – the press depicted the raid as an unexceptional, almost ordinary occurrence. As a leader's comment put it in the regional daily, *Der Mitteldeutsche*, on 18 January 1945: 'Life goes on, even if the worries have become greater. Recently we reported on a trip to the west. What we are going through over here right now has been happening over there every day for months and years.'[40]

---

[34] Overmans, *Deutsche militärische Verluste*, pp. 237–9.

[35] Compare Heidelmayer, 'Magdeburg 1945', pp. 112–44; Schmiechen-Ackermann, 'Magdeburg als Stadt des Schwermaschinenbaus', pp. 812f. For contemporary responses to the Soviet offensive see Kempowski, *Das Echolot. Fuga furiosa*.

[36] Rudolf Sparing, 'Der Tod von Dresden. Ein Leuchtzeichen des Widerstandes', *Das Reich*, 4 March 1945. On the propaganda campaign more generally and its impact on post-war memory see Neutzner, 'Vom Alltäglichen zum Exemplarischen'.

[37] *Berichte des Oberkommandos der Wehrmacht*, vol. V, 17 January 1945, p. 480.

[38] Goebbels, *Tagebücher* II/15, 18 January 1945; 21 January 1945.

[39] For a copy of the report see NA II RG 243 E6 # 39 9 (box 383). The summary report does contain a lengthy appendix with a list of damaged buildings and industries.

[40] 'Zupacken', *Der Mitteldeutsche*, 18 January 1945, p. 1.

A comparison of confidential mood reports on Kassel and Magdeburg further underlines the extent to which different contexts influenced
processes of memory formation. In his report of 9 December 1943,
the provincial high court judge (*Oberlandesgerichtspräsident*) for Kassel
averred that 'the impact of the heaviest terror raid on any German city
so far overshadows everything else'.[41] Two months later, the situation
was not much changed, according to a report by the provincial attorney
general (*Generalstaatsanwalt*): 'In comparison to the two terror raids and
their far-reaching effects on the population and the administration, other
events in my district have naturally taken a back seat.'[42] By the end of
April, the provincial high court judge stressed that the overall situation
in the district was still very much affected by the consequences of the
'terror raid of 22 October 1943'.[43] By contrast, the provincial attorney
general for Magdeburg wrote in a report despatched only a fortnight after
16 January 1945, 'The recent military events on the Eastern Front have
created a situation against which all previous difficulties and crises recede
in the background and fade.'[44] On the bombing, all the attorney general
had to say was that 'life and work go on as normal, even in places like
Dessau and Magdeburg, where the recent heavy terror raids have caused
considerable damage and disruption'.[45]

Considering the dramatically altered context in the spring of 1945, it is
little surprise that comparatively few contemporary records survive from
Magdeburg. Despite the efforts by several generations of local historians,
no more than a handful of reports, letters and diary entries were discovered. In view of the acceleration of events, it is perhaps more than mere
coincidence that at least one diary from Magdeburg breaks off altogether
in early 1944. The writer, a middle-class academic who, in September
1939, had blamed Britain for the outbreak of war and by January 1944
still put faith in the Nazi leadership, did not return to his diary until early
1947. By this time, the fire bombing featured prominently in his summary account of the past three years.[46] The first collection of eyewitness
reports was not compiled until the autumn of 1950, at a time when the
SED regime had discovered the propaganda value of the air war in the
new global confrontation of the Cold War.[47]

---

[41] BA Berlin, R 3001/3371, fo. 130, 'Lagebericht des Oberlandesgerichtspräsidenten',
9 December 1943.
[42] Ibid., fo. 138.   [43] Klein (ed.), *Lageberichte*, p. 108.
[44] BA Berlin, R 3001/3380, fos. 131f., 'Lagebericht des Generalstaatsanwalts', 29 January
1945.
[45] Ibid.   [46] StAM, ZG 122.6 (9), Tagebuch Dr. Trimborn.
[47] StAM, ZG 55.3, Akte 16. Januar.

The evidence suggests that by the spring of 1945 the memory cultures of the air war stood at different developmental stages. In Kassel, the air raid of 22 October 1943 was well established as a local *lieu de mémoire*. In Magdeburg, by contrast, the raid of 16 January 1945 had not yet spawned its own memory culture, but was just one – albeit particularly terrifying – episode in the upheavals that engulfed the local community in the final phase of the war.

Yet what was the experiential foundation of memory, and what was the relationship between individual experiences and broader narratives? Whose stories mattered in the construction of memory places, and whose voices were marginalised? The following sections will analyse the immediate responses to the big air raids and reconstruct the emergence of a set of themes that stood at the centre of the evolving memory cultures.

Kassel and the air raid of 22 October 1943

During the war, the most powerful agent of memory was the Nazi regime. With control over the official channels of information, Nazi propagandists stood in a unique position to influence public responses to the air war. Not only did they offer an interpretive framework that helped to structure experiences, they also furnished the very idiom with which to talk about events that, with the exception of the rather limited air raids of World War I, colonial uprisings and the Spanish Civil War, were without precedent before the onset of World War II. The National Socialist authorities had a variety of media at their disposal to underline their interpretation of the air war, including the press, rallies, exhibitions and commemorations, not to speak of the coercive means to suppress dissenting voices. Yet, even before the escalation of strategic bombing in the spring of 1942, official propaganda did not go unchallenged but was contested by semi-public voices that drew heavily on pre-war apocalyptic fantasies of airborne destruction.[48] In a way, stories of urban catastrophe had arrived long before the bombs themselves.[49] By the summer of 1943, they were steadily fed in cities such as Kassel by a trickle of rumours about the experiences of people who had been subjected to area bombing elsewhere.[50] This section briefly surveys the main themes of Nazi propaganda. It then zooms in on the air raid of 22 October 1943,

---

[48] On the pre-war imagination see Fritzsche, 'Machine Dreams'; Fritzsche, *A Nation of Fliers*; Süß, 'Tod aus der Luft', p. 44.

[49] Compare Saint-Amour, 'Air War Prophecy and Interwar Modernism', 158.

[50] On the impact of eyewitness accounts on 'morale' as registered by the SD see Boberach, 'Auswirkungen'; and on popular opinion more generally, Steinert, *Hitlers Krieg*; Stöver, *Volksgemeinschaft*.

identifies the propaganda response and examines semi-public undercurrents of popular opinion.

National Socialist propaganda and the air war

The war in the skies over the Reich was not a war that the National Socialist regime wanted to fight; it was a war that was forced upon it. Not only did the air war swallow up vast material and human resources that were desperately needed elsewhere.[51] Exposing the vulnerability of the German homeland and the helplessness of the regime, strategic bombing also posed something of a dilemma for propaganda, as Joseph Goebbels himself acknowledged repeatedly.[52] Nazi propagandists responded to the challenge in a haphazard fashion, oscillating between outrage, 'realism' and denial.[53] Underlying this response was an attempt to counter that which German analysts considered to be the primary objective of strategic bombing: the undermining of German civilian morale. As the confidential press directives issued by Reich Press Chief Otto Dietrich explained on 5 March 1943, 'The press must react to the systematic terror raids against German cities, which are aimed at the weakening [Zermürbung] of the German people, with the opposite strategy: the strengthening of communal bonds among the population and the doubling of hatred against the enemy.'[54] To this end, three themes were employed, which for the sake of analytical clarity may be identified as 'crime', 'community of fate' and 'war'.[55]

With the onset of indiscriminate bombing in the spring of 1942, National Socialist propaganda focused on the allegedly criminal nature of the allied conduct of the air war.[56] The air raids were denounced as *Terrorangriffe* or 'terror attacks' which aimed to destroy German (and, indeed, European) *Kultur* and to slaughter women and children.[57] According to a press directive from 12 March 1943, British pilots were in future to be

---

[51] Overy, *Why the Allies Won*, pp. 101–33.

[52] Compare Boelcke (ed.), '*Wollt ihr den totalen Krieg?*', p. 231; Goebbels, *Tagebücher* II/7, 14 March 1943, 16 March 1943, 20 March 1943.

[53] See the quantitative analysis compiled by the USSBS, 'Percentage of Space (or Time) Given by German Newspapers (or Radio) to Air War', in NA II RG 243 E 6 # 64b g (2) (box 580).

[54] BA Koblenz, ZsG 109/41, fo. 71, 'Vertrauliche Informationen 57/43', 5 March 1943.

[55] See the post-war analysis by the USSBS, *Effects of Strategic Bombing on German Morale*, vol. I, pp. 73–9.

[56] Compare BA Berlin, R55/20898, fos. 43–51, 'Pressekonferenzen im Reichspropagandaministerium', 30 March 1942, 31 March 1942.

[57] BA Berlin, NS 18/1058, fo. 110, 'Propagandistische Auswertung des Angriffs auf Köln', 30 June 1943; BA Berlin, NS 18/772, fos. 1–8, 'Behandlung des Luftkriegs in der Propaganda', 1943. See also the booklet by Winkelnkemper, *Der Großangriff auf Köln*.

labelled 'arsonists' only.[58] In practice, the press also applied the tags of 'gangster' and 'pirate of the air', which all served to recast military operations as criminal activities.[59] While the general outline of this theme is well known, its specifically anti-Semitic dimension has only recently been studied more fully.[60] According to Nazi propaganda, the strategic air war was no mere atrocity; it was part of a 'war of annihilation' that 'World Jewry' had forced upon the German people.[61] It was no coincidence, therefore, that when Joseph Goebbels, in the summer of 1942, spoke publicly about the 'extermination of the Jewish race in Europe and beyond', he did so in the context of an article that dealt with the air war.[62] 'Behind the bombing terror of our enemies lies the irreconcilable Jewish hatred against German life,' as the Nazi district leader of *Magdeburg-Anhalt*, Rudolf Jordan, declared in typical fashion in January 1944.[63] The term 'terror attack' carried more than the prima facie connotation of an '(air) attack aimed at terrorizing the population'; it formed the semantic bridge between the allied air war and the phantasm of 'the Jew'.[64]

While the overall intention of the theme of 'air war as crime' – the vilification of the enemy as a reinforcing bond for the racial 'community of fate' – seems clear enough, three points are worth noting. Firstly, Nazi propaganda pursued the so-called 'guilt question' with great confidence,[65] engaging and dismissing the argument that the Luftwaffe had initiated area bombing by its raids on Warsaw and Rotterdam in 1939/40. Secondly, in day-to-day propaganda, a curious discrepancy developed between the theme's overall content and the prioritisation of the cultural over the human costs of the air war. This was in part because Goebbels was extremely concerned that too realistic a depiction of the horrors of aerial warfare would spread panic among the population, with devastating consequences for the reputation of the Nazi leadership.[66]

---

[58] BA Koblenz, ZsG 109/41, fo. 88, 'Vertrauliche Informationen 63/43', 12 March 1943.
[59] Compare, for example, *Völkischer Beobachter* (Berlin edition), 3 March 1943, 14 March 1943, 31 March 1943, 7 April 1943, 11 April 1943, 30 April 1943, 18 May 1943, 27 May 1943, 30 May 1943, 2 June 1943, 8 June 1943, 9 June 1943, 19 June 1943, 20 June 1943, 30 June 1943, 2 July 1943, 7 July 1943, 20 July 1943; *Magdeburgische Zeitung*, 24 January 1944; *Der Mitteldeutsche*, 23 January 1944, 6 February 1944.
[60] Stargardt, 'Opfer der Bomben'; Herf, *The Jewish Enemy*.
[61] See, for example, Hans Schlitzberger, 'Warum? Juda und die modernen Vernichtungskriege', *KLZ*, 18 November 1944.
[62] Joseph Goebbels, 'Luft- und Nervenkrieg', p. 350.
[63] Gauleiter Rudolf Jordan, 'Der Bombenkrieg', *Der Mitteldeutsche*, 23 January 1944.
[64] See also Seibert, 'Der jüdische Krieg', *Völkischer Beobachter*, 2 June 1943; Hans Schlitzberger, 'Der jüdische Terror', *KLZ*, 13 October 1943.
[65] BA Koblenz, ZsG 109/41, fo. 71, 'Vertrauliche Informationen 57/43', 5 March 1943.
[66] BA Berlin, NS 18/1333, fos. 73–5, 'Propagandamaßnahmen im Zusammenhang mit dem Luftkrieg', 28 June 1943.

Finally, Nazi coverage was anti-cyclical: the impact of comparatively minor raids of the early years was dramatised whereas the heavy area attacks of later years went comparatively underreported.

The theme of 'air war as crime' played an important role in domestic propaganda, but it was not the only contextualisation. The second theme can be labelled 'community of fate'. This frame was self-consciously modelled, albeit with characteristically National Socialist inflections, on the example of British domestic propaganda during the German Blitz of 1940/1 when, in Goebbels' view, the heroism of the population had been put at the centre of the reporting and a 'myth' been made out of the city of London.[67] Accordingly, the air war was conceptualised as a supreme test of resilience, as a chance for the local community to show their mettle and prove themselves equal to the example of the soldiers fighting at the front.[68] It was expressed in characteristic fashion by the Nazi district leader of Kurhesse, Karl Weinrich, on the occasion of a party-organised funeral service in early August 1943: 'If, however, we prove worthy in this hour and counter the brutal will of annihilation of our enemies with a defiant "in spite of everything", then we will overcome these difficult hours and harvest after victory the sweetest fulfilment of our being.'[69] As the conditional sentence structure indicates, there were inscribed in this theme echoes of the deep suspicion of the Nazi movement towards the civilian in war – the trauma of November 1918. Far from undermining morale, the indiscriminate nature of the bombing served to draw regime and people closer together, or so the propagandists wanted to make their audiences (and themselves) believe.[70] The ability, and indeed, willingness of Germans to sacrifice property and life for the 'interests of the *Reich* and the entire *Volksgemeinschaft*' became the yardstick against which the commitment to the war effort was measured.[71]

Finally, propaganda was at pains to point out that there was still a war being fought in the skies over the Reich, a war that German fighter planes and anti-aircraft guns were winning by causing the enemy bomber planes insufferable losses; and a war whose course would change

---

[67] Boelcke (ed.), '*Wollt Ihr den totalen Krieg*', pp. 269f., 11 August 1942.

[68] 'Magdeburg bestand die erste Probe der Bewährung', *Magdeburgische Zeitung*, 24 January 1944; 'Magdeburgs Bevölkerung hat sich bewährt', *Der Mitteldeutsche*, 23 January 1944; 'Heimat in höchster Bereitschaft', *Magdeburgische Zeitung*, 12 May 1944.

[69] 'Durch Opfer zum Sieg', *KLZ*, 5 August 1943.

[70] Compare Rudolf Jordan, 'Der Bombenkrieg', *Der Mitteldeutsche*, 23 January 1944; Jordan, 'Warum das alles? Gedanken über die Möglichkeit der Luftschutzbereitschaft in der Heimat', *Der Mitteldeutsche*, 6 January 1944. On the 'trauma' of November 1918 see Bessel, *Nazism and War*, pp. 7–34.

[71] Compare Hans Hertel, 'Die größere Opferfähigkeit', *KLZ*, 16 August 1943, pp. 1f.; Joseph Goebbels, 'Führen wir einen totalen Krieg?', *Das Reich*, 2 July 1944, pp. 1f.

dramatically once the fabled secret weapons were ready to wreak retaliation on Britain.[72] As late as February 1945, the regional daily for Magdeburg, *Der Mitteldeutsche*, produced a headline which claimed that no fewer
than 1,389 enemy 'terror bombers' had been shot down in the previous
month.[73]

> *'Let hatred be our watchword': the propagandistic treatment of the*
> *fire raid on Kassel*

In the national media,[74] the area attack on Kassel received very limited
coverage only.[75] On 23 October 1943, the German High Command
spoke in the daily communiqué of a 'heavy terror raid against the city
of Kassel'. Emphasis was placed on damage to 'residential districts',
while 'losses among the population' were acknowledged but no figures
were given. The communiqué claimed that forty-eight bombers had been
shot down.[76] Three days later, a short article in the *Völkische Beobachter*
stressed the success of the German air defences in the battle over the
city.[77] That was all.

By comparison, for the local media to ignore an air raid that had
destroyed much of the urban environment and killed thousands of residents was not an option. The attack and its impact dominated local
press coverage throughout the early autumn of 1943. The very fact that a
'joint emergency edition' could be published at all was just as important
as the content of the reporting. It underlined the central message that
the regime intended to send out to the population: this was a message
of new beginnings in the face of catastrophe. The newspaper not only
provided a channel of information through which emergency relief measures could be relayed to the population, such as where to obtain food,
clothing, documents and the like.[78] It was also crucial for demonstrating
to the population that the Nazi authorities were coping and in control.[79]
In contrast to the communiqué by the German High Command, the
local media made no attempt to gloss over the scale of the devastation.
Adopting a posture of hard realism, they spoke of the 'vast sea of debris'

---

[72] Compare, for example, *KLZ*, 11 October 1943, p. 1; 12 October 1943, p. 1; 16/17
October 1943, p. 1. On retaliation propaganda see Kirwin, 'Waiting for Retaliation'.
[73] *Der Mitteldeutsche*, 6 February 1945, p. 1.
[74] 'Hass muss die Parole sein' ('Let hatred be our watchword'), in 'Terror wird uns zu
keiner Zeit beugen!', *KLZ*, 6/7 November 1943, p. 2.
[75] StAK, S8 B2, Britische Geheimdienstberichte über Kassel.
[76] *Berichte des Oberkommandos der Wehrmacht*, vol. IV, pp. 259f.
[77] 'London gibt 44 Verluste beim Angriff auf Kassel zu', *Völkischer Beobachter*, 26 October
1943.
[78] Compare, for example, 'Hier gibt es Verpflegung!' and 'Einsatzfähige Lebensmit-
telgeschäfte', both *KLZ*, 26 October 1943.
[79] Compare *KLZ*, 25 October 1943, p. 1; *KLZ*, 28 October 1943, *passim*.

that Kassel had become, and on one occasion at least, 'of many thousands of deaths'.[80] The term 'disaster' was employed several times in order to describe the impact of the attack on the city.[81] Unlike in Hamburg the previous July, there appears to have been no intervention from above to avoid any such diction.[82] Yet, while catastrophe was acknowledged, the emphasis of the reporting rested elsewhere.

A close look at the front page of the first 'joint emergency issue' can help to identify the main themes by which local propaganda hoped to regain control over the situation. The page headline was borrowed from the High Command communiqué and read, 'The heavy terror raid on Kassel – forty-eight enemy bombers shot down last night'. In addition to the full communiqué, and in accordance with a confidential directive on 'the deployment of the press after heavy air raids' dating from August 1942,[83] the page featured a proclamation by the district leader and two editorials. There was also a report on developments on the Eastern Front. Taken together, the articles employed all of the three propaganda themes explored above. While the headline stressed the success of the air defences, the district leader denounced the attack as criminal and promised that the Nazi party would do everything in its power to assist the suffering 'racial comrades'. Meanwhile, the editorial by Rolf Seutter von Loetzen insisted that the population had passed the test of resilience, averring that 'in spite of everything . . . our courage and our will are unbroken'. The second editorial viewed present developments through the lens of the recent past: it compared the bombing war to the mass unemployment of the Weimar Republic, and emphasised that redress for the material losses suffered in the bombing was inextricably linked to a victorious outcome of the war.[84]

In the days that followed, the Nazi press wove the individual threads into broader patterns of meaning in which the air raid took on a cathartic quality. In his editorial 'Madmen' (*Amokläufer*), leading propagandist Hans Schlitzberger readily conceded that the fire raid had devoured 'bodies . . . , apartment flats, churches, castles and monuments'. But he was adamant that the attack had failed to exterminate the 'spirit' out of which all of this had grown. On the contrary, the cataclysmic event had welded together individuals into a community that

---

[80] 'Terror wird uns zu keiner Zeit beugen!', *KLZ*, 6/7 October 1943, p. 1.

[81] 'Kasseler Volksgenossen!', *KLZ*, 25 October 1943, p. 1; 'Anordnung des Kreisleiters', *KLZ*, 26 October 1943, p. 1; 'Der neue Anfang', *KLZ*, 6/7 October 1943, p. 1.

[82] The term was banned in December 1943. See Blank, 'Kriegsalltag und Luftkrieg', p. 373.

[83] BA Koblenz, ZsG 109/36, fos. 83f., 'Vertrauliche Informationen, 219/42 (1. Erg.)', 26 August 1942.

[84] On the significance of the Nazi promise of material redress for the cohesion of the home front see Süß, 'Nationalsozialistische Deutungen', pp. 102–4.

was held together not only by bonds of solidarity but also by 'flames of hatred': 'Nobody knew one week ago how much he hated the enemy. Now everybody knows,' Schlitzberger averred. He went on to claim that Britain stood accused of 'atrocities that bear no comparison in world history'. It was not Great Britain, however, for which he reserved his most venomous comments, but the phantasm of 'the Jew'. With reference to allied declarations about a forthcoming Big Three meeting at Tehran, he concluded: 'About the true aims of our enemies others might be deceived; but they won't deceive us, for we have looked in the true face of our enemy, we have looked in the despicable grimace of the Jew.'[85] Not only had the air raid made soldiers out of civilians, it had also opened their eyes to the necessity of leading a war of annihilation against the Jews. There was no end, just a new beginning – these were the central lessons that Nazi propaganda wanted the population to learn from the cataclysmic event.[86]

Yet there was a fundamental problem with this propaganda response to airborne catastrophe in Kassel. For while local Nazi leaders lavished praise on the population, the leaders themselves were found wanting by their superiors. Whereas the civilian population had passed the trial of strength, Nazi district leader Karl Weinrich in particular had failed. This at least was the opinion of Propaganda Minister Goebbels, who in his diary spoke of 'dreadful conditions' in Kassel where things had been 'allowed to slip'. Weinrich, who had sustained an eye injury during the raid trying to save his own house from the flames, cut an 'appalling' (*jämmerlich*) figure – he was 'utterly helpless', a 'complete failure', as Goebbels recorded.[87] Although Weinrich in the aftermath of the raid tried to make good his reputation by presenting himself as a man of action who exercised strong leadership – a series of photographs shows him at the head of rubble clearance detachments and talking to residents – it was too late (Fig. 2).[88] Goebbels had secured Hitler's ear on Weinrich's alleged failure, and after another intervention with the powerful head of the party chancellery, Martin Bormann, Weinrich was forced to step down. To save face, Weinrich declared publicly on 22 November that the Führer had granted him a 'lengthy recreational vacation', but according to a mood report by the provincial high court judge, most people well understood that Weinrich had left for good.[89]

[85] Hans Schlitzberger, 'Amokläufer', *KLZ*, 27 October 1943, p. 1.
[86] See also Hans Schlitzberger, 'Der neue Anfang', *KLZ*, 6 November 1943, p. 1.
[87] Goebbels, *Tagebücher* II/10, 23 October 1943, 25 October 1943.
[88] See the collection in StAK, photo archive.
[89] *KLZ*, 22 November 1943; Klein (ed.), *Lageberichte*, p. 103. Weinrich's case was not helped by the findings of an official enquiry that was launched some time after his

Figure 2. Nazi district leader Weinrich, to the left, reviewing the progress of the mass burial in the main cemetery. Shortly afterwards, he was deposed. Notice in the background the Italian POWs who were made to dig the graves (1943).

'Kassel is no more!': semi-public voices

What was the impact of this propaganda rhetoric on the city population of Kassel? To what extent did the conceptualisations of Nazi propaganda, which dominated the public sphere, structure the experience of allied bombing, and survive, perhaps in slightly altered form, into the post-war years? The evidence from documents that provide insights into the ways in which ordinary residents recorded and communicated their experiences, such as diaries, letters and eyewitness accounts, suggests that propaganda was both successful and a failure. It was successful in so far as many residents seem to have made the Nazi idiom their own and to have accepted key elements of the National Socialist conceptualisation of the air war. Yet, at the same time, Nazi propaganda was singularly unsuccessful in establishing an overarching framework into which

dismissal. In his diary, Goebbels spoke of 'shocking' revelations and commented acidly, 'What Weinrich got up to in the leadership of his Gau simply beggars description. We have got rid of a real *wash-out*.' See Goebbels, *Tagebücher* II/10, 31 December 1943.

a host of harrowing and often disparate experiences could be integrated meaningfully.[90] While many people, for want of an alternative idiom, used the term 'terror raid' and shared in the condemnation of the enemy as criminal, they found little consolation in such invective. To many residents, the wholesale destruction of the spatial and social environment signified not catharsis but death. While propaganda dwelt on resilience and new beginnings, many residents saw nothing but rupture and loss.

Underneath the veneer of official propaganda, the area attack was frequently conceptualised as a catastrophe that had violently torn asunder continuities in time, space and identity. Yet the ubiquitous use of the term should not obscure the fact that 'catastrophe' could mean different things to different people. At the risk of oversimplification, individual perceptions and responses may be typified according to the categories of place, function, gender and race.

Firstly, there was the spatial dimension, the nature of the locality in which the individual experienced the raid – on the street, in a bunker, a public shelter or a tenement basement – and the relative proximity of this place to the epicentre of the bombing in the old town. Secondly, political persuasions and assigned duties in the civil defence organisation mattered. A trained air raid warden who was expected to secure the survival of the 'shelter community' through the exercise of strong leadership experienced the bombing differently from an elderly couple who were enjoined to follow the orders that they were given. A committed National Socialist was likely to put a different gloss on events than would an old Social Democrat. Closely related were gender roles and expectations, for while women on occasion assumed very active roles in civil defence, they were, in accordance with traditional ideas about femininity, generally considered by their male compatriots to be especially susceptible to nervous breakdowns. Finally, and cutting across all the other distinctions, there was the racial dimension in the 'racial state' that was the Third Reich. Access to bunkers and public air raid shelters, for example, was forbidden to Jews and Eastern workers,[91] while detachments of concentration camp inmates and (after the exit of Italy from the war in September 1943) Italian POWs were regularly deployed for the clearance of unexploded bombs and the retrieval of corpses.

---

[90] For an instructive exploration of the ways in which propaganda messages are critically appropriated by their recipients, see Bussemer, *Propaganda und Populärkultur*.

[91] Blank, 'Kriegsalltag und Luftkrieg', p. 409. But compare BA Berlin, R 55/447, fos. 57f., 'LK-Mitteilung no. 26', 19 August 1943, which stipulates that there are 'no special regulations, in particular no bans', with regard to the access of 'foreign workers' to bunkers and public air raid shelters.

The view from the outside

One of the most revealing ego-documents is a detailed war diary by Gebhard Niemeyer, a sixteen-year-old, middle-class grammar school pupil from Kassel.[92] This young man had been called up in February 1943 to serve as an auxiliary following Hitler's decree on the deployment of German youth at the home front.[93] Together with his fellow class-mates, Niemeyer was stationed at a heavy anti-aircraft defence system near the village of Niedervellmar just to the north of Kassel. Niemeyer was a prolific diarist who supplemented his daily notes with press cut-tings and lengthy excerpts from the Nazi press. Judging from the diary, the young man harboured no qualms about Germany's war, which he regarded as a mixture of personal adventure and rite of passage into adulthood.

On several occasions, Niemeyer entered upon detailed reflections on events deemed of particular importance. One such event was the air raid of 22 October 1943 and its aftermath, to which he devoted no fewer than thirty-two pages. Personally, the raid constituted something of a triumph for the young auxiliary, who for the first time participated in an enemy engagement as a soldier on active duty. His pride and elation at the suc-cessful 'baptism of fire' echoed strongly in his diary, where he described the sight of burning enemy aircraft as 'the proudest moment'.[94] Initially, Niemeyer watched the spectacle of the burning city with a mixture of awe and fascination, without being too worried about the fate of his parents and sister who lived in the Upper New Town (*Oberneustadt*). Yet a sense of unease grew the following morning when Niemeyer heard rumours that the chief of the Luftwaffe, Field Marshal Hermann Goering, was planning to visit the city – an unmistakable sign that the attack must have been very heavy indeed. When, later in the morning, he learned about the scale of the destruction in his immediate neighbourhood, he grew alarmed and applied for special leave to search for his parents. Together with a friend, Niemeyer embarked on a journey into the city, entering from the north and travelling south-westward on the periphery of the zone of devastation before crossing into the epicentre of the attack, where he found his home at Königstor 32 burnt out but his family alive

---

[92] StAK, S8 E15, diary Gebhard Niemeyer. Excerpts have been published in Dettmar, *Zerstörung*, pp. 210–13.

[93] For the background, see Noakes (ed.), *Nazism*, pp. 409–15.

[94] A British operational analysis attributed the loss of forty-two aircraft to fighter inter-ception rather than to flak. See NA, Kew AIR 14/413, Operational Research Section, report no. 89: 'Analysis of Navigation – Raid against Kassel October 22/23rd, 1943'.

and well.[95] Niemeyer's account of this journey, of what he saw, smelt and felt, is worth looking at in some detail, for it contains key elements of a semi-public discourse of which the emphasis differed markedly from the official coverage in the Nazi press.

As the young man approached the city on a country road, the first thing that struck his eye was the sight of a trail of refugees coming in his direction, 'dishevelled, the eyes reddened', 'a terrible sight', as he remarked. This was followed by disbelief at what his senses recorded as he entered the city. With obsessive detail Niemeyer chronicled the material destruction that he encountered, diligently recording every devastated street and every ruined landmark:

I only mention these single buildings by name because they used to be familiar landmarks, but don't believe that they are the only sites of destruction, no, everything! . . . I pass through the Untere Königsstraße, and my blood runs cold: death and destruction! More and more I reach the conclusion: Kassel is no more! In a single dreadful night, Kassel has been razed to the ground![96]

This sense of rupture, finality almost, expressed by Niemeyer through the exclamation 'Kassel is no more!', found an echo in many private accounts of the time. Georg B., for example, witnessed the raid from the distance of the nearby village of Oberkaufungen, where he spent long hours of painful uncertainty over the fate of his wife and child, who he feared (wrongly, as it turned out) had been killed. In his account, Georg B. emphasised the overwhelming impression that the devastation had made on him, speaking of the 'annihilation' (*Vernichtung*) of 'our beautiful city of Kassel'. Similarly, a letter from a father to his son opened with the line, 'Kassel used to be [*sic*] a beautiful little town – we must say today. Dear Karl, Kassel has been annihilated.'[97] Interestingly, another writer invoked the devastation in the Soviet Union as a point of comparison to underline her claim that 90 per cent of Kassel had been 'annihilated, a dead city': 'Soldiers on leave from Russia all said that they had not seen a single town in Russia which was as devastated as Kassel.' To this she added emphatically, without noting the contradiction, 'a second Stalingrad'.[98]

The conviction that Kassel had been 'annihilated' by the RAF was not just communicated privately but also found expression in cultural arte-facts that were disseminated semi-publicly. The elegiac poem 'Thus Died My Home Town' was the most prominent example. The text appears to have circulated in many different contexts, the workplace, the camps of

[95] See Map 1 for the route that Niemeyer took into the city.
[96] StAK, S8 E15, diary Niemeyer, 22 October 1943.
[97] StAK, S8 C51, Karl H., 'Abschrift vom Original Schreiben'.
[98] StAK, S8 C51, Asta R., 'Terrorangriff! 23.10.1943'.

the children's evacuation programme, and according to one memory, was even reprinted on a leaflet.[99] At around the same time, another commemorative artefact appeared, of which far fewer traces have survived. The '*Kasseler Heimat* Song' (*Kasseler Heimatlied*) or, as it was alternatively called, 'The Song of the Sorely Afflicted Kassel' (*Das Lied vom leidgeprüften Kassel*) was modelled on the example of the popular *Pommernlied*, a melancholy turn-of-the-century tune of longing for home.[100] In contrast to the original, the adaptation from Kassel struck up a tone that was sarcastic rather than elegiac, as the first lines illustrate: 'Where the roofs are lying on the streets / ... / there is my home town, there I am at home'. Like the anonymous poem, the song focused on the local dimension of material and human loss. It implied that the (air) war had destroyed the very assets for whose preservation the war was allegedly being fought, the *Heimat*.

> Where the wicked Tommy murders wife and child
> Where so many victims are lamented
> . . .
> Where great pain cries out to heaven
> Where everything for miles around has been reduced to rubble
> Where I have sacrificed all my possessions
> Kassel, my home, I love like my blood.[101]

The excerpt illuminates two important aspects of the semi-public 'disaster' narrative. Firstly, lamentation of loss, while in a state of tension with official propaganda, could be made irrespective of political persuasion. It was not by itself indicative of nonconformity with or even opposition to the Nazi regime. Indeed, frequently the opposite was the case. As often as not, lamentation went hand in hand with a passionate denunciation of the allies, as in the lines on the 'wicked Tommy' committing 'murder'. Even propaganda minister Joseph Goebbels, by all measures an unlikely candidate for political nonconformity, spoke in his diary of the 'shattering' impression that Kassel had made on him. After his visit to the city on 6 November, he dictated the following: 'The entire centre and the greatest part of the suburbs have been completely destroyed. [The city] offers a terrible sight to the beholder. The scale of devastation can only be compared to Hamburg. A fire disaster [*Brandkatastrophe*] of the greatest order has raged here.'[102] The propaganda minister held Nazi district leader Weinrich responsible for the catastrophe, and since

---

[99] Compare StAK, S8 E5, Margarete L. to Amt für Kulturpflege, 8 October 1983; S8 E3, Alwin K. to Werner Dettmar, 28 April 1983.
[100] StAK, S8 C53, Literarische Verarbeitung. For the text plus translation see Appendix 2.
[101] Ibid.   [102] Goebbels, *Tagebücher* II/10, 6 November 1943, p. 238.

he worked actively for Weinrich's removal, it is of course possible that he underlined the scale of the devastation in order to justify his intrigue in the light of history, to which his diaries were tailored. Still, there is little reason to doubt that Goebbels' entry also recorded a genuine sense of shock at what he witnessed in Kassel.

Secondly, even for the outside view, 'death' was not just a metaphor for widespread material destruction, but also a reality which came in the shape of rows of corpses, charred bodies and body parts – 'burnt, resembling pieces of charcoal, asphyxiated, suffocated, in grotesquely contorted positions', as one contemporary observer put it.[103] Indeed, too little attention has been paid to the extent to which the dead were visible in the aftermath of area attacks.[104] Niemeyer first came upon dead bodies on his initial visit to the city on the afternoon of 23 October, when he saw about fifty corpses arranged in a row on the Friedrichsplatz, Kassel's traditional parade ground. He noted that men, women, children, soldiers and POWs lay next to one another, all 'very dirty' and 'making for a sorry sight'.[105] This was not a singular occasion. The diary entries of the following days mention rows of corpses repeatedly, ten in one place, a hundred in another.[106] On one occasion Niemeyer watched rescue workers recovering corpses from an air raid shelter and transferring them to a waiting lorry. 'The lorry was half-filled already! A dreadful sight,' he commented.

It was not only the number of deaths that exercised the young man's imagination but also the terrible condition of the bodies, to which he reacted with a mixture of revulsion and curiosity. On the sight of twenty-five burned corpses in the main shopping street, the Untere Königstraße, he wrote in his notes, 'I do not want to turn away; I want to apprehend the misery in its full scale. This sight will make me bitter and make me hard!! Then the stench of the corpses hits me so I need to turn away.'[107] In his detailed account of the day's events, Niemeyer revealed just how closely he had examined the mutilated corpses, describing in detail their various states of decomposition. Confronted with mass death in all its visual and sensory immediacy, the 'cool poise' that the young man tried to muster quickly failed him.[108] No Nazi upbringing in the world could have prepared him for what he saw.

Niemeyer's experience was shared, to various degrees, by many, per-haps most, visitors to the city in the first week or so after the air raid,

---

[103] StAK, S8 C51, Karl H., 'Abschrift vom Original Schreiben'.
[104] A similar point is made by Bessel, 'The Shadow of Death'.
[105] StAK, S8 E15, diary Niemeyer, 23 October 1943.
[106] Ibid., 24, 27, 28 and 29 October 1943.   [107] Ibid., 28 October 1943.
[108] Stargardt, *Witnesses of War*, p. 233.

causing intense sense impressions and leaving memory traces that were
communicated over and over again in ego-documents and would resur-
face in retrospective eyewitness accounts.[109] The presence of the dead
in Kassel was such that even the local branch of the Nazi party grew
alarmed. In a letter to the deputy mayor, dated 25 October 1943, a local
party functionary wrote, 'I know how much work we all have to do.
But please do everything within your power to remove the corpses from
the streets and squares immediately. The sight is shocking and dreadful
scenes occur in front of the uncovered corpses.'[110] Although the responsible authorities tried to speed up the process of removal and burial, even
ordering mass burial in double layers, the chief of police, in his experience
report, defended the practice of leaving the dead at the site of recovery
on the grounds of facilitating their identification.[111]

Whatever the merits of the chief of police's reasoning, the sight of hundreds of corpses lent credibility to stories that vastly inflated the number
of deaths. While, on 3 November, the local press published an insipid disclaimer, asserting that the death toll was not as high as might have been
feared, no precise figure was given.[112] The SD in its summary report
of 18 November 1943 acidly commented that 'just like in Hamburg . . .
exaggerated rumours' were circulating that spoke of '40,000, 60,000
and more victims'. Given that the city only had a pre-war population
of 220,000 people, these figures were remarkable indeed.[113] They were
echoed in some contemporary accounts, such as a letter to Ms Asta R.
from 25 November 1943, in which the writer averred that 'one generally expects 40,000 dead and 150,000 homeless'. Ominously, he added,
'Please do not speak publicly about those figures. You well know how
easily this can be used against one.'[114] Another writer put the death
toll at 20,000, while Niemeyer in his diary spoke rather more realisti-
cally of 'at least 10,000', but added that much higher figures were in
circulation.[115]

So far, this section has concentrated on those impressions and perceptions that were made irrespective of personal involvement – the view from
the outside into the devastated city. Such a perspective helps to illuminate important contours of a semi-public discourse on the air war. Great

---

[109] Compare StAK, S8 C51. For a different view see Stargardt, *Witnesses of War*, pp. 233,
242.
[110] StAK, S8 C50, Opfer Diverses, NSDAP Kreisleitung Kassel to Bürgermeister Schim-
melpfeng, 25 October 1943.
[111] StAK, S8 C40, p. 29.   [112] 'Die Opfer in Kassel', *KLZ*, 3 November 1943.
[113] *Meldungen*, vol. XV, p. 6024, 'SD-Berichte zu Inlandsfragen', 18 November 1943.
[114] StAK, S8 C53, Asta R., 'Terrorangriff! 23.10.1943'.
[115] StAK, S8 C53, Karl H., 'Abschrift vom Original Schreiben'; S8 E15, diary Niemeyer,
26 October 1943.

as the actual destruction was, with the loss of 60 per cent of the built-up environment, and high as the mortality rate was at 3.9 per cent of the pre-war population, in the view of many an eyewitness Kassel had been annihilated, while as much as one-quarter of the population were thought to have died. Fed on personal sense impressions that, in effect, grossly overestimated the impact of the air raid on the city, a narrative emerged at the centre of which stood the attempt to come to terms with a (partly imaginary) level of devastation that appeared beyond all comprehension.

The extrapolation of an 'outside view' is no more than a heuristic device. In reality, things were rather more complex. After all, Gebhard Niemeyer was no disinterested observer but a concerned relative whose journey was motivated by apprehensions about the fate of his loved ones. The only reason he was able to consider the grotesquely mutilated bodies with such a mixture of revulsion and curiosity was because he knew that his immediate family had come out of the conflagration alive. Many others were not so lucky. Karl H., for example, whose father had written to him about the 'annihilation' of the once beautiful city, also had to learn that among the corpses were the mortal remains of his mother and sister. For Niemeyer, the collapsed building at Königstor 32 was evidence not just of one crime or another, but of a home destroyed in which he had lived since he was a little child. If Kassel had ceased to exist as a city, then also the physical, social and symbolic environment that he had known had disappeared.

Yet there was a crucial difference between observers from the outside and observers from the centre. While the former looked upon the material and human wreckage that the bombers had left in their wake, the latter were part of it.[116] While the former, for all the misery and death that they encountered, had not themselves been exposed to mortal danger, the latter were survivors in a very direct sense: they had escaped the bombs, but often only just. It is to their stories that we must now turn. In Kassel, 'inside' stories originated from an area of approximately 4.7 square kilometres in size, comprising much of the historic town on both sides of the river Fulda and being roughly demarcated by Murhardstraße to the west, Wolfhagerstraße to the north, Mönchebergstraße to the east and Arndtstraße to the south (Fig. 3).[117] Here, the individual fires had combined into one massive conflagration that made survival dependent on timely escape.

---

[116] A similar observation is made by Klaus Latzel with reference to the soldiers' experience of trench warfare during World War I. Compare Latzel, 'Die Soldaten des industrialisierten Krieges', p. 129.

[117] StAK, S8 C40, 'Erfahrungsbericht', 7 December 1943, pp. 6f.

town centre

destroyed
damaged

0 60 100 150 200m

Planning Department 1968

Figure 3. The map gives an indication of the zone of conflagration. It was produced on the twenty-fifth anniversary of the raid in 1968 and also served to underline the idea of 'total' destruction.

Views from the centre

Recent scholarship has shown an increased readiness to describe aspects of the German war experience as traumatic.[118] If 'trauma' is understood as a 'distressing' event 'outside the range of usual human experience', then the term is without doubt applicable to the exposure to incendiary

[118] Gregor, 'Is He Still Alive?'; Naumann (ed.), *Nachkrieg*; Bessel and Schumann (eds.), *Life after Death*.

bombing.[119] Yet the heuristic value of the concept remains limited as long as it is used as a label rather than as a tool. In the early 1950s, the German psychiatrist Friedrich Panse examined the experience of 'dread and terror' in the air war on the basis of roughly one hundred eyewitness accounts.[120] According to Panse, typical bodily reactions to aerial bombing were tremor and loss of tonus, sometimes in the form of a 'terror stupor', while in psychosomatic terms, a narrowing of perspective, emotional paralysis, a sharpening of instinctive impulses and a heightened suggestibility were common. Often, there also occurred a change in the subjective sense of time.[121] Air raids, the psychiatrist observed, were usually followed by apathy, occasionally also by euphoria, with increased sensitisation as a long-term effect.

Both the author and his study are deeply problematic. While during the war Panse had gained a doubtful reputation for his brutal treatment of shell-shocked soldiers and, worse still, had been involved directly in the Nazi killing programme of the disabled, the post-war study was written with the explicit purpose of limiting the indemnity claims of German civilians. Not surprisingly, Panse found that area bombing generally had had no lasting debilitating effects. Where mental disabilities occurred, the reason lay in the weak constitution of the person concerned rather than in the exposure to bombing.[122] While there are good reasons to call into question such overall findings, the observations on short-term effects can none the less improve our understanding of the peculiar nature of accounts that were often written only hours or days after the bodily exposure to the overwhelming violence of a concentrated incendiary attack.

The psychiatrist identified the need to talk about the bombing as the most 'conspicuous mass-psychological phenomenon' of the war years.[123] Interestingly, this observation contrasts sharply with the subjective feeling of many survivors of airborne attack, who held that what they had gone through was, in essence, not communicable.[124] Despite this, there were many social contexts in which the victims of area bombardment talked about their experiences, and indeed, were required to do so. Each of these contexts had important repercussions on the ways in which the myriad perceptions and sense impressions were ordered into meaningful narratives. While all accounts bore the imprint of the society in which

---

[119] Förster and Beck, 'Post-Traumatic Stress Disorder', p. 15.
[120] Panse, *Angst und Schreck.*   [121] Ibid., pp. 174–85.
[122] On the context of Panse's study see Ebbinghaus, 'Deutschland im Bombenkrieg', 119f.; Süß, 'Tod aus der Luft', pp. 563–7.
[123] Panse, *Angst und Schreck*, p. 175.
[124] StAK, S8 C51, 'Mein liebes gutes, heiliges Kind', 26 October 1943.

they were produced, the categories of gender, function and race provided important fault lines.

Gender, function, race

When the chief of police, in his summary report of 7 December 1943, tried to account for the high number of fatal casualties in the attack, he employed a highly gendered argument. In the most heavily affected areas, the report explained, the residents' only chance of survival had lain in leaving the air raid shelters before the individual fires had combined into a general conflagration. As this narrow window of opportunity had closed before the raid was over, the chief of police thought it 'understandable' that 'many people . . . had not found the courage to leave the air raid shelter . . . in time'.[125] In particular, he singled out women and children for this sin of omission, adding that in many cases 'husbands managed neither by means of persuasion nor by brute force to induce their wives to leave the air raid shelters'.[126] As a lesson for future attacks, the report recommended the strengthening of 'air raid communities' through the retention of able-bodied men with strong leadership qualities. It emphasised that 'only in exceptional circumstances will a woman be capable of such action'.[127]

Underlying the chief of police's reasoning was a traditional gender model that conceived of men as active and rational protectors and women as passive and emotional sufferers.[128] In Kassel – and one may surmise, also elsewhere – many people still seem to have subscribed to this binary model, the propaganda glorification of 'female fighters' (*Kämpferinnen*) on the home front and the active involvement of many women in civil defence notwithstanding.[129] Traditional ideas about separate spheres rather than the social reality of their progressive erosion shaped expectations of the other sex's behaviour during the attack. The account that Elfriede Niemann gave to Dr Paetow of the Enquiry Office for the Missing may serve to illustrate this point.[130] At the time of reporting, four months after the raid, Niemann was still desperately trying to locate the whereabouts of her only daughter, who had gone missing on 22 October. The young mother was scathing about the men she had encountered

---

[125] StAK, S8 C40, 'Erfahrungsbericht', 7 December 1943, p. 18.
[126] Ibid., p. 17.   [127] Ibid., p. 13.
[128] On the genesis of this binary model in the late eighteenth century see Kühne, 'Männergeschichte als Geschlechtergeschichte', p. 11.
[129] Kramer, 'Mobilisierung', p. 73; 'Das Herz auf dem rechten Fleck. Melderin beim Terror-Angriff / Bewährung eines tapferen Mädels', *KLZ*, 27/28 November 1943, p. 3.
[130] *Überlebensberichte*, pp. 25–8 (no. 10).

during the raid. They had been 'complete failures', she told Paetow. In particular, she was contemptuous of the conduct of a certain Kühlmann, air raid warden in her basement shelter, who, she claimed, had selfishly left her daughter and another child behind in order to save his own skin.[131]

Whatever the justification for Elfriede Niemann's harsh verdict, her report was informed by a gendered perspective in which men were expected to live up to the role models that they had fashioned for themselves. Men too had deeply internalised these role models, and accordingly tended to structure their accounts by the binary opposition of 'success' (*Bewährung*) and 'failure' (*Versagen*). Not infrequently, the stories told by male eyewitnesses carried a defensive undertone, in particular when they were written by air raid wardens who had been among the sole survivors of particular shelter communities. The language was borrowed from the war experience at the front, or rather, from the Nazi jargon that professed to communicate that experience to the home front. An account by Willi Heimbächer, air raid warden at Franziskusstraße 1 in the centre of the old town, is perhaps an extreme but not altogether untypical example. Heimbächer praised the discipline of his own shelter community while denigrating the crowd from the adjacent apartment building for their signs of nervousness. Likewise, he contrasted the 'cowardice' and 'panic' of some of the men surrounding him with his own superior judgement and leadership, which was exercised in the face of extreme adversity for the benefit of those who had been put in his care.[132]

Next to function and gender, race was crucial. Kassel in late 1943 was not just an urban community at total war, but also a hierarchically structured racial society in which 22,300 foreigners were forced to live and work, mainly in the armaments industry.[133] By that time, the destruction of the 3,000-strong Jewish community had largely been completed. After the deportations to the ghetto of Riga, the extermination camp at Majdanek and the concentration camp at Theresienstadt in 1941 and 1942, only a small number of 'privileged' Jews remained in the city.[134] Among them were the physician Lilli Jahn and her five half-Jewish children, who had moved into a flat in the city district of Vorderer Westen after her non-Jewish husband had divorced her in late 1942.[135] The divorce left her extremely vulnerable to the extermination politics of the regime, and in late August 1943, she was arrested and sent to Breitenau

---

[131] Ibid., p. 25.   [132] StAK, S8 C51, Willi Heimbächer, 'Memento Mori'.
[133] Krause-Vilmar, 'Ausländische Zwangsarbeiter', p. 73.
[134] Prinz, 'Judenverfolgung in Kassel', pp. 149, 207.
[135] Doerry, *'Mein verwundetes Herz'*. For a careful reading see Fritzsche, *Life and Death*, pp. 231f.

work camp, where she stayed until she was deported to Auschwitz in March 1944. Lilli John died three months later.

Throughout the time of her imprisonment, her two eldest daughters, Ilse, aged fourteen, and Johanna, aged thirteen, tried desperately to stay in touch with their mother by telling in writing of their daily lives, of what they had done, felt and hoped for. In great detail, their letters also covered the air raid of 22 October 1943, which the children had experienced in the cellar of their apartment building at Motzsraße 3, to the west of the main target area. They were bombed out completely but, other than that, remained unharmed. At first sight, the young girls' accounts do not differ much from the reports by the non-Jewish majority population. There is an emphasis on the scale of the destruction, the many deaths are deplored, and in great detail the children's personal fortunes are related.[136] Unlike Victor Klemperer in his diary entry on the destruction of Dresden,[137] there is no hint in the letters at the idea of just retribution. While the uttering of any such rationalisation would, of course, have been very dangerous in correspondence that was monitored by the Gestapo, precaution cannot quite explain why the eldest daughter Ilse adopted the propaganda idiom of 'mean terror bombers' in order to refer to the allied pilots.[138] And yet, on closer reading, there emerges a sense that the bombing, for all the material deprivation that it had wrought, was of limited significance to the children in comparison with the pain of separation from their mother and the uncertainty over her fate.

As for the forced workers living in the city who longed for Germany's defeat in the war,[139] bombing was a deeply ambivalent experience, threatening death and promising liberation in equal measure. In a very immediate sense, allied bombing increased the vulnerability of slave labourers in at least two respects. For one, inadequate shelters left them very exposed to the dangers of airborne attack, as several post-war accounts by Dutch forced labourers confirm. Many camps were equipped only with fortified ditches (*Splittergräben*), which accorded no protection against high-explosive bombs. Moreover, as a perceived threat to internal security, the labourers became vulnerable to arbitrary measures by the local authorities. In an intermediate report from 30 October 1943, the chief

---

[136] Doerry, '*Mein verwundetes Herz*', pp. 205–11.
[137] Klemperer, *Ich will Zeugnis ablegen* (1945), 17 February 1945, p. 45.
[138] Doerry, '*Mein verwundetes Herz*', p. 184.
[139] Compare Informationsstelle zur Geschichte des Nationalsozialismus in Nordhessen (Infostelle), N 145, P. Mom to Gert Meyer, 25 November 1986; N 135, M. J. Goosen to Krause-Vilmar, 22 November 1986. On the context: Herbert, *Fremdarbeiter*, pp. 335–41.

of police informed his superiors that seven foreigners had been hanged for the alleged offence of plundering, while three had been deported to a concentration camp.[140] In addition, the forced labourers, too, had to cope with fear and loss in their myriad forms.[141]

Overall, there is evidence to suggest that, regardless of their hatred of the Germans, some slave labourers also found the experience of airborne violence overwhelming. Forty years after the event, the Dutch poet and Socialist Wim de Vries associated the area raid not with liberation but with death. 'De dood, vertel mij niets. / Ik zag hem in het groot. / En kolossale dod, de / hoofden maaiend als de / boer het gras', he wrote in a poem that carried the title 'Kassel, 22 October 1943'.[142] At the same time, bombing not only demonstrated Germany's declining fortunes in the war but could also open up unexpected routes of escape. Several instances are documented in which Dutch forced labourers were able to exploit the chaos and disorder following the attack in order to return home, where they went into hiding until the end of the war.[143]

The category of race also informed reports by members of the urban racial community. Else Dietzel, who worked for the Enquiry Office for the Missing, offers a case in point. In detail, the woman described the pain and agony that she saw mirrored in the faces of people who called in to the Enquiry Office, which she felt 'gave nobility and dignity even to non-distinguished physiognomies'. Significantly, Frau Dietzel did not invoke universal categories to explain her observation. Rather, she found confirmed a dictum by the nineteenth-century poet Wilhelm Raabe that ascribed to the 'pensive' German race (*Volk*) a special quality of coping with death.[144]

Although race was significant, the case of Kassel offers no conclusive evidence to support Nick Stargardt's thesis that bombing led to a hardening among the majority population of attitudes towards racial outsiders.[145] While one post-war account by a Dutch former forced labourer related how ordinary residents turned ever more hostile as the bombing escalated – 'as if this was our fault!'[146] – other evidence points

---

[140] StAK, S8 C40, 'Lagebericht zum Luftangriff am 22.10.1943. 5. Ergänzung', 30 October 1943.

[141] Infostelle, N 167, A. van Rosmalen to Gert Meyer, 17 September 1988; *Überlebensberichte*, pp. 39f. (no. 20).

[142] 'Don't speak of death to me. I saw the Grim Reaper in all his power. He cut down people like a peasant cuts down grass.' Vries, *Zurück nach Kassel*, p. 43.

[143] Infostelle, N 142, Jacobus Wallraave, no date [1986].

[144] BGM Kassel, NL 7, Stiftung Karl Paetow (Bad Oeynhausen), 57. Mappe, fos. 47–50, Else Dietzel, 'Erlebnisse auf der Vermisstensuchstelle', 10 April 1944.

[145] Stargardt, 'Opfer der Bomben'.

[146] Infostelle, N 160, A. B. to Gert Meyer, 22 November 1988.

in a different direction. Quite a few of the accounts that were collected by Paetow mentioned with approval the rescue efforts by Dutch and French labourers, who seem to have been considered by many as fellow sufferers.[147] The same, however, did not apply to POWs and forced labourers from the Soviet Union, Poland or Italy, who were ignored at best but generally treated with suspicion. On balance, the accounts seem to reflect less a sudden 'nazification' of mindsets due to bombing than a more gradual internalisation of the Nazi racial hierarchy.

Loss

Despite their differences, the autobiographical texts from the centre of the attack negotiate, in one way or another, the personal dimension of urban catastrophe. Airborne disaster could take on many forms, threatening the individual body and mind no less than the social and spatial environment. The degree to which elements of the threat materialised differed considerably, depending on a combination of institutional, social and individual factors on the one hand, chance and coincidence on the other. The view from the centre shared with the view from the outside the emphasis on catastrophic rupture, but explored the theme in its personal dimension. Often, the experience of loss was balanced against the experience of survival, as this, of course, was the precondition for texts from the centre to be written at all. In no small measure, autobiographical accounts reflected the narrowing of perspective that Panse has identified as a typical reaction to the emotional pressures of aerial bombing. The realisation that personal disaster formed part of a wider catastrophe was frequently delayed, and could either be experienced as shocking or alternatively as comforting.[148]

A close reading of a letter by an unnamed mother to her adolescent daughter who had just embarked on a year of compulsory social service somewhere out of town can help to illuminate important elements of the view from the centre.[149] The text was written a few days after the attack. It describes the journey of the mother, her husband and two younger children from their home in the conflagration zone to the relative safety of the periphery.

[147] Compare, for example, the reports nos. 1, 29, 31, 36, 39, 61, 87, 89, 92, 100 and 108 in *Überlebensberichte* for favourable mentions of French and Dutch POWs and forced labourers. Similar reactions were recorded by the SD in its report on the 'Battle of Berlin'. See *Meldungen*, vol. XV, p. 6103.

[148] Compare *Überlebensberichte*, pp. 90 (no. 65) and pp. 146–8 (no. 98) for the second perspective.

[149] StAK, S8 C51, 'Mein liebes, gutes, heiliges Kind', 26 October 1943.

Typically, the account operates with a number of stark juxtapositions: a scene of peaceful everyday activity is contrasted with the family's panic-stricken flight through smoke-filled air raid cellars and burning streets. Similarly, initial stillness is contrasted with the noise of exploding bombs and frantic screams. At the time of writing, the writer still seems to have been struggling with the idea that the family had indeed survived the bombing unharmed. 'Oh, it was terrible, hardly conceivable that we escaped alive,' she emphasised. Not until the next morning did the family grasp the full dimensions of the air raid's impact on the city – a realisation described as a shocking epiphany: 'Then the horror: everything *kaput* in Kassel . . . In the old town nothing but death.'

Significantly, the general picture of urban devastation and mass death is immediately linked back to the personal environment. The woman lists by name the nineteen casualties who were found in the cellar of a nearby grocer. The dead are not anonymous corpses but individuals who were known personally to the correspondents. In contrast to the detailed description of mass death, the loss of 'our beautiful happy home' is mentioned in passing only, to be followed by the rationalisation that 'it does not matter: the hand of God has preserved us and kept us together'. The letter closes with a passionate plea for the daughter to return home. Clearly, this family tried to compensate for the destruction of their social environment by a strengthening of familial ties.

Altogether, roughly 150,000 residents were made homeless by the attack. While most, such as the family above, could draw comfort from the fact that they had survived without any serious physical harm, others were not so lucky. According to the summary police report, 11,671 people had sustained physical injuries, of which 800 were serious.[150] One case is documented of a nineteen-year-old woman who incurred such severe burns to her knees, hands and face that she was left permanently disabled. According to a letter written by her husband fifty years after the event, the woman became clinically depressed, contributing to what her husband considered her premature death in 1993.[151]

Next to injury, there was death on a scale without parallel in local memory. In a single night, between 6,000 and 8,500 people were killed, leaving behind tens of thousands of residents who had to cope with the premature deaths of their loved ones. The encounter with the death of close kin was frequently experienced as arbitrary and intensely shocking. A woman in her thirties recalled how her sister-in-law was struck dead by burning debris in front of her very eyes while they were trying to

---

[150] StAK, S8 C40, 'Erfahrungsbericht', 7 December 1943, p. 3.
[151] Compare *Überlebensberichte*, pp. 136f. (no. 92), annotation 4.

escape from an air raid cellar. The same woman later found herself regaining consciousness in another shelter among scores of dead and dying occupants.[152] Others were haunted by memories that they had been powerless to prevent the deaths of loved ones while being forced to witness. In an undated letter to an acquaintance, Frau Sch. told of how she, her husband and one of her children had been buried alive in their air raid cellar on Wilhelmshöher Allee 29. She recalled how she had heard her son cry out, 'help, mum, help'. The woman was rescued, but her son and husband were not. Their bodies were not recovered until three weeks later. 'It is horrible. I always hear my dear son cry for help,' Frau Sch. confided to her correspondent.[153]

The death of loved ones appears to have been particularly hard to accept when there was no body to mourn over. In his report to Paetow, the 44-year-old police constable L. B. detailed how he had searched for traces of his family by sieving through the rubble of several burnt-out air raid cellars: 'I have found many wedding rings, but not the one of my wife. I have held in my hand children's vertebrae and skulls . . . But I have found no trace of my family.'[154] In a letter to the mayor, Karl Giermann enquired on behalf of his mother about the memorial provisions for those residents who were confirmed dead but whose bodies had not been recovered. He explained that his mother had been hard hit by the loss of her son and his family, but simply was unable to understand that nothing had been found of them.[155] The bereaved often preferred to have their loved ones buried separately or in family graves whenever possible. Sometimes, relatives would go as far as to intervene with the authorities in order to reverse burial procedures, as is documented for the electrician L. S., who turned to the head of the administrative district (*Regierungspräsident*) to have his wife reburied in the nearby town of Fritzlar.[156] The request was refused, but around the same time the Nazi district leader ordered that in principle families should be allowed to bury their relatives privately.[157]

While thousands were confronted with the deaths of loved ones, others had to live with uncertainty. As of 7 December, as many as

---

[152] *Überlebensberichte*, pp. 103–5 (no. 74). See also ibid., pp. 93f. (no. 68) and 117–19 (no. 81).

[153] BGM Kassel, NL 7, 'Stiftung Karl Paetow (Bad Oeynhausen)', 61. Mappe, fo. 20, Frau Sch. to Rektor Leinius, no date.

[154] *Überlebensberichte*, pp. 88f. (no. 63).

[155] BGM Kassel, NL 7, 'Stiftung Karl Paetow (Bad Oeynhausen)', 61. Mappe, fos. 30f., Karl Giermann to mayor, 20 January 1944.

[156] StAK, S8 C50, Regierungspräsident to lord mayor, 28 October 1943; lord mayor to Herrn S., 28 October 1943.

[157] *Überlebensberichte*, pp. 105–9 (no. 75), here: p. 108.

3,000 people were unaccounted for, while 1,800 bodies had been buried without proper identification.[158] In the first few months after the raid, thousands called in at the Enquiry Office in order to find out about the fate of their loved ones, sometimes several times a week. Elfriede Niemann, mentioned above, would carry on the search for her nine-year-old daughter for years, following up every spurious lead that presented itself.[159]

Casting blame

Who then did the citizens of Kassel hold responsible for the catastrophe that had come upon their city? Who did they credit with their survival? Did they accept the official rationalisation of the air raid as a crime, perhaps even in its anti-Semitic form as a 'Jewish crime', or did they consider the area attack a legitimate act of war? Did the emergency relief lead to a strengthening of the affective bonds between the Nazi regime and the local population, to a second 'seizure of power', as is sometimes claimed?[160] Or did, on the contrary, the inability of the Third Reich to defend the *Heimat* erode the consensual spheres between regime and ordinary citizens, as Ian Kershaw and others have argued?[161]

The case of Kassel in late 1943 does not offer conclusive answers to these much-debated points but suggests, rather, that the questions might be misplaced. From a local perspective, the nation state and the regime were only two knots in a web of accountability that was more complex than has been recognised by historians who focus exclusively on the impact of bombing on the 'morale' of the population. The available data further support the thesis that Nazi propaganda provided an idiom that was readily accepted by many, perhaps most, local residents as a means to express what they had experienced. At the same time, there are few indications that the adoption of a National Socialist idiom translated into a strengthening of the consensual spheres between the Nazi regime and the local population. Rather, the loss of the *Heimat*, family and friends appears to have raised existential questions about life that ran deeper than political loyalties towards party and state.

The most important sphere of accountability was local. Survivors credited courageous individuals with their rescue, be they air raid wardens,

---

[158] StAK, S8 C40, 'Erfahrungsbericht', 7 December 1943, pp. 2f.

[159] BGM Kassel, NL 7, Stiftung Karl Paetow (Bad Oeynhausen), 58. Mappe, fos. 47–50, Else Dietzel, 'Erlebnisse aus der Vermisstensuchstelle'; *Überlebensberichte*, pp. 25–9 (no. 10); 'Ein Schicksal des 22. Oktober 1943: Eine Mutter weiß: Mein Kind lebt!', *HN*, 22 October 1952.

[160] Compare, for example, Friedrich, *The Fire*, p. 390.

[161] Kershaw, *The 'Hitler Myth'*, pp. 200–25; Gregor, 'A *Schicksalsgemeinschaft*?'.

soldiers, POWs, forced labourers, civilians or members of their own families.[162] Likewise, they blamed people in their immediate environments for the deaths of relatives, because they had led them in the wrong direction, abandoned them in the hour of need or refused shelter.[163] Individual behaviour during the attack came under so much scrutiny not only because this could make the difference between death and survival, but also because there were conflicting opinions about the right course of action. By the autumn of 1943, the recognition that British advances in fire-raising techniques had turned air raid cellars from shelters into potential death traps had not yet become general knowledge. Many residents still acted according to the received wisdom by which it was safe to remain in the cellars until the raid was over, appropriate to the high-explosive bombings of 1940/1 but no longer to the incendiary raids of 1942/3. Among them were men who – in the words of the chief of police – 'should have known better', and in particular soldiers on leave, who would use their authority to prevent others from leaving the shelters when there was still time, thus exposing them to death by carbon monoxide poisoning.[164]

The bitterness engendered by the loss of loved ones could be such that some residents tried to sue their neighbours for criminal dereliction of duty. In a letter to the district attorney general of 26 November 1943, the engineer Erich H. claimed that the cellar at Rothenditmolderstraße 19, in which his wife and two children had perished, had resembled a 'crematorium' rather than a shelter because of criminal neglect by the owner and his caretaker. Moreover, the air raid warden had abandoned the shelter community during the raid in order to save his own skin. In sum, H. averred, 'allegations, mistakes and neglect add up to enormous guilt . . . that calls for atonement'.[165] The example illustrates just how divisive the air raid could be. Next to this micro-level, people credited a supernatural being – God – or simply a miracle with their survival.[166] By comparison, the relief efforts of the party and state authorities were acknowledged and sometimes commended, but they also corresponded to widespread expectations.[167]

Contemporaries made frequent use of the vocabulary provided by official propaganda, as is borne out by an analysis of the obituaries published

---

[162] Compare *Überlebensberichte*, pp. 48f. (no. 29), 71–3 (no. 49).
[163] Compare *Überlebensberichte*, pp. 17f. (no. 4), 37f. (no. 18), 85–7 (no. 62).
[164] StAK, S8 C40, 'Erfahrungsbericht', 7 December 1943, p. 17.
[165] StAK, S8 C49, Erich H., 'Wen trifft die Schuld?', 26 November 1943.
[166] Compare *Überlebensberichte*, pp. 15–17 (no. 3), 117–19 (no. 81).
[167] Compare *Überlebensberichte*, pp. 78 (no. 54), 85–7 (no. 62), 101–3 (no. 73), 113f. (no. 77).

in the local newspaper. While, of course, certain statements would have been inadmissible in a newspaper controlled by the Nazi state, the leeway for the wording of private death notices appears to have been considerable. One widow spoke in her obituary of the 'air raid on Kassel' which had caused their house to collapse, 'burying all my loved ones'. Next to her husband and her three children the woman also commemorated their eighteen-year-old Polish worker who had died as well, referring to her as 'our loyal and dear housemaid'.[168] At the other end of the spectrum, a widow thought it appropriate to announce the death of her husband and eight other family members by quoting the Nazi dictum of 'Germany must live even if we have to die!', insisting that her kin had died 'a sacrificial death for an eternal Germany'.[169] While these two examples illustrate the range of possibilities, the vast majority of obituaries referred to the attack as a 'terror raid' without explicitly invoking the Nazi rationale for violent death.[170]

Some private accounts also denounced the RAF raid as criminal and gave vent to expressions of hatred. Gebhard Niemeyer, for one, spoke in his diary of his hatred 'towards the murderers that bombed Kassel into rubble and ruins',[171] while the *Kasseler Heimatlied* contained the line 'where the wicked Tommy murders wife and child'. Likewise, the elegy 'Thus Died My Home Town' mentioned 'flames of hatred' that would 'fall back on England'. By contrast, not a single contemporary document has been preserved that explicitly blames the Nazi regime. Unlike the previous summer, when the SD, in a special report, registered across the Reich an upsurge in critical comments and small gestures of nonconformity, in Kassel, in the autumn of 1943, several party faithful commented on the absence of public or semi-public grumbling.[172] There also appear to have been no stories in circulation, such as were picked up by the regime's informants in mostly Catholic cities such as Würzburg or Munich, that considered the bombing as acts of retribution for Germany's treatment of the Jews.[173]

While it would certainly be rash to infer from the lack of documentary evidence that there was indeed nobody at all who held the Nazi regime responsible, the absence attests to a social climate in which

---

[168] StAK, S8 C50, Opfer Diverses.   [169] Ibid.
[170] See StAK, S8 C62, which consists of an album containing thousands of obituaries.
[171] StAK, S8 B6, diary Niemeyer, 24 October 1943.
[172] Compare *Meldungen*, vol. XIV, pp. 5445f., 'Auflockerungserscheinungen in der Haltung der Bevölkerung', 8 July 1944; BGM Kassel, NL 7, Stiftung Karl Paetow (Bad Oeynhausen), 61. Mappe, fo. 138; *Überlebensberichte*, pp. 132–5 (no. 90), here p. 134.
[173] See Dov Kulka and Jäckel (eds.), *Die Juden in den geheimen NS-Stimmungsberichten*, p. 528 and *passim*; BA Berlin, NS 18/1333, fos. 34–6, 'Gerüchte anläßlich des Terrorangriffs auf München', 28 September 1942.

critics kept their thoughts to themselves. If a reminder of the necessity of such a cautious approach was needed, then this was furnished by the new party district leader in his inaugural speech on 21 November 1943. Karl Gerland spoke of his determination 'to exterminate all inferior elements', among which he explicitly included 'the bearers of foolish rumours'.[174]

What some documents do express is a sense of war weariness. In her letter quoted above, Frau Sch. spoke of war as 'murder', which she hoped would 'someday come to an end'.[175] The elegy 'Thus Died My Home Town' circulated most widely in a variant that concluded with the line 'war is madness', while the *Kasseler Heimat Song* in one version contained the verse, 'Kassel, my home, say, it is enough'.[176] In his last interview before his suspension, even district leader Weinrich spoke of a 'just peace' as the most desirable outcome of the war – an indication, perhaps, of the extent to which the highest local representative of the regime had been demoralised by the air raid and the allegations levelled against him.[177]

With hatred of the enemy and war weariness expressed in approximately equal measure, the evidence on the impact of the air raid on morale remains inconclusive. While there are few signs that the Nazi authorities benefited from the area raid politically, there can equally be no question that the regime remained firmly in control despite the widespread devastation. It must, however, be open to doubt whether an interpretive framework that implicitly adopts the evaluative categories of Nazism can do justice to the emotional impact of area bombing. The assumption that political loyalties stood at the centre of the repercussions of air raids seems questionable. Rather, the scale of the material, social and emotional disruption was such that some residents – temporarily at least – appear to have despaired of life altogether, while others refocused their energies on their immediate social environment, above all the family, and day-to-day survival.[178] In the letter to her daughter analysed above, the anonymous woman wrote, 'we promise to keep

---

[174] 'Und nun Kopf hoch! Wir gehören dem Leben!', *KLZ*, 23 November 1943, pp. 1f.

[175] BGM Kassel, NL 7, Stiftung Karl Paetow (Bad Oeynhausen), 61. Mappe, fo. 20, Frau Sch. to Rektor Leinius, no date.

[176] StAK, S8 C53, 'Das Lied vom leidgeprüften Kassel', line 16.

[177] 'Stark im Ertragen – Mutig im Kämpfen. Eine Unterredung mit dem Gauleiter', *KLZ*, 10 November 1943, p. 1.

[178] Compare *Überlebensberichte*, pp. 57 (no. 35), 83f. (no. 60), 121f. (no. 83), 144f. (no. 97). See also BGM Kassel, NL 7, Karl Paetow (Bad Oeynhausen), 58. Mappe, fos. 47–50, Else Dietzel, 'Erlebnisse auf der Vermisstensuchstelle'; 61. Mappe, fo. 20, Frau Sch. to Rektor Leinius, no date.

our heads down and lead a modest life if only we can have life, because we have you children'.[179]

As the discussion has shown, two powerful agents of memory operated in Kassel in the aftermath of the air raid. The first was Nazi propaganda, which dominated the public sphere and produced a narrative that revolved around the notion of *Terrorangriff* or 'terror raid'. Nazi propaganda denounced the attack as criminal, extolled the resilience of the racial community and stressed the cathartic quality of the catastrophe, which, it was claimed, had ushered in a new, truly National Socialist beginning. The second agent was the local population, whose personal experiences engendered a semi-public undercurrent that revolved around the notion of *Schreckensnacht* or 'night of horror'. This undercurrent comprised many different voices but generally shared in common an emphasis on loss and rupture.

The hold of the cataclysmic event on the collective imagination was such that on the eve of the first anniversary in the autumn of 1944, two-thirds of the population left the city for fear of a repeat of the catastrophe.[180] In his diary, Gebhard Niemeyer wrote on 22 October 1944, 'The first anniversary of the dreadful destruction of Kassel. With the help of my diary entries, I again relived the events of the night of horror.'[181] In the light of this evidence, the decision by the regional Nazi party to mark the first return of the day of 22 October by way of a small commemoration may thus be considered less an attempt at fostering the creation of a memory place than a tacit acknowledgement of the extent to which the date had already attained such a status in collective consciousness.[182]

After the downfall of the Third Reich, the new Social Democratic power holders in the city did not, at first, take up the practice of their Nazi predecessors. Instead of singling out '22 October', they preferred to commemorate 'all the victims of this great murder of nations' on the traditional day of mourning, the last Sunday in November.[183] The reasons for this manifest hesitation in embracing the memory place in the immediate post-war period are not as obvious as it may seem. In contrast to other cities such as Heilbronn, Darmstadt or Dresden, no attempts

---

[179] StAK S8 C51, 'Mein liebes, gutes, heiliges Kind', 26 October 1943.
[180] NA II RG 243 E6 # 64b k21, Background reports of German cities (Kassel), p. 18 (evacuation).
[181] StAK, S8 E15, diary Niemeyer, 22 October 1944.
[182] 'Das Vermächtnis der Toten', *KLZ* 15/249, 23 October 1943, p. 4. See also chapter 2 below.
[183] 'Kassel gedenkt seiner Toten', *HN*, 28 November 1945; StAK, A.1.00, vol. 1, Council Meeting, 2 December 1946; vol. 2, Council Meeting, 13 November 1947.

were made to gain permission from the allied occupation authorities for
an official ceremony in memory of the bombing.[184] Quite simply, the civil
administration seems to have seen no way of integrating '22 October' into
a meaningful narrative that would speak of things other than death. In
Magdeburg, across the inner-German border, the situation was rather
different. Here, the very extent of the disaster served to connect the
present to the past.

Magdeburg and the air raid of 16 January1945

In Magdeburg, the subject of aerial warfare had occupied a prominent
place in local propaganda and civil defence long before the city suffered
its 'solar plexus blow' in early 1945.[185] Owing to the evacuation measures adopted by the civic authorities following the bombing of Hamburg
in the summer of 1943, only about half of the 340,000 residents were
directly exposed to the attack of 16 January 1945. Moreover, by early
1945, general attention had shifted from the air war to the dramatic
developments on the Eastern Front, where the Red Army had launched
a major offensive. The extent to which the regional party leadership was
preoccupied with issues other than the air war in the winter of 1945 may
be gauged from the curious circumstance that, in his post-war memoirs,
the Nazi district leader of Magdeburg-Anhalt, Rudolf Jordan, wrongly
claimed that Magdeburg was destroyed in late February 1945, 'a few
days after' Dresden.[186]

Yet, despite the wider shock of the winter of 1945, the evidence does not
support the assumption that the memory place of '16 January' was wholly
a post-war invention. As contemporary ego-documents make clear, many
individuals perceived the fire bombing as marking a rupture in their personal lives as well as in the history of the city at large. 'As long as we may
live, we'll never forget what we've gone through in the past week,' a young
nurse wrote a few days after the attack in a letter to her parents.[187] True,
the population had experienced heavy raids throughout 1944, some of
which had caused considerable damage and killed hundreds of people,
but the attack of 16 January 1945 was different in transforming Magdeburg into a 'heap of rubble . . . that can no longer be called a city'. 'You'll
be speechless about the way it looks [here]; there's no city left,' wrote

---

[184] Compare Arnold, 'Beyond Usable Pasts'.
[185] See, for example, 'Kampf dem Terror! Aufruf des Gauleiters und Reichsverteidi-
gungskommissars Rudolf Jordan zur Luftschutzwoche im Gau Magdeburg-Anhalt ',
Magdeburgische Zeitung, 12 May 1944, p. 1.
[186] Jordan, *Erlebt und erlitten*, p. 232.
[187] KHM Magdeburg, A 5499 b, Erna to her parents, 21 January 1945.

another Magdeburg citizen in a letter to a relative on 18 January 1945.[188] Within the body of private documents produced in the months following the attack, the death toll was estimated at figures between 5,000 and 40,000 people, that is, between 1.5 per cent and 12 per cent of the pre-war population.[189] As in Kassel fifteen months earlier, the view from the outside communicated the impression that the destructive impact of the air raid had, in effect, annihilated the city as a social space and built-up environment.

Likewise, the view from the inside negotiated, in one way or another, the personal dimension of urban catastrophe. This could take the form of deep gratitude, elation almost, at unexpected survival in desperate circumstances, as in the case of an anonymous writer who managed to escape from a collapsed shelter and found his relatives alive and well amidst the death and devastation surrounding him. The report concluded on a hymnal praise of God.[190] At the other end of the spectrum, personal accounts could convey a sense of deep despair at the loss of loved ones, combined with feelings of self-reproach at having failed them in their hour of need. In a number of letters to a confidant, a mother from the city district of Cracau recounted how her adolescent daughter had gone missing in the raid while she was out of town. Upon her return, the woman not only had to realise that her daughter was among the dead but also had to cope with the ostracism by her neighbourhood, who threatened to report her to the police.[191]

While the immediate responses of ordinary Magdeburger to the incendiary attack were broadly similar to the reactions in Kassel in the autumn of 1943, the quick succession of catastrophic events in the spring of 1945 forestalled the creation of a web of interrelated stories in which the bombing was singled out. Whereas in Kassel, the memory place evolved 'from below', in Magdeburg, the *lieu de mémoire* was to a greater extent the result of memory politics 'from above'. In the years 1945 to 1947, this was as yet due not to the emerging Cold War but to efforts at a communal level to foster a sense of civic identity among a population that was dispirited, disoriented and divided, suffering from cold and hunger as well as from ongoing infringements by the Soviet occupation forces.[192]

---

[188] StAM, Rep. 41/481, 'Liebe Erna', 18 January 1945.
[189] Compare KHM Magdeburg, 'Erinnerungen an die Magdeburger Bombennacht', 28 January 1945 (5,000); ibid., A 5499 b, Erna to her parents, 18 January 1945 (14,000); '16. Januar 1945: Vernichtungsangriff', 2 December 1945 (40,000).
[190] KHM Magdeburg, '16. Januar 1945: Vernichtungsangriff', 2 December 1945.
[191] StAM, Rep. 41/481, 'Liebe Lissy', 20 January 1945.
[192] Compare the evidence collected in StAM, Rep. 41/116, Schriftwechsel mit der Bevölkerung, auch Beschwerden, 1947.

Rupture as continuity: 10 May 1631 and 16 January 1945

In an undated post-war text on the impact of World War II bombing, Ernst Martin, preacher at Magdeburg cathedral, tells of a textual
reminder of urban catastrophe that he kept in his study: 'Memento! 10.
V. 1631 / 16. I. 1945', read a framed sheet of paper on the wall opposite
his desk.[193]

History was crucial for the emergence of '16 January 1945' as a memory place. In the nineteenth century, the city of Magdeburg had been
associated, in the minds of the educated middle classes, with urban disaster. The name of the city conjured up the so-called 'marriage of blood' of
10 May 1631 when, after a prolonged siege, imperial Catholic troops had
razed Magdeburg to the ground and slaughtered 20,000 inhabitants.[194]
In typical fashion, an art guide from 1929 emphasised that the catastrophe at the height of the Thirty Years War had left a lasting imprint on
the city's development. 'There exists a Magdeburg before the destruction
and a Magdeburg after the destruction,' it declared.[195] Throughout the
nineteenth century and beyond, '10 May 1631' was of significance to
German national memory, and in particular to national Protestant memory. Locally, the date occupied a prominent place in the school cur-
riculum, leading generations of pupils to 'shed tears over 10 May', as a
newspaper article expressed it in 1931.[196]

When the three-hundredth anniversary was celebrated at the height
of the Great Depression in 1931, Magdeburg was a city bitterly divided
along confessional and class lines.[197] To the Protestant middle classes,
'10 May 1631' signified the martyrdom of the nation past and present.
In 1631, the citizens of Magdeburg had heroically sacrificed their lives
for the cause of 'German' Protestantism against 'foreign' Catholicism.
'There can be no doubt that the Protestant form of piety for which they
fought . . . was born out of the Germanic spirit,' Prof. Dr Brandenburg,
historian at Leipzig University, told his audience at the civic celebration
in the city hall.[198] At the Church-sponsored commemoration the night
before, Protestant pastor Alfred Frantz spoke of the destruction as a

---

[193] Martin, 'Memento', p. 57. On the role of Martin in the Third Reich see Czubatynski,
'Domprediger Ernst Martin'.
[194] See Cramer, *The Thirty Years' War and German Memory*, pp. 141–77; Ballerstedt, 'Die
Zerstörung der Stadt am 10. Mai 1631'.
[195] Niebelschütz, *Magdeburg*, p. 6.
[196] 'Magdeburger Jungen weinen um den 10. Mai', *Magdeburger General-Anzeiger*, 10 May
1931.
[197] Compare Tullner, 'Modernisierung und mitteldeutsche Hauptstadtpolitik'.
[198] '1631 – Magdeburgs Schicksalstag – 1931. Die Gedenkstunde in der Stadthalle',
Magdeburger General-Anzeiger, special supplement, 12 May 1931.

'heroes' song of faith and *Heimat*' that could serve as a historical example to the crisis-ridden present. 'Remember 10 May 1631! Out of the past, this song [of faith and *Heimat*] speaks to the bitter misery of our days – to the pain out of which the German soul cries for uprising and salvation.'[199]

Although the 'marriage of blood' was in the first instance a memory place of German Protestantism, the local Social Democrats, too, laid claim to the symbolic date – an indication of both their numerical strength and their integrationist politics in a city that was known among the Left as a 'red' town. The lord mayor, Hermann Beims (SPD), frequently invoked the day of remembrance in order to stress the resilience of the population in the face of adverse circumstances. Just as the murder and destruction in the Thirty Years War had failed to 'deliver a fatal blow', so too had two hundred years of authoritarian Prussian rule, Beims declared in 1927 in order to give historical legitimacy to his ambitious goal of making Magdeburg into the capital of 'middle Germany'.[200]

In 1945, with the three-hundredth anniversary celebration still within living memory, Nazi propagandists, too, made an attempt to draw on the historical precedent in order to put present devastation into context. In an article published a week after the bombing in a provincial edition of the regional daily, the unnamed author emphasised the suffering of Magdeburg by drawing a comparison with the city's iconic destruction in the Thirty Years War. 'On 16 January, [the cathedral] witnessed worse things [than on 10 May 1631],' he maintained. Employing Christian imagery, the author claimed that the city had been made to wear a 'crown of thorns' more painfully than most other German cities. None the less, the residents did not despair but persevered, or so he maintained. In so doing, they lived up to the example of their medieval forefathers who had thrown back the 'wolves of the steppe' under Emperor Otto I, the 'greatest Magdeburger'. The article concluded thus: 'This is the eternal admonition of Magdeburg: the way that the city has gloriously risen from the rubble over and over again is a symbol and admonition for the Reich.'[201]

The motif of phoenix-like rebirth, initially popularised by the Social Democrats in the 1920s but first applied to the air war by Nazi propaganda, played a prominent role in the politics of memory of the early post-war period. In the process, the raid of 16 January 1945 was

---

[199] Alfred Frantz, 'Das Magdeburger Heldenlied von Glauben und Heimat', *Magdeburger General-Anzeiger*, 10 May 1931.

[200] Magistrat der Stadt Magdeburg (ed.), *Magdeburg*, pp. 5f.; Tullner, 'Modernisierung und mitteldeutsche Hauptstadtpolitik', p. 754.

[201] 'Magdeburg im Januar 1945', *Der Mitteldeutsche. Haldensleber Tageszeitung – Wolmirstedter Tageszeitung*, 24 January 1945, p. 1.

transformed from a particularly horrifying episode in the city's recent catastrophic past into a memory place. This creation of a *lieu de mémoire* was in large measure due to the initiative of the second post-war administration under Rudolf Eberhard (1891–1965), a pragmatic Social Democrat in an emerging Socialist dictatorship.[202] Appointed by the Soviets on 28 January 1946, Eberhard turned for inspiration to the work of his predecessor, Hermann Beims, whose portrait he put up in his office.[203] From Beims, Eberhard adopted the visionary element as well as the integrationist approach to municipal politics. In Eberhard's view, a civic community spirit formed the necessary precondition for the city to overcome the daunting legacy of the war.[204] To this end, the mayor, rather than preach class struggle, made an effort to reach out to the middle classes, whose political representatives, the LPD and the CDU, had picked up 47 per cent of the vote in the municipal elections of 1946. He also organised a number of ambitious exhibitions and rallies in which an integrationist politics of memory played an important role.

The first such event, the mass rally dubbed 'The Rebuilding of Magdeburg', was held on 12 May 1946. The civil administration had chosen the date deliberately to coincide with the 315th anniversary of the city's destruction in the Thirty Years War. At the centre of the event stood two speeches, one by the mayor, the other by the municipal building officer, Erich Koß. Whereas Koß spoke on the technical details of organised rubble clearance, Eberhard drew a broad sketch of municipal history. 'On 16 January 1945 . . . a building was destroyed on the Breite Weg that bore the inscription, "remember 10 May", a sign in memory of 10 May 1631, the day of Magdeburg's destruction three hundred years ago,' Eberhard told his audience. In opening thus, he linked Magdeburg's iconic fate in the Thirty Years War, 'the biggest catastrophe in the Occident since the downfall of the cities of antiquity', to the recent devastation in World War II.[205] Although the mayor was adamant that he did not intend to equate 'our misfortune' to the 'calamity of 10 May 1631', he still insisted that the past held out consolation for the present, for 'despite great misery . . . new life' had always prevailed.

In a press release prepared for the big dailies of the Soviet Zone of Occupation, the *Neue Deutschland* and *Tägliche Rundschau*, the parallels between the two events were made even more explicit. For a supra-local

---

[202] On Eberhard see the study by his daughter, Meyer-Eberhard, *Rudolf Eberhard*.

[203] Ibid., pp. 76, 166.

[204] Compare Schmiechen-Ackermann, 'Magdeburg als Stadt des Schwermaschinenbaus', p. 814; Meyer-Eberhard, *Eberhard*, p. 42.

[205] Rudolf Eberhard, 'Magdeburg in Kriegsnot und erfolgreicher Arbeit', in 'Was Wahnsinn vernichtet hat, wird wieder errichtet', *Freiheit*, 14 May 1946, p. 5.

audience, the municipal press office tried to distinguish Magdeburg as 'the city that had been destroyed twice over'.[206] 'Comparable to the calamity of 10 May 1631 is the catastrophe that befell Magdeburg on 16 January 1945,' the text read. This 'special position... among Germany's war-torn cities', the authors claimed, would be interpreted by the resident population as a 'call of fate' to double their efforts for the reconstruction of the city and the renewal of Germany.

In the summer of 1947, the theme of death-as-rebirth was developed further in an elaborate exhibition, 'Magdeburg is Alive!', in which the mythical bird of Greek mythology, the phoenix, figured as the official symbol. The city administration did not just intend the event as a showcase for the first architectural designs for reconstruction. They also sought to foster a civic community spirit, to 'replant in the hearts of the Magdeburger the love of their city', as a leaflet put it.[207] One way to achieve this was to integrate the present into the past: eight of the twenty-three exhibition rooms were devoted to Magdeburg's history, creating a colourful tapestry of local events from prehistoric times to the present. One room was devoted to the seventeenth-century *burghermaster* and scholar Otto von Guericke, who in local historiography was widely credited with saving the city from ruin after the disaster of the Thirty Years War (Fig. 4). By contrast, local Socialist traditions were conspicuously played down.

While the Third Reich was not represented, an entire chamber was devoted to the air raid of 16 January 1945, which formed the bridge between room number six, 'Dear old *Heimat*', and room number eight, 'The end: chaos'. In the party paper of the Christian Democratic Union (CDU), *Der Neue Weg*, there appeared a vivid description of this 'chamber of horror' (Fig. 5),

The sound of sirens leads the way to a darkened room which symbolises through the use of optical and acoustic effects the second day of horror in Magdeburg's history: a hand of death built from bombs, a glowing iron girder, the crackle of fire and the drone of planes recall memories of the horrors that the population of our cities suffered in the days and nights of the air raids.[208]

In order to accompany the exhibition, the city council organised a festive commemoration that was called 'Magdeburg's Day of Fate as Reflected through Art'. The event ostentatiously dealt with literary

---

[206] StAM, Rep. 41/112, Aufbau kriegszerstörter Städte, fos. 18–21, 'Die Stadt die zweimal zerstört wurde'.

[207] StAM, Rep. 41/92, Vorbereitung und Durchführung der Ausstellung 'Magdeburg lebt', leaflet, 'Magdeburg lebt', June 1947.

[208] 'Magdeburg lebt', *Der Neue Weg*, 4 July 1947, p. 1.

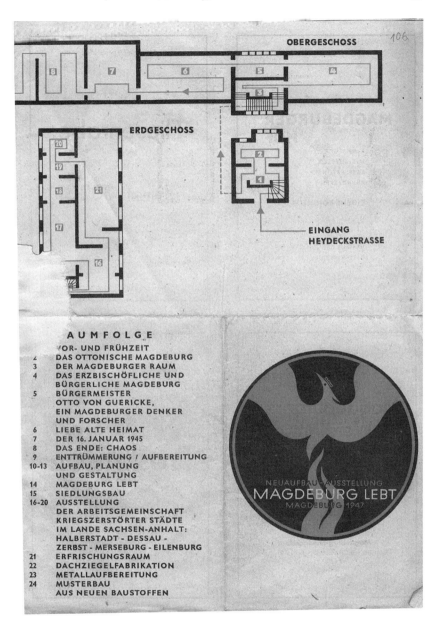

Figure 4. Excerpt from the official exhibition guide, 'Magdeburg is Alive! (1947).

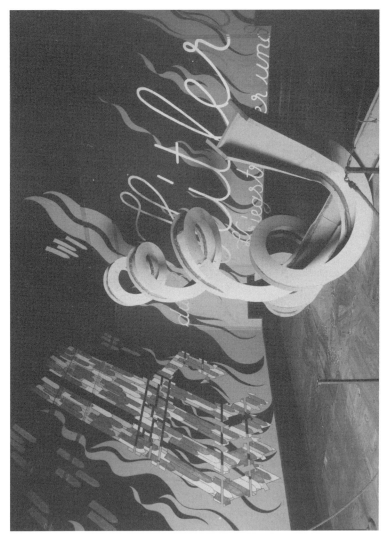

Figure 5. The 'chamber of horror' (1947).

representations of Magdeburg's first destruction. Its real subject, however, was not the past but the present, as Mayor Eberhard made clear in
his address, '10 May 1631 and 16 January 1945'. The destruction of the
city in the recent war found its parallel in the Thirty Years War. And just
as Magdeburg was reborn in the eighteenth century, so it would be again
in the twentieth.[209] In telescoping the multiple experiences of six years
of war, mass death and destruction into a single day, the post-war civil
administration played a pre-eminent role in creating the *lieu de mémoire*
of '16 January 1945'.

It is not easy to determine how much of an impact these efforts had on
ordinary residents. Doubtless, many were preoccupied with day-to-day
survival in an environment of deprivation, violence and black-marketeer
on which the Swiss writer Max Frisch has famously commented that
'the likes of us, suddenly thrust into this life, would perish within three
days'.[210] Accordingly, one response to the exhibition was that of cyni-
cism. Rumours circulated which alleged that the city administration had
paid 10,000 Reichsmarks for the design of the exhibition poster.[211] Likewise, visitors were overheard commenting that the displays were no more
than 'propaganda' and the whole exercise 'pointless'.[212] At the same
time, the fact that around 50,000 residents made the effort to attend
the exhibition, that is, nearly one in five of the resident population as
it stood in 1947, indicates that there existed broad popular demand for
visions of the rebuilding and the future more generally.[213] For one visitor
at least, there was comfort in the fact that the city's history played such
a prominent role in the exhibition. In a warm letter of support to the
mayor, Helmut W. wrote that he had countered the critical remarks of
other visitors by pointing to the city's first destruction in 1631 and the
rebirth that followed.[214] In this case at least, the city administration's
politics of memory had clearly served its purpose.

Conclusion

The resident populations of Kassel and Magdeburg did not experience
the area raids of 22 October 1943 and 16 January 1945 in a vacuum,

---

[209] StAM, Rep. 41/92, Vorbereitung und Durchführung der Ausstellung 'Magdeburg lebt',
fos. 56–63, 'Der 10. Mai 1631 und der 16. Januar 1945'.
[210] Frisch, *Tagebuch*, November 1947, reprinted in Enzensberger (ed.), *Europa*, p. 260.
[211] StAM, Rep. 41/116, Schriftwechsel mit der Bevölkerung, fo. 275, Georg R. to mayor,
3 July 1947.
[212] Ibid., fo. 370, Helmut W. to mayor, 19 June 1947.
[213] StAM, Rep. 41/92, Vorbereitung und Durchführung der Ausstellung 'Magdeburg lebt',
fo. 71, 'Statistik über Besuch der Ausstellung', 10 August 1947.
[214] StAM, Rep. 41/116, Schriftwechsel mit der Bevölkerung, fo. 370, Helmut W. to mayor,
19 June 1947.

but made sense of the events by drawing on the mental structures and referential frames available to them. Nor were the air raids experienced in isolation from their respective political and military contexts. In the minds of many Kasseler, the date of 22 October 1943 denoted the city's 'death' or 'annihilation' despite the frantic efforts of Nazi propaganda to ascribe a cathartic quality to the event. Many Magdeburger, by comparison, did not single out the air raid of 16 January 1945 to the same extent, but viewed it as one particularly harrowing episode in a chain of catastrophic events that was engulfing their environment in the spring of 1945.

The dominant agents of public memory in the two cities – the local Nazi elites during the war and the civil administrations after 1945 – were not free to construct present-centred *lieux de mémoire* as they saw fit, but had to engage with *milieux de mémoire* that fed on a dense web of primary experiences. As a consequence, public memory in both cities came to revolve around a set of recurring motifs and themes: death, destruction and survival. Given the impact of larger referential frames on processes of memory formation, there also emerged significant differences. Whereas the Magdeburg civil administration under Rudolf Eberhard (SED) actively fostered – or one could go further and say 'invented' – the memory place of '16 January' in order to construct a historical analogy with the city's infamous destruction in the Thirty Years War, the Kassel administration under Willi Seidel (SPD) saw little benefit in institutionalising a memory place that seemed to denote nothing but unprecedented catastrophe.

Part I

Commemorating death

2 'Soldiers of the *Heimat*': commemorating the dead, 1940–1945

Introduction

'Why such a terrible fate, why so many victims?' asked the Nazi district leader of Kurhesse, Karl Gerland, in a public rally on 22 October 1944.[1] On the first anniversary of the heavy air raid against the city of Kassel, representatives of the Nazi party, detachments of the army, the labour service (*Reichsarbeitsdienst*) and civilians assembled in an open space in order to commemorate the dead. When a brass band struck up the tune of 'The Song of the Good Comrade' (*Das Lied vom Guten Kameraden*), the flags were lowered and ceremonial words were spoken in honour of the 'fallen'. This was followed by the district leader's speech, which climaxed in a vow that 'none of the dead of this war' had made their 'sacrifice' in vain.[2] Finally, the Hitler salute and the departure of the flags marked the closure of a commemoration in which different groups of participants took part in a public performance.[3] Through music, ritual and speech, the ceremony spoke to the emotions just as much as to the mind.[4] It acknowledged emotional needs among the audience while seeking to channel and to control them.[5]

Commemorations are one medium through which the public memory of the air war has been conveyed. The organisation of commemorative events requires a degree of organisational skill, financial resources and social influence which tends to make them the preserve of powerful interest groups and above all the political and religious elites. They are not celebrated in a socio-political vacuum but reflect the distribution of power in society. By way of commemorations, hegemonic narratives are developed

---

[1] 'Das Vermächtnis der Toten. Gedenkfeier für die Terroropfer der Gauhauptstadt – Der Gauleiter über den Sinn des Opfers', *KLZ*, 23 October 1944, p. 4.
[2] Ibid.   [3] Behrenbeck, *Kult*, p. 276.
[4] On Nazi rituals and the attendant hero myth see Behrenbeck, *Kult, passim*; on the centrality of the cult of the fallen warrior for the Nazi world view Lurz, *Kriegerdenkmäler*, vol. V; and more generally on the connection between nationalism and death in war, Mosse, *Fallen Soldiers*.
[5] Essbach, 'Gedenken oder Erforschen', p. 135.

and popularised through verbal as well as non-verbal modes of communication. In order to invoke feelings and to convey meaning, music, symbols and rituals are just as important as the spoken word. Commemorative addresses can therefore not be interpreted in isolation from their rich non-verbal context. They are not scholarly enquiries into historical subject matter but part of a cultural practice of public remembrance.[6] While the available rites, symbols and tropes are limited, commemorative formats are still subject to historical change.[7]

Through their violent deaths, the civilian casualties of the air war shared in the fate of soldiers killed in battle. Indeed, the deliberate targeting of enemy non-combatants may be considered as one of the 'most significant hallmarks' of 'total war'.[8] Yet, despite the wide-scale erosion of the traditional protective barriers in the actual conduct of warfare, there still existed residual knowledge among both the Axis powers and the anti-Hitler coalition that the killing of unarmed men, women and children was not quite the same as the killing of soldiers in battle. Such action needed to be justified (or at least to be denied) lest the killing be considered an atrocity rather than a legitimate act of war.

Just as other European societies, Nazi Germany largely lacked commemorative practices that would endow the violent death of civilians with meaning.[9] Such modes of representation as had been developed since the beginning of the nineteenth century revolved mainly around the citizen-soldier who was said to have given his life for the greater cause of the nation.[10] But could the same be said of civilians killed in war? The answers that German society developed to this problem during the war were first and foremost the answers of the Nazi regime. While the affective bonds between 'ordinary' Germans and Nazism may have been unravelling by the time the question was posed with urgency from 1943, the regime still wielded enough power to establish a cultural framework that integrated German air raid casualties into the Nazi cult of death.

Although during World War II non-combatant deaths from the air occurred on a scale that found parallels only in the literary imagination of the inter-war period, the phenomenon itself was not without precedent in Germany. During World War I, the Entente powers had dropped 15,700 bombs on the German Reich, resulting in the deaths of some 740 people,

---

[6] Compare Eschebach, *Öffentliches Gedenken*, pp. 9–59.
[7] Compare Koselleck, 'Einleitung'.   [8] Stig Förster, 'Introduction', p. 8.
[9] In societies victimised by Germany the problem of representing civilian death posed itself in different ways but generally with much greater urgency, not to speak of the Jewish community. For a comparative approach see Lagrou, 'The Nationalisation of Victimhood'.
[10] Koselleck and Jeismann (eds.), *Der politische Totenkult*; Winter, *Sites of Memory*.

most of whom were civilians.[11] In south-western cities such as Karlsruhe and Freiburg, which were particularly hard hit, public funeral ceremonies had been staged repeatedly in which clerics and local dignitaries had tried to console the bereaved and to rally the local population behind the war effort. To this end, they had denounced the air raids as atrocities against innocent civilians, and at one and the same time insisted on the soldierly character of non-combatant death. As the lord mayor of Freiburg, Dr Thoma, put it during a burial ceremony that was held a few days after an air raid had claimed the lives of twelve residents on 14 April 1917, 'The victims have died for the fatherland just like the heroes out at the front.'[12] In some respects, therefore, Nazism could draw on commemorative patterns that were already in place when, from 1940 onwards, regional and local functionaries were confronted with the problem of imparting meaning to non-combatant death in the air war. Yet these practices had been developed for rather isolated instances that typically involved no more than a dozen casualties, not for the massive loss of life all across Germany's urban topography that was characteristic of area bombing in World War II.

This chapter argues that the origins of post-1945 commemorative traditions can be traced to the public funeral ceremonies of the local Nazi elites during the war. Memory cultures of allied bombing originated from the public commemoration of death in war.[13] While the cultural enunciation of death had long antecedents,[14] it was Nazism that first applied these practices and traditions to mass death in aerial warfare. Any examination of the trajectory of public memory must therefore begin with a close reading of the narrative themes and cultural forms that the Nazi authorities employed in order to integrate catastrophic rupture into the National Socialist world view.[15]

While the Nazi elites laid total claim to the public expression of loss and bereavement suffered in war, their factual dominance remained precarious. Throughout the period 1940 to 1945, they had to contend with the rivalry of the Christian churches, which had been curtailed in their

[11] Geinitz, 'The First Air War against Noncombatants', p. 207. German strategic bombing of the British Isles between 1914 and 1918 resulted in the deaths of 1,400 civilians. See Schmidt, 'Luftkrieg', p. 688.

[12] 'Die Bestattung der Fliegeropfer', *Freiburger Zeitung*, 18 April 1917. For a careful reading of the ceremony see Chickering, 'Ein Begräbnis in Freiburg 1917'.

[13] Compare also the remarks by Ranft and Selzer (eds.), *Städte aus Trümmern*, pp. 9–25.

[14] On the tradition of public funeral ceremonies in Germany see Ackermann, *Nationale Totenfeiern*; on death as a social phenomenon Fischer, *Geschichte des Todes*; and the pioneering work by Ariès, *Geschichte des Todes*.

[15] For a methodological plea to integrate the experience of death into studies of military history see Geyer, 'Eine Kriegsgeschichte, die vom Tod spricht'.

capacity for public expression but not been eliminated as an autonomous voice.[16] As a 'societal group' to which more than 90 per cent of the German population owed at least formal allegiance, the churches had long developed a complex set of rituals, symbols and meanings that accompanied the life cycle of the individual. They boasted special expertise in dealing with the anthropological certainty of death.[17] With the Catholic All Souls' Day and the Protestant Memorial Sunday, both denominations also possessed well-established remembrance days on which to commemorate death as a collective phenomenon – a practice that was easily adapted to the problem of premature mass death in war.[18] Indeed, the very decision of the Nazi party to extend the Nazi cult of death to all casualties of World War II reflected concern over the rising influence of the Church on the cultural enunciation of death.[19]

This chapter examines the commemorative activity of the local elites of Church and state between 1940 and 1945 as a cultural practice in which power relationships were brought to bear on the public memory of violent death in war. According to the hegemonic narrative of the Nazi regime, the dead were both victims of a criminal deed and sacrificers for a higher goal. The mourning of loss did not stand at the centre of this narrative, but rather hatred of the enemy and commitment to the war effort. By contrast, the Christian churches foregrounded the notion of affliction. Through death and destruction, God had spoken and revealed himself as both wrathful and merciful, or so they claimed.

'Never has a sacrifice been more worthwhile': civilian death as heroic sacrifice

Between the summer of 1940 and the spring of 1945, the city of Kassel was subjected to forty air raids,[20] at least half of which caused losses among the population.[21] Yet, throughout the period, the regional Nazi party organised only four funeral services for the dead, in 1940, 1941, 1943 and 1944 respectively. In Magdeburg, too, there was a discrepancy between the number of air raids and party activity. Eight of twenty-eight

---

[16] For a balanced summary of the role of the churches in the Third Reich see Hehl, 'Die Kirchen in der NS-Diktatur', and more recently, Kösters, 'Christliche Kirchen'.

[17] Compare the acid comment in SD summary report no. 325 of 12 October 1942, in: *Meldungen*, vol. XI, p. 4313.

[18] See Hausen, 'The "Day of National Mourning" in Germany', p. 131.

[19] Compare Behrenbeck, *Kult*, pp. 492–502.

[20] 'Never has a sacrifice been so worthwhile.' Kreisleiter Hans Tichy in his Magdeburg commemorative address of 28 January 1944, in 'Sie starben, damit Deutschland lebt', *Magdeburgische Zeitung*, 28 January 1944, p. 1.

[21] Figures according to Dettmar, 'Kassel im Luftkrieg', pp. 18–20.

attacks were publicly marked by way of commemorations, all but one in 1944. In neither city was there a positive correlation between severity of the air raid and propagandistic investment on the part of the local Nazi party. If anything, the opposite was the case.

The apparent inconsistencies appear to reflect shifting realities on the ground as well as sudden changes in direction from above. Throughout the period, Nazi propaganda never found a consistent approach to the challenges of the air war, oscillating between exaggeration, 'realism' and denial. While official silence flew in the face of the primary experience of millions of Germans, any attempt at exploiting the propagandistic potential of indiscriminate bombing ran the danger of admitting to the regime's helplessness in preventing the progressive destruction of Germany's ability to wage war.[22] Despite the inconsistencies, a pattern emerges which indicates an inverse relationship between the escalation of the air war and the commemorative activity of the Nazi party.[23]

In Kassel, the NSDAP held regular funeral ceremonies for the victims of the air war throughout the period from 1940 until the summer of 1943.[24] After 22 October 1943, such activity was scaled back dramatically. Rather than organise a special commemoration for the thousands of residents who had been killed on that day, the local Nazi representatives used the twentieth anniversary of Hitler's failed putsch, on 9 November 1943, and, to a lesser extent, Heroes' Memorial Day in March 1944, in order to incorporate civilian mass death into the Nazi cult of death. With the exception of the anniversary commemoration of 22 October 1944, no public ceremonies were organised in the autumn and winter of 1944 despite a string of heavy attacks in this period.[25]

In Magdeburg, a similar trend can be observed. Here, the commemorative activity of the Nazi party reached its climax in the summer and autumn of 1944 when six public commemorations were staged in quick

---

[22] A history of the air war as a propaganda war remains to be written. On the central theme of 'retaliation' see Kirwin, 'Waiting for Retaliation'.

[23] The same pattern can be observed in other German cities that were subjected to a string of attacks escalating in severity over the course of several years. Compare, for example, the cases of Darmstadt and Heilbronn. Compare also the remarks in Süß, 'Tod aus der Luft', p. 531.

[24] The biggest funeral ceremony of the entire war was organised on 4 August 1943 in order to mark the death of 188 Germans and forced labourers in two USAAF daytime raids. See 'Rede des Gauleiters bei der Gefallenenfeier am 4. 8. vor dem Rathaus in Kassel', *Soldatenbrief der Gauleitung Kurhessen der NSDAP* (September 1943), pp. 4f.

[25] Between September 1944 and March 1945, 13,000 tons of bombs were dropped on to the city in twenty-four air raids, representing two-thirds of the overall bomb load of 18,000 tons. See NA (Kew) AIR 14/3792, Operational Research Section Bomber Command, report no. 242: 'The Effect of Air Attack on the City and District of Kassel', summary.

succession. Two commemorations in June responded to comparatively insignificant attacks, and followed in the wake of a party-driven 'week of anti-aircraft defence' in mid-May 1944. It appears that the regional leadership had seized on the raids as propagandistic support of its efforts to evacuate the densely populated inner city. In August, another public funeral ceremony was organised in order to commemorate the most destructive and deadly attack thus far, which had claimed 683 lives. After this, the commemorative interest of the local Nazi party declined and appears to have ceased altogether with the indiscriminate air raid of 16 January 1945. No evidence survives of a public funeral service to commemorate the roughly 2,000 casualties of that night, or of any of the raids that followed.

The semiotics of commemoration

As a cultural practice, the 'funeral ceremonies' in honour of the casualties of allied bombing combined elements of the two most important events of the Nazi calendar: 'Heroes' Memorial Day' in March and the anniversary celebrations of the failed Munich putsch of 1923 in November. Both events drew on the bourgeois festive culture of the nineteenth century, military ceremonial and above all the liturgy of the (Catholic) Church. The commemorations of 9 November re-enacted the founding myth of the Nazi movement, emphasising death and sacrifice. Replete with references to the Nazi trauma of the German revolution of November 1918, they revolved around the 'martyrs' of the Nazi party. Although originally dedicated to the followers of the Nazi movement who had been killed during the 'time of struggle' (*Kampfzeit*), the propagandists of the Nazi party increasingly turned '9 November' into a memorial day for the general population.[26] By contrast, 'Heroes' Memorial Day' was dedicated to the memory of the fallen soldiers of World War I, and from the early 1940s, also those of World War II. It was celebrated not as a day of mourning but as a day of rebirth and triumph.[27]

The funeral ceremonies brought together four groups of participants in a public space, demonstrating to a wider public the close connection between all of them: the dead, the bereaved, the Nazi party and the people. First of all, there was the group around whom the celebration ostensibly revolved, the dead. Their presence could be either real or symbolic.[28] In Magdeburg, the NSDAP generally placed great importance on the

---

[26] 'Toten- und Ahnengedenktag'. See 'Unsere Feier', *Die neue Gemeinschaft* 8/10 (1944), p. 337.

[27] This paragraph is based on Behrenbeck, *Kult*, pp. 195–447.

[28] See 'Gedenkfeier der NSDAP für Opfer des Luftkrieges', *Die neue Gemeinschaft* 8/10 (1944), p. 374.

physical presence of the dead. A photograph taken at the commemoration of 27 January 1944 shows long rows of coffins lined up in the ballroom of the city hall (Fig. 6).[29] The arrangement recognised certain distinctions but generally aimed at the creation of a homogeneous victim group. The great majority of coffins were draped in swastika flags. The arrangement and decoration of the coffins deindividualised the victims, suggesting that the 122 casualties had died not as individuals but as members of a group united in a common purpose.

In Kassel, the regional leadership pursued a slightly different approach although the goal was identical. It generally refrained from the physical presence of the corpses and preferred symbolic means of representation instead. In the commemoration of 13 September 1941, for example, the dead were symbolised by a catafalque on which a sacrificial bowl was placed. The arrangement was completed by a giant silver swastika on the wall behind the catafalque.[30] When the number of casualties rose to several hundred, practical necessities forced a shift in Magdeburg as well. In the funeral ceremony on 10 August 1944, the audience faced a black makeshift memorial bearing a silver laurel wreath with an iron cross.[31]

Next to the dead, the bereaved stood at the centre of the formal arrangement of the funeral ceremonies. They attended by special invitation and were generally seated in front, facing the podium and the dead.[32] They were at one and the same time central and marginal to the ceremony. Dressed in black, they were the recipients of condolences by the local political elites and the addressees of the commemorative address by the party functionary.[33] Without them, no 'funeral ceremony' could have been staged with any claim to credibility. Yet they did not speak but were spoken to. Their grief was expressed, interpreted and channelled by others while they were publicly visible and highly vulnerable in their emotional expressions.[34] Just as much as they may have drawn comfort from the presence of a large congregation of mourners, they became instrumental to an official narrative of racial community and paternalistic care which they may or may not have shared.

In contrast to the passivity of the bereaved, the third group of participants played an active role. The formal delegations from party, state and

[29] For the photograph see *Der Mitteldeutsche*, 17 June 1944, p. 5. Coffins were also present at the ceremonies of 31 May 1944 and 24 June 1944.

[30] See the photograph in *KP*, 15 September 1941; *KNN*, 15 September 1941, p. 1.

[31] 'Sie sind unsterblich geworden . . . ', *Magdeburgische Zeitung*, 10 August 1944, p. 4.

[32] Compare *Der Mitteldeutsche*, 26 January 1944, p. 3 and 28 January 1944, p. 1; *KLZ*, 4 August 1943, p. 1 and 5 August 1943, p. 1. See also 'Gedenkfeiern der NSDAP für Opfer des Luftkrieges', *Die neue Gemeinschaft* 12/10 (1944), pp. 572ff.

[33] On colours of mourning see Stubbe, *Formen der Trauer*.

[34] 'Sie starben, damit Deutschland lebt', *Magdeburgische Zeitung*, 28 January 1944, p. 1.

Figure 6. Coffins draped in swastika flags at a funeral ceremony in Magdeburg on 27 January 1944.

army were the genuine bearers of the ritual action such as the ceremonial entry and exit or the lowering and raising of the flags. As 'guards of
honour', they were placed around or behind the bereaved and the dead,
symbolically enacting a role which they were less and less able to perform
in the real world: party and army as shield and protector of the racial community and upholder of the values for which the dead were said to have
given their lives (Fig. 7).[35] Even more important was the representative
from the local party elite, usually the regional or district leader (*Gauleiter*
or *Kreisleiter*), who delivered the commemorative address. Assuming the
role of pastor, he delivered the official interpretation of events to the
congregation and – via the local media – to a wider public.

Finally, there were the private citizens, who were generally informed
about the funeral ceremony and urged to attend via appeals in the local
press. The local press reported attendance figures ranging from several
hundred to several thousand. While these figures cannot be taken at face
value, surviving photographs support the assumption that the obsequies
were generally well attended.

The Nazi party certainly intended the commemorations to be well
attended, and was prepared to subordinate considerations of public safety
to the propagandistic benefits of large public gatherings. Despite the constant risk of new bomb attacks, the commemorations were generally held
in central urban spaces, rarely at the cemeteries themselves. The organisers preferred large halls such as the ballroom of the city hall (*Stadthalle*),
or even better, central public squares such as the Alte Markt in Magdeburg or the space in front of the town hall (*Rathaus*) in Kassel. The
choice of location was indicative of central themes of the party-organised
events. 'This was not a funeral ceremony in the usual sense of the word,'
the *Magdeburgische Zeitung* commented in an article on 28 January 1944.
'Beyond pain and suffering, it demonstrated the will and determination
to draw new strength from their sacrifice for the struggle for victory,' the
paper claimed. The ceremonies were about neither individual death nor
mourning, but ostentatiously about the life of the racial community. This
interpretation was adhered to even after the events of 22 October 1943
had demonstrated the ability of the Western air forces to put not just
the survival of individuals in danger but that of the local community as a
whole. Unwittingly, perhaps, the *Kurhessische Landezeitung* acknowledged
the growing discrepancy between claim and reality when commenting on
the ceremonial closure of the commemoration on 7 November 1943 in

---

[35] See, for example, 'Sie starben im Gesetz, das Deutschland heißt', *Der Mitteldeutsche*,
24 June 1944, p. 5. For a visual representation see 'Die Trauerfeier für die Gefallenen
des Luftangriffs vor dem Kasseler Rathaus', *KLZ*, 5 August 1943, p. 1.

Figure 7. Delegations from party and army as shield and protector of the racial community. Public commemoration for the casualties of the air war in front of Kassel town hall, 4 August 1943.

the following way: 'The guards of honour march off with drums beating through the devastated streets in which all life seems to have died but which are still full of life.'[36]

In all ceremonies, spatial and acoustic markers were used to delimitate the 'sacred' sphere of the ceremonial space from the 'profane' sphere of the everyday. This was a common practice which derived from church liturgy as well as from bourgeois festive culture.[37] In their choice of music, the Nazi functionaries clearly sought to distinguish the secular commemoration from a typical Christian funeral service. The church bells remained silent during the ceremonies, and only once, in August 1940, was a hymn performed.[38] The organisers preferred serious music from the German romantic tradition that tempered mourning with the heroic. Very popular was Beethoven's symphony no. 3, *Sinfonia Eroica* (Heroic Symphony), extracts from which were performed in half of the ceremonies under consideration here.[39] Beethoven's *Egmont* was also used. Next to Beethoven, Richard Wagner featured prominently, in particular his *Twilight of the Gods* and *Rienzi*. Even more important, however, were the two national anthems and 'The Song of the Good Comrade', which formed part of the standard repertoire at every commemoration. While the *Deutschlandlied* and the *Horst-Wessel-Lied* established a link between local events and the National Socialist nation, the military tune of 'The Song of the Good Comrade' identified the civilian casualties of bombing as combatants.[40]

Just as with music, the Nazi party sought to emphasise the non-Christian, heroic character of the ceremonies by means of symbols. Prominent were the national flag bearing the swastika, the Iron Cross, and pylons. Wreaths played a role as well but appear to have been less important than might be assumed. The swastika flag not only demonstrated the official character of the commemoration. Its ceremonial lowering during the 'honouring of the dead' also indicated a reciprocal relationship

[36] *KLZ*, 8 November 1943, p. 1.   [37] Compare Behrenbeck, *Kult*, pp. 313–25.

[38] *Kasseler Sonntagsblatt*, 25 August 1940, p. 12. This early ceremony was unusual in the participation of Pastor Wüstemann, who would later become the first post-war bishop of the state church of Kurhesse-Waldeck. It was held at the open graves in the cemetery of Kassel-Wehleiden. The hymn was 'Da unten ist Frieden'.

[39] Compare entry 'Eroica Symphony', *The Oxford Dictionary of Music*, p. 278; Schleuning, '3. Symphonie Es-Dur Eroica op. 55'. On the political uses of Beethoven see Dennis, *Beethoven in German Politics*; on music and German national identity in general Applegate and Potter (eds.), *Music and German National Identity*. See also the suggestion for pieces of music in *Die neue Gemeinschaft* 8 (1940), pp. 23ff.

[40] The *Lied vom guten Kameraden* was based on the poem by Ludwig Uhland, 'Ich hatt' einen Kameraden' (1809), and composed by Friedrich Silcher. By the time of World War II, the song had become a traditional element of military funeral ceremonies. See Stein, *Symbole und Zeremoniell*, p. 283.

between the dead and the living: just as the commemorated had died for the Third Reich, the commemorators acknowledged their death as a binding sacrifice.[41] The Iron Cross, meanwhile, identified the dead as combatants, as 'soldiers of the *Heimat*', as the *Magdeburgische Zeitung* put it on 28 January 1944.[42] Finally, the pylons once more underlined the sacrificial aspect of violent death under the bombs.[43]

Although the use of music and symbols was designed in order to emphasise the non-Christian character of the official ceremonies, at the same time crucial elements were adopted from the Christian model. This was most obvious in the formal arrangement. Typically, the reading of a Führer proclamation (*Vorspruch*) was followed by a speech from the Nazi district leader, which was succeeded by a proclamation of faith in the Führer and German victory. This was the psalm reading, the sermon and the creed of the Christian liturgy. At the centre of the ceremony stood the formal tribute to the dead (*Totenehrung*), which the Nazi party had also taken over from the Christian churches, where special intercessory prayers for fallen soldiers had been introduced since the beginning of the war.[44] If fatalities were in the range of several dozens, the name of each person was read out to lowered flags and to the tune of 'The Song of the Good Comrade'. Sometimes, a minute's silence followed. In Kassel, after 22 October 1943, the sheer number of fatalities – an exact figure was never officially acknowledged – necessitated a change in procedure. On 7 November 1943, the names of the 'martyrs' of the failed 1923 putsch stood in for the thousands of local residents, while on 22 October 1944 a speaker referred in general terms to the 'fallen soldiers of this war' and to the 'women, men and children of the city of Kassel' who had fallen 'victim to the bombing terror of our enemies'.[45]

Themes

If the interpretation of the Nazi funeral ceremony as a secularised church service is valid, then the party functionary may be said to have assumed

---

[41] The symbol goes back to 1813 when William III of Prussia founded a medal awarded for bravery in the form of an iron cross. See Stein, *Symbole und Zeremoniell*, pp. 48–50, 54–63.

[42] 'Sie starben, damit Deutschland lebt', *Magdeburgische Zeitung*, 28 January 1944, p. 1.

[43] On the popularity of pylons in the Third Reich see Behrenbeck, *Kult*, p. 409.

[44] Compare Behrenbeck, *Kult*, pp. 492–501. For Magdeburg, see the example of the Protestant Domgemeinde. AKPS, Rep. J1, no. 3290, Kanzelabkündigungen 1936–49; for Kassel, the example of the Protestant congregation of Kassel-Wilhelmshöhe. See Apel, *In Memoriam*.

[45] *KLZ*, 8 November 1943, p. 1; *KLZ*, 23 October 1944, p. 4.

the role of high priest.[46] By virtue of his calling, he acted as a mediator between the dead and the living, the Führer and his people, the *Heimat* and the front. He claimed to possess special authority to put local catastrophe in context and to impart meaning to violent death. The idea of the 'sleeping dead', which had played such a prominent role in the commemorations of the inter-war period, stood at the centre of this practice.[47] 'We believe that the dead are not dead but live with and amongst us,' the district leader of Kurhesse, Karl Weinrich, declared in typical fashion at the commemorative address on 4 August 1943. The dead were not dead but still alive, and the Gauleiter was the mouthpiece through which they spoke, 'They call upon us . . . to grow hard and strong in this period of trial before fate.'[48] The claims of the National Socialist regime on the population were couched in terms of a personal obligation of the living to the dead; that is, of the local residents to their very own deceased acquaintances, relatives and loved ones. Likewise, failure to live up to the demands was presented as treason towards the community of the dead past and present. 'The failure of our nation would be treason towards the meaning of our history,' as Weinrich put it.

By the same token, the functionary acted as an intermediary between the local population and the Führer, bestowing praise and censure. 'The Gauleiter instructed Dr Goebbels to tell the Führer that the population of Kassel . . . had shown exemplary and heroic bearing in this hardest night of the city's history,' the local press reported when the propaganda minister visited Kassel in November 1943.[49] One year later, Weinrich's successor, Karl Gerland, used the first anniversary commemoration to insinuate that the people of Kassel had partly themselves to blame for the high loss of life on 22 October 1943. Their suffering was punishment for a double sin of omission: just as 'some amongst us' had failed to grasp the nature of this war as a war of annihilation, 'far too many' had been disobedient to the party 'admonition' to be evacuated. In addition, '22 October has taught Kassel that there is no humanity and chivalry in the conduct of war by our supposedly civilised enemies,' as the district

---

[46] Attempts to understand Nazism as a political religion go back to Voegelin, *Die politischen Religionen*. For a critique of recent adaptations see Gregor, 'Nazism – A Political Religion?'

[47] Winter, *Sites of Memory*, pp. 15–28; Goebel, *Great War*, pp. 254–74. Compare also Flex, *Der Wanderer zwischen beiden Welten*, pp. 78–83.

[48] 'Deutschland muss sein, trotz Sorgen und Not', *KLZ*, 5 August 1943, p. 4; 'Die Rede des Gauleiters bei der Gefallenenfeier am 4. 8. vor dem Rathaus in Kassel', *Soldatenbrief der Gauleitung Kurhessen der NSDAP* (September 1943), pp. 4f.

[49] 'Terror wird uns zu keiner Zeit beugen! Reichsminister Dr. Goebbels sprach in Kassel / Kundgebung eines unerschütterlichen Siegeswillens', *KLZ*, 6/7 November 1943, p. 1.

leader summed up the official lesson of the air raid.[50] Modern notions of the chain of responsibility were thus reversed. Here, the population was accountable to the leadership, not vice versa.

During the early years of the war, representatives from the party and the army were wont to seize on air raids in order to remind the 'home front' of a moral obligation to the soldiers fighting at the front. In an undated speech of 1940 or 1941, the district leader of Magdeburg-Anhalt, Rudolf Jordan, came close to welcoming the loss of life in the *Heimat* as some kind of educational measure:

And this is why I maintain – and I pray not to be misunderstood – that it is good that in this war life is sacrificed on the home front as well. It is good that in this war the home front can likewise say that tonight someone may be hit, and tonight myself, and tonight the neighbour, and tonight somebody else. It is good that Germany's front will thus be united in common endeavour through blood.[51]

In a similar vein, the commanding general of the garrison in Kassel declared in a commemorative speech in November 1941 that 'the events of this night direct our eyes to the front where the soldier fights under much harder conditions and continual willingness to die'.[52] As the examples illustrate, the spectre of a repeat of 'November 1918' was never far from the minds of the National Socialist elites. It resonated through their attempts to bestow meaning on the death of non-combatants in the air war.[53]

In order to make sense of material destruction and violent death, contextualisation was a crucial strategy. 'There is no need to elaborate on the misfortune to you who have become not just witnesses but sufferers,' Goebbels declared in Kassel on 5 November 1943. 'I will [therefore] confine myself to the definition and explanation of the *fundamental principles* governing the present situation,' the propaganda minister continued.[54] Three months earlier, district leader Weinrich had explained the present war with reference to 'two thousand years of our struggle for the creation of a *Reich* and *Volk*'. At the same time, the bombing of the home town served him as evidence of a 'Jewish will of annihilation' towards the German people.[55] However much the enemy had demonstrated his ability to destroy the locality, however many lives had been lost, the nation had

---

[50] *KLZ*, 23 October 1944, p. 4.   [51] Rudolf Jordan, *Wir und der Krieg*, p. 21.

[52] 'Tod und Trauer, doch stärker ist der Ruf des Lebens', *KP*, 15 September 1941.

[53] On the importance of the myth of '1918' for the Nazi world view see the classic treatment by Mason, 'Erbschaft der Novemberrevolution', as well as Hitler, *Mein Kampf*, pp. 221–5.

[54] Goebbels' speech of 5 November 1943 is reprinted under the title of 'Appell der Kasseler Amtswalter', in *Goebbels-Reden*, vol. II, pp. 259–85, here pp. 259f.

[55] *KLZ*, 5 August 1943, p. 4

become stronger and the racial community more united – this was the mantra of the official interpretation of the air war. The individual, the locality and the present were thus subordinated to the *Volk*, the nation and the eternal. 'Our enemies can destroy cities and kill Germans, but our people will live forever,' Weinrich declared on 4 August 1943.[56]

At the centre of the National Socialist treatment of the violent death of non-combatants in the air war stood a process of double identification that was inherently paradoxical. The civilian casualties of allied bombing were identified as defenceless civilians who had fallen victim to a (war) crime. At the same time, they were lauded as 'soldiers of the *Heimat*' who had sacrificed their lives for a greater cause.[57] Early in the war, in August 1940, the *Kasseler Neueste Nachrichten* acknowledged something of this contradiction in an article that treated the first two deaths of local residents in a British air raid. Speaking of 'senseless murder', the article none the less insisted that the casualties had died a 'sacrificial death'. 'As meaningless as it may seem that the . . . father and the daughter . . . had to lose their lives by the blind hatred of enemy fliers, their death has strengthened the community of those for whom they have died,' the article claimed. As much as the Nazi regime sought to exploit the deaths of German civilians in order to denounce the allied conduct of the war, the underlying distinction between combatants and non-combatants ran counter to the National Socialist understanding of the war. In the self-proclaimed 'total war', there was no space for civilians standing aside.[58]

Thus the tension between the non-combatant status of the majority of air raid casualties and the official hero cult of voluntary sacrifice remained unresolved. The calling out of the names of the dead in the funeral ceremonies to the tune of 'The Song of the Good Comrade' – borrowed from military ceremonial – clearly identified them as 'comrades' and 'soldiers of the *Heimat*'. On this understanding, the allied air war was a supreme and necessary trial on the way to redemption through victory: 'Never has a *Volk* achieved victory without sacrifice,' the Nazi district leader for Magdeburg, Tichy, stated apodeictically on 27 January 1944.[59]

---

[56] Ibid.

[57] 'Mord-, Brand- und Vernichtungswillen', *KLZ*, 23 October 1943, p. 4. The phrase 'soldiers of the *Heimat*' was used at a Magdeburg funeral service on 9 August 1944. See 'Sie sind unsterblich geworden . . .', *Magdeburgische Zeitung*, 10 August 1944, p. 4. Compare also LA Magd. LHA, Rep. C 127 Oberlandesgericht Naumburg (Saale). Rep. C 127 Nr. 1291. Luftschutz, Bd. 2 1941–45, fo. 140: 'Betrifft: Änderung der Bezeichnung für "getötete" und "verletzte" Zivilpersonen bei Luftangriffen', 15 June 1943.

[58] See Echternkamp, 'Im Kampf'.

[59] 'Magdeburg nahm Abschied von seinen Gefallenen', *Der Mitteldeutsche*, 28 January 1944, p. 1. Compare 'Sie starben, damit Deutschland lebt', *Magdeburgische Zeitung*, 28 January 1944, p. 1.

In a similar vein, party functionaries urged the populace to consider the destruction of the home town as a mark of distinction. 'When the few remaining church bells . . . announce victory, you will happily walk through the ruins of this city . . . Nobody will be able to say of this city that victory has been earned undeservedly,' Goebbels told his audience in Kassel on 5 November 1943.[60]

The second strand of interpretation coexisted uneasily with the idea of 'death as sacrifice'. Just as the civilian casualties of allied bombing were praised as 'soldiers of the Heimat', they were also identified as victims of a (war) crime. Their death was interpreted as evidence of a 'Jewish' war of annihilation being waged against the German people as a whole, not just Nazism. 'This night, in which English planes destroyed large parts of our city and murdered many German men, women and children, has shown us that the hatred and will of annihilation of our enemies is not just directed against the National Socialist leadership, the National Socialist idea but against German life as a whole, against every family and kinship group,' district leader Weinrich declared on 7 November 1943, to give just one example of this line of interpretation.[61] From 1943 onwards, allied air raids were summarily referred to as 'terror raids', allied strategy denounced as 'flying murder' and 'air terror', while the pilots themselves were labelled 'arsonists' and 'gangsters of the air'. Common to Nazi propaganda as a whole, such vocabulary featured most prominently in the daily press. Although the speakers at the ceremonies used denunciatory rhetoric as well, their linguistic efforts were arguably directed elsewhere, at the creation of an aural atmosphere in which to affirm the Nazi ethical canon of struggle, sacrifice and racial communalism.[62]

The vocabulary of commemoration

The language of the official commemorations was the language of the Third Reich as famously described by Victor Klemperer in his *Lingua Tertii Imperii*.[63] The rhetoric of the funeral ceremonies was marked by the frequent use of metaphors, superlatives, qualifying adjectives and fixed expressions. It made use of sudden changes between the archaic and the contemporary, the vulgar and the literary. The language was expressive and appellative, striking a heroic tone and addressing the emotions. The press invariably described the various ceremonies as 'edifying' (*erhebend*), 'moving' (*ergreifend*) and 'dignified' (*würdig*). The most revealing term

---

[60] Goebbels, 'Appell der Kasseler Amtswalter', p. 285.
[61] 'Wir hüten das Erbe unserer Gefallenen', *KLZ*, 8 November 1943, p. 1.
[62] Compare Koonz, *The Nazi Conscience*, pp. 4–16.   [63] Klemperer, *LTI*.

was 'solemn' (*weihevoll*), the adjectival form of 'to consecrate' (*weihen*), 'to make holy' (*heilig machen*), which evoked associations of the sacred, holy and eternal. Through the use of such terms, the press reports endowed party-organised funeral rallies with a semi-religious aura. They provided a spiritual frame in which the morale-boosting slogans of the local party functionaries took on the meaning of eternal laws and onto-logical truths.

To emphasise the heroic, the commemorative language of Nazism made frequent use of archaisms and literary expressions. The brass band marched 'with drums beating' (*mit klingendem Spiel*), delivering 'airs' (*Weisen*).[64] Meanwhile, armed conflict was described as a 'struggle' (*Ringen*) in which the Germans responded to the challenge of the bomb-ing attacks with an 'obstinate' (*trutzig*) attitude. The dead were com-memorated on a 'field of honour' (*Ehrenstätte*). In a similar vein, stock phrases from the national (*völkisch*) tradition stressed timeless heroism.[65] The daily *Der Mitteldeutsche*, for example, applied the epigram 'The glo-rious deeds of the dead last forever' (*Ewig ist der Toten Tatenruhm*), even to the non-combatant casualties of the air war, whose only glorious deed had been to be in the wrong place at the wrong time.[66] The same article also modified a famous dictum from the poem *Soldatenabschied* by the First World War poet Heinrich Lersch. The line 'Germany must live even if we have to die' was adapted to read, 'they died so Germany can live'.[67]

The casualties of allied bombing had died in accordance with a 'nat-ural law' that was invariably prefixed by the adjective 'brazen' (*ehern*). The term derived from the Old German *ērīn* which described the qual-ity of bronze but was also used figuratively to denote toughness and the eternal.[68] Their deaths commanded an attitude of collective 'rever-ence' (*Ehrfurcht*), which stressed the awe-inspiring aspect of their alleged heroism.[69] Here as elsewhere, the commemorative language made fre-quent use of the superlative. On 7 November 1943, Gauleiter Weinrich spoke of the air raid as the 'hardest stroke of fate' that obligated the liv-ing to the 'deepest gratitude' and 'highest performance of duty'.[70] The

---

[64] *KLZ*, 8 November 1943, p. 1.

[65] See the collection of poems and epigrams in *Die neue Gemeinschaft* 8 (1940), pp. 36–48.

[66] The epigram was taken from the Edda, a collection of mythological Old Norse poems made in the twelfth century.

[67] *Der Mitteldeutsche*, 28 January 1944, p. 1. On the popularity of these slogans see Lurz, *Kriegerdenkmäler*, vol. V, pp. 15–19, 210.

[68] Compare *Trübners Deutsches Wörterbuch*, vol. II, p. 133 (entry *ehern*); *Duden. Das Herkun-ftswörterbuch*, p. 170.

[69] Compare *Trübners Deutsches Wörterbuch*, vol. II, pp. 133f (entry *ehre*); *Deutsches Wörterbuch*, p. 67 (entry *Ehrfurcht*).

[70] *KLZ*, 8 November 1943, p. 1.

'legacy' (*Vermächtnis*) of the dead was described in terms of the Nazi ethical canon of 'faith, volition, deed', or, in a variation on Benedict of Nursia's famous sixth-century dictum of 'ora et labora', by means of the injunction 'to work, fight, and believe'.[71] The emotional extremes of love and hate played an important role in this canon. While the term 'love' carried positive connotations and was usually reserved for the Führer, hatred could be either positive or negative. Whereas allied bombing was described as an expression of 'blind' hatred, the racial community was said to respond with 'glowing' or 'flaming' hatred. In the words of district leader Weinrich, 'We devote all our love to him [i.e. Hitler] . . . The passion of all our hatred, however, will be directed against the enemy. Our love and our hatred must match the importance of the historic hour.'[72]

The commemorative language revolved around a binary opposition between 'us' and 'them' that was expressed in moral categories. The ceremonial language was the language of moral righteousness: 'chivalry' and 'humanity' were said to be lacking from the allied conduct of the (air) war just as 'honour' and 'dignity' were said to characterise the 'bearing' (*Haltung*) of the German people. References to the allied 'air terror' were frequently prefixed by the adjective 'wicked' (*ruchlos*) rather than the more common 'criminal' (*verbrecherisch*). A literary term, 'wicked' did not just denounce the air war in legal terms but carried connotations of a violation of the sacred, of sacrilege and desecration.[73] In the same vein, every mention of England was preceded by the adjective 'hypocritical'. By contrast, Germany was associated with notions such as 'faith', 'honour' and 'comradeship'.[74]

The language of the speeches oscillated between paternalistic praise that ostentatiously used the first person plural as the signature of community, and open and veiled threats against 'them', the enemies without and within. 'Let us hate our enemies in the belief that one day we will take merciless revenge for all the suffering they have brought upon us,' district leader Weinrich declared with reference to the Western powers on 4 August 1943. In equally unmistakable terms, Goebbels, on 5 November 1943, addressed those racial comrades who might be having second thoughts about the heroism of death under the bombs. 'All I can say is this: a person who lends an ear to the catchwords of the enemy in such a

---

[71] 'To work, fight, and believe – be this our will and oath in this hour before the fallen soldiers at the front and at home.' Gauleiter Weinrich on 4 August 1943. The speech is reprinted in *KLZ*, 5 August 1943, p. 4.

[72] *KLZ*, 8 November 1943, p. 1.

[73] *Trübners Deutsches Wörterbuch*, vol. V, pp. 458f. (entry *ruchlos*).

[74] Collated from Gauleiter Weinrich's speeches of 14 September 1941 and 4 August 1943. *KP*, 15 September 1941; *KLZ*, 5 August 1943, p. 4.

situation lacks in esprit de corps . . . We will cut off his head.' According to the transcript of the speech, the audience reacted with applause.[75]

'Come, and let us return unto the Lord': catastrophic rupture as affliction

While the secular sphere – the public square, the assembly hall and the news media – was firmly controlled by Nazism, the spiritual sphere of the Church provided a space in which pastors rather than party functionaries expounded the meaning of death in war.[76] Although this difference held for the commemoration of violent death in general, it was particularly relevant to the treatment of non-combatant death in aerial bombing. In a summary mood report of July 1945, an unnamed cleric from the state church of Kurhesse-Waldeck described an inverse relationship between Nazi commemorative activity and the severity of the air war in Kassel: 'Until 1943, the party claimed a special place in funeral ceremonies for the victims of bombing. Later, this activity declined and ultimately ceased altogether.'[77] While the second part of the comment was clearly an overstatement, the observation correctly expressed a general trend. As the propaganda activity of the local Nazi functionaries decreased after 22 October 1943, the voice of the Church gained in audibility, contributing to the remarkable revival of ecclesiasticism that was to become a characteristic feature of the early post-war period.[78]

To some extent, the rise in importance of the Church vis-à-vis the Nazi state was a question of logistics. With two-thirds of the city population made homeless by the air raid, Kassel-based ceremonies such as the commemorations of 7 November 1943 and of 22 October 1944 reached only a limited number of people. By contrast, the church of Kurhesse-Waldeck could rely on individual pastors to conduct decentralised commemorative services. In addition, the church leadership could draw on the intact organisation of the surrounding countryside in order to reach out to the church-going evacuee population. Evidence survives of a range of memorial and funeral services that were held by pastors in the half-year or so following the air raid of 22 October 1943. On 14 November 1943, pastor Paul Velbinger of the severely affected parish of the

---

[75] Goebbels, 'Appell der Kasseler Amtswalter', p. 282.
[76] 'Come, and let us return unto the Lord.' Hosea 6.1.
[77] StAK, A.1.10. no. 70, Police Situation Report, July 1945.
[78] Kleßmann, 'Kontinuitäten und Veränderungen', p. 403. Compare also the comment by Pastor D. Johannes Steinweg in 1953: 'As a factor in public life, the church is held in higher regard than at any time during the past 200 years'; 'Die evangelische Kirche Kassels', p. 19.

Lutherkirche conducted a special service for the Kassel evacuees in the town of Hannover'sch Münden.[79] On 22 February 1944, Velbinger's colleague at the Lutherkirche, Dr Preger, commemorated the dead from the parish in a funeral service at the Diakonissenhaus in Kassel, to which the congregation had temporarily moved after the destruction of the church building.[80] The parishioners of the Freiheiter Gemeinde and Altstädter Gemeinde likewise held special commemorative services in early 1944.[81] For the territory of the state church of Kurhesse-Waldeck as a whole, the church leadership (*Landeskirchenausschuss*) published a special announcement that was read from all pulpits on Christmas Day 1943.[82]

By means of home visits, blessings and memorial services, the Church assumed its customary role as dispenser of pastoral care, offering consolation, orientation and meaning to a population that had been subjected to the disruptive effects of extreme violence.[83] In so doing, the Church also demonstrated its own survival amidst the catastrophe. The places of worship may have been destroyed in the air raid, but as a social network, the Church had survived, ready to assemble the dispersed parishioners around the word of God. This was the message that the commemorations communicated to the bombed-out and bereaved above and beyond the content of the individual sermons.[84] Continuity in rupture was underlined further by formal elements. While the memorial services were usually held on Sunday, the customary day of worship, their liturgy followed the traditional service, with the sermon at the centre, communal hymn singing and prayer.

Themes

'Why? Why does God allow for such a misfortune to happen? Why do we have to suffer so much?' asked pastor Paul Velbinger in his first sermon after the air raid, conducted for the evacuees of Kassel in the small town of

[79] Archiv der Lutherkirche Kassel, Paul Velbinger, 'Predigten', pp. 192–7: 'Erster Gottesdienst nach dem Unglück für die Kasseler Bombengeschädigten in der St. Blasienkirche zu Hannover'sch Münden am 14. Nov. 1943.'

[80] Stolze, '. . . *es soll uns doch gelingen*', p. 53.

[81] Schwab (ed.), *Kreuz und Krone*, p. 23; Archiv Altstädter Gemeinde Kassel, Sitzungsprotokolle Kirchenvorstand: 'Erste Sitzung der Altstädter Kirchengemeinde nach dem Terrorangriff auf Kassel (22.10.1943)', 23 January 1944.

[82] *Kirchliches Amtsblatt. Gesetz- und Verordnungsblatt der Evangelischen Landeskirche von Kurhessen-Waldeck* 58/10, 15 December 1943, p. 66.

[83] See the post-war accounts by Protestant pastors from Kassel: Steinweg, 'Die evangelische Kirche Kassels', p. 15; Buchenau, *Aus dem Schatz*, pp. 18–20, 27–34; Preger, 'Aus meiner Kasseler Amtszeit', p. 33.

[84] Compare the pamphlet *Zerstörte Kirchen – lebende Gemeinde*.

Hannover'sch Münden on 14 November 1943.[85] Faced with catastrophic rupture, clerics struggled to give answers to questions that doubtless were on the minds of many residents, about the ultimate reasons for the catastrophe. It is indicative of the extent of the disaster that clerics and Nazi functionaries alike wrestled with the same problem.

The Church did not prove immune to the interpretive frames of Nazi propaganda. Pastors adapted phrases and concepts of the secular narrative to a spiritual context. Yet the emphasis of the spiritual narrative rested elsewhere. Whereas Nazi propaganda oscillated between the denunciation of the air war as a crime and the extolling of death under the bombs as a sacrifice, the Church put the notion of 'affliction' (*Heimsuchung*) at the centre of its efforts to make sense of what had happened. Carrying strong transcendental connotations, the term described an intervention by God in worldly affairs. Grimm's German Dictionary defined *Heimsuchung* as a 'visit by the punishing God', making the word into a synonym of 'punishment' or '(divine) judgement'.[86] Through the air raid, God had spoken to the population – this was the common thread running through otherwise disparate utterances by representatives of the Protestant Church in Kassel in the aftermath of 22 October 1943.

Partial adaptation of the Nazi propaganda narrative was most pronounced in a statement that was both widely accessible and vulnerable to state censorship, a proclamation on the air raid by the church leadership of Kurhesse-Waldeck, which was published in the church gazette in order to be read from all pulpits on Christmas Day 1943.[87] The text, 'Light shines in the Darkness', referred to the air raid in the interpretive categories of official propaganda, using the propaganda term 'terror raid' and representing the casualties of allied bombing as victims of a crime. 'In deep sorrow we remember those who were murdered in the terror raid on Kassel of 22 October 1943, and their bereaved families,' the statement read. On a surface level, the text thus appeared to corroborate the official propaganda: allied bombing was not an act of war but a criminal deed pure and simple.

Yet there was an inter-textual dimension to the statement that subtly subverted its surface meaning. In order to give expression to the emotion of sorrow, the text invoked quotations from the Old Testament prophets of Ezekiel and Jeremiah. 'Oh that my head were waters, and mine eyes a fountain of tears, that I might weep day and night for the slain of the

[85] Archiv der Lutherkirche Kassel, Paul Velbinger, 'Predigten', pp. 192–7, here p. 195.
[86] *Deutsches Wörterbuch*, vol. X, column 883 (entry *Heimsuchung*).
[87] *Kirchliches Amtsblatt. Gesetz- und Verordnungsblatt der Evangelischen Landeskirche von Kurhessen-Waldeck* 58/10, 15 December 1943, p. 66.

daughter of my people!' (Jer. 9.1), the text read. In so doing, the statement not only provided a language of mourning to the congregation but also shifted the emphasis from the character of the deed to the question of agency. It thus offered an alternative reading of the catastrophic event that was decipherable by regular churchgoers. In the Old Testament, the prophets Jeremiah and Ezekiel predict the destruction of Jerusalem as divine punishment for the wilful violation of God's law.[88] By analogy, the destruction of Kassel might therefore be understood not just as the result of a criminal deed at the hands of the enemy but as a (divine) affliction brought on the city by the residents themselves.

In the pulpit proclamation, the interpretive frame of divine punishment was not spelled out but required an inter-textual exegetic effort in order to be recognised. On the whole, faith in transcendental salvation played a larger role than any deliberation on the ultimate causes of the disaster. While the reasons for this restraint may or may not have been due to fears about state repression, the internal correspondence of the signatory of the text, Kirchenrat D. Happich, showed a marked difference in emphasis. Not only did Happich explicitly use the term 'affliction', he also refrained from adopting the idiom of Nazi propaganda. In a circular letter to the leaders of the other Protestant state churches of 27 October 1943, Happich used the phrase 'horrible bombing night' rather than 'terror raid' in order to refer to the attack. He also begged his addressees to pray for the 'heavily afflicted district'.[89]

A close reading of two commemorative sermons by Lutheran pastor Paul Velbinger may help to delineate further the ways in which Protestant clerics employed the concept of *Heimsuchung* in order to provide consolation in distress and to explain the disaster to believers. The notion served less to explore the causal nexus between an aggressive foreign policy and domestic destruction than to stabilise a spiritual world view that was in danger of being eroded by the extent of the catastrophe. Born in 1882, Velbinger was in many respects a typical representative of German Protestantism in the early twentieth century.[90] Socialised to a middle-class background in Wilhelmian Germany, Velbinger had enthusiastically welcomed the demise of the Weimar Republic and the advent of the Third Reich.[91] In May 1933, he joined the Nazi party and became involved with the 'German Christians', the pro-Nazi pressure

---

[88] Compare Siegfried Herrmann, 'Jeremia / Jeremiabuch', *TRE* vol. XVI, pp. 568–86.
[89] LKA Kassel, Sammlung Kirchenkampf no. 24, D. Happich to the members of the Church Council, 27 October 1943.
[90] On the context see Vollnhals, 'Der deutsche Protestantismus'.
[91] See Stolze, 'Lutherkirche', pp. 38–41.

group among the clergy that had been formed in May 1932. He served briefly on the board of the Kommissarische Kirchenregierung, the organisational spearhead of the ill-fated attempt to install a pro-Nazi church leadership in the church of Kurhesse-Waldeck.[92] Although a process of gradual disillusionment with Nazism had set in by late 1933, Velbinger remained strongly nationalist in his outlook, conceiving of the Christian faith in *völkisch* categories.[93]

In his preaching on the air raid, Velbinger sought to reassure his parishioners in their Christian faith by emphatically reasserting the omnipotence of God in the face of the catastrophic event. The pastor conceived of the air raid as a 'trial of faith' (*Anfechtung*) which put the believer to the test and exposed popular misconceptions about God. In his sermon of 14 November 1943, Velbinger declared, 'The worst that could happen to us is to lose faith in God because of all the horror that we have gone through. If we turned away from God now, we would have failed in our trial of faith. We would be deserters to the flag. The deserter, however, has lost his right to live.' As the excerpt shows, there were clear echoes of both the idiom and the interpretive frame of Nazi propaganda, such as the analogy between the believer/apostate and the soldier/deserter, the notion of the air raid as an 'opportunity to prove one's worth' (*Bewährungsprobe*), and the threat of annihilation should the individual fail this test. Yet, as a Lutheran pastor, Velbinger was concerned foremost not with shoring up the home front against the corrosive impact of the air war but with salvaging a Christian understanding of the world from the rubble and death that surrounded him. God was still in charge, reigning well, Velbinger maintained emphatically. If God ruled the world omnipotently, then the catastrophe of the air raid must be of God as well. 'Who is he that saith, and it cometh to pass, when the Lord commandeth it not?' Velbinger asked his audience by way of an inter-textual reference to Lamentations 3.37 in his remembrance service of 22 October 1944. The suffering of the present, Velbinger argued, could not be explained with reference to categories such as coincidence or fate but must be understood as an affliction sent by a God who was not only the benevolent father of the New Testament but also the stern judge of the Old Testament.[94]

[92] Waßmann, *Evangelische Pfarrer*, p. 336. On the local 'church struggle' see Slenczka, *Die evangelische Kirche von Kurhessen-Waldeck*.

[93] Compare Velbinger's comments in a sermon on 18 November 1936: 'We carry three proud names. We are Germans . . . We are Christians . . . And we are Protestants.' In Velbinger, 'Predigten', pp. 221–5, here p. 223.

[94] Velbinger, 'Predigten', p. 195.

There was enormous critical potential in a reading of events that identified the misdeeds of the 'we-group' as the ultimate cause for the disaster. In his anniversary sermon of October 1944, Velbinger invoked the
Lamentations of Jeremiah 3.22–32 in order to draw an analogy between
the biblical past and the present. He declared, 'The prophet admonished
the people with great seriousness, but it was in vain. They listened to
the words of false prophets and seducers. This was their undoing.'[95]
To quote from the Lamentations of Jeremiah in the autumn of 1944,
at a time when the Nazi regime was making a frantic last-ditch effort
at the total mobilisation of the home front, certainly spoke of an erosion of affective ties between the speaker and Nazism. More importantly,
the analogy offered up a way to think of the catastrophe in terms of
cause and effect rather than in the propaganda categories of sacrifice and
victimhood.

Yet it appears that the main function of this argument was theological
rather than political. The notion of *Heimsuchung* shored up the idea of an
omnipotent and benevolent higher being against the problem of theodicy.
Although unfathomable, God's judgement was just, as Velbinger maintained in his sermon on 14 November 1943. The extent to which even
Protestant clerics could struggle with the problem of making sense of an
unparalleled catastrophe is well illustrated by a prayer that Pastor Brien of
the Altstädter Gemeinde spoke at the first post-raid meeting of the parish
council in January 1944. 'Distressed we stand before you because you
have spoken to us,' he declared, in order to continue, 'How unfathomable
are your ways, how unfathomable are your judgements. Help us so we
may not despair.'[96] In contrast to this admission of confusion, Velbinger
took recourse to the notion of God's ultimate benevolence. However
much the congregation had been punished, the promise of salvation still
held. To underline this idea, Velbinger based his first post-raid sermon on
Hosea 6.1: 'Come, and let us return unto the Lord: for he hath torn, and
he will heal us; he hath smitten, and he will bind us up.'[97] On this reading, the suffering incurred in the air raid fulfilled a near-eschatological
function by strengthening the congregation in their faith. However much
Velbinger challenged the interpretive frame of Nazi propaganda, in practical terms, he advocated a kind of quietist patience in the face of adversity
that undoubtedly played into the hands of the Nazi regime.

---

[95] Ibid., p. 198.
[96] Archiv der Altstädter Gemeinde Kassel, Sitzungsprotokolle Kirchenvorstand: 'Erste
Sitzung der Altstädter Kirchengemeinde nach dem Terrorangriff auf Kassel
(22.10.1943)'.
[97] Velbinger, 'Predigten', p. 192.

Conclusion

In the period 1940 to 1945, the public commemoration of civilian death in aerial warfare was expressed through the cultural repertoire of Nazism; or, to be more precise, through an older idiom inherited from the nineteenth century and World War I into which Nazism had inserted itself successfully. Just like the Reich leadership, the local political elites never developed a consistent approach to the challenge of allied bombing, oscillating between propagandistic overstatement of minor raids and silence in the face of unprecedented urban destruction. Generally speaking, however, the commemorative activity decreased in the same measure as the severity of the raids escalated. By way of public commemorations, the regional Nazi party leaderships enacted through ritual what they were ever less able to provide in the real world: the protection of the racial community against the consequences of the self-proclaimed total war. Likewise, the local Nazi elites employed verbal and non-verbal modes of communication in order to reaffirm the myth of a 'community of fate' in the face of ever-intensifying social disruption and dissolution. They did so by drawing on the standard themes of the mythical world view of Nazism. The mostly civilian casualties of strategic bombing were incorporated into the cult of heroic death. Having fallen victim to a sacrilegious crime, the dead had also heroically sacrificed their lives.

The rituals and themes that the Nazi party employed in Kassel and Magdeburg were repeated across the cities and towns of the German Reich whenever local branches organised official ceremonies for the casualties of the allied air war. Although the propaganda leadership did not issue official 'suggestions' on the arrangement of the commemorations until August 1944,[98] there was a remarkable degree of conformity in both format and content throughout the period. Regardless of whether the ceremonies were held in Freiburg, Wuppertal, Hamburg, Darmstadt or Heilbronn, the central tenets remained the same: speakers would condemn and praise, admonish and rally, incite and promise.[99]

To the post-war world, Nazism left a commemorative tradition that was shot through with the rhetoric of heroism and hatred while identifying the casualties of allied bombing as 'soldiers of the *Heimat*' in an eschatological struggle of annihilation and at the same time as victims of a heinous crime. Yet the discursive power of the Nazi regime began to be eroded well before the war was over. As the commemorative activity

---

[98] 'Gedenkfeiern der NSDAP für Opfer des Luftkrieges', *Die neue Gemeinschaft* 10/8 (August 1944), pp. 374–81.
[99] On Hamburg, see the careful analysis in Thießen, *Eingebrannt ins Gedächtnis*, pp. 60–70. Compare also Arnold, 'Beyond Usable Pasts', pp. 27–9.

of the NSDAP declined in the face of unprecedented urban disaster, the Church gained in influence, resuming its customary role as the dispenser of care and consolation in times of distress. From the pulpit, pastors delivered a reading of events that put the notion of divine affliction at the centre. While eschewing the identification of the dead as either victims of crime or voluntary sacrificers, the Church interpreted the air war as a punishment for sins against God. At the same time, the Church held out the Christian promise of salvation to the bereaved.

3 'In quiet memory'?: post-war memory cultures, 1945–1979

Introduction: a usable past?

> Today, we remember all the dead whose lives were over so suddenly. We remember the dead whose graves we can adorn; we remember those who vanished without a trace and whose graves nobody knows. We remember the mourning relatives of those who were swept away by the storm of fire.[1]

Seven years after the devastating air raid on Kassel and six years after his first commemorative service, Lutheran pastor Paul Velbinger returned to the subject of death under the bombs. In a memorial service that he held on 22 October 1950 in a makeshift church, Velbinger conceptualised the attack as an affliction, taking the rubble as evidence of God's judgement as well as his grace.[2] The Lutherkirche was not the only parish to mark the day by means of a special commemoration. It was joined by other Christian congregations across the city of Kassel.[3] In the afternoon, 5,000 residents had gathered in the main cemetery in order to attend a secular memorial celebration that had been organised by the local branch of the Central League of Air Raid Victims (*Zentralverband der Fliegergeschädigten*).[4] Wreaths were laid and words of commemoration spoken. Across the border, in the city of Magdeburg, commemorative activity was also noticeable. On 16 January 1950, the SED convened a 'mass rally' to mark the fifth anniversary of what it referred to as the 'Anglo-American destruction of Magdeburg'.[5] In the

---

[1] Archiv der Lutherkirche, Paul Velbinger, 'Predigten', no. 37, 'Gedächtnisgottesdienst zur Erinnerung an den Bombenangriff auf die Stadt Kassel', 22 October 1950, pp. 202f.

[2] For the context see Stolze (ed.), '. . . *es soll uns doch gelingen*', pp. 56–66.

[3] Compare Archiv der Christuskirche, Kassel, Abkündigungen 1945–50, 22 October 1950. The first post-war commemorative service was held the previous year, on 22 October 1949, by Pastor Buchenau of the Auferstehungsgemeinde. See *Evangelische Sonntagsbote*, 6 November 1949, p. 405.

[4] *Kasseler Sonntagsblatt*, 29 October 1950.

[5] 'In der nationalen Front dem Frieden dienen. Großkundgebung am 5. Jahrestag der Zerstörung Magdeburgs', *Volksstimme*, 17 January 1950.

parish of the Domgemeinde, meanwhile, an hour of commemoration was held in memory of the bombing.[6]

Five years after the bombs had stopped falling, different groups and institutions in Kassel as well as Magdeburg turned to commemorating the civilian casualties of the allied air war. Although the dead of World War II had been remembered on various occasions and in different ways in the immediate post-war years as well, the singling out of the air raid victims was a novel development in the commemorative cultures of the two cities. Elsewhere, in heavily bombed places such as Darmstadt, Heilbronn, Würzburg or Dresden, annual funeral ceremonies had been institutionalised earlier, from 1945/6 onwards.[7] But here as well as in Kassel and Magdeburg, official and popular investment in public ceremonies rose considerably during the early 1950s.

The upsurge in commemorative activity occurred at a historical juncture when influential agents of public memory in both German states turned to constructing selective narratives of World War II that were designed to be 'usable' in the struggles of the day. As West Germans reversed the results of allied denazification in a process that has been described as a 'politics of the past',[8] an emphasis on German suffering replaced the earlier debate on the suffering occasioned by the Germans.[9] The emerging myth of German victimhood served both to integrate the one-time supporters of Nazism into the West German state and to dissociate the nascent Federal Republic from its 'totalitarian' predecessor as well as the 'other Germany' east of the zonal border. Meanwhile, the GDR extended the anti-fascist credentials of its ruling elites to the population at large, stressing the heroic and ultimately victorious struggle against a dictatorship that had allegedly held the German people captive.[10]

To some extent, the institutionalisation of memory cultures of the air war in the 1950s can be accounted for in terms of usability as well. After all, the death and destruction wrought by allied bombing comprised an aspect of World War II in which Germans had stood at the receiving end of terrible violence. The bombs had killed, injured and scarred regardless of the individual's political persuasion and involvement in the crimes of the Nazi regime, thus turning potentially all Germans into victims. In

---

[6] AKPS, Rep. J 1, no. 3291, Kanzelabkündigungen 1950–4, 15 January 1950. The first post-war commemorative service was held on 16 January 1948. See ibid., no. 3290, Kanzelabkündigungen 1936–49, 11 January 1948.

[7] See Arnold, 'Beyond Usable Pasts'; Seiderer, 'Würzburg, 16 März 1945', pp. 147f.

[8] Frei, *Vergangenheitspolitik*, pp. 7–24; Brochhagen, *Nach Nürnberg*, pp. 19–172; Wolfrum, *Die geglückte Demokratie*, pp. 169–86.

[9] Moeller, *War Stories*; Frei, *Vergangenheitspolitik*, pp. 133–306.

[10] Fulbrook, *German National Identity*, pp. 28–36; Herf, *Divided Memory*, pp. 162–200.

other respects, however, the subject matter of aerial warfare was far from usable. Deeply disruptive, touching on primary experiences of a generally traumatic nature and burdened with the semantic, topographical and interpretive frames of Nazism, mass death under the bombs was not easily adapted to the political confrontations of the post-war world. For the mainstream elites of West Germany, there was no political advantage to be gained from reviving memories of the uncompromising ways in which the Western allies had pursued their fight not just against Nazism but against the German people as a whole. Moreover, the legal and moral problems raised by indiscriminate bombing appeared to furnish arguments for 'you did it too' apologetics, which rested uncomfortably with the 'anti-Nazi foundation consensus' of the Federal Republic.[11] At the same time, the partial adaptation of the Nazi 'terror raid' narrative by the East German SED raised the suspicions of the 'anti-totalitarian' mainstream of West German political opinion.[12] Meanwhile, even the Communist elites of the GDR, while eager to exploit the propaganda potential of the air war, had to be cognisant of the uncontrollable effects of stoking up emotions that had their experiential basis in deeply disturbing primary experiences.

In light of these observations, the institutionalisation of commemorative practices east and west of the inner-German border cannot be explained solely in terms of the battle lines of the Cold War, which had entered a new phase with the outbreak of hostilities in Korea on 25 June 1950. While the geopolitical confrontation had important repercussions for local memory cultures, the evidence presented in this chapter does not support the claim that the air war was the exclusive preserve of the East.[13] Any analytical approach that conceives of public memory in functional terms only runs the risk of neglecting the existential dimension of memory.[14] It is true that sites of memory were constructed by political 'agents' as sites of political mobilisation and social integration. But they also functioned as sites of mourning and consolation – in post-1945 Kassel or Magdeburg no less than in post-1918 London or Paris.[15]

---

[11] Frei, *Vergangenheitspolitik*, p. 23. For an example of *tu quoque* apologetics see ibid., pp. 282f. For the use of this argument by the German defence in the Nuremberg trials see Bloxham, *Genocide on Trial*, pp. 149–53.

[12] See Groehler, 'Dresden'. In Kassel, Bishop Wüstemann opened his commemorative address of 22 October 1951 with the following disclaimer: 'Here in Kassel, so close to the inner-German border, we have no intention whatsoever at this commemorative hour to become political in the wrong sense.' In LKA Kassel, SB Wüstemann, no. 22, 'Ansprache am 22. Oktober', 22 October 1951.

[13] Naumann, 'Leerstelle Luftkrieg', 13. Compare also Moeller, *War Stories*, p. 5.

[14] This argument is developed more fully in Arnold, 'Beyond Usable Pasts'.

[15] Winter, *Sites of Memory*.

In Kassel and Magdeburg, the casualties of allied bombing were publicly remembered with great intensity and a high degree of popular participation throughout the 1950s and 1960s. They formed one of the most visible victim groups of World War II. In a social environment in which thousands of residents mourned the deaths of loved ones and tens of thousands personally remembered the terror of aerial warfare, the agents of public memory – whatever their political agendas and persuasions – were not free to construct any narrative they saw fit, but were obliged to address a set of questions that had been raised by the events themselves. Why so much death and suffering? Does mass death hold any meaning? What lessons can be learned from the catastrophe? Opinion makers in both cities tried to channel and control the public enunciation of memory but had to contend with primary experiences and local traditions in their efforts to construct usable pasts.

In Kassel, the initiative for the institutionalisation of a public memory culture originated from below, from the local section of the Central League of Air Raid Victims, Evacuees and Victims of the Currency Reform (*Zentralverband der Fliegergeschädigten, Evakuierten und Währungsgeschädigten*). The organisation had been founded in Heidelberg in September 1947 on the initiative of school inspector Adolf Bauser (1880–1948), who held a seat in the state parliament of Württemberg-Baden for the CDU. The Central League was a special interest organisation whose active membership peaked at 250,000 in 1951. It cooperated closely with federal and state authorities in order to secure the restitution of damage which had been incurred in the bombing war and the currency reform, and to press for the repatriation of evacuees to their home towns.[16] The organisation enjoyed an uneasy relationship of rivalry and cooperation with other pressure groups, in particular the expellee organisations, which proved much more successful in mobilising their constituencies and in pressing their grievances in the political arena. In part in order to reverse this trend, the Central League encouraged its local sections to engage in an active politics of memory, and to organise public commemorations on the anniversaries of heavy bombing raids as well as special 'days of the evacuees' in their respective communities.[17]

The Air Raid Victims enjoyed a strong presence in post-war Kassel, where they were also represented in the city parliament by way of

---

[16] Krause, *Flucht vor dem Bombenkrieg*, pp. 234–41; *Dokumente deutscher Kriegsschäden*, vol. I, pp. 489–504.

[17] Hauptstaatsarchiv Stuttgart, Q 3/43, Vorstandsakte, 'Entwurf für die Festansprache', 26 November 1966; 'Fliegergeschädigte gründen Zentralverband', *Selbsthilfe*, 15 September 1947; 'Zusammenarbeit der Geschädigtenverbände', *Selbsthilfe*, 22 November 1952, p. 1; 'Zerstörtes Kulturgut', *Selbsthilfe*, 18 September 1954, p. 2.

association with the parliamentary arm of the expellees, the Bund der Heimatvertriebenen und Entrechteten (BHE). In the summer of 1949, a 'day of the evacuees' was held, and on 22 October of the same year, the group organised a wreath laying. By the early 1950s, the Air Raid Victims were starting to put pressure on the Church and the city council to give greater public recognition to the victims of the air war, to which demand the political and religious elites responded with a policy of semantic pacification. They attempted to depoliticise and decontextualise the memory of 22 October 1943 while re-Christianising the format of the commemorations. To that end, they put forward a number of interpretations that were noteworthy for their blind spots as well as for their emphases: the lamentation of a (natural) disaster; the mercy of silence; the admonition of 'never again'. In comparison with the local politicians, the churches put a stronger emphasis on exploring the relationship between cause and effect. Within an overall context that conceptualised the air raid as an affliction for past wrongdoings, individual pastors also raised the issue of a causal link between the treatment of the Jews in the Third Reich and the destruction of the home town in World War II. Meanwhile, challenges to the consensus narrative were mounted by the radical Left, which attempted to repoliticise the iconic event and turn the memory of allied bombing into a weapon in their fight against the rearmament of the Federal Republic.

In Magdeburg, the political elites remembered the air raid less as a disaster than as a (war) crime – a crime of World War II and of the Cold War. Strongly influenced by the national *lieu de mémoire* of 'Dresden', official remembrance recontextualised and repoliticised the air war while making heroes of its victims. The political elites produced a set of interpretations that were designed to foster the active identification with the new social order and to cultivate a culture of hatred towards the old and new enemy.[18] The prime mover was the SED, which employed the party press, the city council, the Regional Peace Council (*Kreisfriedensrat*) and the umbrella organisation of the National Front as agents of dissemination. The churches, meanwhile, kept their distance, refusing to lend their support to the official interpretation.[19] They put forward an alternative reading of events that, just as in the West, placed the notion of 'affliction' at the centre. Above all, the churches, together with the satellite Christian Democratic Party (Ost-CDU), attempted to shift the

---

[18] For the context compare Bessel, 'Hatred after War'.
[19] See Schultze (ed.), *Berichte der Magdeburger Kirchenleitung*, pp. 64, 73, 77, 97; AKPS, Rep. A, gen. 3026, Kirche und Staat. Nationale Front. Generalia und Einzelfälle, 1949/50; ibid., gen. 3600, Kirche und Staat. Volksbefragungen am 3.–5. 6. 1951 und 27.–29.6.1954.

commemorative focus from the field of political agitation back to the field of mourning.

Focusing on the memory of mass death, this chapter examines the institutionalisation of local *lieux de mémoire* in the formative period of the 1950s. It looks at the ways in which the dead were identified and commemorated by the protagonists of public memory in the two cities. In both Kassel and Magdeburg, the chapter argues, the emergence of annual commemorations and of mnemonic topographies resulted in the stabilisation of public narratives about allied bombing. In Kassel, the political elites pursued a policy of semantic pacification that was characterised by a tendency towards depoliticisation, decontextualisation and re-Christianisation. In Magdeburg, by contrast, the SED and its subsidiaries repoliticised and recontextualised the subject matter while de-Christianising the format of the commemorations. Whereas in Kassel, the casualties of the air war were remembered as victims of a (natural) disaster, in Magdeburg they were commemorated as victims of a crime. This chapter traces the emergence of these narratives and assesses the extent to which they reached hegemonic status in the memory cultures of the two cities.

Identifying the dead

One of the most difficult tasks facing the local authorities in the wake of indiscriminate area raids was the retrieval and identification of thousands of corpses. Because identification required the active participation of the population, thousands of local residents were brought face to face with mass death, with potentially devastating consequences for popular morale.[20] Acutely aware of this danger, in the aftermath of 22 October 1943 the Kassel chief of police ordered that burial of the corpses be given priority over identification, allegedly on the grounds of public health.[21] As a consequence, 1,800 of the 5,830 recovered bodies were buried anonymously.[22] In Magdeburg, only 1,930 casualties of the January raid had been found by early March 1945, whereas 3,591 people were still missing.[23] While the retrieval and identification of individual corpses was fraught with enormous difficulties, the collective identity of the dead

---

[20] Compare StAK, S8 C40, 'Erfahrungsbericht', 7 December 1943, pp. 27–33, in particular p. 28; StAK, S8 C50, Opfer Diverses, Kreisleitung Kassel to mayor, 25 October 1943. See also BA Berlin, R 55/447, fo. 132, 'LK-Mitteilung no. 72. Betr.: Leichenbergung', 18 December 1943.

[21] *Überlebensberichte*, pp. 105–9 (no. 55).

[22] StAK, S8 C40, 'Erfahrungsbericht', 7 December 1943, p. 2.

[23] NA II RG 243 E-6 # 399 (box 383), 'Erfahrungsbericht', 5 March 1945.

was more straightforward. In their experience reports, the chiefs of police distinguished between Germans and 'foreigners', subsuming both groups under the label of 'soldiers killed in action' (*Gefallene*). Nazi propaganda, meanwhile, identified the German casualties both as victims of a crime and as sacrificers for the fatherland.

Graves

With the military defeat of the German Reich, official plans to turn the sites of mass burial into 'fields of honour' that would convey the Nazi conceptualisation of death were abandoned.[24] Throughout the years of the occupation, the work of memory was largely left in the hands of mourning families and friends. While local authorities contented themselves with the superficial denazification of the provisional burial sites,[25] the bereaved commemorated the dead not as members of a collective – be this as 'soldiers of the *Heimat*' or as 'victims of crime' – but as individuals, as deceased brothers, sisters, mothers, fathers, neighbours, friends. To this end, they erected sites of memory that functioned as sites of mourning. Drawing on well-established Christian traditions, they adorned the real and imagined graves of their loved ones with wooden crosses, wreaths and flowers. While this practice focused on the cemetery, it was also employed to mark the places of death in the city itself. Indeed, makeshift memorials erected on collapsed buildings constituted one of the most conspicuous features in the memory landscape of the rubble years.

Sometimes, these private sites of mourning consisted of simple wooden crosses that still bore the insignia of a militarised people's community. At other times, they could also come in the form of elaborate memorial slabs (Fig. 8). In the old town of Kassel, for example, a wooden grave marker had been erected that bore the following inscription:

In the unforgettable night of October, our dear loved ones, Marta Trube, née Kirsten, and her brother-in-law, Karl Trube, moved towards an inexplicable fate / Your future lies in darkness but we will not forget you.

To this was added the poem, 'The sound of angels' tears / quietly blows around the tomb / Ghostlike ruins stare into the empty air.'[26]

---

[24] On these plans see StAK, A.4.41, Neugestaltung von Ehrenfriedhöfen, 1943–4.
[25] StAM, Rep. 18/4, Ra 4, Dezernentenbesprechung, 'Entfernung der Hakenkreuze an den Grabkreuzen der Gefallenen auf dem Westfriedhof', 28 January 1946; Rep. 18/4, Ausschußsitzungen 1945–53, Ausschuss für Garten- und Friedhofsangelegenheiten, As 4, fos. 360–2; As 5, fos. 482–4; As 6, fos. 125–8, 137.
[26] See StAK, Fotoarchiv, Gedenkstätten auf Trümmern.

Figure 8. Private site of mourning in Kassel, after 22 October 1943.

In another instance, a family had put up a placard on the rubble, show-ing Kassel before the destruction, together with a wreath that commem-orated 'seventeen fallen comrades [*Hausgenossen*]' in 'quiet memory'.[27] Although a phrase such as 'fallen comrades' testified to the lasting impact of Nazism on the post-war enunciation of loss, private sites of mourning may still be read as an attempt to detach the memory of the dead from the

---

[27] Ibid. The image is reprinted in Klaube, '*Kassel lebt!*', p. 82.

total claims of the National Socialist regime or any other state authority. As sites of mourning, the makeshift memorials reaffirmed the individual identities of the deceased as civilians.

With the institutionalisation of a post-war memorial culture in the 1950s, this attempt at reclaiming the civilian identities of the dead came to an end. As the rebuilding got under way, the private sites of memory were cleared from the cityscape. Likewise, the cemeteries were subjected to redevelopment measures that severely curtailed the ability of relatives to tend the graves of loved ones individually. In Kassel, the mass grave was redesigned as a 'cemetery of honour', replacing 'the confusion of the different crosses made from wood and stone . . . with a beautiful and solemn arrangement' of two hundred identical gravestones, each bearing fifteen to twenty names, as the weekly *Kasseler Sonntagsblatt* commented. In future, the graves were to be 'tended collectively in order to stress the communal aspect that unites all the people who have found their last place of rest here'.[28] In the name of a 'dignified appearance', the municipal authorities created a collective identity for a disparate group of people who often, in truth, had shared nothing more in common than having been in the wrong place at the wrong time. Not unlike the fallen soldiers of the Wehrmacht, who lay buried in military formation in 'fields of honour', the (civilian) casualties of aerial warfare were pressed into an imaginary community even in death (Figs. 9 and 10).[29]

Memorials

One way to explore continuity and change in the collective identity of the dead is to look at war memorials. As Reinhart Koselleck has argued in a now classic essay on memory and identity, war memorials embody 'a double process of identification'. They identify the dead as the bearers of certain ideals and in turn oblige the living to fulfil their legacy. This section argues that in Kassel as well as Magdeburg, there emerged a broad and unquestioned consensus that the casualties of the air war formed part of a community of victims. If there was broad agreement on this across party political as well as ideological lines, the nature of this 'victimhood' was less clear. Whereas the democratic Left in Kassel tended to subsume the dead under the rubric of 'victims of fascism', Conservatives preferred to speak of 'victims of war'. The Church went furthest in stressing a causal relationship between the casualties of aerial warfare and the deeds of the

---

[28] 'Zum 22. Oktober 1953: Der neue Ehrenfriedhof', *Kasseler Sonntagsblatt*, 25 October 1953.

[29] See Lurz, *Kriegerdenkmäler*, vol. VI, pp. 132–4.

Figure 9. The design for the 'cemetery of honour' in Kassel from 1953. Individual sites of mourning have been replaced by an arrangement of identical crosses. The pietà-style sculpture was not executed.

Figure 10. Wreath-laying at the 'cemetery of honour' in 1983.

Germans in World War II. Some representatives suggested that, in truth, the dead had fallen victim to the Germans themselves. In Magdeburg, by comparison, the dominant view, as popularised by the SED and its subsidiaries, held that the casualties of the air war were victims of a crime. Not unlike Nazi propaganda during the war, they spoke of deliberate murder caused by the allied bombs.

On 5 November 1948, the SPD faction in the city council of Kassel tabled a motion that called for the erection of a 'dignified site of memory for the victims of fascism'.[30] In his defence of the motion, city councillor Goethe emphasised that the monument was intended not to deepen divisions among the citizenry but rather to serve as a general warning 'never again to rule by the use of violence'. In order to underline the conciliatory purpose, Goethe employed the broadest definition of 'victims of fascism' conceivable. This definition encompassed the dead and the living, ranging from the victims of Nazi political, racial and religious persecution to the fallen soldiers of 'all countries'; from the expellees to the 'bombed out' (*Ausgebombte*) and the victims of war (*Kriegsbeschädigte*); from the conservative resisters who had plotted to assassinate Hitler on 20 July 1944 to the Socialist anti-fascists, both in Germany and in Republican Spain.

Such an inclusive definition met with sharp criticism from Councillor Reinbach of the Communist party, who insisted that only those who had 'actively fought against fascism' deserved to be called 'victims of fascism', while those who had become victims 'by accident' did not qualify. His, however, was a minority view, and when the city council passed the stipulations for the design competition in January 1951, the SPD's inclusive definition was adopted. 'Victims of fascism' were not only those 'Kassel citizens' who had languished in the Nazi concentration camps but also the soldiers of the Wehrmacht, who were said to have been 'forced' to serve under the flag, and the victims of the bombing.[31]

If, according to the council, the dead and survivors of the air raids were thus to be identified as 'victims of fascism' together with all other victims of war, then this point was lost on the parliamentary representative of the League of Air Raid Victims, Konrad Fülling (BHE/PWG). In a council debate on the restoration of the city's central World War I 'warrior monument' in 1952, Fülling remarked that the memorial to the victims of fascism had excluded 'the victims of the two world wars, and in

---

[30] StAK, A.0, Stadtverordnetenversammlung, 5 November 1948, pp. 26–33. On the official unveiling of the memorial in 1953 see StAK, A.1.10, no. 186.
[31] StAK, A.4.41, no. 54, 'Wettbewerb zur Erlangung von Entwürfen für den Bau eines Denk- und Mahnmals (Opfer des Faschismus)', 3 January 1951.

particular the many victims of the bombing war'.[32] In an earlier debate, Fülling had endorsed an FDP motion for restoration but added that he wished to see the 'victims of the city of Kassel', and in particular the 'victims of the bombing', included.[33] He was supported in this by the Social Democrats, who argued that the World War I monument should be renamed 'Memorial site for the victims of both world wars'. Both council factions thus identified the dead of the air war as 'victims of war', albeit for different reasons. While the BHE tried to secure public recognition for the casualties of aerial warfare, the SPD sought to redefine the meaning of the 'warrior monument' altogether, turning it into a site of mourning and admonition. To FDP councillor Kaltwasser, meanwhile, the monument was not about victimhood at all but about the honour of the German soldier in World War II, which he tried to separate from the guilt of Adolf Hitler as the commander-in-chief.[34]

Although both the 'memorial to the victims of fascism' (*Mahnmal*) and the reopened 'warrior monument' (*Ehrenmal*) included the civilian casualties of aerial warfare among the commemorated groups, the second half of the 1950s witnessed the erection of half a dozen memorials that were exclusively dedicated to the dead of the air war. While the memorial to the victims of fascism had been a secular affair, the memorials in memory of the air war were largely created on the initiative of the Protestant Church. Their creation was indicative of the important place of this group of casualties in the memory culture at large. Through their iconography and inscriptions, the memorials also revealed the attributes which the founders ascribed to the dead, and by implication, to themselves. In them was inscribed not only the Church's conceptualisation of the air war as an affliction but also a message of consolation and transcendental hope.

The memorials were usually erected on the mass burial sites in the various cemeteries. They displayed Christian iconography and inscriptions. In the city districts of Bettenhausen, Wahlershausen and Harleshausen, they took the shape of large crosses adorned with Bible verses, while at Wehleiden cemetery and at the church of the Brüderkirche in the centre of town, the memorials depicted angels. Significantly, three memorials showed survivors rather than casualties, invariably represented as female

---

[32] StAK, A.0, Stadtverordnetenversammlung, 15 December 1952, pp. 5–12, here p. 8. On the history of the Kriegerehrenmal in Kassel see Adamski (ed.), '*Glücklich die Stadt, die keine Helden hat*'; StAK, A.1.10, no. 416, Ehrenmal in der Karlsaue 1957–70; Lurz, *Kriegerdenkmäler*, vol. VI, pp. 77f., as well as *passim* for the context.

[33] StAK, A.0, Stadtverordnetenversammlung, 30 June 1952, pp. 20–7, here p. 25.

[34] Ibid., pp. 22f. On the myth of a 'clean' Wehrmacht in the 1950s see Frei, *Vergangenheitspolitik*, pp. 133–308; Brochhagen, *Nach Nürnberg*, pp. 21–130; Müller and Volkmann (eds.), *Die Wehrmacht*.

Figure 11. Detail of the memorial to the victims of the air raid at the Brüderkirche in Kassel, dedicated on Memorial Sunday in 1958. The photo was taken in 2010.

or as children. While in Rothenditmold city district, a pietà-style sculpture was depicted in silent prayer for her deceased loved ones, the central monument in the main cemetery, dedicated on Memorial Sunday 1956, showed a relief of 'five women and three children trying to take shelter from the inexorable war', as the weekly *Kasseler Sonntagsblatt* described the scene (see Fig. 10).[35]

The iconography and inscriptions of the Church-sponsored memorials identified the casualties of aerial warfare – the deceased as well as the survivors – as helpless victims of a divine judgement. They offered consolation in the transcendental promises of the Christian faith: 'Behold, I send an Angel before thee, to keep thee in the way, and to bring thee into the place which I have prepared' (Exodus 23.20), read the inscription on the memorial in the Brüderkirche in the old town, dedicated on Memorial Sunday 1958 (Fig. 11). While the central message of the

[35] 'Weihe des Ehrenmals für die Bombenopfer', *Kasseler Sonntagsblatt*, 2 December 1956, p. 16.

Church was one of hope and consolation in the face of catastrophic loss and bereavement, the notion of affliction also established a connection between victimhood and agency. 'The dead have a right to be remembered by us because none of us can wash our hands of [their death],' Pastor Schwab declared at the official opening of the memorial in the main cemetery in 1956.[36] On this interpretation, the casualties of allied bombing, rather than having fallen victim to Nazism or the war, were victims of the Germans themselves, who had brought divine affliction on to the city by their wrongdoings. At the consecration of the new cemetery in 1953, the Catholic pastor Ludwig Wiegand asked the congregation of mourners, 'Were we not part of this wretched crowd that once shouted "yes" when asked, "Do you want total war?"'[37]

Within this context, several clerics also raised the issue of a possible connection between death in the air war and the persecution of the Jews. In his address at the commemorative service of 1949, Pastor Wiegand told his audience of a Jewish mother who had begged him to look after her daughters when she received her deportation order for 23 October 1943. The family was killed in the air raid, which, according to the pastor, had saved them from an even worse type of death in the Nazi extermination camps.[38] Whatever the factual basis of the anecdote – and there are reasons to doubt its accuracy – the address contained an unusually critical potential. It served as a reminder that the casualties of aerial warfare were not the only victims of World War II, that indeed, there had been different and worse forms of victimhood than being killed in an air raid.

Although only implicit in Wiegand's address, the notion of retribution featured prominently in the memoirs of several religious ministers in the 1950s. Pastor Preger of the Lutherkirche, for example, likened the flight of the bomb-stricken population from the devastated city to the 'exodus of the children of Israel' in the deportations. His Magdeburg colleague, cathedral preacher Ernst Martin, compared the image of burning churches in the air war to the image of burning synagogues in the November pogrom of 1938.[39] Although the ecclesiastical authorities invariably conceived of retribution as an act of God rather than of mankind, the conceptualisation easily combined remnants of anti-Semitic stereotypes about the power of 'International Jewry' with philo-Semitic notions about the singularity of Jewish suffering.[40]

---

[36] Ibid.   [37] 'An den Gräbern der Bombenopfer', *HN*, 26 October 1953.
[38] 'Kassel trauerte am Grabe der Opfer des 22. Oktober 1943', *HN*, 24 October 1949, p. 5.
[39] Preger, 'Aus meiner Kasseler Amtszeit', p. 30; Martin, 'Memento', p. 60.
[40] See Stern, *Im Anfang war Auschwitz*, pp. 25–39, 267–98.

While the identification of the dead of the air raid as 'victims of fascism', 'victims of war' or 'victims of divine judgement' remained controversial, the consensus formula that served to cover up the dissension was the identification of the dead as 'our fellow citizens', as mayor Willi Seidel (SPD) wrote in a public appeal on the tenth anniversary in 1953.[41] Striking a similar chord, Protestant bishop Adolf Wüstemann declared in a commemorative address in October 1951, 'We commemorate the dead as those who have shared their lives with us in this city.'[42] The dead were defined in relational and spatial terms, not in the categories of agency and responsibility. Whoever was to blame for their death and however much they themselves might have had a hand in their own undoing, they were 'our dead' – an imagined community that included soldiers as well as women and children, the rich and the poor, avid supporters of the Nazi regime as well as its opponents. Even ninety foreigners and forced labourers from nine nations who had died in the air raid and been buried in the mass grave in the main cemetery were tacitly subsumed under this category.[43]

Among the political elites of Magdeburg, too, the identity of the air raid casualties as victims was not in doubt. Although initially, local KPD functionaries, echoing the proclamation by their central committee of 11 June 1945,[44] had drawn a sharp distinction between the minority of the 'anti-fascist freedom heroes' and the majority of the German population who 'had cheered the false messiah',[45] mayor Rudolf Eberhard, a Social Democrat, pursued an integrationist approach in his politics of memory. In this, he differed little from his Social Democratic colleagues west of the border. At the formal opening of the 'grove of honour' (*Ehrenhain*) for the 'victims of fascism' in the main cemetery in June 1947 – a site ostensibly dedicated to the (Socialist) resistance fighters against Nazism – Eberhard took great pains to include the civilian casualties of aerial warfare as well as the Wehrmacht soldiers in his commemorative address. He subsumed both groups under the category of 'victims of Hitler's war'. With regard to the dead of the air war, he turned explicitly against the Nazi notion of sacrifice, maintaining that they had died as innocent victims.[46]

---

[41] *KP*, 15 October 1953; *HN*, 18 October 1953.

[42] LKA Kassel, SB Wüstemann, 'Ansprache am 22. Oktober 1951', p. 3.

[43] Compare Friedhofsamt Kassel, Kriegsgräberlisten und Gräberlisten Hauptfriedhof; Pasche, Diefenbach and Wegner, *Todtenhof und Nordstadtpark*, pp. 21–3.

[44] 'Aufruf der Kommunistischen Partei Deutschlands', 11 June 1945, in Michaelis and Schraepler (eds.), *Ursachen und Folgen*, pp. 255–61.

[45] Walter Kassner, 'Unsterbliche Opfer', *Freiheit*, 21 June 1947; 'Den Opfern des Faschismus', *Amtliches Mitteilungsblatt*, 2 October 1945.

[46] 'Ehrenhain für die Opfer des Faschismus', *Amtl. Mitteilungsblatt*, 27 June 1947. Compare also StAM, Rep. 41/610, Die Einrichtung für die OdF auf dem Westfriedhof, 1946–50.

By the 1950s, this had changed: now the dead of 16 January 1945 were no longer victims of a past war, but those of a present war. After the arrest of Mayor Eberhard on charges of financial embezzlement and his replacement with the Communist Philipp Daub in the summer of 1950 – both symptom and consequence of a broader transformation in the political culture of the GDR from an 'anti-fascist-democratic' new order with strong local self-government into a centralised Socialist dictatorship[47] – the dead were reappropriated for the global confrontation between the forces of the 'world peace camp' (*Weltfriedenslager*) and 'Anglo-American imperialism'.[48] Nor were the dead any longer victims of war in the usual sense. Rather, they had become victims of crime, of 'bestial' mass murder, as the lead article in the *Volksstimme* put it on 4 May 1950.

The present-centred nature of the official conception of victimhood was well reflected in the stipulations for a competition that the city administration held in 1959 in order to obtain designs for a 'memorial to the victims of 16 January 1945'.[49] Although the memorial was to be erected on the site of mass burial in the cemetery, it was not intended primarily as a site of mourning but as a site of 'indictment' and 'appellation', as city councillor Meyer reminded the jury before they entered into deliberations.[50] During the selection procedures, Meyer again pointed out that the design should convey a sense of human beings having been 'senselessly murdered regardless of their persuasion'.[51] Accordingly, designs that were likely to invite contemplation and mourning on the part of the observer carried little favour with the jury. For example, sculptor Eberhard Rossdeutscher's suggestion that a cemetery called for a 'site of memory' (*Gedenkmal*) rather than a 'memorial' (*Mahnmal*) was rejected. Similarly, the idea of a pictorial representation of the mythical bird the phoenix was criticised as an 'idealised depiction of an eternal cycle of war and peace'.[52] By contrast, the jury commended a proposal that projected a massive neo-realist bronze sculpture of a 'falling person' raising the left arm in defiance. 'The gesture of resistance and indictment is commendable, and expresses well the central idea of the monument,'

---

[47] On the erosion of local self-government in the GDR see Schneider, 'Kommunalverwaltung und Verfassung'; Großbölting, 'Das Bürgertum auf dem Rückzug'. On Eberhard's arrest see Ingrun Drechsler, 'Eberhard, Rudolf', in *Magdeburger Biographisches Lexikon*, p. 152; on the broader context see Weber, *Geschichte der DDR*, pp. 163–212.

[48] La Magd., LHA, Rep. P 16, SED-Stadtleitung Magdeburg. Sekretariat, no. IV/5/1/ 45 A, Arbeitsrichtlinien der Kreisleitung der SED Magdeburg für die Monate Januar und Februar 1951.

[49] StAM, Rep. 41/2466, fos. 137–86, 'Künstlerischer Ideenwettbewerb "Mahnmal der Opfer des 16. Januar 1945"', 25 April 1959.

[50] Ibid., fo. 158.   [51] Ibid., fo. 162.   [52] Ibid., fo. 160.

the jury commented, for '[the sculpture] shows at once helpless annihilation and a strong will to live' (Fig. 12).[53]

Although neither design was realised owing to shortages in the supply
of raw materials and financial difficulties, the jury decisions reflected the
official identification of the dead in the Magdeburg of the late 1950s. The
casualties of allied bombing were victims of a crime but they were cast
less as helpless victims than as defiant accusers who, in some respects,
resembled the (Socialist) resistance fighters against Nazism.

Commemorating the dead

Differences in identification found expression in the format and content
of the commemorations, which (re-)emerged in both cities in the 1950s.
These ceremonies were held on or around the anniversaries of heavy
air raids. In many ways, they formed the backbone of public memory,
not only providing a public forum for opinion makers but also eliciting extensive coverage in the local media, on both the historical events
themselves and the commemorative rituals surrounding their return. In
confronting large segments of the population with the recent catastrophic
past, commemorations stabilised the status of '22 October' and '16 January' as collective *lieux de mémoire*. They provided occasions for private
citizens to revisit their personal fortunes during the 'nights of horror',
to share amongst themselves stories of death and survival, and to search
their attics for personal documents relating to the air war.[54] Yet, not only
individual lives but also the commemorations had a history that reached
back into the war. As a cultural practice, they were permeated with the
topographical, semiotic and semantic choices of Nazism – a deeply problematic past in its own right that was rarely acknowledged by the post-war
arbiters of public memory.

In Kassel, public ceremonies were carried out by the local section of
the Central League of Air Raid Victims, the civil administration and
the churches. In comparison with the official funeral ceremonies during the war, the post-war commemorations were marked by strong re-
Christianising tendencies which accorded a prominent role to the pastor and the rituals of the Christian funeral service (Fig. 13). Whereas
in Kassel, a convergence of secular and spiritual narratives took place,
in Magdeburg a strict separation between state and Church persisted.
While the SED and its affiliated organisations mainly drew on the indigenous tradition of the Socialist protest rally, they also incorporated narrative elements of Nazism into the secular ceremonies. Confined to the

[53] Ibid., fo. 158.   [54] See Thießen, 'Der "Feuersturm" im kommunikativen Gedächtnis'.

Figure 12. Successful design for the memorial in the main cemetery, Magdeburg, from a competition held in 1959. The design was never realised.

HN. 25. 10. 1954

Kränze für die Toten des 22. Oktober

Feierstunden auf dem Hauptfriedhof und auf dem Friedrichsplatz

Kassel. (*) „Meinen Frieden laß' ich euch", unter diesem Bibelwort versammelten sich viele hundert Kasselaner, um auf dem Hauptfriedhof in einer schlichten Feier der Opfer des Bombenkrieges zu gedenken. Aus der Trauer dürften nicht Haß oder Gleichgültigkeit wachsen, sondern Liebe, sagte Pfarrer G i e h l, der die Toten beider Konfessionen in sein Gebet einschloß. Bei der Feierstunde, die vom Kreisverband Kassel der Fliegergeschädigten veranstaltet wurde, legten ein Vertreter des Volksbundes Deutscher Kriegsgräberfürsorge, Stadtverordneter Hermann Ziegler für die Fliegergeschädigten, Stadtrat Heinrich Cornelius im Auftrage des Magistrats der Stadt Kassel und Stadträtin Edith Hellermann für die Heimatvertriebenen Kränze nieder.

Stadtrat C o r n e l i u s betonte, jeder einzelne habe die Verpflichtung, die Toten nicht zu vergessen, deren Opfer nur dann einen Sinn gehabt haben könne, wenn die Lebenden alles hergeben, um den Frieden zu erhalten.

Die Feierstunde wurde durch einen Posaunenchor umrahmt. Nachdem die Anwesenden das Lied vom guten Kameraden gesungen hatten, beteten sie gemeinsam das Vaterunser. Viele Angehörige verweilten an den Gräbern ihrer Lieben, die durch ein grausames Schicksal vor elf Jahren hinweggerafft worden waren.

Am Freitagabend hatten sich mehrere hundert Kasselaner bewegten Herzens auf dem Friedrichsplatz vor dem in rotes Licht getauchten Museum Fridericianum zu einer Stunde des Gedenkens an die Opfer des Angriffs versammelt, der elf Jahre zuvor um diese Zeit begonnen hatte. Keiner, der sich der Gewalt der Erinnerung an die Schrecken dieser Nacht hätte entziehen können.

Stadtrat Hans N i t s c h e und der 1. Vorsitzende des Kreisverbandes der Fliegergeschädigten, Hermann Z i e g l e r, gedachten in schlichten, ergreifenden Worten der Opfer, deren Schicksal uns Ueberlebenden Mahnung bleiben müsse alles zu tun, um

Elf Jahre nach der schrecklichsten aller Bombennächte gedachte Kassel seiner Toten. Unser Bild zeigt Pfarrer Giehl bei der Gedenkansprache; zweiter von links Stadtverordneter Hermann Ziegler; rechts vorn Stadtrat Cornelius. (Aufn. HN/Z)

die Wiederholung einer solchen Katastrophe abzuwenden. Stadtrat Nitsche versprach, daß die Stadt alles daransetzen werde, um den Evakuierten, die noch immer fern ihrer geliebten Heimatstadt leben müßten, die Rückkehr zu ermöglichen.

Von der Chorgruppe Heinrich Wilke (Männergesangverein „Frohsinn", Henschelchor) und „Schubertbund") klang das „Heilig, heilig, heilig ist der Herr …" machtvoll zum nächtlichen Himmel auf. Auch diese eindrucksvolle Feierstunde war vom Bund der Fliegergeschädigten veranstaltet worden.

In allen Kasseler Kirchen fanden Gedenkgottesdienste statt.

Figure 13. In the 1950s, the format of the commemorations was re-Christianised in Kassel, the Nazi functionary replaced by a pastor. The article appeared on the eleventh anniversary of the bombing in 1954.

spiritual space of the church building, the churches, meanwhile, employed the format of the 'memorial hour' (*Gedenkstunde*) in order to remember the dead.

Different adaptations of wartime traditions had repercussions for the topography of memory. In Kassel, the cemetery replaced the public square as the most important site of memory. The change of place was indicative of a semantic shift away from the *imitatio heroica* of the Nazi cult of death to the *memento mori* of the Christian faith.[55] Although

---

[55] See Lurz, *Kriegerdenkmäler*, vol. VI, p. 266.

commemoration re-entered the public square in the early 1950s, the practice of holding secular ceremonies in the city itself proved short lived. With the erection of a memorial in the main cemetery in 1956, secular commemorations returned to the resting place of the dead, where they would be performed annually until the end of the 1960s and beyond. In Magdeburg, by contrast, the trajectory of memory took the opposite direction. Prioritising appellation over contemplation, the secular elites initially focused on the public squares but moved certain rituals to the cemetery when they encountered challenges to their politics of memory. In comparison, the activity of the Church remained confined to the spiritual sphere of the church building.

In Kassel, the inception of an institutionalised culture of memory did not originate from above but grew out of the activities of the local branch of the League of Air Raid Victims. The League was an organisation of the living, not the dead, whose goal was to gain compensation for material losses incurred in the air war by means of federal law (*Lastenausgleich*).[56] However, the Air Raid Victims also pressed for public memory of the dead, both as a tool in domestic politics and, perhaps, in order to answer an emotional need amongst their members. In the summer of 1949, the local section organised a meeting of Kassel's evacuees, which drew a crowd of approximately two thousand people.[57] The central event was billed as a 'memorial service' (*Totengedenkfeier*), but sported the motto 'Forgotten victims of bombing demand their rights!' The main speech was given by the chairman of the Central League (*Zentralverband*), Dr Wilhelm Mattes (1892–1952), who had succeeded the organisation's founder, Adolf Bauser, after the latter's death in the autumn of 1948. In his speech, Mattes drew a bleak picture of the social situation of the war-damaged and evacuees four years after the end of the war and presented a catalogue of their demands. Throwing invectives at all political parties, he invoked the dead as the guardians of the evacuees' interests: 'The admonition of the dead of World War II to remember the dispossessed has already been forgotten. This is why today the war-damaged

56 Compare Adolf Bauser, 'Gerechtigkeit: Gerechte Lastenverteilung!', *Selbsthilfe. Unabhängige Zeitschrift für Politik, Kultur und Wirtschaft*, no. 1, 1 April 1946, p. 1; 'Hilfe für die Fliegergeschädigten', *Selbsthilfe*, no. 2, 15 April 1946, p. 1.; 'Was wir wollen. Ziele und Aufgaben des Bundes der Sparer und Fliegergeschädigten', *Selbsthilfe*, no. 7, 1 July 1946, p. 1.
57 'Partei der Kriegsgeschädigten auf dem Treffen der Ausgebombten Nordhessens angekündigt', *HN*, 13 June 1949, p. 1; 'Evakuierte bleiben Kasselaner', *HN*, p. 5; 'Für die Opfer des 22. Oktober', *HN*, 13 June 1949; StAK, A.1.00, vol. XIII, 'Treffen der Ausgebombten und Evakuierten aus Nordhessen', 19 May 1949; ibid., 'Ankündigungen', 2 June 1949; StAK, NL Seidel, Tagebuch 2, 11/12 June 1949, p. 206.

are forced to voice their demands and to proclaim their loss of faith in justice.'[58]

The event in Kassel formed part of a broader political campaign on the part of the Zentralverband in the run-up to the first Bundestag elections on 14 August 1949. Under their new chairman, the League had adopted a sharply confrontational stance towards the established political parties, and in cooperation with the expellee organisations, decided to contest the elections by founding a political party of its own that would press its claims in the federal parliament. The initiative was stalled when the allied occupation authorities withheld their licence, and as a consequence, the League had to resort to fielding independent candidates, with limited success.[59]

While the League's weekly journal, the *Selbsthilfe*, hailed the evacuee meeting in Kassel as an 'impressive mass rally', the mixture of radical rhetoric and funeral ceremony drew sharp public criticism from the established political elites. In a letter to the local press, a regional SPD luminary spoke of an 'abuse of memory', accusing the Air Raid Victims of having 'take[n] advantage of the good-will of their fellow citizens' for self-interested political gain.[60]

Despite the criticism, the Air Raid Victims continued to invoke the legacy of the dead in order to lend greater legitimacy to their grievances. In the autumn of 1949, the local section revived a wartime practice of the Nazi party, the public commemoration of the casualties of aerial warfare. On 22 October, one thousand citizens gathered at the main burial site in the main cemetery for a 'funeral service with religious participation', as the press announcement put it.[61] The format revolved around the commemorative address by two clergymen, to be followed by wreath laying and prayer.[62] As rites of demarcation, a brass ensemble performed hymns that were taken up by the congregation. Although the ceremony had been organised by a political pressure group, issues of mourning and consolation rather than politics stood at the centre. The ceremony

---

[58] 'Geschädigte demonstrieren für ihr Recht', *Selbsthilfe*, 1 July 1949, p. 2.
[59] 'Millionen Deutsche ohne Menschenrecht', *Selbsthilfe*, August 1949; Krause, *Flucht vor dem Bombenkrieg*, pp. 235f.; on the hard-fought first federal election of 1949 more generally see Benz, *Auftrag Demokratie*, pp. 439–62.
[60] 'Eine missbrauchte Totenehrung', *HN*, 14 June 1949, p. 3; 'Dem Eigennutz ist jedes Mittel recht. Böse Entgleisung auf dem Kasseler Evakuiertentreffen', *Hessischer Sonntag. SPD Informationen*, 19 June 1949, p. 3.
[61] '22. Oktober ✝', *HN*, 21 October 1949.
[62] 'Kassel trauerte am Grabe der Opfer des 22. Oktober 1943', *HN*, 24 October 1949; 'Kränze als Zeichen der Verbundenheit', *KZ*, 24 October 1949; 'Den Toten des 22. Oktober 1943 zum Gedächtnis', *Der evangelische Sonntagsbote*, 6 November 1949, p. 405.

provided an institutional frame to the informal practice of visiting the graves of loved ones on the anniversary of the day of their death, which had been established for years.[63]

The Air Raid Victims played a crucial role in the institutionalisation of annual commemorations in Kassel. Proceeding with a mixture of obstinacy and street pressure, they not only organised ceremonies on their own but also lobbied the council and the Church for greater involvement. In this, the local section seems to have followed a shift in policy at the federal level, where the Zentralverband abandoned its early confrontational stance after the failure at the Bundestag elections in order to seek greater cooperation with the established political elites.[64] Although reluctant to comply with the demand by the Air Raid Victims for official commemorations on 22 October,[65] the council preferred to take control of developments that it could not prevent. When the Air Raid Victims enlisted the support of a broad coalition of private citizens and local organisations for the celebration of a 'memorial service' in the centre of town in 1951, the council granted institutional support but decided to take over the organisation and implementation of the event in the future.[66] As with the political elites, the Protestant Church, too, was of the opinion that public rituals had best be presided over by the established institutions of Church and city. When approached by the Air Raid Victims in the autumn of 1951, Bishop Wüstemann agreed to deliver the commemorative address but proposed that in future the commemorations be held in one of the church ruins in such a way as to forestall 'any appeal to nationalist feelings of hatred', as he remarked in a note for the files.[67]

The remark may have reflected the bishop's concern over the strong presence of groups with grievances against the post-war settlement in the 'citizen's committee' that was responsible for the commemorative event. Next to such established institutions as the German Red Cross or the Society of Housewives, there functioned as cosignatories also the Interest Group of the Victims of Occupation (*Interessengemeinschaft der*

---

[63] See *KZ*, 24 October 1949.
[64] The evidence is sketchy but see 'Empfang durch den Bundeskanzler', *Selbsthilfe*, July 1951, p. 1; 'Bundes-Innenminister auf der Großkundgebung in Hannover', *Selbsthilfe*, February 1952, p. 1.
[65] See StAK, A.1.10, Magistratsprotokolle, 16 October 1950.
[66] StAK, A.1.10, no. 398, Trauerfeier am 22.10. (1951–68), council resolution, 18 October 1951.
[67] LKA Kassel, SB Wüstemann, no. 22, 'Stellungnahme des Bischofs zur Gedenkfeier für die Kasseler Bombenopfer am 22. Oktober 1951', 27 September 1951; see also ibid., Fülling to Wüstemann, 'Betr.: Gedenkfeier am 22. Oktober ds. Js. für die Bombenopfer', 12 October 1951.

Besatzungsgeschädigten), the League of the Expellees, and the League of Wehrmacht Veterans (*Bund ehemaliger Wehrmachtsangehöriger*). By comparison, organisations of the political Left, such as the trade unions, were conspicuously absent, as were the Victims of Nazism (VVN) and the Jewish community.

While the Air Raid Victims were successful in putting '22 October' on the official calendar, their say in shaping the commemorative format was progressively curtailed. When in 1952 the Church offered to hold special anniversary services in all Protestant churches, the parliamentary representatives of the Air Raid Victims withdrew a council motion that had proposed to declare 22 October an official 'day of remembrance'.[68] The following year, the city took over the organisation of the tenth-anniversary commemoration but proved reluctant to repeat the effort thereafter. Among the council, reservations persisted both about the day of remembrance in general and the role that the Air Raid Victims played in its implementation in particular. In a council meeting of October 1954, deputy mayor Grenzebach (FDP) argued that the ghosts of the bombing had better not be raised year after year. Instead, he suggested that the casualties of aerial warfare be commemorated together with all the other victims of war on the People's Day of Mourning or on Memorial Sunday. Councillor Goethe (SPD), meanwhile, took exception to the special interest politics that the speakers of the League of Air Raid Victims advocated during their funeral ceremonies.[69]

Constant renegotiations between the Air Raid Victims on the one hand and council and Church on the other had a considerable impact on the actual implementation of the ceremonies, forestalling the emergence of a central site of commemoration in the city. At the same time, the protracted process put limits on the extent to which Nazi-era liturgical elements were restored in post-war Kassel. In 1952, the Air Raid Victims held the secular commemoration in the same place where the Nazis had conducted their largest funeral ceremony of the war, the 'square of honour' in front of the town hall. The following year, however, the city assumed responsibility and shifted commemorative activity to the square in front of the ruins of the Martinskirche, popular symbol of Kassel and also a target of Bomber Command on 22 October 1943. In 1954 and 1955, the Air Raid Victims organised ceremonies on the Friedrichsplatz, the city's traditional parade ground. In 1956, the secular

---

[68] StAK, A.1.10, no. 398, Trauerfeier am 22.10. (1951–68), 'Antrag auf Einrichtung des 22. Oktober als ständigen Gedenktag der Kasseler Bombenopfer', 20 June 1952. For the debate in the Stadtverordnetenversammlung see StAK, A.0, 30 June 1952, pp. 34–9.

[69] StAK, A.1.10, no. 398, 'Mitteilungen: Gedenkfeier für die Opfer des 22. Oktober 1943', 25 October 1954.

ceremony was moved from the centre of town to the 'cemetery of honour' in the main cemetery, where a memorial was unveiled the same year.[70] The Church, meanwhile, held annual memorial services in most parish churches until the fifteenth anniversary in 1958. After that, commemorative activity was centralised in the city's largest church, the recently rebuilt Martinskirche.[71]

In comparison to the funeral ceremonies during the war, the secular commemorations of the 1950s were distinguished by the reintroduction of formal elements from the Christian liturgy. This was most strongly reflected by the prominence that was given to the church bell as the most important acoustic marker. In the 'memorial hour' on 22 October 1953, for example, the church bells were sounded both as an opening rite and as a closing rite, taking up no less than twenty-five minutes of the sixty-minute commemoration.[72] Likewise, church hymns and spiritual music by baroque composers such as Johann Sebastian Bach, Georg Friedrich Händel and Wilhelm Friedemann Bach – often performed by a church brass ensemble – replaced the predilection for the romantic music of Beethoven and Wagner that had been characteristic of the Nazi-era funeral services. Finally, there was the central role assigned to representatives of the Church. Even at the secular ceremonies, a clergyman, rather than a functionary or politician, tended to deliver the central commemorative address. The re-Christianising of memory found its institutional expression in the agreement between Church and council to hold an ecumenical church service rather than organise two separate events on the occasion of the fifteenth anniversary in 1958.[73]

Next to religious elements, the ceremonies also contained elements of commemorative idioms that, although dating back to the nineteenth century, had been successfully adapted by Nazism during the war, and which appeared especially, but not exclusively, in the formal repertoire of the League of Air Raid Victims. In October 1952, for example, the Air Raid Victims not only selected the same public square for commemoration as the Nazi party had done in 1943, they also erected a 'grove of honour' and made use of pylons in order to symbolise the alleged sacrifice of those who had perished in the bombing. In so doing, the Air

---

[70] 'Bombenopfer sind unvergessen. Gedenkfeier auf dem Ehrenfriedhof', *KZ*, 22 October 1956.

[71] LKA Kassel, Dekanat Kassel-Mitte no. 17, Gedenkgottesdienste in der Martinskirche. Jahrestag der Zerstörung Kassels, 1952–83, Dean Schwab to editors of *HA* and *KP*, 20 October 1959.

[72] Ibid., Schwab to parish pastors, 19 October 1953.

[73] See StAK, A.1.10, no. 398, Trauerfeier am 22.10. (1951–68), note for the files, 13 October 1958; 'Magistrats Mitteilungen', 21 October 1958.

Raid Victims provided for the continuity of central elements of the Nazi cult of death into the post-war world. Three years later, the Air Raid Victims used Wagner's *Twilight of the Gods* and Beethoven's *Egmont* as demarcation rites, thus unwittingly, perhaps, ascribing a heroic quality to the dead of the air war that directly echoed the National Socialist conceptualisation of the civilian casualties as 'soldiers of the *Heimat*'.[74]

By contrast, the SPD-led city council was much more cautious about the use of music and symbols that bore associations with any military tradition, past or present. This stance reflected the suspicion on the part of many leading Social Democrats, both in the city and in the country at large, towards the rearmament of the Federal Republic, which the Conservative Adenauer government was pursuing as a cornerstone of its policy of Western integration.[75] Although, in 1953, formations from the Federal Border Guard as well as the police and the fire brigade gave the ceremony a stately air, in 1957 the council emphasised that in order 'to avoid any military appearance', the official wreath would be carried by civil servants rather than police officers.[76] Caution notwithstanding, the city also approved of one central element of continuity between the ceremonies of the war years and of the 1950s: 'The Song of the Good Comrade' (*Das Lied vom guten Kameraden*).[77] The song, which had a history stretching back beyond World War II to the Weimar Republic and the Second Empire,[78] was reintroduced in 1950 as background music to the ceremonial honouring of the dead. On a symbolic level, the song identified the non-combatant casualties of the air war as soldiers, and in so doing, perpetuated an important element of the Nazi cult of death.

While the organisation and implementation of the ceremonies lay in the hands of the local elites and the Air Raid Victims, there is much evidence to suggest that the public commemorations enjoyed broad popular support in post-war Kassel. On the occasion of the tenth anniversary in 1953, for example, commemorative services were held in no fewer than twenty-six Protestant parishes, while the press reported an attendance of 10,000 people at the secular commemoration that followed. In a letter to the mayor, a resident spoke of the 'deep emotions' [*tiefe Ergriffenheit*]' with which he had listened to the mayor's speech, and emphasised

[74] Compare 'Mahnende Glocken und Posaunen', *HN*, 23 October 1952; 'Mahnende Flammen', *KZ*, 23 October 1952; ' Kassel gedachte der Bombenopfer', *KP*, 24 October 1955.
[75] On the context see Large, *Germans to the Front*.
[76] StAK, A.1.10, no. 398, 'Vermerk', 23 October 1957.
[77] For an insightful reading of *Das Lied vom guten Kameraden*, see Kühne, *Kameradschaft*, pp. 30–3.
[78] On the history of the song see the comments by Dietmar Klenke in Maier and Schäffer (eds.), *'Totalitarismus' und 'Politische Religionen'*, vol. II, p. 66.

that many fellow citizens had expressed 'genuine and heart-felt words of appreciation'.[79] Although the year of the tenth anniversary no doubt represented a special case, participation was considerable in other years as well. Approximately 5,000 Kasseler attended the commemoration in the main cemetery in 1950, while the following year, some 1,200 people packed the assembly hall of the Friedenshof in order to listen to the commemorative address by Bishop Wüstemann.[80] With the passing of time, attendance waned, levelling off in the range of several hundred, but on special occasions, such as the consecration of two new church bells in 1962, the commemorative service was still able to attract more people than the largest city church, the Martinskirche, could hold.[81]

In the 1950s, '22 October' mattered, equalling in importance the People's Day of Mourning and surpassing by far the commemorative events organised in memory of the victims of Nazism.[82] It appears that participation was particularly high among two groups for whom the war did not easily pass into history, the bereaved and the evacuees. With 9,202 non-combatant deaths in the air war, the first group comprised tens of thousands of people, while by the early 1950s there were still 70,000 former residents living in small towns and villages in the Hessian countryside who had not been able to return.[83] On the anniversaries, relatives adorned the graves of their loved ones with fresh flowers and attended the ceremonies, not infrequently shedding tears in public.[84] The evacuees, for their part, took the official commemorations as an occasion to revisit the city of their birth and their longings, welcoming the opportunity of free travel that the city granted them on at least one occasion. Nearly two decades after the end of the war, some evacuees were still living in financial circumstances so precarious that they could ill afford the 'luxury of an extraordinary expense' for the journey home, even if they lived no more than a hundred kilometres away.[85]

Whereas in Kassel, the format of the commemorations showed a tendency towards re-Christianisation, in Magdeburg public memory remained a strictly secular affair, drawing on the tradition of the Socialist

[79] StAK, A.1.10, no. 398, Schluckebier to mayor, 23 October 1953.

[80] *Kasseler Sonntagsblatt*, 29 October 1950; 28 October 1951, p. 12.

[81] 'Die Osanna-Glocke rief zum Gedenken', *HA*, 23 October 1961.

[82] On the history of the People's Day of Mourning see Kaiser, 'The *Volkstrauertag* (People's Day of Mourning)'.

[83] 'Die zahlenmäßigen Veränderungen unter den Kasseler Bürgern, die während der Kriegszeit evakuiert wurden, nach Ergebnissen der Volkszählungen', in *Statistischer Bericht der Stadt Kassel* (1/1952), pp. 29–35, here p. 30.

[84] 'Kassel trauerte am Grabe der Opfer des 22. Oktober 1943', *HN*, 21 October 1949.

[85] StAK, A.1.10, Trauerfeier am 22.10. (1951–68), correspondence between evacuee Konrad K. and mayor, 17 October 1963; 18 October 1963; 24 October 1963.

mass rally while integrating elements of the Nazi cult of death. Whereas in Kassel, 'existential' consolation and 'functional' integration stood side by side, in Magdeburg the secular events were tilted much more heavily towards the 'functional' side of memory, as catalysts for political mobilisation and social integration. Here, secular commemorative rituals did not emerge as the result of pressure 'from below', but were implemented 'from above' by the SED and its associated organisations. Yet, due to the highly centralised nature of the SED-state and fluctuations in the Cold War, the commitment of the Socialist power holders to a local memory place such as '16 January' was half-hearted at best. This resulted not only in inconsistencies in the annual implementation but also in room for manoeuvre for other agents who were concerned about the 'existential' side of memory, such as the churches and the bereaved.

During the 'anti-fascist-democratic upheaval' of 1945 to 1949, '16 January 1945' had been created by the city council as a *lieu de mémoire* that would put the destruction in World War II on a par with Magdeburg's iconic 'marriage of blood' during the Thirty Years War. From 1948 onwards, with the erosion of local self-government, this began to change.[86] When the SED-leadership in Berlin discovered the potential value of strategic bombing for the propaganda struggles of the Cold War, '16 January 1945' became subordinated to '13 February 1945', the date of the Dresden raids.[87] This official prioritising not only led to a rewriting of indigenous experiences in the light of the model of Dresden – an 'import of memory', so to speak – but also delayed the emergence of annual rituals.

The new politics of memory divested allied bombing of its original context of World War II and recontextualised the campaign as the first act of imperialist aggression in the Cold War. According to this reinterpretation, strategic bombing had made no contribution to the destruction of German fascism. Without any military objective, the allied air war had aimed deliberately to destroy the territory of the future GDR. A leader's comment in the *Volksstimme* summed up the main themes of the new narrative in May 1950 thus:

The German people will celebrate this day [the German surrender on 8 May 1945] with heartfelt gratitude to the victorious Soviets . . . to whom alone we owe the liberation from fascist slavery and tyranny. But what did the Anglo-American imperialists do? As the Red Army rushed from victory to victory all the way from Stalingrad to the river Oder, the Anglo-American imperialist bombers . . . unleashed an insane orgy of destruction . . . The devastation served

---

[86] See Großbölting, *SED-Diktatur und Gesellschaft*.
[87] See Margalit, 'Der Luftangriff auf Dresden'; Neutzner, 'Vom Anklagen zum Erinnern'.

only one purpose: to leave a scene of devastation, a dead zone, to the inexorably advancing Red Army.[88]

Drawing on core elements of Nazi wartime propaganda, the air war was conceptualised as a senseless atrocity, as 'murder, despicable treacherous murder', as a leader in the party paper of the CDU, *Der Neue Weg*, put it.[89]

Although the Magdeburg SED recognised the potential inherent in the symbolic date for the political mobilisation of the population, '16 January' at first occupied only a subordinate place in the annual calendar. On the occasion of the fifth anniversary in 1950, a public meeting was held that did not explicitly deal with the air war but with the creation of the umbrella organisation of the National Front, in which all political parties as well as mass organisations such as the Free German Youth or the trade unions were represented.[90] In the following year, propagandistic treatment remained largely confined to the press.[91] In a meeting of SED cadres on 22 January 1951, the first secretary of the regional party organisation (*Kreisleitung*) commented on the disappointing progress of the 'peace work' in the city and pointed to the neglect of the memory place. 'We did not make enough use of 16 January. On this day especially we could have mobilised the masses.'[92]

The following year, the local political elites decided to put the *lieu de mémoire* to better use, proposing to commemorate the day as a 'memorial day in the memory of the victims of the terror raid'.[93] Although the decision was reached unanimously,[94] it did not at first meet with the approval of the local Peace Council, which argued that priority should be given to the national over the local, to Dresden over Magdeburg. 'Our objections that 13 February 1952 – the day of the destruction of Dresden – has been selected by the German Peace Council in Berlin as the national commemoration day went unheeded,' an internal report noted with some irritation.[95] The memorial celebration that followed inaugurated a

[88] 'Der Befreiungstag ein Tag des Gedenkens', *Volksstimme*, 4 May 1950, p. 1.

[89] *Der Neue Weg*, 16 January 1950.

[90] 'Die Nationale Front handelt. 3000 Magdeburger auf der Großkundgebung der Nationalen Front', *Volksstimme*, 17 January 1950, p. 1; 'In der Nationalen Front dem Frieden dienen. Großkundgebung am 5. Jahrestag der Zerstörung Magdeburgs', ibid., p. 3.

[91] StAM, Rep. 41, no. 917, Chronik der Stadt Magdeburg, 16 January 1951.

[92] LA Magd., LHA, Rep. P 16, SED-Stadtleitung Magdeburg, no. IV/5/1/45, fos. 7–21, here fo. 19, Sekretariatssitzung, 22 January 1951.

[93] LA Magd., LHA, Rep. P 1, Landesfriedenskomitee Sachsen-Anhalt, no. 33, fo. 117, Monthly Report for January 1952.

[94] Ibid.

[95] LA Magd., LHA, Rep. P 1, Landesfriedenskomitee Sachsen-Anhalt, no. 33, fo. 117.

tradition of secular remembrance that has continued to the present day
(Fig. 11). Already some years earlier, in 1948, the Protestant Church had
marked the return of the day by means of an 'hour of commemoration' in
the cathedral refectory.[96] The extent to which Church and state pursued
separate politics of memory in the 1950s was illustrated by the refusal
of the Church to comply with an official request to ring the church bells
during the ceremonial minute of silence on 16 January 1952.[97]

In the files of the Peace Council, a detailed report has been preserved
that provides insight into the meticulous planning of the ceremonies at
the height of the Cold War.[98] The 'Plan on the Organisation of 16 January
1953' aimed at the comprehensive and yet closely supervised mobilisation
of the citizens of Magdeburg for the political goals of the SED-regime.
The plan distinguished between a preparatory phase and the organisation
of the event proper. In the run-up to the day, the National Front was
expected to make frequent references to the upcoming anniversary, while
the Peace Committee would publish a proclamation together with a string
of articles and eyewitness accounts in the press. In addition, there were
plans to put up slogans in public places and window displays, while the
political parties and affiliated organisations agreed to commit themselves
to a 'campaign of education' about the meaning of 16 January 1945.
On the day itself, short commemorations were to be held in all schools,
factories and offices, to be followed by a central rally in the public square
of Alter Markt at four o'clock. Afterwards, delegations would march to a
makeshift monument in the ruins of the theatre of the Kammerlichtspiele
on Breiter Weg, where they would lay wreaths. Until the fall of night,
members of the state youth organisations would stand guard. It was
planned to sound air raid sirens at midday, during which traffic was
expected to come to a standstill. The population and the administration
were expected to drape their windows with flags.

In a summary report written a few days after the event, the Peace
Committee gave an ambivalent assessment. While most measures had
been implemented as planned, the pasting up of public slogans and the
decoration of shop windows had left much to be desired. On the central
rally, the report noted that attendance had reached a figure of 3,500
to 3,800 people. The report was critical of the speech by city councillor

---

[96] AKPS, Rep. J1, Ev. Domgemeinde, nos. 3290–1, Kanzelabkündigungen, 1936–54.
[97] Schultze (ed.), *Berichte der Magdeburger Kirchenleitung*, p. 97 (report by Bishop D. Ludolf
Müller, 11 January 1952); LA Magd., LHA, Rep. P 1, Landesfriedenskomitee Sachsen-
Anhalt, no. 33, fo. 117, 6 February 1952.
[98] LA Magd., LHA, Rep. P 2, Bezirksfriedensrat Magdeburg, no. 54, Berichte, Statistiken,
Arbeitspläne und Presseartikel des Kreisfriedensrates Magdeburg, fos. 336–9, 'Bericht
über die durchgeführte Gedenkkundgebung am 16. Januar 1953', 22 January 1953.

Figure 14. Secular commemoration in Magdeburg on the tenth anniversary of the air raid in 1955.

Bösche, who was censured both for its excessive length and for the failure to address the 'world struggle for peace' in any detail. As a consequence, the protest resolution against a trial for espionage in the United States had received insufficient attention, the report noted critically. In conclusion, the Peace Council suggested that, in future, 'instruction' and 'inspection' be intensified.[99]

Although certain rituals and symbols – such as the wreath-laying as a symbolic offering of the living to the dead – were drawn from the same cultural repertoire as in Kassel, there were important differences. This was no accident but reflected the strong emphasis that the bearers of the ritualised action in Magdeburg placed on mobilisation and indictment rather than on consolation and integration. In the secular commemorations of the 1950s, the Christian element, so prominent west of the border, was absent. Not only was the commemorative address made by a political functionary rather than a pastor, hymns, prayer and the symbol of the cross were missing as well. Instead, the commemorations of the early 1950s bore the imprint of the Socialist mass rallies, featuring flags, banners, uniformed youth and workers' delegations. The recitation of poems by working-class poets, the reading of protest resolutions and the observance of ceremonial minutes of silence also stemmed from the same tradition. At the same time, the ceremonies adopted formal elements from the Nazi funeral ceremonies, showing a tendency to invest the ritual action with an aural atmosphere and tending to make heroes of the casualties of aerial warfare. In 1953, for example, the makeshift memorial was framed by 'guards of honour' who stood by as the official delegations laid their wreaths to the tune of Beethoven's funeral march from symphony no. 3, *Eroica*.[100] Another example was the prominent role of the national anthem, which, as in the Third Reich, invested local events with national significance.

While the secular commemorations emphasised determination and protest, emotional outlets for grief were tightly circumscribed. Yet the marginalisation of mourning did not go unchallenged. On the semi-public level, ordinary citizens turned the makeshift memorial into a personal site of memory when they put down wreaths that were dedicated to their loved ones.[101] On the institutional level, the Protestant Church likewise called for a renegotiation of the meaning of '16 January'. In

---

[99] All quotes in ibid.
[100] 'Unser Gelöbnis: Nie wieder ein 16. Januar 1945!', *Der Neue Weg*, 20 January 1953, p. 3.
[101] LA Magd., LHA, Rep. P 2 Bezirksfriedensrat Magdeburg, no. 54, Berichte, Statistiken, Arbeitspläne und Presseartikel des Kreisfriedensrates Magdeburg, fo. 336f. Compare also Lüdtke, 'Histories of Mourning'.

November 1953, a regional synod passed a motion that called on the city council to declare the day a specially protected 'day of remembrance' on which all festivities should stop.[102] The appeal was taken up by the Ost-CDU and popularised in the CDU party paper, *Der Neue Weg*,[103] At stake was nothing less than a reorientation of the official memorial culture, from an emphasis on protest to an emphasis on mourning, as was clearly recognised by the SED-controlled city council. In the meeting of 13 January 1954, the council rejected the motion, arguing that the institutionalisation of '16 January' as a 'special day of repentance' was wrong.[104] Remarkably, the council responded by radically curtailing commemorative activity altogether. The commemoration of the dead was moved from the place of death, the centre of the city, to the place of burial, the Westfriedhof, where the council confined the ritualised action to simple wreath laying.[105] The city space itself, by contrast, was reserved for the celebration of the reconstruction effort, as was made clear by the decision of 1955 to hold a special 'voluntary work action' on the day of 16 January.[106]

Serving the dead: *mortui viventes obligant*

'The meaning of this death cannot be understood and cannot be explained rationally,' declared Kassel deputy mayor Wilhelm Grenzebach (FDP) as he laid a wreath in memory of the dead on the tenth anniversary of the bombing in 1953. He went on to deplore the 'destruction' of millions of 'defenceless human beings . . . in our time', concluding on a note of deep anthropological pessimism: 'The graves . . . raise the issue of justice. The answer is: Mankind is evil from the beginning.'[107]

In the radical refusal to make sense of violent death in war, the speech was unusual. While the post-war protagonists of public memory no longer

---

[102] AKPS, Rep. A Spec. K. 2351, 'Verhandlungsniederschrift', 12/13 April 1953.

[103] 'Was ist nun eigentlich mit dem 16. Januar? Wir warten immer noch auf eine Verordnung des Rates der Stadt', *Der Neue Weg*, 12 January 1954, p. 3; 'CDU beantragt den Schutz des 16. Januar. Verbot aller Lustbarkeiten an dem Schreckenstag Magdeburgs gefordert', *Der Neue Weg*, 13 January 1954, p. 3. On the role of the East German CDU in the formative period of the GDR see Richter, *Die Ost-CDU*.

[104] StAM, Rep. 18/4, Ra. 30, Ratssitzungen, Dezember bis Januar 1954, fos. 4f., 13 January 1954.

[105] Ibid.

[106] See StAM, Rep 18/4, Ra. 41, Ratssitzungen Januar 1955. Niederschrift, 5 January 1955; LA Magd., LHA, Rep. P 13, SED-Bezirksleitung, no. IV/2/3/40, p. 004, Bürositzungen, 'Vorschläge für den 16. Januar', 6 January 1955.

[107] 'Kranzniederlegung für die Toten des 22. Oktober', *KZ*, 24 October 1953. Compare also 'Kassel wird sie nicht vergessen', *KP*, 24/25 October 1953; 'Kranzniederlegung für die Bombenopfer', *HN*, 24 October 1953.

demanded of the living to emulate the dead, as the Nazis had done, they rarely abandoned the underlying premise of a reciprocal relationship between the dead and the living. In the 1950s, the nineteenth-century notion of an obligation of the living towards the dead – typically expressed through the Latin tag, *mortui viventes obligant* – still formed the conceptual basis for most attempts at imparting meaning to premature death.[108] The conceptual frame endured not least as a result of its ability to posit a connection between the bereaved and the deceased across the rupture of death. 'Admonition' and 'obligation' remained crucial terms in the discourse on violent death, despite the fact that the precise nature of this *Mahnung* and the purpose of the *Verpflichtung* had become unclear. What, then, was the obligation that the living owed to the dead in a world in which the idea of heroic succession had become discredited?

In Kassel, the local elites tried to provide a number of answers that were all premised on the identification of the dead as 'our dead'. The first obligation revolved around the act of remembrance itself: 'Our dead admonish us never to forget them,' Catholic pastor Wiegand declared in typical fashion in 1949.[109] Two years later, at the commemoration in 1951, the same idea was expressed through the words of a popular nineteenth-century poem, 'Requiem' by Friedrich Hebbel. 'Soul, do not forget them / soul, do not forget the dead!', an actor from the state theatre recited.[110] While the act of remembrance was considered as the fulfilment of an obligation in itself, the carriers of the mnemonic discourse insisted that the dead also held a more specific lesson for the living, the admonition of 'never again'. No longer demanding of the living to carry on the fight on their behalf, the dead called on the survivors to prevent another war from ever happening again. Such concern over peace had played a prominent role in the rhetoric of the Republican war veterans' organisation of the Reichsbanner during the Weimar Republic, but by the 1950s the injunction was no longer the preserve of an embattled minority of democratic socialists.[111] It was embraced across the political spectrum and also by the churches. In the post-war period, the admonition of 'never again' formed the lowest common denominator in the attempt to derive meaning from the carnage of the war in general and the bombing in particular.[112]

---

[108] Koselleck, 'Kriegerdenkmale', p. 255. On the cultural context see Baumgartner, 'Christliches Brauchtum'.

[109] 'Kränze als Zeichen der Verbundenheit', *KZ*, 24 October 1949.

[110] Friedrich Hebbel, 'Requiem', in *Deutsche Gedichte*, pp. 214f.

[111] On the memory politics of the Reichsbanner see Ziemann, 'Republikanische Kriegserinnerung', 388f.

[112] Compare also Bessel, 'War to End all Wars', p. 92.

While the injunctions 'to stop forgetting' and of 'never again' were equally popular among the secular and religious authorities, there were differences of emphasis. Pastors were eager to stress the close connection between God's judgement and the obligation of a Christian renovation. 'Make sure that the rubble of your cities will be turned into steps that lead to God,' as Lutheran pastor Velbinger declared at a memorial service in 1950.[113] At the same time, they were careful to avoid the impression that the dead had in any way deserved their fate because they had become guilty before God. 'The issue of guilt is not related to death or survival,' as an unsigned memorandum emphasised in 1953. While God had judged the citizenry of Kassel – and humankind more generally – for transgressions of the First Commandment, he had made no distinction between the innocent and the guilty in his wrath. Survival was no sign of righteousness but demanded penance and a return to God.[114]

The secular representatives of the city administration, meanwhile, combined the general injunction of 'never again' with an attempt to harness the memory of the dead to the immediate task at hand, the reconstruction. The extent to which public statements on death oscillated between tradition and innovation, between apologia and critical engagement, is well illustrated by the commemorative speech that the SPD mayor Willi Seidel delivered on the tenth anniversary of the air raid in 1953.

Before an audience of 10,000 residents, Seidel universalised the legacy of 'our dead' by drawing a pacifist conclusion from the catastrophe. Echoing the Weimar-era peace movement, the mayor insisted that the carnage of World War II taught the present never again to start another war.[115] Although Seidel spoke in oblique terms of the 'megalomania and craving for power of a few irresponsible men' that were responsible for the present situation, he refused to explore the nexus between aggressive war and domestic destruction in any detail. 'Let us not search hatefully for the culprits in the past,' he told his audience. Instead, he proposed to lay the past to rest for the sake of reconciliation in the present, declaring,

---

[113] Archiv der Lutherkirche, Paul Velbinger, 'Predigten', no. 37, 'Gedächtnisgottesdienst zur Erinnerung an den Bombenangriff auf die Stadt Kassel, 22–10–50', pp. 202–6, here p. 206.

[114] LKA Kassel, Dekanat Kassel-Mitte, no. 17, Gedenkgottesdienste in der Martinskirche. Jahrestag der Zerstörung Kassels, 1952–1983, unsigned manuscript, no date [1953].

[115] StAK, NL Seidel, Ansprachen 3 [nos. 48–93], pp. 1201–5, 'Trauerfeier vor der Martinskirche aus Anlass des 10. Jahrestages der Zerstörung Kassels', 22 October 1953; for the quotation p. 1204. On the history of the slogan 'Nie wieder Krieg', see Lütgemeier-Davin, 'Basismobilisierung gegen den Krieg'.

'We must and want to draw a line below the past. Let the spirit of peace and reconciliation enter between us.'[116] In line with this demand, Seidel decontextualised the air raid in terms of a 'natural disaster' that had struck 'our poor city' seemingly out of nowhere.[117]

The semantic ambiguity of the German term *Opfer* made it easy for the mayor to characterise the dead as innocent victims and at one and the same time turn them into guardians of the reconstruction. The dead had not only *been* sacrificed but they had also *made* a sacrifice – a sacrifice that obliged the living to join hands in the 'reconstruction of our beloved city of our fathers'. In his concluding paragraph, Seidel even spoke of the dead as 'having given their blood for us so that we can live'. In so doing, he echoed the official conceptualisation of violent death during the Nazi years, which had typically been expressed through the phrase 'Germany must live even if we have to die'.[118]

In many respects, Seidel's public statement can be considered typical of a dominant strand of West German public memory in the 1950s.[119] Seidel's speech was an indictment of the cruelty of war in general, shirking for the sake of internal and external reconciliation any confrontation with either the specific nature of the German war of 1939–45 or the strategic air war of the Western allies of 1942/3–45. At the same time, it demonstrated not only the present-centred uses of memory but also the lasting relevance of interpretations that derived from the pre-1945 world, be this the invocation of Weimar-era pacifism or of a notion of sacrifice that – although of long standing – had been used to excess during the Third Reich.

Five years later, in 1958, Seidel's successor, Lauritz Lauritzen (SPD), placed greater emphasis on the historical context, speaking of mass death as a 'hard indictment of all those who were in positions of political responsibility back then'. According to Lauritzen, the 'most disastrous of all wars' was the end of a German special path that could be traced from the failed Hitler putsch of 1923, through the accession to power of the 'Hitler tyranny' in 1933 to the destruction in World War II. While the mayor's address reflected wider shifts in emphasis in the public discourse on Nazism that characterised the late 1950s,[120] he still upheld the distinction between 'them' – the Nazi rulers – and 'us', the victims. 'In a megalomaniac military adventure they wanted to conquer the world.

---

[116] Seidel, 'Trauerfeier', p. 1204.   [117] Ibid., p. 1201.
[118] The phrase derived from a poem by Heinrich Lersch, 'Soldaten-Abschied' (1914).
[119] Compare the famous observations of Arendt, 'Aftermath of Nazi Rule', 343.
[120] See Gregor, *Haunted City*, pp. 227–45.

With their catastrophic downfall they brought boundless misery over all of us,' he declared before his audience in the Martinskirche.[121]

While the universalising and self-victimising tendencies of the post-war memory culture have been well documented in recent research,[122] less attention has been paid to the deep divisions which lay just below the surface of a consensus slogan such as 'Never again'. In Kassel, these divisions were exposed in the controversy about the rearmament of West Germany, which formed an integral part of Adenauer's policy of Western integration.[123] Locally, the various stages of the drive for the establishment of Federal Armed Forces were bitterly contested by the radical Left, and at grass-roots level, also by the moderate Left and non-affiliated sections of the population.[124] Publicly, the opposition found expression in mass rallies, petitions for a referendum and forms of direct action.[125] In Kassel, the issue was deeply divisive for at least two reasons. Firstly, the critics feared, the establishment of a West German army would deepen the partition of Germany, from which the city, situated a mere fifty kilometres west of the border, suffered disproportionately. Secondly, an army would bring back soldiers into a city that had long served as a 'garrison town', contributing to a remilitarisation of society and above all putting the city at enormous risk in the event of another war.[126] Kassel had been a military target in World War II, and would be a target again in a future war, the critics argued.

Against this backdrop, the radical Left tried to divest the injunction of 'Never again' from the depoliticised commemorative context and to reclaim the formulation for the rallying of mass protest against rearmament.[127] 'No more tiger tank city, never again another 22 October 1943,' a banner read on a protest march in Kassel, which drew on the *lieu de mémoire* in order to posit a connection between armament and destruction – past and present.[128] According to this reading, the destruction of World War II had been a direct consequence of Kassel's importance as an armaments centre and military garrison in the Third Reich. Just as the 'remilitarisation' of the Adenauer government

---

[121] StAK, A.1.10, no. 607, Reden OB Lauritzen, no. 53, 22 October 1958, no pagination.

[122] Niedhart, "So viel Anfang war nie", pp. 16f.; Dubiel, *Niemand ist frei von der Geschichte*, pp. 37–77; Moeller, *War Stories*, pp. 21–50.

[123] See, for example, Wolfrum, *Die geglückte Demokratie*, pp. 96–143.

[124] On the context see Geyer, 'Der Kalte Krieg, die Deutschen und die Angst'.

[125] See Osuch, 'Remilitarisierung'.

[126] For a detailed discussion of the controversy see Arnold, "Kassel mahnt".

[127] On the genesis of the rallying cry 'Nie wieder Krieg' in the early Weimar Republic see Holl, *Pazifismus*, p. 144.

[128] See the photograph in Osuch, 'Neubeginn im Rüstungszentrum Kassel', p. 63.

re-enacted the rearmament of the Third Reich, so would the city again meet the fate of World War II in a future war, the argument went.[129] From this angle, the Communist Left attacked the politics of memory of the local elites. The 'true culprits... of the past and instigators of a new misfortune [in the present]' were glossed over in the commemorations, the *Sozialistische Volkszeitung* alleged in typical fashion on the tenth anniversary. On this view, the dead obliged the living neither to return to God nor to rebuild the city. Rather, they admonished them to get involved in radical political action with the goal of 'putting a stop to the activities of the culprits... forever'. The latter were identified by the newspaper as a coalition of American capitalists and German militarists.[130] In 1954, the *Sozialistische Volkszeitung* went one step further, presenting the Communist party as the 'most determined fighter against an even worse 22 October'.[131]

Interestingly, the debate in the city did not subside when the new federal army came into existence in 1955. In contrast to the nationwide Paulskirche initiative against rearmament, which quickly fizzled out once the federal parliament had passed the Paris Treaties on 27 February 1955,[132] controversy in the city intensified. Should Kassel become home to detachments of German troops or did the bitter experience of airborne destruction preclude any revival of the tradition as a garrison town? This was the question that exercised the local public in the spring of 1956 as no other issue. When the *Hessische Nachrichten* asked its readers to voice their opinion in a readers' poll in February 1956, the response was overwhelming. Within the course of little over a week, 1,501 letters had reached the editors,[133] 90 per cent of which opposed the stationing of troops in the city. Just as remarkable as the result was the pre-eminent role that memories of the bombing played in the debate. As a 'symbol of a painful experience', the 'magical date' of 22 October cropped up again and again, the editors wrote in their introduction. While the proponents of a West German army pointed towards the financial benefits of a garrison, the opponents invoked the memory of 22 October in order to underline their claim that the garrisoning of troops would put the city at additional risk in a future war. 'Kassel has suffered enough,' was the

---

[129] See Anonymous [Willi Belz], '22. Oktober 1943 – Ewige Mahnung zum Frieden. Kassel gedenkt der Opfer der Bombenangriffe. Niemals darf sich das Grauenvolle wiederholen!', *SVZ*, 22 October 1951, p. 4.

[130] [Willi Belz], 'Der 22. Oktober mahnt Kassel', *SVZ*, 22 October 1953, p. 4.

[131] 'Kassels Zerstörung am 22. Oktober 1943', *SVZ*, 23 October 1954, p. 6.

[132] See Large, *Germans to the Front*, pp. 227–33.

[133] *HN*, 18 February 1956. All the published reactions are reprinted in Osuch, 'Remilitarisierung', documentary appendix.

rationale that informed this argument.[134] Or, as another contribution put it,

Tens of thousands of *Kasselaner* had to witness how thousands of their relatives were roasted to death in the flames, painfully perished in smashed ruins and suffocated in blocked air raid shelters . . . Those were the advantages of a 'garrison city'! That was the end of the 'tank city of Kassel'. That was the 'wiping out' of the 'tiger [tank] city'! We've had enough for ever . . .

The issue exposed the deep cleavages running through post-war Kassel, pitting the working-class parties of the SPD and KPD, the trade unions and the left-leaning *Hessische Nachrichten* against the middle-class parties of the CDU and FDP, the veterans' organisations and the conservative *Kasseler Post*. It climaxed in a passionate debate in the city council in March 1956, during which the SPD pushed through a motion that protested against the revival of the city's tradition as a garrison town.

In Magdeburg, 'memory', 'peace' and 'rebuilding' were central terms in the secular discourse as well but were invested with connotations quite different from their usage in Kassel. 'Peace' was the 'fight for peace', be this, as in 1954, for the success of the Berlin Four Power Conference or, as in the following year, against the ratification of the Paris Treaties.[135] The term 'rebuilding', meanwhile, conveyed more than the physical reconstruction of the city, encompassing the creation of the new society of the GDR. In the secular memory culture of Magdeburg, the admonition of 'never again' was premised on the identification of the dead as 'victims of crime' and accompanied by specific interpretive guidelines. 'Never again' equalled the active 'struggle for peace', which in turn was synonymous with the identification with and active support of the Socialist 'world peace camp'. This interpretation was popularised through all the channels available to the SED, its affiliated organisations, and the 'agents of transmission' (Hermann Weber), the National Front and the Peace Committees.

On 1 September 1949, the daily *Volksstimme* published a small article called 'The last letter'. The piece formed part of the special coverage on the tenth anniversary of the outbreak of World War II.[136] The article reported on a letter of farewell which an old carpenter had scribbled on a piece of wood in a makeshift air raid shelter shortly before his death on

---

[134] Quote from a letter by Willy Orth, in *HN*, 18 February 1956: 'Wo werden die Streitkräfte stationiert?'

[135] 'Ich habe den 16. Januar nicht vergessen!', *Volksstimme*, 16 January 1954, p. 1; Werner Guse, 'Auferstanden aus Ruinen', *Volksstimme*, 15 January 1955, p. 4.

[136] '41 Millionen Tote mahnen', *Volksstimme*, 1 September 1949, supplement.

16 January 1945. While the letter was a document of despair in the face of imminent death, the newspaper professed to know what the old man would have written if he had had more time. It claimed that 'he surely would have added: "Fight for a better world of peace" '. In a similar vein, the article 'Mass Death in the Beer Cellar' on the same page concluded with the admonition 'always to remember and to join the peace front! Citizens of Magdeburg, you owe this to yourselves, your children and to the 16,000 dead of this dreadful winter night.'[137] The same message was conveyed by the makeshift monument erected on the ruins of a theatre in January 1953, which carried the inscription 'Never again another 16 January. That is why you must fight for peace!'[138]

The legacy of the dead was uncompromising. Gestures of conciliation were eschewed in favour of a rekindling of hatred towards the enemy past and present. The living were enjoined to stand up against 'Anglo-American imperialism', the 'deadly enemy of the German people', as one headline from January 1950 put it.[139] As in other fields of mass mobilisation and propaganda, the SED and its subsidiaries were remarkably unconcerned about perpetuating Nazi propaganda techniques and narratives.[140] In 1952, for example, the *Volksstimme* ran a picture series of postcard images from pre-war Magdeburg that carried the title 'Do you still remember? Before Ami-gangsters destroyed our city.'[141] During the war, the Nazi press had run a similar series, called 'From the criminal records of the gangsters of the air.'[142]

Yet there is some evidence to suggest that among the affiliated bourgeois parties, and in particular the Ost-CDU, reservations persisted well into the 1950s about a politics of memory that revolved around the institutionalisation of hatred. In an article that appeared in the CDU party paper, *Der Neue Weg*, on the seventh anniversary of the air raid in 1952 the author expressed his hope that the church bells would admonish the readers 'to remember this day in a new spirit, without opening up old wounds and inciting new hatred; without sowing new strife but . . . to work for true peace'. But at the same time, the paper, if anything, even surpassed the SED in its denunciation of the air war as a crime. In a lead article of 1951, it insisted that what had happened on 16 January

---

[137] Ibid.
[138] 'Unser Gelöbnis: Nie wieder ein 16. Januar 1945!', *Der Neue Weg*, 20 January 1953, p. 3.
[139] 'Der schwarze Tag von Magdeburg: Heute sehen viele klarer als 1945 / Der anglo-amerikanische Imperialismus – der Todfeind des deutschen Volkes', *Volksstimme*, 16 January 1950, p. 4.
[140] See Ranke, 'Linke Unschuld?'   [141] See *Volksstimme* of 1952.
[142] See, for example, *Völkischer Beobachter*, 2 June 1943, p. 3.

1945 in Magdeburg was 'murder, common treacherous murder [*gemeiner Meuchelmord*]'.[143]

Conclusion

An exploration of the ways in which the dead were publicly remembered highlights the differences in the commemorative cultures of Kassel and Magdeburg. The identification, in Kassel, of the dead as 'our dead' goes some way in explaining the emergence of a memory culture that centred on rites of mourning which depoliticised, decontextualised and re-Christianised its subject matter. The public conversation was characterised by a number of formulae that were designed to restore 'dignity' to the victims of the air war and impart some kind of meaning to their premature death. The consensus, however, remained fragile, as the controversy over rearmament showed. Moreover, depoliticisation avoided rather than engaged with the rhetoric of National Socialist propaganda, thus ensuring that many tropes continued to linger just below the surface.

By contrast, the official identification of the dead in Magdeburg as 'victims of crime' stood at the centre of a memory culture that recontextualised and repoliticised the air war. Public commemorations revolved around protest while representations of death were used as evidence of crime and indictment of the criminal alike. In Magdeburg, elements of Nazi propaganda did not just linger on semi-publicly but were openly embraced by the Socialist Unity Party (SED) as the dominant agent of memory in the city. The 1950s memorial culture not only shared with Nazi propaganda the indictment, it also marginalised issues of private grief and mourning. To this, local citizens responded by looking for semi-public outlets, such as the laying of unauthorised wreaths.

The evidence presented in this chapter suggests that some historiographical positions on the cultural impact of the air war need to be reconsidered. The memory of the air war was not the exclusive prerogative of the East German state. Allied bombing was just as intensely remembered in a West German city as in its East German counterpart, if not more so. Likewise, the preoccupation in memory research with the myth of victimhood has tended to obfuscate the very real differences in the commemorative practices of East and West German urban societies.[144] Nor does the evidence bear out the view that post-war (West) German

---

[143] 'Wenn heute alle Glocken läuten...', *Der Neue Weg*, 16 January 1952, p. 3.; 'Ein düsterer Schatten: Magdeburg – 16. Januar 1945', *Der Neue Weg*, 16 January 1951, p. 3.

[144] Groehler, 'Dresden'.

memory prioritised the material and cultural losses of the air war over its human costs.[145] Despite their absence in visual representations, the dead were central to the 1950s memorial culture of Kassel. Indeed, the intense concern with questions of piety, dignity and bereavement suggests that the famous dictum of the German 'inability to mourn' needs to be critically revisited.[146] For émigrés such as Alfred Döblin or Hannah Arendt revisiting their country of birth after the war, Germans seemed at first sight to be perplexingly unconcerned about the catastrophe that they had brought upon themselves, 'moving through the dreadful rubble as if nothing had happened', mailing 'each other picture postcards still showing the cathedrals and market places, the public buildings and bridges that no longer exist'.[147] Yet, upon closer inspection, Alfred Döblin for one noticed a different kind of behaviour: 'I frequently saw people climb on top of the heaps of rubble. What did they do there? Were they looking for something? They carried flowers in their hands. On the hills they had erected crosses and placards. There were graves. That's where they put down the flowers, kneeled and prayed.'[148]

The sites, rituals and narratives that were established during the 1950s determined the trajectory of public memory in the decade that followed. Throughout the 1960s, the syntax of memory changed but little. In the city of Kassel, the day was typically commemorated by a recurrent set of activities. In the morning, representatives of the city laid wreaths 'in quiet memory' at the memorial in the main cemetery. This was followed, in the afternoon, by an 'hour of commemoration' at the cemetery, which was organised by the League of Air Raid Victims with the participation of the Church. At night, there was an ecumenical church service in the Martinskirche, which climaxed in the ceremonial ringing of the big church bell on the hour that the air raid had commenced in 1943. On the major anniversaries of 1963 and 1968, the mayor gave the central commemorative address, while on ordinary anniversaries, this task was performed by a Protestant or Catholic pastor from Kassel.

In Magdeburg, the SED and affiliated organisations focused their commemorative activity on the cemetery, where they held a ceremony in which wreaths were laid and the mayor, or one of his deputies, made a speech. On major anniversaries, the SED also organised additional events in the city itself. In 1965, the city council was convened for a special session, which guests from other war-torn cities were invited to attend. In

---

[145] Heinemann, 'The Hour of the Woman', 368–70.
[146] Mitscherlich and Mitscherlich, *Die Unfähigkeit zu trauern*, pp. 36–42.
[147] Alfred Döblin, 'Schicksalsreise', p. 188f.; Arendt, 'Aftermath of Nazi Rule', 342.
[148] Döblin, 'Schicksalsreise', pp. 190f.

addition – and this was a novel development – representatives from the Church took part as well. Five years later, the SED held a so-called 'peace rally' on Karl Marx Street, the former Breite Weg, in the centre of town. The Church, meanwhile, commemorated the historical event by holding memorial services in the cathedral, although this practice was no longer observed on an annual basis by the mid-1960s.

Throughout the 1960s, commemorations mattered, attracting between several hundred and several thousand people and eliciting regular, and at times extensive, coverage in the local media. Yet there were unmistakable signs that the observance of the annual day of remembrance was taking on a routine, almost perfunctory character. The bombing, it seemed, no longer exercised the minds and hearts of those involved in commemorative activity to quite the same extent as had been the case in the previous decade of the 1950s. Despite the regular invocation of the 'unforgotten bombing victims', Lethe, the river of forgetfulness of Greek mythology, appeared slowly to swallow up the dead. As the *Hessische Allgemeine* remarked in 1966 with reference to the memorial service in the main cemetery in Kassel, 'The circle of those taking part in the commemorations gets smaller year after year.'[149] There were both socio-cultural and socio-demographic reasons for this development.

Unlike other aspects of Germany's catastrophic past, the air war did not stand at the centre of the political and mnemonic controversies that transformed (West) German society in the 1960s.[150] In some respects, the subject had been pacified too successfully by the local elites. True, there were attempts, on the part of the Kassel branch of the War Resisters International,[151] to divest the memory place of the grip of elite politics and turn it into a pacifist symbol. In 1963, for example, the war resisters organised a ceremony that was dedicated to the 'victims of the inferno of 22 October 1943'. Sporting the motto 'Never again bombs on Kassel', the event was followed by a torchlight procession of one hundred activists through the streets of Kassel.[152] In Magdeburg, meanwhile, the SED on occasion used the *lieu de mémoire* in order to denounce the American war in Vietnam. At the 'peace rally' on 16 January 1970, for example, a regional SED functionary declared, 'When we commemorate this night

---

[149] 'Bombenopfer sind unvergessen', *HA*, 24 October 1966.
[150] Schildt, Siegfried and Lammers (eds.), *Dynamische Zeiten*; Reichel, *Vergangenheitsbewältigung in Deutschland*, pp. 138–81; Jarausch, 'Der nationale Tabubruch'; Jarausch, *Umkehr*, pp. 133–242; Winkler, *Weg nach Westen*, pp. 206–314.
[151] On organised pacifism in post-war Germany see Holl, *Pazifismus*, pp. 220–37.
[152] 'Feierstunde und Schweigemarsch der Kasseler Kriegsdienstgegner', *HA*, 23 October 1963.

[of the bombing], parallels come to mind with the criminal conduct of the American war in Vietnam.'[153]

On the whole, however, these attempts at putting the memory of World War II bombing to the service of a pacifist politics or a state-sponsored protest against American foreign policy were pursued only half-heartedly. In Kassel, the war resisters failed to establish an annual commemorative tradition, while the Magdeburg SED generally used other channels than the memory place of '16 January' to revile the American engagement in Vietnam. As Mary Nolan has argued, the (West) German student movement did not compare the carpet bombing of the American Air Force in Vietnam to indiscriminate area bombing in World War II.[154]

By and large, the same held true of the other defining issue of the 1960s, the 'return' of the Nazi past.[155] Although an opinion survey found in 1968 that one-third of the (West) German population thought that the conduct of the allied air war to some extent atoned for genocidal war and Judaeocide,[156] relativising rhetoric found no expression in the public memory culture of Kassel. Here, the political elites repeatedly referred to '22 October' in order to gain popular acceptance for alternative memory places that addressed Nazi crimes. When, for example, the opening of an exhibition on Jewish children's drawings from Theresienstadt concentration camp fell on 22 October 1961, Mayor Lauritz Lauritzen (SPD) seized the opportunity in order to legitimise the engagement with the Nazi past through the invocation of the well-established day of remembrance. In his opening address, he emphasised that this coincidence was of more than just symbolic significance, for it underlined the 'misery that a wrongheaded political system' had brought 'upon the world'.[157] Although Lauritzen, in problematic fashion, equated the German victims of war with the (German-) Jewish victims of German genocide, he did so in order to raise awareness of other, worse forms of suffering (and dying) than those encountered by the we-group in the air war.

Whereas in Kassel, the hierarchy of victimhood was starting to change by the 1960s, slowly displacing 'our dead' from the pre-eminent position that they had enjoyed in the previous decade, in Magdeburg the status of the air raid casualties changed but little throughout the period. While they continued to be depicted as victims of a crime, there was a reorientation in the labelling of the criminal. With the inception of a propaganda campaign that aimed at exposing the continuities between the

[153] 'Friedenskundgebung', *Der Neue Weg*, 17/18 January 1970, p. 1.
[154] Nolan, 'Air Wars, Memory Wars', 19, footnote 47.
[155] Siegfried, 'Zwischen Aufarbeitung und Schlussstrich'.   [156] Ibid., p. 102.
[157] StAK, A.1.10, no. 607, Reden [OB Lauritzen], 'Ansprache anlässlich der Eröffnung der Ausstellung "Hier fliegen keine Schmetterlinge"', 22 October 1961, p. 1.

Third Reich and the Federal Republic,[158] a greater share of the blame in the destruction of Magdeburg was assigned to the 'swastika-rats' of Nazism.[159] As Mayor Sonnemann (SED) declared at the ceremony on the twentieth anniversary in 1965, 'Despite our achievements, we are worried about developments in Western Germany, where the same people occupy influential positions again who also bear a great share of the responsibility for the destruction of Magdeburg.'[160]

The second reason for the progressive ossification of public memory in the 1960s and 1970s lay in the gradual erosion of the *milieu de mémoire* that had sustained commemorative activity in the 1950s. 'It is our fate to become ever lonelier in our pain,' Kassel mayor Karl Branner (1910–97) declared on the thirtieth anniversary of the air raid in 1973.[161] He thus gave expression to a sentiment that was frequently voiced in Kassel and Magdeburg throughout the period, the belief that the memory group comprised the eyewitnesses of the cataclysmic events, with the bereaved and evacuees at its core, but did not extend to the post-war generation. Such a view appeared to be borne out by the development of the League of Air Raid Victims. Despite their claim to have been the 'first expellees' of the war, the League, in contrast to the expellee organisations, never managed to foster a group identity that would appeal to the descendants of the experience-generation. Although the Kassel group still boasted approximately 1,000 members in 1963, ten years later there were only 150 left. By the time of the thirtieth anniversary in 1973, they no longer possessed the influence to pressurise the city into organising a commemorative event that would have had a 'certain propagandistic effect', as an internal letter put it.[162] By the mid-1970s, the Air Raid Victims were in inexorable decline, and so was public memory of the air war, or so it seemed.

---

[158] Lemke, 'Instrumentalisierter Antifaschismus'.
[159] 'Hakenkreuzratten', in 'Nie mehr diese Verbrechen zulassen! Magdeburger Bürger gedachten der zahllosen Opfer des Bombenangriffs vor 15 Jahren', *Der Neue Weg*, 19 January 1960, p. 6.
[160] 'Unsere Stadt soll blühen', *Volksstimme*, 18 January 1965.
[161] StAK, A.1.10., Reden [OB Branner], no. 669. IV. 75–101 (1973), no. 100, 'Ansprache Gedenkgottesdienst zur 30. Wiederkehr des 22. Oktober 1943', 22 October 1973.
[162] Hauptstaatsarchiv Stuttgart, Q 3/43, Bund der Fliegergeschädigten hessen, Kreisgruppe Kassel to Zentralverband, 15 August 1973; 16 October 1973.

4 The return of the dead: the renaissance of commemoration, 1979–1995

Introduction: shifting contexts

In September 1987, the *Stattzeitung*, an alternative city guide for Kassel, carried a cover that showed a grisly scene of mass death: dozens of scattered corpses and body parts formed an undifferentiated landscape of death from which a single body stood out in the shape of an inverted crucifix.[1] The image derived from a photograph that had been taken a few days after 22 October 1943. It depicted the retrieval of dead bodies from the public shelter of the Bürgersäle, which had turned into a mass grave on the night of the air raid.[2] Significantly, the photo reporter of the *Stattzeitung* had not unearthed the motif from an archive but had discovered it in his immediate environment – in the form of a giant poster covering the entrance door of a World War II brick bunker (Fig. 15).[3]

The display was the work of a group of local activists, the 'Tenacious Doves' (*Zähe Tauben*), who had reintroduced this apocalyptic visualisation of mass death into urban space and established three referential frames by way of textual commentaries.[4] On the first level, they situated the photograph within the context of World War II. A small caption located the image in time and space, indicating where and when the corpses had been found. On the second level, a large headline established a connection between the past and the present, linking the image from World War II to the arms race of the 1980s. The pun 'Dead certainly CERTAIN DEATH' made a point about the futility of civil defence measures in the age of the atomic bomb. Finally, on the third level, the slogan 'Stop the Stationing of US Atomic Missiles' drew a connection between the local and the national, between grass-roots opposition and federal security policy. Through a combination of visual and textual elements, the montage raised the spectre of a return of the catastrophic past. As

---

[1] *Stattzeitung* (September 1987), title page.　　[2] See Dettmar, *Zerstörung*, p. 167.
[3] 'Bunker in der Gräfestraße', *Stattzeitung* (October 1987), p. 6.
[4] See the reporting on the action in the daily press, *HNA*, 4 June 1987; 5 June 1987; 22 August 1987.

141

Figure 15. Image of World War II mass death on the title page of the 'counter-culture' city guide, the *Stattzeitung* (1987).

the primary victims of such a development, ordinary people were not only justified in resisting the policies of their government but had an existential duty to do so, the Tenacious Doves suggested.

The example illustrates a characteristic trend in the public memory of the 1980s and 1990s: the return of the dead. The casualties of

World War II bombing re-entered the urban space by means of visual representations and exhibitions, through eyewitness accounts and public commemorations. The dead stood at the centre of a revival of interest in the experience of indiscriminate bombing in both Kassel and Magdeburg. This was because the living, teetering on what appeared to be the brink of atomic annihilation, had seemingly forgotten the injunction of the dead 'never again' to allow another war to break out; because the residents of 1980s Kassel and Magdeburg inhabited and moved through the very spaces in which thousands of their fellow residents had died a generation before; and because for those who were born before 1945, death in the air war still formed part of lived experience.

The renaissance of commemoration took place in an environment in which political developments intersected with broader cultural and generational trends to produce a peculiar dynamic to the 'process of double identification' that characterises the memory of premature violent death.[5] It revolved around two related but distinct issues, security and identity, or more precisely, around the questions of peace and of guilt. Both may be understood as contemporary reformulations of problems that had troubled the protagonists of public memory ever since the 1940s – questions about causes, identifications and meanings. The dead of World War II bombing were invoked as a prelude to an 'atomic Holocaust' at the very moment that their collective identity as innocent victims was called into question by a growing acceptance of the historical Holocaust as the central 'civilisation rupture' (Dan Diner) of the twentieth century.[6]

On both counts, the year 1979 may be considered a turning point. As the year of the Soviet invasion of Afghanistan and the NATO 'double-track' decision to deploy a new generation of intermediate-range ballistic missiles should negotiations fail, 1979 marked the end of détente in international relations and made the preservation of peace the defining political issue of the 1980s.[7] As the year of the first screening of the TV series *Holocaust* and the fortieth anniversary commemorations of the outbreak of World War II, 1979 forced a critical reappraisal of the historic identity of Germans at both national and local level.

The debate was underpinned by generational changes that altered the link between primary experience and discursive power, with important repercussions for local discourses on the Nazi past. By the early 1980s, the generation from which the functional elites of the Third Reich had

[5] Koselleck, 'Kriegerdenkmale', p. 255.
[6] Kelly, 'In der Tradition der Gewaltfreiheit', p. 313; Diner (ed.), *Zivilisationsbruch*.
[7] See the ongoing research project sponsored by the GHI Institute, Washington, DC, in cooperation with the Universities of Augsburg and Heidelberg, at http://nuclearcrisis.org [16 June 2010].

been recruited – the age cohorts born around 1905 – reached the end of their biological lives while the 'sceptical generation' of those born around 1925 neared retirement age. At the same time, the first post-war generation of those born around 1945 – the generation of '68 – moved into positions of influence, gradually gaining prominence in the public enunciation of the past.[8]

As the introductory example indicates, politics played an important role in the return of the dead in the 1980s. With their dramatic gesture, the Tenacious Doves protested against the consequences of the NATO 'double-track' decision of 12 December 1979.[9] The Tenacious Doves formed part of a broad, heterogeneous coalition of dissident Social Democrats, Greens, Communists, Christians and independents that is commonly referred to as the peace movement, which combined utopian visions of communitarian living with apocalyptic fears about the future of humankind in an age of nuclear deterrence and environmental pollution.[10] As the slogan 'Stop the Stationing of US Atomic Missiles' illustrates, the politics of many activists were as one-sided as their modes of expression were unorthodox. They aimed to shock the public through the confrontation with mass death.[11]

In Kassel, but also in other West German communities such as Hamburg, Würzburg or Pforzheim,[12] the fight against the twin-track decision may be considered the political catalyst for the renaissance of interest in World War II aerial bombing.[13] With the ascendancy of the peace movement came the rise to dominance of a narrative that had been confined to the orthodox Left in the 1950s: the conceptualisation of the air war as a prelude to total annihilation. In Kassel, this development was given further impetus by the broad support of the Social Democratic power holders in the city, who infused the established commemorative consensus formula of 'Never again' with a political edge.

---

[8] Frei, *1945 und wir*, p. 27; Herbert, 'Drei politische Generationen'. On the heuristic value and limits of the concept of 'generation' see Jureit and Wildt (eds.), *Generationen*.

[9] For the context see Rödder, *Bundesrepublik*, pp. 59–74.

[10] Wirsching, *Abschied*, pp. 79–106; Rödder, *Bundesrepublik*, pp. 213f.; Breyman, *Why Movements Matter*, p. 36; and for a comparative perspective, Ziemann, 'Situating Peace Movements'.

[11] On the anti-American undercurrent of the peace movement see Ziemann, 'The Code of Protest', 248f. (with further references); on East German attempts at exploiting the potential of mass protest in the Federal Republic, Knabe, *Die unterwanderte Republik*, pp. 234–60.

[12] Thießen, *Eingebrannt ins Gedächtnis*, pp. 255–60; Seiderer, 'Würzburg, 16 März 1945', pp. 159f.; Groh, '"Was Pforzheim angetan wurde!"', p. 190.

[13] A similar point is made by Domansky, 'A Lost War'. But see for an alternative view Nolan, 'Air Wars, Memory Wars', 24, footnote 63; Huyssen, 'Air War Legacies', 164f.

In different yet parallel ways, the second Cold War of the 1980s also marked a turning point for the memory culture of Magdeburg. In their executive meeting of 13 December 1979, the local SED made a conscious decision to harness local memories of mass death to the political issue of the day: '16 January' was to be revived as a 'fighting day [*Kampftag*]' against the NATO double-track decision.[14] Out of concern over the course of international developments, the Protestant Church in the GDR, too, put a new emphasis on the peace question. Locally, this led to the reinstitution in 1980 of annual commemorative services in memory of 16 January 1945.

The renaissance of interest in World War II bombing occurred within the context of a larger commemorative turn in the political cultures of the two Germanys.[15] Between 1983 and 1995, German society relived the twelve years of the Third Reich as a sequence of fiftieth-anniversary events.[16] This was accompanied by an empirical turn towards the history of the everyday in general, and of the Third Reich in particular. For the first time, National Socialist rule was explored as lived experience within a concrete environment – which gave the Nazi past, in the words of Eckart Conze, 'a new and lasting, very specific and often haunting presence'.[17] Whereas this endeavour was often undertaken on the initiative of grass-roots history workshops, in Kassel the research into the local history of Nazism received early institutional support from a town council resolution that commissioned professional academics from the local university.[18] At the same time, the 'spiritual-moral renewal' (*geistig-moralische Wende*) that the new centre-right Kohl government proclaimed in 1982 brought in its wake the attempt of revisionist historians to 'normalise' German history by relativising the singularity of the crimes committed during the Third Reich. In the public controversy that ensued, the views of the revisionists were discredited, resulting not in a normalisation of National Socialism but in a prioritisation of the Holocaust as the pivotal civilisation rupture of the twentieth century.[19]

Finally, political and cultural shifts intersected with generational change. By the 1980s, the common experiential basis between the protagonists of public memory and their audiences – a characteristic feature

---

[14] LA Magd., LHA, Rep. 16, SED-Stadtleitung Magdeburg. Sekretariat. No. IV/D-5/1/068, fos. 2f., 13 December 1979.

[15] Frei, *1945 und wir*, p. 9.   [16] Naumann, *Der Krieg als Text*.

[17] Conze, *Suche nach Sicherheit*, p. 655.

[18] StAK, A.0, Stadtverordnetenversammlung, vol. 140. IX. LP, pp. 32–41, 7 May 1979.

[19] The literature on the politics of memory of the Kohl government and the famous *Historikerstreit* is vast. For a dispassionate evaluation twenty years after, see Herbert, 'Der Historikerstreit'. On the politics of memory of the Kohl government compare Niven, 'Introduction: German Victimhood at the Turn of the Millennium', pp. 5–7.

of the memory culture of the 1950s and 1960s – had become fractured.[20]
The narratives of the local elites were increasingly expounded by members of age cohorts who had been socialised in the post-war world. When
Kassel mayor Hans Eichel, born in 1941, addressed the citizenry on the
occasion of the fortieth anniversary of the air aid in October 1983, he
had no personal experiences of aerial warfare on which to draw. But
among his audience in the tightly packed Martinskirche, there were still
many contemporaries of the iconic event. On the local level, the 'official'
enunciation of World War II had passed into the hands of a generation
socialised in the two post-war Germanys, whereas contemporaries of the
events turned to the historical recreation of the air war in order to preserve 'their' memories – a trend that would be repeated on the national
level ten years later.[21] In no small measure, this transition from 'communicative' to 'cultural' memory accounted for the peculiar dynamic of the
urban memory culture in the 1980s and 1990s.[22]

This chapter unravels the impact of political, cultural and generational
shifts on the form and content of the commemorative practices in Kassel
and Magdeburg in the 1980s and 1990s. The period not only witnessed
the revival of interest in the experience of area bombing. It also ushered
in a critical reappraisal of the role of local communities in World War II.
While a core set of rituals remained stable throughout the period, the
semantics of commemoration were modified in two potentially conflicting directions. During the second Cold War of the early 1980s, influential
protagonists tended to draw on the memory place in order to illustrate
the dangers of an atomic war, thereby displacing the narrative of successful overcoming that had dominated public memory in the decade
from the mid-1960s to the late 1970s. In this new perspective, World
War II bombing featured no longer as a symbol of a dark and distant
past but as a warning from history with direct relevance to the present.
Mass death by conventional weapons in World War II was a harbinger of
mass annihilation in the atomic war of the future. Such an interpretation,
while challenging some of the silences of the 1950s and 1960s, ultimately
reaffirmed a narrative that conceived of local communities as victims of
forces beyond their control.

Yet the emergence of local Holocaust memory, and even more so,
the receding of the threat of atomic annihilation due to the easing of
tensions between the superpowers after Mikhail Gorbachev had become
general secretary of the Soviet Communist Party in 1985, forced a critical

---

[20] A similar point is made by Süß, 'Tod aus der Luft', pp. 611f.   [21] See chapter 8 below.
[22] J. Assmann, *Das kulturelle Gedächtnis*, pp. 48–66; Niethammer, 'Diesseits des "Floating Gap"'.

re-evaluation of the prominence given to local victimhood past and present. In the minds of an increasing number of clerics, politicians and journalists, the memory of mass death in World War II bombing no longer allowed for the construction of a collective identity of martyrdom but called for a historically sensitive exploration of the nexus between local disaster and broader developments.

Between 'day of struggle' and 'prayer for peace': commemorative formats in the 1980s

In their executive meeting of 13 December 1979, the leadership of the Magdeburg SED discussed the consequences of the recent shift in Western defence policy. According to the minutes, the party cadres were in agreement that the NATO double-track decision represented a 'decisive climax' in the 'preparation [of Western imperialism] for war'.[23] 'Through extensive political mass agitation amongst all workers and the population at large', the minutes emphasised, 'the NATO decision must be used as an opportunity to expose the whole brutality of imperialism, in particular the imperialism of the USA and FRG.' To this end, the SED decided to revive '16 January' as a 'day of struggle' (*Kampftag*) that was designed to demonstrate 'the will for peace of the population of Magdeburg'.[24] The organisation of the thirty-fifth anniversary in January 1980 was put in the hands of the 'Section Agitation/Propaganda', which produced a detailed plan on the semiotics of commemoration.[25] The conception (*Ablaufkonzeption*) drew in part on established formats as practised since the 1950s but also showed elements of contemporary mass mobilisation.[26]

In 1980, commemoration returned to its place of origin. While in the morning, representatives of the SED, the associated parties and others laid wreaths at the cemetery, in the afternoon the central event was held on Old Market Square (*Alter Markt*) in the centre of town. This was the same space where the Nazi party had staged the first public commemorations in 1944. In comparison with the 1940s and 1950s, the thirty-fifth anniversary celebration was far larger in scale. Whereas in the 1950s a few thousand people had assembled at an improvised memorial, the

---

[23] LA Magd., LHA, Rep. 16. SED-Stadtleitung Magdeburg. Sekretariat. No. IV/D-5/1/068, fos. 2f., 13 December 1979.
[24] Ibid., fo. 3.   [25] Ibid., fos. 82, 87, 170–2.
[26] LA Magd., LHA, Rep. P 13, no. IV/E-2/3/120, fos. 64f., 'Konzeption für die Großkundgebung am 9. September 1984 in Magdeburg', 8 August 1984; StAM, Rep. 18/4. Ra 634. 4, 'Jahreskulturplan 1985 der Stadt Magdeburg', 17 January 1985. For the context see Danyel, 'Politische Rituale als Sowjetimporte'.

local press, in 1980, reported an attendance figure of 70,000 residents, one in four of the entire city population.[27] The 'mass rally' reflected the hierarchical structure of GDR society. While regional functionaries from party and state were seated on a VIP rostrum, ordinary residents had to stand throughout the event.[28] As an 'organised mass', they witnessed the formal opening by a trade union functionary as a demarcation rite. After that, they listened to a commemorative address by the mayor and the reading out of a 'workers' declaration'. As a closing rite, they joined in the singing of the hymn of the International Workers' Movement, 'Brothers, to Sun, to Freedom'. The inclusion of representatives from the Red Army as guests of honour – an element of protocol insisted on by the regional SED leadership – underlined that this was not a pacifist rally but a 'day of struggle' against the West.[29]

The SED organised a similar, if less bellicose, mass rally on the fortieth anniversary five years later, but generally kept a lower profile on ordinary anniversaries when commemorative activity was restricted to the traditional wreath laying and a remembrance concert.[30] In 1985, the rally was even bigger in size than in 1980, with the local press reporting attendance figures of 80,000 people.[31] More significant was the attempt to broaden the public appeal by recruiting speakers from different generations and walks of life. At the rally, 'For Peace and Détente – against NATO Arms Build-Up', the keynote speech was delivered by the first secretary of the SED city leadership, Heinz Hanke, but superintendent Dietrich Schierbaum from the Protestant Church was also invited to speak.[32]

The end of détente led not only to renewed investment in the *lieu de mémoire* on the part of the political elites but also to a revival of commemoration by the Protestant Church. Encouraged by an episcopal appeal to conduct a rogation service for peace, the Magdeburg church resurrected a tradition that had been discontinued since 1965.[33] On 16 January 1980, a prayer for peace was held in the Wallonerkirche,

---

[27] 'Machtvolle Demonstration gegen Raketenbeschlüsse der NATO', *Volksstimme*, 17 January 1980, pp. 1, 7.

[28] LA Magd., LHA, Rep. 16. SED-Stadtleitung. Sekretariat. No. IV/D-5/1/068, fo. 172, 'Ablaufkonzeption', 2 January 1980.

[29] LA Magd., LHA, Rep. 13. SED-Bezirksleitung Magdeburg. No. NID-2/3/119, fo. 5, 'Beschluss-Nr. 3/1', 9 January 1980.

[30] See *Volksstimme*, 17 January 1981, p. 8; 17 January 1984, p. 6; 17 January 1987, p. 8; 17 January 1989, p. 1.

[31] *Volksstimme*, 17 January 1984, pp. 1, 3.

[32] LA Magd., LHA, Rep. P13. SED-Bezirksleitung. No. IV/E-2/3/129, fos. 119f., 9 January 1985.

[33] On the appeal by Bishop Krusche see Neubert, *Geschichte der Opposition*, pp. 382f.

Figure 16. Worshippers at the 'prayer for peace' light candles in front of the World War I memorial by Ernst Barlach in Magdeburg cathedral on 16 January 1985.

from where the practice moved permanently to the cathedral the following year.[34] With few exceptions, the 'prayer for peace' was conducted in the form of a short half-hour 'commemorative worship' (*Gedenkandacht*) held in front of an anti-war memorial by Ernst Barlach from the time of the Weimar Republic (Fig. 16). Typically, the liturgy consisted of a short address by the pastor, a meditative section that sometimes involved the memorial, communal singing of church hymns and prayer. After the blessing a period of ceremonial silence followed, to be

[34] See Archiv der Ev. Domgemeinde, Magdeburg, Monatliche Mitteilungen der Domgemeinde, 1964–72, January 1965; Mitteilungsblatt, 1975–95, 16 January 1980.

succeeded by the pealing of the cathedral bells on the hour that the bombs had started falling in 1945.[35] Attendance figures are only recorded for 1985 when the congregation numbered about six hundred worshippers.[36] While this was less than 1 per cent of the number of people who had attended the SED-organised commemoration on Old Market Square the same day, the 'prayer for peace' offered an alternative interpretation, the popular resonance of which increased in the same measure as the SED coopted the Protestant Church in the official 'struggle for peace'.

Just as in Magdeburg, in Kassel too, the NATO double-track decision of December 1979 provided the catalyst for a revival of interest in the local day of remembrance. Here, local peace activists recognised the opportunity to broaden the mass appeal of the movement by reaching out to the memories of the war generation. In a programmatic article in the alternative *Stattzeitung*, activist Dieter Wollenteit argued that the Left had shied away from tapping collective memories of World War II for fear of stoking revanchism – a reluctance which, the author maintained, had played into the hands of the ruling elites. Accordingly, Wollenteit went on to call on fellow activists to recognise 'the sleeping potential' that those people carried who had experienced 'Stalingrad and the expulsion from the east', and suggested harnessing their fears to the cause of peace.[37] To this end, the Kassel Workshop Peace Week (*Arbeitskreis Friedenswoche*) seized the opportunity when, in October 1983, the fortieth anniversary of the bombing coincided with the pinnacle of nationwide movement activity against the Euro missiles. To the nationwide slogan, 'Say No! No new atomic missiles in our country', the local groups added, 'Kassel 1943 admonishes. Never again bombs on our city.' This was underlined visually by a photomontage that showed an image of war-torn Kassel together with a mushroom cloud.[38]

Similar analogies were drawn by grass-roots activists in other West German cities such as Hamburg, Heilbronn, Würzburg or Pforzheim, but at the national level, references to the bombing of German cities appear

[35] Archiv der Ev. Domgemeinde, Magdeburg, Domprediger Quast. Sammlung Friedensgebete, 'Mahnung zum Frieden – Gebet um Frieden' [1983]; 'Gedenkandacht vor dem Barlachmal am 16.1.1989'; 'Gebet am Barlachehrenmal 16.1.1990'; 'Gedenken der Zerstörung Magdeburgs 16.1.1991'; 'Friedensgebet 16.1.1992'; 'Gebet um Frieden und Versöhnung 16.1.1993'; 'Friedensgebet 50. Jahrestag Magdeburg 16.1.1995'. I would like to thank Pastor Giselher Quast for making these texts available to me.

[36] *Die Kirche*, 10 February 1985.

[37] Dieter Wollenteit, 'Wider den falschen Konsens. Anmerkungen zur Friedensbewegung', *Stattzeitung* (October 1981), pp. 20f.

[38] For a reproduction see *GhK publik*, 9 November 1983; on the iconography of the peace movement more generally, Ziemann, 'Code of Protest'.

to have been, if not wholly absent, of secondary importance only.[39] The atomic bombing of Hiroshima and Nagasaki of August 1945 featured more prominently in the rhetoric of the national peace movement than did the strategic air war against the German Reich. During the so-called 'double-track' debate in the federal parliament on 22/23 November 1983, for example, the peace activist and member of parliament for the Greens, Christa Nickels, wore around her neck a garland which she claimed had been made in Hiroshima. The necklace consisted of paper cranes, which, according to Ms Nickels, served both as a memory artefact of the atomic bombing and as a symbol of hope not to repeat the mistakes of the past.[40]

The prioritisation at the national level of 'Hiroshima' and 'Nagasaki' over 'Dresden' and 'Hamburg', or for that matter, 'Kassel' and 'Magdeburg', was in large measure a consequence of the use of atomic rather than conventional weapons in the destruction of the Japanese cities. The international orientation of the peace movement may have played a role as well, calling for global rather than national or local *lieux de mémoire*. Aside from this, there appears to have been a certain reluctance among peace movement activists at a national level, who often belonged to a generation born after 1945, to engage their older political opponents on grounds that for many of them still formed part of the experience of their childhood or early adolescence. As Chancellor Kohl, who was fifteen years old in 1945, emphasised in the same debate in which Christa Nickels, born in 1952, spoke, 'In our people, in our families, and within us, the memory of the wounds lives on that the reign of terror and the war have caused . . . Never will we know exactly how many people died back then – in the cellars of the lawless regime, in the battles of the war, in the bombing nights at home.'[41]

Locally, the situation was different, in particular in cities such as Kassel where peace movement protests met with the sympathy of the Social Democratic power holders. Drawing on the social practices of earlier protest movements, the Struggle against Atomic Death of the 1950s and the Vietnam protest movement of the 1960s,[42] the Kassel activists sought to take the commemoration of mass death out of the confines of church and cemetery into the public square.[43] As an opening event

---

[39] Thießen, *Eingebrannt ins Gedächtnis*, p. 259; Karl-Heinz Kimmerle, 'Tapferkeit', *Heilbronner Stimme*, 9 December 1983; Seiderer, 'Der Luftkrieg im öffentlichen Gedenken', 349; Groh, '"Was Pforzheim angetan wurde!"', p. 190.

[40] The speech is reprinted in Druve (ed.), *Die Nachrüstungsdebatte im deutschen Bundestag*, pp. 157–61.

[41] The speech is reprinted in ibid, pp. 11–32; for the quotation, p. 31.

[42] Breyman, *Why Movements Matter*, pp. 154, 162.

[43] For the context see ibid., pp. 177–209.

to the 'action [and] resistance week' (*Aktions- und Widerstandswoche*) of 15–23 October 1983, a 'die-in' was staged on the large Friedrichplatz, followed by a 'stand-up for peace'.[44] In another square, a one-week vigil 'in memory of the dead of the Kassel bombing night' was conducted as a warning against the dangers of atomic war. This message was underlined symbolically by setting up crosses and images of war-torn Kassel. On the day of remembrance itself, peace activists lit 10,000 candles in the vicinity of the Lutherkirche, each light symbolising a casualty of strategic bombing. Meanwhile, inside the church, all-night fasting and prayer were accompanied by communal singing of the civil rights hymn 'We Shall Overcome'.[45] Five years later, in 1988, three hundred activists with torches formed a human peace sign on Königsplatz. The square had been selected on purpose because of its association with mass death in October 1943, when it had functioned as a collecting ground for retrieved corpses.[46]

In order to make their cause heard, peace activists also interfered with the established rituals of wreath laying and ecumenical church service. On the fortieth anniversary, a heckler challenged Bishop Hans-Gernot Jung to speak out on the issue of nuclear disarmament during his sermon in the Martinskirche. The next day, peace activists sported a banner reading 'Kassel 1943 Admonishes', during the official ceremony at the cemetery (Fig. 17).[47] In memory of the casualties of allied bombing, activists placed a thousand red roses on the graves. While the impact of peace movement activity was considerable on the major anniversaries of 1983 and 1988, its long-term influence on the semiotics of commemoration should not be overstated. By and large, official commemoration remained in the hands of the political and spiritual elites. The Church, in particular, proved unwilling to adapt traditional liturgy to the demands of lay activists.[48] Core elements of the annual remembrance service included a meditative overture played on the organ as an introductory rite; psalm reading and bible lesson; the singing of hymns and chorals by the choir and the congregation; a sermon by the pastor, to which, on major anniversaries, was added an address by the mayor; and

[44] See StAK, uncatalogued material, 'Kassel 1943 mahnt: Nie wieder Bomben auf unsere Stadt. NEIN. Keine neuen Atomraketen in unser Land', no date [October 1983]; *Stattzeitung* (October 1983), p. 23.

[45] StAK, S5 C126, Friedensbewegung, '22. Oktober 1943/22. Oktober 1983'.

[46] 'Zeitzeugen erinnern und mahnen zum Frieden', *HA*, 24 October 1988.

[47] Jung, *Rechenschaft der Hoffnung*, p. 161; *HA*, 24 October 1983.

[48] See Dekanat Kassel-Mitte, Akte Martinskirche, correspondence between Deacon Hans Feller and Dieter Wollenteit, 'speaker of the peace workshop at the congregation of Kirchditmold', 7 September 1988; 26 September 1988.

Hauptfriedhof: Kranz für Bombenopfer niedergelegt

Sie gedachten der Bombenopfer des 2. Weltkriegs: Offizielle, Mitglieder der Friedensbewegung und Kasseler Bürger. Ein jeder auf seine Weise. Stadtverordnetenvorsteher Günter Kestner und Bürgermeister Heinz Hille legten ebenso wie die Vertreter des Ausländerbeirates der Stadt Kassel schweigend einen Kranz am Ehrenmal auf dem Hauptfriedhof nieder. „Kassel 1943 mahnt: Sagt nein! Keine neuen Atomraketen in unserem Land" appellierten Mitglieder der Friedensbewegung, für die der Kasseler Arzt Dr. Hans Greiner, Augenzeuge jener Bombennacht vor 40 Jahren, deutlich zu machen versuchte: „Jeder Krieg ist ein Raubkrieg, und auch der nächste wird wieder einer sein." Seine Forderung: „Wir müssen uns aus der atomaren Umklammerung der Großmächte befreien." Die Aufstellung welcher Waffen auch immer nannte er „ein Verbrechen gegen uns alle, die Natur, den Schöpfer".

Im Anschluß daran legten Mitglieder der Friedensbewegung und Kasseler Bürger rote Rosen an den Gräbern der Toten nieder.

(smt/Foto: Haun)

Hessische Allgemeine 24.10. 1983 SS P97

Figure 17. Peace movement activists sport a banner at the traditional wreath-laying in the main cemetery in Kassel. The banner reads 'Kassel 1943 admonishes. Say "No"! No new missiles in our country' (October 1983).

finally, prayer and blessing. The service in the Martinskirche concluded with the pealing of a single church bell as a closing rite.[49]

Between harbinger and retribution: the semantics of commemoration

This section explores change and continuity in both synchronic and diachronic perspective by way of a close reading of central anniversary celebrations in Kassel and Magdeburg. Throughout the 1980s, the

---

[49] Feller, '"Gedenket aber der früheren Tage"', p. 52.

semantics of commemoration revolved around three interrelated issues;
security, group identity and personal identity.[50] Whenever the concern
over peace stood at the centre of memory, the historical experience of
indiscriminate bombing was easily harnessed to the construction of a collective identity of shared victimhood. The catastrophic past seemed to
confer special legitimacy on urban communities for assuming the moral
high ground from which to speak out on the security questions of the day.
In characteristic fashion, the Magdeburg mayor, Werner Herzig (SED),
used Magdeburg's destruction in World War II to justify his participation
in an international conference of 'martyr cities' in 1987.[51] To the extent,
however, that, from the mid-1980s onwards, fears over an 'atomic Holocaust' receded and the historical Holocaust was increasingly recognised
as an unparalleled civilisation rupture, 'peace' was displaced by 'guilt'
as the central problem that called for answers in the commemorative
culture. At the same time, and in some respects independent of these
shifts, public commemorations remained a space in which the protagonists of memory addressed the impact of aerial warfare on the individual,
calling attention to the mental and physical scars that the exposure to
extreme violence had left on individual biographies. For contemporaries
of the events in particular, public memory retained – and, in some cases,
regained – a strong existential dimension next to its functional side.

Meaning depends on context. To speak of 'guilt' and 'atonement' in the
sacral setting of the church is different from using the same vocabulary
in the secular space of the market square. The observation helps to
bring into focus a fundamental difference in the memory cultures of
Kassel and Magdeburg. In Kassel, the central space of commemoration
was the church. Even when politicians were invited to deliver keynote
speeches, their words were embedded in the liturgy of a church service.
In Magdeburg, the situation was different. Here, the most important
commemorative space was the secular framework of the public square.
This held true even when representatives of the Church agreed to make
a contribution, as was the case in 1985.

*'Great Carthage waged three wars': mass death as harbinger of
atomic annihilation*

The fortieth-anniversary commemoration in Kassel was celebrated on
22 October 1983 at the height of the controversy over the NATO arms

---

[50] On the distinction between collective identity and personal identity see Straub, 'Personale und kollektive Identität'.
[51] StAM, Rep. 41/701, 'Rede des Oberbürgermeisters auf der Konferenz der
Märtyrerstädte vom 27.4. bis 29.4.1987 in Madrid'.

build-up.[52] The 'Worship for Peace' was held in the town's biggest sacral space, the Martinskirche.[53] It attracted an audience of approximately 1,800 people. The Protestant bishop of Kurhesse-Waldeck, Hans-Gernot Jung, conducted the liturgy while the Social Democratic mayor, Hans Eichel, delivered the commemorative address. The problem of peace was central to both of them, but the sacral narrative of the bishop invested the term with a different meaning from the secular narrative of the politician: for the church man, the term had an eschatological dimension; for the politician, peace was a political issue.[54]

The bishop expounded a sacral narrative that drew on religious texts in order to prescribe a cycle of despair and lamentation, of recognition and salvation.[55] To this end, the opening rite of an organ meditation was followed by an Old Testament reading from the Lamentations of Jeremiah, 1.1–11, 'How doth the city sit solitary that was full of people!'[56] In recalling Kassel's destruction in World War II through the words of Jeremiah, Jung provided an idiom of mourning to the congregation. At the same time, he offered an explanation for catastrophic rupture that found the root cause for urban destruction in the misdeeds of the 'we-group'. Jerusalem was destroyed by its enemies in AD 587 because of its sins against God (1.8), and so was Kassel in October 1943, the bible reading appeared to suggest. Rejecting any interpretation that explained the events with reference to fate, the narrative posited divine judgement as an explanation for urban catastrophe, and offered repentance as a way towards redemption.[57] In so doing, the bishop took up an interpretation of the historical events that had been expounded by individual pastors since the 1940s.[58]

The two hymns that followed turned the motif of lamentation from the specific to the general, from the mourning over a historical event to a universal condition of human existence. Sung by a choir, the first song was a modern variation of the seventeenth-century hymn 'Alas, how transitory, alas how vain is the life of man'.[59] Everything was vain, material possessions no less than life; hope rested with God alone, the lyrics suggested. The second hymn, the sixteenth-century 'When We are

---

[52] On 22 October 1983, altogether some one million West Germans protested against the Euro missiles in several regional gatherings and at a central rally in Bonn. See Breyman, *Why Movements Matter*, p. 193; Wirsching, *Abschied*, pp. 103–6.

[53] 'Zehntausend Lichter zum Gedächtnis der Toten', *Blick in die kirche* 11 (1983), p. 17.

[54] Compare Huber, 'Frieden IV', in *TRE* XI, p. 636.

[55] Dekanat Kassel-Mitte, Akte Martinskirche, 'Samstag, 22. Okt. 1983, 20 Uhr, Martinskirche Kassel. Gottesdienst für den Frieden am 40. Jahrestag der Zerstörung Kassels'.

[56] I have used the Authorised or King James Version of 1611.

[57] Gunther Wanke, 'Klagelieder', in *TRE* XIX.   [58] See chapter 2 above.

[59] *Evangelisches Kirchengesangbuch* (*EKG*), no. 327: 1, 8. The variation was written by Wolfgang Fortner (born 1907).

in Deepest Pain', developed further the motif of divine consolation.[60] The lyrics explicated the belief that there was double consolation in God – both as a confidant of sorrow and as the locus of forgiveness: 'This is why we come to you, oh Lord, and lament all our pain because we are forlorn in our sorrow and affliction.' Within the overall structure of the service, the hymns functioned as a prelude to the sermon as the core of the sacral narrative.

Hans-Gernot Jung based his address on Paul's epistle to the Romans 5.1: 'We who have become justified through faith / have peace with God through our Lord, Jesus Christ.' The passage explicated the Pauline (and Protestant) gospel of 'salvation through grace' and 'justification by faith'.[61] In taking the passage as his point of reference, the bishop invested 'guilt' and 'peace' with transcendental meaning. Just as all humankind stood in need of divine grace, 'peace' described the relationship between God and justified believers. Turning against a worldly reading of Romans 5.1, Jung insisted that 'peace with God' was not a slogan to be used in the political debates of the day but a reminder of Christ's sacrifice for the sake of humans. Accordingly, the bishop refused to comment on the NATO double-track decision when challenged to do so by a heckler. He emphasised that his task was not to 'advocate a single opinion that could be considered binding upon the conscience' but to stand up for mutual respect.[62] In so doing, Jung implicitly criticised a grass-roots movement among the clergy of his own state church, who had drawn on the same passage in order to justify their uncompromising opposition to the Euro missiles.[63] With his rejection of the argument of a 'no [to the Euro missiles] without any yes' in favour of a 'no with a conditional "still"', the bishop supported the position of the Council of the Protestant Church in Germany (EKD) against the declaration by the Reformed Church (*Moderamen des Reformierten Bundes*), which in June 1982 had declared even temporary toleration of the system of nuclear deterrence as incompatible with the Christian faith.[64]

---

[60] *EKG*, no. 282: 1–5.   [61] Compare Balz, 'Römerbrief', *TRE* XXIX.

[62] 'Zehntausend Lichter zum Gedächtnis der Toten', *Blick in die kirche* 11 (1983), p. 17. Unfortunately, the text of the sermon has not been preserved. But see Jung, 'Unter dem Evangelium'.

[63] 'Frieden und Gerechtigkeit. Eine Erklärung von Pfarrerinnen und Pfarrern der Evangelischen Kirche von Kurhessen-Waldeck', *Blick in die kirche* 10 (1983), p. 17.

[64] For the quotations: Hans-Gernot Jung, 'Unser Friedensauftrag ist Predigt, Seelsorge und Unterricht', *Blick in die kirche* 10 (1983), pp. 13f. See also 'Konflikt um die "Nachrüstung" – Was soll die christliche Gemeinde tun?', ibid; Landeskirchenamt Kassel, Generalakten, Kirchliche Friedensaktivitäten, vol. 4, circular letter by the bishop, 26 September 1983. The declarations of the EKD are collected in Evangelische Kirche in Deutschland, *Die Denkschriften der EKD*, vol. I/3. For the context see Silomon, 'Verantwortung für den Frieden'.

In contrast to the bishop, the Social Democratic mayor, Hans Eichel, engaged more directly with both the political issues of the day and the legacy of the bombing war. Eichel was a typical representative of the age cohort of the so-called 'grandchildren' of legendary party chairman and chancellor Willy Brandt. He formed part of a group who sought to modernise the SPD after the breakdown of the social-liberal coalition government in 1982, by displaying greater sensitivity to widespread concerns about the use of nuclear energy, environmental pollution, social and gender inequalities, and the threat of nuclear war.[65] Born in 1941, Eichel had joined the SPD as a student in 1962 and risen through the ranks of the youth organisation of the Young Socialists (*Jungsozialisten*), before becoming mayor of Kassel in 1975 at the very young age of thirty-three. In 1981, he was re-elected with the help of the Green party faction after the SPD had lost its absolute majority in the council elections of March in the same year.[66]

In his commemorative address in the Martinskirche on 22 October 1983, Eichel invoked the memory of Kassel's destruction in World War II in order to make a passionate plea for unilateral disarmament.[67] Drawing on the late Bertolt Brecht, Eichel argued for active pacifism as the lesson to be learned from the carnage of World War II. 'For mankind is threatened by wars against which the wars of the past are no more than pitiful attempts; and they will come if we do not smash the hands of those who prepare them openly,' he quoted from a text that Brecht had written in the context of the debate over the rearmament of the Federal Republic in the early 1950s.[68] Within the mayor's argument, '22 October' featured above all as a warning from history, as a harbinger to total annihilation facing the city in a future atomic war: '[Speculations on a winnable atomic war] have forced us to look back. To look back at the unbelievable misery of the women, children and old men back then in October 1943 . . . But all of this was little compared with the terror that would face us today.'[69] Eichel briefly referred to the place of the air raid within the larger historical context but did not dwell upon it. In his address, he made clear that the city's destruction belonged in the context of the history of National Socialism but made no attempt to explicate the precise relationship between the two. Instead, he posited that both subjects had been shrouded in taboo until very recently because of

---

[65] Wirsching, *Abschied*, pp. 148f.
[66] 'In Kassel arrangieren sich die Grünen mit der SPD', *HA*, 3 June 1981.
[67] For the text of the speech see StAK, A.1.10, no. 715. 'Ansprache Martinskirche', 22 October 1983.
[68] Brecht, 'Zum Kongress der Völker für den Frieden', in *Werke*, vol. XXIII, pp. 215f.
[69] StAK, A.1.10, no. 715, 'Ansprache Martinskirche', 22 October 1983.

'the misery, our guilt, complicity through inaction'.[70] For the highest political representative of the city in 1983, the question of peace clearly took precedence over the problem of guilt.

The speech was followed by two hymns, which returned to the sacral narrative, calling on God for 'His peace'. In particular the second song, 'Give us Peace Gracefully', a Reformation hymn traditionally sung at the closing of the service, could also be understood as an implicit comment on the mayor's speech and as a subtle criticism of his politics.[71] Eichel had concluded on a plea for action 'for each one of us', stressing that 'our efforts are needed'. By contrast, the lyrics put faith in God alone, 'for there is no one else who could fight for us'. Whereas the mayor called for direct action, the hymn made a plea for acquiescence. This difference was even more pronounced in the second stanza, which was not sung on this occasion but was probably familiar to regular churchgoers. Stanza two explicated the traditional Lutheran doctrine of Two Kingdoms, calling on God to give 'peace and good government' to 'all authority so we may lead a still and quiet life' – a far cry from the Brechtian injunction 'to smash the hands of those who prepare for war'.

Whereas in Kassel, commemorative activities on the fortieth anniversary revolved around the problem of peace, in Magdeburg 'peace' and 'guilt' entered into a much closer relationship. For the political elites of the SED, the renaissance of the memory place went with a revival of the political rhetoric of the 1950s. The theorem of 'imperialism' allowed for a narrative that equated the German war of aggression with the (Western) allied efforts to end this war. 'German monopolists' had been responsible for World War II while Anglo-American 'imperialists' stood accused of the destruction of Magdeburg, as a leader's comment put it in the *Volksstimme* on 16 January 1980.[72] The construct also provided for a dimension that linked the past to the present: 'Then and now, imperialist policy always stays the same,' the article declared.

In his commemorative address of the same day, mayor Werner Herzig (SED) took this line of interpretation even further, extending the responsibility of imperialism to the city's first destruction in the Thirty Years War. Magdeburg, he maintained, had twice been victimised by 'the ruthless rulers of the oppressor societies', in 1631 no less than in 1945.[73] Within this crude historical-materialist frame, Herzig interpreted the air raid of 16 January 1945 as the final attempt on the part of imperialism to

---

[70] Ibid.   [71] *EKG*, no. 139.
[72] Günter Honig, 'Gedanken zu diesem Tage', *Volksstimme*, 16 January 1980, p. 1.
[73] StAM, Rep. 41/531, 'Rede des Oberbürgermeisters auf der Großkundgebung am 16. Januar auf dem Alten Markt', p. 4.

stop the coming of a 'new historic age' of peace and socialism. Although this plan had been thwarted by the 'glorious . war of liberation' of the Red Army, 'imperialist armament and expansion plans' were again threatening peace and humankind – an 'unholy alliance [of] USA, FRG, and NATO', 'today as always', as the mayor stressed ominously.[74] Interestingly, Herzig invoked Bertolt Brecht as well, citing from his Open Letter of September 1951 the passage about 'Great Carthage' that had waged three wars and become uninhabitable after the third – a problematic analogy that not only drew an implicit parallel between the German conduct in World War II and the military feats of Hannibal in the Second Punic War. It also cast Germany in the role of victim by imperialist aggression.[75]

Five years later, the SED put a greater emphasis on the positive aims of the foreign policy of the GDR, as the paratactic structure of the official motto for the mass rally indicated. The marchers were said to be 'in favour of peace and détente' just as much as they were said to be 'against the NATO arms build-up'. This was an expression of a certain shift in the foreign policy of the SED-leadership since 1982, which out of both practical considerations and, it appears, genuine concern over the future, gave priority to the peace problem and made efforts to continue the dialogue with the Federal Republic despite misgivings from Moscow.[76] At the same time, there was, at least within the context of air war memory, a strong continuity in a self-serving rhetoric of finger-pointing. Before an audience of 80,000 people, the first secretary of the Magdeburg SED, Heinz Hanke, declared on 16 January 1985, 'Never will we forget who was responsible for this cruel deed of destruction and barbarism: it was imperialism, the bane of humanity.'[77] The evocation of the past served to cultivate a politics of hatred in the present. While Hanke spoke of 'anger' when recalling the 50 million casualties of World War II, another speaker, a 21-year-old chemist, provided a present-centred channel for these emotions. 'I hate those imperialist forces in the world, those reactionary circles in the USA and in the NATO states who are again preparing the destruction of entire cities and countries, indeed of our planet,' she cried out.[78] Whereas the speakers evoked feelings of hatred towards the trans-historical villain of 'reactionary imperialism', they drew on the dead in order to oblige the living to strengthen state Socialism in order

[74] Ibid., pp. 5f., 7.
[75] Brecht, 'Offener Brief an die deutschen Künstler und Schriftsteller', in *Werke*, vol. XXIII, pp. 155f.
[76] Compare Siebs, *Die Außenpolitik der DDR*, pp. 306–11.
[77] *Volksstimme*, 17 January 1985, p. 1; *Neues Deutschland*, 17 January 1985, pp. 1f.
[78] *Volksstimme*, 17 January 1985, p. 2. On the politics of hatred in the GDR see Bessel, 'Hatred after War'.

to secure peace. 'The stronger Socialism, the more secure is peace,' was the formula that connected past and present, the dead of World War II with self-obligations 'to attain high production figures'.[79]

Yet, embedded in this secular narrative of Socialist fight for peace and imperialist atrocity was the speech of a representative from the Protestant Church who approached the issue from a very different angle. The very presence of superintendent Dietrich Schierbaum at the anniversary commemoration was indicative of shifts in state-Church relations in the country at large, which had taken on a more conciliatory nature after an official meeting between the Board of the Protestant Churches in the GDR (*Konferenz der Evangelischen Kirchenleitungen, KKL*) and the head of state Erich Honecker in March 1978.[80] Politically, the willingness of the Church to cooperate in the ceremony no doubt played into the hands of the SED, which sought to demonstrate the broad appeal of its peace politics to audiences at home and abroad. Successful cooptation, however, came at the price of allowing an alternative interpretation of '16 January 1945' to be voiced outside the confines of the church.

In his speech, Schierbaum did not speak of atrocity but put the term 'affliction' at the centre of his reflections on the meaning of mass death in aerial warfare.[81] Affliction, Schierbaum explained, was a biblical term that reminded Christians of their guilt. Remarkably, the superintendent did not refer to the Christian understanding of guilt in its transcendental meaning but spoke of the historical guilt of Germans who had destroyed many cities in the 'Soviet Union and in England . . . long before a single bomb had fallen on Magdeburg'.[82] Responsibility for World War II rested with the Germans not with abstract concepts, making the destruction of Magdeburg the logical consequence of aggression. 'People reap what they sow,' Schierbaum maintained with reference to the Old Testament metaphor of Hosea 8.7. Echoing a central passage from the Stuttgart Confession of Guilt of 19 October 1945,[83] he located the root cause for the city's destruction in the events of 1933, and more specifically, in the failure 'not to have confessed more courageously, prayed more faithfully . . . and believed more strongly'.

Schierbaum not only differed from his fellow speakers by situating the air war in the historical context of the war of aggression that had been launched by Nazi Germany, he also refrained from blaming 'imperialism' for the dangers facing the world in the 1980s. Instead, he spoke of 'mutual

79 *Volksstimme*, 17 January 1985, p. 2.
80 For a concise summary of the controversial debate about state–Church relations in the GDR see Dähn, 'Die Kirchen in der SBZ/DDR'.
81 StAM, Rep. 41/481, 'Rede des Superintendenten', 16 January 1985.   82 Ibid.
83 The text is reprinted in Kleßmann, *Die doppelte Staatsgründung*, p. 378.

respect' and counselled that 'on the issue of peace, everybody needs to start sweeping at his own door'.[84] With his emphasis on German guilt rather than imperialist atrocity and his plea for mutual respect instead of hatred, the superintendent expressed a solitary opinion within the framework of the secular commemoration. The self-critical potential of the address was safely contained by three speakers who all toed the party line. None the less, his contribution was significant in illustrating the gradual erosion of the discursive power of the SED in the 1980s.[85] It pointed to the Church as the most important locus of an alternative interpretation of the meaning of urban destruction, and indeed, of the future of state Socialism more generally.

'Judgements that we bring on to ourselves': mass death as retribution

On 16 January 1985, the Protestant Church celebrated its traditional 'prayer for peace' in the Magdeburg cathedral in the form of an ecumenical service. Next to members of the local Protestant and Catholic clergy, there also took part in the liturgy delegations from Rotterdam, Moscow, Poland and Frankfurt am Main. At the centre of the service stood the idea of a special responsibility for peace born out of Germany's responsibility for World War II. In emphasising this connection, the Church in Magdeburg drew on the 'word on peace' which the Protestant churches of the GDR and the Federal Republic of Germany had published jointly in 1979 on the occasion of the fortieth anniversary of the outbreak of war.[86] The central symbol of the commemoration was a candle bearing the Latin inscription: 'Dona nobis Pacem' (Give Us Peace). It was lit during the service, to be sent on a 'pilgrimage of commemoration, reconciliation, and prayer for peace' through those cities of the GDR that had suffered similar destruction in aerial warfare to Magdeburg. While the symbolism of the 'prayer for peace' established a national context, the inclusion of representatives of war-torn cities from across Europe consciously provided for an international dimension. The lamentation of loss was tempered by a confession of guilt, which was considered a necessary precondition for an intervention in the peace debate of the present.

As in Kassel in 1983, the service started with a demarcation rite that drew on the Lamentation of Jeremiah. In Magdeburg, however, the nexus of loss and guilt was not universalised but applied to the specific historical context. In her introduction, cathedral preacher Waltraud

---

[84] StAM, Rep. 41/481, 'Rede des Superintendenten', 16 January 1985.
[85] Sabrow, 'Einleitung'.
[86] 'Wort zum Frieden', in *Kirche als Lerngemeinschaft*, pp. 260–2.

Zachhuber described the 'suffering [and] misery' of Magdeburg on 16 January 1945 as the outcome of a 'long history of failure, forgetfulness, and guilt', which she specified in three respects.[87] Firstly, she singled out the Jews of Magdeburg who had experienced 'expulsion, flight and destruction' long before the town had been destroyed. Secondly she reminded the congregation of the 'German armies' and 'soldiers from Magdeburg' who had spread 'suffering, pain, and death' throughout Europe. Finally, the preacher pointed to the destruction of Germany's cityscapes and the division of the nation. Speaking for the congregation at large, Zachuber acknowledged 'our complicity' in the crimes against Jewry and other nations while ascribing a redemptive power to the act of remembrance.[88]

The introduction was followed by a prayer that developed further the theme of redemption through memory, imploring God 'to let us learn from your judgements that we bring on to ourselves'. The prayer also introduced the second theme of the sacral narrative, 'peace' – defined not as the fulfilment of one's duties towards the Socialist state but as the liberation of the individual from fear, mistrust and deceitfulness through the grace of God. The transcendental dimension in this understanding of peace was underlined by the hymn 'Thou Art the Duke of Peace', which was sung by the whole congregation after the prayer. The lyrics celebrated Jesus Christ as the source both of consolation and of intercession with God, suggesting that despite 'all our sins and guilt', there was hope for redemption.[89] On the level of liturgy, the promise of forgiveness was reinforced by the presence of representatives from nations victimised by Germany, who indicated their willingness to meet the admission of guilt in a spirit of conciliation through their active participation.

The greetings (*Grußworte*) were followed by the core of the sacral narrative, the sermon, in which Superintendent Schierbaum spoke on Ephesians 2.14. The opening line, '[Christ] is our peace', was central to church interventions in the political debate on rearmament in the 1980s. It featured prominently in the joint 'word on peace' of September 1979.[90] Within the context of the secular society of the GDR, the Christological dictum rejected the simple equation of peace and Socialism. Instead, it emphasised the distinctive contribution of the Christian faith to the problem of peace.[91] At the same time, the epistle addressed the relationship between guilt and redemption, professing confidence in the divine promise of salvation through faith alone.[92] 'There is no guilt too great

[87] For the text see Archiv der Evangelischen Domgemeinde, Magdeburg, 'Eine Kerze unterwegs im Zeichen von Frieden und Versöhnung', unpublished manuscript [1985].
[88] Ibid.   [89] *EKG*, no. 391.
[90] 'Wort zum Frieden', in *Kirche als Lerngemeinschaft*, pp. 260f., here p. 261.   [91] Ibid.
[92] Compare Mußner, 'Epheserbrief'.

that cannot be forgiven by Him on the Cross,' as Schierbaum reassured his congregation in the sermon.[93]

In his address, the superintendent acknowledged the Holocaust as the pivotal crime of World War II, and constructed a hierarchy of suffering in which the air raid on Magdeburg occupied a subordinate place. The 'inferno' of Magdeburg's destruction had been without precedent in local history, but it was an 'affliction' that had been brought upon the city by its residents. Repeating a core passage from his earlier address at the secular ceremony, Schierbaum found the root cause for the night of 16 January 1945 in January 1933, and more generally, in a turn-away from Jesus Christ. The fate of Magdeburg in World War II called for 'compassion', but even more for 'shame'. After all, the 'madness of mutual annihilation' had originated 'from us'. For Schierbaum, 'Auschwitz' eclipsed 'Magdeburg', guilt outweighed lamentation, as he made clear by putting the memory place of 16 January in relation to the *lieu de mémoire* of 9 November.

The memory of the so-called 'Night of Broken Glass' (*Kristallnacht*) of 1938, in which about a hundred Jews were killed and thousands sent to concentration camps, had gained in importance within the Protestant churches in the GDR since the 1970s, and in this reorientation, the Magdeburg church had played a prominent role.[94] Yet – Schierbaum maintained – even the guilt of genocide could be forgiven, as he saw illustrated in the gesture of conciliation that a Jewish rabbi had shown towards the superintendent when both had prayed together in the Jewish cemetery on the fortieth anniversary of the pogrom in 1978.[95]

Although the reflections on the place of the Holocaust were embedded in a problematic narrative of lamentation, recognition and forgiveness, the Protestant Church in Magdeburg preceded the Church in Kassel by several years in making the genocide of European Jewry the pivotal event of the commemoration of aerial warfare. While Schierbaum, in 1985, constructed a hierarchy of suffering, his counterpart in Kassel, Dean Hans Feller, equated mass death in the extermination camps with mass death under the bombs. In an address on 23 October 1983, he employed a paratactic construction to speak of the 'innocent suffering of Kassel *and* Auschwitz'.[96] Within the context of the annual memorial

---

[93] Archiv der Evangelischen Domgemeinde, Magdeburg, 'Eine Kerze unterwegs im Zeichen von Frieden und Versöhnung', 'Ansprache im Gedenkgottesdienst in Magdeburg', 16 January 1985.

[94] See Schmid, *Antifaschismus und Judenverfolgung*, pp. 76–103.

[95] Archiv der Evangelischen Domgemeinde, Magdeburg, 'Eine Kerze unterwegs im Zeichen von Frieden und Versöhnung', 'Ansprache im Gedenkgottesdienst in Magdeburg', 16 January 1985.

[96] Feller, '"Gedenket aber der früheren Tage"', p. 56, emphasis added. The sermon was delivered on Sunday, 23 October 1983, not, as erroneously stated in the reprint, on 22 October 1983. Letter of Hans Feller to author, February 2006.

service in Kassel, the nexus between extermination and destruction was not explored in any detail until the fiftieth anniversary of the anti-Semitic pogrom in 1988 had put the persecution of German Jewry at the centre of the local memorial culture,[97] and equally importantly, until German reunification had raised fears of a resurgent xenophobic nationalism.[98] The first time that the memory place was used to address the fate of Kassel Jewry was in October 1991, in a sermon by Pastor Udo Luest (born in 1928).

'Why memory?' was the opening question of an address that took Matthew 5.9 as a starting point for a reflection on the meaning of 22 October 1943, its connection with 7 November 1938 (the day of the pogrom in Kassel) and the lessons for the present. In his sermon, Luest employed the visual as a memory trigger, showing slides of pre-war Kassel in order to take the congregation (and himself) back to the days of their youth: 'Some of us will recognise [the historic Old Town]. Memories of youth and adolescence come awake – dreams of quiet peacefulness'.[99] Yet the visual revelling in the beauty of old Kassel was brought to an abrupt end when the pastor proceeded to show images of the burning city and the landscape of ruins – images 'that we have erased from our memory', as he insisted. He went on to describe the bombing night as a somatic experience that had the power to bring back memories of sounds, smells, fears and hopes almost fifty years after the event. 'Who [amongst us] does not have the images in front of his eyes, the smell of smoke in his nose, of the swath of fire and the firestorm?'[100]

Luest spoke as much in his capacity as an eyewitness as in his pastoral role, engaging in an intra-generational dialogue with his audience, many of whom like himself still held personal memories of the war. It was also this personal approach through which he chose to establish a connection between the symbolic dates of 22 October 1943 and of 7 November 1938.[101] 'Do both belong together – the Martinskirche and the synagogue – does this commemoration belong in this evening hour?' he asked. As the rhetorical question made clear, to speak of the fate of the Kassel Jewry when speaking of the air raid of 22 October 1943 was still far

[97] See the press clippings in StAK, S5 R5, Judenpogrom 'Kristallnacht', 7.-9. Nov. 1938. For a critical analysis of the blind spots of 'Kristallnacht'-memory in the 1980s see Domansky, 'Kristallnacht'; and more fully Schmid, *Erinnern an den Tag der Schuld*.

[98] See the special issue, 'Christen und Juden', *Blick in die kirche* 11 (1988); *Kassel kulturell* no. 8 (November 1988); StAK, Best. A.1.10 [OB Eichel], no. 964. II. 1987, 88, 89, 90.

[99] Udo Luest, 'Gottesdienst 22.10.1991'. I would like to thank the pastor in retirement for making available a copy of the sermon to me.

[100] Ibid.

[101] On the anti-Semitic looting and burning of November 1938 in Kassel see Kropat, *'Reichskristallnacht'*, pp. 56–78.

from self evident in 1991. Whatever his audience may have thought, the
pastor clearly believed that both dates did belong together. Recalling personal memories of the sudden disappearance of his Jewish classmate in
the autumn of 1941, he stated reproachfully, 'Nobody explained it to us.'
In so doing, he intimated that his generation had been made complicit
in a crime for which they were too young to bear personal responsibility
but the consequences of which had haunted them ever since. 'Perhaps
we still ask tonight, where were we in November 1941 when the largest
group of Jews were deported?'

To Luest, confronting the past was necessary not only as a moral obligation towards the victims but also, and perhaps more so, as a warning
to the present. Echoing a dictum by Alexander Mitscherlich, he maintained that 'whoever represses his past is compelled to repeat it'.[102] On
this interpretation, violent assaults on asylum seekers in recently reuni-
fied Germany were a direct consequence of the failure to engage with
the legacy of the Third Reich. As Luest declared, 'Aren't there reasons enough to look back? Day after day we experience how minorities
are marginalised in the recently enlarged Germany, with brutal violence
according to the motto, one human life, one foreigner does not count
for much'. Consequently, the pastor wished the Bible verse of Matthew
5.9, 'Blessed are the peacemakers', to be understood as an injunction for
the individual to stand up for a civil society, 'to speak out for peace, to
raise our voice for the persecuted and the threatened, as well as for the
foreigners'. 'We must be watchful and be on our guard against hatred,'
he maintained.[103]

By the time of the fiftieth anniversary in 1993, the understanding that
the destruction of Kassel was not a single event but a gradual process that
had started with the persecution of the Jews in 1933 – still controversial
in 1991 – had become a standard element of the public memory culture.
In his commemorative address of 22 October 1993, for example, the new
mayor, Georg Lewandowski (CDU), referred matter of factly to 1933 as
the year in which the destruction of the urban community had set in.[104]

'Mine eyes do fail with tears': dealing with pain

As important as questions of collective identity – the we-group as a victim
of war vs the we-group as an integral part of a perpetrator society – were

---

[102] The idea of the compulsion to act out the repressed goes back to Freud, 'Erinnern,
Wiederholen und Durcharbeiten', in *Studienausgabe. Ergänzungsband*, pp. 206–15, here
p. 210.

[103] Luest, 'Gottesdienst 22.10.1991'.

[104] 'Versöhnter Umgang schenkt Zukunft', *Bonifatiusbote*, 31 October 1993, p. 17. See also
Esther Hass, 'Die Zerstörung begann 1933', *HNA*, 22 October 1993.

for the memory culture in the 1980s and 1990s, this was not the whole story. Anniversary commemorations also provided a space in which the protagonists of public memory as well as ordinary residents reflected on the long-term impact of the experience of extreme violence on individual biographies, not least of all their own. Likewise, commemorative ceremonies were not just a locus for rational deliberation on the causes, consequences and lessons of mass death in aerial warfare. They were also a space for public mourning, in which contemporaries and their descendants came face to face with grief and loss. Functional aspects stood side by side with the existential side of memory. Throughout the period, the Church saw itself as much as consoler as educator, in particular vis-à-vis those members of the congregation who held primary memory traces of the traumatic events. It is likely that despite generational change, this group still made up the majority of attendants up until the turn of the century. By drawing on the Bible, hymns and selected secular literature, the Church offered a language of public mourning. Kassel pastor Klaus Röhring, for example, made an excerpt from the Lamentations of Jeremiah 2.11 into a *leitmotif* of his remembrance service of 1990: 'Mine eyes do fail with tears, my bowels are troubled.'[105] Dean Hans Feller, in 1983, recalled the lyrics of the hymn no. 349, 'The Radiant Morning of Eternity', which one of his predecessors had intoned on the morning of 23 October 1943.[106]

For the negotiation of loss in the 1980s and 1990s, the central issue was the rupture between past and present. In his Sunday service of 23 October 1983, Dean Hans Feller remarked, 'Whoever looks at the old photographs . . . will observe . . . [that the] paper fades but the faces don't grow older. When I see the faces of my killed brothers-in-law, of the perished friends and classmates, a feeling of alienation comes over me. Their sons have grown older than the fathers ever were!' Feller's feeling of alienation had its natural basis in the growing temporal distance between the historical event and the present but was reinforced by the modernising reconstruction and the social and mental shifts or *Wandlungsprozesse*[107] of German society since the end of the war. 'Alien the faces, alien the style of the letters and thoughts – as if from a different world which is so far away!' he exclaimed.

Yet, as the dean knew, traumatic experiences of the kind encountered in aerial bombing tended to return as *mémoires involontaire*, as unwanted

---

[105] 'Gottesdienst zum Gedächtnis der Zerstörung Kassels am 22. Oktober 1943'. I would like to thank Oberlandeskirchenrat i.R. Klaus Röhring for making a copy available to me.
[106] Feller, '"Gedenket aber der früheren Tage"', pp. 54–8.
[107] Herbert (ed.), *Wandlungsprozesse in Westdeutschland*.

memories that 'broke forth' unexpectedly, as one crossed a street, heard
a sound or smelled a scent. Feller described this phenomenon, which is
well known from clinical psychiatry, in the following terms:

All of a sudden, an image, a memory, a smell: and the pain is back, the memory
and the thoughts! You walk across the new Kurt-Schumacher-Avenue and suddenly you remember: the cars pass over the collapsed cellars of the Old Town.
How many corpses might still be lying there? Suffocated, buried, forgotten?

The answer that the Church gave to this problem in the 1980s and 1990s
was 'to risk looking back', to confront consciously one's personal memories. As the dean readily conceded, this was a painful process that opened
up old wounds and involved 'pain and doubt [*Anfechtung*]'. Facing the
past, however, was necessary to avoid the danger of emotional and mental
'sclerosis', on both an individual and a societal level.[108] The underlying
premise was the notion that returning to the past would help in mastering
the present – a central assumption of psychoanalysis, of course, which
was typically, and, within the context of post-fascist German society,
problematically, expressed through the cabbalist dictum, 'The secret of
salvation is memory.'[109]

Yet, for many of those who had lived through the bombings themselves,
there was memory, but there was little salvation in looking back. 'It's been
fifty years on 16 January 1995, and year after year one relives this dreadful night,' wrote 87-year-old Wilhelm F. in response to a public appeal
for eyewitness accounts that was published in the local media of Magdeburg in the run-up to the fiftieth anniversary of the bombing.[110] True,
among the 140 or so letters that members of the war generation sent in
to the municipal archive, there were stories in which apparently successful attempts were made to integrate the lived experience of the air war
meaningfully into an autobiographical narrative. Joachim H., for example, who was a sixteen-year-old Hitler Youth serving with the fire brigade
in early 1945, emphasised the disillusionment with the Nazi regime and
the political conversion that the raid on Magdeburg had occasioned in
him. Looking back from the vantage-point of the mid-1990s, he defined
his experience in the smouldering city as one of the crucial moments of
his life, teaching him the difference between mediated representations of
violence and the immediacy of personal, lived experience. Echoing the
Socialist rhetoric that had permeated the public memory of Magdeburg

---

[108] Feller, '"Gedenket aber der früheren Tage"', pp. 55–7.
[109] On the problematic usage of the dictum in 1980s West German Holocaust memory see
Brumlik, 'Gedenken in Deutschland'.
[110] StAM, ZG 133.9 (24), account by Wilhelm F.

for much of the second half of the twentieth century, he spoke of the 'social political insights' about the 'meaning of fascism' that must be preserved for the future. Others lent coherence to their stories by stressing that the destruction must never be repeated.[111]

But for every 'good story', for every emphasis on social solidarity in times of distress and every consoling notion of lessons finally learnt, there was a tale that spoke of anguish and abiding loss, of lives cut short and biographies deformed. 'With bitterness I look back on World War II, which has brought so much pain on mankind and has stolen the best years of life from those born between 1920 and 1925,' wrote seventy-year-old Margot D.[112] The old lady was adamant that the bombs were still falling in her mind's eye, and that for her, the fear of a return of the past was an abiding emotion. Resentment could be felt towards very different agents: the Nazi authorities, the 'Anglo-American bombers' with their 'criminal terror raids',[113] but significantly also towards fellow residents whose actions and/or inactions nearly half a century ago were still held responsible for the deaths of loved ones. 'I simply cannot forgive the fellow house occupants from back then for what they did. My mother could have lived on for years to come [after the raid],' confessed Margot D. in her account.[114]

The sense of a dreadful past that continued to haunt the present is perhaps best captured in a crude poem that one resident sent in to the archive. The piece was called 'The War-blind' and spoke of the inability to leave the past behind: 'I walk blind among the seeing / I can see neither petals and flowers nor happy children's faces / But what I do see in my lonely hours / with bitter sorrow and twisting mouth / is the horror of war: / raging flames in the dark night; / humans set alight like torches / cracking bombs and death screams.' This scene of horror, the lyrical 'I' insisted, was 'the picture that never faded / like a monument inside of myself'.[115] In view of images like these, it is perhaps not surprising that some eyewitnesses longed not for memory but for forgetting. 'Please understand that . . . I would rather repress the dreadful experiences of the bombing night,' wrote Otto St. in 1993 in reply to a request from the municipal archive in Kassel to revisit his experiences, which had first been recorded by Karl Paetow as early as 1944.[116] In the raid, both Otto St. and his wife, Margarete St., had suffered severe burns, from which

---

[111] StAM, ZG 133.9 (31), account by Joachim H., 5 January 1995.
[112] StAM, ZG 133.9 (19), account by Margot D.
[113] StAM, ZG 133.10 (12), Gert K. and Rolf K.
[114] StAM, ZG 133.9 (19), account by Margot D.
[115] STAM ZG 133.11 (18), Irmgard Sch., 'Des Kriegsblinden Bild'.
[116] See chapter 1 above.

the woman in particular had never fully recovered.[117] The voices of people like Otto and Margarete St. tend to go unnoticed in an oral-history historiography that gives perhaps undue emphasis to 'good stories' of successful overcoming.[118]

'Or does memory . . . resist the changes of today?': commemoration in the 1990s

What happens to local memory when the political and social environment changes as dramatically as was the case in Magdeburg, and to a lesser extent, Kassel, between 1989 and 1995?[119] Did the end of the Cold War, the collapse of the SED dictatorship and German reunification leave established commemorative patterns and practices in place? And if so, was this because of a conscious effort to retain markers of continuity amidst sweeping change or because longer-term generational and cultural factors proved more important than short-term socio-political rupture? This section explores this problem with a special emphasis on Magdeburg as a city that not only underwent revolutionary political change but whose socio-economic and demographic basis was also altered profoundly in the period. Politically, the city without doubt benefited from unification. Magdeburg was made into the capital of the new state of Saxony-Anhalt, not to speak of the new democratic freedoms. There was also continuity in so far as the Social Democrats managed to regain some of the political dominance that they had enjoyed in the 1920s. Economically and demographically, however, the unification process proved a disaster. Magdeburg's heavy industries collapsed, leading to structural unemployment hovering around the 15 per cent mark and a dramatic contraction of the resident population, which declined by approximately 10 per cent between 1990 and 1995, from 290,000 to 260,000.[120]

This section looks at elements of change and continuity in the topography of memory between the mid-1980s and the mid-1990s. It argues that the trajectory of commemoration in the post-GDR environment may be described as a process of selective appropriation of pre-1989 traditions. Politicians, clerics and artists drew on some elements while discarding

---

[117] StAK, A.4.415, no. 357/1: 50. Jahrestage, correspondence between municipal archive and Otto St., 9 June 1993 and 24 June 1993.

[118] Thießen, 'Der "Feuersturm" im kommunikativen Gedächtnis', p. 331.

[119] 'Or does memory . . . resist the changes of today?' Archiv der Evangelischen Domgemeinde, Magdeburg, 'Friedensgebet 16.1.1992 Barlachehrenmal'.

[120] Köhler, 'Bevölkerungsstruktur von Magdeburg', p. 33; Schoch, 'Economic Development'.

others, seizing on the memory place in order to reformulate a civic identity amidst the turmoil of the 'unification crisis'.[121]

On the most general level, continuity prevailed in Kassel as well as Magdeburg. In both localities, the subject of allied bombing retained a prominent place in the memory culture, forming an important element in the commemorative cycle of 1983 to 1995. The fiftieth anniversaries in 1993 and 1995 were commemorated with an extraordinary investment of time and effort, spawning special 'committees' that coordinated the activities of the administration, the Church, artists and ordinary citizens.[122] Given the prominent role that the SED had played in the shaping of the *lieu de mémoire* since the 1950s, this finding might be surprising with regard to Magdeburg. Yet, unlike most other dates, '16 January' did not disappear from the commemorative calendar with the demise of Socialism.[123] On the contrary; against the backdrop of dramatic political and socio-economic changes, the memory place steadily gained in importance in the early 1990s, climaxing in a three-day commemorative marathon in January 1995 that surpassed even the state-sponsored mass rallies of the 1980s.[124] In a temporal perspective, two phases may be distinguished: firstly, the unification years of 1989 to 1990, in which the air war was rediscovered as a common experience of Germans on both sides of the crumbling Berlin Wall; secondly, the years of 1991 to 1995, in which the 'woman of the rubble' was conjured up as a historical example to a crisis-ridden present.

'Two cities – one fate': the air war as national founding myth

'For the first time, the memory of the victims of 16 January 1945 has united Magdeburgers and citizens from the twin city of Braunschweig,' wrote the *Volksstimme* on the forty-fifth anniversary of the bombing in 1990.[125] The previous day, an official delegation from Braunschweig had participated in the commemoration on Old Market Square, where the deputy mayor of the West German twin city,[126] Brigitte Freifrau Grothe, addressed a crowd of several hundred residents. She reminded

---

[121] Kocka, *Vereinigungskrise.*

[122] For Kassel see StAK, A.4.415, no. 357/1: 50. Jahrestage; for Magdeburg: StAM, Rep. 18/4 StR 56, 6 September 1994.

[123] The protest marches in memory of Rosa Luxemburg and Karl Liebknecht have a similar post-1989 history. See Sabrow, 'Kollektive Erinnerung und kollektiviertes Gedächtnis'; Könczöl, *Märtyrer des Sozialismus*, pp. 320–3.

[124] 'Dreitägiges Gedenken zur Mahnung an die Bombennacht', *Volksstimme*, 5 January 1995, p. 11. Landeshauptstadt Magdeburg (ed.), *Magdeburg 16. Jan. 1945–16. Jan. 1995.*

[125] 'Gemeinsames Gedenken in Magdeburg', *Volksstimme*, 17 January 1990, p. 1.

[126] Alfred Heidelmayer, 'Zwei Städte – ein Schicksal', *Volksstimme*, 16 January 1990, p. 8.

her audience that 'once before... on 16 January 1945, citizens from Braunschweig came to the rescue of the burning Magdeburg'. Speaking of the air war as a 'common fate', the baroness employed the first person plural in order to invoke a national identity grounded in a past of shared catastrophe.[127] In 1945, Braunschweigers had helped Magdeburgers in coping with urban destruction, just as western Germans were coming to the rescue of their impoverished eastern relatives today, her analogy suggested.

In contrast to the optimism of the Braunschweig deputy mayor, local superintendent Almuth Noetzel struck a cautionary tone. Exhibiting an acute awareness of the patronising undercurrent in the Western politician's speech, she warned in her address, with a view to the future just as much as to the past, 'Let us listen carefully to the words of those who now intend to assume responsibility for our country. Let us not be awed by well-sounding phrases.'[128]

Contrary to appearances, the joint ceremony was not a direct result of the revolutionary upheaval of the autumn of 1989. It reached back to the politics of memory of the SED. Since the 1950s, the East German political elites had tried to use the common experience of the air war as a lever to engage West German communities in political debates about the future of Germany – an endeavour that finally came to fruition under the different political conditions of the late 1980s. On 1 September 1988, the forty-ninth anniversary of the outbreak of World War II, the Magdeburg mayor welcomed an official delegation from Braunschweig, with which an official partnership had been established the year before. On 16 January 1989, the forty-fourth anniversary of the iconic attack, representatives from the two cities met again to commemorate death in war.[129]

Such selective continuation of pre-1989 commemorative formats for post-unification nation building could be observed in other communities as well.[130] The most prominent example was Dresden, the destruction of which on 13 February 1945 soon attained the status of an 'all-German memory place', as was evident in the commemorative address that the head of state, Federal President Roman Herzog, gave at the fiftieth-anniversary commemoration in 1995.[131] Hand in hand went attempts to establish 'Dresden' as a global symbol of both the destructiveness of war

---

[127] Ibid. See also *Der Neue Weg*, 16 January 1990, p. 6.
[128] Almuth Noetzel, '"Nie wieder soll der Himmel über Magdeburg brennen!" Ansprache auf dem Alten Markt am 16.1.1990'. I would like to thank Pastor Almuth Noetzel for making available to me a copy of this speech.
[129] StAM, Rep. 41/703, vol. I: 'Rede des OB anlässlich der Gedenkveranstaltung zum 44. Jahrestag der Zerstörung Magdeburgs im 2. Weltkrieg am 16.1.89'.
[130] Compare Naumann, 'Leerstelle Luftkrieg', 12.
[131] Naumann, *Der Krieg als Text*, p. 35.

and the power of reconciliation, in particular by way of an international appeal for funds to rebuild the eighteenth-century Frauenkirche.[132]

'The same confidence and commitment': the woman of the rubble as example

The process of appropriation and redefinition is best described with reference to the fate of the Socialist-era monuments in Magdeburg. Within the city's mnemonic topography, two monuments had been dedicated specifically to the memory of the air war, the first in 1968, the second in 1983.[133] Together, they functioned as visual signifiers in the cityscape of central narrative strands of the official memory up until 1989. The first was a memorial that marked the central gravesite in the main cemetery where approximately 2,400 casualties lay buried.[134] The design was much more modest than the projected idea of 1959.[135] The monument came in the form of a simple memorial slab on which the inscription admonished viewers 'to remember' and 'to fight for peace' (Fig. 18).[136]

The second monument, by the nationally renowned sculptor Heinrich Apel, was dedicated on 9 May 1983 in order to commemorate the thirtieth anniversary of the start of the reconstruction in the old town (Fig. 19). It consisted of two sculptures that were placed in front of the only partially restored Johanniskirche, where a permanent exhibition on Magdeburg's destruction had been housed since 1979.[137] An additional element was a relief that formed one of the bronze doors to the church. While one sculpture showed a mother sheltering her child from the falling bombs, the other depicted a rubble woman clearing debris. By way of historical context, the relief depicted apocalyptic scenes from the firestorm. Furthermore, the relief established a link between past and present by pointing an accusatory finger at those 'who had not learned from history'.[138] The ensemble by Heinrich Apel visualised the theme of triumph over criminal adversity, as was clearly recognised by Mayor Herzig, who in his unveiling speech praised the work for striking a balance

---

[132] Fache, 'Gegenwartsbewältigungen'.
[133] For a survey of the topography of memory see Gerling, *Denkmale der Stadt Magdeburg*; Buchholz and Ballerstedt, *Man setzte ihnen ein Denkmal*.
[134] Grünflächenamt (ed.), *100 Jahre Westfriedhof*.   [135] See chapter 3 above.
[136] 'Zum mahnenden Gedenken', *Volksstimme*, 16 January 1968, p. 8; Gerling, *Denkmale der Stadt Magdeburg*, p. 17.
[137] KHM Ordner Johanniskirche, 'Konzeption zur Neugestaltung der "Mahn- und Erinnerungsstätte für die Zerstörung Magdeburgs" in der ehemaligen Johanniskirche', p. 2. I would like to thank Ms Karin Grünwald for making this material available to me.
[138] Gerling, *Denkmale der Stadt Magdeburg*, p. 7 shows the relief and the rubble woman but leaves out the mother sheltering her child.

Figure 18. 'In admonishing memory of 16th January 1945. Fight for Peace,' read the inscription on the Socialist-era memorial slab in the Westfriedhof that was removed in 1995.

between accusation and optimism, between the atrocity of the 'Anglo-American terror bombers' and the achievements of the 'activists of the first hour'.[139]

In post-dictatorial Magdeburg, the memorial in the cemetery was replaced while the ensemble in front of the Johanniskirche remained. Whereas the formulaic admonition to 'fight for peace' was discarded owing to its close association with the propagandistic vocabulary of the SED, the semantic potential of the sculptures proved flexible enough to be adapted to the conditions of the post-1989 world.

In the run-up to the fiftieth-anniversary commemorations, the town council initiated a competition for a redesign of the gravesite in the cemetery, from which a design by sculptor Wieland Schmiedel emerged victorious (Figs. 20 and 21). In contrast to the straightforward inscription on the old memorial, the new design refrained from codifying a central message. It invited meditation instead of admonition, as a press report

---

[139] StAM, Rep. 41/534, 'Rede des Oberbürgermeisters anlässlich der Übergabe des plastischen Ensembles', 9 May 1983, pp. 6f.

Figure 19. Sculptural ensemble in front of the Johanniskirche by Heinrich Apel. The sculptures were unveiled in 1983. They survived the regime change of 1989/90. The photo was taken in 2010.

Figure 20. The memorial in the Westfriedhof by sculptor Wieland Schmiedel that replaced the Socialist-era memorial slab in 1995.

Figure 21. Detail of the new memorial.

put it.[140] Using stone and steel, geometrical forms and open space, the arrangement was based on the ground plan of a cathedral. The prospective visitor entered through the nave and proceeded to the apse, where the site of mass burial was located. On the way, he or she came across a marble plate that bore the inscription '16 January 1945'. Reaching the aisle, the visitor encountered an open space in which a dislocated cube was framed by steel girders that afforded no protection against the sky. Finally, in place of the altar, a marble stele stood next to a steel girder from which a rusted steel ball was hanging, evoking associations of both church bell and wrecking ball.[141] In a press conference, Schmiedel stressed that he had attempted to create a memorial that left room for individual thoughts and feelings, conveying not just pessimism but also a promise of hope. 'One can rebuild, one can hear the bell; the space can be closed, and the cube be put right,' he explained.[142]

While the political injunction 'to fight for peace' had thus disappeared from the memory landscape of Magdeburg, the accusatory tone and the celebration of perseverance remained. Shorn of their Socialist connotations, both narrative strands played an integral part in the memorial culture of post-dictatorial Magdeburg. Not only was there continuity on the level of narrative, the protagonists of post-1989 public memory also availed themselves of the same symbolic repertoire as their predecessors.

On 16 January 1991, the Magdeburg city council made a last-minute effort to prevent the outbreak of hostilities in the Persian Gulf where a United Nations military coalition had assembled to drive Iraqi forces out of occupied Kuwait. In a symbolic gesture, the council sent telegrams to the heads of state of Germany, Iraq and the United States which urged them to refrain from the use of violence. The initiative, while of no practical consequence for the course of events in the Persian Gulf, was remarkable for the rationale that underpinned it. As a community that had been exposed to the kind of aerial bombardment that the United Nations was widely (and incorrectly) expected to unleash on Iraq, the councillors felt that their suffering in World War II put them in a strong moral position to plead for a peaceful resolution of the conflict. 'On 16th January 1945, the last war brought great suffering and death over our city,' the telegram read. In two additional dispatches the following day, the signatories expressed their 'sadness' (*Betroffenheit*) and 'angst' at the

---

[140] Renate Wähnelt, 'Mahnmal aus Marmor und Metall erinnert an die Toten', *Volksstimme*, 11 January 1995, p. 14.

[141] See 'Faltblatt zur künstlerischen Neugestaltung der Gedenkstätte für die Opfer des Luftangriffs vom 16. Januar 1945'. Text: Norbert Eisold (Magdeburg, 1995).

[142] Renate Wähnelt, 'Mahnmal aus Marmor und Metall erinnert an die Toten', *Volksstimme*, 11 January 1995, p. 14.

outbreak of hostilities through the words of the church inscription by Heinrich Apel. 'We appeal to political reason worldwide. "We accuse all those who still have not learned from history, and who continue to sow hatred and dissension" – is written on the door of the Johanniskirche.'[143] Here, opposition to the Gulf War was couched in language that had been coined at the height of the second Cold War in the 1980s. In this tradition, the accusatory finger of the 'we' was directed against 'those' who 'still [had] not learned from history', in 1945 no less than in 1983 or in 1991, the reference suggested. Implicitly, a community of 'pain' and 'suffering' was juxtaposed to 'hating' and 'quarrelsome' forces of aggression, which were identified as Anglo-American then and now.

While the use of the inscription points towards strands of continuity in the secular memory culture of Magdeburg across the caesura of 1989/90, another usage illustrates the extent to which public symbols could be reloaded with different meanings in different contexts. Against the backdrop of an upsurge in xenophobic violence in the early 1990s, a committee of liberally minded politicians, clerics, journalists and citizens chose the memory place in order to launch an appeal for a 'chain of light against war, violence, and xenophobia'. The initiative brought together a crowd of approximately 50,000 Magdeburgers on 16 January 1993.[144] As a commentary on the events, the *Volksstimme* again quoted from the inscription, presenting Apel's memento against the misdeeds of 'imperialism' as an admonition for the creation of a civil society.[145]

Of equal, if not greater, importance to the post-1989 memory culture was the sculpture of the 'rubble woman' from the ensemble in front of the Johanniskirche, which, during the unveiling ceremony of 1983, had been praised as a monument to perseverance in the face of criminal adversity. It was the potential for positive identification that made the figure attractive to the first post-unification administration under mayor Willi Polte (SPD), which had to cope with an imploding industrial base and the moving away of about 30,000 residents in the half-decade between 1989 and 1995.[146]

As early as 1991, Polte had declared that he 'wished . . . for all Magdeburgers today [to have] the same confidence and commitment that many citizens showed in the face of death and rubble back then'. In addition to furnishing a historical precedent, the idolisation of the woman of the rubble also served another purpose. It provided a way of salvaging the

---

[143] StAM, Rep. 18/4, StVV 6. Sitzung, 17 January 1991.
[144] 'Heute Lichterkette: Machen Sie mit', *Volksstimme*, 16 January 1993, p. 1. See also ibid., p. 3, and 17 January 1993, pp. 1, 3.
[145] *Volksstimme*, 16 January 1993.
[146] Compare Bettecken, '"Dann jagen uns die Bürger gleich wieder aus dem Rathaus"'.

lives' work of the 'reconstruction generation' from the discrediting of the political system in which they had spent most of their lives. 'What you, dear Magdeburger, have achieved for our city, for your home town, is not forgotten,' Polte declared in the town hall during a special 'honouring of rubble women' that opened the string of commemorative activities in January 1995.[147] Quoting from an eyewitness account, he continued, 'Only those who have seen what Magdeburg looked like after 16 January 1945 can judge how much reconstruction effort is visible in the face of the city today.'[148] With a view to critics who tried to turn the memory place into a discursive space for reflecting on the cultural and human costs of forty years of SED rule, Polte added, 'Some seem to have forgotten already.'[149]

In important respects, the political elites of the early 1990s pursued a memory politics that resembled the memory politics of the late 1940s. Just as the civil administration under Rudolf Eberhard (SED) had constructed a *lieu de mémoire* of aerial bombing in order to infuse the citizenry with a sense of confidence in the reconstruction effort, the administration under Willi Polte (SPD) drew on the memory place in order to present the 'will to survive' of the post-war years as an example from history to the present. Underlying both approaches were notions of victimhood and perseverance that tended to marginalise questions about complicity and agency. On an iconic level, the historical parallel was symbolised by the re-emergence of the sculpture of 'Magdeburg in Mourning', which was returned to the ruins of the Johanniskirche in 1989. It quickly regained its place as the defining icon of the 'night of horror'.[150] The sculpture invited emotions that had been largely missing from the official memorial culture of the GDR. At the same time, it called for empathy with a city that had been victimised repeatedly but also persevered in suffering.

Whereas local journalists and the civil administration selectively appropriated elements of the pre-1989 discourse to the post-dictatorial environment, the Protestant Church drew on the tradition of the annual

---

[147] Büro des Oberbürgermeisters, Magdeburg, Willi Polte, 'GW zur Ehrung von Trümmerfrauen (16. Januar 1995, 9.30 Uhr, Rathaussaal)'. See also Alfred Heidelmayer, 'Der große Irrtum einer amerikanischen Zeitung', *Volksstimme*, 16 January 1992, p. 14.

[148] Büro des Oberbürgermeisters, Magdeburg, Willi Polte, 'GW zur Ehrung von Trümmerfrauen (16. Januar 1995, 9.30 Uhr, Rathaussaal)'.

[149] See Peter Dömeland, 'Es begann mit der Sprengung der Türme von St. Ulrich', *Volksstimme*, 13 January 1993, p. 9; 'Zum 16. Januar: Bilder einer doppelten Zerstörung in unserer Stadt', *Volksstimme*, 17 January 1993, p. 10.

[150] Starting in the 1980s, the discussion on the return of the sculpture preceded the collapse of the SED dictatorship. See StAM, Rep. 41/604, Kirchenfragen Sicherung der Ruine Johanniskirche und Auswahl eines Standortes für die Plastik 'Trauernde Magdeburg', 1987–9; Rep. 12U 44, Nachlass Gerling. Plastik 'Trauernde Magdeburg', 1987–92.

'prayer for peace', which continued throughout the early 1990s. Thematically, the Church kept its distance from the political elites, commenting critically on the social and cultural changes in the wake of unification, as the following example from 1992 illustrates. 'Has [unification] also changed the memory of the casualties of war; the recognition that we as Germans were guilty and that this guilt was paid back through the bombing terror of the Americans and British?' asked cathedral preacher Giselher Quast in his commemorative address.[151] Drawing attention to the introduction of the People's Day of Mourning in Magdeburg, Quast took exception to the military ceremonial that accompanied the new ritual, in particular the language of honour that was employed by the political elites. 'On 16 January we do not honour the dead in Magdeburg because their death was not honourable but painful,' he stressed. With reference to the dead soldiers of World War II, he added, 'We do not honour them because they did not die on the field of honour but on the field of German guilt – we pity them as agents of an unlawful system against which they could not or would not stand up, and who were torn from their families and our people.' According to Quast, the only Christian way was one of 'emphatic pacifism', which was not commensurable with any politics. '[Pacifism] will always be a provocation' – in the GDR no less than in unified Germany, he concluded.

Conclusion

Recent literature on 'air wars, memory wars' has suggested that there was something distinctly novel about 'the invocation of bombings past to critique bombings present' in early 21st-century Germany.[152] Andreas Huyssen, for example, has argued that, in its opposition to the Iraq War of 2003, the German peace movement 'for the first time . . . bolstered its position by referring directly to the experience of strategic bombings of German cities in World War II'.[153] As this chapter has shown, such a thesis is untenable. On the level of local culture, the renaissance of interest in World War II bombing preceded the 'turn of the tide' in the German memory culture of the early 2000s by at least two decades.[154] In Kassel no less than in Magdeburg, the NATO double-track decision of December 1979 provided the political catalyst for new investment in

---

[151] Archiv der Evangelischen Domgemeinde, Magdeburg, 'Friedensgebet 16.1.1992: Barlachehrenmal'.

[152] Nolan, 'Air Wars, Memory Wars', 25.

[153] Huyssen, 'Air War Legacies', 164f. See also Nolan, 'Air Wars, Memory Wars', 24, footnote 63.

[154] Frei, '1945 und wir', p. 21.

a memory place that had been institutionalised in local culture since the early 1950s.[155] A set of meanings and rituals was still in place when local politicians, clerics and peace activists infused the *lieu de mémoire* with new political relevance in the 1980s. In Magdeburg, 80,000 residents attended a state-sponsored mass rally on 16 January 1985, which turned the fortieth anniversary of the bombing into a 'day of struggle' against the 'NATO arms build-up'. Meanwhile, in Kassel, on 22 October 1983, more than 1,800 residents crammed into the city's central church in order to attend a commemorative service on the fortieth anniversary of the cataclysmic air raid, while in a nearby church, peace activists staged all-night prayer and fasting.

While there was remarkable continuity throughout the 1980s and 1990s in the basic format of commemoration despite the ebb and flow of peace movement activity and, in Magdeburg, regime change, there were important shifts in content. The period witnessed the gradual erosion of the dominant status of an interpretation of events that had stressed the victimhood of the local community in World War II aerial bombing. By the mid-1980s, discursive power had passed into the hands of a generation that, unburdened by personal responsibility for the catastrophic past, showed a greater sensitivity for the historical context and a greater receptivity to the memory of the Holocaust. For members of the generation of '68, but also of the older 'sceptical generation', mass death in World War II bombing no longer attested, first and foremost, to the victimhood or martyrdom of the memory group but, increasingly, also to their complicity in the crimes of Nazism.

---

[155] Compare also Malte Thießen's findings for Hamburg: 'Gedenken an "Operation Gomorrha"', 56.

Part II

Confronting destruction

5   'What we have lost': framing urban destruction, 1940–1960

Introduction

The sun starts her daily round
She rises in eternal beauty.
But quickly she covers her face,
Looking for a town that cannot be found.[1]

Thus concludes the anonymous poem, 'Thus Died My Home Town', which circulated widely among the residents of Kassel in the months following the attack of 22 October 1943.[2] The metaphor of the sun covering her face derives from an observation that was made frequently in the aftermath of heavy fire bombings. The thick concentration of smoke particles in the air tended to blot out the sun, casting the devastated cityscape in an eerie twilight. In employing the imagery of sentimental poetry, the text not only renders a disconcerting experience consumable, it also gives expression to a sense of irredeemable loss. The term 'death' is used both descriptively and metaphorically, referring to the destruction of human life and material objects as well as of the 'home town' as a place of belonging. The example serves as a reminder that bombing did not just terminate the lives of thousands of residents, but transformed the urban environment beyond recognition.

A certain prevalence of material destruction in post-war representations of the air war has often been noted, and sometimes been taken as evidence of a prioritisation of the cultural over the human losses in German post-war society.[3] Less often has the notion of destruction itself been analysed. What did Germans think they had lost in the air war? How did they conceptualise the impact of aerial warfare on their material, social and imagined environment? What kind of language did they use to talk about it, and to what purpose?

[1] 'So starb meine Heimatstadt'. See introduction and Appendix 1.
[2] The title of this chapter comes from 'Was wir verloren haben . . .', *KZ*, 22 October 1953, p. 1.
[3] See Heinemann, 'The Hour of the Woman'.

This chapter argues that German city-dwellers of the mid-twentieth century responded to the devastation by turning to two concepts that were readily available to them: to the concepts of *Heimat* and *Kultur*. As 'historical ideas', both had been in use since the early nineteenth century to define ways of belonging and distinction, to lay claim to the unique and the universal, and to construct images of the self and the other.[4] Although Germans tried to make sense of what had happened to the locality by framing their perceptions in traditional ways, there were significant changes over time.[5] An analysis of the evolution of the two ideas in the period 1940 to 1960 can help to illuminate continuities and ruptures in the memory cultures of Kassel and Magdeburg as well as identify parallels and differences between them.

The connection between the notions of *Kultur* and *Heimat* on the one hand and strategic bombing on the other was established during the war. From early on, Nazi propaganda denounced allied bombing as a wilful assault on German culture, insinuating that the destruction of cultural monuments was a means to the end of annihilating the racial identity of the German *Volk*.[6] By comparison, the idea of *Heimat* was less often invoked in the official propaganda but featured prominently in a semi-public undercurrent of popular opinion that drew on primary experiences. Stripped of their *völkisch* connotations, both ideas retained an important place in local discourse beyond the watershed of 1945. Indeed, the flexibility and positive connotation of both concepts made them attractive to influential agents of memory in both Kassel and Magdeburg. Owing to its inclusive nature, *Heimat* became a crucial category for the post-war world: the term was drawn upon to articulate feelings of longing and belonging, to invoke ideals of common endeavour and social harmony, and to reflect on rupture and continuity. While rooted in the locality, the notion could also be constructed as an 'interchangeable representation' of the region and the nation.[7] Most important of all, perhaps, *Heimat* was by definition at the receiving end of organised violence: *Heimat* could be defended in war, it could endure and suffer, but it could not go to war itself.[8] The same was true of *Kultur*, which

---

[4] On the idea of *Heimat* see Applegate, *A Nation of Provincials*; Confino, 'Nation as Local Metaphor'; Confino, *The Nation as Local Metaphor*; Confino, 'This Lovely Country'. On the notion of *Kultur* as used in Germany since the late eighteenth century see Fisch, 'Zivilisation, Kultur'.

[5] For the relationship between continuity and change in German memory since 1870 see Koshar, *From Monuments to Traces*, pp. 1–14.

[6] Echoes of this narrative have recently been repopularised by Friedrich, *The Fire*, p. 466: 'Potsdam was destroyed in order to annul the history of Prussian militarism.'

[7] Confino, 'Nation as Local Metaphor', 50.

[8] Ibid., p. 73. For a contrasting reading that stresses the 'masculine' qualities of the institutionalised *Heimat* movement see Oberkrome, *'Deutsche Heimat'*, p. 144.

remained important as an indicator of loss, a marker of civic identity, and a bridge between the locality and the wider world. Both concepts thus provided ways for urban societies to talk about the allied air war without talking about local investment in the German war of aggression and genocide.

In Kassel as well as Magdeburg, the impact of aerial warfare on *Kultur* and *Heimat* was explored by way of three narrative codes or languages. The carriers of public memory quantified loss by producing figures, spoke of 'their' town in anthropomorphic metaphors, and visualised urban destruction through photographs and drawings. While, at first, there were only minor differences in the ways that these codes were used in Kassel and Magdeburg, this changed with the escalation of the Cold War from 1948/9. Whereas in Kassel loss tended to be discussed in affective and aesthetic categories – condensed in the nostalgic image of the 'beautiful old town' – in Magdeburg political usages dominated a public discourse that revolved around the twin themes of criminal destruction and heroic rebuilding.

Establishing the parameters, 1940–45

*'Bombs on a thousand years': urban destruction as a
'crime against Kultur'*

In response to allied air raids, Nazi propaganda habitually pointed to the great damage that the attacks had caused to cultural monuments such as historic buildings and churches.[9] This was a stock propaganda response, which allowed the Nazi media to talk about strategic bombing without saying much. The emphasis on *Kultur* served to conceal the real extent of the destruction – including war industries – while providing a lever with which to indict the allied conduct of the air war as criminal.[10] *Kultur* was an important term in the *lingua tertii imperii* for several reasons. The politicisation and nationalisation of the concept in the wake of World War I allowed Nazism to pose as defender of the material and spiritual values of the nation against the threat of materialist nihilism (*Unkultur*).[11] Moreover, the term was easily infused with ideas of racial supremacy, as *Trübners* German Dictionary in its 1943 edition illustrates. The entry defined *Kultur* in the words of Joseph Goebbels as the 'highest expression

---

[9] German M. Vonau, 'Bomben auf 1000 Jahre [Bombs on a Thousand Years]', *KLZ*, 12 November 1943, p. 1.
[10] Compare BA Berlin, R 55 / 20898, fos. 43f., press conference, 30 March 1942; ibid., NS 18/1058, fo. 110, 'Propagandistische Auswertung des Angriffs auf Köln', 30 June 1943.
[11] Fisch, 'Zivilisation, Kultur', pp. 759–66.

of the creative forces of a people'. It went on to present the activities of German paramilitaries after World War I – and by implication the present war of aggression – as a defensive war on behalf of 'European culture' against the 'threat of annihilation from the east'.[12]

The propaganda theme of strategic bombing as a deliberate attack on Germany's cultural heritage was adapted to the local circumstances of Kassel in the aftermath of 22 October 1943. This was above all the work of two local propagandists, Hans Schlitzberger (1902–78) and German M. Vonau (1900–56), who published a string of articles on the subject in the official Nazi newspaper, the *Kurhessische Landeszeitung*, in the autumn of 1943. Schlitzberger, a rabid anti-Semite, was the paper's editor and second in command of the regional propaganda office;[13] Vonau was a conservative fellow-traveller of Nazism who gained in importance in regional propaganda as the war progressed, featuring as editor in chief of the *Kurhessische Landeszeitung* by the autumn of 1943.[14]

In a leader of 6 November 1943, 'The New Beginning', Schlitzberger developed a narrative that revolved around a number of sharp opposites: matter versus spirit; creativity versus nihilism; good versus evil.[15] The 'criminal destruction by nihilist forces' had destroyed material goods, but 'the eternal German spirit of research' (*der ewige deutsche Forschergeist*) had survived. Clearly, the article was designed to boost the morale of the local population, to stress survival over death and continuity over rupture. In so doing, the author revealed something of the ambivalence with which Nazism viewed the air war. According to Schlitzberger, the 'catastrophe' was not to be regretted. For 'together with all the good and great things that have been destroyed, much that was superfluous and a hindrance has been weeded out as well'. Foremost among the latter was 'the spirit of the big city (*Geist der Großstadt*) that has caused so much damage to our racial (*völkisch*) soul'.[16] In its stead, 'the spirit of the front' had entered the devastated city. In Schlitzberger's interpretation, then, fire bombings functioned as a cathartic force that destroyed matter but purified the racial spirit. On balance, gain outweighed loss.[17]

---

[12] *Trübners Deutsches Wörterbuch*, vol. IV, pp. 298–300.

[13] See BA Berlin, R 55/645, fo. 14, Hans Schlitzberger to Ministerialdirektor Berndt, 7 July 1943; Schlitzberger was Gauverlagsleiter of the Gauverlag Kurhessen GmbH.

[14] Vonau is also listed as editor in chief of *Der Propagandist: Mitteilungsblatt der Gaupropagandaleitung* after the relaunch in June 1944. See BA Berlin R 55/610, fo. 85; on his life and career see also StAK, S1 no. 2379, German M. Vonau.

[15] Hans Schlitzberger, 'Der neue Anfang', *KLZ*, 6 November 1943, p. 1.

[16] Compare also Schlitzberger's comments in 'Zerstörerkraft gegen Schöpfergeist', *KLZ*, 13/14 November 1943, p. 1. On the hostility of Nazism towards the big city see Marchand, 'Nationalsozialismus und Großstadtfeindschaft', and more generally Bergmann, *Agrarromantik und Großstadtfeindschaft*.

[17] See also, with reference to the bombing of Dresden, Robert Ley, *Der Angriff*, 3 March 1945, p. 1.

In contrast to Schlitzberger, Vonau put a different emphasis on urban destruction. To be sure, he was no less vitriolic in his condemnation of the allied conduct of the air war. But in his leader of 12 November 1943, 'Bombs on a Thousand Years – Terror has Destroyed the Historic Face of Kassel', there was none of Schlitzberger's indifference to the fate of cultural monuments.[18] On the contrary, the destruction of *Kultur* was the linchpin around which Vonau's argument revolved. Drawing on the popular distinction between Western civilisation as the gratification of material needs and European *Kultur* as the material expression of spiritual values, Vonau accused the Western allies of ignorance and hypocrisy. He, too, worked with a number of stark opposites: the air war was a war of 'merciless terror' and 'fanatical hatred' against 'awe-inspiring', 'noble' and 'holy' cultural monuments. Their destruction amounted to a desecration, an 'irreplaceable loss to all of cultured mankind [*Kulturmenschheit*]' that left 'human beings conscious of history and culture speechless'.[19] Giving a detailed description of the destroyed architectural monuments of Kassel, Vonau depicted the city as a living organism of which the 'historic face' had been disfigured and the 'body' been trampled on by an 'enemy on a rampage of blood and destruction'.[20]

Without doubt, Vonau's emphasis on the extent of the cultural loss served to accentuate the greatness of the alleged crime. Within the overall argument, the fate of the locality mattered not so much for its own sake but as an illustration for the war as a whole. This conceptualisation, however, also allowed the author to express a sense of shock: the air raid of 22 October amounted to an irredeemable loss of the city's architectural heritage, and by implication, of local identity, '[The enemy] has burnt down and blown up the indefinable magic of the thousand-year-old town, which we try to capture in the words of culture, tradition, art, and history.'[21] In lamenting the loss of the 'indefinable magic' of Kassel, Vonau articulated a sense of belonging. The 'thousand-year-old town' was a metaphor for the nation; it was also *Heimat*.

---

[18] German M. Vonau, 'Bomben auf 1000 Jahre', *KLZ*, 12 November 1943, p. 1. The article first appeared under the title 'Kulturschänder am Pranger', in *Die Innere Front. Pressedienst der NSDAP*, 11 November 1943, pp. 1f. See also Vonau, 'Das Haus an der Wildemannsgasse', *KLZ*, 8 November 1943, p. 3; as well as the series 'Stätten im Herzen der Kasselaner', *KLZ*, 23/24 October 1943, p. 3; 25 October 1943, p. 4; 27 October 1943, p. 3; 28 October 1943, p. 3; 6 November 1943, p. 5.

[19] Vonau, 'Bomben auf 1000 Jahre'.

[20] Ibid. For a detailed description of war losses and post-war reconstruction and neglect of architectural monuments in Kassel see Beseler and Gutschow, *Kriegsschicksale Deutscher Architektur*, vol. II, pp. 856–86. For Magdeburg see Eckardt (ed.), *Schicksale deutscher Baudenkmale*, vol. I, pp. 247–70.

[21] Vonau, 'Bomben auf 1000 Jahre'. On the importance of the notion of the 'beautiful old town' for regional identities in Germany see Paul, 'Der Wiederaufbau der historischen Städte', pp. 119f.; Beyme, *Der Wiederaufbau*, pp. 13–22.

'Heimat Remains!'?

Grimm's German Dictionary of 1877 defined *Heimat* in relation to place, either real or imagined. *Heimat* was 'the land or region where one was born or lived permanently', the 'place of birth or permanent residence', the 'parental home or estate', or, in a transcendental perspective, heaven.[22] If *Heimat* resided in place, then what happened to the idea when the place itself was radically transformed? The answer that local propagandists gave to this question was unequivocal: '*Heimat* Remains!' was the characteristic title of a poem by the local poet Willi Lindner, which appeared in the *Kurhessische Landeszeitung* on 3 November 1943.[23] On the whole, however, Nazi propaganda preferred not to dwell too much on the impact of allied bombing on *Heimat*.

After all, the regime had led the nation into an aggressive war on the understanding that the *Heimat* would provide for the material and immaterial needs of the front, but would not itself be turned into a war zone.[24] The confident boast ascribed to Hermann Göring from the summer of 1939 that no enemy plane would penetrate the borders of the Reich illustrated this understanding. And as late as June 1943, the party chancellery objected to a proposal by the propaganda ministry to use the term 'air war areas' in relation to the cities of the heavily bombed Ruhr region.[25] On a more general level, Nazism was deeply suspicious of any idea of *Heimat* that did not encompass the neologism of '*Heimatfront*'.[26] While drawing on the patriotic fervour and communitarian idealism, Nazi propagandists despised the love of provincialism and the tolerance of diversity that stood at the core of the historic enunciation of the idea.[27] *Trübners* German Dictionary of 1939 remarked critically that the term, while carrying connotations of the Latin *patria*, lacked the 'political significance' of the younger term, *fatherland*.[28]

It was therefore no coincidence that public reflections on the impact of allied bombing on *Heimat* as a place of belonging played only a marginal role in Nazi propaganda, and were typically left to the medium of lyrical poetry. Willi Lindner in 'Heimat Remains!' insisted that *Heimat* rested

---

[22] *Deutsches Wörterbuch*, vol. X, pp. 864f.
[23] Willi Lindner, 'Die Heimat bleibt bestehen!', *KLZ*, 3 November 1943, p. 3. Compare also Karl Holzamer, 'Heimat ohme Heim', *Reichsrundfunk* 9, December 1943, pp. 175f.
[24] Compare 'Und Du?', *Die neue Gemeinschaft* 44, August 1940, pp. 1f.
[25] BA Berlin, NS 18/500, fo. 74, Bormann to Goebbels, 18 June 1943.
[26] See, for example, 'Propaganda der Tat. Schnappschüsse vom Frontabschnitt "Heimat"', *Der Propagandist. Mitteilungen der Gaupropagandaleitung Kurhessen* 1 (1944), 18–21. For the historical roots of this suspicion see the classic treatment by Mason, 'Erbschaft der Novemberrevolution'.
[27] Compare Applegate, *A Nation of Provincials*, p. 212.
[28] *Trübners Deutsches Wörterbuch*, vol. III, pp. 387f.

in nature and was indestructible as long as there were affective bonds between the people and their locality.[29] A week later, the writer Fritz Stuck unwittingly demonstrated the helplessness of official propaganda in the face of unprecedented devastation with his poem 'My Kassel' (*Mein Kassel*).[30] The text revolves around a 'holy oath' to home town and fatherland that the lyrical 'I' renews after the bombing. Drawing on the stock repertoire of Nazi phraseology, the 'I' of the poem commemorates the dead as 'heroes' who sacrificed their lives and invokes the archetypal 'Hessian loyalty', which 'stands guard' in the rubble. Any recognition of the scale of the destruction is immediately countered by professions of faith in victory and the city's phoenix-like rise from the rubble in an indefinite future. The poem concludes with the conjuring up of a 'proud ring of forests' that performs what the Nazi regime was unable to do: 'to guard the soil of the *Heimat*'.[31]

While National Socialist propaganda privileged notions of cultural loss over those associated with *Heimat*, there were private voices that told a very different story. Far from subscribing to the optimistic rhetoric of official propaganda, these voices contemplated the possibility that the bombs might have destroyed not only material goods and an unprecedented number of residents but the very idea of *Heimat* itself.[32] It is indicative of the force of these voices that they found collective expression in the cultural artefacts of anonymous lyrical poetry.[33] The most prominent, 'Thus Died My Home Town', established a link between *Heimat* and death in its very title, while local renditions of the popular 'Friesenlied' adopted a tone that was sarcastic rather than elegiac, as the first stanza of the 'Kasseler Heimatlied' illustrates:[34]

> Where the roofs lie scattered in the streets
> . . .
> Where bombers circle in the skies at night
> Where entire city districts burn from time to time
> Where ruins stand in empty fields
> There is my home, Kassel on the river Fulda.

Interestingly, between the two versions of the 'Friesenlied' in circulation in Kassel, there existed noteworthy differences in the ways that the impact of the bombing was described. While the 'Heimatlied' insisted that suffering had strengthened the affective ties towards the *Heimat*,

---

[29] Willi Lindner, 'Die Heimat bleibt bestehen!', *KLZ*, 3 November 1943, p. 3.
[30] For the full text plus translation see Appendix 3.
[31] Fritz Stück, 'Mein Kassel', *KLZ*, 11 November 1943, p. 3.   [32] See chapter 1.
[33] See introduction.
[34] For the text plus translation see Appendix 2. On the popularity of the 'Friesenlied' see Max Kuckei, '"Wo de Nordseewellen"', *Niederdeutsche Welt* 15/6, June 1940, pp. 94f.

the second rendition, 'The Song of the Sorrowful Kassel' (*Das Lied vom leidgeprüften Kassel*), spoke of disbelief rather than affection: 'Kassel, my home, I don't recognise you anymore.'[35] Whereas the 'Heimatlied' concluded on a note of determination – 'Kassel, my home; I love like my blood' – the second version resignedly had 'Kassel, my home, say, "It is enough!".'

In Magdeburg, the local Nazi media likewise habitually denounced strategic bombing in terms of a desecration of *Kultur*. On occasion, propagandists also used the concept to legitimise the German war of conquest as a defensive campaign on behalf of Occidental culture, which united the peoples of Continental Europe against the combined threat of Bolshevist and Anglo-American 'nihilism' (*Unkultur*).[36] In comparison with Kassel, however, the theme was not adapted to local circumstances with quite the same intensity. This was no surprise, given that Magdeburg was not subjected to indiscriminate area bombing until January 1945. By that time, the official media no longer provided an outlet for purely local developments. Similarly, the notion of the air war as the destruction of *Heimat* played an important role in private correspondence, but by early 1945 no longer found expression through cultural artefacts as it had done in Kassel fifteen months earlier.

Articulating loss, 1945–60

Kultur and *Heimat* remained crucial concepts for the framing of urban destruction across the watershed of May 1945. In important ways, they provided bridges for elements of the wartime narrative into the post-war world. Shorn of their overtly racial connotations, both furnished important frames for articulating feelings of loss, bereavement and resentment. Next to continuity, there was also change. With the collapse of the nation state, *Heimat* displaced *Kultur* from its dominant position. This shift reflected the extent to which the semi-public counter-narrative of the war years filled the vacuum that was left by the discontinuation of Nazi propaganda in the spring of 1945. Equally importantly, local societies developed new 'languages' in which to discuss the material impact of aerial warfare: these were the languages of figures and images. While both had roots in the war years, they rose to public prominence only under the altered conditions of the post-war world.

---

[35] StAK, S8 C53, Literarische Verarbeitung.
[36] 'Um die Kultur des Abendlandes', *Magdeburgische Zeitung*, 8/9 April 1944, p. 1. See also Rudolf Jordan, 'Der Bombenkrieg', *Der Mitteldeutsche*, 23 January 1944, p. 1.

The language of figures

'The only authority that has so far been able to create order out of rubble . . . is the statistician,' wrote Carl Otto Hamann in the regional daily *Hessische Nachrichten* in the autumn of 1945. 'The bare figures draw a portrait of the destroyed city, recording for the present and the future the horrifying picture of a tormented community that has been sacrificed to the madness of an idea,' the journalist continued.[37] The excerpt attests to the importance that statistical data gained in the post-war discussion of urban destruction. Creating a semblance of order out of chaos, they promised to provide objective criteria for measuring the material impact of aerial warfare. The language of figures was the language of the political and planning elites, who ascertained and promulgated statistical data in order to demonstrate both their expertise and the 'sacrifice' of the local community. Figures provided the basis for petitions to the occupying powers and claims on supra-local authorities for the allocation of much-needed funds.[38] At the same time, control of the statistical data immunised post-war city planning against critical interventions 'from below'.

On a more general level, the language of figures shaped ways of perception. In both Kassel and Magdeburg, the impact of allied bombing was measured by three criteria that shared in common their exclusive focus on civilian loss and hardship: firstly, the post-war population as compared with the 1939/43 population figure; secondly, the number of civilian dwellings damaged or destroyed; and finally, the amount of rubble in cubic metres or cubic metres per capita.[39] This is not to deny that there were perfectly legitimate reasons for the city administration to do so. After all, rubble clearance was a necessary prerequisite for any rebuilding work while the shortage of housing constituted the most pressing social problem of the post-war years. It is, however, to argue that all three criteria lent weight to an interpretation of the allied air offensive that reduced strategic bombing to indiscriminate area bombing, and area bombing in turn to a deliberate attack on civilian infrastructure.

In the immediate post-war period of 1945–8, there were only marginal differences in the ways that local political elites in Kassel and Magdeburg

---

[37] Carl Otto Hamann, 'Zahlen zwischen Trümmern', *HN*, 14 November 1945, p. 3.
[38] Compare *Verwaltungsbericht der Stadt Kassel 1945–1949*, pp. 153–6; StAK, NL Seidel, Reden, vol. I, pp. 659–67, 'Kassel baut auf', 5 May 1946; StAK, A.1.10, no. 53, Berichte an den Regierungspräsidenten, Staatsministerien, Minister & Militärregierung, *passim*; StAK, A.0, Stadtverordnetenversammlung, vol. V, pp. 20f., minutes, 28 July 1947.
[39] For the extraordinary problems connected with any attempt at establishing reliable figures of loss see the discussion in Hohn, *Zerstörung*, pp. 34–50.

presented and utilised their figures of loss. In Kassel, mayor Willi Seidel (SPD) set the tone in a public speech that he gave on the opening of the exhibition 'Kassel is Rebuilding!' in May 1946. Before an audience of planning experts, regional and state-level government representatives and the occupation authorities, Seidel ranked Kassel among those cities that had been 'most severely destroyed in our German fatherland'. 'All that has remained of Kassel except for the unique landscape and thousand years of history is a heap of rubble,' he continued. In order to illustrate the extent of loss, Seidel emphasised that only 16,000 dwelling units had survived the war out of a pre-war figure of 65,000.[40]

The mayor left the details to the municipal architect (*Baurat*), Erich Heinicke (SPD), who likewise stressed the exceptional nature of the local situation: 'From the study of the figures anybody will realise that our city has suffered exceptional destruction under the impact of total war in comparison with other German cities.' This claim of negative distinction was based on the criterion of rubble per capita. Heinicke produced figures that put Kassel well ahead of all other cities, with 27 cubic metres per person as compared with 20 for Cologne, 18 for Frankfurt and 9 for Hamburg. He went on to stress that the figures were deceptive because they had been calculated on the basis of the pre-war population. If, however, one took the present city population into the equation, Kassel would bear an even higher rate of rubble per capita. Heinicke's remarks were no mere play on numbers but served the explicit purpose of underlining 'the real situation in our city' before an audience of influential decision makers.[41] One year later, the city received official confirmation of its exceptional status within the state of Hesse. The state ministry of reconstruction authorised figures that put the level of destruction in Kassel at 77.6 per cent, placing the city well ahead of Darmstadt with 46.7 per cent and Frankfurt with 32.7 per cent.[42]

If the language of figures was used to draw attention to the plight of the town, it also served to legitimise the reconstruction and silence potential critics. Post-war urban planning in Kassel derived from blueprints that architects working for the bureau of reconstruction under Albert Speer had drawn up in 1944/5. Premised on the assumption of near-total destruction, the plans combined elements from the early 1940s, when it was intended to transform the city into a representative regional capital

---

[40] StAK, NL Seidel, Reden, vol. I, 'Kassel baut auf', 5 May 1946.

[41] The speech is reprinted in Durth and Gutschow, *Träume*, vol. II, pp. 807–10.

[42] StAK, A.0, Stadtverordnetenversammlung, vol. V, p. 20, minutes, 28 July 1947; 'Das Wohnungsproblem in Zahlen', *HN*, 2 August 1947; *Verwaltungsbericht der Stadt Kassel*, p. 153. Hohn, *Zerstörung*, puts the figure for Kassel at 60 per cent; see p. 271 (table 42).

(*Gauhauptstadt*), with the modernist ideal of a structured and relieved city.[43] Both approaches shared in common a profound disregard for the historical urban space.[44] Post-war continuity of these ideas was personified by Heinicke himself, who had headed the planning department since 1941 and was kept in office by the new administration despite the demands of the American occupation officer to dismiss him on account of his Nazi past.[45] Heinicke argued that the destruction was so vast as to necessitate, and indeed, to provide 'a unique opportunity to create a new healthy organism and a very far reaching new ordering', as he declared in 1946.[46]

A city-sponsored damage chart from July 1945 supported the municipal architect's claim about the near-total disappearance of the pre-war city in the air war. The chart placed many buildings in the category of total destruction (70–100 per cent) which earlier assessments had categorised as near total (70–80 per cent).[47] When the reconstruction exhibition 'Kassel is Rebuilding!' attracted heavy public criticism for showing blueprints from the time of the Third Reich, Mayor Seidel justified the exhibits by pointing to the level of destruction. On the occasion of a meeting of the Hessian Council for Reconstruction, he emphasised, 'I believe that the critics . . . overlook the fact that urban planning needs to make a distinction between moderately damaged cities on the one hand and cities that have suffered near-total destruction on the other. Kassel, unfortunately, belongs in the second category.'[48]

In Magdeburg, statistical data likewise were used to document the extent of material destruction. As in Kassel, the second civil administration of 1946–50 under mayor Rudolf Eberhard (SED) emphasised that the city had suffered exceptionally during the war. 'Among Germany's big cities, there are only a few that showed an image of destruction as desolate as in Magdeburg by the end of Hitler's war,' wrote the mayor in

---

[43] On the post-war reconstruction of Kassel see Lüken-Isberner, 'Kassel: Neue Stadt auf altem Grund'; König, 'Konflikt'; Durth and Gutschow, *Träume*, vol. II, pp. 791–809. For the context see Durth and Gutschow, *Träume*, vol I, pp. 161–220; Beyme *et. al.* (eds.), *Neue Städte*, pp. 9–31. Compare also, for an example of reconstruction under conservative auspices, the insightful study on Munich by Rosenfeld, *Munich and Memory*.

[44] For the general context see Durth and Gutschow, *Träume*, vol. I, pp. 237–80.

[45] See StAK, NL Seidel, Tagebuch, pp. 63f., 25 April 1946; ibid., p. 65, 6 May 1946.

[46] The speech is reprinted in Durth and Gutschow, *Träume*, vol. II, pp. 807–10, here p. 809.

[47] König, 'Konflikt', p. 101. A copy of the damage chart of July 1945 can be found in StAK, NL Kaltwasser, folder 42.

[48] 'Großhessischer Aufbaurat in Kassel', *HN*, 4 June 1946, p. 4. For a contemporary assessment of the public protests see Wolff, 'Kassel baut auf!'.

1946.[49] One year later, at a public rally, Eberhard put the tally of destruction for the most severely affected districts at 77.3 per cent, whereas the damage for the city as a whole was given as 60 per cent.[50] Yet it was not percentage points as in Kassel but the absolute number of destroyed dwelling units that became the most popular indicator of loss in Magdeburg. 'Through Hitler's war, 40,677 dwelling units have been totally destroyed, 5,499 lightly damaged and 1,295 severely damaged,' as the municipal architect Erich Koß (1899–1982) informed his audience at a public rally in the summer of 1947.[51]

In contrast to Kassel, in Magdeburg the tally of destruction was usually presented as the result of a historical cause. Where the Kassel mayor, Seidel, in the speech quoted above, had obliquely referred to a 'foolish system' that had caused 'wounds' and 'guilt', the Magdeburg political elites usually mentioned Hitler's name in connection with the balance-sheet of loss. For example, in 1947, Mayor Eberhard subtitled the section on urban destruction in a written report on the work of the civil administration with 'What Hitler cost us'. One year earlier, a chapter in *Ein Jahr Aufbauarbeit in Magdeburg* carried the title, 'The demolished city – legacy of a criminal leadership'.[52] Here, more strongly than in Kassel, the language of figures also served an educational purpose. In demonstrating the consequences of Nazi rule, it legitimised the 'new beginning' under the SED-led civil administration.

However, with the escalation of the Cold War in 1948/9, the name of Hitler was replaced by the names of the Western allies. In this new context, statistical data became stock figures in the propagandistic repertoire against the West: '40,677 totally destroyed dwelling units' was the headline of an article published in the SED daily, *Volksstimme*, on 16 January 1951. The article drew a direct link between the 'Anglo-American bombing terror' of World War II and contemporary policies of the 'American warmongers', quoting a US senator with a line reminiscent of Hitler's infamous remark about the eradication of British cities.[53] In line with the Socialist cult of numbers, figures formed an integral part of most official statements on the air war throughout the 1950s.[54] In 1952, for example, the commemorative article in the *Volksstimme* contained a

---

[49] *Ein Jahr Aufbauarbeit in Magdeburg*, ed. Magistrat der Stadt Magdeburg, p. 7.
[50] 'Die neue Stadt – das gemeinsame Werk', *Freiheit*, Magdeburger Beilage, 7 June 1947, p. 5.
[51] Ibid.
[52] 'Verehrung dem Alten – Mut zum Neuen', *Freiheit*, 7 June 1947, p. 5; *Ein Jahr Aufbauarbeit*, p. 7.
[53] *Volksstimme*, 16 January 1951, p. 4.
[54] Compare Danyel, 'Politische Rituale als Sowjetimporte', p. 74.

special section entitled 'The Result of 40 Minutes of War', in which detailed figures were given of the numbers and types of bombs used, people killed, housing, public buildings, schools, meeting halls, church buildings, cinemas, theatres, museums and hospitals destroyed.[55] The list had been compiled from the official report of the Nazi chief of police from March 1945, with two significant omissions. The army installations and industrial plant that were listed in the original document were left out.[56]

Figures formed an important element of urban memory cultures. As the preserve of the political elites, they established order out of chaos, provided 'scientific' evidence for claims of negative distinction and positive achievement, legitimised the modernising objectives of reconstruction, and served as ammunition in the propaganda battles of the Cold War. For the memory culture as a whole, however, the visual played an even greater role. Images were the most important medium through which urban societies engaged with urban destruction.[57] In both Kassel and Magdeburg, visual representations were crucial for the way in which institutions, organised groups and individuals remembered aerial warfare.

The language of images

Within a few hours, . . . the *Gau* capital of *Kurhesse* [was turned] into a field of rubble whose ruins accusingly rise up against the sky, bearing witness to the senseless destruction at the hands of the Anglo-American conduct of the air war.[58]

The quotation, from the 'summary report' on the air raid of 22 October 1943, is illuminating in several respects. Not only does it anticipate the central medium of urban memory cultures, the visual, it also draws attention to two important functions of (photographic) visualisations: they are produced and reproduced for their documentary as well as their symbolic value. Photography is a polysemous medium that speaks to the mind and the emotions in equal measure; it is both document and fetish.[59] In the

---

[55] *Volksstimme*, 16 January 1952, p. 4.
[56] See NA RG 243 E-6, file no. 39 9 (box 383), 'Erfahrungsbericht über den schweren Terrorangriff auf den LS-Ort Magdeburg am 16.1.1945', 5 March 1945.
[57] Compare Glasenapp, 'Nach dem Brand'; Glasenapp, *Nachkriegsfotografie*, pp. 100–134. On the importance of the visual for memory see Burke, 'History as Social Memory', p. 101.
[58] StAK, S8 C40, 'Erfahrungsbericht', 7 December 1943, p. 13.
[59] Sekula, 'On the Invention of Photographic Meaning'; Sontag, *On Photography*, pp. 3–27, 153–80; Barthes, *Camera Lucida*; Brink, *Ikonen der Vernichtung*, pp. 9–19.

example, the chief of police attempts to capture the impact of allied bombing by focusing on the image of the 'field of rubble': the ruins are documents of what has happened and at the same time symbols of an allegedly criminal act.

Allan Sekula has influentially argued that photographic communication may be understood as an 'incomplete utterance' the readability of which depends 'on some external matrix of conditions and presuppositions'.[60] Yet, as Susan Sontag has pointed out, the meaning of any visual message remains fragile: even the most straightforward caption cannot guarantee the channelling of reader responses in a certain direction; it privileges only one among several possible ways of reading the image.[61] Recognising the polysemous potential of the medium, Nazi propagandists attempted to restrict the semantic potential of visual utterances by straightforward textual frames. 'Images accuse!' was the headline of a typical article in the *Kasseler Post* of 12 September 1940, which showed three close-ups of bomb damage to civilian dwellings.[62] Yet there was no way of knowing for the propagandists if the photographs were really received in the intended manner or if they also communicated another message, namely, the inability of the Nazi regime to prevent destruction by a superior antagonist. Joseph Goebbels himself acknowledged this conundrum when in the autumn of 1944 he cancelled a propaganda project of special commemorative stamps that were to carry famous cultural landmarks. 'Those images . . . back then [in 1943] were capable of eliciting feelings of anger and revenge, [but] today [they] will only cause resignation,' as his decision was paraphrased in the official document closing the file.[63] Likewise, visual representations in the press were curtailed significantly as actual damage escalated.[64]

This section argues that it was precisely the polysemous nature of visual narratives that accounts for the popularity of photography in post-war memory cultures of the air war. Photos could be invested with multi-layered meanings, document and symbolise very different things. For the same reason, the visual remained a difficult medium for the local political and journalistic elites, presenting them with problems not unlike those

---

[60] Sekula, 'On the Invention of Photographic Meaning', p. 85; Glasenapp, *Nachkriegsfotografie*, p. 27, speaks of 'the deficiency of the medium when it comes to generating meaning'.

[61] Sontag, *On Photography*, p. 109.   [62] 'Bilder klagen an!', *KP*, 12 September 1940.

[63] BA Berlin, R 55/611, Propaganda gegen feindlichen Luftterror durch Sonderbriefmarken, fo. 161, 29 November 1944.

[64] Compare BA Berlin, NS 18/1333, fo. 61, 'Wiedergabe der Aufnahmen von Großschadensstellen in der Presse', 9 October 1942; ibid., fos. 73–6, 'Propagandamaßnahmen im Zusammenhang mit dem Luftkrieg', 28 June 1943. See also Sachsse, *Erziehung zum Wegsehen*, p. 203.

facing their Nazi predecessors. This was particularly the case with rubble photography. For one, post-war visualisations of urban destruction stood in the tradition of the well-established usages of Nazi propaganda. Moreover, there was critical potential in rubble photography that was difficult to control. In Kassel, the civil administration threatened to sue a publisher of an illustrated book depicting ruins for fear of the negative impact on tourism.[65] In Magdeburg, panoramic views of the devastated cityscape drew attention to the spires of church ruins that the SED had earmarked for demolition against the opposition of the Protestant clergy.[66] One consequence was that in neither town were images of urban destruction as dominant in public discourse as has been suggested for post-war Germany as a whole;[67] another was that rubble photography was rarely left to 'speak for itself' but usually integrated into narrative frames. This holds true for both the guided media of Magdeburg as well as for the more pluralistic media of Kassel. Only in private photo albums do we find visual representations of destruction of which the commentary is descriptive rather than normative.[68]

Visual narratives in the two cities shared important features in common. They were made up of three elements, of which rubble photography was but one. Equally important were images of the city before the destruction and after the rebuilding. Indeed, more often than not, rubble motifs were integrated into broader visual (or textual) narratives of 'death' and 'rebirth'. In both cities, the photographic view tended to be selective, subsuming self-inflicted damage in the broad picture of indiscriminate bombing, erasing all visual references to the presence of Nazism, and prioritising the cultural over the industrial dimensions of loss. Finally, visual narratives in both cities showed an intense interest in local landmarks, which suggests that at the centre of local discourses stood the preservation and reformulation of local identities.

Throughout the period 1945 to 1960, visual narratives followed a trajectory that was shaped by the reconstruction. As the new city took shape, the initial juxtaposition of 'before the destruction–after the destruction' gave way to the triad of 'before–after–now', or was replaced with 'destroyed–rebuilt'. While this broader shift occurred in both of the cities under consideration here, differences deepened as a result of the

---

[65] StAK, A.1.00, Magistratsprotokolle, vol. XIII, minutes, 22 September 1949.
[66] AKPS, Rep. A Spec G. A795, St Ulrich; StAM, Rep. 41/416, Heiliggeistkirche; StAM, Rep. 41/918, Katharinenkirche; Reinhardt, *Magdeburg einst und jetzt*, pp. 35f.; Jakobs, 'Wie Phönix aus der Asche', p. 176.
[67] Glasenapp, *Nachkriegsfotografie*, p. 100.
[68] See, for example, StAK, photo archive, Wolf Bür, 'Fotoalbum. Frau Johann Schlieper zum 17.11.49'.

integration of Kassel and Magdeburg into the antagonistic socio-political systems of the Federal Republic and the GDR.

In Kassel, there were several visual narratives that competed with one another. The city administration promulgated a future-centred view that expressed confidence in a successful reconstruction, whereas journalists tended to focus on the desolate present. Publicists, meanwhile, wistfully looked back to a romanticised past. By contrast, the ruling elites in Magdeburg depicted the reconstruction as a quasi-sacral undertaking while they closely linked appeals to nostalgic sentiment with political objectives.

'Like a fellow human being that has left us': nostalgia

On New Year's Eve 1946, a remarkable article appeared in the *Kasseler Zeitung* that carried the title 'In memoriam anno . . . '.[69] The piece was a dream narrative in which a first-person narrator relived the happy days of an end-of-year pub crawl through the narrow alleys of the medieval old town of Kassel. The narrator recalls that his memory became blurred after pub number fourteen, but eyewitnesses assured him that the merry party went on to visit the public houses on the Altmarkt and Renthof. After this, even the eyewitnesses lost count, but according to rumour some made it to Graben, where they had been seen eating herring salad with bread buns. 'Fire crackers exploded, serpents swirled through the air, with paper streamers adding to the merry confusion. Confetti rained down, and the church bells chimed from the nearby Martinskirche. Happy New Year!', the narrator enthusiastically remembers. Then, suddenly, the present intrudes in the form of 'twelve heavy strokes'. He awakes, alone, shivering with cold. Through the half-barricaded window, a field of ruins stares him in the face.[70]

In the Kassel of the late 1940s and early 1950s, one of the most influential responses to the devastation was to close one's eyes and imagine that it had never happened. This is not to suggest, of course, that the residents of post-war Kassel permanently lived in a dream world. Rather, it is to argue for the considerable popularity not of rubble photography but of nostalgic images that dealt in an unscathed city. At the centre of this narrative stood the idea of *Heimat* as captured in the myth of *Alt-Kassel* or 'Old Kassel'. Popularised through a range of diverse media – historical exhibitions, postcard series, calendars, commemorative articles,

---

[69] 'In memoriam anno . . . ', *Kasseler Zeitung*, 30 December 1946. 'Like a fellow human being . . . ': Vonau, *Kassel. Bauwerke einer alten Stadt*, p. 5.
[70] 'In memoriam anno . . . ', *Kasseler Zeitung*, 30 December 1946.

film – nostalgia even spawned its own literary genre, the memory book.[71] With titles like *Kassel – Buildings of an Old Town* or *Kassel before the Firestorm*, these publications were not interested in delineating the causes of the disaster that had struck the city.[72] Nor were they interested in the reality of life in pre-war urban society. They traded in an imagined past of beauty, social harmony and innocence (Fig. 22).

As an influential cultural phenomenon, nostalgia, the 'painful longing for home', has received insufficient attention in studies of the occupation and the early Federal Republic. The evidence from Kassel suggests that the dominant view, according to which there was little regret over the loss of places and a 'relative absence of . . . nostalgia after 1945', needs to be reconsidered.[73] Not only were romanticised images of the 'beautiful old town' far more popular than rubble photography, nostalgia also provided a bridge for elements of wartime propaganda into the post-war world. The continuity across the divide of 1945/9 was not just one of narrative but also of narrator. For Kassel, this was personified by the propagandist, journalist and art critic German M. Vonau. During the war, Vonau, together with Hans Schlitzberger, had set the local parameters for the ways in which the air war was conceptualised as a criminal assault on German *Kultur*. After 1945, accusation turned into lamentation. The theme was divested of its overtly anti-Western tone and adapted to the new political realities. This was in no small measure due to the influence of Vonau himself. Whereas Schlitzberger disappeared from public view in 1945, Vonau joined the conservative daily, *Kasseler Post*, in 1949 and soon re-established himself as an important voice in local journalism. Through his journalistic work as well as a string of popular books, he fashioned himself as one of the most influential guardians of Kassel's cultural heritage.[74]

'How many years lie between us and the Kassel of old?' Vonau lamented in the preface to his *Kassel – Buildings of an Old Town*, published in 1950. 'And yet the city lives in our memory', he continued, 'like a place that we

---

[71] Staatliche Kunstsammlungen, *Alt-Kassel*; *Alt Kassel. Kalender auf das Jahr 1949* (1948); the postcard series 'Kassel – die tausendjährige Stadt' and 'Alt-Kassel, die Heimstatt althessischer Bau- und Handwerkskunst'; Karl Kaltwasser, 'Vergangenes Kassel', *HN*, 20 October 1945; 'Kassel einst und jetzt', dir. Kurt Lange (1938/45).

[72] Helm (ed.), *Kassel vor dem Feuersturm*; Vonau, *Kassel. Bauwerke einer Alten Stadt*; *Cassel und Wilhelmshöhe in alten Stichen und Lithographien* (1955); Kramm, *Kassel* (1951); *Merian* 4/10, 'Kassel'.

[73] Gutschow, 'Stadtzerstörung und Gedenken', pp. 268f.; Betts, 'Remembrance of Things Past', p. 180.

[74] Compare Vonau, *Kassel. Bauwerke einer Alten Stadt*; *Cassel und Wilhelmshöhe in alten Stichen und Lithographien*, text by G. M. Vonau (1955); Helm (ed.), *Kassel vor dem Feuersturm*, 2nd edn, with an afterword by G. M. Vonau (1953); *Hessisches Land*, with a preface by G. M. Vonau (1948); Vonau (ed.), *Führer durch Kassel und Wilhelmshöhe*.

Wehmütige Erinnerungen

Wehmütige Erinnerungen werden in vielen alten Kasseler Bürgern wach, angesichts dieses Aquarells, das der Kasseler Graphiker Kurt W i n t g e n s schuf und das einen Blick auf einen der reizvollsten Winkel der Kasseler Altstadt vor ihrer Zerstörung am schicksalsschweren Abend des 22. Oktober 1943 wiedergibt: Ein Stück der Obersten Gasse mit der Martinskirche zu der Zeit, als ihre spitzen Türme noch ein Wahrzeichen Kassels waren.

Heute jährt sich der Tag wieder, an dem vor elf Jahren dieser Teil und fast die ganze Altstadt in Rauch und Flammen aufging und viele tausend Kasseler Männer, Frauen und Kinder unter den Trümmern den Tod fanden. Ihr Andenken wird unvergessen sein und die Kirche in Gottesdiensten und durch Glockengeläut ihrer schweren Todesnot heute abend gedenken. Wie in jedem Jahr werden darüber hinaus weitere Gedenkfeiern, so die vor der Landesbibliothek auf dem Friedrichsplatz ebenfalls heute abend und am Sonntag auf dem Kasseler Hauptfriedhof, die Erinnerung an Kassels größtes Blutopfer im Lauf seiner tausendjährigen Geschichte wachhalten.

*

Keiner sollte sich ihrer erschütternden Mahnung verschließen, aus dem Bekenntnis zu den Toten aber den um so stärkeren Willen mitnehmen, dem Leben zu geben, was des Lebens ist, damit die letzten Zeugnisse dieser schweren Zeit aus unserer Heimatstadt verschwinden und das begonnene große Aufbauwerk vollendet wird.

Figure 22. 'Melancholy Memories' was the title of a commemorative article that appeared in the *Kasseler Zeitung* on the eleventh anniversary of the air raid. The watercolour drawing of the old town by Kurt Wintgens was a typical example of 1950s nostalgia.

visited years ago and have not yet seen again   like a fellow human being who has left us and of whom pictures and letters still lie on our desk.'[75] In the book, the material was arranged as a series of vignettes in which drawings of historical buildings were accompanied by short sketches of their architectural history. 'We become witness again to the building's hour of birth . . . It is like a discovery, a first rendezvous, even if we will never again see the building in the reality of the cityscape, which has been transformed by a dreadful event [*ungeheuerliches Geschehen*]'.[76]

The book was not a post-war idea but had been conceived during the Third Reich.[77] Indeed, the project stemmed from the time shortly before the city's destruction, and was justified to superior officers with reference to the likely loss of Kassel's architectural heritage in the near future.[78] In view of this, it is of little surprise that central elements of the post-war nostalgic narrative were prefigured in an article that Vonau had written in early November 1943 for the Nazi daily, *Kurhessische Landeszeitung*.[79] The article dealt with the destruction in the recent air raid of the so-called Grimmhaus, a half-timbered Renaissance building in which the two Romantic philologists Jacob and Wilhelm Grimm had lived from 1805 to 1814. 'Buildings have a face like humans,' Vonau declared, anthropomorphising his subject matter. 'In front of the rubble of the Grimmhaus, we stand in front of a beloved being; a beloved being that died, was murdered.' The destruction of the Grimmhaus called for mourning – 'mourning that all people conscious of *Kultur* ought to share'. Yet, in the injunction to mourn was embedded an injunction to hate, for the air war was 'annihilation, destruction, murder . . . extermination at all cost', as Vonau declared. While in 1943, the author had blended sentimental art journalism with Nazi propaganda, by 1950 his ramblings on the criminality of the allied air war had disappeared. For his entry on the Grimmhaus in the memory book, Vonau adapted verbatim only those passages that dealt with the significance of the Grimms' collection of fairy tales 'as the greatest cultural present [for] the German people [and] all of humanity'.

'Old Kassel' was not an invention of the post-war world but derived from the turn-of the century preservationist movement, which had discovered the picturesque qualities of Germany's historical cityscapes – the 'beautiful old town[s]' – as a source of local and national pride and

---

[75] Vonau, *Kassel. Bauwerke einer Alten Stadt*, p. 5.   [76] Ibid., p. 6.

[77] StAK, 41/3, Geplante Veröffentlichungen, 1942–5.

[78] Ibid., Gauleitung Kurhessen to Wirtschaftsstelle des Deutschen Buchhandels, 29 September 1943.

[79] German M. Vonau, 'Das Haus an der Wildemannsgasse. Vor den Trümmern des Grimm-Hauses. Unzerstörbar bleibt der Geist', *KLZ*, 8 November 1943, p. 3.

identity.[80] The most popular of the memory books of the 1950s, *Kassel before the Firestorm*, borrowed its visual inventory from the preservationist manifesto of 1913, *Alt Cassel* by Alois Holtmeyer.[81] Just as with Vonau's *Kassel – Buildings of an Old Town*, the idea for a 'memory book' was first raised during the war when the air war had led to an increased demand for copies of *Alt Cassel*, which was by then out of print.[82] Nor was the attempt to define the city in terms of art and culture a novel phenomenon. Rather, it was a selective appropriation of a tradition that throughout the Third Reich had run parallel to the militaristic image of Kassel as 'City of the Reich Warrior Days' (*Stadt der Reichskriegertage*).[83]

In post-war Kassel, the nostalgic narrative was carried by a group of (self-appointed) custodians of the city's cultural heritage who tended to be middle class in their social disposition and conservative in their political outlook. Before 1945, some of them, such as German M. Vonau, had belonged to the inner circle of power in the city, while others, such as the art critic Karl Kaltwasser or the curator Dr Helm, had established cordial working relationships with the National Socialist power holders. After the war, they often supported the FDP, which, even more than the CDU, was the party of choice for broad sections of the compromised Protestant middle classes.[84] The custodians of the lost past worked together closely with a number of local publishing houses and the conservative press, in particular the *Kasseler Post*. Following in the footsteps of turn-of-the-century preservationism, they depicted 'Old Kassel' as a 'gem of medieval architecture' rather than as an unsanitary, overcrowded district with a distinct proletarian milieu and radical politics. Nostalgia of the 1950s sanitised and depoliticised *Alt-Kassel*.[85]

Despite their idealisation of the beauty of *Alt-Kassel*, the middle-class guardians of the architectural heritage made only half-hearted attempts at exploiting the subversive potential inherent in the notion of the 'beautiful

---

[80] Paul, 'Der Wiederaufbau der historischen Städte', pp. 119f.; Beyme, *Der Wiederaufbau*, pp. 13–24. On Kassel see Holtmeyer, *Alt Cassel*, pp. 5f. and *passim*; Holtmeyer, *Die Bau- und Kunstdenkmäler im Regierungsbezirk Kassel*; *Alt-Cassel*. On preservationism and memory more generally compare Koshar, *Germany's Transient Pasts*.

[81] Compare Helm (ed.), *Kassel vor dem Feuersturm* (1950), pp. 17ff. to Holtmeyer, *Alt Cassel* (1913), pp. 1–96.

[82] StAK, A.4.41/25, Elwert'sche Universitäts- und Verlagsbuchhandlung to Councillor Heilig, 7 January 1944.

[83] See, for example, *Kassel-Wilhelmshöhe, die schöne deutsche Kunst und Parkstadt* (1935); Kramm, *Kassel* (1933).

[84] See FDP-Kreisvorstand Kassel (ed.), *Freie Demokratische Partei*.

[85] In the 1930s, there lived 460 people to the hectare of the Old Town and the Upper New Town. See Kemp and Neusüß (eds.), *Kassel 1850 bis heute*, pp. 16–24. Compare the memoirs of the Communist activist, Willi Belz, *Die Standhaften*. See also Marsen, Kulbarsch and Soltau, *Stadtteilgeschichte*, pp. 152–209.

old town' in order to criticise the brutal modernisation that the SPD-led civil authorities, drawing on the ideas and personnel of Nazi-era city planning, had initiated.[86] To employ Svetlana Boym's distinction, post-war nostalgia was 'reflective' rather than 'restorative'.[87] The myth of Old Kassel was premised on the assumption of irredeemable loss. Although individuals such as Helm and Vonau spoke out in public against the removal of the vestiges of the old city, on the whole the planning elites faced little popular opposition in their pursuit of constructing a 'new city on historic ground'.[88] Local residents attended in great numbers the exhibition '*Alt-Kassel* – The art and history of a beautiful town', which was staged by the State Art Collection in order 'to honour the city's past' in the summer of 1947.[89] Nostalgic sentiment did not, however, translate into political pressure 'from below' for the preservation of what had been left of the old cityscape in the contemporary environment.[90]

With the passing of time, visualisations of 'Old Kassel' were beginning to lose traction with the local public, and by the mid-1950s, were starting to give way to images of the destruction, and even more prominently, to images of the new city under construction. This process, which was closely linked to the idea of a 'rebirth', can best be illustrated with different editions of what was perhaps the most successful of the memory books, *Kassel before the Firestorm*. The first edition of 1950 placed special emphasis on the architectural heritage of the late Middle Ages and the Renaissance, which had for the most part been 'wiped out [by the] dreadful destruction that Kassel suffered in the last war', as the editor, Rudolf Helm, put it in his introductory essay.[91] By contrast, images of the destruction itself were absent, as was rubble photography.

Three years later, on the occasion of the tenth anniversary of the air raid, a new revised edition appeared. An advertisement in the *Kasseler Post* praised the book as a 'memory of the immemorial cityscape', which was a must-have for 'every Kasselaner, whether living at home or abroad'. The advertisement went on to stress that in the second, improved edition the concept of 'Old Kassel' had been extended to include the late

---

[86] On the rebuilding of Kassel as a 'new city on historic ground' see Lüken-Isberner, 'Kassel: Neue Stadt auf altem Grund'.

[87] Boym, *The Future of Nostalgia*, p. xviii.

[88] Rudolf Helm, 'Kassel baut auf', *HN*, 25 May 1946, p. 4; German M. Vonau, 'Die Rettung unserer Städte', *KP*, 8 August 1951.

[89] Staatliche Kunstsammlung, *Alt-Kassel*, p. 3. On attendance see 'Alt-Kassel', *KZ*, 30 May 1947, p. 2.

[90] Compare König, 'Konflikt', pp. 97–115, here p. 102. Ironically, the one notable exception revolved around the preservation of a building that, in a narrow sense, did not form part of *Alt-Kassel* at all, the late Wilhelmian state theatre on the Friedrichsplatz.

[91] Helm (ed.), *Kassel vor dem Feuersturm*, 1st edn (1950), p. 15.

nineteenth-century districts in order to keep alive 'memories of places of happy lives'. Moreover, *Kassel before the Firestorm* in its second edition had also become 'a book for the future', which documented the population's 'will to live'.[92] In a new epilogue, Vonau emphasised the importance of the publication, which did not just preserve 'delightful memories' of what had been lost but also celebrated 'the changed image of a city reborn'. Only in the context of this 'rebirth' did the publishers consider the inclusion of rubble photography opportune – within a pictorial sequence of 'before–after–now'. According to Vonau, rubble photos were to be read both as a 'memento' to the 'hardest fateful hours of our city' and as a sign of confidence in the 'indestructible . . . human will to live'.[93]

Seven years later, in 1960, a third, revised edition appeared, this time in radically altered form under the new title of *Kassel Then and Now*.[94] Only about one-third of the images from the previous edition had been kept. About two-thirds were made up of new photographs that showed views of the contemporary city. On the dust jacket, the editors explained their decision as follows: 'In its present form, the book only records of the old Kassel what seems worthy to pass on to a younger generation that never knew the Kassel of old. After that, we want to focus on the new Kassel.'[95]

In Magdeburg, nostalgia did not play quite the same role as in Kassel. Although the first post-war administration, in January 1946, commissioned the building department (*Bauverwaltung*) to produce visual material from 'old' Magdeburg as well as from the contemporary city, visual representations of the pre-war city generally remained of subsidiary importance in the public narrative on urban destruction.[96] There appear to have been two reasons for this. Firstly, as a city whose medieval and Renaissance architecture had been destroyed in the Thirty Years War, Magdeburg had never commanded the same attention from turn-of-the-century preservationists as had Kassel. While Germany's leading encyclopaedia, the *Brockhaus*, in 1931 spoke of Kassel as 'one of the most beautiful towns in Germany', the entry on Magdeburg emphasised the importance of the city as a modern industrial and communications centre.[97] Similarly, an English-language city guide commented in 1939,

[92] 'Der Wiederaufbau Kassels in Wort und Bild. 20-seitige Sonderbeilage', *KP*, 24/25 October 1953, no pagination.
[93] Helm (ed.), *Kassel vor dem Feuersturm*, 2nd edn (1953), no pagination.
[94] Batz and Mitte (eds.), *Kassel einst und jetzt* (1960).   [95] Ibid., dust jacket.
[96] StAM, Rep. 18/4, Ra. 4, Dezernentenbesprechung, 'Schaffung von Bildmaterial', 2 January 1946.
[97] *Der Große Brockhaus*, 15th rev. edn, vol. IX, pp. 775–7, here p. 776; vol. XI, pp. 754–7.

'Although Magdeburg is one of Germany's oldest towns, it has the outward appearance of a modern German city.'[98] In the 1920s, the Social Democratic city administration self-consciously promoted Magdeburg as a 'young' city that had embraced architectural modernism, coining the slogan 'City of the new building spirit'.[99] By comparison, the phrase 'old Magdeburg' referred to the town as it had existed before 1631 rather than to a 'beautiful town' worthy of admiration and preservation in the present. In short, there was no tradition on which the cultural enunciation of post-war nostalgia could have drawn.

Secondly, public discourse in the city was dominated by the political elites.[100] Only in the immediate post-war period were local artists and photographers able to publish visual representations of the pre-war cityscape, but such production soon ceased.[101] While it appears, therefore, that some demand for romanticised images existed in Magdeburg as well, there was little room for their public expression owing to the restrictions placed upon public memory by the Socialist power holders.[102] After all, the catchword of the SED elites and their associated 'bourgeois' parties was 'to build a new, more beautiful Magdeburg in a new Germany'.[103]

Despite the future-oriented stance of the local elites, there were several occasions on which visual representations of the 'old town' gained limited currency in Magdeburg as well. During the immediate post-war period of 1946/7, the civil administration under the former Social Democrat Rudolf Eberhard regularly invoked the idea of *Heimat* by way of visual representations of the pre-war cityscape. In the exhibition of 1947, 'Magdeburg is Alive!', for example, an entire room was devoted to the theme of 'dear old *Heimat*'. While the cabinets displayed photographs of locally renowned Magdeburger, including poets, socialists, reformers and eccentrics, the walls were decorated with images of Baroque buildings, churches and streets. Marks of ownership (*Hauszeichen*) retrieved from the rubble were placed on pedestals. Meanwhile, the exhibition

---

[98] *Magdeburg. The City in the Heart of Germany.*

[99] Hermann Beims, 'Vorwort', in Magistrat der Stadt Magdeburg (ed.), *Magdeburg*, pp. 5f., here p. 6; Johannes Göderitz, 'Magdeburg, die Stadt des Neuen Bauwillens', in ibid., pp. 26–31. See also Tullner, 'Modernisierung und mitteldeutsche Hauptstadtpolitik', pp. 742–8.

[100] For the broader context see Martin Sabrow (ed.), *Geschichte als Herrschaftsdiskurs.*

[101] H. Friedrich, *Magdeburg. Bildmappe 1 and 2* (Magdeburg, 1946). See also Seegers, 'Kulturelles Leben in Magdeburg', p. 891.

[102] Compare the contrasting example of Dresden: Meinhardt, 'Der Mythos vom "Alten Dresden"'.

[103] On the reconstruction of Magdeburg see Berger, 'Magdeburg: Klassenkampf der Dominanten'; Manz, *Wiederaufbau*; Reuther and Schulte, 'Städtebau 1945–1990'; Landeshauptstadt Magdeburg/Stadtplanungsamt Magdeburg, *Städtebau in Magdeburg.*

room was dominated by a panoramic aerial view of the city from before the war, measuring 3 m × 2.5 m.[104]

The visual narrative as produced by the Magdeburg civil administration during the immediate post-war period differed little from similar narratives by the civil administration in Kassel.[105] Cultural landmarks represented *Heimat* rather than *Kultur*, positioning the present administration in a long tradition of local self-government. While acknowledging the achievements of the 'bourgeois' past, Mayor Eberhard turned sharply against romanticising tendencies. As he stressed in his opening address to the same exhibition, 'We think in admiration of old Magdeburg, the city of our fathers . . . But we refrain from any romantic rapture that only recognises the good in the old and depicts the past as a realm of quiet cosiness.'[106] On the whole, the loss of the Magdeburg of old was no cause for regret but opened up great opportunities. 'We have lost a city and gained the freedom to rebuild her according to our will and our plans,' the mayor declared in a turn of phrase that was reminiscent of the statement by Kassel's municipal architect, Erich Heinicke, from 1946.[107]

As local self-government underwent Stalinisation from 1948 onwards, images of old Magdeburg as visual markers of 'dear old *Heimat*' largely disappeared from public view. Yet, on occasion, they were used in order to illustrate the propaganda campaign against the Western powers, and in particular, the United States. The campaign reached its climax in the spring and summer of 1952 when the *Volksstimme* ran a picture series with photographs of historical buildings from the time before the war. The series was called, 'Do you Remember – Before Ami-barbarians Destroyed our City?' On 22 January 1952, for example, a pre-war image of the Johanniskirche was published with the caption:

Who from Magdeburg does not remember the hill of St John with its honourable church? . . . Never will they forget who reduced their home town to debris and rubble with phosphorous and fire bombs. Imperialist barbarians must never again destroy the cultural possessions of our nation; therefore all peace-loving Germans opt for all-German elections.[108]

---

[104] 'Lieber trocken Brot als Bombenhagel. Wiederaufbaukundgebung und Eröffnung der Ausstellung "Magdeburg lebt!"', *Freiheit*, 9 June 1947, p. 4.

[105] See, for example, Heinicke, 'Kassel – einst – jetzt – später'; Kessler, 'Kassel baut auf. . . !', pp. 3–10.

[106] StAM, Rep. 41/92, Vorbereitung und Durchführung der Ausstellung 'Magdeburg lebt', 1947, here fo. 13: 'Die neue Stadt – das gemeinsame Werk'.

[107] Ibid., fo. 14.

[108] 'Kennst Du es noch? Bevor Ami-Gangster unsere Stadt zerstörten', *Volksstimme*, 6/18, 22 January 1952, p. 4. See also *Volksstimme* 6/19, 6/21, 6/23, 6/24, 6/27, 6/28–30, 6/33–5, 6/37, 6/40–7, 6/49, etc.

In denouncing allied bombing as criminal, the series drew on Nazi wartime propaganda, and more specifically, on a nationwide campaign from the summer of 1943 that had depicted destroyed cultural monuments in their undamaged state under the heading 'From the debt register of the air gangsters'.[109] Whereas in Kassel the cultural enunciation of nostalgia allowed one-time Nazi propagandists to re-establish themselves as honourable art critics mourning the loss of architectural treasures, in Magdeburg the narrators changed but the narrative remained the same. Here, postcard images from old Magdeburg served as evidence for an alleged crime against German *Kultur*.

Visualising the 'disfigured face': rubble photography

The German visual inventory of urban destruction was compiled by professional and private photographers in the decade between 1940 and 1950. During the war, photo reporters and professional photographers worked on the orders of the state, party and military, while amateurs shot private photos in circumvention of official regulations.[110] After the war, the new civil administrations and institutions such as the Church commissioned professionals to take stock of the destruction. At the same time, photo reporters and photo amateurs photographed their transformed environment, sometimes for commercial purposes.[111] In the post-war memory cultures of Kassel and Magdeburg, selected images from the war merged with the rubble photography of the immediate post-war period, subsuming bomb damage from dozens of air raids, demolitions by retreating Wehrmacht units and rubble clearance under the symbolic headings of '22 October 1943' and '16 January 1945'.

Kassel   In Kassel during the period 1945 to 1960, the public usage of rubble photographs was distinguished by the recurrence of

---

[109] 'Aus dem Schuldbuch der Luftgangster', *Völkischer Beobachter*, 2 June 1943, p. 3; 4 June 1943, p. 3; 8 June 1943, p. 3; 28 July 1943, p. 3.

[110] For the context see Deres and Rüther (eds.), *Fotografieren verboten!*; Sachsse, *Erziehung zum Wegsehen*, pp. 202–7; Derenthal, *Bilder der Trümmer- und Aufbaujahre*, pp. 44–86; Glasenapp, 'Nach dem Brand'; Jäger, 'Fotografie – Erinnerung – Identität'; *Deutsche Fotografie*.

[111] In Kassel, the most influential post-war photographer was Walter Thieme, who documented the destruction for the Protestant Church and traded rubble photography commercially, earning him the nickname 'rubble photographer'. See *Leben in Ruinen*, pp. 103–10. In Magdeburg, Paul Gehlert appears to have worked for the city as the official photographer both before and after 1945. See StAM, Fotoalbum P. Gehlert.

certain motifs, the strategy of embedding them in broader contexts and the tendency to 'soften' their visual impact.

Many different photos were taken of the destruction during and after the war, but the motifs that newspaper editors and publishing houses considered suitable for public consumption were limited.[112] The two most prominent were the Christian symbol of the cross and the ruined landmark of the Martinskirche. Both featured together as early as 1947 when the *Hessische Nachrichten* devoted an illustrated article to the memory of '22 October 1943'. The picture on the title page was captioned 'Old Kassel Today'. It was composed around a diagonal line, which stretched from the bottom lefthand corner to the top righthand corner (Fig. 23). In the foreground, the viewer looks upon a heap of rubble, overgrown with weeds. The heap is crowned by a gravestone in the shape of a cross that contrasts sharply against the sky. In the background, the burnt-out towers of the Martinskirche are visible. The church structures the landscape, rendering the transformed urban environment recognisable to the local observer. The motif allows for the moonscape of rubble to be identified as the home town while visualising its 'disfigured face'.

The photograph, and in particular the motif of the cross, was open to contrasting readings. As the Christian symbol of suffering and loss, the cross testified to the 'death' of 'Old Kassel'. In this perspective, the photograph could be read as an indictment – of the 'Hitler madness', as the caption put it, but perhaps also of the Western allies, of whose part in the destruction the residents did not need to be reminded. Alternatively, the image could also be read as a critical comment on the work of the civil administration, which two years after the end of war had made little progress in relieving the scene of utter desolation.[113] Conversely, the cross could be understood as a symbol of overcoming and hope, pointing to survival amidst death and a new beginning that would lead, in the words of the caption, to a 'new Kassel of peace and prosperity'.

Visual representations of the destruction rarely appeared in isolation but were usually put in context. Verbal or visual contextualisation may be understood as an attempt on the part of the local protagonists of public discourse to influence responses to the visual, to structure ways of seeing. Throughout the period, the depiction of the 'disfigured face' was usually linked to a positive message. Often, this was done visually by juxtaposing

---

[112] Friedrich Herbordt, 'Die Nacht, in der Kassels Altstadt unterging', *KP*, 22 October 1949. Compare the similar observation by Naumann, *Der Krieg als Text*, p. 35.

[113] The relationship between the press and the civil administration was strained throughout the late 1940s and early 1950s. See StAK, A.1.10, no. 53, Interior Ministry to Regional Councillor (*Regierungspräsident*), 29 August 1947.

Hessische Nachrichten
Vom 21. 10. 1947
1947

ALT-KASSEL HEUTE ZUR WIEDERKEHR DES 22. OKTOBER

Aus den Schutt- und Trümmermassen Alt-Kassels ragen wie ein Mahnmal die Stümpfe der Kirchtürme von St. Martin empor. Das alte Kassel sank unwiederbringlich am 22. Oktober 1943 dahin. Tausende seiner Bürger fielen dem Hitler-Wahnsinn zum Opfer. Aus Leid und Not ersteht ein neues Kassel des Friedens und der Wohlfahrt. (H.N.)   Aufnahme: Tilcher-H.N.

Figure 23. 'Old Kassel Today' reads the caption of a commemorative photograph that appeared in the *Hessische Nachrichten* on the fourth anniversary of the air raid.

rubble photography with images of the rebuilding.[114] The same effect could also be reached textually, as in the following example. On the fifth anniversary of the air raid in 1948, the *Kasseler Zeitung* marked the day by publishing a photograph and a poem. Both were set off from the

---

[114] Compare, for example, 'Mahnstätte der Grausamkeit – Lichter der Hoffnung. Heute vor neun Jahren raste der Feuersturm über Kassel', *KP*, 22 October 1952.

Fünf Jahre danach — Gedanken zum 22. Oktober

In dem lieben, alten Kassel, an dem schönen Fuldastrand
liegt mein Vaterhaus, das teure, kriegszerstört und ausgebrannt.

Stolze Bauten, schöne Plätze, dichte Straßen dieser Stadt
fanden wie gar viele Menschen, durch den Krieg ein frühes Grab.

Wo ich meinen Blick hinwende, seh' ich Trümmer, Schutt und Not;
Wohlstand, Reichtum sind entschwunden, reiche Ernte hielt der Tod.

Jeder Frohsinn scheint gestorben, tiefster Ernst nahm dessen Platz,
Trauer um ein liebes Wesen, Trauer um den letzten Schatz. —

Gern gedenk' ich froher Kreise, wo gesungen und gelacht,
wo man schmauste ohne Sorgen tief hinein oft in die Nacht.

Einst das Leben in den Straßen pulste wie des Herzens Schlag,
schaffte täglich neue Werte, brachte Freude jeden Tag. —

Dennoch woll'n wir nicht verzagen, fest im Glauben weit und breit!
Uns're Hoffnung soll nicht schwinden, Wunden heilen mit der Zeit.

Hat der Krieg uns auch genommen, was das Leben uns geschenkt:
Soll durch Fleiß uns Neues werden, und die Notzeit wird verdrängt.

Bild: T h i e m e   Eingesandt von August H e l d m a n n

Figure 24. 'Five Years After – Thoughts on 22 October', *Kasseler Zeitung*, 22 October 1948.

surrounding text by a double frame, thus stressing their commemorative character (Fig. 24).[115]

The image took in a panoramic view of the devastated old town, looking from the tower of the Lutherkirche in a south-eastern direction upon a

---

[115] 'Fünf Jahre danach – Gedanken zum 22. Oktober', *KZ*, 22 October 1948. For the text plus translation see Appendix 4.

scene of near-total urban destruction. This impression is underscored further by a number of compositional elements. The frame cuts off the landscape of ruins at the bottom, left and right margins, while the camera focuses on a triangle of ruins in the centre, two of which are important landmarks, the Martinskirche to the left and the Druselturm to the right. Moreover, the slanting angle makes the landscape of ruins appear to extend all the way to the horizon. There is hardly any life visible in the streets, reinforcing the impression of irredeemable desolation and of a violent break with everything that went before it. The photograph, which was taken by the professional photographer Walter Thieme in 1946 or 1947, provided visual confirmation of the notion of 'total' destruction. By the time of its first publication in the local media in 1948, it may already have circulated as a postcard. The image quickly gained iconic status in the local memory culture, which it retained throughout the second half of the twentieth century.[116]

The accompanying poem was called 'Five Years After – Thoughts on "22 October"'. The sixteen verses oscillate between blissful memories of an idealised past and descriptions of a desolate present. The lyrical 'I' introduces the subject matter in the stock phrases of conventional *Heimat* poetry. 'In dear old Kassel, on the beautiful banks of the river Fulda', the first verse reads. In the lines that follow, the 'I' conjures up memories of what has been lost and contrasts them with the present. 'Proud buildings and beautiful squares . . . have found an early grave'; 'rubble, debris and pain' have replaced 'wealth [and] prosperity'; 'grief' has taken the place of 'merriment' and 'excitement'. The bulk of the poem thus reads like a textual commentary on the photograph. Characteristically, however, the poem does not end in resignation but on a note of optimism. 'Despite everything we are not going to despair, strong in our faith everywhere!', the lyrical 'I' intones in verse thirteen, and continues,

> Our hope will not disappear
> Wounds heal with time
> . . .
> Our Diligence will create something new again
> And the time of want will be pushed aside.

The poem provides a good example of the dominant contextualisation of rubble photography in the late 1940s. Images of urban destruction were

---

[116] The image was reproduced in the early 1950s in 'Schicksal unserer Stadt', *KP*, 1 January 1950; 'Mahnstätte der Grausamkeit – Lichter der Hoffnung', *KP*, 22 October 1952; Wolfgang Drews, 'Kassel', *Die neue Zeitung*, 31 December 1952; 'Kassel – Zehn Jahre danach. Zerstörung und Wiederaufbau einer Stadt', *KP*, supplement October 1953.

typically embedded in a tale of hope and confidence – years before actual progress in the physical reconstruction became visible.

Another influential mode of representing the 'disfigured face' in local discourse was to soften the visual impact. This was achieved by drawing on the conventions of idyllic genre painting, presenting nature as a benign force that covered the devastated cityscape with flowers or snow. An early example was published on Whitsun 1946 in the *Hessische Nachrichten* where a photograph showed horses grazing peacefully against a backdrop of bizarre ruinous shapes. Another image focused on wild flowers in full bloom, reaching up to the façade of the severely damaged Wilhelmian government building.[117] While in the press nature was invoked in order to aestheticise the landscape of rubble, the civil administration preferred painting to photography as a medium through which to render the devastation presentable. For the official publication *Kassel is Alive – Despite Everything*, the city council commissioned a local artist to supply watercolour illustrations of the ruins of famous architectural landmarks.[118]

These approaches did not remain confined to the sphere of representations but by the mid-1950s were transferred to the physical cityscape as well. On the occasion of the Federal Flower Exhibition (*Bundesgartenschau*) of 1955, the rubble that had been deposited on the banks of the Karlsaue – a park stretching on the left bank of the river Fulda – was planted with roses and thus transformed into a recreational ground and tourist attraction. Likewise, the severely damaged neo-classical building of the Fridericianum was used to house an international exhibition on modern art, the first 'documenta'.[119]

Magdeburg   In contrast to Kassel, there was no space in the guided media of Magdeburg for romantic rubble photography. Here, visual representations of urban destruction were integrated into two narrative contexts. The first was one of cause and effect, the second of an overcoming of a zero hour.

In public discourse, images of the devastated cityscape were used as documentary evidence of an allegedly criminal deed. By the early 1950s, the SED-controlled media returned to the Nazi propaganda narrative that had used selected images of damaged churches and civilian dwellings to denounce the allied air war as criminal. In so doing, the local media abandoned an earlier interpretation that had named Hitler as the prime culprit for the destruction of the city. Against the

---

[117] 'Kasseler Pfingsten', *HN*, 7/8 June 1946, p. 4. Compare also Vogel, *Die Ruine*.
[118] *Kassel lebt . . . trotz alledem!*.
[119] Compare Burckhardt, 'Blütenzauber auf Trümmern'; Kimpel, *Documenta*, pp. 73–146.

background of the Cold War, Anglo-American 'imperialism' took the place of Adolf Hitler and 'his' war. In January 1952, for example, an image depicting a street of rubble with the damaged Johanniskirche in the background was supplied with the following caption: 'Neither churches nor living quarters were sacred to the Anglo-American air gangsters. Their catchword was to destroy and to murder.'[120] Rubble photography constituted one element within a broader narrative that sought to draw on personal memories of strategic bombing in order to legitimise the policies of the Communist elites. 'The rubble in our city admonishes: what do you do for peace?' was the caption of a drawing depicting Magdeburg cathedral.[121]

Images of urban destruction were employed not just as an accusation but also as a backdrop to demonstrate the success of the reconstruction effort: they visualised the 'zero hour' against which the 'new Magdeburg' contrasted sharply. A visual sequence of three images that were printed in the *Volksstimme* in January 1953 may provide a typical example. Picture one depicts a scene of utter desolation. The façade of a burnt-out building in the foreground draws attention to a street covered in debris, which directs the eye to the damaged towers of the Johanniskirche in the centre-background. While no sign of life is visible in this desolate cityscape, picture two shows workers lifting an iron girder from the rubble, symbolically leading upwards. The positive message is underlined by the caption, which reads 'We tackled the problems.' The final picture focuses on new residential blocks on Karl Marx Street, thereby demonstrating the success of the common effort.[122]

These examples notwithstanding, rubble photography played a rather limited role in the local master narrative of criminal destruction and heroic reconstruction. This was no coincidence but the consequence of a political directive from above. In January 1953, the local SED leadership, cognisant of the slow progress of the actual rebuilding, decided that the press in future should put greater emphasis on the 'perspective of reconstruction' in its annual coverage of '16 January 1945'.[123]

'The new city, more beautiful than ever': Heimat *reborn?*

In both cities, the annual return of the *lieu de mémoire* provided an occasion to review the progress of the rebuilding effort. In Kassel as well as Magdeburg, politicians, journalists and publicists developed a

---

[120] 'Auferstanden aus Ruinen', *Volksstimme*, 16 January 1952, p. 4.
[121] *Volksstimme*, 16 January 1952, p. 4.   [122] *Volksstimme*, 16 January 1953, p. 5.
[123] LA Magd., LHA, Rep. 16, SED-Stadtleitung Magdeburg. Sekretariat. No. IV/5/1/50, fo. 16, minutes, 2 January 1953.

narrative which conceptualised the 1950s reconstruction as a 'rebirth' of the city following its 'death' in the air war. In Magdeburg, the notion of 'rebirth' was invested with quasi-sacral connotations and soon took on a triumphal tone. The city had risen from the rubble and *Heimat* been reborn 'more beautiful' than ever, as local functionaries and the media would stress over and over again.[124] In Kassel, the rhetoric of overcoming the rubble was prominent as well but the tone was celebratory rather than triumphal. Kassel was being rebuilt, but whether *Heimat* would return was another matter. Moreover, the idea itself came under scrutiny: was there, after all, a link between the *Heimat* of old and the catastrophe?

Magdeburg   On the tenth anniversary of the air raid in 1955, the *Volksstimme* carried a commemorative page that was carefully arranged and richly illustrated (Fig. 25). The page was framed by the first lines of the East German national anthem, 'Risen from the ruins / and facing the future'. The quotation did not just make for a nice visual effect but also set the theme for the textual and visual narratives, linking the local to the national. The 'new Magdeburg' was rising from 'the rubble and the graves', in which the combined destructive force of 'Anglo-American air gangsters', 'American monopoly capitalists', 'fascism' and 'German militarism' had thrown the city, as the first secretary of the local SED, Werner Guse, stressed in his programmatic article.[125] The 'new Magdeburg' was not just a city rebuilt but a society transformed. The 'home town' represented a new social order 'where the factories and the residential buildings as well as the new social and cultural facilities are owned by the people': *Heimat* stood for Magdeburg just as much as for the German Democratic Republic and the idea of a 'united, democratic and peace-loving Germany'.[126] But the 'new Magdeburg' was under threat. 'The same American monopoly capitalists who ordered the destruction of our city and bear the responsibility for the unspeakable atrocities that have brought so much suffering on the population are again preparing another war,' Guse warned ominously. The injunction of 'never again

---

[124] 'Aus den Trümmern wuchs ein schöneres Magdeburg', *Volksstimme*, 15 January 1956, p. 5. See also *Volksstimme*, 16 January 1950, p. 3; 16 January 1952, p. 4; 16 January 1953, p. 5; 16 January 1954, p. 7.
[125] 'Auferstanden aus Ruinen / Und der Zukunft zugewandt', *Volksstimme*, 15 January 1955, p. 4. Compare also LA Magd., LHA Rep. P16, SED-Stadtleitung Magdeburg no. IV/5/1/58, fo. 5, 7 January 1955.
[126] 'Auferstanden aus Ruinen / Und der Zukunft zugewandt', *Volksstimme*, 15 January 1955, p. 4.

AUFERSTANDEN AUS RUINEN

Hütet den Frieden!

Tausend Jahre Geschichte
formten das Antlitz der Stadt.
Durch Krieg ward in Stunden zunichte,
was Fleiß einst geschaffen hat.

Die kunstvollen Häuser der Bürger,
die Brücken, der Straßen Zug . . .
Krieg, der grausame Würger,
zerschlug sie im Bombenflug.

Es klagen die Türme Konturen,
es mahnt mancher zerborstenes Haus:
Zehn Jahre löschten die Spuren
des Unheils nicht völlig aus.

Doch über den Krieg siegt der Friede.
Durch ihn wird die Welt licht und schön.
Er singt in der Jugend Liede
von Zukunft und Auferstehn.

Ans Werk drum, Arbeiter, Bauern!
Ans Werk jede schaffende Hand!
Dann wachsen aus Trümmern die Mauern
und blüht im Frieden das Land.

In eure Hand ist gegeben
das Schicksal von Dorf und Stadt.
Hütet wie euer Leben
des Friedens keimende Saat.

UND DER ZUKUNFT ZUGEWANDT

Figure 25. Commemorative page on the tenth anniversary of the air raid of 16 January 1945, *Volksstimme*, 15 January 1955.

another 16 January' thus linked the past with the present, World War II
with the Cold War.[127]

Public memory invested the reconstruction with sacral shades of meaning, as is best illustrated by the visual sequence that occupied the centre
of the page. Three images and a poem were arranged as a triptych, in
which the construction workers on the wings took on the role of disciples
worshipping an apotheosised city. This impression was underscored by
the archway that framed the new city like a halo. The reconstruction
was a sacral undertaking, for which the two workers were prepared to
devote several hundred 'voluntary' reconstruction hours over the next
twelve months. It was, however, not enough to give one's labour; the
city population also needed to identify with the 'fight for peace' in the
'peace state' of the GDR, as the poem at the centre bottom of the photomontage stressed. 'Your hands carry / the fate of village and town /
Preserve like your life / the blossoming seeds of peace,' the poet urged his
readers with great pathos. In extension of this argument, the commemorative article of the following year carried a picture of a paramilitary unit
marching through the streets of the 'more beautiful Magdeburg'. The
article carried the inscription,

We will never allow to be taken away from us what we have built in eleven
years of hard labour, our beautiful residential dwellings, hospitals, child care
units... None of this must again be destroyed by an imperialist aggressive war
that would only serve the interests of profit-hungry money magnates.[128]

The rhetoric of 'rebirth' thus served both as evidence of the superiority
of the new social order and as a means to foster a climate of fear.

Kassel   In Kassel no less than in Magdeburg, the *lieu de mémoire*
of the air war became an occasion that called for celebration. On the tenth
anniversary in 1953, the local media not only covered the official commemoration in great detail but also brought out special supplements that
reviewed the achievements of the reconstruction. This was undertaken
mainly through the medium of photography: '1943 – Kassel on 22 October – 1953. Picture reports from back then and from today' was the title of
a special page by the *Hessische Nachrichten*, which juxtaposed rubble photography with pictures taken in 1953.[129] By way of visual representations,

---

[127] Ibid.
[128] 'Aus den Trümmern wuchs ein schöneres Magdeburg', *Volksstimme*, 14 January 1956,
p. 5.
[129] 'Bildberichte von damals und heute', *HN*, 22 October 1953.

'22 October 1943' was cast as a zero hour whose causes remained unexplored but whose legacy the population was mastering by way of a 'tenacious rebuilding effort'.

The conservative *Kasseler Post* published a twenty-page supplement, 'Kassel Ten Years After: Destruction and Reconstruction of a City', in which the editorial took the progress in the rebuilding effort as evidence of the 'will to live of the Kassel citizenry (*Bürgertum*)'.[130] This was underlined visually by juxtaposing a contemporary aerial view with Walter Thieme's panoramic image of desolation from 1946/7. In contrast to the left-leaning *Hessische Nachrichten*, the *Kasseler Post* did not exclude images of 'Old Kassel' from its pictorial narrative, but in no way linked the picturesque views of 'medieval artistry' to World War II. The air war was depicted as a 'sudden catastrophe engulfing the *Heimat*', the city as a martyr who 'had been forced to drink from the cup of suffering to the full'.[131] On the tenth anniversary of the air raid, it was not so much the actual progress in the physical reconstruction that appeared noteworthy to the editors but the 'rebirth of the will to live': 'A city has found itself again, which had lost with one stroke not just its corporeal substance but its sense of constituting a polity, a centuries-old tradition,' they declared.[132]

In contrast to the other two papers, the liberal *Kasseler Zeitung* struck a less optimistic tone, using the decennial to reflect on the meaning of material destruction. 'What We Have Lost . . .' was the title of an editorial on the front page that stressed the irreversible nature of loss, intimating that even a city rebuilt might not equal the home town reborn. 'No reconstruction plan will ever bring back to life the distinctive atmosphere in the alleys of the old town that once delighted the traveller through Old Kassel.'[133] In a similar vein, the same journalist noted melancholically in his special report 'The *Heimat* Ten Years after the Firestorm – Kassel's Rebirth': 'On 22 October 1943 a city was destroyed. A polity that had grown organically through a thousand years lost its face. People come and go; a city dies only once.'[134]

In subsequent years, the conservative and liberal press repeatedly voiced concern that the reconstruction took too little cognisance of tradition. 'The New City' was the title of an article published in the *Kasseler Post* on the twelfth anniversary of the air raid, in which the journalist

---

[130] 'Zehn Jahre danach. Der Lebenswille des Kasseler Bürgertums', *KP*, supplement, October 1953.
[131] Ibid.   [132] Ibid.
[133] 'Was wir verloren haben . . .', *KZ*, 22 October 1953, p. 1.
[134] 'Die Heimat zehn Jahre nach dem Feuersturm. Kassels Wiederaufstieg', *KZ*, 24 October 1953.

told an anecdote of an old lady who had lived in the city for sixty years but simply was unable to find her way in the rebuilt town. 'Kassel lost its historic face twelve years ago. For the older generation, the city never recovered it,' the piece concluded.[135] If there was some concern that the 'new city' for all its progressive features might never become *Heimat*, local publicists also started to ask more probing questions about the character of the 'thousand-year-old Kassel' that had been destroyed on the night of 22 October 1943.

This re-examination of the 'home town' of old as yet hardly touched upon the most recent past. Although, in the autumn of 1957, the Kassel adult education centre ran a lecture series on the Third Reich under the title of 'Unmastered Past', the connection between Nazism and the locality was hardly drawn: Kassel as home town remained victim, while responsibility rested with supra-local government and institutions, or at most, with certain local individuals.[136] The extent of this consensus is best assessed from its margins. In his memoirs, first published in 1960, the Communist activist Willi Belz firmly anchored the destruction of the home town in the Old Testament parable of 'sowing the wind and reaping the whirlwind'.[137] Deploring the lack of interest among the general public in reflecting on the causes of the disaster, he pointed to the aggressive politics of Nazism in general and the importance of Kassel as a military garrison, armaments centre and traffic junction in particular. Yet even Belz drew a categorical distinction between the locality and the nation: the war had been started 'from German soil', the 'Nazi state' had turned Kassel into an armaments centre – and the 'home town' had suffered.[138]

More influential than this Marxist deliberation on guilt and responsibility was another narrative that probed the meaning of catastrophic rupture for the city's past and future. It was most influentially advanced by Karl Kaltwasser, middle-class scholar and liberal politician. As early as November 1943, Kaltwasser had jotted down some thoughts, which after the war he developed in a commemorative article, 'Bygone Kassel', that appeared in the *Hessische Nachrichten* on 22 October 1945.[139] Twelve years later, the critic returned to the subject in an influential epilogue that

---

[135] 'Die neue Stadt', *KP*, 24 November 1955.
[136] StAK, S4 L15, VHS Kassel, Arbeitsplan Herbst 1957, pp. 4f., 'Unbewältigte Vergangenheit'.
[137] Hosea 8: 7, 'For they have sown the wind, and they shall reap the whirlwind.'
[138] Belz, *Die Standhaften*, pp. 161–6, here p. 161.
[139] Karl Kaltwasser, 'Vergangenes Kassel', *HN*, 22 October 1945, p. 5. Manuscript in StAK, NL Kaltwasser, Mappe 35, 'Kassel. Vergang und Dauer I', 17 October 1945. See also the notes dated 27–11–43, in ibid., Mappe 32.

he wrote for a new edition of Paul Heidelbach's cultural history of the city, *Kassel. a Millennium of Hessian City Culture*.[140]

On Kaltwasser's view, the (air) war had done more than destroy the 'image' of Kassel; it had 'mortally wounded' the city. Here, Kaltwasser saw a crucial difference between Kassel and other German towns. 'Whereas elsewhere, in Frankfurt or Hamburg, life had been buried beneath the rubble, in Kassel life itself was buried.'[141] This was less because of a difference in the severity of the air war than because of the nature of the Kassel of old. Throughout its history, Kassel had been a residential town and a 'city of subjects' (*Untertanenstadt*), which had been defined by and through the state, he argued. In other words, for all its beauty, Old Kassel had lacked a tradition of civic liberties. As a consequence, 'false government' and 'erroneous obedience' had had more disastrous effects on the city than on other German towns.[142] In arguing thus, Kaltwasser shifted the focus from the air war to the broader historical context. Rather than the bombing, the lack of a confident middle-class culture was to blame for Kassel's 'death' in October 1943.

By the end of the 1950s, the *Heimat* of old was taking on new shades of meaning. To the same extent that nostalgia receded, influential protagonists of public discourse came to point to the beneficial effects of the city's 'death and rebirth' in the (air) war, as would become fully apparent in the decade that followed.

Conclusion

As this chapter has demonstrated, urban communities framed unprecedented destruction with the traditional concepts of *Kultur* and *Heimat*. Both parameters were established during the years 1940 to 1945 but after the end of the war were expressed in the novel narrative codes of the figure and the image. While this holds true for both Kassel and Magdeburg, the escalation of the Cold War in 1948/9 reinforced differences in emphasis. While in Kassel, the material impact of aerial warfare tended to be discussed in affective and aesthetic categories, allowing one-time Nazi propagandists to reinvent themselves as guardians of *Kultur*, the protagonists of public discourse in Magdeburg focused on political usages that drew heavily on the themes of Nazi wartime propaganda.

---

[140] Heidelbach, *Kassel. Ein Jahrtausend Hessischer Stadtkultur*, pp. 297–319. For the local reception of the new edition see StAK, NL Kaltwasser, Mappe 36.
[141] Heidelbach, *Kassel. Ein Jahrtausend Hessischer Stadtkultur*, p. 315.   [142] Ibid., p. 316.

6   From celebration to lamentation: dealing with the legacy of the air war, 1960–1995

Introduction

'A Look at the Time of Hopelessness' was the title of a commemorative article that the journalist Wolfgang Hermsdorff wrote for the *Hessische Allgemeine* in 1965 on the occasion of the twenty-second anniversary of the air raid (Fig. 26).[1] The article was accompanied by an image that took the reader back in time, visualising memories of wartime desolation: a street lined by collapsed buildings and burnt-out façades; overhead cables hanging down; rubble clearance detachments at work. 'A desolate picture,' as Hermsdorff summed up the scene in order to continue, 'All the greater are the reconstruction achievements that Kassel and her citizens were capable of in the past two decades.' The return of the day of remembrance elicited mournful reflection but also pride in a collective achievement. Functioning as a foil to a brighter present, memories of urban destruction were integrated into a wider narrative of successful overcoming.[2]

The text may be considered a typical example of the way in which local publicists conceptualised the material legacy of aerial bombing in the 'dynamic' 1960s, at a time when a 'new society' turned to enjoying the fruits of steady economic growth amidst a climate of broad optimism for the future.[3] German chancellor Ludwig Erhard's declaration of the 'end of the post-war period' in 1963 found a local parallel in the staging of an architectural exhibition that proudly proclaimed 'A City has been Rebuilt'.[4] 'The wounds have been healed; the ruins have disappeared,' as municipal press officer Hans Pippert wrote in a special edition of *Hessen Heute*, fusing the technical idiom of city planning with organic metaphors.[5] The 'new face [of the] city of tomorrow' had finally put the ghosts of the air war to rest.[6] Or so it seemed.

---

[1] Wolfgang Hermsdorff, 'Blick in die Zeit der Trostlosigkeit', *HA*, 22 October 1965.
[2] Ibid.   [3] Schildt, 'Materieller Wohlstand'.
[4] StAK, S5 O190, Hessentag 1964, 1980, 1982.
[5] 'Eine Stadt ist wieder aufgebaut', *Hessen Heute* (special edition *Hessentag* 1964), p. 10.
[6] Ibid.

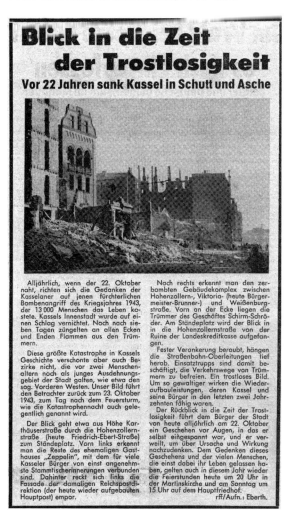

Blick in die Zeit der Trostlosigkeit

Vor 22 Jahren sank Kassel in Schutt und Asche

Alljährlich, wenn der 22. Oktober naht, richten sich die Gedanken der Kasselaner auf jenen fürchterlichen Bombenangriff des Kriegsjahres 1943, der 13 000 Menschen das Leben kostete. Kassels Innenstadt wurde auf einen Schlag vernichtet. Noch nach sieben Tagen züngelten an allen Ecken und Enden Flammen aus den Trümmern.

Diese größte Katastrophe in Kassels Geschichte verschonte aber auch Bezirke nicht, die vor zwei Menschenaltern noch als junges Ausdehnungsgebiet der Stadt galten, wie etwa den sog. Vorderen Westen. Unser Bild führt den Betrachter zurück zum 23. Oktober 1943, zum Tag nach dem Feuersturm, wie die Katastrophennacht auch gelegentlich genannt wird.

Der Blick geht etwa aus Höhe Karthäuserstraße durch die Hohenzollernstraße (heute Friedrich-Ebert-Straße) zum Ständeplatz. Vorn links erkennt man die Reste des ehemaligen Gasthauses „Zeppelin", mit dem für viele Kasseler Bürger von seit angenehmste Stammtischerinnerungen verbunden sind. Dahinter reckt sich links die Fassade der damaligen Reichspostdirektion (der heute wieder aufgebauten Hauptpost) empor.

Nach rechts erkennt man den zerbombten Gebäudekomplex zwischen Hohenzollern-, Viktoria- (heute Bürgermeister-Brunner-) und Weißenburgstraße. Vorn an der Ecke liegen die Trümmer des Geschäftes Schirm-Schröder. Am Ständeplatz wird der Blick in die Hohenzollernstraße von der Ruine der Landeskreditkasse aufgefangen.

Fester Verankerung beraubt, hängen die Straßenbahn-Oberleitungen tief herab. Einsatztrupps sind damit beschäftigt, die Verkehrswege von Trümmern zu befreien. Ein trostloses Bild. Um so gewaltiger wirken die Wiederaufbauleistungen, deren Kassel und seine Bürger in den letzten zwei Jahrzehnten fähig waren.

Der Rückblick in die Zeit der Trostlosigkeit führt dem Bürger der Stadt von heute alljährlich am 22. Oktober ein Geschehen vor Augen, in das er selbst eingespannt war, und er verweilt, um über Ursache und Wirkung nachzudenken. Dem Gedenken dieses Geschehens und der vielen Menschen, die einst dabei ihr Leben gelassen haben, gelten auch in diesem Jahr wieder die Feierstunden heute um 20 Uhr in der Martinskirche und am Sonntag um 15 Uhr auf dem Hauptfriedhof.

rff/Aufn.: Eberth.

Figure 26. Commemorative article on the twenty-second anniversary of the air raid, *Hessische Allgemeine*, 22 October 1965.

Yet, a mere decade later, dissonant voices radically called into question the narrative of the rebuilt city as success story. As the optimistic belief in progress was eroded by a broad sense of crisis in society at large,[7] New Left critics started to articulate their 'dismay' (*Betroffenheit*) over

---

[7] See Rosenfeld, *Munich and Memory*, pp. 229–31; Winkler, *Der lange Weg nach Westen*, pp. 330f.

the urban environment.[8] Subverting the idiom of the 1960s, these voices lamented the 'open [and] bleeding wounds' of the 'heap of rubble' that had yet to become a city again.[9] Contemporary Kassel was in truth still *kaput*: a city that stood as testament to the 'consequences of totalitarian rule'.[10] Lacking in 'urbanity', the city invited no sense of identification, exuding neither 'warmth [nor] intimacy'.[11] According to the critics, post-war city planning had not mastered the air war, but had, on the contrary, cynically exploited the devastation to engineer a 'second destruction' – an 'unprecedented annihilation of history', as the urban planner Dieter Hoffmann-Axthelm wrote in a report that was provocatively called *Die verpasste Stadt* or 'The Failed City'.[12]

Having originated among the New Left, the narrative of reconstruction as second destruction fused with traditionalist nostalgic sentiment, ushering in a renaissance of the idea of *Alt-Kassel* as a 'beautiful town' of social harmony and innocence.[13] By the late 1980s, the force of this critique was such that a prominent leftwing critic could demand the demolition of the post-war city altogether and its rebuilding 'according to the plans prior to 1943'.[14] While this 'radical solution to the dreadful state of Kassel's inner city' was, of course, never implemented, the early 1990s did witness the self-conscious attempt to regain the 'lost city' by way of refounding a historic city district that had been abandoned after 1945.[15]

In Magdeburg, this shift from 'modernist' celebration to 'post-modern' lamentation was discernible as well, albeit with some differences in emphasis and timing. Although, as a rule, realities on the ground lagged

---

[8] Rolf Hanusch, 'Ach Kassel', *Stattzeitung*, 6 (1980), p. 3. For the context: Beyme *et al.*, 'Leitbilder des Wiederaufbaus', pp. 26–30. See also the important contemporary texts: Mitscherlich, *Die Unwirtlichkeit unserer Städte*; Siedler, Niggemeyer and Angress, *Die gemordete Stadt*.

[9] 'Blutende, offene Wunden': Rolf Hanusch, 'Ach Kassel', *Stattzeitung* 6 (1980), p. 36; 'Steinehaufen': Rolf Schwendter, 'Aus dem Steinehaufen Kassel eine Stadt machen', *Stattzeitung* 10 (1976), pp. 6f.

[10] 'Zeugnis der Folgen totalitärer Herrschaft': Joachim Vieregge, 'Zwei Jahre in Kassel: etwas von außen gesehen', *Stattzeitung* 8 (1976).

[11] 'Kulturlose Stadt'; 'kein Hauch von Urbanität': Rolf Hanusch, 'Ach Kassel', *Stattzeitung* 6 (1980), pp. 3, 36; 'Wärme'; 'Intimität': Joachim Vieregge, 'Zwei Jahre in Kassel: etwas von außen gesehen', *Stattzeitung* 8 (1976).

[12] Hoffmann-Axthelm, *Die verpasste Stadt*, p. 6.

[13] On the embrace, and transformation, of the idea of *Heimat* by the New Left see Koshar, *From Monuments to Traces*, pp. 228–37; Moosmann (ed.), *Heimat. Sehnsucht nach Identität* (Berlin, 1980).

[14] Schwendter, 'Thesen zur radikalen Lösung der Innenstadtmisere', p. 51.

[15] *Wege zur Unterneustadt: Wie baut man eine Stadt?* (1994); *Wege zur Unterneustadt: So baut man eine Stadt* (1996). For the quotation: Wisotzki and Wegner, *Auf der Suche nach der verlorenen Stadt*. Compare also the official website of the Society for the Development of the Lower New Town at www.peg-kassel.de [22 December 2009].

seriously behind the ambitious schemes of Socialist city planners, a self celebratory rhetoric of spectacular success formed an integral part of the official narrative until 1989.[16] As in Kassel, the achievements of post-war reconstruction, real and imagined, were described in the idiom of medical surgery.[17] Here, aesthetic rather than functional categories prevailed: the 'new face' of the city was said to be 'beautiful' – indeed, 'more beautiful' than the pre-war city had ever been, as political functionaries and the guided media never grew tired of pointing out.[18] Yet, underneath the official discourse, voices were discernible that spoke of the 'new Magdeburg' not as of a city reborn but as of a city destroyed twice over – voices that increasingly turned to the pre-war city as an imagined alternative to the 'Socialist metropolis' in which they lived. In the process the idea of *Alt-Magdeburg* was born, which from the 1980s onwards also found public expression via exhibitions and photographs. By the time that SED rule collapsed in 1989/90, the narrative of successful overcoming had largely been subverted already. The wholesale denunciation that followed of Socialist city planning as a 'second destruction' drew on sentiments that had been in circulation since the 1960s.[19]

Local debates over the merits and shortcomings of post-war reconstruction were informed by memories of the air war. Despite the differences in political culture, the protagonists of public discourse in both cities drew on similar vocabularies and concepts in order to talk about the material legacy of aerial warfare. They employed organic metaphors to prescribe life cycles of death and rebirth, of faces wiped out and restored, of wounds bleeding, closed up and scarred. From the 1960s to the mid-1990s, the *lieux de mémoire* of aerial bombing served as important points of reference for both the defenders of the post-war rebuilding and their critics: as 'zero hour' of the unprecedented success story of a 'modern' or 'beautiful' city; as 'pretext' to engineer cynically a premeditated assault on the 'visual identity' of the *Heimatstadt*;[20] as symbolic vantage point to initiate belated 'healing' through the restoration of iconic ruins or

---

[16] The difference between plan and implementation is emphasised by Manz, *Wiederaufbau*. On planning inconsistencies see also Berger, 'Magdeburg: Klassenkampf der Dominanten'; Jakobs, 'Wie Phönix aus der Asche'; Landeshauptstadt Magdeburg and Stadtplanungsamt (ed.), *Magdeburg. Architektur und Städtebau*, pp. 29–31.

[17] 'Spaziergang ins Vergangene', *MZ am Wochenende*, 15 January 1965, p. 2.

[18] The phrase *schöner denn je* derived from a pronouncement by Adolf Hitler. It was taken up by general secretary Walter Ulbricht at the SED party conference in 1950, and repeated by state president Wilhelm Pieck in Magdeburg in 1952. Compare Gutschow, 'Stadtzerstörung und Gedenken', p. 269 and StAM, Rep. 41/703, fo. 7.

[19] See, for example, 'Zum 16. Januar: Bilder einer doppelten Zerstörung in unserer Stadt', *Volksstimme*, 15 January 1993, p. 10.

[20] Beyme, *Der Wiederaufbau*, pp. 13–24, here p. 13.

the refounding of historic city districts. Underlying these debates were broader questions about ways of identification and belonging, about the relationship of the residents to their urban environment. How much *Heimat* resided in the 'new' city? How much cultural heritage was necessary in order to feel at home in the urban environment? The answers that institutions, social groups and individuals gave to these questions between the 1960s and the mid-1990s form the subject matter of this chapter.

The 'closed wound': celebrating the city rebuilt, 1960–1975

With the completion of the first phase of the reconstruction in the 1960s, the material legacy of the war gradually began to disappear from the urban landscape. Although in Kassel, and even more so, Magdeburg, war ruins and vacant lots remained integral parts of the urban topography well into the 1990s, they lost their commanding hold on the imagination of contemporaries.[21] Influential protagonists of public discourse celebrated the achievements of the reconstruction, employing various forms and media – exhibitions, books, photographs and music pieces – to declare an end to the rubble years. In both cities, successful overcoming was invested with meaning that extended beyond the practical side of providing housing and social facilities to the resident, and evacuee, population. Stressing renewal over restoration, the political elites of both cities argued that the 'new face' of the cityscape symbolised comprehensive shifts in the political and cultural outlook of the citizenry as well. Through biological imagery, a connection was posited between the 'modern face' of the city and reconfigurations of civic identity. In this rhetoric, the locality, as an 'interchangeable representation' (Alon Confino), also stood in for the nation at large.

In Kassel, the early 1960s marked the turning point when the postwar rhetoric of 'rebirth' gave way to an emphasis on closure. This shift was well reflected in the official city guide, *Führer durch Kassel und Wilhelmshöhe*. In several editions from the second half of the 1950s, mayor Lauritz Lauritzen (SPD) had used the formulation of the 'changing face' in order to refer to the reconstruction as an event in progress.[22] The

---

[21] For Magdeburg, see the photographs in Krenzke and Goldammer, *Magdeburg. Bewegte Zeiten*, especially pp. 62f. In Kassel, the municipal planning office established in 1976 that there were still twenty-six vacant lots in the inner city. See StAK, A.0, Stadtverordnetenversammlung, vol. CXXXIV, session 17, 10 July 1978, p. 40.

[22] See *Führer durch Kassel und Wilhelmshöhe* (4th edn, 1956; 5th edn, 1957; 6th edn, 1958; 7th edn, 1959).

metaphor was dropped in the eighth edition of 1960 in favour of a sentence that indicated that a provisional end-point had been reached. 'After a time of fruitful reconstruction, the new image of our town is nearing completion,' Lauritzen wrote in the preface, which was reprinted verbatim in the following editions of 1961 and 1962.[23] Two years later, the city administration officially declared the reconstruction period to be over. On the occasion of the 1964 *Hessentag* – a cultural festival organised annually in order to promote a sense of common identity among the different regions making up the post-1945 state of Hesse – closure on the post-war years was celebrated through a special exhibition that carried the title 'A City has been Rebuilt'. In his opening address, Lauritzen's successor as mayor, Karl Branner (1910–97) (SPD), declared that the 'epoch of construction' had come to an end, to be followed by a phase of continuous 'extension'.[24]

In Magdeburg, the self-proclaimed goal of turning the city into a 'Socialist metropolis' precluded an overt emphasis on closure in the present.[25] The projected *longue durée* conveniently helped to gloss over planning inconsistencies as well as bottlenecks in the supply of labour and materials that seriously impeded the pace of the reconstruction.[26] Thus, mayor Philipp Daub (SED) could write in the first post-war city guide, published in 1961, that the booklet did not yet depict a 'completed' city because 'stormy Socialist construction' was producing permanent change in all spheres of society as well as in the cityscape.[27] Casting the promising achievements of the present as a prelude to an even brighter future, the mayor emphasised that the 'new construction according to Socialist principles' had made the 'face of the city . . . beautiful and attractive already', but would produce still greater achievements in the future.[28] This emphasis on the ongoing process notwithstanding, the Magdeburg city council also set a symbolic mark of closure. On the sixteenth anniversary of the air raid, in 1961, Beethoven's Ninth Symphony was performed in order to illustrate the progress *per aspera ad astra* or 'through darkness to light' that the city had made since the end of the war.[29] Quickly, the

---

[23] *Führer durch Kassel und Wilhelmshöhe* (8th edn, 1960; 9th edn, 1961; 10th edn, 1962), p. 3.

[24] StAK, S5 O190, OB Branner eröffnete 'Eine Stadt ist wieder aufgebaut', 1964.

[25] Seegers, 'Schaufenster zum Westen', p. 130.

[26] An early example was the controversy in 1952 between central government and local authorities on the reduction of labour and materiel engaged in rubble clearance for the sake of rebuilding Berlin. StAM, Rep. 41/762, fos. 6–8, August 1952.

[27] *Führer durch Magdeburg*, p. 1.   [28] Ibid.

[29] 'Glockengeläut zum Gedenken', *Der Neue Weg*, 19/20 January 1963, p. 7; 'Durch Nacht zum Licht', *Der Neue Weg*, 18 January 1962, p. 5; *Volksstimme*, 7 January 1961; 20 January 1961; *Mitteldeutsche Neueste Nachrichten*, 19 January 1961. See also Magdeburgische Philharmonie (ed.), *100 Jahre städtisches Orchester*, p. 39.

remembrance concert became an integral part of the commemorative activities surrounding the memory place, and even survived the regime change of 1989/90.

Together with the 'new Socialist city' a 'new Socialist human being' had emerged from the rubble and debris of the war, as Friedrich Sonnemann (SED), Philipp Daub's successor as mayor, declared on 16 January 1962.[30] Three years later, Sonnemann drew a parallel between the 'new' Magdeburg and a 'more beautiful', that is, Socialist, Germany.[31] In similar rhetoric, Hessian minister president Georg-August Zinn (SPD) emphasised in a public address of 1964 that the 'renewal' of Kassel encompassed spiritual and cultural aspects just as much as the material reconstruction.[32] Five years earlier, the city council had already issued a publication that underlined this very link between material and spiritual regeneration. The booklet, *Kassel – City of the Documenta*, recast the erstwhile City of Reich Warrior Days (*Stadt der Reichskriegertage*) as a community that had wholeheartedly embraced modernity, playing an avant-garde role in the democratic culture of West Germany as host to the modern art exhibition of the 'documenta'.[33]

Conspicuous in this self-congratulatory rhetoric was the frequent use of vocabulary that implied strong emotional gratification. In 1963, for example, Kassel mayor Karl Branner wrote in response to television coverage of the bombing war, 'We are rightly proud of our new ascendancy that finds a clear expression in the new rise of our cities.'[34] Here, Branner used the adjective *stolz* or 'proud' to refer to a collective state of consciousness – a term that denotes qualities of virility, strength and heroism.[35] Sonnemann, in 1962, spoke of *Genugtuung* or 'satisfaction', thus using a word that implied emotional compensation for previous injuries.[36] The significance of this kind of language becomes apparent when situating the 'end of the post-war period' (Ludwig Erhard) within the context of the 'return' of the 'unmastered past' of Nazi barbarism.[37] At a time when Israeli and German courts confronted the German public with state crimes that triggered a domestic discourse of guilt and shame,

[30] *Der Neue Weg*, 17 January 1662, p. 4.
[31] 'Aber das Herz schlug weiter. Magdeburg – zwanzig Jahre nach der Zerstörung', *Der Neue Weg*, 16 January 1965, p. 8.
[32] StAK, A.4.41, no. 457, Hessentag in Kassel, 'Einleitende Worte des Hessischen Ministerpräsidenten Zinn', 2 July 1964.
[33] *Kassel – die Stadt der documenta* (1959).
[34] StAK, A.1.10, no. 621, Reden [OB Branner] II 1963/41, 'Fernseh-Sendung 22. Oktober 1963', p. 2.
[35] *Deutsches Wörterbuch*, vol. XIX (1957), entry 'stolz (adj.)', cols. 231–66, here col. 233.
[36] Compare *Deutsches Wörterbuch*, vol. V (1897), entry 'Genugtuung', col. 3517.
[37] Siegfried, 'Zwischen Aufarbeitung und Schlussstrich', p. 78.

the achievements of the reconstruction were couched in the language of pride and honour, offering a symbol of positive identification for the 'war generation' turned 'reconstruction generation'. To an extent, the 'heroic' language of the discourse of closure can thus be understood as fulfilling a compensatory function for feelings of humiliation induced by the public discussion about the crimes of Nazism.

Given this connection, it is no surprise that, amid the turmoil of '1968', members of the political establishment would point towards the post-war achievements of the war generation in order to counter charges about their activities during the war.[38] In the autumn of 1968, Kassel mayor Branner did just that at an opening address to the exhibition 'From Ruins to the New City', which was staged to mark the twenty-fifth anniversary of the iconic air raid.[39] According to the mayor, the exhibition was not a self-congratulatory celebration of the post-war rise of Kassel but served the pedagogical purpose of an inter-generational admonition. Here, the sons rather than the fathers stood accused. Branner placed upon the youth of 1968 the obligation to familiarise themselves with the 'incomprehensible destruction' of Kassel's 'zero hour' in order to understand the consequences that resulted from disregarding the lessons of the past. Reversing the customary roles in the inter-generational conflict, he recast the war generation as staunch defenders of democracy against an irrational onslaught of youthful exuberance and ignorance: 'They must learn why the older generation will not tolerate any deliberate or accidental endangering of our democracy and the fruits of many hard years of reconstruction.' Speaking for his generation at large, he postulated a 'right to be proud', while placing on the younger generation the 'duty to acknowledge the achievements [of the reconstruction]'.[40]

Allied bombing as 'zero hour'

Within the larger discursive context of 'reconstruction' and 'renewal', allied bombing as *lieu de mémoire* retained a pivotal place throughout the 1960s. It legitimised the radical break with the pre-war urban environment, and more generally, functioned as a dark foil to the present. In the 1960s, allied bombing took on the meaning of a negative founding myth – the archetypal 'zero hour' – in Kassel as well as Magdeburg. There was both apologetic and critical potential in such an interpretation. Just

---

[38] Compare Rusinek, 'Von der Entdeckung der NS-Vergangenheit'.
[39] StAK, A.1.10, no. 638/78, Reden [OB Branner] 1968, 'Eröffnung der Ausstellung "Von Ruinen zur neuen Stadt"', 27 September 1968.
[40] Ibid., pp. 3f.

as the notion of radical rupture could be used to telescope the years of the Third Reich into a single event, thus obfuscating both local support of Nazism as well as personal and structural – not least of all, city planning – continuities across the watershed of 1945, the notion could also be used as a vantage point for exploring the uncanny aspects of the pre-war *Heimat*.

In Kassel, the connotation of the memory place began to change with the completion of the first phase of the reconstruction. Gradually, the notion of the aerial bombardment as the 'dying day' of *Alt-Kassel* was displaced by the notion of 22 October 1943 as the 'birthday' of the new city – a cathartic catastrophe that had severed the links with a discredited past in order to make way for a brighter future. By the 1960s, a narrative strand thus gained dominance that had first been articulated by committed Nazis in 1943/4, and had subsequently been embraced by city planners and the civil administration: the end was a new beginning; urban destruction a unique opportunity for a thorough new ordering of the city-space. At the same time, the counter-trend of the nostalgic yearning for the city of old – to which the *lieu de mémoire* indicated nothing but catastrophe – as influentially promoted during the war by conservative fellow-travellers of Nazism and popularised by sections of the middle classes in the 1950s, lost in influence.

To be sure, *Alt-Kassel* did not disappear from public discourse in the 1960s. With the spreading of affluence in the wake of steady economic growth, more Kasseler than ever before could afford to spend money on luxury items such as coffee-table books – and the continuous trickle of new publications on the pre-war city suggests that a certain demand existed throughout the period.[41] Yet, as an imagined place of architectural beauty and social harmony, the notion of *Alt-Kassel* reached a low point in the 1960s. 'Whoever has known Old Kassel cannot help but be touched by certain feelings of nostalgia when looking at those photographs,' the editor to a special edition of a nostalgic newspaper series from the 1950s wrote in 1968. But characteristically, he added, 'But he will also acknowledge that the city has become so much healthier and more spacious [since] 1945.'[42] This impressionistic evidence is corroborated by the findings of contemporary public opinion research. According to a poll conducted by the Bad Godesberg Institute of Social Research in 1964, 90 per cent of the population agreed that the civil administration

---

[41] Metz, *Hochfürstlich Hessische Residenzstadt Cassel*; Hermsdorff and Eberth, *Es geschah in Kassel von 1900 bis heute*; *Kassel einst und jetzt* (4th edn, 1966); Lometsch, *Cassel in alten Bildern*; Herbordt, *Bilder aus dem alten Kassel*; Heidelbach, *Casseler Spaziergänge*.

[42] Hessische Brandversicherungsanstalt, Direktor, 'Zum Geleit', in Herbordt, *Bilder aus dem alten Kassel*.

had done a commendable job in rebuilding Kassel after 1945. Only 7 per cent of the sample interviewees were of the opinion that grave mistakes had been made. The social researchers also found that nine out of ten residents felt happy in their 'new *Heimat*', of whom the majority had no personal memories of *Alt-Kassel* because they had been born after the war or moved to the city after 1945.[43]

In light of these figures, a private letter addressed to the mayor in 1964 may claim to carry more than just anecdotal significance.[44] The letter was written by seventy-year-old Elisabeth Riebeling on the twenty-first anniversary of the bombing night. It opened by recounting harrowing scenes from the air raid, and went on to recall feelings of despair and resignation: 'Never will Kassel be a city again I thought to myself... The destruction is just too great.' Past dejection was contrasted to present elation when the old lady continued by praising the rebuilt city: 'Kassel has risen again... more beautiful than ever. A miracle has happened.' Remarkably, Elisabeth Riebeling not only expressed her happiness and gratitude at the fact of the reconstruction itself, she also explicitly commended the modern way in which the city had been rebuilt. Although the old lady admitted to being moved by visual representations of the 'romantic alleys' of *Alt-Kassel*, she was unequivocal in her praise of the new living quarters that allowed for 'sun, wind, and air': 'A good thing it is that the dark and gloomy alleys are gone, with the pale women and the pale little children... It is a good thing that the heart of Kassel has been created in a such a friendly and homely way that everybody loves the new city, visitor and local alike.'[45]

Although preservationists pointed out that some eminent historical monuments of *Alt-Kassel* could have been restored if the political will to do so had existed – that, indeed, buildings like the Nahlsche Haus or the Lutherische Pfarrhaus had fallen victim to post-war city planning rather than the bombing war – their cautious critique of the principles underlying the reconstruction was shared by a minority only.[46] The marginal role of traditionalist sentiment in the period is well illustrated by the fact that the municipal architect Wolfgang Bangert, in 1961, was able to use the official organ of the Heimat League as a platform to celebrate 'Kassel – the new city on old ground'.[47] Here, Bangert not only reiterated

---

[43] 'So sehen die Bürger ihre Stadt', *Unsere Stadt Kassel* (1968), p. 20; Institut für angewandte Sozialwissenschaften (IFAS), *IFAS report Sonderheft Kassel*.

[44] StAK, A.1.10, no. 398, Elisabeth Riebeling to mayor, 22/23 October 1964.

[45] Ibid.

[46] Ganßauge, 'Was blieb vom alten Kassel erhalten?', *Hessische Heimat*, n.s., 11/2–3 (1961), 28–32.

[47] Bangert, 'Kassel – eine neue Stadt auf altem Grund', *Hessische Heimat*, n.s., 11/2–3 (1961), 2–8.

the standard argument of city planning that the 'near-total destruction' of the bombing war had 'cleared the way' for 'healing' the long-ailing organism of the city. He also challenged the preservationist readership of the magazine to leave behind their nostalgia and embrace the new Kassel.[48] 'Among the *Heimat* enthusiasts one can often hear the regretful complaint that all the old beauty has vanished and that our new cities . . . all look the same,' Bangert wrote. Coyly suggesting that the recognition by traditionalists was a central measuring rod for the success of his work, the municipal architect continued, 'And . . . those who have tirelessly worked for the reshaping of the city will feel amply compensated for their efforts when the citizens of Kassel, and in particular the friends of the *Heimat*, will feel – above and beyond the pain for what has been irrevocably lost – affection and love for the newly risen . . . city.'

Whereas in Kassel, the notion of a 'zero hour' finally displaced the old notion of the 'dying day', in Magdeburg there occurred a shift of emphasis rather than a paradigm change. Here, official interpretations remained within the established framework of the dialectic of death and rebirth, which had been a constituent element of the guided discourse ever since the emergence of '16 January 1945' as a memory place in 1946.[49] However, in 1960s Magdeburg too, political functionaries tended to stress the 'new beginning' rather than the death of the old order. 'We are looking to the future,' as Karl Brossmann, local head of the satellite party of the CDU, wrote in a programmatic article on the occasion of the air raid's fifteenth anniversary. 'We remember in order to become aware of how much we have achieved in Magdeburg since 1945,' he proclaimed.[50] In a similar way, mayor Friedrich Sonnemann (SED) five years later celebrated the 'construction achievements' of the present.[51] While acknowledging that 'not all the wounds of the imperialist war have yet been healed', he maintained, 'Today, twenty years after the day of destruction, the eyes and hearts of our citizens are no longer filled with tears. No, blissfully they look upon what they have achieved and their hearts belong to Socialism.'[52]

The pathos of the political elites notwithstanding, there is evidence to suggest that the 'beauty' of the new Magdeburg was not appreciated by all sections of the population. This appears to have been due less to the discrepancy between the self-congratulatory rhetoric and the slow

---

[48] For the quotations see ibid., 2, 4.   [49] See chapter 1.
[50] Karl Brossmann, 'Wir blicken in die Zukunft. Gedanken zum 16. Januar', *Der Neue Weg*, 16 January 1960, p. 1.
[51] Friedrich Sonnemann, 'Aber das Herz schlug weiter', *Der Neue Weg*, 16 January 1965, p. 8.
[52] Ibid.

progress of actual reconstruction than to the official goal of building a
'Socialist metropolis'. In a dictatorship with totalitarian tendencies, conflicting positions on the feasibility of the restoration of historic buildings
quickly took on the character of a power struggle, in particular between
the state and the Church. Throughout the late 1950s and early 1960s,
a bitter controversy raged over the question of whether the numerous
church ruins of the historic Old Town could be integrated into the new
cityscape or whether they had better be torn down. Generally, the state
sought to reduce the presence of ecclesiastical buildings whereas the
Church strove to preserve as many of them as possible, opposing all projected demolitions tenaciously, if unsuccessfully. The issue was particularly contentious where political rather than functional criteria appeared
to motivate the demolition plans, as was the case with the seventeenth-
century Heiliggeistkapelle and the fourteenth-century Katharinenkirche.
After a protracted struggle, the partially restored Heiliggeistkapelle was
torn down in 1959 in order to make way for a mass rally ground.[53]
Five years later, the shell of the Katharinenkirche was demolished as an
'inappropriate' reminder of the past on the modern boulevard of Karl
Marx Street in contravention of an earlier agreement between Church
and state.[54]

A petition that was sent to the City Building Office may help to elucidate some of the ways in which traditionalists used memories of the
bombing in order to make a case for preservation. The letter was written
not by a local resident but by a West German citizen who had heard of
the projected demolition of the Heiliggeistkirche. Legitimising his intervention with a common responsibility of Germans east and west of the
border for the cultural heritage of the nation, he drew on the shared
experience of aerial warfare in order to argue that historic buildings must
be treated as material expressions of a single *Kulturnation* or 'cultural
nation'. On this line of reasoning, the rupture of allied bombing did not
provide a unique opportunity for creating something new, but conferred
a special obligation on the post-war generation to preserve carefully what
was left.[55]

Within Magdeburg, the bitter conflict over the demolition of the church
ruins appears to have functioned as an important catalyst for segments

---

[53] Compare StAM, Rep. 41/416, Heiliggeistkirche, 1956/7; AKPS, Rep. A Spec. G., A
774, Abriss der Heiliggeist-Kirche.

[54] StAM, Rep. 41/918, fos. 1–3, Stadtbaudirektor Ungewitter, 'Begründung über den
Abbruch der Katharinenkirche im Nordabschnitt der Karl-Marx-Straße', 21 January
1964. See also AKPS, Rep. A Spec. G., A 22522, St. Catharinen Bauten (1952 bis
1967).

[55] StAM, Rep. 41/416, W. Patzig to Rat der Stadt – Bauamt, 15 November 1956.

of the old middle classes to turn to the pre-war city as a place of longing. In a dialectic twist, the ruthless policy of creating a 'Socialist metropolis' helped to invest material relics of the past with an emotional significance that they had not hitherto possessed, spawning a notion that had until then existed in rudimentary form only: the idea of *Alt-Magdeburg* as a beautiful city. When the 42-year-old civil engineer Heinz Gerling co-founded the Interest Group for the Preservation of Historical Monuments in 1964, he was motivated in part by the experience of the demolitions.[56] In the same year, 68-year-old Werner Priegnitz, pensioned artisan and associate of the municipal museum, suggested at a board meeting the idea of a photographic exhibition on Old Magdeburg.[57] His recommendation went unheeded, but in an article for the satellite party paper, the *Liberal-Demokratische Zeitung*, Priegnitz described 16 January 1945 as the 'day of destruction' for Old Magdeburg while paying no more than lip service to the notion of rebirth.[58] By this time, the *Heimat* researcher had for some years used the occasion of the day of remembrance in order to give public lectures on 'Magdeburg in the past, present, and future'. Using slides to invite his audience on 'a stroll through the Elbe city of old', he emphasised the 'immeasurable loss' of the bombing war, as the paper of the CDU, *Der Neue Weg*, reported.[59] Was this activity, perhaps, also a veiled comment on the demolition policy of the city council?

Born 'at the moment death [came] over the city':
celebrating the new beginning

Whatever the reservations of traditionalists, their voices played a marginal role only throughout the 1960s. Dominating public discourse was the celebration of the city rebuilt, as a modern 'consumer paradise' and 'city of fine art' in Kassel;[60] as a vibrant 'city of heavy industry' and beautiful 'city of Socialist education and culture' in Magdeburg.[61] The medium of choice for demonstrating the achievements of the reconstruction was the visual. In newspapers, exhibitions and special publications, photographs

---

[56] Kriewald, 'Gerling, Heinz'. In 1997, Gerling was made an honorary citizen for his services to the architectural heritage of Magdeburg.

[57] StAM, Rep. 41/792, Rat der Stadt MD, KHM. Protokolle von Dienstbesprechungen des Museums (1962–70), fo. 52. See the biographical sketch by Maren Ballerstedt, 'Priegnitz, Wilhelm Franz Werner', *Magdeburger Biographisches Lexikon*, pp. 557f.

[58] W. Priegnitz, '16. Januar 1945 – Tag der Vernichtung', *LDZ*, 16 January 1965, p. 3.

[59] 'Gedenken an den 16. Januar 1945', *Der Neue Weg*, 20 January 1958, p. 2.

[60] 'Kassel – Stadt der Kunst', *Hessen Heute*, special edition 1964: *Hessentag. Kassel 3.7. bis 5.7.1964*, p. 16.

[61] *Führer durch Magdeburg*, p. 1.

of the contemporary city were contrasted with rubble photography, both providing 'objective' evidence of post-war progress and serving as potent symbol of the mastering of the past. In using rubble photography as a dark foil for a bright present, the 1960s witnessed the culmination of a trend that had been in evidence since the mid-1950s.[62] Through the visual, the notion of the air war as the 'real zero hour' of the local community was confirmed over and over again.[63]

Next to the visual, there emerged another means of representation that captured both defining notions of the 1960s: the air war as a new beginning and the present as a thriving time of youth. Drawing an analogy between the home town and the life of the individual, the local media became fond of marking the day of remembrance by portraying the lives of young adults who were born on the day that the old city was destroyed. As an illustration of a dialectic relationship between death and life, this mode of representation was particularly popular in Magdeburg. Mayor Sonnemann (SED) even received two residents in order to present them with gifts in advance of their twentieth birthdays on 16 January 1965. In so doing, the mayor symbolically designated the memory place as a day that called for celebration, not mourning.[64]

The first such example appeared in print on the occasion of the thirteenth anniversary of the air raid in 1958. In a *Volksstimme* article, journalist Hans-Georg Noack told a parable that is worth considering at some length. The story took as its subject matter the victory of life over death through the virtues of courage and perseverance. At the centre of the narrative stands machine-fitter Franz W., to whom a son is born 'at the moment that death has come over the city'.[65] While the screams of the newborn inspire hope among the community that is huddled in a shelter, the confident mood gives way to desperation as the building collapses. Whereas the people around him despair, Franz W. remains steadfast, and taking up all his strength, manages to dig a hole through the rubble with his bare hands, rescuing himself and the baby (while apparently leaving behind his wife, who goes unmentioned). 'After countless hours, Franz W. squeezed himself out into the open of a dusky dark day. The bundle with his son he kept tightly pressed to his chest as he stepped over

---

[62] For Magdeburg see, for example, 'Magdeburg 16. Januar 1965: Schön ist unsere neue Stadt', *Volksstimme*, 16 January 1965, p. 1; 'Nach zwanzig Jahren', *MZ am Wochenende*, 15 January 1965, pp. 1f.; for Kassel: Magistrat der Stadt Kassel, press office (ed.), special supplement 'Unsere Stadt 1943 bis 1968', in *Unsere Stadt*, October 1968.

[63] StAK, A.1.10, no. 638, Reden [OB Branner] II 1968/78, 'Eröffnung der Ausstellung "Von Ruinen zur neuen Stadt"', 27 September 1968.

[64] 'Geburtstagskinder beim OB', *Volksstimme*, 18 January 1965, p. 8.

[65] Hans-Georg Noack, 'Der 16. Januar mahnt', *Volksstimme*, 16 January 1958, p. 3.

the rubble that used to be his home in a dark, sunless alley of the Old Town ... [T]hrough the sheets and the coat, he felt the beating of a little heart,' the first part of the narrative concluded, dramatically illustrating the notion of the collapse of the old city – and by extension, the old order – as the birthday of the new. This was followed by another part, which was set in the present: father and son survey the open plain 'that used to be the darkest part of the Old Town'. While the father recalls the misery of life in the back alleys and the 'death of old Magdeburg' in the boy's hour of birth, the son confidently replies, 'We will rebuild, only more beautiful than before!' And with conviction, he adds, 'But we will not allow the new streets to be destroyed by the bombs again.' Here, coincidence was presented as parable – a reading of events to which the guided media would return several times in the years that followed.[66]

In Kassel, the *Hessische Allgemeine*, in 1968, also researched the names of young adults who were born on the night 'that *Alt-Kassel* disappeared forever', but did not invest the subject with quite the same tone of high pathos.[67] Whereas in Magdeburg, birthday girl Elisabeth Bauermeister praised the industry of the reconstruction generation, her counterpart in Kassel, Ingrid Esbach, confessed to amnesia when asked about her memories of the rubble years. 'Kassel before the reconstruction? To be honest, I don't know much about it,' she replied, according to the newspaper. Likewise, when asked about the lessons from the air raid, 25-year-old Jochen Gärtner merely reiterated the general consensus of 'Never again'. By contrast, Elisabeth Bauermeister pointed fingers at the alleged threat originating from West Germany, stressing her determination to fight against 'people in Western Germany ... who are planning even worse deeds'. In Magdeburg, the example suggests, an overt emphasis on closure was precluded by the politicisation of the air war, whereas in Kassel wartime destruction appeared ever more as a distant memory.

Revisiting Alt-Kassel

There was both apologetic and critical potential in the reappropriation of '22 October 1943' as a founding myth for the new city. On the one hand, the emphasis on the notion of a new beginning corroborated a tendency that had been in evidence ever since the formation of a collective memory place in the 1940s: the telescoping of World War II, and more generally,

---

[66] See Rudi Hartwig, 'Als die Nacht vorüber war ...', *Volksstimme*, 16 January 1960; Elisabeth Bauermeister, 'Als ich geboren wurde ...', *Volksstimme*, 16 January 1965, p. 6.
[67] 'Am 22. Oktober 1943: Acht Namen im Geburtsregister', *Hessische Allgemeine*, 22 October 1968.

the Third Reich, into a single event the inherent characteristic of which was victimhood rather than agency. On the other hand, the notion of the 'zero hour' helped to stabilise the democratic political culture of the present. In Kassel, a self-confident sense of collective achievement opened up possibilities for a critical re-engagement with the past. From the vantage point of present closure, influential voices started to revisit *Alt-Kassel*, and what they found bore little resemblance to the town of beauty, innocence and harmony that had been dreamt up in the 1950s.

In Magdeburg, by comparison, continuity prevailed. Here, the guided media tended to look on the pre-war urban environment with ambivalence, just as they had done in the 1950s. Pre-war Magdeburg may have been picturesque in places, but emphasis was placed on the unsanitary living conditions that were taken as emblematic of a corrupt social order.[68]

In Kassel, the notion of the 'zero hour' led to a curious discrepancy in different sectors of the memory culture. At a time when commemorations were starting to link the 'night of horror' of 1943 with the 'domestic policy disaster' of 1933,[69] the official city guide, in a historical sketch of a thousand years of municipal history, telescoped the years of Nazism into the date of 22 October 1943.[70] The same strategy was adopted by the municipal press office on the twenty-fifth anniversary when, in a twelve-page documentary, the iconic event was singled out as a vantage point for a summary sketch of Kassel's 'path from decline to rise' between 1943 and 1968.[71] In comparison, the *Führer durch Magdeburg* of 1961 provided a more detailed – if by no means less problematic – picture of the recent past, listing the 'organised resistance of the workers under the leadership of the KPD' and 'Anglo-American terror raids' as the defining features of local history in the years 1933 to 1945.[72]

While the notion of 'zero hour' provided ample room for evading uncomfortable questions about agency, complicity and continuity, it also furnished an opportunity to explore – from the perspective of a prosperous present – the uncanny side of *Alt-Kassel*. This exploration could take the form of a personal confession, as was the case with novelist Christine Brückner (1921–97), who contributed an essay to the above-mentioned

---

[68] Compare the typical comments in 'Spaziergang ins Vergangene', *MZ am Wochenende*, 15 January 1965, p. 2.

[69] StAK, A.1.10, no. 621, Reden [OB Dr. Branner] II 41/63, '"Deutschlands Städte starben nicht"? – Das alte Kassel *ist* gestorben', 22 October 1963.

[70] 'Tausendjähriges Kassel', in *Führer durch Kassel und Wilhelmshöhe* (9th edn, 1961), pp. 6–10, here p. 10.

[71] Magistrat der Stadt Kassel, press office (ed.), special supplement 'Unsere Stadt 1943 bis 1968', in *Unsere Stadt*, October 1968.

[72] *Führer durch Magdeburg*, p. 6.

special documentary 'Kassel 1943–1968'. It could also take the form of essayistic reflection, as in *Kassel – Portrait of a City* by poet Manfred Hausmann (1898–1986).

In the piece 'The New Kassel is Incomparable', Brückner contrasted adolescent memories of wartime Kassel with her feelings upon moving back to the city in 1960.[73] In her reflections, the air raid occupied a central place, functioning as a violent rupture that separated adolescence from adulthood, the past from the present. 'On that night, all my possessives (*Possessiva*) burnt to ashes,' she declared. Brückner vehemently rejected any notion of 'return'. In 1960, she moved to Kassel, but did not return to the *Vaterstadt* she had left in 1943: 'I did not recognize anything and did not want to recognize anything... I refused to find the old Kassel again... In my memory there was nothing but rubble and death.' To Brückner, *Alt-Kassel* as she knew it was not a postcard idyll but a 'Nazi town... a war town, dark [and] cold' – memories that even with the passing of time, she insisted, took no trace of golden hue. To this, she contrasted the 'incomparable city' she had moved to in 1960, which had broken with the past even in the ordering of the city space. 'Never before', she extolled, 'was the Friedrichplatz as beautiful as today! No more marches, no more space for military parades.' Whereas she remembered the *Alt-Kassel* of her youth as dark and fortified, the new city was light and green, and above all, democratic: 'In the new Kassel, a lot belongs to "us",' she exclaimed.[74]

Adopting the genre of essayistic reflection, Manfred Hausmann concurred with Brückner's central contention in his influential *Kassel – Portrait einer Stadt*.[75] While the bombs had killed and destroyed, they had also liberated the citizenry from the chains of the past. Only through catastrophe had the residents gained the chance to make the one-time *Residenzstadt* or 'capital city' their own, and in the process, evolve from subjects into citizens. 'It seemed as if the catastrophe was necessary in order to set free forces that had always existed but had not been able to make themselves felt due to unfortunate circumstances,' Hausmann wrote.[76] The *Heimat* of old was in truth an uncanny place, while post-war Kassel was built and owned by the citizenry in a way that Old Kassel had never been. Without doubt, there were residents who disagreed with the characterisation of *Alt-Kassel* as advanced here – a review called Hausmann's thesis 'provocative' – but for Hausmann and Brückner to be able

---

[73] Christine Brückner, 'Das neue Kassel ist unvergleichlich', special supplement, 'Unsere Stadt 1943 bis 1968' in *Unsere Stadt*, October 1968. The text is reprinted in Brückner, *Ständiger Wohnsitz*, pp. 70–6.
[74] Ibid.   [75] Hausmann, *Kassel – Portrait einer Stadt*.   [76] Ibid., p. 59.

to articulate such strident criticism in popular coffee-table books at all is indicative of shifts in the ways that notions of belonging were defined in the 1960s.

The 'painful scar': mourning the second destruction, 1975–1995

The celebration of the rebuilt Kassel as functional, youthful and modern proved short-lived. As the dynamism of the 1960s gave way to the stagnation of the 1970s, Kassel as a self-consciously 'modern' city increasingly came to be described in terms of its deficits – as a place lacking in urbanity, beauty and history.[77] A New Left disquiet over the 'sclerosis' of the urban environment merged with the traditionalist idea of *Alt-Kassel*, and by the late 1970s, pitted the imagined beauty and homeliness of the prewar city against the perceived coldness and ugliness of the contemporary environment, eliciting charges of a 'double destruction'.[78]

As the polemical tag indicates, more was at stake in the debate over city redevelopment than technical matters such as the closure of gap sites, the development of public squares and the planting of trees in the inner city.[79] The issue served as a catalyst to discuss wider questions about the relationship between rupture and continuity, loss and mourning, identity and alienation. According to critics such as the urban planner Hoffmann-Axthelm, the contemporary city-space amounted to an 'architectural memory loss' that reflected the inability of the reconstruction generation to face the past. 'Only people who . . . did not love their city were capable of destroying it in such a way,' Hoffmann-Axthelm commented in his report on urban development, 'The Failed City'.[80] What had been lost, he argued, was the identification with the locality as a place where one belonged, of Kassel as *Heimat*: 'The residents of today, wherever they might come from, live in the city as strangers.'[81] In a less polemical but equally damning critique, museum curator Karl-Hermann Wegner argued in 1985 that the 'identity [of the citizens of Kassel] with their own history was lost through the destruction and the reconstruction'.[82]

[77] Rosenfeld, *Munich and Memory*, pp. 229–31.
[78] Mitscherlich, *Die Unwirtlichkeit unserer Städte*; Siedler, Niggemeyer and Angress, *Gemordete Stadt*. For the context see Beyme *et al.* (eds.), *Neue Städte*, pp. 9–31.
[79] See the official leaflet Stadt Kassel–Der Magistrat. Amt für Stadtplanung und Stadterneuerung (ed.), *Zur Diskussion*.
[80] Hoffmann-Axthelm, *Verpasste Stadt*, p. 57.
[81] Ibid., p. 8. See also StAK, A.1.10, no. 894, Stadtentwicklung Innenstadt 1985–9, Axthelm to Amt für Stadtplanung, 6 July 1986.
[82] *Kassel. Moderne Stadt mit Tradition*, p. 6.

Within the context of the larger debate, '22 October 1943' functioned as an important point of reference for both the defenders and the critics of the contemporary cityscape. While the apologists of the 'new city on old ground' sought to legitimise post-war planning by pointing to the allegedly total devastation occasioned by the air war, the critics shifted attention to questions of local agency. They opined that the iconic date did not mark the end point of the city's destruction but rather the beginning of a process that lasted until the 1970s. Hoffmann-Axthelm spoke of the destruction *since* 1943 rather than the destruction *of* 1943, maintaining provocatively, 'The air raids achieved what the city planners had hoped that they would achieve.'[83]

Beneath the surface of the streamlined media, broadly similar developments were discernible in Magdeburg. Although the alleged beauty of the 'new' Magdeburg remained a stock-in-trade of the official rhetoric,[84] here too, memories of the pre-war city – no longer conceived of as a negative foil but imagined as a vibrant and beautiful place – provided a challenge if not an alternative to the contemporary 'Socialist metropolis'. The renaissance of *Alt-Magdeburg* was fostered by the work of local amateur historians of the 'Section Municipal History' in the League for Culture (*Kulturbund*). Led by Alfred Heidelmayer, the group exploited the leeway in the 'heritage' conception of state cultural policy in order to revive 'memories of Magdeburg'[85] by way of public exhibitions that were staged on the anniversaries of the bombing. Although, as a rule, post-war developments occupied considerable space in the exhibitions as well, the presence of large-size photographs of the Baroque splendour of turn-of-the-century Magdeburg tended to let the rupture of the air war appear in a different light: 16 January 1945 was not the day of birth for a bright present but the 'darkest day' in Magdeburg's history, as the paper of the satellite party of the CDU wrote on 16 January 1987.[86] The idea of *Alt-Magdeburg* was well established by the time that SED rule collapsed in 1989/90 and the deficiencies of post-war city planning could be openly addressed.

In post-1989 Magdeburg, no less than in Kassel a decade earlier, the results of the post-war reconstruction were discussed in terms of their

---

[83] Hoffmann-Axthelm, *Verpasste Stadt*, pp. 13, 45.
[84] 'Magdeburg ist heute schöner denn je', *Mitteldeutsche Neueste Nachrichten*, 15/16 January 1983.
[85] This was the title of the first two exhibitions staged in 1983 and 1985. 'Erinnerungen an Magdeburg. Ausstellung der Fachgruppe "Stadtgeschichte" bis morgen geöffnet', *LDZ*, 15 January 1983, p. 8. See on the context Meier and Schmidt, *Erbe und Tradition*.
[86] 'Heute vor 42 Jahren erlebte Magdeburg den schwärzesten Tag seiner Geschichte', *Der Neue Weg*, 16 January 1987, p. 8.

deficiencies as a 'creeping' or 'double destruction'.[87] Nor did the debate
remain confined to technical issues such as the failure of the command
economy to meet building needs and to uphold the urban infrastructure.
Here, too, notions of belonging and questions of identity assumed central
importance. As in Kassel, the *lieu de mémoire* of allied bombing played an
important role in this debate, functioning as a point of reference for those
arguing that Socialist city planning had been driven by the ideological
goal of destroying 'the last remnants of identity' in the city.[88] The date
was equally important for those who defended the lives' work of the
reconstruction generation, if not the results of this work itself.

Lieu de mémoire as site of mourning

'We are going to mourn for four weeks,' was the inscription on a wreath
that was placed in front of the Brüderkirche in Kassel on 22 October 1981.[89] To underline this message, the angel-shaped sculpture on
the church wall, which had been erected in 1958 as a memorial to the
casualties of the air war in the old town, was covered in black cloth.[90]
Responsible for this symbolic action was not the civil administration but
the grass-roots citizens' initiative of the Arbeitskreis für Denkmalpflege
und Sanierungskritik, a group of left-leaning preservationists, architects
and academics living in Kassel. By way of this public gesture, they challenged the hegemonic connotation of the memory place as a day of
birth, and by implication, the underlying narrative of achievement and
progress. According to the activists, '22 October' was a symbol not of
successful overcoming but of continuing loss, calling for mourning, not
celebration. Far from being mastered, the legacy of urban destruction
had been *verdrängt* or 'suppressed', buried under the cold functional-
ity of a car-friendly city-space and the superficial hustle of a mindless
consumer culture. General suppression found concrete expression in the
sorry state of the monument itself, which had been 'covered up by traffic
signs, smudged over by the symbols of a car culture, no longer recognisable as a site of memory and admonition', as the Arbeitskreis wrote in
the *Stattzeitung*.[91]

---

[87] Konrad Mieth, 'Keine Stadt in der Welt sollte es noch einmal erleben müssen...',
Volksstimme, 16 January 1991, p. 17; 'Zum 16. Januar: Bilder einer doppelten Zerstörung
in unserer Stadt', *Volksstimme*, 15 January 1993, p. 10.
[88] Peter Dömeland, 'Es begann mit der Sprengung der Türme von St. Ulrich', *Volksstimme*,
13 January 1993.
[89] 'Der Kasseler Bombenopfer gedacht', *HA*, 24 October 1981.   [90] See chapter 3.
[91] Arbeitskreis für Sanierungspolitik und Denkmalpflege, 'Stört das Denkmal – Denkmalz-
erstörung in Kassel', *Stattzeitung* 10 (1981), pp. 38f.

By the time the activists staged their protest in October 1981, the debate about the deficits of post-war reconstruction had reached the cultural mainstream. As early as 1977, architectural critic Peter Bode, in a special Kassel issue of the popular *Merian* series, had contrasted the 'very beautiful medieval Old Town' and the 'enchanting' Upper New Town of the city before the war with the 'extremely small-minded mediocrity' of the post-war architecture, which, in places, amounted to nothing less than an 'architectural desert' and an 'urban development disaster' (*städtebaulicher Sündenfall*).[92] Here, as elsewhere, *Alt-Kassel* provided the rod against which the shortcomings of the contemporary city were measured. Radical rupture between the past and the present – the absence of a 'thousand years of municipal history' from the contemporary urban space – was identified as the root cause for the present malaise of the inner city, leading, so the argument went, to a lack of identification of the resident population with their urban environment.[93]

There were, of course, also voices that expressed reservations about a revisionist critique that found inspiration in the pre-war city and employed aesthetic rather than functional categories. In a preface to a popular coffee-table book, mayor Hans Eichel (SPD), for example, spoke of the 'pride' that the 'very interesting' inner-city architecture of the 1950s – such as the pedestrian zone of the Treppenstraße – inspired even in 1986. At the same time he turned against the 'transfiguration' of *Alt-Kassel* as 'beautiful' when behind the picturesque façades there had lurked overcrowding and squalor.[94] Yet, by the 1980s, even the apologists of post-war city planning had abandoned the celebratory rhetoric of successful closure that had characterised local discourse in the 1960s. In his preface, the mayor acknowledged 'wounds' that the city still exhibited forty years after the air raid.[95] More than a decade later, Eichel's successor, Georg Lewandowski (CDU), likewise stressed the long-term effects of allied bombing. 'Kassel is a city that still suffers from the wounds of its near-total destruction,' he wrote in a preface to the selected writings of the novelist Christine Brückner.[96]

The return of nostalgia

The extent to which the notion of successful overcoming had been displaced by an accentuation of continued loss is perhaps best illustrated by the shifts of emphasis in the work of poet Manfred Hausmann, who had

---

[92] Bode, 'Von der Hand in den Mund geplant'.
[93] Wegner, *Kassel. Ein Stadtführer*, p. 13.
[94] Hans Eichel, preface, in Brier and Dettmar, *Kassel. Veränderungen einer Stadt*, vol. I, p. 7.
[95] Ibid.   [96] Georg Lewandowski, 'Zum Geleit', in Brückner, *Ständiger Wohnsitz*, p. 8.

played such a prominent role in the celebratory rhetoric of the 1960s,[97] By the late 1970s, the eighty-year-old Hausmann struck a very different tone. In a contribution to the *Merian* special issue on Kassel, the poet revisited the city of his childhood in the spirit of nostalgic yearning.[98] Yes, the old town had been overcrowded and unhealthy, but it had also been full of life and, above all, of incomparable beauty, he wrote in his piece 'The Old Cassel'. In contrast to 1964, there was no more talk of 'broken chains' and new-found liberty. On the contrary, speaking sarcastically of a 'total redevelopment (*totale Sanierung*) of dreadful thoroughness', Hausmann condemned the air raid as 'senseless destruction of a unique . . . treasure' that he called both 'sad' and 'disgraceful'. In 1977, unlike 1964, '22 October 1943' signified nothing but loss – a loss that called for mourning, not celebration: 'One should not mourn what is lost and face the future, a saying goes. This is a very questionable dictum. For anybody who has known the old town . . . will never in his whole life cease to mourn [its] passing . . . Not just Kassel, the whole world has become poorer for it.[99]

The article was richly illustrated with picturesque photographs of the late medieval old town that aimed to impart both the architectural beauty and the charm of which Hausmann had spoken (Fig. 27). This was no coincidence but an indication of the importance that the visual played in the remarkable renaissance of the idea of *Alt-Kassel*. From the late 1970s, a string of illustrated books, postcard series, calendars and booklets appeared that took the pre-war cityscape as subject matter and conveyed – however much the individual publications differed in tone and intention – a sense of irredeemable loss.[100] The evolution of *Kassel before the Firestorm*, renamed *Kassel – Then and Now* in the revised edition of 1960, provides a case in point. In many ways, the seventh edition of 1981 took up the visual narrative of *Alt-Kassel* that had been dropped in the third edition of 1960 and only partially restored in the fourth edition of 1966.[101] Whereas in 1960, the editors had drastically reduced the

---

[97] Hausmann, *Kassel. Portrait einer Stadt*, pp. 7f.   [98] Hausmann, 'Das alte Cassel'.
[99] Ibid., p. 27.
[100] Homburg (ed.), *Kassel in alten Ansichtskarten*; Hermsdorff, *Ein Blick zurück aufs alte Kassel*; Hamecher (ed.), *Kassel in alten Ansichtskarten. Neue Folge*; Marsen, Kulbarsch and Soltau, *Stadtteilgeschichte als Stadtgeschichte*; Willi Friedrich, *Kassel. Zerstörung und Wiederaufbau*; Metz, *Residenzstadt Cassel*; Ausstellung der Fachbereiche Architektur und Stadtplanung der Gesamthochschule Kassel (ed.), *Beiträge zur Stadtentwicklung*; *Kassel einst und jetzt* (7th edn, 1981); Hermsdorff, *Kassel 1900 bis heute* (3rd edn, 1981); Kemp and Neusüß, *Kassel 1850 bis heute*; Lometsch, *Bauten aus dem alten Kassel*; Baumann, *Kassel in alten Ansichtskarten*; Brier and Dettmar, *Kassel. Veränderungen einer Stadt*; Klaube, *Alt-Kassel*; Wegner, *Bilder aus dem alten Kassel*. The trend continues unabated and has, if anything, accelerated in recent years. See, for example, the video *Die Kasseler Altstadt vor ihrer Zerstörung 1943* (2000).
[101] *Kassel einst und jetzt* (1960; 4th rev. edn, 1966; 7th rev. edn, 1981).

Figure 27. *Alt-Kassel* as imagined by the poet Manfred Hausmann in 1977. The visual illustration was adopted from the early twentieth-century preservationist movement. Note the anachronistic spelling of the town as 'Cassel'.

number of photographs from pre-war Kassel in order to make room for the contemporary cityscape, twenty years later the remaining editor included once again many of the images that had been left out in the 1960s. In the seventh edition of 1981, more than half the photographs showed pre-war motifs, as compared with a ratio of one in four in 1960 and one in two in 1966.

In Magdeburg, the restrictive licensing practices of the ruling SED did not allow for the emergence of a body of literature that would have celebrated *Alt-Magdeburg* in quite the same way. It took until after the fall of Communism for nostalgic sentiments to be reflected in illustrated books carrying titles such as *Magdeburg before 16 January 1945* or *Magdeburg – a Lost Cityscape*.[102] Yet post-unification nostalgia had roots that reached back into the 1980s and beyond. The amateur historians of

---

[102] *Was da in Schutt und Asche fiel*, ed. MZ am Wochenende; Stadtarchiv Magdeburg, *Magdeburg. Ein verlorenes Stadtbild*; Buchholz, *Der Breite Weg*; Buchholz, Ballerstedt and Buchholz, *Magdeburg – so wie es war*; Buchholz, Ballerstedt and Buchholz, *Magdeburg in alten Ansichten*; Schütte, *Magdeburg in alten Ansichtskarten* (1990, 1995).

the 'Section Municipal History', in particular, used the *lieu de mémoire* of allied bombing in order to popularise cultural memories of the pre-war city. By way of visual representations and contrasts, several exhibitions in the 1980s shifted the emphasis from the contemporary 'Socialist metropolis' to *Alt-Magdeburg*, and thereby, from successful overcoming to irrevocable loss.

The high point of this activity was reached in 1987 when the amateurs presented an exhibition on the history of the architectural and commercial centre of pre-war Magdeburg, the Breite Weg, which had not only been renamed Karl Marx Street in 1953 but also been changed beyond recognition by the double impact of the bombing war and Socialist city planning. The exhibition, which was staged between 16 and 25 January, met with great popular acclaim. It also received considerable coverage in the press of the satellite bourgeois parties.[103] According to a report in the *Mitteldeutsche Neueste Nachrichten*, nearly three hundred historical photographs illustrated 'why the street had once been famous well beyond the borders of our city as a boulevard of Baroque artistry'.[104] In another report, the *Neue Weg* emphasised the awed reception with which those sections of the exhibition had been met that focused on turn-of-the-century Magdeburg.[105]

Exposing the zero hour as a myth

With the new emphasis on loss came a search for reasons. Why did the old city have to be destroyed, and why did the contemporary environment bear so little resemblance to the pre-war city? In the Kassel of the 1980s, two sets of answers emerged to questions such as these. The first revolved around the nature of World War II, the second around rupture and continuity in urban planning.

To some extent, the accentuation of loss led to a heightened irritation with the conduct of the allied air war. In his reverie on Old Kassel, poet Manfred Hausmann spoke of a 'disgraceful [act of] senseless destruction' with reference to what had happened on 22 October 1943. In doing so, he implicitly drew on elements of Nazi wartime propaganda: indiscriminate bombing was criminal destruction for its own sake, pure and simple. Hausmann did not stand alone. In the late 1970s and early 1980s, the idiom and interpretive frames of Nazism experienced some kind of limited revival. Writers as diverse as novelist Christine Brückner and a

---

[103] See Ballerstedt, 'Daten zur Magdeburger Stadtgeschichte', p. 215.
[104] 'Aus der Geschichte des einstigen Breiten Weges', *MNN*, 13 January 1987.
[105] 'Eine Magistrale offenbart ihre 750 jährige Historie', *Der Neue Weg*, 21 January 1987.

group of postgraduate research students used the propaganda term 'terror raid' in order to refer to the bombing.[106] Brückner even went so far as to insinuate that the ultimate goal of the air war had been the annihilation of *Kultur*: '[22 October 1943 was] one of the terror raids that included the annihilation of the historical and art-historical treasures of a city; the aim was to alienate the population from their city,' she wrote in a contribution to a popular coffee-table book.[107]

Brückner was a committed democrat; so were Hausmann and the university students. Their use of National Socialist idiom should therefore be read not as an expression of a revisionist politics but rather as an indication of the extent to which reflections on the loss of the historic city-space were emotionally charged. In the same piece, Brückner spoke of the 'mourning and confusion' that arose in her when looking at photographs of the bygone city. Author Hans Baumann, in a collection of old postcard motifs, confessed to a 'feeling of profound loss', and of 'anger'.[108]

Despite the occasional use of Nazi rhetoric, the main thrust of this anger was directed not at the Western allies but at the German war generation. In the 1980s, a body of writing emerged that searched for local agency in order to find answers to the question of loss. Reflecting shifts in the wider memory culture, this literature worked from the broad consensus that the bombing must be considered a 'logical reaction to the premeditated launching of war, genocide and Holocaust', as university professor Folckert Lüken-Isberner stated emphatically in an exhibition catalogue in 1993.[109] Critical attention, however, was turned elsewhere: at a tradition in urban planning that had welcomed the destruction of the air war as a 'unique opportunity'.[110] While some knowledge of the fabricated character of the underlying claim of 'total' destruction had existed throughout the reconstruction period, it was in the 1980s that the notion of the air war as a 'zero hour' was systematically exposed as a myth. Of crucial importance in this process was the work of a research group from Kassel University, the Arbeitsgruppe Stadtbaugeschichte, who popularised their findings on the ideological roots of post-war city planning in a number of publications and exhibitions.[111]

---

[106] Marsen, Kulbarsch and Soltau, *Stadtteilgeschichte als Stadtgeschichte*, p. 195: 'On the night of 22/23 October, British bombers flew a terror raid against the inner city of Kassel that razed the Old Town to the ground.'

[107] *Kassel. Moderne Stadt mit Tradition*, pp. 7–25, here p. 8.

[108] Baumann, *Kassel in alten Ansichtskarten*, introduction.

[109] Lüken-Isberner, 'Von der Gauhauptstadtplanung zur Gigantomie', p. 173. Compare also Baumann, *Kassel in alten Ansichtskarten*, introduction.

[110] Stadtbaurat Erich Heinicke in 1947.

[111] Petra Wettlaufer-Pohl, 'Ausstellung zur Stadtplanung in Kassel: "Stunde Null" gab es nicht', *HA*, 27 November 1987; Lüken-Isberner, 'Kassel: Neue Stadt auf altem Grund';

According to the revisionist argument, the contemporary cityscape was the result less of radical rupture in the air war than of personal and conceptual continuities in urban planning between the Third Reich and the post-war period. The notion of total destruction was a 'fable' that had been cynically invented by urban planners in order to legitimise and implement Nazi-era ideas that deliberately broke with the historic city-space.[112] Contemporary Kassel, in short, was the result of continuity rather than of rupture, of an insufficient break with Nazism in the post-war period and not of any total destruction suffered in the air war. Although some attempts were made to salvage the notion of total devastation against this revisionist challenge, the apologist interventions were defensive in tone, indicating the extent to which a central legitimising plank of the post-war years had been eroded by the 1980s.[113] As a consequence, not just the pre-1945 activities of the 'fathers of the reconstruction', municipal architect Erich Heinicke (1892–1964) and chief of the municipal planning bureau Werner Hasper (1911–93), were brought into sharp focus but also those of the reconstruction generation at large.

Indeed, 'generation' indicated an important fault line in this debate.[114] Most revisionist critics were born during or after the war, and by addressing the issue of continuity across 1945, highlighted the double identity of their fathers and grandfathers as members of both the reconstruction generation and the war generation. In a preface to a collection of pre-war photographs, Hans Baumann, born in the late 1940s, spoke of the ambivalence of 'respect' and 'anger' that he felt towards his father's generation, who 'proudly point towards their rolled-up sleeves' but had left behind a legacy of 'urban planning barbarism'.[115] Apologists of the contemporary city likewise recognised that inter-generational conflict played an important role in the debate. Journalist Wolfgang Rossbach, for example, used the forty-sixth anniversary of the bombing in order to intervene on behalf of the reconstruction generation. In a commentary that appeared in the *Hessische Allgemeine* on 22 October 1989, he warned against 'rash judgement [that accuses] a whole generation of a lack of competence and vision'.[116]

　　Lüken-Isberner, 'Von der Gauhauptstadtplanung zur Gigantomie in Trümmern'; König, 'Konflikt'; Hoffmann-Axthelm, *Verpasste Stadt*, pp. 13–24. See also Durth and Gutschow, *Träume in Trümmern*, vol. II, pp. 791–809.

[112] Hoffmann-Axthelm, *Verpasste Stadt*, p. 23.

[113] See for example the contribution by Werner Noell, after the wartime head of the building construction office (*Hochbauamt*), '"Die Zerstörung unserer Stadt war so vernichtend gewesen . . .". Gedanken zu Kassels Wiederaufbau', *HA*, 17 June 1985.

[114] On the concept of 'generation' see Jureit and Wildt (eds.), *Generationen*; Reulecke (ed.), *Generationalität und Lebensgeschichte*.

[115] Baumann, *Kassel in alten Ansichten*, introduction.

[116] Wolfgang Rossbach, '22. Oktober 1943 – 46 Jahre danach', *HNA*, 21 October 1989.

Whereas in Kassel, the highly emotional debate reached its climax in the second half of the 1980s, in Magdeburg similar questions could not be raised until after the demise of SED rule. When the debate did finally erupt in the early 1990s, the experience of the second German dictatorship assumed centre stage. While in Kassel the critics pointed to the personal and ideological links between the (early) Federal Republic and the Third Reich, in post-Communist Magdeburg the ideological goals of the SED regime – rather than any continuities between the Third Reich and early post-war planning – were held responsible for the 'un-Magdeburgian' appearance of the contemporary city.[117] Here, the inclusion of Magdeburg in the centralised planning of the Nationales Aufbauwerk in August 1952 made it easy for the post-dictatorial public to construct a simple dichotomy between commendable indigenous efforts on the one hand and catastrophic outside interventions on the other. This interpretation allowed for acknowledging the deplorable state of the urban environment while paying tribute to the efforts of a resident population who increasingly saw their lives' work slandered by the wholesale discrediting of the GDR in post-unification Germany.[118]

Sites of memory as sites of 'healing'

The controversy over urban planning to some extent diminished the importance of the air war as a historical event. If the notion of 'total devastation' was an ex-post rationalisation that had served to legitimise a deliberate break with the city of old, then the schemes of urban planners rather than the bombing raids were responsible for the absence of the past in the contemporary urban environment. The growing recognition of this connection did not, however, diminish the importance of the air war as a memory place. On the contrary, the *lieu de mémoire* turned into a symbolic space in which the disparate events of total war and of domestic urban planning were commemorated jointly. The civil administrations, in collaboration with citizens' initiatives, chose the day of remembrance in order to lay the foundation for restorative projects that were intended, at long last, 'to heal the wounds' in the urban topography that had been caused by allied bombs and reckless city planning.[119]

In Kassel in 1993, the fiftieth anniversary of the air raid witnessed not only unprecedented commemorative activity but also the inaugural event of an ambitious urban development project, the refounding of the thirteenth-century Lower New Town (*Unterneustadt*). On 23 October 1993, politicians, city planners and residents assembled

---

[117] Jakobs, 'Wie Phönix aus der Asche', p. 175.   [118] Ibid., pp. 172f., 176.
[119] Hellweg, 'Wiedergründung der Unterneustadt', p. 6.

in the Brüderkirche to open up a discussion process that aimed at 'closing . . , one of the last great wounds' of the war, as the municipal building officer, Uli Hellweg, stressed in a pamphlet documenting the event.[120] Like few other urban spaces, the 'lost city district' of the late medieval Lower New Town appeared to epitomise the lasting impact of the 'double destruction' to which the city had been subjected:[121] devastated by fire in the air raid of 22 October 1943, the city district was abandoned by post-war city planners and never rebuilt. Fifty years later, the once densely built-up area functioned as an exhibition ground while a four-lane federal road cut across the ground on which the district church had once stood. Through 'critical reconstruction', the project sought to found anew the Lower New Town – not by way of a one-to-one replication of the pre-war city but through the critical 'reappropriation' of the historic city-space, as Dieter Hoffmann-Axthelm explained in his introductory address.[122] In so doing, the project not only addressed – and to some extent sought to undo – loss but also reflected on the legacy of 'fifty years of not knowing how to deal with the destruction, fifty years of unrealised mourning over the lost city'.[123]

The urban development project of the Lower New Town self-consciously used '22 October' in order to regain that which, according to an influential strand of public opinion, had been lost through the air war and the post-war reconstruction: civic identity (*Bürgersinn*). Whatever the factual merits of a diagnosis that identified a lack of historical consciousness as the root cause for the socio-economic problems bedevilling late twentieth-century Kassel, the same line of reasoning motivated the Magdeburg city council to undertake a similar, if less ambitious, project. On 13 December 1990, the city council passed a CDU motion on the 'conceptual rebuilding' of the ruin of the late medieval Johanniskirche, which had, since 1979, functioned as a memorial site to the destruction in World War II.[124] As city councillor for culture R. Löhr explained in a letter to preservationist Heinz Gerling, the oldest parish church and traditional market church not only symbolised the 'civic self-confidence' (*bürgerliche Selbstbewußtsein*) of the old city but also stood as a symbol of 'defiant resistance [to the] ignorance of the past decades', that is, the shortcomings of Socialist city planning.[125]

---

[120] *Wie baut man eine Stadt*, preface. See also the official homepage, www.peg-kassel.de [15 June 2010].

[121] Wisotzki and Wegner, *Auf der Suche nach der verlorenen Stadt*.

[122] Hoffmann-Axthelm, 'Die Idee der kritischen Rekonstruktion'.   [123] Ibid.

[124] StAM, Rep. 18/4, 'Antrag der CDU-Fraktion vom 19.9.1990: Wiederaufbau der Johanniskirche', 13 December 1990.

[125] StAM, Rep. 12U, NL Gerling, no. 124, Kuratorium für den Wiederaufbau der Johanniskirche 1990–5, fos. 173–5, here 173, Stadtrat für Kultur to H. Gerling, 20 December 1990.

Although the projected rebuilding sought to reverse the impact of post-war neglect no less than that of the air war, the *lieu de mémoire* of allied bombing – rather than any date connected to Socialist city planning – was chosen to initiate this process. In post-Communist Magdeburg, no less than in Kassel, memories of the destruction wrought by allied bombers were less divisive than memories of the post-war destruction brought about by domestic city planners, and thus more suitable for the 'common work of reconciliation'.[126] On 16 January 1991, the Committee for the Reconstruction of the Johanniskirche held its inaugural meeting in the council chamber of the city hall.[127] It was convened in order to raise public awareness of the project and to coordinate fundraising activities. The following year, the committee jointly co-organised the commemoration of '16 January 1945' with the city council.[128] 'Healing', not confrontation, was the premise underlying the reconstruction – of Magdeburg's silhouette, the deficit in civic identity, and the division of the nation, as mayor Willi Polte (SPD) made clear in the preface to a fundraising publication. Ironically, this 'new beginning' drew on a memory place whose history was indelibly linked with the past that it sought to overcome.[129]

Conclusion

As this chapter and the previous one have shown, the discourse surrounding the legacy of urban destruction made up a second vector in urban memory cultures of the air war. Here, the use of the term 'death' stood in as a metaphor for the radical transformation of the built-up environment that had been occasioned by area bombing. In order to make sense of rupture, political and planning elites in the two cities, public intellectuals and ordinary citizens resorted to the familiar ideas of *Heimat* and *Kultur*. Conceptualising the city as an organism, they employed organic metaphors in order to speak about the material impact of aerial warfare, produced statistics on the extent of the destruction, and drew on visual representations both to celebrate and to discredit what had been lost and what was erected in its stead. In the two cities, the trajectory

[126] StAM, Rep. 12U, NL Gerling, no. 124, fo. 57, 'Gemeinsames Versöhnungswerk': in 'Zur Geschichte der Johanniskirche', unsigned manuscript, 10 May 1992.
[127] See 'Magdeburg gedachte der Opfer des 16. Januar', *Volksstimme*, 17 January 1991, p. 16; StAM, Rep. 12U, NL Gerling, no. 124, fos. 173–5.
[128] StAM, Rep 12U, NL Gerling, no. 124, fos. 69–80.
[129] Willi Polte, 'Grußwort zur Bildmappe Johanniskirche', in Kuratorium für den Wiederaufbau der Johanniskirche zu Magdeburg (ed.), *Die Johanniskirche*. Compare also Magdeburgische Gesellschaft von 1990 zur Förderung der Künste, Wissenschaften und Gewerbe e.V., *Festreden zur Eröffnung der Johanniskirche am 2.10.1999.*

of memory was determined by local traditions, the pace and nature of the reconstruction, and shifts in the wider political, socio-cultural and generational parameters.

Whereas the period of 1940 to 1960 was distinguished by the attempt to master the legacy of urban destruction through 'modern' reconstruction, the period of 1960 to 1995 was marked by the celebration of closure and the subsequent lamentation of continued loss. Although, by the mid-1960s, the material impact of the air war appeared to have been overcome, a mere ten years later dissonant voices started to perceive the rebuilt city in terms of its deficits, alleging that post-war city planning had, in effect, completed what the bombers had begun. In Kassel, this radical critique of the contemporary urban environment originated among the New Left, which appropriated the nostalgic idea of *Alt-Kassel* in order to formulate a positive vision of the city as a place of belonging. In Magdeburg, sections of the old middle classes likewise turned to the pre-war city in order to posit a visual alternative to the emerging 'Socialist metropolis'. In doing so, they invested the idea of *Alt-Magdeburg* with affectionate and aesthetic qualities that it had not possessed in the immediate post-war period. After the political watershed of 1989/90, both cities – now part of a single nation – initiated ambitious urban development projects that were intended to reconcile the past to the present. Both the 'critical reconstruction' of the Lower New Town in Kassel and the rebuilding of the Johanniskirche in Magdeburg were designed to make visible again elements of the pre-war city in the contemporary cityscape.

As a *lieu de mémoire*, the air war served as an important point of reference in the public debate on the merits and demerits of the post-war reconstruction, and the wider discourse about ways of belonging and modes of identification. In the period up until 1960, the conceptualisation of the memory place as a 'unique opportunity' and a 'new beginning' – as promoted by Nazi propagandists during the war and by the local political elites and city planners after the war – contended with an alternative view, according to which the *lieu de mémoire* denoted nothing but catastrophic loss and metaphoric 'death'. In the 1960s, with the first phase of the reconstruction complete, the first interpretation attained hegemonic status. Politicians, publicists and ordinary citizens drew upon the iconic air raids as founding myths for a bright present, as a 'zero hour' that threw into sharp relief the achievements of the 'reconstruction' generation. From the 1970s, however, different groups in the two cities started to embrace the second interpretation, challenging and, finally, displacing the notion of the 'new beginning'. According to the revisionist challenge, the memory of the air war called for mourning, not celebration, marking the beginning, not of a successful reconstruction, but of a process of continuous destruction that stretched from the Nazi years to the present. By the 1990s, the *lieu de mémoire* of allied bombing had thus turned into a symbol of cultural loss that had been brought about by allied bombs and urban planning in equal measure.

Part III

Writing histories

7   Reconstructing the 'night of horror': local histories of allied bombing, 1940–1970

Introduction

'In many accounts and stories, the memory of the night of horror lives on,' observed the author of an article that the *Hessische Nachrichten* published on 21 October 1950 in order to mark the seventh anniversary of the big air raid on Kassel. The piece was called '22 October 1943 – From the Secret Report of the Chief of Police'. It made available to the local public excerpts from the confidential experience report that had been compiled by the chief of police in December 1943.[1] Although the journalist contended that the document contained 'comprehensive statistical material' that offered a broadly reliable picture of the extent of the catastrophe, he expressed severe reservations about the number of casualties that the report mentioned.[2] He argued that the chief of police must have had an interest in downplaying the deaths. Instead he proposed to accept a figure that lay somewhere in between the official death toll of 5,830 and the rumoured figure of 70,000–80,000.[3] When, three years later, the article was reprinted in the SPD weekly, *Hessischer Sonntag*, the editors inserted an annotation that went further in privileging the 'subjective truth' of personal memory over the documentary evidence.[4] 'Nobody who has lived through the destruction of the old town is willing to believe those figures,' they averred emphatically.[5]

The episode sheds light on the 'interdependence' of history and memory that characterises contemporary history in general but is of special

---

[1] '22. Oktober 1943. Aus dem Geheimbericht des Kasseler Polizeipräsidenten', *HN*, 21 October 1950.

[2] For a copy of the report see StAK, S8 C40, 'Erfahrungsbericht zum Luftangriff vom 22.10.43 auf den LO I. Ordnung Kassel', 7 December 1943.

[3] '22. Oktober 1943', *HN*, 21 October 1950.

[4] A. Assmann, 'Wie wahr sind Erinnerungen?', p. 104. Compare also, with reference to Dresden and the controversy over fighter planes strafing civilians, Welzer, 'Bilder der Macht'; Bergander, 'Vom Gerücht zur Legende'; Schnatz, *Tiefflieger über Dresden?*

[5] 'Gedenken und Mahnung: Der Feuertod raste durch die Stadt', *Hessischer Sonntag*, 18 October 1953.

relevance to the sub-discipline of local history.[6] Here, journalists and lay historians produce historiographical texts for a local audience of which they themselves are an integral part. In the case of aerial bombing, the post-war attempts at writing authoritative accounts of what 'really' happened were undertaken in the context of myriad 'subjective truths' and popular legends that had their origins in an interplay of personal experiences, rumours and the stories put into circulation by Nazi propaganda. The problem of continuity between wartime narratives and post-war historiography extended to the very documents that served as historical source material. As the example of the experience report by the chief of police illustrates, post-war accounts often had to draw on the documentary evidence that had been produced under the auspices of Nazi authorities during the war.

This chapter and the following one will chart the local historiography on the air war between 1940 and 1995 as a third vector of memory. They conceive of local history as a distinct genre that is concerned just as much with present-centred considerations of finding 'usable' pasts as with observing the professional standards of academic history.[7] Who wrote about the air war, and what did the authors want to know about it? How did they contextualise their subject matter, and what functions did these historiographical narratives play in the context of the broader memory culture?

In order to analyse local history writing as an integral part of memory, it is helpful to make use of a typology that was proposed by Friedrich Nietzsche in the second of his *Untimely Meditations* in 1874.[8] In 'On the Use and Disadvantages of History for Life' the philosopher famously distinguishes between three conceptions of history, which he terms 'monumental', 'antiquarian' and 'critical'. Monumental history, according to Nietzsche, subordinates the 'individuality' of the past to the demands of the present.[9] It turns history into a storehouse from which 'the resourceful and the powerful' derive heroic examples for their actions.[10] By contrast, the antiquarian approach is concerned not so much with the exemplary character of the past but with the pious collection of historical detail for the sake of preservation.[11] Finally, critical history puts the past on trial, seeking to explode myths by bringing to bear on to received knowledge the analytical tools of rational enquiry and source criticism.[12]

---

[6] Jarausch, 'Zeitgeschichte und Erinnerung'; Hockerts, 'Zugänge zur Zeitgeschichte'. Compare Hans Rothfels' famous definition of 'contemporary history' as 'the epoch of contemporaries and its scholarly treatment'. Rothfels, 'Zeitgeschichte als Aufgabe', 2.
[7] Moeller, *War Stories*.   [8] Nietzsche, *Vom Nutzen und Nachteil*.   [9] Ibid., p. 258.
[10] Ibid., pp. 258–65, here p. 258.   [11] Ibid., pp. 265–9.   [12] Ibid., pp. 269f.

This chapter argues that during the war, Nazism projected a history of the allied air war that was monumental in conception. Nazi propagandists stressed the exemplary conduct of the 'racial comrades' and the Nazi party under aerial bombardment, seeking to preserve and to create documentary evidence that would bear out their interpretation of the unfolding events. In so doing, Nazism influenced the documentary base and the analytical parameters of post-war histories as well. After the demise of Nazism, the task of writing about the air war fell within the remit of local journalists, who produced stories that projected no longer heroism but suffering. Despite individual attempts at writing critical histories, an inverted monumental historiography prevailed that sought to render a disconcerting past commensurable to the sensibilities of the present. While this trend was discernible both east and west of the Iron Curtain, there were also differences. Whereas in Kassel journalists produced historical accounts that exhibited a tendency towards external and internal pacification, in Magdeburg the historiographical narratives were put into service in the cause of mass mobilisation. The dominance of monumental conceptions of history lasted until the 1970s when a number of antiquarian endeavours got under way that also incorporated critical elements, albeit to a limited degree.

'The true culprits of this bloody world war': allied bombing as anti-Semitic parable, 1940–1945

'When the history of this war is written, a special chapter... will have to be reserved for the Anglo-American bombing war,' the Nazi district leader of Magdeburg-Anhalt, Rudolf Jordan, declared in a programmatic article that was published in the local press of Magdeburg in January 1944.[13] The remark may serve as a good starting point for a discussion of the place of allied bombing in Nazi ideas about the historiography of World War II. It underlines the extent to which key protagonists of the Third Reich self-consciously viewed the present as a future past. Bernd Wegner argues, indeed, that during the final phase of the war, Nazi leaders were motivated above all by a concern about their place in history, and to this end purposefully stage-managed their demise as 'heroic downfall'.[14] Even if one does not follow Wegner all the way, there can be little doubt that the political elites of the Third Reich attempted

---

[13] 'The true culprits of this bloody world war': Gauleiter Rudolf Jordan, 'Der Bombenkrieg', *Der Mitteldeutsche*, 23 January 1944, pp. 1f.; *Magdeburgische Zeitung*, 24 January 1944, pp. 1f.

[14] Bernd Wegner, 'Choreographie des Untergangs'. See also Geyer, 'Endkampf 1918 and 1945'.

to influence future histories of the war during their lifetime. In January 1943, for example, Jordan ordered the founding of a regional archive in order to collect 'documentary evidence' for writing the 'history, development and politics' of the Nazi party, and 'contemporary history' more generally.[15] The attempt to shape the historiography of the future was not confined to the creation, preservation and destruction of documents, but extended also to setting the parameters for the analysis of the historical source material.

As the quotation from Jordan's piece on the bombing war indicates, the Nazi leadership intended to accord a prominent place to the strategic air war against the German Reich in a future history of World War II. While confronting Nazi propagandists with a host of difficulties in the daily representation of the unfolding events,[16] the strategic air war, at the same time, appeared to furnish them with a profitable subject for a future historical treatment of the war. As a theatre of action in which the Western allies systematically violated the spirit – if not the letter – of the rules of war as laid down in the Hague Convention of 1907,[17] the air war was deemed an ideal topic for addressing the moral and legal side of the conflict as a whole. It was singled out in order to illustrate the National Socialist meta-narrative of World War II as a 'world revolutionary struggle' in which chivalrous German soldiers faced cowardly enemies bent on wanton destruction and murder.[18]

In the early summer of 1943, Goebbels finalised plans for publishing a governmental white book that focused on the legal side of aerial bombing.[19] The booklet was issued in July by the Foreign Office under the title, 'Documents on the Sole Responsibility (*Alleinschuld*) of England for the Bombing War against the Civilian Population'.[20] In several respects, the publication differed markedly from the Nazi propaganda

---

[15] BA Berlin, NS 18/985, Gaupropagandaleitung Dessau, fos. 73–90, here fo. 73, 'Anordnung', 15 January 1943. On the relationship between cultural memory and the archive see A. Assmann, *Erinnerungsräume*, pp. 343–407.

[16] See Boelcke (ed.), '*Wollt Ihr den totalen Krieg?*', pp. 269f., 280, 289.

[17] Naumann, *Der Krieg als Text*, p. 34; Hays Parks, 'Air War and the Laws of War'; Messerschmidt, 'Strategic Air War and International Law'. More recent scholarship has shown an increased readiness to go further still and to label indiscriminate bombing, or at least individual raids such as the one on Dresden, as 'war crimes'. Compare Bloxham, 'Dresden as a War Crime'; Langenbacher, 'The Allies in World War II'; Grayling, *Among the Dead Cities*.

[18] Jordan, 'Der Bombenkrieg', *Der Mitteldeutsche*, 23 January 1944, p. 1. Compare also 'Luftkrieg: Die Kriegführung der Minderwertigen', *Völkischer Beobachter* (Berliner Ausgabe), 11 March 1943, p. 1.

[19] BA Berlin NS 18/1058, fo. 127, 'Re: Weißbuch über die rechtliche Seite des Luftkrieges', 1 July 1943.

[20] Auswärtiges Amt, *Dokumente über die Alleinschuld*. On Goebbels' reaction see Goebbels, *Tagebücher*, II/9, 1 July 1943, 8 July 1943.

as disseminated in the daily press. Academic in tone, the text professed to offer an objective evaluation of the issue of guilt on the basis of the available documentary evidence.[21] Moreover, the publication claimed to provide a historical dimension to contemporary problems by stressing continuities in German and British foreign policy that reached back beyond the Nazi takeover of power in 1933. According to the white book, the present administration stood in a long tradition of German attempts at civilising the conduct of war through binding international agreements. In so doing, the text exonerated the Nazi leadership not only from any responsibility for the escalation of the air war but, by extension, for the conflict as a whole: 'This barbarisation (*Verwilderung*) of war could have been avoided if Germany's present enemies had heeded the Führer's endeavours for the humanisation of war... The German attempts foundered on the will of our enemies to employ the air terror as a detailed plan for the annihilation of Europe.'[22] The referential frame was thus extended both spatially and temporally. Strategic bombing was not a course of action pursued to weaken the enemy in a military conflict but formed part of a premeditated scheme 'to annihilate Europe', or so the white book claimed. Likewise, the rhetoric of 'main guilt' (*Hauptschuld*) and 'sole responsibility' (*Alleinschuld*) echoed (and inverted) the controversial article 231 of the treaty of Versailles of 1919, in which Germany had been forced to accept 'the responsibility... for causing all the loss and damage' suffered by the allies during World War I.[23] Thus, the air war took on a significance that went beyond the narrow issue of deliberate or accidental bombing of civilian targets: it was presented as a parable for trans-historical 'truths' about the world as conceived by Nazism.

If Nazi propagandists thought that the strategic air war provided them with a lever to deflect attention from their responsibility for the outbreak of war and their genocidal conduct of this war, the subject matter appeared attractive for two additional reasons. It was used to privilege the role of the Nazi party on the 'home front' and to illustrate a central plank of the Nazi world view, the alleged culpability of 'the Jew'.

In a circular letter of July 1944, Joseph Goebbels informed high-level state and party functionaries of a special Air War Archive, requesting them to supply 'written and visual documents on the air war'. The propaganda minister justified the initiative with reference to the 'heroism' shown on the home front: 'Party and state are engaged in magnanimous

---

[21] See also the press coverage, 'Englands Alleinschuld am Bombenterror. Die Verbrechen der britischen Regierung im Lichte der Dokumente', *Völkischer Beobachter*, 7 July 1943, p. 1.

[22] Auswärtiges Amt, *Dokumente über die Alleinschuld*, p. 17.

[23] Department of State, *The Treaty of Versailles*, p. 413.

relief efforts for the population . . . Deeds are performed that will one day provide witness to stunned posterity of the bearing and the achievements of our generation.'[24] In emphasising the 'heroic bearing' of the population under the impact of strategic bombing, the propaganda minister projected a kind of historical writing that might be called monumental in the Nietzschean sense. He envisioned a heroic tale of a racial community welded together by the wanton destruction of allied bombing, triumphing over enormous odds through the leadership of the Nazi party. As a mode of enemy action directed at the 'home front', strategic bombing yielded material for a history of the war in which the Nazi party rather than the army took centre stage. The general absence of mass panic and unrest in the wake of area bombardments could be seized upon as evidence for the effectiveness of Nazi wartime domestic policy. The subject of the air war seemed well suited to legitimise the domestic 'war deployment' (*Kriegs-Einsatz*) of the Nazi party, strengthening its prestige among the population and vis-à-vis the army and providing retrospective justification for the transformation of German society since the takeover of power in 1933.[25]

Finally, Nazi propagandists used the bombing war as a parable for a central tenet of Nazi political culture – the obsessive belief that the anti-Hitler coalition was held together by 'International Jewry', which was said to have instigated the war with the sole purpose of destroying its world-historical antagonist, the Aryan race.[26] In the leader 'The Bombing War', district leader Jordan stressed the unprecedented nature of strategic bombing, which in his view marked a rupture in the 'history of warfare of civilised nations'.[27] At the same time, Jordan strongly opposed any interpretation that viewed the escalation of the air war as accidental. Instead, he claimed that 'the barbaric application of the bombing terror against a defenceless civil population' revealed a deeper truth about the nature of this conflict, bringing to light the characteristic features of those 'diabolical forces' that must be considered 'the invisible but genuine progenitors of this bloody world war'. In Jordan's view, the bombing war was but the contemporary expression of 'a bloody age-old attempt on the

---

[24] BA Berlin, R 55/447, Luftkriegsmitteilungen des Interministeriellen Luftkriegsschäden-Ausschusses beim RMVP, fos. 238f., 'LK-Mitteilung 151', 14 July 1944. See also ibid., fo. 246, 'LK-Mitteilung 158', 4 August 1944.

[25] On the unpopularity of the Nazi party in general and the demise of Hitler's popularity in the second half of the war see the classic treatments by Kershaw: *Popular Opinion* and *The 'Hitler Myth'*, pp. 169–224.

[26] Compare Herf, '"Der Krieg und die Juden"', who stresses the importance of anti-Semitism as a central narrative frame in Nazi political culture against a functionalist interpretation that focuses on the political usefulness of anti-Semitic propaganda.

[27] Jordan, 'Bombenkrieg', p. 1.

part of the Jewish race to annihilate the substance of the Aryan races'[28] Nazism thus turned the strategic air war into an anti-Semitic parable that professed to hold ontological truths about the origins and nature of the present conflict.[29]

The 'special chapter' that Jordan had envisioned in his leader of January 1944 was never written. What remained, however, were the conceptualisations of Nazi propaganda as well as a wealth of written documents, collected as raw material for present propaganda purposes and future histories.[30] Put in the categories of source criticism, the German sources originating from the sphere of party and state were not just relics but often contained elements of tradition. In part, they were written and preserved not only for the present but also for history. The extent to which such documents were produced in the first place and remained available to local historiography after the end of the Third Reich could differ considerably, depending on the timing of the air raids, the extent of allied post-war confiscations, and, not least, coincidence. In this respect, Kassel and Magdeburg represented opposite cases. The bulk of the documents produced in Kassel in the wake of the October raid survived the end of the war, whereas in Magdeburg few primary sources were produced in the first place, and fewer still remained available after 1945.

In Kassel, the production of documents was clustered around two time periods – the immediate aftermath of the big air raid, and the spring and summer of 1944. Into the first phase fell the various situation reports and experience reports that were composed by local functionaries for superior offices. Naturally, they were prompted foremost by the concerns of the day. In a letter to the mayor of 7 November 1943, the chief of police stressed that 'the experience report about the air raid of 22 October 1943 will be of great importance to other cities (*Luftschutzorte*)'.[31] The resulting document ran to fifty-two pages, containing a wealth of detailed information about the raid itself as well as the rescue and relief measures of the local administration. As much as the report was written with the exigencies of the present in mind, it was also self-consciously drawn up as a historical document. In their general introduction, the authors

---

[28] Ibid.

[29] See also Joseph Goebbels, 'Der Luft und Nervenkrieg', *Das Reich*, 14 June 1942; 'Die Juden sind schuld', *Das Reich*, 16 November 1941; Hans Schlitzberger, 'Der jüdische Terror', *KLZ*, 13 October 1943, p. 1; 'Amokläufer', *KLZ*, 27 October 1943; 'Zerstörerkraft gegen Schöpfergeist', *KLZ*, 13/14 November 1943, p. 1.

[30] This transitional stage is documented in *Der anglo-amerikanische Bombenkrieg. Tatsachen und Stimmen (aus der Presse des In- und Auslandes)*.

[31] StAK, S8 C44, chief of police to mayor, 7 November 1943.

lamented the loss of the city's cultural heritage, turning the ruins into 'witnesses [of a] senseless anger of destruction'.[32]

In the second phase of the spring and summer of 1944, the creation of documents as historical source material played a larger role. In the spring, the city employee and trained art historian Dr Karl Paetow started collecting personal accounts as related by local residents who had lived through the air raid. At the time, Paetow was serving as head of the Enquiry Office for the Missing, but his initiative appears to have been a result of his earlier function as Kassel's 'municipal researcher' (*Stadtforscher*), in which position he had emphasised the strong affinity of his research with the ideas of Nazism.[33] In a complementary move, the city administration in July requested all departments to submit a report on the 'perceptions, experiences and actions' following the 'terror raid of 22 October'.[34]

By contrast, no similar initiatives were undertaken in Magdeburg after 16 January 1945. Here, the air raid elicited no more than routine responses. The obligatory experience report by the local chief of police of 5 March 1945 was a case in point. It consisted of no more than two pages, plus a lengthy appendix. This was in all likelihood due to the rapidly deteriorating military situation as well as to the lack of interest of superior offices in an event that was repeated almost daily all over the Reich. Whereas the post-war historiography in Kassel could thus draw on a wealth of contemporary documents that bore, in one way or another, the imprint of Nazism, history writing in Magdeburg was, in theory, less burdened with this legacy. At the same time, it faced the difficult task of reconstructing the past on the basis of ex-post accounts. Yet, in practice, the interpretive categories of Nazism played an equally, if not more important role in the local post-war historiography of Magdeburg than in Kassel.

Serving the present: monumental history between pacification and mobilisation, 1945–1960

In the academic scholarship of the early Federal Republic, the strategic air war played a negligible role only.[35] Although in 1956 the *Vierteljahreshefte für Zeitgeschichte* carried an article by Anton Hoch which showed that the raid on Freiburg of 10 May 1940 had been accidentally carried out by

---

[32] StAK, S8 C40, 'Erfahrungsbericht', 7 December 1943, p. 13.
[33] StAK, A.4.41, no. 455, Karl Paetow, 'Drei Jahre Stadtforschung', no date [1938].
[34] See the reports collected in StAK, S8 C48.
[35] Benda-Beckmann, 'Eine deutsch-deutsche Katastrophe?', p. 297.

the German Luftwaffe,[36] the subject of World War II bombing remained largely outside the purview of professional history. As a consequence, the war in the air became the preserve of non-professional writers, such as former civil defence functionaries,[37] Luftwaffe generals,[38] war correspondents[39] and lawyers.[40] Between 1958 and 1962, the Ministry of Expellees, Refugees and War Damaged published the multi-volume *Documents of German War Losses*,[41] which was supplemented with a collection of experience reports and newspaper articles about the bombing war.[42] In partial adaptation of the wartime propaganda narrative, the volumes drew a picture of a 'community of fate' engaged in a 'heroic defensive battle'. But in contrast to the earlier propaganda, 'non-political' civil defence functionaries replaced Nazi party activists and the impersonal dynamics of modernised warfare took the place of human agency.[43]

While the historiographical landscape of the Federal Republic in the 1950s was characterised by a wealth of popular literature and very limited professional research, GDR historiography paid even less attention to the strategic air war.[44] Despite the significance of the subject in the official rhetoric, no historical study was published in order to legitimise the claims of state propaganda. The leading historical journal of the GDR, the *Zeitschrift für Geschichtswissenschaft*, was content with issuing a riposte to Hoch's article about the Freiburg raid. Interestingly, the author, Dietrich Zboralski, did not attack Hoch's findings about the accidental bombing as a whitewash of the Western conduct of the air war – as might have been expected in the light of the political rhetoric of the 1950s – but insisted on the plausibility of the earlier thesis that had indicted Hitler for ordering the attack on Freiburg.[45]

In Kassel and Magdeburg, historical enquiries into the air war started to appear from the late 1940s and the early 1950s, respectively. The most

---

[36] Hoch, 'Der Luftangriff auf Freiburg'. Compare also Süß, '"Massaker und Mongolensturm"', 536–43.

[37] See the publications by Hans Rumpf, during the war Generalinspektor des Feuerlöschwesens with the rank of major general: *Der hochrote Hahn*; 'Luftkrieg über Deutschland'; *Das war der Bombenkrieg*.

[38] Galland, *Die Ersten und die Letzten*.   [39] Bartz, *Als der Himmel brannte*.

[40] Spetzler, *Luftkrieg und Menschlichkeit*; Czesany, *Nie wieder Krieg gegen die Zivilbevölkerung*.

[41] *Dokumente deutscher Kriegsschäden*.

[42] *Dokumente deutscher Kriegsschäden. Beiheft I: Aus den Tagen des Luftkrieges und des Wiederaufbaues: Erlebnis- und Erfahrungsberichte* (1960); *Beiheft II: Der Luftkrieg im Spiegel der neutralen Presse* (1962). Vol. I contained also a summary account of the course of the air war by Georg W. Feuchter, 'Der Luftkrieg über Deutschland'.

[43] Compare Süß, 'Erinnerungen an den Luftkrieg', pp. 20f.

[44] Paulus, 'Zur Verfälschung der Geschichte des Zweiten Weltkrieges', does not mention the air war.

[45] Zboralski, 'Zum Luftangriff auf Freiburg'.

important forum was the local press where journalists not only reported on the commemorative activities of the local elites but also produced historical accounts of their own.

In Kassel, the history of the bombing was written from a local perspective, without taking much heed of the larger West German 'master narrative of the air war'.[46] Partly, this was because none of the national accounts dealt in any detail with the events in Kassel. More importantly, local enquiries were motivated by a different set of questions from the national literature. Here, the air war was conceptualised as a disaster, not an opportunity for heroism: 'Want and horror, thousands of deaths, loss of *Heimat* and possessions, the destruction of a town of a thousand years... This is the balance sheet of 22 October 1943,' the journalists Herta Pehnt and Wilhelm Blank wrote in characteristic fashion in an article in the local *Hessische Nachrichten* on 21 October 1947.[47] Local lay researchers were less interested in generals' tales about the alleged tragedy of the German fighter force or casuistic deliberations on the legality or otherwise of area bombing than in the reconstruction of events as they unfolded on the ground. At the same time, they balanced the 'disciplined quest for truth' (Hans Rothfels[48]) of scholarly history against what they considered palatable to the sensibilities of their local readership, aiming at semantic pacification in the present rather than at confrontation with the past.

In Magdeburg, local journalists shared in the attempt to reconstruct the events of the air war as they occurred in the locality. They sought to achieve this goal through the systematic collection of memories ex post – an initiative that was both triggered and made irrelevant by the emergence of 'Dresden' as a national memory place in the early 1950s.[49] With the escalation of the Cold War, local events were retold in a national context, local experiences displaced by the parameters of the Dresden narrative. The results of local enquiries were ignored in favour of a largely fictional account that placed Magdeburg second to Dresden. Rather than at semantic pacification as in Kassel, the historiographical stories aimed at mass mobilisation.

---

[46] Süß, 'Erinnerungen an den Luftkrieg', p. 20. For example, the efforts by Hans Rumpf to rehabilitate the anti-Semitic propaganda term 'terror raid' as a technical term for indiscriminate area bombing found little resonance among the protagonists of the local historiography. See Rumpf, *Das war der Bombenkrieg*, p. 39.

[47] Herta Pehnt and Wilhelm Blank, '4 Jahre danach', *HN*, 21 October 1947, p. 4.

[48] Rothfels, 'Zeitgeschichte als Aufgabe', p. 5.

[49] On Dresden see Groehler, 'Dresden'; Margalit, 'Der Luftangriff auf Dresden'; Neutzner, 'Vom Anklagen zum Erinnern', pp. 139–44.

In both cities, the dominant approach to the past thus remained monumental in the Nietzschean sense, albeit in inverted form. Where Joseph Goebbels had envisioned a tale of collective heroism, the local post-war historiography constructed a tale of collective suffering. The most important medium in this process was the eyewitness account, which was used to homogenise different experiences and to legitimise a narrative that focused on the effects of allied bombing rather than its causes.

'An individual fate that speaks for many thousands of others': the eyewitness as collective mouthpiece

In both cities, publicists relied on eyewitness accounts in order to tell the events of the air war 'from below'. Rather than approach these documents with the tools of source criticism, asking who speaks when, where and why, they tended to use the accounts selectively as a medium through which to construct a collective experience. Local historiography showed a strong tendency to replace the first-person pronoun with the collective singular, to recast individual memories as an experience shared by the memory-group as a whole. 'An individual fate that speaks for many thousands of others' was a typical subtitle, which appeared in the *Volksstimme* on the sixth anniversary of the air raid on Magdeburg in 1951.[50] In Kassel, the above-mentioned article by Pehnt and Blank from 1947 used the impersonal 'one' (*man*) to describe attitudes and reactions on the ground.[51] The text formed part of the broader coverage of the anniversary in the local *Hessische Nachrichten*, which devoted a whole page to '22 October 1943' under the heading of 'Four Years After'.[52] The article merits closer consideration because it contains many elements that were typical of the early historiography of the bombing in general.

Pehnt and Blank tell the events of 22 October as a story of collective overpowering. In their account, routine disintegrates in the face of unprecedented catastrophe, giving way to disjunctions between subjective time and external time, sense perception and cognition. Characteristically, they adopt a point of view 'from below'. Larger developments are taken into consideration only in so far as they help to elucidate local developments. In employing the construct of the 'ordinary Kasselaner', the journalists draw a picture of non-political city-dwellers standing at the receiving end of extreme violence, targeted by the impersonal forces

---

[50] '"Mein Mann verbrannte nebenan". Ein Einzelschicksal, das für viele Tausend spricht', *Volksstimme*, 16 January 1945, p. 4.
[51] Pehnt and Blank, '4 Jahre danach', p. 4.   [52] Ibid.

of mechanised warfare, deceived and in fear of the Nazi leadership. As a structural device, the text employs juxtapositions to translate extreme perceptions into coherent narratives: the beauty of an autumn day is contrasted to the inferno of the night; the silence among the air raid community to the thundering roar of the approaching bombers; the darkness in the shelter to the glow of the fires in the streets.[53]

In the account by the two journalists, the air raid does not come unexpectedly. The authors speak of an 'angst psychosis' among the population, caused by the recent raids on Hamburg and Hanover.[54] Precautionary measures by the Nazi welfare organisation (NSV) and the police only serve to heighten this state of collective anxiety. Pehnt and Blank go on to describe collective responses as the futile attempt to bring the 'social knowledge' of a militarised population to bear on unprecedented violence:[55] while the sound of the sirens elicits the usual precautionary measures and customary 'jokes against the Führer', routine soon gives way to trepidation. Confronted with an existential threat, the social cohesion of the shelter community disintegrates into smaller units as purposeful activity gives way to helpless coping strategies: 'Mothers clasp their children; frightful crying, loud prayers.' In those conditions, survival becomes dependent on personal determination, chance and – the text implies – recklessness. The narrative does not develop the ethical implications of personal survival that depends in part on the indifference to the fate of others but prefers to remain descriptive. 'One cannot breathe any more and must try to save oneself through the burning house, over the burning street, through the firestorm. Many hesitate – and pay for their hesitation with their lives.'[56] In the Kassel of the late 1940s and early 1950s, eyewitness accounts formed an important element in the attempts to describe the events of 22 October 1943 historically. The majority were drawn from the collection of 'survivors' reports' that Paetow had produced in the spring of 1944. The circumstances of their origin privileged those voices that had lost close relatives and friends over those who had lived through the raid without suffering personal injury. Moreover, the collection reproduced the racial segregation of the Third Reich between the 'racial comrades' on the one hand and 'community aliens' (*Gemeinschaftsfremde*) on the other. In so doing, it denied a voice to the thousands of foreign slave labourers, the remaining Jews and the imprisoned

---

[53] See the example of other cities and time periods, Arnold, 'Sammelrezension Bombenkrieg'.
[54] Pehnt and Blank, '4 Jahre danach', p. 4.
[55] On the concept of 'social knowledge' see Latzel, *Deutsche Soldaten – nationalsozialistischer Krieg?*, p. 92 (with further references).
[56] Pehnt and Blank, '4 Jahre danach'.

opponents of Nazism.[57] From a collection of one hundred accounts, only one was by a foreigner, a Dutch national from Rotterdam.[58] To Paetow, the (eastern European) forced labourers and the Italian military internees were not subjects to be interviewed, but objects to be photographed.[59]

Yet the wartime accounts were not transferred verbatim into the post-war memory culture. Rather, newspaper editors subjected them to varying degrees of revision. When the conservative *Kasseler Post*, for example, published a statement by the industrialist Sch. in October 1950, the text was heavily edited, doing away with all elements that stressed purposeful fire-fighting activity. Moreover, the term 'terror raid' was dropped from the account, as was an invective against Churchill that had served to categorise the air raid in the original.[60] In cleansing the account of both agency and political bias, the editing illustrated the extent to which the historical source material was made to conform to the sensibilities of the local public.

In subsequent years, all three of the local newspapers repeatedly returned to the 'survivors' reports' of 1944, reworking them to fit the emphases and silences of the larger memory parameters. In 1953, on the tenth anniversary, the left-leaning *Hessische Nachrichten* published a special commemorative page, 'Ten Years Ago in Kassel', which contained three accounts drawn from Paetow's collection.[61] The reports were not reproduced in the I-narration of the original but related in the more neutral third person. Harrowing anecdotes found in the original source material were left out, as in the case of Clara H., who had given the following nightmarish account to Paetow about her experiences in a collapsed shelter where she had fallen unconscious:

[When I regained consciousness] I realised that I was in the shelter. I tried to rise up and reach behind me; but it was very slippery . . . I didn't know what it was. I had a torchlight in my pocket, took it out and switched it on. Then I saw that I had touched two dead people. Their heads were green and there was foam in front of their mouths . . . When I reached the drain, I got a big scare: the strong iron plate had been removed from the hole. A woman was lying in the drain; she was dead. There was a chair placed on top of the woman and a man was sitting on the chair; he was alive.[62]

---

[57] See the classic study by Peukert, *Volksgenossen und Gemeinschaftsfremde*.

[58] Compare *Überlebensberichte*, no. 20 (pp. 39f.).

[59] See the images reproduced in *Leben in Ruinen*, pp. 75f.

[60] 'Schicksal eines Hauses in der Wolfhager Straße', *KP*, 21/22 October 1950, p. 6. Compare the original text in *Überlebensberichte*, no. 70 (pp. 95–9).

[61] 'In Kassel vor 10 Jahren: Erlebnisberichte Kasseler Einwohner', *HN*, 22 October 1953. Compare the original accounts in *Überlebensberichte* nos. 74 (pp. 103–5), 81 (pp. 117–9), 60 (pp. 83f.). The special commemorative page featured also three contemporary interviews with a physician, a pastor and a trade unionist.

[62] See *Überlebensberichte*, no. 74 (pp. 103–5), here p. 104.

By comparison, the same scene was rendered in 1953 as follows: 'When she regains consciousness . . . she reaches for the torchlight in her pocket: there are dead bodies above and below her.'[63] Such editing was not confined to the *Hessische Nachrichten* but was carried out by the other Kassel dailies as well. In the reproduction of an account by a local tailor, for example, the editors of the conservative *Kasseler Post* replaced the phrase 'killed in action' with 'deceased'.[64] From the same document, they left out a reference to Jewish residents who had been caught up in the raid.

There was a broad consensus among the local media concerning the cleansing of personal accounts of both politically compromising aspects and the horrific details of death. This consensus extended beyond the realm of written documents to the visual sphere as well. The early post-war representation of Kassel during the Third Reich bore no resemblance to the 'City of Reich Warrior Days' of the 1930s and early 1940s. The absence of the insignia of Nazism denazified the local community and recast them as victims of a natural catastrophe. Equally important, the local press refrained from reproducing images of the dead despite their easy availability in the municipal archive. In an illustrated article of 1949, the journalist Friedrich Herbordt justified the selective use of visual material with considerations of propriety. 'Of the many dreadful pictures which the photographer took on the day after the disaster, only a few are fit for publication,' he maintained.[65]

The year before, the *Hessische Nachrichten* had published a drawing that illustrated both the priorities and the boundaries of the mnemonic discourse as practised in the daily newspapers (Fig. 28).[66] The drawing depicts a dramatic scene of escape in which a woman with panic-stricken features clutches three children and runs in the direction of the observer on a street littered with debris, the wide-open eyes suggesting that the experience will leave scars for life. The band of four is framed by crumbling buildings ablaze with raging fires. Theirs is not an optimistic survival story but a tale of escape by the skin of one's teeth from an apocalyptic event.

While the local media as a whole manipulated eyewitness accounts in order to make them conform to contemporary sensibilities, the

---

[63] 'Der Sohn hörte ihr Klopfen zuerst', *HN*, 22 October 1953.

[64] Compare 'Schicksalstag der tausendjährigen Stadt', *KP*, 22 October 1953, with *Überlebensberichte*, no. 98, p. 146.

[65] '22. Oktober 1943. Die Nacht, in der Kassels Altstadt unterging', *HN*, 22 October 1949, p. 3. The one exception that I have found appeared in the SPD-weekly *Hessischer Sonntag*, in the context of a polemic against the conservative press. See 'Zwei Rezepte – ein Doktor', *Hessischer Sonntag*, 15 January 1950.

[66] *HN*, 22 October 1948, p. 1.

22. Oktober 1943! Dies Datum bleibt den Kasselanern als das der schrecklichsten der Schreckensnächte für immer in Erinnerung. In dieser Nacht sank Alt-Kassel unwiederbringlich dahin. Einen Eindruck der Szenen, die sich auf offener Straße abspielten, gibt hier die Zeichnung von Rainer H a r t m e i z wieder.

Figure 28. 'Never Again!' reads the caption of an illustration of the 'night of horror' that appeared in the *Hessische Nachrichten* on 22 October 1948.

conservative press in particular utilised source material in yet another way. The *Kasseler Post* and the *Kasseler Zeitung* on occasion reprinted Nazi wartime documents without any editorial comment. In 1953, for example, the *Kasseler Post* published, as part of the extensive special coverage of the tenth anniversary, the official communiqué of the German High Command of 23 October 1943.[67] By letting the sources 'speak

---

[67] 'Der Wehrmachtbericht meldet', *KP*, 22 October 1953, p. 4.

for themselves', the newspaper reintroduced the vocabulary of the war into public discourse, opening up the referential frames of Nazism without explicitly disclaiming them. On occasion, this idiom also entered the language of contemporary press reports, as in a short article on the same page that used the term 'terror raid'.[68] Against the backdrop of the debate over the armament of the Federal Republic, both middle-class papers also revived a (denazified) version of the 'heroic' wartime narrative. They stressed the relief efforts of the Wehrmacht and emphasised the 'unknown heroism' of 'ordinary Kasselaner'.[69]

In Kassel, local publicists sanitised wartime eyewitness accounts in order to tell tales of suffering that fit the mnemonic parameters of the 1950s. In Magdeburg, the evidence of eyewitness accounts was likewise subordinated to the demands of the present. Here, the accounts were created ex post and subsequently rewritten in order to fit revisions in the official interpretation of the event as they occurred with the escalation of the Cold War in 1948/9. The extent to which the same source material could be made to serve different contexts is well reflected by an experience report that appeared in the *Volksstimme* of 15 January 1948, and again, in the *Volksstimme* of 1 September 1949. In 1948, the account by the restaurant owner Otto K. formed part of the press coverage on the third anniversary of the 'night of horror', which was headed 'Memento: Magdeburg, 16 January 1945'.[70] In September 1949, a modified version appeared on a special page that marked the tenth anniversary of the outbreak of World War II with the headline '41 Million Deaths Admonish'.[71]

In the article of 1948, Otto K. relates his odyssey through the burning city under the heading of 'A Man is Looking for his Wife'.[72] Otto K. is presented as a purposeful man who overcomes tremendous obstacles in order to be reunited with his wife. After having dug himself out of a collapsed shelter, the protagonist rescues fellow Magdeburgers who have lost their nerve. Otto K. watches fire-fighters being condemned to idleness due to the lack of water, and residents frantically escaping from their shelters underneath burning buildings. At the end of his journey through the burning city, he finds that his home has been destroyed but is reunited with his wife. This is a survival story with a happy ending,

---

[68] 'Der 16. Angriff auf Kassel', *KP*, 22 October 1953, p. 4.
[69] 'Helfer in bitterster Not: 24000 Soldaten. Die Wehrmacht bei den Rettungsarbeiten in Kassel – Hilfeleistung in eigener Verantwortung', *KP*, 21/22 October 1950; 'Kradmelder im Feuersturm. Wassergassen in der brennenden Kasseler Altstadt – Oberfeuerwehrmann Kollien berichtet für viele', *KZ*, 22 October 1953, p. 4.
[70] 'Memento: Magdeburg, 16. Januar 1945', *Volksstimme*, 15 January 1948, p. 4.
[71] '41 Millionen Tote mahnen †', *Volksstimme*, 1 September 1949.
[72] 'Wie sie es überlebten / Berichte von der Schreckensnacht', *Volksstimme*, 15 January 1948, p. 4.

full of optimism despite the loss of material goods. As such it fitted well with the rationalisation of '16 January 1945' as it had been developed by the civil administration in the immediate post-war years: the built-up environment had collapsed, but Magdeburg as a social formation had survived, free to embark on a new beginning: 'One final glance at the smouldering grave of my possessions, one last sigh, then a determined about-turn, and – the woman who I thought dead is standing in front of me,' the text concludes.[73]

Eighteen months later, the same experience was retold in the same newspaper in a very different register.[74] Under the heading of 'The Night of Hell in Magdeburg', the narrator emphasises death, not survival, relating harrowing tales of residents who try in vain to escape from air raid shelters by using their bare nails and teeth. He thus evokes an image that might have been familiar to some readers from the American picture reports about the atrocity at Gardelegen in April 1945 where concentration camp prisoners had been locked up in a barn und burnt alive.[75] Whereas in the 1948 account, Otto K. is motivated by the desire to find his wife, in the rendition of September 1949 he is presented as an anti-fascist resistance fighter who escapes from his 'dungeon prison' amidst 'the smell of gas'. Not only does he bear witness to a dying world around him, saving fellow Magdeburgers from self-destruction, but he also demonstrates to the world that 'during the Nazi years there were two types of people, brown beasts and fighting anti-fascists'.[76] In the version from 1949, K.'s reunification with his wife becomes a mere footnote. Instead, a scene takes centre stage in which Otto K. reveals himself to a group of forced labourers from France, Belgium and the Netherlands who are searching for him in the rubble. He 'sheds tears over their loyalty and sacrifice for the little bit of love that I had given to them as a restaurant owner'.[77]

Under the double impact of domestic Stalinisation and the escalating Cold War, eyewitness accounts in Magdeburg started to abound with anecdotes of violent mass death. The shift from an emphasis on survival to an emphasis on death was reflected in the visual sphere as well, as a look at the photographs that accompanied the two accounts by Otto K. in the *Volksstimme* illustrates. In 1948, the textual narrative was illustrated with three images, all of which stressed survival: residents leaving the city after an air raid; a deserted street lined with ruins; and a frontal view

---

[73] Ibid.   [74] 'Die Höllennacht in Magdeburg', *Volksstimme*, 1 September 1949, p. 5.
[75] Compare Amerikanisches Kriegsinformationsamt, *KZ*; Brink, *Ikonen der Vernichtung*, pp. 46–82.
[76] 'Höllennacht', *Volksstimme*, 1 September 1949, p. 5.   [77] Ibid.

of the sculpture of 'Magdeburg in Mourning'[78] One and a half years later, the iconography of survival had given way to the iconography of death. 'The Night of Hell in Magdeburg' showed two images. The first was an atrocity photograph, depicting a row of dead children stretching in a diagonal line across the frame.[79] The caption read 'After 16 January 1945: children's corpses accuse!', suggesting that this was the scene of a crime. The second image depicted a farewell letter carved into a piece of wood by an eighty-year-old carpenter who had been trapped in a burning shelter. The engraving read 'There's no more hope. The place is burning down from above, and one is suffocating.'[80] Both motifs became part of the stock visual representation of the 'night of hell' in the 1950s.

Next to the creation of inverted monumental histories, there were also attempts in both cities to reconstruct the events from a more critical perspective. These efforts were faced with different preconditions. Whereas in Kassel, a substantial amount of documentary evidence had survived into the post-war era, in Magdeburg the primary source base was thin, and appears to have been diminished further by the activities of the United States Strategic Bombing Survey in the summer of 1945.[81] In Kassel, local journalists strove to make available to a wider public the official documents produced during the war, while their colleagues in Magdeburg were faced with the difficult task of retrieving information from post-war recollections.[82]

Reconstructing the 'night of horror' as critical history?

In Kassel, the first historian of the air raid was the journalist Friedrich Herbordt (1899–1958). In some respects, Herbordt was an unusual candidate for writing about a subject that, on the national level, was used by the Far Right in order to downplay the crimes of Nazism.[83] As a middle-class intellectual with Socialist convictions, Herbordt had spent more than six and a half years in prison during the Third Reich for alleged 'preparation of high treason'. After the end of the war, he joined the staff of the American-licensed *Hessische Nachrichten*, where he specialised in

---

[78] 'Memento: Magdeburg, 16. Januar 1945', *Volksstimme*, 15 January 1948, p. 4.
[79] On the history of atrocity photography see Knoch, *Die Tat als Bild*, pp. 49–75.
[80] 'Höllennacht', *Volksstimme*, 1 September 1949, p. 5.
[81] See the material collected on Magdeburg by the USSBS in NA II RG 243 E-6, files 394–9.
[82] See Friedrich Herbordt, 'Aus dem Geheimbericht des Kasseler Polizeipräsidenten', *HN*, 21 October 1950.
[83] Gerhard Zumbach, 'Todesmühlen und öffentliche Meinung', *HN*, 13 March 1946, p. 1.

art criticism and local history.[84] On the occasion of the sixth anniversary of '22 October' in 1949, he published a piece of investigative journalism that may be considered the first serious attempt at treating the events historically. Despite his personal experiences under Nazism, Herbordt – in his public statements at least – did not think of the air raid as having made any contribution to the defeat of the Third Reich. Without any regard to the broader context, the journalist situated the event firmly in municipal history, unequivocally categorising 22 October 1943 as the 'darkest day in the thousand-year-old history of the city of Kassel'.[85]

Adopting a perspective 'from below', Herbordt focused on a single episode. In his article, he attempted to reconstruct the events in the public air raid shelter underneath the restaurant Zur Pinne, which on 22/23 October 1943 had turned into a mass grave, with the loss of almost four hundred lives. Anticipating the objectives of contemporary history as famously formulated by Hans Rothfels in 1953,[86] Herbordt aimed to dispel 'rumours and legend' by means of a critical enquiry. On the basis of the available documentary evidence, interviews with survivors and a visit to the scene, Herbordt argued for structural defects and unfortunate chance as the cause of mass death. The journalist took great pains to exonerate the air raid warden from any blame, declaring with the authority of the historical evidence, 'Rumours have circulated about his [i.e., the air raid warden's] bearing during the night in question, which the accounts of the survivors show to be pure invention.'[87]

In a similar vein, Herbordt assured his readers that the victims had died painlessly, with death coming as deadly sleep in the wake of carbon monoxide poisoning. 'The physician confirms that this state does not cause any unpleasant feelings or ailments. In darkness and silence death walked the cellars of the Pinne.' In arguing thus, the journalist ignored those eyewitness accounts which had spoken of an erupting panic in the shelter as smoke entered the cellar.[88] For all his careful research, Herbordt carefully balanced historical knowledge against the presumed sensibilities of his audience. Through his enquiry, he sought to heal internal divisions and to console mourning residents. In 1950s Kassel, even critical approaches to the past did not challenge the larger mnemonic parameters, as Herbordt himself acknowledged in the introduction to his

---

[84] On Friedrich Herbordt see StAK, S1 no. 184, containing a copy of the sentence by the Kassel district court of 1937; Buttlar, *Trauerrede für Friedrich Herbordt*.
[85] Friedrich Herbordt, '22. Oktober 1943. Die Nacht, in der Kassels Altstadt unterging', *HN*, 22 October 1949.
[86] Rothfels, 'Zeitgeschichte als Aufgabe', 5.   [87] Herbordt, '22. Oktober 1943'.
[88] See *Überlebensberichte*, nos. 43 (p. 65), 55 (p. 79). Compare also report by chief of police of 20 July 1945, in NA II RG 243 E-6 # 64b p (3) (box 575).

article where he declared, 'About the horrifying individual and collective fates no survivor can bear witness. They will forever be shrouded in merciful darkness.'[89]

While the investigative journalism of Herbordt approached the subject analytically, two contrasting tendencies characterised developments in Magdeburg. On the one hand, the local archive launched a public appeal in the autumn of 1950 that called on the population to send in eyewitness accounts. In so doing, it sought to establish the empirical basis that was necessary for any historical research on the subject. On the other, the guided media popularised a sensational tale that freely combined historical knowledge with unsubstantiated rumour.

On 13 October 1950, the *Liberal-Demokratische Zeitung*, the paper of the satellite Liberal Party (LDP), published an article called 'The Destruction of the City of Magdeburg in 1945'.[90] The article appeared two days before the general election to the People's Chamber (*Volkskammer*), which set the seal on the establishment of a Stalinist dictatorship as the electorate was asked to cast their votes openly on the basis of unified lists of candidates.[91] Within this context, the newspaper drew on the past in order to legitimise the present, as the introductory paragraph made clear:

The Magdeburg night of horror of 16 January 1945 must be preserved to keep alive the hatred against war for generations to come . . . Today we publish some scenes of the dreadful annihilation to drive home to every Magdeburger why he must attend elections on Sunday.[92]

Written by a young teacher and freelance journalist Manfred Rolle (1929–2005), the article established a mode of representation that remained influential in the local historiography well into the post-unification period.[93] Emotive in tone, the piece offered scenic description instead of analysis, freely combining established knowledge with rumour and invention. The text fell into three parts, plus an introduction.

---

[89] Herbordt, '22. Oktober 1943'.
[90] Manfred Rolle, 'Die Zerstörung der Stadt Magdeburg 1945', *LDZ*, 13 October 1950, p. 3.
[91] Weber, *Geschichte der DDR*, p. 174; Neubert, *Geschichte der Opposition*, pp. 55–9; Staritz, *Geschichte der DDR*, pp. 75–84.
[92] Rolle, 'Zerstörung', p. 3.
[93] The article was reprinted, abridged and revised in *LDZ*, 15/16 January 1955 under the title of 'Als das Inferno über Magdeburg hereinbrach'. Compare also by the same author, 'Magdeburg überwand den Tod', *Volksstimme*, 16 January 1959; the series 'Großangriff auf Magdeburg – Hilfe!', *Mitteldeutsche Neueste Nachrichten*, 16, 19, 20, 21, 22, 23, 26, 27, 28, 29 and 30/31 January 1965; 'Die Nacht des Grauens', *Volksstimme*, 16 January 1970; '"Stadt in Flammen". Eine Serie von Manfred Rolle', *Bild*, January 1995; 'Die Schreckensnacht', *Magdeburger Kurier* 12 (1/2005), p. 9.

Part one, 'The Way It Began', stressed the element of surprise, suggesting somewhat implausibly that the population of one of the major industrial towns of central Germany was taken by complete surprise by the raid of 16 January 1945. To support his claim, Rolle argued that many residents erroneously believed that they would be spared because of the strong Socialist traditions of the town. Interestingly, he made this point not – as might perhaps be expected – in order to accuse the Western allies for attacking the wrong target, but in order to criticise the behaviour of the resident population: 'Despite the warning by the Gauleiter headquarters . . . , parts of the population did not deem it necessary to go to the shelters.'[94]

This was followed by two scenes that emphasise death and human agency. They form the centre of the narrative. The first, 'Tragedy of the Jakobi Bunker', recounts an episode in which the doors of a bunker situated next to the Jakobikirche in the north of the old town were shut well before all the residents of the surrounding area had found shelter, leaving hundreds of latecomers exposed to the falling bombs. In desperation, they huddle in front of the bunker and fall victim to the attack. Their dead bodies obstruct the door, preventing the people crammed into the bunker from leaving their prison shelter. 'Only when the corpses are violently ripped apart from the outside, the way opens,' Rolle writes. While the author may have exaggerated the death toll, the incident itself appears to have been factual, featuring prominently in several eyewitness accounts.[95]

By contrast, the second scene, 'In the Cathedral', had little evidence to support it.[96] The episode makes a point about human agency that was aimed at the Protestant middle-class readership of the *Liberal-Demokratische Zeitung*. In drastic language, the text tells of the death by falling debris of the Christian congregation in their place of worship on the night of 16 January 1945: 'Ripped apart and torn to pieces are all the people who had looked for shelter in this house of God from the satanic deeds of humans.' Despite the faith of the believers, God had been powerless to protect his flock from an atrocity that 'no devil could have initiated . . . but humans did', Rolle declared. In so doing, he presented a morality tale in the guise of history. The scene might also have served the additional purpose of delegitimising a popular tale that told

[94] Rolle, 'Zerstörung', p. 3.

[95] See StAM, ZG 55.3, Akte 15. Januar, Erwin Stapel, 'Brandnacht 1945', undated; Erich Tambourek, 'Die Hölle über Magdeburg am 16. Jan. 1945', 29 October 1950.

[96] The cathedral was hit on 16 January 1945 but the cathedral pastor, Ernst Martin, makes no mention of any casualties in his memoirs. See Martin, 'Memento'; cathedral preacher Giselher Quast to author, 1 October 2009.

a very different story. According to several eyewitnesses, the interior of another church, the burnt-out Katharinenkirche, had served as a place of refuge amidst the conflagration for hundreds of people fleeing their shelters in the Old New Town (*Alte Neustadt*).[97]

Within the context of the propaganda campaign surrounding the general election, the guided media not only published the first historical account of the 'night of horror'. They also initiated steps to collect documentary evidence about the events of the air war. In August 1950, October 1950 and again in May 1952, the city archive published appeals in the local papers for eyewitnesses to come forward and write up their experiences for a city chronicle.[98] The goal was political, as the press notice of October 1950 emphasised: 'Magdeburger, what did you experience during the night of horror of 16 January 1945? Write it up for the city chronicle! It must become a memento to peace. Grandchildren and great grandchildren must know about it!' Altogether about forty reports were sent in to the archive over the course of the autumn and winter of 1950/1. 'There must be many more reports about the day of the destruction,' an internal assessment noted with some disappointment.[99] While the unnamed commentator opined that perhaps not enough time had passed since the catastrophic event, he refused to entertain the idea that the limited response might perhaps also have been a reflection of the legitimacy deficit of SED rule in the city. Instead, the assessment criticised a number of accounts for their failure to live up to the expectations as laid out in the press appeal. In particular, the assessment deplored the disappointing response from former civil defence functionaries. Just one official had replied, and his report 'bore all the traces of an adulation of superior offices'.[100]

The commentator conceived of the air raid as a deterrent example, a 'memorial for peace', but wondered whether one could really learn lessons from the past. After all, he objected, the people of Magdeburg had had a similar memento before, the destruction of 1631; 'Therefore everybody had been warned; and still the misfortune happened again.' Adopting a historical-materialist stance, he concluded from the local example that one had to change the fabric of society if there was to be a chance of putting an end to the cycle of destruction. 'Our task must be to build a social order which no longer knows the word "war", or any other term describing the murder of nations and the annihilation of human life.'[101]

---

[97] For the Katharinenkirche serving as a shelter for survivors see StAM, ZG 55.3, Akte 15. Januar, reports by Frieda Hillemann, 24 August 1950; H. Müller, 14 September 1950.

[98] StAM, ZG 55.3, Akte 15. Januar, cover sheet, no date.   [99] Ibid.   [100] Ibid.

[101] Ibid.

The evaluation did not just take exception to the lack of political awareness among the respondents. It also wondered about the factual value of the accounts, noting that they contained many different – and at times – contradictory claims and observations. 'These differences may lead one to the conclusion that the truth is not always honoured,' the commentator remarked. Yet he asserted that, despite their differences, all the reports concurred in their assessment of the air raid as a 'crime against humanity':

This mad deed cannot be justified as a necessary act of war because the war was already decided at this moment. Perhaps the explanation lies in the . . . carving out of occupation zones, and on the part of America and England there was no interest in preservation but on the contrary in total annihilation.

Among the respondents, a substantial number had indeed employed the interpretive frame of 'air war as crime' in order to contextualise their personal memories. Some explicitly invoked the official terminology of the ruling elites, mixing the jargon of Nazi propaganda with the idiom of class warfare. They spoke of 'gangsters of the air', lauded the 'peaceful Soviet army' and condemned the 'war mongers', while stressing the lesson of 'never again'.[102] Eighty-year-old Bernhard M., for example, insisted that owing to the absence of any effective air defence in 1945, the air raids had turned into 'harmless Sunday rides of murder and annihilation', 'a sadistic show' that no longer bore any resemblance to war.[103] Some saw the press appeal as a chance to draw attention to present grievances. Paul L., while denouncing the 'flying murderers in their lust for blood', added shrewdly that he was still without a flat of his own six years after the end of the war.[104] Others appear to have been motivated by a genuine desire to make a contribution to peace. Anni K., for example, wrote that the traumatic events of the bombing night had turned 'many people into fanatical fighters for peace', and concluded on the rallying cry: 'Let us always remember and never allow another war to happen.'[105]

As a whole, the accounts not only accorded insights into the wealth of narrative strategies that eyewitnesses used to communicate their experiences, into the different literary genres and idioms that they employed – from lyrical poetry to prose report, from affective mode of writing to neutral description. They also furnished a quarry of personal memories from

---

[102] StAM, ZG 55.3, Akte 15. Januar, *passim.*
[103] StAM, ZG 55.3, Akte 15. Januar, Bernhard M., 'Brandnacht 1945', no date.
[104] StAM, ZG 55.3, Akte 15. Januar, Paul L., 1 November 1950; see also ibid., Walter B., 13 April 1951.
[105] StAM, ZG 55.3, Akte 15. Januar, Anni K., 'Betrifft 16. Januar 1945', 20 November 1950.

which a wealth of factual information could have been retrieved if the local authorities had so desired.[106] The death toll provides a case in point. By the early 1950s, the political elites had started to emphasise that on 16 January 1945 16,000 people had died. In so doing, they popularised a figure that may have been rumoured in the immediate aftermath of the attack but lacked any documentary evidence to substantiate it.[107] One of the people to send in a report was Erwin Stapel, gardener at the main cemetery during the war. In his account, he spoke of 1,700 burials at the cemetery, thus producing a figure that anticipated the findings of the early 1990s.[108] In a similar vein, the ex-police captain, Peter M., declared that as of April 1945, 2,900 casualties had been buried while 2,000 people were still considered missing.[109] Yet the evidence contained in the local accounts was not allowed to interfere with the official figures and rationalisations, which had more to do with the dominance of 'Dresden' in the national memorial culture than with historical knowledge based on empirical research.

In Magdeburg, the antiquarian initiative of the city archive did not lead to a critical re-evaluation of the received narratives; the factual information contained in the forty or so eyewitness accounts remained unused throughout the 1950s. In Kassel, too, even the critical approach of Friedrich Herbordt legitimised rather than challenged the larger mnemonic parameters.

Continuity and change: the 1960s and the rise of the 'documentary account'

In the 1960s, local histories of the 'night of horror' were produced against the backdrop of shifting 'memory regimes' as well as broader social, cultural and generational changes in both German societies.[110] Just when some kind of provisional closure had been reached on the social and material legacy of World War II,[111] a number of anti-Semitic scandals and

---

[106] On the value of retrospective eyewitness accounts as historical source material see Markowitsch, 'Die Erinnerung von Zeitzeugen'.

[107] A private letter of 21 January 1945 gives a figure of 14,000 deaths. In KHM, A 5499b.

[108] StAM, ZG 55.3, Erwin Stapel, 'Brandnacht 1945', no date.

[109] StAM, ZG 55.3, 'Protokoll des ehemaligen Luftschutzkommandeurs von Magdeburg', 14 September 1950.

[110] For the term 'memory regimes' see Langenbacher, 'Changing Memory Regimes'. Recent literature locates the West German turning point from a restorative return to 'normalcy' to the embrace of 'modernity' in the second half of the 1950s. See Schildt, 'Nachkriegszeit', pp. 573f.; Sywottek, 'Wege in die 50er Jahre'.

[111] See Schildt, Siegfried and Lammers (eds.), *Dynamische Zeiten*; Wolfrum, *Die geglückte Demokratie*, pp. 187–326; Wolle, *Aufbruch in die Stagnation*.

a series of well-publicised trials against low- and mid-level SS perpetrators ushered in the 'return' of the Nazi past,[112] putting, for the first time since the early post-war period, the Nazi politics of annihilation at the centre of public perceptions of World War II.[113] While historians from the Institute of Contemporary History acted as expert witnesses in the first Auschwitz trial of 1963–5,[114] philosophers and psychoanalysts raised broader questions about Germany's 'unmastered past'.[115] Meanwhile, academic historians debated the thorny question of a catastrophic 'special path' in German history in the Fischer controversy, while lamenting a general 'loss of history'.[116]

What, if any, was the impact of these broader shifts on the local air war historiography of Kassel and Magdeburg? Did, as Gilad Margalit has speculated with reference to the memory of the Dresden bombings, a subtext enter local narratives that aimed to relativise 'Auschwitz' by pointing to the death toll in the air war?[117] Or did the local historiography remain the same despite the changes in the broader memory culture?

In the 1960s, the protagonists of local historiographical discourse made no attempt to play off the bombing war against the Nazi Judaeocide. Although, in Kassel in particular, the gradual shift in the supra-local culture from a preoccupation with German victimhood to a concern with the victims of the Germans had local repercussions, '22 October' served to legitimise rather than to obstruct these developments.[118] While this tendency was most pronounced in the commemorative practices of the political elites, the historical representations of the air war continued to neglect the larger context of Nazi genocidal policy, focusing instead on local catastrophe, and increasingly, on military history.

In Magdeburg, likewise, there was a considerable degree of continuity between the 1950s and the 1960s despite the fact that the public culture of the GDR had undergone a shift of emphasis from the denunciation of 'Western imperialism' to the uncovering of the allegedly fascist roots

---

[112] Siegfried, 'Zwischen Aufarbeitung und Schlussstrich', p. 83; Reichel, *Vergangenheitsbewältigung in Deutschland*, pp. 138–81.

[113] Gregor (ed.), *Nazism*, pp. 335f.; Herbert, 'Vernichtungspolitik', pp. 13–19; Frei, 'Deutsche Lernprozesse', pp. 34–7; Knoch, *Die Tat als Bild*, pp. 589–916; Lemke, 'Instrumentalisierter Antifaschismus und SED-Kampagnepolitik'; Groehler, 'Der Holocaust in der Geschichtsschreibung der DDR'.

[114] Buchheim *et al.*, *Anatomie des SS Staates*; compare Berg, *Holocaust*, pp. 311–22.

[115] Adorno, 'Was bedeutet: Aufarbeitung der Vergangenheit?'; Arendt, *Eichmann in Jerusalem*; Mitscherlich and Mitscherlich, *Die Unfähigkeit zu trauern*.

[116] Heuss, *Verlust der Geschichte*. See Assmann and Frevert, *Geschichtsvergessenheit*, pp. 212–14. On the Fischer controversy see Jarausch, 'Der nationale Tabubruch'.

[117] Margalit, 'Der Luftangriff auf Dresden', p. 205.

[118] See chapter 3 above, conclusion.

of the Federal Republic.[119] To a limited degree, these changes impacted the local historiography of the air war. This was despite the fact that the lay journalist Manfred Rolle remained the authoritative voice on the subject. Throughout the 1960s, his scenic account of October 1950 formed the backbone of historical writing on the 'night of horror'. The article was reproduced, with small but significant alterations, in 1959, 1961, 1962, 1965, and again in 1970. In the version of 1959, 'Magdeburg Has Overcome Death', some of the gross exaggerations of earlier editions had disappeared, while the death toll was revised to conform to the official figure of 16,000.[120] Although all versions retained the anti-transcendental bias of the original text, later editions introduced the Nazi leadership as additional villains alongside the Western bomber crews. 'Murderers had arrived by plane, but murderers were also [amongst us] in the town,' as the version from 1965 put it.[121] By 1970, Rolle went so far as to concede that, with the air raid, the violence of war had returned to its place of origin. Here, the destruction had become a 'consequence of a mad war instigated by German imperialists and fascists'.[122]

In Kassel, shifts in the larger memory regime of the Federal Republic had local repercussions but a very limited influence on the historiography of the air war. As early as the autumn of 1957, the adult education centre (*Volkshochschule*) ran a lecture series on Germany's 'Unmastered Past', with individual papers by distinguished scholars such as Werner Conze, Karl Dietrich Bracher, Hans Buchheim, Helmut Krausnick and Hans Rothfels, amongst others.[123] In 1960, the Communist activist Willi Belz published his memoirs on the (Communist) resistance in Kassel during the Third Reich.[124] In the following year, the Society for Christian–Jewish Cooperation, in cooperation with the adult and youth education centres, presented an exhibition on the fate of Jewish children at Theresienstadt concentration camp.[125] Yet the impact on local culture of these early confrontations with the Nazi past should not be overestimated.[126] The archivist Robert Friderici, who started collecting material for a 'future

[119] Lemke, 'Instrumentalisierter Antifaschismus'.
[120] 'Magdeburg überwand den Tod', *Volksstimme*, 16 January 1959, p. 3.
[121] 'Magdeburg am 16. Januar 1945 (Schluss). Bomben verschonten Rüstungswerke', *MNN*, 30/31 January 1965, p. 6.
[122] Manfred Rolle, '16. Januar 1945. Die Nacht des Grauens', *Volksstimme*, 16 January 1970, supplement.
[123] StAK, S4 L15. 1947–58, Volkshochschule. Herbst Trimester 1957, pp. 4f.
[124] Belz, *Die Standhaften*.
[125] StAK, A.1.10, no. 607, Reden [OB Lauritzen] 39, 'Eröffnung der Ausstellung "Hier fliegen keine Schmetterlinge"', 22 October 1961.
[126] For a critical re-evaluation of *Vergangenheitsbewältigung* as 'success story' see Gregor, '"The Illusion of Remembrance"'.

municipal history' in the early 1960s, was the same person who, in 1943, had been charged by the Nazi mayor with documenting the history of Kassel during the war.[127]

With regard to air war historiography, change came not from inside the local culture but from outside. In the 1960s, scenic description – not unlike the work of Manfred Rolle in Magdeburg – replaced the analytical approach as practised by Friedrich Herbordt in his investigative journalism. At the same time, the purely local perspective receded in favour of a greater emphasis on the military context. This shift was only in part a result of Herbordt's premature death in 1958. More important was the influence of a popular history of strategic bombing, *Und Deutschlands Städte starben nicht*, by the young British freelance historian David Irving.[128] Before its publication in monograph form, the so-called documentary report had already been serialised in the illustrated weekly *Neue Illustrierte*. Two instalments dealt with the events of October 1943 in Kassel.[129] A local advertisement, possibly produced for newsagent stalls, carried an image of the ruins of the Martinskirche that was coloured in red, together with the sensational title 'Carpet Bombs on Kassel, From the Secret Archives of the Royal Air Force'.[130]

Irving's account quickly became the defining historical text on the destruction of Kassel. On the occasion of the twentieth anniversary in 1963 and again on the twenty-fifth anniversary in 1968, the local press published special reports, copying verbatim long passages from the documentary account.[131] In 1968, the city-sponsored publication *Unsere Stadt* simply reprinted Irving's article in a special section that was designed to document the city's 'success story' 'from downfall to rise'. In doing so, the city turned the piece into the authoritative historical treatment of the bombing of Kassel.[132] Irving's work must be considered the single most influential text in the local memory culture of Kassel, with a decisive impact on the indigenous research that got underway in the following decades. Why was this? As a close reading will suggest, the popularity of Irving's 'documentary report' was due to the ways in which the text appeared to reaffirm, with the authority of the international scholar,

---

[127] StAK, A.4.415, no. 152, mayor to Friderici, 18 October 1943.
[128] Irving, *Und Deutschlands Städte starben nicht*.
[129] *Neue Illustrierte* 17/10 (1962), pp. 28–35; 17/11 (1962), pp. 28–35.
[130] StAK, S5 P97.
[131] Wolfgang Hermsdorff, '22.X.43. 20 Jahre danach', *HA*, 22 October 1943; *KP*, 22 October 1963; Egon E. Vogt, 'Heute vor 25 Jahren: So starb Kassel. Der 22. Oktober 1943', *HNA*, 22 October 1968; *KP*, 22 October 1968. See also Mohr, 'Bombenkrieg und Kassels Zerstörung 1943'.
[132] See David J. Irving, 'Das Chaos einer Nacht', in Magistrat der Stadt Kassel, press office (ed.), special supplement 'Unsere Stadt 1943 bis 1968' in *Unsere Stadt*, October 1968.

central tenets of the local memorial culture, while relocating local catas
trophe within the context of an 'honourable' war.

The text drew on British and German primary sources as well as
the standard research literature of the time. It was carefully composed,
describing the course and consequences of the air raid from different per-
spectives – the British air staff, the local civilian population, the bomber
crews and the Nazi leadership. As its main compositional elements, the
text employed juxtaposition and scenic description. In the first instalment, 'Carpet Bombs on Kassel', the introduction described 22 October
1943 as the 'dying day' of Kassel, thus confirming a well-established
conceptualisation of the air raid. In order to lend authority to this assessment, Irving quoted from the 1952 memoir by the General Inspector
of Fire Prevention during the war, Hans Rumpf, which had spoken of
a 'funeral pyre' and 'crematorium'.[133] Shifting perspective, the text also
quoted from the official British history and Goebbels' diaries in order to
establish 'objectively' the destructiveness of the raid.[134]

For the sake of illustration, Irving cited extensively from an eyewitness
account by Clara H. that was drawn from the collection by Karl Paetow.
Sanitised excerpts of her harrowing story of survival amidst mass death
had already been used by the local press in 1953, but Irving remained
largely – although not entirely – faithful to the original document, thereby
pushing the boundaries of what could publicly be said about the circumstances of death under the bombs.[135] The break with received notions of
propriety was even more pronounced in the sphere of the visual, where
images of the dead entered public memory in the wake of Irving's documentary report.[136]

Yet the text did not just validate local voices with the help of the
national literature. It also offered an answer to a central question of local
enquiries, the reasons for the catastrophe. Unlike Herbordt in 1949, who
had looked for structural defects in the civil defence provisions, Irving's
explanation in 1963 focused on the 'war of the air waves'. He gave a
dramatic description of British attempts at deceiving the German night
fighter force through intercepting their radio intelligence. Kassel, the
argument went, had fallen victim to British officers imitating the German
officers on the wireless (*Funkleitoffiziere*). This thread was taken up in the

---

[133] Rumpf, *Der hochrote Hahn*, pp. 102f., reads, 'From the high furnace of this murder fire
[*Mordbrand*], not many managed to escape.' Irving quoted the passage but left out the
term *Mordbrand*.
[134] Webster and Frankland, *Strategic Air Offensive against Germany*, vol. II, pp. 161f., 267f.
[135] See pages 265f. above.
[136] Compare Egon E. Vogt, 'Heute vor 25 Jahren: So starb Kassel. Der 22. Oktober 1943',
HNA, 22 October 1968.

second instalment, 'Kassel in the Zero Hour', in which Irving gave an account of a confrontation between a bomber crew and a German fighter plane. In order to illustrate the devastating impact of the raid, he quoted extensively from the police report of 7 December 1943 and lauded the German fire police for their courage. The article concluded by dealing with the issue of guilt. It stressed that ultimate responsibility for the destruction of Kassel lay with Hitler for starting the war, as well as with Goebbels for allegedly suppressing knowledge about its destructiveness.

In his account, Irving retold the air raid as part of a confrontation between British bomber crews on the one hand and the German Luftwaffe and civilians on the other, in which honourable exploits were performed on both sides. The role of the villain, by contrast, was assigned to the Nazi leadership. Thus, the text shifted the emphasis back from a purportedly natural disaster to a military confrontation and its consequences. At the same time, Irving reaffirmed the central conceptualisation of the local memorial culture. In an air war waged in isolation from World War II, the city was depicted as a victim of forces beyond its control. In the serialised version, the narrative went so far as to claim that even in the 1960s, Kassel still suffered from the wartime secrecy campaign of Joseph Goebbels: '22 October 1943 is the day of death of a German city, whose annihilation was covered up by Goebbels so effectively that even today many Germans have no idea of the extent of this horrifying bombing raid.'[137]

Conclusion

If academic history can be said to function as a 'rational check' on collective memory, then the reverse held true for the local historiography of the air war in the first decades after 1945.[138] Here, collective memory disciplined history. In Kassel no less than in Magdeburg, local journalists, in their endeavours to recreate the past, manipulated the historical source material and homogenised disparate experiences in order to tell stories that they deemed palatable to the political and emotional sensibilities of their local audiences. In both cities, the historiography of the 1950s may be characterised as an inversion of the monumental conception that had characterised the Nazi years: the privileging of the heroic gave way to an emphasis on victimhood; the inspiring example to deterrent example. The most important building block for this kind of history was the eyewitness account, the 'individual fate that speaks for many thousands', which

---

[137] 'Bombenteppiche auf Kassel', *Neue Illustrierte* 17/10 (1962), p. 30.
[138] Jarausch, 'Zeitgeschichte und Erinnerung', p. 21.

symbolised the experiences of the memory-group as a whole. Whereas in Kassel, local historiography was put to the service of pacification, in Magdeburg local history served the task of mobilisation.

Local air war historiography did not stand at the centre of the mnemonic controversies that slowly reconfigured the broader cultural parameters in the 1960s. In both cities, local historiography continued to emphasise the victimhood of the local community, without paying much attention to the broader context in which the air raids had taken place. Next to continuity, there was also change. In Magdeburg, the central text on the air raid was modified in order to cast blame for the destruction of the city on German fascism as well as on American imperialism. In Kassel, meanwhile, the impact of David Irving's work led to a recontextualisation of local disaster within the history of the air war as a military confrontation.

8 The 'greatest event in municipal history': local research as antiquarian endeavour, 1970–1995

Introduction

The process of ossification and decline that characterised the memorial culture in the 1970s did not affect all vectors of memory in equal measure. Despite the scaling back of commemorative activity in both Kassel and Magdeburg, the air raids retained their significance as important points of reference for local historiography.[1] When Herfried Homburg published his cultural history *Kassel: the Intellectual Profile of a Thousand Year Old Town*, in 1969, he dedicated his work 'in memory of 22 October 1943'.[2] The same perspective was shared by the Communist Willi Belz, who explicitly invoked 'the tragedy of 22 October 1943' in the preface to his autobiographical study of local resistance to Nazism.[3] In Magdeburg, too, the bombing remained an important marker in local historical writing, although perhaps not quite to the same extent as in Kassel. The official *History of the City of Magdeburg*, published by the city council in 1975, devoted a subchapter to the attack of 16 January 1945.[4]

More remarkably, both cities witnessed attempts to write authoritative local histories of the air war at the very moment that the social dynamics of public memory had reached a low point. These efforts were undertaken by members of the 'sceptical generation' of the age cohorts born in the decade between 1925 and 1935, who had lived through the war as anti-aircraft auxiliaries, young soldiers or adolescents.[5] In February 1975, Werner Dettmar (born 1927), an employee with the city of Kassel, went public in the *Hessische Allgemeine* with an appeal for documents about the events of 22 October 1943. One month earlier, the journalist Rudi Hartwig (born 1932) had published preliminary results of his

---

[1] The quotation in this chapter's title comes from Werner Dettmar, in Manfred Schaake, 'Alt-Kassel ging in einem Feuersturm ohne Beispiel unter', *HA*, 16 October 1982.
[2] Homburg, *Kassel – das geistige Profil*, p. 3.   [3] Belz, *Die Standhaften*, p. 6.
[4] Asmus, *Geschichte der Stadt*, pp. 320–31.
[5] Frei, 'Deutsche Lernprozesse', p. 27. The term derives from the sociologist Helmut Schelsky, *Die skeptische Generation*. Compare also Schörken, *Luftwaffenhelfer und Drittes Reich*; Moses, 'Die 45er'.

investigation into the air raid of 16 January 1945 in the *Volksstimme*.[6] Local initiatives mirrored developments in the field of academic history where in both East and West the first serious scholarly treatments of the air war started to appear in the 1970s.[7] Although local research efforts were conceived in the same decade, they came to fruition in the fundamentally different political and historiographical climate of the 1980s, amidst a flourishing peace movement and a turn to 'the history of the every day'.[8]

This chapter argues that the mid-1970s marked a turning point in the historiography on the air war. Drawing, in part, on the earlier writings of David Irving, the period spawned two modes of representation that were to dominate the 1980s and 1990s: the documentary account and the historical exhibition. On the conceptual level, historical writing no longer functioned as crude legitimisation for the narratives that had been developed by the protagonists of public memory. In Nietzschean terms, the monumental conception of the 1950s and 1960s gave way to an antiquarian approach, which sought to document, but not necessarily to explain. In some respects, historical re-creation became a mode of engagement in which the experience generation sought to preserve 'their' memories against the paradigm shift in public commemorations, where a younger generation had started to frame local disaster within the broader context of the German war of annihilation. Yet, for the 1980s at least, this tension should not be exaggerated. Against the backdrop of a cultural climate in which fears over an 'atomic Holocaust' existed side by side with the (re-)discovery of the historical Holocaust, this flak auxiliary historiography coexisted easily with critical studies of Nazism.[9] This was to change only after the end of the Cold War, when the antiquarian approach to aerial warfare came under increasing criticism as revisionism in disguise.

---

[6] 'Phasen der Bombennacht nachgespürt. Werner Dettmar sammelt Dokumente über Zerstörung Kassels im Jahr 1943', *HA Stadtausgabe*, 15 February 1975; Rudi Hartwig, 'In der Glut des Feuersturms. Untersuchung des Luftangriffs auf Magdeburg am 16. Januar 1945', *Volksstimme*, 17 January 1975, supplement, p. 2.

[7] Benda-Beckmann, 'Eine deutsch-deutsche Katastrophe?', p. 303.

[8] On the history of the every day see Lindenberger, '"Alltagsgeschichte"'; Peukert, 'Das "Dritte Reich" aus der "Alltags"-Perspektive'.

[9] Dettmar cooperated to some extent with a group of academics and students from Kassel University who were working on a critical history of National Socialism. On the gestation of this city-sponsored project see StAK, A.4.415, no. 163, Forschungsprojekt 'Kassel in der NS-Zeit' II (1979–82); ibid., no. 174, Stadtgeschichtliches Forschungsvorhaben: Kassel unter dem Nationalsozialismus I (1979–87). The results were published in 1984 and 1987 in the two-volume *Volksgemeinschaft und Volksfeinde*, ed. by Frenz, Kammler and Krause-Vilmar.

Air war historiography as documentary account

In the Kassel of the late 1970s, there were several contenders for writing a definitive account of the city's destruction on 22 October 1943. Next to the city employee Werner Dettmar, there were the art historian and former 'municipal researcher' Dr Karl Paetow (1904–93) and the local resident Horst Wagner (born 1926). Only Dettmar succeeded, while the efforts by Paetow and Wagner did not progress beyond the manuscript stage. Despite these differences, they shared two features in common which set them apart from a group of academics from Kassel University who had embarked on studying the history of the every day under Nazism. Born between 1904 and 1927, they had lived through World War II as adults or adolescents. They also held personal memories of the air raid of 22 October, Dettmar as a flak auxiliary on duty, Wagner as a young marine on holiday leave, and Paetow as a city employee.

In many respects, Dr Karl Paetow was the obvious candidate for writing the history of Kassel's destruction in World War II. As a university-educated art historian with a publishing record, he possessed the relevant experience and skills. Moreover, as the city's official 'researcher' during the Third Reich and head of the Enquiry Office for the Missing in 1944, he had collected more than a hundred eyewitness accounts that could have furnished the empirical basis for a history 'from below'. Possibly encouraged by the great success of David Irving's writings on Dresden and other German cities, Paetow started work on a local history of the bombing in the 1970s.[10] In an undated outline, the art historian sketched the central ideas of a project that he called 'Kassel in the Melting Furnace of Time' (*Kassel im Schmelzofen der Zeit*).[11]

In this projected story of an 'end of a thousand-year-old history' and the 'beginning of a new epoch', the eyewitness accounts from 1944 were to occupy centre stage. In addition, the visual was to play an important role as well, as a handwritten addition makes clear. By contrast, Paetow planned to avoid any discussion of responsibility, as he emphasised with the injunction, 'Do *not* throw up the issue of guilt!' Rather, Paetow insisted on the 'non-political' nature of the book, which he wanted to be understood as a 'town chronicle'. To this purpose, he invoked a trans-historical 'law of fate' as an explanation for the destruction of the city in World War II.[12]

---

[10] See Paetow's collection of press clippings on Irving and others in BGM Kassel, NL 7, Stiftung Karl Paetow, folder 58, 'Kassel im Schmelzofen der Zeit, Die Stadt in der Hölle, Zeitungsartikel, masch. & hs', fos. 1–8.

[11] Ibid., fo. 10.   [12] All quotations ibid.

In the finished manuscript, Paetow indicated the temporal and conceptual frame of his project with the subtitle 'The Destruction and Reconstruction of a City'.[13] In the preface, he spoke of a 'peaceful community' that had suddenly been engulfed by history. His book was to give testimony to 'the capacity of suffering [and] the will to survive' of a town that had been forced into 'a tragedy of the greatest scale [by] the destructive force of modern weaponry'. Paetow conceptualised the air raid in familiar terms as the destruction of *Heimat* by a (natural) disaster, suggesting that the eyewitness accounts be read as the 'swan song' of Kassel, which had found 'her poet...in destruction'. Clearly, Paetow was not interested in analysing his source material critically. Instead, he apotheosised the collection as the voice of the people, casting himself as a chronicler who had merely arranged the source material. While he insisted that no meaning could be derived from the air raid, Paetow still contended that the deaths of '12,000 innocent victims' could have a cathartic effect on posterity. Might not, he asked, 'yield the self-destructing madness of humanity...to the warm recognition of shocked hearts? May this be the message of Kassel.'[14]

As the preface indicated, Paetow had no intention of writing a scholarly history or of producing a critical edition of historical documents. Rather, he wanted the collection of eyewitness accounts to be understood as a folk tale, as 'the voice of the common people' that had been collected and saved from oblivion just as the Brothers Grimm had collected their fairy tales in the nineteenth century. Whatever the appeal of such a romantic conception of history to a scholar whose main research interest lay with German fairy tales, Paetow's prospective publishers at the Motorbuch Verlag were not impressed. In a letter on 16 November 1981, a lector told Paetow that he only saw chances for publication if excerpts from the reports were 'integrated into a broader frame which does not only touch on human experiences but also on all other aspects of the air war...as preparation of the attack, relief measures, organisation, technical issues, and so on'.[15] Not the blatant self-victimisation but the disregard of the military context stood in the way of publication. What the publisher looked for was local military history as, for example, Hans Brunswig had written about Hamburg, rather than a folk tale.[16] Despite the setback, Paetow pursued the project for some time after that, but when attempts at cooperating with Dettmar did not materialise and the mayor of Kassel,

---

[13] Ibid., fo. 11.   [14] Ibid., fos. 13–15.
[15] Ibid., fos. 62, 1–19, 'Briefwechsel und geplante Veröffentlichung', 1981–2, here fo. 7.
[16] Compare Brunswig, *Feuersturm*.

Hans Eichel (SPD), refused to support the project financially, he finally abandoned his plans in 1982.[17]

At about the same time that Paetow offered his 'Kassel in the Melting Furnace of Time' to Motorbuch Verlag, Horst Wagner finished a draft manuscript that shared in common the underlying perspective.[18] Like the art historian, Wagner sought to describe the experience of the air raid 'from below'. Rather than sifting through a private archive as Paetow, Wagner searched his own memory, producing an autobiographical text that recalled his experiences as a young marine on home leave in mid-October 1943.

'The Firestorm' (Der Feuersturm) was the personal account of a man nearing retirement age who looked back on his youth during the war. The text was scenic rather than analytical, and despite the objectifying third person, brimmed with strong emotions, extreme judgements and present-centred reflections. Of the two hundred manuscript pages, only about a third dealt with the experiences of the protagonist during the air raid, while the bulk of the manuscript offered a dense description of a seventeen-year-old negotiating different social roles and attitudes: Horst as proud marine on leave, looking down on the 'auxiliary soldiers' of the Heimat (fo. 36) and bragging to his family about his knowledge of air raid damage in other cities; Horst as rebellious youth in pursuit of pleasure, unwilling to accept the hierarchies of old; and Horst as teenager falling in love with his childhood sweetheart in time of war.

Just like Paetow, Wagner embedded his story in a broader context, which served to demonstrate the relevance of his experiences to the present. In his preface, he constructed an analogy between the concept of nuclear deterrence of the 1980s and German rearmament in the 1930s, and concluded with a bizarre logic: 'Despite his enormous rearmament efforts, Hitler was unable to prevent the war.'[19] Employing an interpretation that distinguished between government and the governed but recognised no historical causation, he contended that politicians of all countries had unwittingly led their peoples into a war that had known 'only losers, and those were the common people'.[20] Within this conceptualisation, the (allied) air war became nothing but deliberate 'murder of human beings'.[21] If this interpretation illustrated that the paradigm of 'air war as crime' was by no means the preserve of the official politics of memory of the GDR, Wagner went further still, drawing a parallel between

---

[17] StAK, S8 E5, Ausstellung 1983 (III), Paetow to Motorbuch Verlag, 5 April 1982; BGM Kassel, NL 7, Stiftung Karl Paetow, folder 62, fos. 11–15.

[18] StAK, S3, no. 379, Horst Wagner, 'Der Feuersturm', unpublished manuscript (c. 1982).

[19] Wagner, 'Feuersturm'.   [20] Ibid., fo. 3.   [21] Ibid., fo. 2.

the allied air war, the Holocaust and the expulsion of the Germans from the east.

Wagner demanded that the 'millions of victims of bombing' ought to be considered equal 'to the cruel genocide in the KZ's [*Konzentrationslager*] [and] the millions of deaths among the refugees and expellees in all the world', and went on to lament what he perceived to be a difference in the public representation of the various victim groups: 'To us Germans, the last epoch of German history has been suppressed for years. But instead [we have been] confronted again and again with the atrocities of the Third Reich. Still today, on Memorial Sunday, there are no more than a few meaningless words of remembrance about the innocent victims of the bombing war.'[22] Problematic as this line of reasoning was, it revealed more than the author's unwillingness to recognise the categorical difference between victims of war and victims of genocide. It illustrated the extent to which the parameters of public remembrance were changing in the 1980s. Wagner no longer compared the casualties of allied bombing to soldiers killed in action, as was common in the 1950s, but likened them to the victims of the Nazi genocide. Even in denial, Wagner acknowledged the extent to which the Holocaust had assumed a pivotal place in the public memory culture of the Federal Republic.[23]

Yet, throughout the second Cold War of the 1980s, fears of an 'atomic Holocaust'[24] loomed just as large in public consciousness as concerns over the historical Holocaust. The popularity of a pacifist sentiment that condemned war in general as an act of mass murder made it easy for writers such as Wagner to fuse critical comments about the contemporary East–West confrontation with apologetic revisionism of World War II. Contrasting what he perceived to be the 'mastered past' of Nazi genocide with the 'unmastered past' of the bombing war, he asserted, 'The person responsible for the genocide has been sought and found. About the murder of human beings [*Menschenmorden*] there is embarrassed silence.' Wagner went on to draw his own conclusions, intimating that there existed a link between the alleged suppression of the air war and the arms race: 'This murder of defenceless civilians has apparently long been forgotten. How else is it possible that today games are played again with the strategic and tactical possibilities of modern means of destruction?'[25] Despite Wagner's insistence on the criminality of the air war, he wanted his account to be read as a memento for the future rather than as an indictment of the past. He dedicated the text to the

---

[22] Ibid.   [23] See chapter 4 above.
[24] For the term see Kelly, 'In der Tradition der Gewaltfreiheit (1983)', p. 313.
[25] Wagner, 'Feuersturm', fo. 2.

'many innocent victims of the air war', remembering in particular his own mother and sister who had died in the attack. In the epilogue, Wagner defined the victim group he had in mind. In an 'interchangeable representation' (Alon Confino) of the locality and the nation, the suffering of the resident population represented 'the suffering and the pain' of all Germans.[26]

However widespread Wagner's sentiments may have been, there was no space for this blend of autobiographical memoir and apologetic revisionism in the public historiography of Kassel in the 1980s. The personal experience report remained unpublished, although Wagner himself continued to play a role in the public conversation about the air war. He deposited his manuscript in the municipal archive and also collaborated with Werner Dettmar on his project of a historical exhibition.[27] While the failure to have the manuscript published may not be regretted, the text deserves attention not just as a document of the local memory culture, revealing the amalgam of apologetic revisionism and emotional intensity with which contemporaries retold the bombing of their home town forty years after the event. The memoirs also contained a wealth of observations that could have provided valuable material for a social history of the war. On page 140, for example, Wagner describes the carping that he overheard in a shelter immediately after the attack. 'Some were just sitting there and sobbing quietly. Others swore at the Tommies, the Nazis, the grandfathers and grandmothers . . . They swore at everybody and everything, even at God, who was responsible for everything. Only they were making no efforts to help themselves.'[28] What the observation suggests is that grumbling was a (helpless) way of coping with the emotional and physical stress of bombing, while the object of the invective was interchangeable, and to a large degree, irrelevant.

Neither Paetow's romanticising apotheosis of the 'voice of the people' nor Wagner's revisionist memoirs progressed beyond the manuscript stage. Local historiography of the air war came, instead, to be associated with the name of Werner Dettmar. During the course of the late 1970s and early 1980s, this employee of the Bureau of Cultural Affairs established himself as an authority on strategic bombing whose advice and comment were sought whenever the subject aroused public attention. Like Paetow and Wagner, Dettmar was a local resident and an eyewitness of the air raid. In the autumn of 1943, he had been deployed as a young anti-aircraft auxiliary in the vicinity of Kassel but experienced the attack

---

[26] Ibid., epilogue, fo. 191.
[27] See also StAK, S8 C51, Horst Wagner to HNA Lokalredaktion, 8 October 2003.
[28] Wagner, 'Feuersturm', fo. 140.

in a shelter north of the city centre because he was on weekend leave.[29] Yet, unlike his fellow historians, Dettmar did not make personal memories the centre point of his historical writing. Instead, he approached the subject from an 'objective' angle, aiming to produce a 'comprehensive documentation [of the] destruction of Kassel in October 1943', as the dust jacket of his 1983 publication put it.[30]

To this end, Dettmar went public as early as February 1975 with a newspaper appeal for contemporaries to come forward.[31] While Dettmar sought to tap local knowledge, he showed no interest in retrospective eye-witness accounts. He positioned himself as a scholar who approached the subject dispassionately, undertaking research trips to British archives, collecting and sifting through historical documents in order to find answers to such technical questions as the position of the anti-aircraft batteries around Kassel.[32] There was no emotional language in Dettmar's public appeal, no talk of the 'voice of the people' or 'war crimes'. In the objectified language of the scholar, Dettmar described the air raid of 22 October 1943 as 'the biggest event in the city's history'.[33]

Drawing on the (popular) research literature of his time and a wealth of primary sources, Dettmar wrote the history of the destruction as a blend of *Heimat* history and military history. In his documentation, *The Destruction of Kassel in October 1943* (1983), chapters on 'Old Kassel in Old Postcards' were followed by sections on the German air raid defences. The text dealt with the strength and tactics of British Bomber Command but also contained a casualty list of all 6,000 registered victims of the bombing raid. Following David Irving, Dettmar put the air raid in the context of the history of air warfare, without paying any attention to the genocidal character of the German (land) war of 1939–45.[34]

Remarkably, the historians' voice was barely audible in Dettmar's text. Making no overt attempt at interpreting the events of October 1943, he documented but did not offer historical explanations. In the preface, for example, Dettmar posed the question about the reason for 'all those deaths' but neither the section on the industrial importance of Kassel nor the chapter on the local civilian defence offered any answers.

---

[29] See 'Chronist der Zerstörung. Werner Dettmar: Ausstellungsmacher und Autor', *Kassel Kulturell* (October 1993), pp. 8–12.

[30] Dettmar, *Zerstörung*, dust jacket. The book was based on the exhibition of the same name. See below.

[31] 'Phasen der Bombennacht nachgespürt. Werner Dettmar sammelt Dokumente über Zerstörung Kassels im Jahr 1943', *HA*, 15 February 1975.

[32] Ibid. See the visual illustration of the article: Dettmar was shown studying documents.

[33] Ibid.

[34] Of the forty footnotes, nineteen referred to *Von Guernica nach Vietnam* (1982) by David Irving.

He abstained from subjecting the source material to critical analysis, suggesting that the documents 'speak for themselves' (p. 54). Yet, as Detlev Peukert has pointed out, conventional explanations tend to take over where the historians refrain from doing their job.[35] Here, this was particularly the case with the rich visual material, which suggested a narrative of a 'beautiful' town (pp. 10–26) being defended by child soldiers and men of retirement age (pp. 27–48), but overwhelmed by a superior enemy whose crews shared much in common with the youthful defenders (pp. 84–117). The air raid resulted in unprecedented human suffering (pp. 160ff.), the destruction of the cityscape (pp. 201f.) and the legacy of mass death (pp. 257ff.).

In analogy to Nicolas Berg's characterisation of German contemporary history as a 'fellow traveller narrative' (*Mitläufer-Erzählung*), one might speak of a flak auxiliary historiography which reproduced the contemporary fascination with the technical apparatus of destruction while accepting the (air) war as a 'natural' aspect of life.[36] Characteristically, the diary entries of the flak auxiliary Gebhard Niemeyer were the central ego-document of a text that mainly reproduced official documents such as the British post-raid assessments and the experience report by the German police.[37] The narrative exhibited an equal if not greater degree of empathy with the British bomber crews as with the local resident population. Quoting from an unreferenced source (Irving?), Dettmar depicted the British crews as a mirror image of the German flak auxiliaries: 'Thus most of them started night after night with fear in their hearts to do no more and no less than was their mission.'[38]

While the historiography of Kassel in theory aimed at integrating catastrophic rupture into the continuum of municipal history, and in practice, offered description rather than analysis, the historiography of Magdeburg was both more ambitious in scope and less concerned with the empirical evidence. It sought to link local developments to a world-historical context, to uncover the motive forces of the strategic air war and to answer the issues of guilt and responsibility, past and present. When the journalist Rudi Hartwig published his account of the air raid on Magdeburg in 1975, he cast his piece as an 'enquiry', arguing that Magdeburg was destroyed for political rather than military reasons.[39] Here, as elsewhere, local events were made to fit a political master narrative that had been developed for the national *lieu de mémoire* of 'Dresden'.

[35] Peukert, 'Das "Dritte Reich" aus der "Alltags"-Perspektive', 538f.
[36] Berg, *Holocaust*, p. 424; Schörken, *Luftwaffenhelfer und Drittes Reich*, pp. 36, 121–32.
[37] Dettmar, *Zerstörung*, pp. 76f., 210–13.   [38] Ibid., p. 84.
[39] Rudi Hartwig, 'In der Glut des Feuersturms', *Volksstimme*, 17 January 1975, supplement.

The function of historical research in the GDR as self-avowedly 'biased' (*parteilich*) scholarship was to provide 'scientific' legitimacy for the historical narrative of the political elites.[40] Thus Olaf Groehler, the leading air war historian of the GDR, argued that during the final phase of World War II, strategic bombing was no longer aimed at defeating Nazi Germany but had turned into a political campaign for pre-empting the spread of Communism in the post-war period.[41] In his *History of Air Warfare, 1910–1975*, he put his case succinctly: 'The nature of the Western-allied war effort began to change. Instead of remaining a part of the just campaign of the anti-Hitler coalition, it turned increasingly into an instrument of the anti-Soviet plans for world domination of the most reactionary forces of American and British imperialism.'[42] For Groehler, the Dresden raids of 13/14 February 1945 constituted both the symbol and climax of this campaign. He argued that in late January 1945 allied strategy underwent a decisive shift. In the light of the stalemate on the Western Front and the simultaneous disintegration of the German armies on the Eastern Front, the British and American air staff revived plans for a decisive knock-out blow from the air, code-named 'Thunderclap'. These plans, Groehler claimed, focused deliberately on the cities in the future Soviet zone of occupation, being motivated by the political consideration of demonstrating to the Soviet Union the strength of Western air power. The result, according to Groehler, was a 'massacre from the air', as evidenced in the Dresden raids of February 1945.[43]

Whatever the heuristic strengths and weaknesses of a 'political' explanation of the Dresden raids,[44] the anachronistic assumptions underwriting Groehler's interpretation were all too obvious: World War II strategic bombing had been recontextualised as an aggressive act of the Cold War.[45] For Magdeburg, there existed the additional problem that the city played no role in this narrative. In his standard history, Groehler made no mention of 16 January 1945, and subsumed attacks on Magdeburg under the rubric of 'similar terror raids'.[46] Local historians were thus faced with the impossible task of integrating the raid of 16 January 1945

---

[40] On the *Parteilichkeit* of historical research in the GDR see Sabrow, 'Einleitung'. For the context see Iggers *et al.* (eds.), *Die DDR-Geschichtswissenschaft*.

[41] Groehler, *Geschichte des Luftkrieges*.

[42] Ibid., pp. 453f. Compare also Margalit, 'Der Luftangriff auf Dresden', p. 201.

[43] Groehler, *Geschichte des Luftkrieges*, pp. 456ff.

[44] For good discussions of the decision-making process of the Dresden raids see Bergander, 'Vom unattraktiven zum besonders lohnenden Ziel'; Cox, 'The Dresden Raids'.

[45] Compare Groehler's own post-1989 critical comments in *Bombenkrieg*, pp. 450f.; Groehler, 'Dresden'.

[46] See Groehler, *Geschichte des Luftkriegs*, p. 458: 'Similar terror raids were directed against Magdeburg, Chemnitz, Dessau, Leipzig, Halle and Bitterfeld.'

into a politically licensed frame that had been developed for a different historical setting. While Dresden may or may not have been an important military target in the spring of 1945, Magdeburg clearly was, boasting key war industries of the highest priority. Dresdeners may or may not have been thinking that they inhabited an 'oasis of peace', but Magdeburgers had no reason to do so, with more than five hundred alarms and constant raids throughout 1944.[47]

Local historiography sought to resolve this tension between national master narrative and empirical evidence by rearranging the chronology of the historical events. In his 'enquiry', Hartwig pre-dated Groehler's thesis about a shift in allied policy to November 1944, selectively quoting from a Bomber Command target list dated the first of that month.[48] Moreover, he constructed a causal link between target selection and the allied agreement of September 1944 on the joint occupation of post-war Germany: 'These cities [from the target list] were situated on the territory of the future Soviet zone of occupation . . . Harris knew of the government agreement of 12 September 1944 where the allied powers had agreed on the borders of the future zones of occupation.'[49] By contrast, the emphasis in allied documents on the industrial and military importance of Magdeburg was dismissed as mere rhetoric, as a 'cover-up', as Hartwig claimed.[50] In order to underline the significance of the city in the overall political design, he construed a further link, between the raid of 16 January 1945 and allied plans to bring the war to an end through air power alone. Where Groehler had argued that the raid on Berlin of 3 February 1945 was the first implementation of Operation 'Thunderclap', Hartwig simply exchanged the Reich capital for the city on the river Elbe, stating that Magdeburg had become the first victim of this strategy.[51] Echoing Groehler's verdict on the Dresden raid, he claimed that Magdeburg had been destroyed for 'power-political' reasons.

[47] The Junkers aero-engine works and the Krupp Gruson works were rated 1+ targets in the 'Bomber's Baedeker', the Polte gun manufacturer was rated 1 while the Bergius hydrogenation plant Braunkohle (Brabag) was a primary oil target. See the information collected by the USSBS in NA II RG 243 E-6 # 39 1–19. See StAM, ZG 122.6 (9), Tagebuch Trimborn, entry of 30 January 1947, for contemporary rumours that sought to account for the absence of devastating raids in 1944.

[48] Webster and Frankland consider the directive of 25 September 1944, which accorded priority to oil and transport, as a turning point that ushered in 'the beginning of the final air offensive'. By comparison, they regard the directive of 1 November 1944 to have 'closely followed' the lines of its predecessor. Webster and Frankland, *Strategic Air Offensive*, vol. III, pp. 42–74; for the quotations pp. 63, 73. For the wording of the November directive see ibid., vol. IV, pp. 177–9. It demanded that 'particular emphasis' be given to targets in the Ruhr area. For the Bomber Command target list of 1 November see Groehler, *Bombenkrieg*, p. 356.

[49] Hartwig, 'In der Glut des Feuersturms'.   [50] Ibid.

[51] Groehler, *Geschichte des Luftkriegs*, p. 457; Hartwig, 'In der Glut des Feuersturms'.

Local historiography thus legitimised the claims that were made by the political elites during commemorative ceremonies. In elevating the raid of 16 January 1945 from a local event to an important turning point in world history – the first aggressive act of the Cold War – historical writing also provided the municipal authorities with a powerful myth that was useful to position the city on the international stage. Mayor Werner Herzig (SED), for one, derived special authority from Magdeburg's purportedly special role in World War II in order to speak out at an international conference of so-called 'martyr cities' in 1987.[52] However, for the voice of the city to be raised with confidence in international affairs, it was not enough to show that Magdeburg had been singled out as a target. Historiography also needed to demonstrate that the city had suffered exceptionally in the air war, that, indeed, Magdeburg's destruction was on a par with the most ravaged cities in World War II and history.

This was unproblematic for the local historiography in so far as the material devastation was concerned. In his article of January 1975, Hartwig put the index of destruction for Magdeburg third among the cities of the former German Reich, 'behind Dresden and Cologne but before Berlin'.[53] With regard to the human cost of the air war, however, the empirical results of historical research came into conflict with the political narrative of the SED. Interestingly, this was as much due to a growing intransigence on the part of the local elites as to fresh insights from empirical research. By the early 1980s, there had long existed a certain degree of incongruity between the official death toll of 16,000 casualties and the empirically verifiable figure. Interviewees in 1950 had spoken of 2,000–4,000 deaths, and Manfred Rolle, in the same year, had put the death toll for 16 January 1945 at 8,223.[54] As long as these figures remained confined to archives and to the media of the satellite parties, the local SED was prepared to tolerate the apparent inconsistency.

Conflict ensued when the parameters of the memory culture began to change in the 1980s. At a time when the discursive power of the SED came under challenge by an increasingly vocal opposition that found institutional support among the Christian churches,[55] the local leadership turned to the 'victim identity' of Magdeburg in order to raise the profile of the city nationally and internationally. The figure of 16,000

---

[52] Compare StAM, Rep. 41/701, 'Rede des Oberbürgermeisters auf der Konferenz der Märtyrerstädte vom 27.4. bis 29.4.1987 in Madrid'.
[53] Hartwig, 'In der Glut des Feuersturms'.   [54] See chapter 7 above.
[55] For the context see Neubert, *Geschichte der Opposition*, pp. 335–903; Sabrow, 'Einleitung'.

casualties was crucial in this effort to establish the city second to Dresden as the 'Nagasaki' of the GDR.[56] When Hartwig in 1985 challenged this central plank on the basis of his findings, pointing out that the verifiable number of fatalities was 2,680, the SED intervened and stopped the delivery of the official fortieth anniversary publication, *Magdeburg in a Storm of Fire*.[57] In spite of the historical evidence, the official casualty rate was upheld until the demise of the SED regime in 1989.[58] Surprisingly, perhaps, the mythical figure of 16,000 refused to go away even in unified Germany, provoking a minor controversy in 1995.[59] Characteristically, post-reunification historians played down the significance of the death toll, treading very quietly where the SED regime had produced a lot of noise before 1989.[60]

The rise of the exhibition, 1983–1995

Next to the 'documentary account', the historical exhibition became the central medium through which the subject of allied bombing re-entered historical discourse in the latter decades of the twentieth century. Both cities staged public displays on the occasion of the fortieth anniversaries in 1983/5 and again on the fiftieth anniversaries in 1993/5, each time to spectacular success.[61] Exhibitions are modes of representation that put material objects rather than texts at the centre, inviting the audience to

---

[56] This argument is developed more fully in Arnold, '"Nagasaki" in der DDR'.

[57] Rudi Hartwig, 'Magdeburg verglühte im Feuersturm', *Volksstimme*, 11 January 1985, supplement, p. 2; Hartwig, 'Bomben auf Frauen und Kinder', 7; Hartwig and Wille, *Magdeburg im Feuersturm*, p. 69. Author's conversation with Prof. Manfred Wille, 21 January 2005; conversation with Ms Karin Grünwald, Kulturhistorisches Museum, 16 February 2005; letter of Rudi Hartwig to author, 29 December 2005. Compare also Groehler, *Bombenkrieg*, p. 451.

[58] See for example, StAM, Rep. 41/699, 'Interview des OB mit der Zeitschrift "Panorama/ Kommunal" zum Thema "Die Stadt für den Frieden"', anlässlich des 40. Jahrestages der Zerstörung Magdeburgs', no date [January 1985].

[59] See 'Dann färbte sich der Himmel blutrot', *Volksstimme*, 10 January 1995; 'Hintergrund: 16.000 oder 2.000 – wie viele starben am 16. Januar 1945?', *Volksstimme*, 16 January 1995; 'Studium des Buches der Bombenopfer. Wieviele Menschen starben am 16. Januar 45?', *Volksstimme*, 27 January 1995.

[60] To give a recent example: Ballerstedt and Buchholz, *Es regnet Feuer*, p. 43.

[61] In 1983/5: Stadt Kassel, 'Die Zerstörung Kassels im Oktober 1943. Eine Dokumentation im Bürgersaal des Rathauses', 22.10.1983–10.11.1983 (extended until 20 November 1983); Rat der Stadt/Kulturbund/Haus der DSF, 'Erinnerungen an Magdeburg – der 16. Januar 1945'; Museen der Stadt Magdeburg, 'Mahn- und Erinnerungsstätte für die Zerstörung Magdeburgs', permanent exhibition. In 1993/5: Stadtmuseum Kassel, 'Leben in Ruinen. Kassel 1943 bis 1948', 22.10.1993–22.10.1994; Kulturhistorisches Museum Magdeburg, '"Dann färbte sich der Himmel blutrot..." Die Zerstörung Magdeburgs am 16. Januar 1945', 15.1.1995–14.5.1995. Compare also the similar developments in Hamburg: Thießen, 'Gedenken an "Operation Gomorrha"', 54ff.

experience the past through its relics. '[The exhibition] wants to give the visitor the opportunity to comprehend through the visual,' as a draft paper by the Kassel City Museum expressed the idea in characteristic fashion in 1993.[62] Public displays aim to reach historical understanding through the senses just as much as through the mind. Eliciting affective responses, they invite the audience to see, feel and imagine.[63] 'Sensual perception should stand at the beginning of all learning and experience in this historical exhibition,' the above-mentioned paper asserted.[64] As Ute Frevert has argued, the public display of material objects is a medium that allows the audience to engage with the past 'creatively', to respond to the exhibits in a variety of ways that cannot be anticipated or controlled by the goals and intentions of the exhibition makers.[65] In their polyvalence, they resemble photographs, and indeed, visual representations often form a core element in displays on contemporary history.[66]

The local exhibitions of the 1980s and 1990s drew on several influ-ences, reflecting recent shifts in supra-local culture as well as indigenous traditions. Firstly, there was the impact of contemporary developments: since the late 1970s, the exhibition as a medium of historical representa-tion had experienced a spectacular revival, silencing cultural critics that had lamented a lack of interest in the national past. In 1977, the public display about 'The Times of the Hohenstaufen' in Stuttgart attracted around 700,000 visitors. Four years later, half a million people trav-elled to Berlin in order to see material relics of the state of Prussia.[67] Secondly, there was an element of continuity on the local level. Munici-pal authorities had long used the medium to document transformations in the cityscape – the 'death' and 'rebirth' of the material environment – and to foster a sense of civic identity. In 1946/7, the post-war plans for reconstruction had been presented to the public in the form of elabo-rate displays, and some twenty years later, the city administrations had returned to the medium to document the successful rebuilding.[68] Finally, there was a more sinister influence as well, going back to the wartime efforts of the Nazi party to mobilise the population and to strengthen their morale in the face of strategic bombing. In early 1942, an 'air raid protection' exhibition was staged in Kassel. Two years later, in March

---

[62] Stadtmuseum Kassel (StMK), Ausstellungen, 'Leben in Ruinen. Kassel 1943–1948', Planung/Organisation [I], 'Kassel vor 50 Jahren. Leben in Ruinen. Zur Konzeption einer Ausstellung', p. 2. I would like to thank Dr Alexander Link for making this material available to me.

[63] Frevert, 'Geschichte als Erlebnis'.   [64] StMK, 'Kassel vor 50 Jahren', p. 2.

[65] Frevert, 'Geschichte als Erlebnis', p. 252.

[66] The most prominent example is the exhibition Verbrechen der Wehrmacht by the Hamburg Institut für Sozialforschung.

[67] Frevert, 'Geschichte als Erlebnis', p. 251.   [68] See chapter 6 above.

1944, the Nazi district leader for Magdeburg opened the travelling exhi
bition 'The Terror from the Air'.[69] Both used material objects, and in
particular air war ammunition, in much the same way as the exhibitions
of the 1980s would four decades later: as symbolic illustration of the
threat from the air and 'war trophy' alike.[70]

While a combination of factors thus predisposed the exhibition as the
favoured medium for historical representations of the air war, another
factor was crucial for its popular success: the curators involved the local
public, their core audience, in the making of the exhibitions. In appeal-
ing for source material in the local press or through informal channels,
the organisers turned all contemporaries of the war into potential eyewitnesses, personal memories into historical documents, and everyday
material objects into precious exhibits.[71] In Kassel in 1983 and 1993,
and in Magdeburg in 1995, and to a lesser extent also in 1985, the
public representation of the past was thus 'created' by a large number
of local residents who had contributed their memories and relics. This
was a reciprocal process: just as individuals influenced the overall make-
up of the exhibition through their personal artefacts, the event in turn
prompted other residents to search their attics and write down their
memories.

'Petting instead of Pershing': contexts

Why this unusual degree of public interest and personal investment in
the reconstruction of an event that only a decade earlier seemed to have
become all but irrelevant to urban culture? An examination of the popular responses to one well-documented example from Kassel, the city-
sponsored display of 1983, 'The Destruction of Kassel', may help to
sketch some of the personal motives and social contexts that accounted
for the revival of interest in aerial warfare in the late twentieth century.
Although 'The Destruction of Kassel' had little more to offer than some
World War II bombs, miniature models and old photographs, the exhibition was a spectacular success, attracting close to 90,000 visitors in

---

[69] 'Der Luftterror. Eine Ausstellung in Magdeburg', *Magdeburgische Zeitung*, 21 March
1944, p. 3; Ballerstedt and Buchholz, *Es regnet Feuer*, p. 31.
[70] See, for example, *Kasseler Sonntagsblatt*, 25 January 1942, p. 5.
[71] See 'Unterlagen und Zeugen gesucht', *HA*, 16 October 1982; 'Leben in Ruinen. Kassel '43 bis '48', *HNA*, 24 May 1993, p. 23; 'Als die "Halifax" die Weihnachtsbäume
brachten...', *Volksstimme*, 22 December 1984; 'Ausstellung zum 16. Januar in Vorbereitung: Museum sucht Zeugen des Bombenüberfalls', *Volksstimme*, 17 January 1994;
'Zeitzeugen gesucht', *Volksstimme*, 13 January 1995.

the course of four weeks, statistically almost one in two of the resident population.[72]

On the basis of an examination of the visitors' book and letters to the exhibition's organiser, this section argues that the resurgence of interest in aerial warfare was due to a complex interplay of generational, cultural and political factors, making the subject relevant to different age cohorts and political persuasions for different reasons.[73] Broadly speaking, three modes of engagement may be distinguished. The first was personal, deriving its impetus from primary experience; the second was cultural, reacting to recent shifts in the public representation of World War II; and the third was political, responding to the potential threats of the re-escalating Cold War.

On 30 October 1983, a driving school instructor, Heinz R. (born 1927), wrote a letter of thanks to Werner Dettmar, the exhibition's curator: 'The exhibition and your book . . . have left a deep impression on me – no, I wasn't just impressed but deeply moved, shaken even!' The writer went on to provide a synopsis of his war experiences, starting with childhood memories of a 'wonderful time' between 1939 and 1942. He continued by telling of his experiences during the air raid when he lost his home, and concluded by outlining his service as an anti-aircraft auxiliary, labour service draftee, Luftwaffe soldier, and finally, prisoner of war.[74]

To people like Heinz R., the exhibition on Kassel's destruction was a deeply emotional affair, actualising personal memories of events that stretched back half a lifetime. These memories could be intensely painful, as with Maria A. (born 1923), a native-born Kasseler now living in the GDR, who wrote in after having listened to a radio feature on the subject. 'I personally experienced the dreadful night of 22 October 1943. The tears are welling in my eyes as I write.'[75] In a similar vein, pensioned civil servant Erwin S. told Dettmar that he often took the exhibition catalogue in hand, looking at the images and reading through the casualty list 'with the many names of people who are still alive in [my] memory'. He proceeded to relate memories that he insisted he had never talked about before. These were memories about his work at the municipal cemetery where he had been charged with retrieving valuables from the corpses by sawing off their body parts.[76]

---

[72] Figure according to StAK, S8 E12, Dettmar to Adolf Sp., 29 November 1983.
[73] This section is based on fifty or so letters collected in StAK, S8 E3–5, Ausstellung 1983.
[74] StAK, S8 E4, H.R. to Dettmar, 30 October 1983.
[75] StAK, S8 C51, Maria A. to city council, 21 October 1983.
[76] StAK, S8 E5, Regierungsdirektor retd Erwin S. to Werner Dettmar, 12 March 1984.

The renaissance of interest in the historical subject matter in Kassel was carried by members of the 'sceptical generation' of the age cohorts born between 1925 and 1935, who had lived through the catastrophic raid as young adults or adolescents. Nearing retirement age by the mid-1980s, they were old enough to find the spare time to revisit their past and young enough to make an active contribution to the memory culture of their day. The bulk of the eyewitness accounts, photographs and other memory artefacts were sent in by members of this generation. As much as some contributors stressed that they had been motivated by the wish to prevent future wars, their primary motivation appears to have been personal rather than political. They were driven by the desire to 'record for posterity' their personal memories, that is, to have primary experiences recognised as historical documents. This actualisation of personal memories could come without further contextualisation, but could also go with a violent denunciation of the air war, as the following examples make clear.

Indeed, some residents used the public eyewitness appeal as an opportunity to engage in a full-scale attack on the emerging prioritisation, since 1979, of Holocaust memory, and more generally, on the culture of *Vergangenheitsbewältigung* as it had been institutionalised since the early 1960s.[77] In a letter of 22 November 1982, retired lieutenant Karlheinz K. spoke of the 'Holocaust in Kassel', called the air raid a 'war crime' and offered to pass on the fruits of his 'basic research'.[78] Voicing a variation on the theme of 'you did it too' apologetics, Curt H. sent in twenty manuscript pages about the 'criminal terror raids in World War II', claiming that the raids on Dresden alone had cost 300,000 lives.[79] A third writer accused the exhibition of a leftist bias, asserting that the Western allies had been motivated by the desire 'to annihilate the German people' long before the onset of World War II. Construing a Babylonian captivity of a *Volk* 'betrayed [and] ridiculed' by the 'enemy re-education [and] plagiarising money historians', he posed as defender of a 'tortured people' against 'bootlickers [and] traitors'.[80] Another writer indignantly rejected any suggestion of a historical parallel between the November pogrom of 1938 and the air raid on Kassel. Giving free rein to his anti-Semitic sentiments, he went on, 'But for the Jews "shalom" is totally inappropriate. Impudently they still build more settlements, despite all agreements.'[81]

---

[77] Compare Frei, 'Deutsche Lernprozesse'.
[78] StAK, S8 E3, Karlheinz K. to Werner Dettmar, 22 November 1982.
[79] StAK, S8 E3, Curt H. to Werner Dettmar, 20 October 1982; ibid., 'Anlage zum Brief'.
[80] StAK, S8 E5, Toni W. to Werner Dettmar, 24 October 1983.
[81] StAK, S8 E3, M.W. to Werner Dettmar, 23 October 1983.

These voices, too, came from members of the war generation. While they made up a rather small minority of the letters preserved in the city archive, it must remain an open question just how widespread their views really were. There are, however, a number of indications which suggest that the legal categorisation of the air raid was not a primary concern for the majority of local residents, even when they believed that a war crime had been committed. Annemarie A., for example, agreed that the air raid was appropriately labelled 'insane mass murder', but wrote to commend Dettmar on his efforts 'to document a sad piece of the history of our home town' and to share lived experiences of survival amidst mass death.[82] Furthermore, all the above examples carried a clear defensive undertone: however widespread their revisionist views may have been among the population of Kassel, the point is that the writers *felt* marginalised. Curt H. complained that for the past twenty years he had tried in vain to place 'enlightening articles' in the newspapers, while M.W. sent off his anti-Semitic diatribe in response to an article by the local deacon, which had explored the causal link between anti-Semitism and urban destruction. Even Karlheinz K.'s explicit use of the term 'Holocaust' may be read as an indication of the extent to which the genocide of European Jewry had been established as a central mnemonic reference point by the early 1980s. Indirectly, Curt H. also acknowledged this shift when in 1979 he responded to tabloid coverage of the TV series 'Holocaust' with the rhetorical question, 'Why does no one produce movies that publicly denounce the dismal crimes of Germany's wartime enemies?'[83]

Through their active involvement, members of the 'sceptical generation' revisited the air raid as a historical event that had left a deep impact on their biographies during a formative phase of their lives. To some extent, the revisionists focused on the past as well, trying to renegotiate the balance sheet of World War II between German crimes and alleged crimes against Germans. Yet the spectacular success of the exhibition 'The Destruction of Kassel' cannot solely be explained with reference to generational factors. It struck a chord because many residents felt that the subject matter of 'apocalyptic destruction' was of relevance to their present, regardless of personal involvement in the historical event. Several writers commented on the large number of adolescents attending the exhibition, while teachers arranged guided tours for their pupils. To people concerned about the dangers of atomic deterrence, the destruction

---

[82] StAK, S8 E3, Annemarie A. to Werner Dettmar, 17 October 1982.
[83] StAK, S8 E3, Curt H. to Dettmar, 20 October 1982, p. 19, 'Bezugnahme auf den Artikel der BILD-Zeitung v. 24.1.1979'.

of Kassel in World War II featured above all as a warning to the present. Among them were members of the experience generation, as for example, Ursel Martin (born 1927), who handed over Dettmar's book to the American delegation at the Geneva Disarmament Conference of 1983.[84] On the whole, however, the peace movement was a youth movement, which drew its supporters from a generation that had been socialised in the post-war world.[85]

In a letter, a representative of the 'Kasseler Citizens for Peace' (*Kasseler Bürgerinnen und Bürger für den Frieden*) commended Dettmar on the exhibition and proceeded to draw a link between the past and the present. '[The exhibition] has demonstrated the horror of the past destruction but has also raised the question: what has happened since then ... in order to prepare another – in all likelihood final – war? ... We are of the opinion that the look back must open our eyes for the contemporary dangers of war.' He went on to suggest that Dettmar participate in a public discussion about the present relevance of past destruction.[86] A present-centred view on the dangers of nuclear destruction made up the decisive political context for the reception of the exhibition in the 1980s. The visitors' book was filled with slogans from the peace movement, such as 'Petting instead of Pershing', 'Waffles instead of weapons' or 'Sexual intercourse instead of federal army' (*Geschlechtsverkehr statt Bundeswehr*). Here, (nuclear) war in itself was a crime, regardless of its goals and intentions. Espousing a present-centred view of the past, the peace movement was interested in the causes and consequences of strategic bombing only in so far as this helped to further their goals of (nuclear) disarmament. 'Nothing is more important to us than peace,' the manual of the Third Kassel Peace Week stated in a problematic formulation that set 'peace' as a moral absolute.[87]

It appears that similar generational factors were at work in Magdeburg, although the dearth of documentary evidence makes empirically sound conclusions difficult. Seventy-six residents responded to an appeal in the *Volksstimme* in December 1984 to write down their memories of the air raid of 16 January 1945.[88] Unfortunately, these letters have not been preserved. As in Kassel, a number of contemporaries of the war used

[84] For the text of the covering letter, signed by mayor Hans Eichel, see StAK, S8 E12, 'To the delegation of the United States of America at the Geneva Disarmament Conference', no date.

[85] For the different groups that made up the organised peace movement in Kassel see AG Kasseler Friedenswochen (ed.), *3. Kasseler Friedenswochen. Vom 6. bis zum 27. November 1982. Programmzeitung der Arbeitsgemeinschaft Kasseler Friedenswochen*, p. 8.

[86] StAK, S8 E5, Ulrich Schedensack to Dettmar, 23 November 1983.

[87] AG Kasseler Friedenswochen (ed.), *3. Kasseler Friedenswochen*, p. 2.

[88] See 'Leser schreiben zum 16. Januar', *Volksstimme*, 15 January 1985, p. 8.

the media coverage to send in personal memory artefacts to the archive, most notably Lucien Ranson, a Belgian painter who had experienced the attack as a forced labourer.[89] The exhibitions' organisers, however, did not respond to suggestions 'from below' to quite the same extent as in Kassel. Ranson's memories, for example, did not gain public currency until ten years later when a German translation was published.[90]

Themes

If the analytical focus is changed from the reception of the exhibitions to their contents, then different emphases within broadly similar modes of representation are thrown into sharp relief. In Kassel, the exhibition of 1983 revolved around two major themes. The first was the irretrievable loss of human life and the built-up environment as a consequence of aerial bombing. The second theme was aerial warfare as a military confrontation, a stand-off between youthful defenders and equally youthful bomber crews. By contrast, the two exhibitions that were organised in Magdeburg on the occasion of the fortieth anniversary of the city's destruction revolved around a double narrative of cause and effect and 'destruction as opportunity'. The two exhibitions were, however, not identical in their points of view, illustrating the extent to which the political culture of the late GDR had diversified. The first, 'Memories of Magdeburg', was produced by amateur historians organised in the Section Municipal History of the Culture League (*Kulturbund*), while the second, a permanent exhibition housed in the ruin of the Johanniskirche, was conceived by the professionals of the municipal museum.[91] In stressing the allegedly criminal nature of the raid, the professional curators remained wedded to the political narrative of the 1950s and 1960s. By comparison, the amateur historians situated the attack in the context of the 'imperialist war policy of German fascism'. With the air raid, they argued, violence had finally 'returned' to its place of origin.[92]

Kassel

The characteristic features of the Kassel exhibition in 1983 are best illustrated by its core exhibits. Upon entering the exhibition room, the visitor

[89] StAM, Rep. 41/481, Lucien Ranson to mayor, 7 November 1984.
[90] Ranson, *Vom Zwangsarbeiter zum Freund.*
[91] I owe this information to Ms Karin Grünwald, Kulturhistorisches Museum, Magdeburg. I would like to thank her for making available to me uncatalogued material from the museum.
[92] KHM, Ordner Johanniskirche, 'Konzeption zur Ausstellung "Erinnerungen an Magdeburg – der 16. Januar 1945"', no date.

was confronted with a large-size photograph of two bombed-out survivors of the air raid, which was fixed to a partition wall. Taken by a German photographer in the aftermath of the October raid, the picture derived from an album deposited in the Imperial War Museum in London, and was (re-)introduced into the local memory culture by the curator Werner Dettmar after one of his archival research trips (Fig. 29).[93]

The camera focuses on two unknown female figures, both sitting on suitcases. The woman to the right looks straight at the photographer, and thus at the observer, clutching a gas mask in her left hand and a bundle of blankets under her arm. Her facial expression is one of distress and exhaustion. Next to her sits another woman, burying her head in her hands. In the background, other air raid victims are visible against a backdrop of buildings covered in smoke. Reproduced on both the official invitation cards and the dust jacket of the accompanying publication, in the 1980s the motif became the central image of Kassel's destruction. In displacing Walter Thieme's 1946/7 panorama view of the destroyed city (which was reproduced on the same partition in smaller size), the photograph reflected a shift in the visual representation from the material to the human costs of the air war. It invited positive identification with the war generation as 'survivors' of an apocalyptic event that had caused wounds that 'even today, after forty years [had] not healed', as the introductory text on the same partition informed the reader.[94]

While the image asked the local audience to empathise with the victims of the bombing of 22 October 1943 – that is, with themselves and/or their mothers, fathers, grandparents as 'survivors' and 'witnesses' – the photograph was unspecific enough (the two women were never identified) to extend its meaning both in space and time. 'When British bombers destroyed Kassel on 22 October 1943, 50,000 Britons had already lost their lives in German air raids and over 50,000 Germans in British raids,' the text explained. Suffering had been a universal characteristic of World War II, and so it would be of future wars, the narrative went on to suggest. The destruction of Kassel had been the consequence of an air raid with 'conventional weapons', the text pointed out, adding that 'meanwhile the technical advances . . . have led to an unimaginable rise in the capacity for destruction'. In opening up the referential space of nuclear apocalypse, the text linked the past to the present.[95]

While the exhibition emphasised death and scarred survival as a consequence of bombing, it did not neglect the material consequences, depicting the destruction through a host of photographs as well as an

---

[93] IWM, London, GSA 387, Air Raid Damage in Germany 1943, RAF raids on Kassel, July and October 1943, HU 43974.
[94] For the text see StAK, S8 E9, [Textvorlagen].   [95] Ibid.

Werner Dettmar
Die Zerstörung Kassels im Oktober 1943
Eine Dokumentation

Hesse GmbH

Figure 29. An image of dishevelled survivors after the air raid of 22 October 1943, reproduced on the cover of Werner Dettmar, *Die Zerstörung Kassels* (1983).

architectural model of the devastated cityscape.[96] By comparison, images of the post-war reconstruction were conspicuously absent. This was not a triumphal narrative of successful overcoming but rather a melancholic view of past beauty irretrievably lost.

[96] See StAK, Bildarchiv, Ausstellung 1983.

If the exhibition was characterised by an emphasis on loss, it also put great stress on operational planning and the technical side of urban destruction, showcasing original bombs as used by RAF Bomber Command in World War II, and presenting miniature models of British heavy bombers, German fighter aircraft and anti-aircraft positions. The bombing war, the exhibition suggested, was also a military confrontation, in which youthful defenders faced youthful bomber crews. Rather than casting blame (or looking for responsibilities), the visual and textual narratives stressed the common war experience of German and British crews and flak auxiliaries, even introducing the crew of a British aircraft that had participated in the raid. The central exhibit of this technical narrative was a glass cabinet containing one incendiary bomb and 400,000 matches as symbolic visualisation of the number of incendiary bombs dropped on Kassel.

Magdeburg

While the Kassel exhibition offered a detailed description of operational procedures as an explanation for the city's destruction, both Magdeburg exhibitions showed less concern for technical details but presented a coherent meta-narrative. In contrast to 'The Destruction of Kassel', they also gave broad space to the reconstruction, affirmatively emphasising 'the great achievements of the Magdeburg workers under the leadership of the workers' party in rebuilding Magdeburg as a blossoming socialist city', as the draft paper of 'Memories of Magdeburg' by the Section Municipal History put it.[97]

While the draft paper insisted that the destruction had been 'pointless', it showed a keen awareness of cause and effect, conceptualising the raid as 'the consequence of the imperialist war policy of German fascism'.[98] This was reflected in the selection and arrangement of the exhibits: according to the conception, the first exhibition room showed photos and documents of the effects of German air raids on 'cities destroyed by German fascism, as for example Warsaw, Leningrad, Rotterdam, Coventry'.[99] In addition, the room emphasised the importance of Magdeburg as an armaments centre, providing a chart of local war industries.

By contrast, the professional exhibition in the ruins of the Johanniskirche continued to speak of the 'Anglo-American air terror' and explicitly denounced the attack of 16 January 1945 as a 'terror measure'.

---

[97] KHM, Ordner Johanniskirche, 'Konzeption zur Ausstellung "Erinnerungen an Magdeburg – der 16. Januar 1945"'.
[98] Ibid., p. 2.   [99] Ibid.

It construed a crude opposition between 'German fascism', 'monopoly industries' and the 'air terror' on one hand and the 'Red Army' and 'the people' on the other. As the textual commentary put it, 'This toll of lives that the people had to pay to the fascists was increased by the victims of the air war.'[100] Whereas 'Memories of Magdeburg' focused on World War II and its aftermath, the permanent exhibition drew a link between the city's first destruction in the Thirty Years War and the second destruction in World War II, interpreting the town's ruptured history until 1945 as evidence of the 'inhumane nature of the exploiter societies'.[101]

Professionalisation and differentiation: the 1990s

The exhibitions of the 1980s set a precedent for the historical representation of the air war in the 1990s. In both cities, costly exhibitions formed the core around which an increasingly diverse historiographical discourse – lecture series, film screenings, discussion evenings, student competitions – revolved.[102] On the fiftieth anniversary of the bombing, the Kassel City Museum opened an exhibition called 'Life in Ruins, Kassel 1943–1948', which ran for twelve months and consisted of a permanent exhibition plus complementary special exhibitions. Fifteen months later, the Kulturhistorisches Museum Magdeburg embarked on a similar venture, opening the doors to 'When the Heavens Turned Crimson Red . . .', which was scheduled to run until May but was later extended until July owing to public demand.

In both cities, there were considerable continuities between the fortieth anniversary and the fiftieth anniversary exhibitions despite the sociopolitical rupture of 1989. This was in part due to the medium itself. Core exhibits of the 1980s were again given prominent places in the 1990s. The 1993 Kassel exhibition, for example, reserved an entire room for the miniature model of the city in ruins which had already featured in 1983. The room was decorated in order to strike a balance between 'historical documentation . . . and the solemn atmosphere of a memorial', as the conception described it.[103] In Magdeburg, as well, central exhibits of the permanent exhibition of the 1980s were used again ten years later.[104] Moreover, an element of continuity rested also with the protagonists of historical research. In Kassel, Werner Dettmar contributed the article

---

[100] Ibid., 'Texte: Ausstellung Johanniskirche'.   [101] Ibid., 'Konzeption', p. 1.
[102] Compare Kulturamt Kassel (ed.), *50. Jahrestag der Zerstörung Kassels*; Landeshauptstadt Magdeburg (ed.), *Magdeburg 16. Januar 1945/16. Januar 1995.*
[103] StMK, Ausstellungen, 'Leben in Ruinen. Kassel 1943–8'. Planung, Organisation [I], 'Anmerkungen zu Aufbau und Gestaltung der Ausstellung', p. 2.
[104] KHM, Ordner Johanniskirche, 'Grundriß Gruft St. Johannis'.

on the bombing war in the exhibition catalogue to 'Life in Ruins'.[105] Despite the demise of the GDR, this was also the case in Magdeburg where Manfred Wille, co-author of the 1985 documentary account by Rudi Hartwig and historian at the teacher training college, wrote an essay on the air war for the exhibition catalogue.[106]

At the same time, there were important changes: firstly, increased professionalism; secondly, a turn towards a social historical approach; and finally, a diversification of opinions and responses.

In the run-up to the fiftieth-anniversary commemorations, the local political and cultural elites took the representation of the past firmly in their hands. In Kassel, the town councillor for culture, Ms Schleier, convened a committee made up of representatives from the Bureau of Culture, the City Museum, various archives, Werner Dettmar and others in order to coordinate the various projects well in advance.[107] A similar step was taken in Magdeburg.[108] Whereas the exhibitions of the 1980s had derived in large measure from the efforts of amateurs, the historical exhibitions of the 1990s were conceived and implemented by professionals at the municipal museums. This shift did not just result in improved standards of representation, including the publication of catalogues, but also provided the financial resources for further research. Thus, the material compiled by the USSBS in the summer of 1945 was made available to the local public of Magdeburg through a research trip by the director of the Magdeburg Museum to the National Archives in Washington, DC.

Professionalisation also entailed an increasing convergence between academic scholarship and local history. In Kassel, Dettmar's emphasis on the operational planning of the attack gave way to a social historical approach that sought to document aspects of the everyday life in the wake of catastrophe. In accordance with shifting research paradigms in scholarly history, the time period under investigation changed as well. The rubble years of 1943 to 1948 rather than a single day came into focus.[109] Although the conception stressed emphatic identification with the 'pain' and 'suffering' of the war generation as one goal, the cooperation with specialists from Kassel University ensured that the representation of urban war society no longer remained confined to the Nazi *Volksgemeinschaft*. Reflecting the recent empirical turn in the scholarly research on Nazi extermination politics, the exhibition catalogue devoted

---

[105] Dettmar, 'Kassel im Luftkrieg'.   [106] Wille, 'Tod und Zerstörung'.
[107] Compare the minutes in StMK, Ausstellungen, 'Leben in Ruinen. Kassel 1943–8', Planung, Organisation [I]. See also StAK, A.4.415, no. 357/1, 50. Jahrestage.
[108] StAM, Rep. 18/4, Stadtverordnetenbeschlüsse, 'Sitzung des Komitees zur Vorbereitung der Gedenkfeierlichkeiten der Zerstörung Magdeburgs am 12.9.94'.
[109] See Broszat, Henke and Woller (eds.), *Von Stalingrad zur Währungsreform*.

a separate chapter to the practice of forced labour in Kassel, while the exhibition documented extensively the spheres of local consent and coercion during the Third Reich.[110]

In Magdeburg, too, the exhibition of 1995 adopted the perspective of the everyday, claiming 'for the first time to place the destruction of Magdeburg in a larger historical context'.[111] Here, the meta-historical props of GDR historiography were quietly abandoned while individual elements of this narrative remained. In the preface, the Social Democratic mayor, Dr Willi Polte, mentioned the British target list of November 1944 just as Hartwig had done twenty years earlier, but no longer claimed that this date marked a decisive turning point in the strategic air offensive. In comparison to Kassel, the representation of hitherto marginalised groups remained underdeveloped. The exploitation of forced labour, for example, was documented with a few exhibits, the main function of which appears to have been to absolve ordinary Magdeburger from any blame. In an echo of the Socialist narrative of international solidarity, the exhibition catalogue stressed that Magdeburg workers helped 'their foreign colleagues' by secretly passing on food to them.[112]

It was indicative of changes in the political culture of the 1990s that traditional historical representations of the air war no longer went unchallenged. In Kassel, Werner Dettmar's contribution to the exhibition catalogue, in which he sought to trace the development of aerial warfare from 1918 through to 1945, was subjected to harsh criticism in an article in the alternative city magazine, *Stattzeitung*. The author, Peter Adamksi, argued that Dettmar – unwittingly or not – had contributed to a German myth of victimhood by downplaying the Luftwaffe raids of 1939 to 1941 and neglecting the broader historical context.[113] In another intervention, Esther Hass, museum educationalist for the history of the Jews in Kassel,[114] stressed the significance of the year 1933, arguing that the history of destruction needed to be written with that date in mind.[115] In a similar way, critical voices in Magdeburg contended that the exhibition had failed to live up to the self-professed goal of documenting the ultimate causes of the destruction. Ironically, those criticisms came from the successor organisation of the SED, the Party of Democratic

---

[110] See *Leben in Ruinen*, pp. 57–88. On the 'empirical turn' in academic scholarship on Nazism since the mid-1980s see Herbert, 'Vernichtungspolitik', pp. 19ff. Compare also the same author's pioneering study on forced labour, Herbert, *Fremdarbeiter*.

[111] *'Dann färbte sich der Himmel blutrot . . . '*, p. 5.

[112] Ibid., p. 197.

[113] Peter Adamski, 'Anmerkungen zum Sieg im Luftkrieg', *Stattzeitung* (November 1993), p. 2.

[114] Museumspädagogin für die Geschichte der Juden in Kassel

[115] Esther Hass, 'Die Zerstörung begann 1933', *HA*, 22 October 1993.

Socialism (PDS), which claimed a critical tradition for itself without reflecting on the political usage of the subject in the GDR.[116] To be sure, these critical voices remained a minority, but they were indicative of the extent to which some residents were no longer prepared to treat the destruction of the home town in isolation from the larger context of Germany's genocidal conduct in World War II.[117]

Conclusion

By the early 1980s, the ossified memory of allied bombing had become infused with a new dynamic that resulted from a complex interplay of generational, cultural and political factors. Against the backdrop of new tensions between the superpowers, the 'sceptical' generation revisited a formative experience of their adolescence and made available their memories of urban destruction as 'authentic' memory artefacts to a receptive public in fear of atomic annihilation. To some contemporaries of World War II, the revival of interest in aerial warfare also accorded an opportunity to voice their resentment against shifts in the broader memory culture, which, since the late 1970s, had started to confront the history of Nazism in the locality and to prioritise the memory of the Holocaust.

With the renaissance of the 1980s, the relationship between different vectors of memory changed as well. Whereas in the 1950s and 1960s, history had served collective memory, in the following decades history attained a degree of autonomy in the memory culture. Historical writing in the 1980s and 1990s no longer followed a monumental approach that modified the historical evidence to accommodate the sensibilities of the present. Instead, the historiography of the 1980s and 1990s tended to be antiquarian in nature, collecting documents and letting the source material 'speak for itself'. Yet, more often than not, such an approach resulted in the unwitting perpetuation of conventional narratives that homogenised urban war society and universalised victimhood.

---

[116] F. Berfelde, '"Dann färbte sich der Himmel blutrot..." Fragen nach einem Ausstellungsbesuch', *PDS-Journal*, 20 January 1995.
[117] Compare Naumann, *Der Krieg als Text*.

Conclusion

This study has distinguished between three discursive fields or 'vectors' of air war memory. While such a model is useful for situating different responses to the human and material impact of indiscriminate bombing within their respective traditions and contexts, it is important to remember that, in practice, the various discourses could frequently overlap. For example, the bishop of Kurhesse-Waldeck, in an address on 22 October 1951, commemorated the 'Kassel victims of the bombing' but emphasised that mourning extended to the 'end [of] our city' as well. In the same speech, he also referred to the people who had first-hand experiences of the 'dreadful night' and were compelled 'over and over to tell about the most dreadful [experiences] of all the horrors' that they had gone through.[1]

By way of conclusion, this chapter pulls together the different commemorative threads in order to sketch the evolution of the memory cultures in Kassel and Magdeburg in the period from the mid-1940s to the mid-1990s. After that, some remarks will be offered about the trajectory of memory in the decade that followed, and an attempt made to situate the case study within a broader context.

Experience and memory

Indiscriminate area raids as carried out by the RAF against Kassel on 22 October 1943 and against Magdeburg on 16 January 1945 confronted the resident populations with death and destruction on a scale that was without precedent in living memory. Catastrophic rupture was, however, experienced not by ahistorical 'civilians' within a socio-political vacuum, but by members of a brutalised society whose hegemonic voice was Nazism, the very force that had been responsible for the unleashing

---

[1] LKA Kassel, SB Wüstemann, no. 22, 'Ansprache', 22 October 1951.

of a world conflagration in the first place.[2] Although individual responses to the bombing varied considerably, depending on religious and political dispositions, the place of the individual within the Nazi racial hierarchy and a set of circumstantial factors, there was a tendency to frame the catastrophe in 'traditional languages', that is, in the interpretive categories and with the cultural repertoire that was available to German city-dwellers of the mid-twentieth century.

Wherever possible, the dead were retrieved from the rubble, identified and buried, while their graves – real and imagined – were adorned with symbolic offerings and their days of death commemorated. Meanwhile, the catastrophic transformation of the built-up environment was conceptualised in terms of the 'home town', that is, a place of belonging, destroyed. Finally, attempts were made to narrate lived experiences, to tell stories about what had happened and why. While all of these coping strategies fed on well-established traditions – the Christian cult of the dead, *Heimat* discourse, local historiography – their wartime enunciation occurred within the context of a culture that was permeated with the idiom, ideas and practices of Nazism.

In public commemorations, the dead were collectively identified as victims of a 'Jewish crime', while their obituaries and graves bore the insignia of a militarised racial community. Local propagandists both denounced the destruction of *Heimat* as a crime against German culture and celebrated it as proof of the resilience of the home front. Meanwhile, city planners were busy exploiting the material impact of aerial warfare as an unprecedented opportunity for reordering the historic city-space. Finally, state and party officials seized on the legal and ethical problems of indiscriminate bombing in order to present World War II as an eschatological struggle of annihilation between a 'chivalrous' Aryan race and its 'criminal' antagonist of 'World Jewry'. At the same time, initiatives were undertaken to create, collect and preserve historical documents that told a heroic tale of triumph over adversity.

Although Nazism enjoyed hegemonic status in the public articulation of the meaning of death and destruction throughout the duration of the war, the double conceptualisation of allied bombing as a criminal 'terror raid' and a supreme 'test of resilience' did not go unchallenged. The Christian churches embraced an interpretation that put the notion of 'affliction' at the centre of their attempts to explain what had happened. By this view, local catastrophe was a punishment by a wrathful God for sins on the part of the we-group. Focusing on the nexus between

---

[2] See Dietmar Süß's critique of Jörg Friedrich's use of the term 'civilian' (*das Zivil*) in Süß, 'Massaker und Mongolensturm', 525, footnote 17.

cause and effect, such an interpretation carried subversive potential but served primarily to shore up the idea of an all-powerful and ultimately benevolent higher being against the problem of theodicy. Meanwhile, a semi-public undercurrent or counter-narrative prioritised the catastrophic impact over questions of causation. This perspective 'from below' was captured in the term 'night of horror', which conveyed a horrifying experience from which there was no escape, without making any references to agency.

In their endeavours to overcome the legacy of the air war, the postwar agents of public memory were thus faced not only with vast-scale material and social devastation but also with a plethora of circulating idioms, stories and interpretations. In other words, the search for usable pasts took place within the context of a *milieu de mémoire* that was saturated with personal memory traces, popular legends and the fragments of Nazi propaganda. In consequence, the post-war protagonists of public memory were not free to construct any narrative they saw fit, but were compelled to address a set of recurring questions about the reasons for the catastrophe, its meaning and the lessons that could be drawn from it. Moreover, the range of possible answers was limited not only by audience expectation and present expediency but also by the boundaries and traditions of the discursive fields in which they were given. A commemorative speech that addressed a mourning congregation about the loss of loved ones belonged to a different genre from a historical enquiry that sought to uncover the reasons for the massive loss of life. A lecture by a city planner on the reconstruction drew on different narrative traditions from a lyrical poem that mourned the loss of the built-up environment.

Cycles of memory

In a temporal perspective, two cycles of memory may be distinguished, which roughly corresponded to broader political, socio-cultural and generational shifts in both German societies. Cycle one extended from the early 1950s to the late 1960s; cycle two stretched from the 1970s to the 1990s. While cycle one witnessed the institutionalisation of a set of commemorative practices that revolved, first and foremost, around the commemoration of mass death, cycle two was characterised by a greater emphasis on the historical reconstruction of events. Although developments in Kassel and Magdeburg followed a broadly similar trajectory, there were also important differences. By the end of the war, the air raid of 22 October 1943 had attained the status of a collective memory place in Kassel, whereas in Magdeburg the emergence of '16 January 1945' as a *lieu de mémoire* was to a large degree the result of post-war developments.

Next to differences in timing and local tradition, there was the impact of the Cold War. With the escalation of international relations in 1948/9, the carriers of public discourse in Magdeburg sought to tap local memory in order to mobilise the resident population in the 'struggle for peace', whereas their counterparts in Kassel aimed at a 'quiet remembrance' in which questions of historical causation were subordinated to a politics of pacification.

In the public memory culture of the 1950s and 1960s, there were two main protagonists: on the one hand, the local elites, and on the other, a broad section of local society that comprised people who had suffered emotional and/or material injury in the air war, in particular the bereaved and the evacuees. In Kassel, this second group was crucial in establishing an annual commemorative tradition that formed the backbone of public memory. Through their organisational voice, the League of Air Raid Victims, the bereaved and evacuees pressurised the reluctant elites of Church and state into commemorating '22 October' on an annual basis. Whereas in Kassel, the institutionalisation of the memory place was the result of pressure 'from below', in Magdeburg annual commemorations were introduced 'from above' in response to the emergence of 'Dresden' as a national memory place in the GDR.

In both cities, the protagonists of public discourse identified the casualties of aerial warfare, and by extension, the local community at large, as victims of forces beyond their control rather than as agents in a war of conquest and annihilation that Germany had unleashed. Commemorative practices in both cities drew on older traditions, which were of Christian, Socialist and, at times, also of Nazi origin. They also reflected the political and ideological battle lines of the Cold War. In Kassel, the political and religious elites aimed at semantic pacification through the decontextualisation, depoliticisation and re-Christianising of commemoration. In Magdeburg, by contrast, the SED-led elites recontextualised and repoliticised public memory in order to mobilise the local population for a politics of hatred against Western 'imperialism'. Whereas in Kassel, all the dead of the air war – be they, in the Nazi terminology of the Third Reich, 'racial comrades' or 'racial aliens' – were homogenised under the category of 'our dead', in Magdeburg the casualties were depicted both as victims of a crime and as (Socialist) sacrificers.

While public remembrance of the dead constituted a vector of memory in which local politicians and clerics sought to impart meaning to premature violent death and to console the bereaved, the discourse on the material legacy of the air war revolved around a different set of issues, involving a slightly different set of protagonists. Here, memories of the air war and the pre-war cityscape informed the debate on the progress and result of the post-war reconstruction, which affected the resident and evacuee populations in equal measure. Positing a zero hour, city planning experts and local politicians argued that the impact of the bombing on the urban environment must be considered less a catastrophe than a unique opportunity to rebuild the home town in a modern and functional way – 'more beautiful than ever', as a popular phrase in Magdeburg expressed it. Although the progressive rhetoric of the Socialist planning elites in Magdeburg and of the Social Democratic elites in Kassel met with little popular opposition, sections of the population turned to idealised representations of the pre-war city. This kind of reflective – rather than restorative – nostalgia was particularly pronounced in Kassel, where a group of middle-class intellectuals, some of whom had had strong affiliations with Nazism prior to 1945, drew on turn-of-the-century notions of *Alt-Kassel* in order to imagine the pre-war city as a place of beauty, harmony and innocence. In Magdeburg, by comparison, the notion of *Alt-Magdeburg*, which had been of marginal importance in pre-war discourse, did not gain wider currency until the 1960s when the demolition of several inner-city churches provoked opposition from sections of the old Protestant middle classes.

In comparison with the commemoration of the dead and the debate on the reconstruction, the historical recreation of the past played a subservient role in public memory throughout the period. The local historiography was produced not by specialists but by journalists who manipulated and sanitised their sources in order to produce narratives that fitted in with the broader mnemonic parameters of their environments. Eyewitness accounts that spoke of overpowering and suffering, but also of perseverance in the face of adversity, were used in order to construct a collective experience of a homogenous community victimised by forces beyond its control. In short, the local historiography in the period functioned not as a critical corrective to collective memory but in order to stabilise a narrative that stressed collective victimhood.

Involving – through personal experience and personal loss – broad sections of urban society, the air war occupied an important place in the broader discourse on the recent past throughout the 1950s, and to a lesser degree, in the 1960s. As *lieu de mémoire*, bombing did not only play a role east of the Iron Curtain, as a popular thesis would have it, but also, on the local level, in western Germany. In Kassel, where 10,000 people attended the central commemorative ceremony on the tenth anniversary in 1953, '22 October' rivalled the People's Day of Mourning in importance, surpassing any commemorations that were held in memory of the victims of Nazism. In Magdeburg, attendance at the commemorations was lower, especially when considered against the backdrop of mass mobilisation on other occasions. But the eagerness with which the local political elites sought both to tap memories of the bombing and, at the same time, to circumscribe gestures of mourning, attests to the importance that the memory place held for many Magdeburgers as well.

By the mid-1960s, the first cycle of memory was coming to an end. Although a core set of ritual practices continued to be performed annually, the much proclaimed 'end of the post-war period' turned memories of urban destruction into a foil against which to measure the achievements of the present, while the emergence of Auschwitz as a symbol of Nazi criminality was starting to re-centre attention from German victims to the victims of the Germans. In both cities, public memory of the air war reached a low point in the 1970s. The following decade, however, ushered in a renaissance of local memory cultures that stretched until the fiftieth anniversary commemorations of the mid-1990s. This second cycle of memory resulted from a combination of political, cultural and generational factors that, in different ways, had repercussions on all three vectors of memory.

Within the context of rising anxiety over the possibility of an all-out atomic war, the commemoration of indiscriminate mass death in aerial warfare attained a new relevance for many contemporaries in the 1980s. In Magdeburg, the local SED responded to the NATO twin-track decision of December 1979 by reinventing the *lieu de mémoire* as a 'fighting day' of organised mass protest, which involved an unprecedented number of local residents in the anniversary commemorations of 1980 and 1985. In Kassel, the pacifist potential of '22 October' was rediscovered by the peace movement, which cast the events of 1943 as a prelude to the atomic annihilation facing the present. In this, the peace movement was supported by the Social Democratic city administration, whereas the local church leadership was more cautious about the merging of memory and protest.

Although the resituating of World War II bombing within the context of the second Cold War initially reaffirmed the emphasis on victimhood that had been characteristic of the memory culture of the 1950s, the simultaneous emergence of Holocaust memory called into question the nexus between destruction and victimhood. In both Magdeburg and Kassel, it was the Church that first addressed this issue within the context of public commemorations. Drawing on an older interpretive framework that had conceptualised local catastrophe as an affliction, clerics explored the connection between the persecution and deportation of local Jewry and the destruction of the home town. Increasingly, they came to represent indiscriminate bombing as some kind of retribution suffered for the misdeeds of the (non-Jewish) local community during the Third Reich.

While the second Cold War provided the political catalyst for a revival of interest in the human costs of World War II bombing, a post-modern concern over the 'inhospitality' (A. Mitscherlich) of the modern city redirected attention to the material legacy of the air war. In Kassel, a New Left critique of the contemporary cityscape fused with the traditional idea of *Alt-Kassel*, leading to a radical re-evaluation of the reconstruction of the 1950s and 1960s. Rather than representing an achievement, the 'new city on historic ground', the critics argued, amounted to nothing less than a denial of history and identity. Worse, the deplorable state of contemporary Kassel was the result less of a total destruction brought about by aerial bombing than of personal and conceptual continuities between Nazi-era city planning and post-war city planning. In short, the 'zero hour' was a myth – cynically invented by the post-war planning elites to engineer a second destruction in the name of modernity. Although, in Magdeburg, SED control of the public sphere did not allow for the emergence of an equally critical discourse, here too, the notion of *Alt-Magdeburg* gained in popularity in the 1980s. In public exhibitions, amateur historians pushed the boundaries of the 'discursive prison' (M. Sabrow) of the GDR by presenting the pre-war city as a visual alternative to the 'Socialist metropolis' of the present. The slogan of the second destruction, current among Magdeburgers living in West Germany since the 1960s,[3] entered local discourse after the demise of SED rule, where it referred to the goals and practices of Socialist city planning rather than, as in Kassel, to the continuities across the watershed of 1945.

Finally, the second cycle of memory was characterised by an upsurge of interest in the historical recreation of the past. In both cities, historical exhibitions were staged on the occasion of the fortieth anniversary in the mid-1980s, and again on the fiftieth anniversary in the mid-1990s, each time to exceptional popular success. The historical engagement with the past, while no longer wholly subservient to collective memory, may be characterised as a flak auxiliary historiography that was antiquarian rather than critical in nature. It was carried by the contemporaries of the historical events, who made an effort to preserve 'their' memories against the backdrop of generational change. Whereas in Kassel lay historians produced documentary accounts that oscillated between the genres of military history and *Heimat* history, parallel efforts in Magdeburg were both more ambitious and more ideologically loaded. They sought to explain where their counterparts in Kassel were content merely 'to let the sources speak for themselves'.

Although local historiography in Magdeburg remained wedded to the anachronistic view according to which World War II strategic bombing

---

[3] Laeger, *Vereinigtes Dom- und Klostergymnasium*, pp. 142f.

was but the first act of aggression in the Cold War, the empirical find
ings also challenged received wisdom, most notably on the issue of mass
death in the air raid of 16 January 1945. As with the renaissance of *Alt-
Magdeburg*, the 1980s marked a turning point for local historical writing,
eroding the discursive dominance of the SED and sowing the seeds for
developments that came to fruition in the 1990s when the historiogra-
phies in both cities developed a greater receptivity to the questions and
findings of academic history. As a consequence, there was both a broad-
ening of the temporal perspective – an effort to situate local catastrophe
within the continuum of history – and a greater willingness to take into
account the experiences of those sections of urban society who had been
victimised by the racial community, in particular foreign slave labour
and local Jewry. Yet, at the same time, the uncritical hypostatising of the
'authentic' voice of the eyewitness provided for the continuation of narratives that accentuated the victimhood and suffering of ordinary residents
in 'ordinary' communities.

A 'turn of the tide'?: continuity and change in the early twenty-first century

Since the late 1990s, the air war has become something of a 'collective
obsession' in Germany,[4] playing a prominent role in a larger discourse
on German wartime suffering, which, according to some observers, is
reconfiguring the wider mnemonic landscape. In the view of one prominent critic, this 'turn of the tide' threatens to marginalise once again
the victims of the Germans, and thus to undo thirty years of self-critical
engagement with Nazism, genocidal war and Judaeocide.[5]

If one considers the contemporary boom in representations of German wartime suffering from a local perspective, then many elements of
continuity, rather than new departures, strike the eye. In the early 2000s,
the residents of cities such as Kassel or Magdeburg did not suddenly
discover a long-tabooed subject. Rather, they commemorated the sixtieth anniversaries of particularly devastating bombing raids within the
continuity of well-established *lieux de mémoire*. When, for example, the
local *Hessische Niedersächsische Allgemeine*, on 22 October 2003, devoted
a special page to the memory of the air raid on Kassel, the newspaper did
so by printing a (sanitised) version of the poem 'Thus Died My Home
Town'. Moreover, the same page reproduced two photographs that had
long been integral elements of the local memory culture (Fig. 30). The
first was a panoramic view of the devastated city, taken by Walter Thieme
in 1946 and reproduced many times since then. The second image was a

[4] Nolan, 'Air Wars, Memory Wars', 8.   [5] Frei, '1945 und wir', p. 21.

Figure 30. Commemorative page in the local newspaper on the sixtieth anniversary of the bombing of Kassel (2003).

close-up of two dishevelled female survivors, which had been popularised by Werner Dettmar in the 1980s. Likewise, when two archivists from the Magdeburg municipal archive, in 2003, put together an illustrated book on the raid of 16 January 1945, they used the well-established term 'night of horror' (*Schreckensnacht*) in order to refer to the experience of bombing.[6]

While there was nothing new or unexpected about many of the historiographical and commemorative activities that surrounded the sixtieth anniversaries of heavy bombing raids, there were, at the same time, other developments that transcended the established boundaries of public discourse. These developments were marked by the refusal to ascribe any cathartic function to indiscriminate bombing: the destruction of Kassel or Magdeburg did not provide an opportunity for the building of a 'modern' or 'more beautiful' city, nor did the suffering in the air war atone for any of the crimes committed by the Germans during World War II. By this view, the memory place stood for irredeemable loss, nothing else.

Carried by the generation of '68 and their fellow contemporaries who had rediscovered (and reconciled) themselves as 'war children', this narrative fused the 1950s emphasis on victimhood with the tone of moral righteousness that had characterised the New Left interventions of the 1980s in the debate about the shortcomings of the post-war reconstruction. Although the historical connection between German genocidal war and domestic destruction was freely acknowledged, embraced even, the main thrust of the irritation was directed no longer at Nazism – whose culpability was taken for granted – or at continuities in domestic city planning, but at the allied conduct of the air war. 'Ambassador, when are you going to pull down the statue to Bomber Harris?', a heckler called to the British ambassador as he left the auditorium after his commemorative address on the sixtieth anniversary of the bombing of Kassel. The heckler, who may have been in his forties or fifties, added, 'After all, we don't put up a statue to Hermann Goering, either.'[7] Although the challenge may be seen as an instance of relativising apologetics, the underlying assumption appears to have been that post-war Germany had faced its criminal past whereas Britain still had a good deal of work to do.

While an opening up of the memory culture towards a critical discussion of indiscriminate bombing may be considered a welcome

---

[6] Ballerstedt and Buchholz, *Es regnet Feuer.*
[7] Quoted from personal memory. I attended the ceremony on 22 October 2003 in the Kassel City Hall. See also Helmut Dick, letter to the editor, 'Die Taten anderer. Zur Diskussion um Schuld und Sühne', *Werra Rundschau*, 23 December 2003.

development,[8] the events in Magdeburg two years later showed just how susceptible such tendencies were to the politics of the extreme Right. Here, the initiative 'Against Forgetting' (*Initiative gegen das Vergessen*), which was supported by Neo-Nazi 'comradeships' from all over the Federal Republic, used the occasion of the sixtieth anniversary of 16 January 1945 to stage a 'funeral march' through Magdeburg.[9] Although a broad coalition of the local elites, citizens' initiatives and Leftists organised a number of counter-events that eventually succeeded in cutting short the march, the Neo-Nazi slogans were closer to some of the positions advanced in the recent debate on the 'bombing war' than the anti-Nazi demonstrators were wont to admit. Moreover, banners such as 'The Bombing Holocaust Must Never be Repeated' or 'Allied Terror since 1943 – Murder Remains Murder' also fed on local traditions of memory as they had been expounded throughout the time of the GDR.

Some tentative generalisations

To what extent, then, can the findings of this comparative case study be generalised? Were Kassel and Magdeburg typical of other cities east and west of the German border, or was there something distinct about them? Not enough comparative work has been done to provide a definitive answer but a few tentative suggestions may be offered on the basis of the available literature.

On a surface level, much of what happened in the two urban communities under consideration here was played out elsewhere as well. In West German cities such as Hamburg, Pforzheim, Wurzburg, Heilbronn, Freiburg and many others, airborne destruction in World War II spawned vibrant memory cultures of long duration that crystallised around the experience of particularly devastating air raids. East of the inner-German border, too, in Dresden but also in towns such as Halberstadt, similar *lieux de mémoire* emerged. Death in the air war was remembered on a regular basis, the destruction of the lived environment conceptualised in terms of *Heimat* lost, regained (and lost again), while everywhere attempts were made to tell stories about what had happened and why. Although there were considerable differences in the intensity of commemorative activity, by and large the commemorative cycles that have been identified for Kassel and Magdeburg could be observed

---

[8] See, for example, Maier, 'Targeting the City', 443.

[9] For an account of the march from the perspective of the extremist activists, see www.gedenkmarsch.de/magdeburg/?p=98 [6 July 2010]; for the general background Virchow, 'Provocation, Mimicry, Authenticity'.

elsewhere as well: the 1940s through to the mid-1960s saw the first cycle, the mid-1970s through to the mid-1990s the second, with a third stretching from the 1990s into the present.

With the important exception of Dresden, and to some extent also Hamburg, air war memory remained rooted in the locality. Just as a particular attack could be the defining moment in a town's history and at the same time merit less than a footnote in the history of the air war, let alone the war as a whole, a day of remembrance could be of vital importance to a particular community and be virtually unknown outside the locality. Memory cultures of the air war were acted out in spaces that had been directly affected, and often irretrievably changed, by bombing, and this sense of place gave them their peculiar quality. Urban memory cultures cannot be adequately understood if they are viewed as mere local variations of national developments. Rather, they constituted a field of engagement with Germany's catastrophic past in which national political, cultural and generational patterns intersected with specifically local traditions and concerns.

Yet, for the many similarities that can be observed all over Germany's heavily bombed cities, on closer inspection an important fault line emerges. There were urban communities that managed to transform airborne catastrophe into 'good stories' of successful overcoming.[10] In others, a sense of rupture prevailed. Freiburg im Breisgau and Hamburg, for example, fall in the first category; Kassel, Halberstadt, and to some extent also Magdeburg, in the second. The distinction was, in the first instance, a matter of perceptions shared by an unquantifiable number of residents living in the respective communities, and not a direct consequence of either the severity of airborne attack or the pace of postwar recovery. Yet it appears that a sense of irredeemable loss remained strongest in cities that, although they had largely been defined through their architectural heritage before the war, tried to make a virtue out of destruction by self-consciously embracing a modernity for which they lacked the resources to make a lasting contribution.[11] The result was not a city reborn but an identity destroyed. In 1931, *Brockhaus* encyclopaedia praised Kassel as one of the 'loveliest towns' in Germany. Twenty-four years later, in the first post-war edition, the epithet had vanished. It was never to appear again.[12]

---

[10] Arnold, Süß and Thießen, 'Tod, Zerstörung, Wiederaufbau', p. 10.

[11] Compare Neumann, 'Lange Wege der Trauer', pp. 217f.

[12] *Der Große Brockhaus*, vol. IX (15th edn, 1931), pp. 775–7, here p. 776; *Der Große Brockhaus*, vol. VI (16th edn, 1955), pp. 281–2.

Appendices

Appendix 1
'So starb meine Heimatstadt Kassel' (Thus Died My Home Town of Kassel)

Line	
1	*Frau Chasalla trägt schmerzvoll ein Trauerkleid,*
	Frau Chasalla wears a mourning dress,
2	*in ihren Mauern birgt sie unsagbares Leid*
	In her walls she harbours unspeakable pain
3	*was Menschengeist einst ersonnen*
	What the human spirit once conceived
4	*Was fleiss'ge Hände einst vollbracht*
	What industrious hands once accomplished
5	*vor tausend Jahren schon begonnen*
	What was started a thousand years ago
6	*vernichtet war's in einer Nacht*
	Has been annihilated in a single night
7	*O Nacht voll Schrecken und voll Grauen,*
	Oh night of horror and terror,
8	*viele Riesenvögel musste sie schauen*
	Many giant birds she was forced to see
9	*sie nahten mit unheimlichem Dröhnen und Klingen*
	They approached with frightful rumbling and noise
10	*Tod und Verderben der Stadt zu bringen,*
	To bring death and ruin to the city,
11	*zwar krachen und donnern die Flakhaubitzen*
	The flak artillery thunders and rumbles
12	*deutsche Jungen möchten die Heimat beschützen*
	German youths want to protect the homeland
13	*sie kämpften tapfer mit Heldenmut*
	They fought bravely with the courage of heroes
14	*viele vergossen ihr junges Blut.*
	Many shed their young blood.
15	*Doch die Übermacht war riesengroß*
	But the superior strength was overwhelming

This transcript is based on the version 'So starb meine Heimatstadt Kassel', signed 'Kassel, 23rd October 1943' (henceforth, A1).

Line	
16	*Und bald brach die reinste Hölle los,*
	And soon all hell broke loose,
17	*am Himmel grellroter Feuerschein*
	In the sky the red reflection of fire
18	*unzählige Brandbomben schlugen bald ein*
	In no time countless incendiary bombs struck
19	*Ein Zittern der Erde, ein Wanken und Schwanken*
	The earth trembled, swayed and shook
20	*Sprengbomben, dass die Häuser zusammen sanken*
	High explosive bombs made the buildings cave in
21	*Tausende gerieten in bittere Not.*
	Thousands were plunged into severe anguish.
22	*Tausende fanden den Flammentod*
	Thousands suffered death by fire
23	*Tausende für die es keine Rettung mehr [gab]*
	Thousands who could not be rescued
24	*fanden unter den Trümmern ein ewiges Grab*
	Found an eternal grave under the rubble
25	*Feuerstürme toben die Straßen einher*
	Firestorms rush through the streets
26	*das Herz der Stadt gleicht einem Feuermeer*
	The heart of the city equals a sea of fire
27	*In der Unterstadt das gleiche Entsetzen*
	In the Low Town soon the same horror
28	*Flammen, Flammen, die Menschen hetzen*
	Flames, flames, people rush
29	*zum Friedhof, da könnte noch Rettung sein,*
	To the churchyard where rescue might still be possible,
30	*dort drang der Feuersturm nicht ein*
	The firestorm did not enter there
31	*Der Rauch, der auch hier fast den Atem nahm*
	In smoke, which made breathing difficult here as well
32	*lagen sie frierend bis endlich der Morgen kam*
	They lay shivering until the morning broke at last
33	*Schmerz wurde tausendfach geboren,*
	Pain was born a thousand times,
34	*drei Kleine haben die Mutter verloren*
	Three young children lost sight of their mother
35	*sie faßten sich tapfer bei der Hand*
	They bravely took each other by the hand
36	*und suchten nach Ihr in Rauch und Brand*
	And looked for her in smoke and flames
36a	*[Die Not des Ältesten war riesengroß!]*[1]
	[The anguish of the oldest was enormous]

---

[1] Only in the variant, 'So starb meine Heimatstadt' (henceforth, A2).

Line

37	*Doch ließ auch der Tod selbst die Kleinen nicht los*[2]
	But even death would not let go of the little ones
38	*noch angefaßt, die blonden Löckchen versengt*
	Still holding each other, the blond curls scorched
39	*die Füsschen verkohlt, so hat man sie später herausgeholt*
	The little feet charred – thus they were later pulled from the rubble
40	*Kindergesichtchen vom Schmerz und Entsetzen entstellt*
	Children's faces disfigured by pain and agony
41	*Ergreifende Anklage dieser Welt!*[3]
	Moving indictment of this world
42	*Ein Mann trägt keuchend Frau und Kind*
	A man breathes heavily carrying woman and child
43	*Gottlob, dass sie geborgen sind*
	Praised be God that they are safe
44	*doch wehe nicht die vertrauliche Stimme klingt an sein Ohr*
	But woe, not the familiar voice reaches his ear
45	*eine Fremde trägt er zum Leben empor.*
	A stranger he has carried to life.
46	*Der starke Mann wankt, hört kaum noch wie sie stammelnd ihm dankt,*
	The strong man shakes and hardly hears her thanking him,
47	*längst eilt er den Weg noch einmal zurück,*
	He has long since hurried back,
48	*zu spät, nur Trümmer begraben sein Liebstes, sein Glück.*
	Too late – rubble has covered his dearest, his happiness.
49	*Ein Soldat der freudig auf Urlaub kam*
	A private, happy to be on leave
50	*der Flammentod Frau und Kinder ihm nahm*
	Death by fire has taken wife and children from him
51	*Erschüttert*[4] *steht er am Sarg*
	Shocked, he stands by the coffin
52	*der all seine Lieben auf einmal barg*
	That keeps all his loved ones
53	*Ein anderer von Feuersglut umloht*
	Another surrounded by fire
54	*vor ihm sein Haus, das mit Einsturz droht*
	His house is threatening to collapse in front of him
55	*da liegt am Wege, hab Erbarmen, ein Säugling gefallen*
	There by the wayside, have mercy, a baby
56	*aus Mutterarmen, sein Koffer oder ein junges Leben,*
	Has fallen out of her mother's arms – his luggage or a young life
57	*ein langes Besinnen darf es nicht geben,*
	There can be no hesitation,

[2] A2 has *Doch ließ er im Tod selbst die Kleinen nicht los* [But even in death he would not let go of the little ones].

[3] A2 reads *Ergreifenste* [sic] *Anklage des Mordes dieser Welt!* [The most moving indictment of the murder of this world!]

[4] *Erschüttert* in A2. A1 reads *erschütternd* [shocking].

Line	
58	*schnell hebt er das Kindlein zu sich empor*
	He quickly picks up the child
59	*zwar weiß er, dass er alles verlor*
	Although he knows that he has lost everything
60	*Vielleicht, dass einer Mutter Freudentränen*
	Perhaps a mother's tears of joy
61	*mit seinen Opfern ganz versöhnen*
	Will reconcile him with his sacrifice
62	*Menschen stehen auf den Straßen umher,*
	People are standing on the streets,
63	*Sie retten ihr Leben und sonst nichts mehr.*
	They have saved their lives but nothing else.
64	*Im Herzen die Sorge um all Ihre Lieben*
	In their hearts they worry about all their loved ones
65	*Angst, dass allein man ist übrig geblieben*
	They fear that they alone have remained
66	*Des Phosphors gierige Flammen zerbrachen Menschenglück*
	Phosphorous flames have destroyed human happiness
67	*sie schlagen als Hasses-Flammen [auf England]*[5] *zurück*
	As flames of hatred they fall back [on England]
68	*Der Hass in solch einer Nacht geboren*
	Hatred born out of such a night
69	*hat zur Gemeinschaft uns erst recht verschworen*
	Has welded us into one community
70	*Die Funken wirbeln wie toll umher*
	Sparks are flying through the air
71	*denn Häuserrisse bersten nur schwer*[6]
	Because cracked buildings break slowly only
72	*Nach Stunden erst ist die Vernichtung vollbracht*
	Only hours later the destruction is complete
73	*Öde Fensterhöhlen zeugen vom Schrecken der Nacht*
	Empty window frames are witness to the horror of the night
74	*Dann beim ersten Morgengrauen*
	With the first crack of dawn
75	*sind überall rauchende Trümmer zu schauen*
	Smoking heaps of rubble are everywhere
76	*Ein Bersten und Krachen erfüllt die Luft*
	The air is filled with the sounds of bangs and crashes
77	*Ein Bild des Jammers, das nach Vergeltung ruft!*
	A picture of misery that calls for retaliation!
78	*Die Sonne beginnt ihren Tageslauf*
	The sun starts her daily round

[5] Only in A2.

[6] A2 has *die Häuserriesen wanken nur schwer* [the high-rise buildings sway only slowly]; another variant reads *denn Häuserriesen sterben nur schwer* [because high-rise buildings die only slowly].

Line	
79	*In ewiger Schönheit steigt sie auf*
	She rises in eternal beauty
80	*doch schnell verhüllt sie ihr Gesicht*
	But quickly she covers her face
81	*Sie sucht eine Stadt und findet sie nicht!*
	She looks for a town but cannot find it!
82	*Nur Trümmer hört sie zum Himmel schrei'n*
	Rubble cries out to heaven
83	*'Krieg kann nur der Wahnsinn der Menschheit sein'*[7]
	'War is madness.'

[7] Lines 82f. are not found in either A1 or A2 but in half a dozen other variants collected in StAK S8 C53. The lines could either be a later addition or they may have been left out in some versions for fear of reprisals by the authorities.

Appendix 2
'Kasseler Heimatlied' ('Das Lied vom leidgeprüften Kassel') ('Kasseler Heimat Song' ['The Song of the Sorely Afflicted Kassel'])

Line	
1	*Wo die Dächer liegen auf den Straßen rum* Where the roofs are lying on the streets
2	*Wo man hört der Flieger feindliches Gebrumm* Where you hear the hostile droning of the aeroplanes
3	*Wo man muss verdunkeln, löscht die Lampen aus* Where one blacks out, extinguishes the lamps
4	*Da ist meine Heimat, Kassel an der Fuld.* There is my home, Kassel on the river Fulda.
5	*Wo die Bomber kreisen nachts am Firmament* Where the bombers circle on the firmament at night
6	*Wo mitunter ein ganzer Stadtteil brennt* Where entire city districts burn down from time to time
7	*Wo Ruinen stehen auf weitem Feld* Where ruins are all around
8	*Da ist meine Heimat, Kassel an der Fuld.* There is my home, Kassel on the river Fulda.
9	*Wo der böse Tommy mordet Frau und Kind* Where the wicked Tommy murders wife and child
10	*Wo so viele Opfer zu beklagen sind* Where so many victims are lamented
11	*Wo die feuchten Augen sind so tränenschwer* Where the wet eyes are heavy with tears
12	*Oh, du meine Heimat, wie lieb ich dich so sehr.* [*Kassel, meine Heimat, dich kenn ich nicht mehr.*] O my home, I love you so much. [Kassel, my home, I don't recognize you any more.]
13	*Wo die große Not zum Himmel schreit* Where great pain cries out to heaven

StAK S8 C53. There are two copies, with slightly different wording. The transcript is based on the variant 'Kasseler Heimatlied' (B1), while significant variations in the version 'Das Lied vom leidgeprüften Kassel' (B2) are given in square brackets. Both are based on a popular song, the so-called 'Friesenlied' from 1908/9.

Line

14	*Wo in Trümmern liegt alles weit und breit*
	[*wo die Menschen sind so voller Kummer, Leid*]
	Where everything for miles around has been reduced to rubble
	[Where the people are in so much pain and sorrow]
15	*Wo ich hab' geopfert all mein Hab und Gut*
	Where I have sacrificed all that I possessed
16	*Kassel, meine Heimat, lieb ich wie mein Blut.*
	[*Kassel, meine Heimat, sag: 'Es ist genug'.*]
	Kassel, my home, I love like my blood.
	[Kassel, my home, say, 'it is enough'.]

Appendix 3
'Mein Kassel', by Fritz Stück, *KLZ*, 11 November 1943, p. 3

Line	
1	*Den Toten Dank und Abschiedsgruß zuvor,* Thanks and Farewell to the Dead,
2	*den Helden, die mit ihrem Leben zollten;* To the heroes who paid with their lives;
3	*ein Händedruck dem Freunde, der verlor,* A handshake to the friend who lost
4	*was ihm als Liebstes, Teuerstes gegolten!* His most beloved, his dearest!
5	*Durch Deine Straßen zieht der grause Tod;* Dreadful death walks your streets;
6	*in Deinen Trümmern wacht die Hessentreue.* In your rubble Hessian loyalty stands guard.
7	*Ich liebe Dich in dieser tiefsten Not;* I love you in this deepest sorrow;
8	*sie weckt den heil'gen Schwur, den ich erneue:* It calls forth the holy oath that I renew:
9	*Nicht Mordlust je, noch der Vernichtung Wahn* Neither lust for murder nor the madness of annihilation
10	*bereiten uns'rem Vaterland das Ende,* Will spell an end on our fatherland,
11	*kein Feuermeer hemmt uns'res Aufbaus Plan;* No sea of flames will stand in the way of our reconstruction;
12	*frei vor uns tagt des Siegesmorgens Wende!* The morning of victory is in sight!
13	*Mein Kassel wird einst, einem Phönix gleich,* One day, my Kassel will rise, like a phoenix,
14	*aus Trümmern, Schutt und Asche rings entsteigen:* From the rubble, debris and ashes all around:
15	*mein Kassel, Stadt an selt'ner Schönheit reich,* My Kassel, rich in rare beauty,
16	*vor der sich noch die Enkel stolz verneigen.* The grandchildren will bow proudly before you.
17	*Ging auch verloren, was jahrhundert'lang* Although we have lost what for centuries

Line

18	*uns heiligstes Vermächtnis war geworden,* We regarded as our holiest legacy,
19	*nicht eine Stunde naht uns, zukunftsbang* We are not afraid, not even for a single hour
20	*und Leben wächst aus dem Verbrechen, Morden.* And new life rises from the crime, the murder.
21	*Mein Kassel lebt! Sein stolzer Wälderkranz* My Kassel is alive! Its proud ring of forests
22	*umschirmt der Heimat schmerzbelad'ne Erde* Guards the *Heimat* earth, heavy with pain
23	*Doch aus dem grauenhaften Totentanz* But out of the dreadful dance of death
24	*wird Leben blühen und ein neues 'Werde'!* New life will blossom!

Appendix 4
'Fünf Jahre danach – Gedanken zum 22. Oktober', by August Heldmann, *KZ*, 22 October 1948

Line	
1	*In dem lieben, alten Kassel, an dem schönen Fuldastrand*
	In dear old Kassel, on the banks of the beautiful Fulda river
2	*liegt mein Vaterhaus, das teure, kriegszerstört und ausgebrannt*
	There lies my dear father's house, war-ravaged and burnt-out,
3	*Stolze Bauten, schöne Plätze, dichte Straßen dieser Stadt*
	Proud buildings, beautiful squares, narrow alleys of this city
4	*fanden wie gar viele Menschen, durch den Krieg ein frühes Grab*
	Found an early grave through the war, just like so many people
5	*Wo ich meinen Blick hinwende, seh' ich Trümmer, Schutt und Not*
	Wherever I turn my eye, I see nothing but rubble, debris and want
6	*Wohlstand, Reichtum sind entschwunden, reiche Ernte hielt der Tod*
	Prosperity, wealth have disappeared; death had a rich harvest
7	*Jeder Frohsinn scheint gestorben, tiefster Ernst nahm dessen Platz*
	Happiness seems to have died, seriousness took its place
8	*Trauer um ein liebes Wesen, Trauer um den letzten Schatz.*
	We mourn a beloved being, we mourn the last treasure.
9	*Gern gedenk' ich froher Kreise, wo gesungen und gelacht,*
	I remember happy company, where we sang and laughed,
10	*wo man schmauste ohne Sorgen tief hinein oft in die Nacht.*
	Where we feasted without sorrow until deep into the night.
11	*Einst das Leben in den Straßen pulste wie des Herzens Schlag*
	Once upon a time life in the streets pulsated like the beat of a heart
12	*schaffte täglich neue Werte, brachte Freude jeden Tag.*
	Brought forth valuable objects every day, brought forth happiness every day.
13	*Dennoch woll'n wir nicht verzagen, fest im Glauben weit und breit!*
	But we must not despair, faithful everywhere!
14	*Uns're Hoffnung soll nicht schwinden, Wunden heilen mit der Zeit.*
	Our hope must not fail us; wounds heal with time.
15	*Hat der Krieg uns auch genommen, was das Leben uns geschenkt:*
	Although war has taken from us what life had given:
16	*Soll durch Fleiß uns Neues werden, und die Notzeit wird verdrängt.*
	Diligently we will build anew, and the time of want will be pushed aside.

Bibliography

PRIMARY SOURCES

ARCHIVES

Kassel
Archiv der Altstädter Gemeinde, Kassel
    Sitzungsprotokolle Kirchenvorstand

Archiv der Christuskirche, Kassel
    Abkündigungen, 1945–50

Archiv der Ev. Freiheiter Kirchengemeinde St. Martin
    Verhandlungsbuch des Kirchenvorstandes

Archiv der Lutherkirche, Kassel
    Paul Velbinger, 'Erlebtes und Erlittenes. Aus meinem Leben',
        unpublished manuscript
    Paul Velbinger, 'Predigten', unpublished manuscript (1992)
    Gemeindebrief der Ev. Gemeinde der Lutherkirche

Brüder Grimm Museum Kassel (BGM Kassel)
    Nachlass 7: Stiftung Karl Paetow (Bad Oeynhausen)

Dekanat Kassel-Mitte
    Akte Martinskirche

Friedhofsamt Kassel
    Kriegsgräberlisten und Gräberlisten Hauptfriedhof

*Informationsstelle zur Geschichte des Nationalsozialismus in
Nordhessen (Infostelle)*
    N. Ausländische Zwangsarbeiter in Kassel

Landeskirchenamt Kassel
    Generalakten R 173. Komitee für Frieden, Abrüstung und Zusam-
        menarbeit
    Generalakten R 195. Kirchliche Friedensaktivitäten
    Gerneralakten R 190. Kirche und Öffentlichkeit

Landeskirchliches Archiv Kassel (LKA Kassel)
     Dekanat Kassel-Mitte
     Ev. Gesamtverband Kassel
     Sammlung Kirchenkampf
     Sekretariat Bischof (SB) Wüstemann

Staatsarchiv Marburg
     Best. 165. Preußische Regierung Kassel (bis 1945)
     Best. 401. Regierungspräsident Kassel (nach 1945)

Stadtarchiv Kassel (StAK)
     A.0 Stadtverordnetenversammlung
     A.1.00 Magistratsprotokolle
     A.1.10 Oberbürgermeister
     A.4.41 Kulturpflege
     A.4.415 Stadtarchiv
     NL Betting
     NL Kaltwasser
     NL Schulz
     NL Seidel
     S1 Personen
     S3 Handschriftliche Quellen
     S4 Periodika
     S5 Zeitgeschichtliche Sammlung
     S8 Luftkrieg
     Statistisches Amt und Wahlamt der Stadt Kassel (ed.), 'Ver-
          waltungsbericht der Stadt Kassel 1945–1949', unpublished
          manuscript (1950)

Stadtarchiv Kassel, Fotoarchiv
     Allgemeine Zerstörung
     'Alt-Kassel, die Heimstatt althessischer Bau- und Handwerk-
          skunst', postcard series
     Ausstellung 1983
     Fotoalbum. Frau Johanna Schlieper
     Gedenkstätten auf Trümmern
     Gauleiter Weinrich besichtigt Zerstörung
     'Kassel – die tausendjährige Stadt', postcard series
     Luftaufnahmen. Gesamtansichten
     Opfer

Stadtmuseum Kassel (StMK)
     Ausstellungen. Leben in Ruinen. Kassel 1943–8

Magdeburg
Archiv der Kirchenprovinz Sachsen (AKPS)
     Rep. A gen. Kirche und Staat
     Rep. A Spec. G Akten betr. Bauten

Rep. A Spec. K Kirchenkreis Magdeburg
Rep. J1 Evangelische Domgemeinde

Archiv der Ev. Domgemeinde, Magdeburg
Abkündigungsbuch, 1961–84
Gemeindekirchenrat der Domgemeinde Magdeburg (ed.) 'Eine Kerze unterwegs im Zeichen von Frieden und Versöhnung', unpublished manuscript (1985)
Herbert Martin (ed.), 'Ernst Martin: Aus seinem Leben', unpublished manuscript (Bad Harzburg, 1979).
Monatliche Mitteilungen der Domgemeinde, 1964–72
Mitteilungsblatt, 1975–95
Domprediger Quast, Sammlung Friedensgebete, 1982–95

Büro des Oberbürgermeisters, Magdeburg
Ansprachen Willi Polte, 1995

Kulturhistorisches Museum Magdeburg (KHM)
Briefe
Ordner Johanniskirche

Landesarchiv Magdeburg, Landeshauptarchiv (LA Magd., LHA)
Rep. C 20 I Oberpräsident, Allgemeine Abteilung I b
Rep. C 127 Oberlandesgericht Naumburg (Saale)
Rep. P 1 Landesfriedenskomitee Sachsen-Anhalt
Rep. P 2 Bezirksfriedensrat Magdeburg
Rep. P 4 Nationale Front, Bezirksausschuss Magdeburg
Rep. P 13 SED-Bezirksleitung Magdeburg
Rep. P 16 SED-Stadtleitung Magdeburg
Rep. P 26 Fotosammlung des SED-Bezirksparteiarchivs
Rep. P 31 Sammlung Fotoalben

Stadtarchiv Magdeburg (StAM)
Fotoalbum P. Gehlert
N. Fotosammlung des Stadtarchivs Magdeburg
NG. Fotosammlung des Stadtarchivs Magdeburg
Rep. 12U 44 Nachlass Gerling
Rep. 18 Protokolle der Stadtverordnetenversammlung und des Rates 1945–90
Rep. 41 Rat der Stadt Magdeburg ab 1945
Rep. 44 Der Oberbürgermeister der Stadt Magdeburg 1933–45
ZG Zeitgeschichtliche Sammlung

Other
Bundesarchiv Berlin (BA Berlin)
NS 18 Reichspropagandaleiter der NSDAP
R 22 / alt 3001 Reichsministerium der Justiz
R 55 Reichsministerium für Volksaufklärung und Propaganda

Stiftung Archiv der Parteien und Massenorganisationen der DDR im Bundesarchiv Berlin (SAPMO)
NY 4243 Nachlass Philipp Daub

Bundesarchiv Koblenz (BA Koblenz)
ZsG 109 Sammlung Oberheitmann

Hauptstaatsarchiv Stuttgart
Q 3/43 Bund der Fliegergeschädigten

National Archives II, College Park, Maryland (NA II)
RG 243 United States Strategic Bombing Survey (USSBS)

Imperial War Museum, London (IWM)
Photograph Archive GSA 387 Air Raid Damage in Germany 1943
RAF raids on Kassel, July and October 1943

National Archives, Kew
AIR 14 Royal Air Force: Operational Reports

Stadtarchiv Darmstadt
Best. ST 24.11 Kulturamt Nr. 4/166. Feier zum Gedächtnis der
   Toten der Fliegerangriffe

Stadtarchiv Heilbronn (StA Heilbronn)
Akten der Verwaltungsregistratur betr. Gedenkfeier für die Opfer
   des 4. Dez. 1944

Stadtarchiv Stuttgart (StA Stuttgart)
Bestand Luftschutz

MANUSCRIPTS IN PRIVATE COLLECTIONS

Becker, Michael, Pfarrer. 'Ansprache am 22. Oktober 1995'
Giesler, Erhard, Prälat i.R. 'Ökonomischer Gottesdienst 22. 10. 1995'
Kapp, Johannes, Weihbischof. '50. Jahrestag der Bombennacht in Kassel'
Lüst, Udo, Pfarrer i.R. 'Gedenkgottesdienst 22.10.1991'
Noetzel, Almuth, Pfarrerin. 'Ansprache auf dem Alten Markt am 16.1.1990'
'Ansprache im Magdeburger Dom, 16.1.1991'
Röhring, Klaus, Oberlandeskirchenrat i.R. 'Gottesdienst zum Gedächtnis
   (1990)'
Temme, Willi, Pfarrer. 'Gottesdienst am 22.10.1998'

PERIODICALS

Amtliches Mitteilungsblatt. Milit. Govern. in Deutschland
Amtsblatt der Ev. Kirche der Kirchenprovinz Sachsen

Angriff, Der. Tageszeitung der Deutschen Arbeitsfront
Bild
Blick in die kirche. Informationen aus der Ev. Kirche von Kurhessen-Waldeck
Bonifatiusbote
Das Reich: deutsche Wochenzeitung
Die neue Zeitung: die amerikanische Zeitung in Deutschland
Evangelische Sonntagsbote, Der. Für die Gemeinden der Ev. Landeskirche von Kurhessen Waldeck
Freiburger Zeitung
Freiheit. Mitteldeutsche Tageszeitung. Organ der Sozialistischen Einheitspartei Deutschlands für die Provinz Sachsen-Anhalt
Gemeindebrief der Ev. Kirchengemeinde Christuskirche
Gemeindebrief der Martinskirche
GhK publik. Kasseler Hochschulzeitung
Heilbronner Stimme
Heimat-Schollen. Blätter zur Pflege hessischer Art, Geschichte und Heimatkunst
Hessen heute
Hessenland. Zeitschrift für die Kulturpflege des Bezirksverbandes Hessen
Hessische Allgemeine (HA). Überparteiliche Tageszeitung für Kassel und Nordhessen
Hessische Heimat. Veröffentlichungen des Landesvereins für Heimatschutz für Kurhessen und Waldeck
Hessische Nachrichten (HN)
Hessische Niedersächsiche Allgemeine (HNA)
Hessischer Sonntag. SPD Informationen. Ausgabe Hessen-Nord
Informationen, Kultur für alle. Theaterzeitung. Kasseler Kulturkalender
Innere Front, Die. Pressedienst der NSDAP
Karlskirche, Die. Nachrichtenblatt der Karlskirchengemeinde Kassel
Kassel kulturell
Kasseler Kulturkalender
Kasseler Post (KP). Hessische Post & Stadtanzeiger
Kasseler Sonntagsblatt. Christliches Volksblatt für Deutschland
Kasseler Zeitung (KZ). Überparteiliche Tageszeitung für Nordhessen
Kirche, Die. Evangelische Wochenzeitung
Kirchlicher Anzeiger der Altstädter Gemeinde Kassel, Brüderkirche
Kirchliches Amtsblatt. Gesetz- und Verordnungsblatt der Ev. Landeskirche von Kurhessen-Waldeck
Kontakte. Ökumenischer Gemeindebrief Adventskirche, St. Elisabeth, Karlskirche, Lutherkirche, Martinskirche, Wehleiden
Kurhessische Landeszeitung (KLZ). Gau-Organ der NSDAP
Liberal-Demokratische Zeitung (LDZ). Organ der Liberal-Demokratischen Partei für die Provinz Sachsen-Anhalt
Magdeburger Generalanzeiger
Magdeburger Kurier
Magdeburgische Zeitung
Merian

Mitteldeutsche, Der. Tageszeitung für nationalsozialistische Weltanschauung

Mitteldeutsche Neueste Nachrichten (MNN). Ausgabe des Bezirksvorstandes Magdeburg der National-Demokratischen Partei Deutschlands

Monatliche Mitteilungen der Domgemeinde

MZ am Wochenende. Das Blatt des Magdeburgers

Neue Gemeinschaft, Die

Neue Illustrierte

Neue Weg, Der. Tageszeitung der Christlich-Demokratischen Union

Neues Deutschland. Sozialistische Tageszeitung

PDS-Journal

Propagandist, Der. Mitteilungsblatt der Gaupropagandaleitung Kurhessen

Reichsrundfunk. Hrsg. von der Reichsrundfunk – Gesellschaft Berlin

Selbsthilfe. Unabhängige Zeitschrift für Politik, Kultur und Wirtschaft

Soldatenbrief der Gauleitung Kurhessen der NSDAP

Sozialistische Volkszeitung (SVZ). Eine deutsche Zeitung für die hessische Bevölkerung

Stattzeitung. in und um kassel. Hrsg. Verein zur Förderung der sozialen Infrastruktur Kassels

Unsere Stadt Kassel

Völkischer Beobachter (VB)

Volksstimme. Organ der Sozialistischen Einheitspartei Deutschlands in Sachsen- Anhalt

SECONDARY SOURCES

Ackermann, Volker, *Nationale Totenfeiern in Deutschland. Von Wilhelm I. bis Franz Josef Strauß. Eine Studie zur politischen Semiotik* (Stuttgart: Klett-Cotta, 1990).

Adamski, Peter (ed.), *'Glücklich die Stadt, die keine Helden hat'. Über Denkmäler in Kassel*, vol. I (Kassel: Geschichtswerkstatt, 1993).

Addison, Paul and Jeremy A. Crang (eds.), *Firestorm: the Bombing of Dresden, 1945* (London: Pimlico, 2006).

Adorno, Theodor W., *'Ob nach Auschwitz sich leben lasse'. Ein philosophisches Lesebuch*, ed. Rolf Tiedemann (Frankfurt am Main: Suhrkamp, 1997).

'Was bedeutet: Aufarbeitung der Vergangenheit?' [1959], in: Rolf Tiedemann (ed.), *Gesammelte Schriften, vol. X.2. Kulturkritik und Gesellschaft II* (Frankfurt am Main: Suhrkamp, 1977), pp. 555–72.

AG Kasseler Friedenswochen (ed.), *3. Kasseler Friedenswochen. Programmzeitung der Arbeitsgemeinschaft Kasseler Friedenswochen* (Kassel, 1982).

Alt-Cassel. Federzeichnungen von Ernst Metz (Melsungen: Heimatschollen Verlag, [1922]).

Alt Kassel. Kalender auf das Jahr 1949 (Kassel: Karl Winter, 1948).

Amerikanisches Kriegsinformationsamt im Auftrag des Oberbefehlshabers der Alliierten Streitkräfte, *KZ. Bildbericht aus fünf Konzentrationslagern* (no place: no date [1945]).

Der anglo-amerikanische Bombenkrieg. Tatsachen und Stimmen (aus der Presse des In- und Auslandes). Materialsammlung (no place: no date [Oct.(?) 1944]).

Apel, Karl, *In Memoriam. Gefallene und Vermisste 1914–1918 und 1939–1945. Ev. Kirchengemeinde Kassel-Wilhelmshöhe. Die Gedenkstätte in der Christuskirche* (Kassel: Hausdruckerei Bruderhilfe, 1995).

Applegate, Celia. *A Nation of Provincials: the German Idea of Heimat* (Berkeley, Los Angeles and Oxford: University of California Press, 1990).

Applegate, Celia and Pamela Potter (eds.), *Music and German National Identity* (University of Chicago Press, 2002).

Arendt, Hannah, 'The Aftermath of Nazi Rule: Report from Germany', *Commentary* 10 (1950), 342–53.

Eichmann in Jerusalem. Ein Bericht von der Banalität des Bösen (Munich and Zurich: Piper, 1992 [first edn 1964]).

Zur Zeit: politische Essays, ed. Marie Luise Knott (Hamburg: Rotbuch, 1986), pp. 43–69.

Ariès, Philippe, *Geschichte des Todes*, 8th edn (Munich: dtv, 1997).

Arnold, Jörg, 'Beyond Usable Pasts: Rethinking the Memorialization of the Strategic Air War in Germany, 1940 to 1965', in: Niven and Paver (eds.), *Memorialization in Germany*, pp. 26–36.

'"Kassel mahnt . . ." Zur Genealogie der Angst im Kalten Krieg', in: Bernd Greiner, Christian Th. Müller and Dierk Walter (eds.), *Angst im Kalten Krieg* (Hamburg: HIS, 2009), pp. 465–94.

'"Nagasaki" in der DDR: Magdeburg und das Gedenken an den 16. Januar 1945', in: Arnold, Süß and Thießen (eds.), *Luftkrieg*, pp. 239–55.

'A Narrative of Loss'. Review of Jörg Friedrich, *Der Brand. Deutschland im Bombenkrieg 1940–45*', H-German, H-Net Reviews, November 2003. www.h-net.msu.edu/reviews/showrev.cgi?path=280291070845163 [19 January 2011].

'Sammelrezension Bombenkrieg', *Historische Literatur* 2/2 (2004), pp. 17–38.

Arnold, Jörg, Dietmar Süß and Malte Thießen (eds.), *Luftkrieg. Erinnerungen in Deutschland und Europa* (Göttingen: Wallstein, 2009).

'Tod, Zerstörung, Wiederaufbau: Zu einer europäischen Erinnerungsgeschichte des Luftkrieges', in Arnold *et al.* (eds.), *Luftkrieg*, pp. 9–24.

Asmus, Helmut, *Geschichte der Stadt Magdeburg*, ed. Rat der Stadt Magdeburg and a team of authors under the leadership of Helmut Asmus (Berlin: Akademie Verlag, 1975).

Assmann, Aleida, *Erinnerungsräume. Formen und Wandlungen des kulturellen Gedächtnisses* (Munich: Beck, 2003).

'Wie wahr sind Erinnerungen?', in: Harald Welzer (ed.), *Das soziale Gedächtnis. Geschichte, Erinnerung, Tradierung* (Hamburger Edition, 2001), pp. 103–22.

Assmann, Aleida and Ute Frevert, *Geschichtsvergessenheit. Geschichtsversessenheit. Vom Umgang mit deutschen Vergangenheiten nach 1945* (Stuttgart: DVA, 1999).

Assmann, Jan, 'Das kollektive Gedächtnis zwischen Körper und Schrift. Zur Gedächtnistheorie von Maurice Halbwachs', in: Hermann Krapoth and Denis Laborde (eds.), *Erinnerung und Gesellschaft. Mémoire et Société: Hommage à Maurice Halbwachs (1977–1945)* (Wiesbaden: Verlag für Sozialwissenschaften, 2005), pp. 65–83.

Das kulturelle Gedächtnis. Schrift, Erinnerung und politische Identität in frühen Hochkulturen, 4th edn (Munich: Beck, 2002).

'Die Lebenden und die Toten', in: Assmann, Maciejewski and Michaelis (eds.), *Der Abschied von den Toten*, pp. 16–36.

Assmann, Jan, Franz Maciejewski and Axel Michaelis (eds.), *Der Abschied von den Toten. Trauerrituale im Kulturvergleich*, 2nd edn (Göttingen: Wallstein, 2007).

Ausstellung der Fachbereiche Architektur und Stadtplanung der Gesamthochschule Kassel (ed.), *Beiträge zur Stadtentwicklung in Kassel zwischen Jahrhundertwende und Wiederaufbau* (Kassel: Gesamthochschule Kassel, 1981).

Auswärtiges Amt, *Dokumente über die Alleinschuld Englands am Bombenkrieg gegen die Zivilbevölkerung* (Berlin: Franz Eher Nachf, 1943).

Ballerstedt, Maren, 'Daten zur Magdeburger Stadtgeschichte', in: Landeshauptstadt Magdeburg and Landesheimatbund Sachsen-Anhalt e.V. (ed.), *Magdeburg. Portrait einer Stadt*, 2nd edn (Halle an der Saale: Janos Stekovics, 2004), pp. 161–224.

'Die Zerstörung der Stadt am 10. Mai 1631 im öffentlichen Bewusstsein Magdeburgs', *Sachsen Anhalt. Beiträge zur Landesgeschichte* 16 (2000), 34–55.

Ballerstedt, Maren and Konstanze Buchholz, *Es regnet Feuer. Die Magdeburger Schreckensnacht am 16. Januar 1945* (Gudensberg-Gleichen: Wartberg, 2003).

Balz, Horst, 'Römerbrief', *TRE* vol. XXIX, pp. 291–308.

Bangert, Wolfgang, *Kassel: Aufbau von 1955–62* (Stuttgart: AWEG, 1962).

'Kassel – eine neue Stadt auf altem Grund', *Hessische Heimat*, n.s., 11/2–3 (1961), 2–8.

Kassel. Zehn Jahre Planung und Aufbau (Stuttgart: AWAG, 1955).

Barthes, Roland. *Camera Lucida: Reflections on Photography* (London: Cape, 1982).

Bartz, Karl, *Als der Himmel brannte. Der Weg der deutschen Luftwaffe, 1940–45* (Hanover: Sponholtz, 1955).

Batz, Wilhelm and Kurt Mitte (eds.), *Kassel einst und jetzt* (Kassel: Schneider & Weber, 1960).

Baumann, Hans D., *Kassel in alten Ansichtskarten* (Zaltbommel: Europäische Bibliothek, 1985).

Baumgartner, Jakob, 'Christliches Brauchtum im Umkreis von Sterben und Tod', in: Hansjakob Becker *et al.* (eds.), *Im Angesicht des Todes: ein interdisziplinäres Kompendium*, vol. I (St Ottilien: EOS-Verlag, 1987), pp. 91–133.

Beaumont, Roger, 'The Bomber Offensive as a Second Front', *JCH* 22/1 (1987), 3–19.

Beck, Earl R., 'The Allied Bombing of Germany, 1942–1945, and the German Response: Dilemmas of Judgement', *German Studies Review* 5/3 (1982), 325–37.

Behrenbeck, Sabine, *Der Kult um die toten Helden. Nationalsozialistische Mythen, Riten und Symbole 1923 bis 1945* (Vierow bei Greifswald: SH-Verlag, 1996).

Belz, Willi, *Die Standhaften. Über den Widerstand in Kassel 1933–45* (Ludwigsburg. K. J. Schromm, 1960).

Benda-Beckmann, Bas von, 'Eine deutsch-deutsche Katastrophe? Deutungsmuster des Bombenkriegs in der ost- und westdeutschen Geschichtswissenschaft', in: Arnold, Süß and Thießen (eds.), *Luftkrieg*, pp. 297–311.

Benz, Wolfgang, *Auftrag Demokratie: Die Gründungsgeschichte der Bundesrepublik und die Entstehung der DDR 1945–1949* (Berlin: Metropol, 2009).

'Nachkriegsgesellschaft und Nationalsozialismus. Erinnerung, Amnesie, Abwehr', *Dachauer Hefte* 6 (1990), 12–24.

Berg, Nicolas, *Der Holocaust und die westdeutschen Historiker. Erforschung und Erinnerung* (Göttingen: Wallstein, 2003).

Bergander, Götz, 'Vom Gerücht zur Legende. Der Luftkrieg über Deutschland im Spiegel von Tatsachen, erlebter Geschichte, Erinnerung, Erinnerungsverzerrung', in: Thomas Stamm-Kuhlmann, Jürgen Elvert, Birgit Aschmann and Jens Hohensee (eds.), *Geschichtsbilder. Festschrift in honour of Michael Salewski* (Stuttgart: Steiner, 2003), pp. 591–616.

'Vom unattraktiven zum besonders lohnenden Ziel. Dresden in den Luftkriegsplanungen der Alliierten', in: Reinhard, Neutzner and Hesse (eds.), *Das rote Leuchten*, pp. 44–57.

Berger, Hans, 'Magdeburg: Klassenkampf der Dominanten', in: Beyme *et al.* (eds.), *Neue Städte*, pp. 299–312.

Bergmann, Klaus, *Agrarromantik und Großstadtfeindschaft* (Meisenheim am Glan: Hain, 1970).

Berichte des Oberkommandos der Wehrmacht 1939–1945, Die, 5 vols. (Munich: Verlag für Wehrwissenschaften, 2004).

Beseler, Hartwig and Niels Gutschow, *Kriegsschicksale Deutscher Architektur. Verluste – Schäden – Wiederaufbau. Eine Dokumentation für das Gebiet der Bundesrepublik Deutschland*, vol. II (Neumünster: Karl Wachholtz, 1988).

Besier, Gerhard, *Der SED-Staat und die Kirche 1969–1990* (Frankfurt am Main: Propyläen, 1995).

Bessel, Richard, *Germany 1945: From War to Peace* (New York: HarperCollins, 2009).

'Hatred after War: Emotion and the Postwar History of East Germany', *History and Memory* 1/2 (2005), 195–216.

Nazism and War (London: Phoenix, 2005).

'The Shadow of Death in Germany at the End of the Second World War', in: Confino, Betts and Schumann (eds.), *Between Mass Death and Individual Loss*, pp. 51–68.

'The War to End All Wars: the Shock of Violence in 1945 and its Aftermath in Germany', in: Lüdtke and Weisbrod (eds.), *No Man's Land of Violence*, pp. 71–99.

Bessel, Richard and Dirk Schumann (eds.), *Life after Death: Approaches to a Cultural and Social History of Europe during the 1940s and 1950s* (Cambridge: German Historical Institute and Cambridge University Press, 2003).

Bettecken, Winfried, '"Dann jagen uns die Bürger gleich wieder aus dem Rathaus"', in: *Magdeburg. Die Geschichte der Stadt*, pp. 933–50.

Betts, Paul, 'Remembrance of Things Past: Nostalgia in West and East Germany, 1980–2000', in: Betts and Eghigian (eds.), *Pain and Prosperity*, pp. 178–207.

Betts, Paul and Greg Eghigian (eds.), *Pain and Prosperity: Reconsidering Twentieth-Century German History* (Stanford University Press, 2003).

Beyme, Klaus von, *Der Wiederaufbau. Architektur und Städtebaupolitik in beiden deutschen Staaten* (Munich and Zurich: Piper, 1987).

Beyme, Klaus von, Werner Durth, Niels Gutschow, Winfried Nerdinger and Thomas Topfstedt (eds.), *Neue Städte aus Ruinen. Deutscher Städtebau der Nachkriegszeit* (Munich: Prestel, 1992).

'Leitbilder des Wiederaufbaus in Deutschland', in: Beyme *et. al.* (eds.), *Neue Städte*, pp. 9–31.

Biess, Frank, *Homecomings: Returning POWs and the Legacies of Defeat in Postwar Germany* (Princeton University Press, 2006).

Blank, Ralf, 'Jörg Friedrich: Der Brand. Deutschland im Bombenkrieg. Eine kritische Auseinandersetzung', *Militärgeschichtliche Zeitschrift* 63 (2004), 175–86.

'Kriegsalltag und Luftkrieg an der "Heimatfront"', in: Echternkamp (ed.), *DRZW*, vol. IX/1: *Die deutsche Kriegsgesellschaft: 1939 bis 1945. Politisierung, Vernichtung, Überleben* (Stuttgart: Dt. Verlag-Anst, 2004), pp. 361–461.

Bloxham, Donald, 'Dresden as a War Crime', in: Addison and Crang (eds.), *Firestorm*, pp. 180–208.

Genocide on Trial: War Crimes Trials and the Formation of Holocaust History and Memory (Oxford University Press, 2001).

Boberach, Heinz, 'Die Auswirkungen des alliierten Luftkrieges auf die Bevölkerung im Spiegel der SD-Berichte', in: Klaus-Jürgen Müller and David N. Dilks (eds.), *Großbritannien und der deutsche Widerstand 1933–1944* (Paderborn: Schöningh, 1994), pp. 229–41.

Bode, Peter M., 'Von der Hand in den Mund geplant. Verpasste Chancen beim Wiederaufbau', in: *Merian* 30/3: Kassel, 10–21.

Boelcke, Willi A. (ed.), *'Wollt ihr den totalen Krieg?' Die geheimen Goebbels-Konferenzen 1939–1943* (Munich: dtv, 1969).

Boog, Horst (ed.), *The Conduct of the Air War in the Second World War: an International Comparison* (New York and Oxford: Berg, 1992).

Bourke, Joanna, 'Introduction: "Remembering" War', *JCH* 39/4 (2005), 473–85.

Boym, Svetlana, *The Future of Nostalgia* (New York: Basic Books, 2001).

Braese, Stephan, 'Bombenkrieg und literarische Gegenwart. Zu W.G. Sebald und Dieter Forte', *Mittelweg* 36 1 (2002), 4–24.

Brecht, Bertolt, *Werke. Große kommentierte Berliner und Frankfurter Ausgabe*, 30 vols. (Berlin, Weimar and Frankfurt am Main: Aufbau/Suhrkamp, 1993).

'Offener Brief an die deutschen Künstler und Schriftsteller', in: Brecht, *Werke*, vol. XXIII, pp. 155f.

'Zum Kongress der Völker für den Frieden', in: Brecht, *Werke*, vol. XXIII, pp. 215f.

Breyman, Steve, *Why Movements Matter: the West German Peace Movement and US Arms Control Policy* (State University of New York Press, 2001).

Brier, Helmut and Werner Dettmar, *Kassel. Veränderungen einer Stadt. Fotos und Karten 1928–1986*, 2 vols. (Fuldabrück: Hesse, 1986 [2nd edn 2001]).

Brink, Cornelia, *Ikonen der Vernichtung. Öffentlicher Gebrauch von Fotografien aus nationalsozialistischen Konzentrationslagern nach 1945* (Berlin: Akademie Verlag, 1998).

Brochhagen, Ulrich, *Nach Nürnberg. Vergangenheitsbewältigung und Westintegration in der Ära Adenauer* (Berlin: Ullstein, 1999 [1st edn Hamburg, 1994]).

Broszat, Martin, Klaus-Dietmar Henke and Hans Woller (eds.), *Von Stalingrad zur Währungsreform: Zur Sozialgeschichte des Umbruchs in Deutschland*, 3rd edn (Munich: Oldenbourg, 1990).

Brückner, Christine, *Ständiger Wohnsitz. Kasseler Notizen*, 2nd edn (Berlin: Ullstein, 1999).

Brumlik, Micha, 'Gedenken in Deutschland', in: Platt and Dabag (eds.), *Generation und Gedächtnis*, pp. 115–30.

Brunswig, Hans, *Feuersturm über Hamburg. Die Luftangriffe auf Hamburg im 2. Weltkrieg und die Folgen* (Stuttgart: Motorbuch, 1978).

Buchenau, Werner, *Aus dem Schatz einer Kirchenchronik (1943–1949)* (Kassel: Kasseler Dr-u. Verlagshaus, 1949).

Buchheim, Hans, Martin Broszat, Hans-Adolf Jacobsen and Helmut Krausnick, *Anatomie des SS Staates. Gutachten des Instituts für Zeitgeschichte*, 2 vols. (Olten u.a.: Walter-Verlag, 1965/6).

Buchholz, Ingelore, *Der Breite Weg – Magdeburg: Geschichten einer Straße* (Magdeburg: Helmuth Block, 1990).

Buchholz, Ingelore and Maren Ballerstedt, *Man setzte ihnen ein Denkmal* (Calbe: Cuno-Druck, 1997).

Buchholz, Ingelore, Maren Ballerstedt and Konstanze Buchholz, *Magdeburg in alten Ansichten* (Zaltbommel: Europäische Bibliothek, 1992).
Magdeburg – so wie es war (Düsseldorf: Droste, 1991).

Burckhardt, Lucius, 'Blütenzauber auf Trümmern. Die Bundesgartenschau von 1955', in: *Kassel 1955. Die Stadt im Jahr der ersten documenta*, pp. 77–83.

Burke, Peter, 'History as Social Memory', in: Thomas Butler (ed.), *Memory: History, Culture, and Mind* (Oxford University Press, 1989), pp. 97–113.

Burleigh, Michael, *Die Zeit des Nationalsozialismus. Eine Gesamtdarstellung* (Frankfurt am Main: Fischer, 2000).

Bussemer, Thymian, *Propaganda und Populärkultur. Konstruierte Erlebniswelten im Nationalsozialismus* (Wiesbaden: Deutscher Universitäts-Verlag, 2000).

Bütow, Tobias and Franka Bindernagel, *Ein KZ in der Nachbarschaft: Das Magdeburger Außenlager der Brabag und der 'Freundeskreis Himmler'* (Cologne: Böhlau, 2003).

Buttlar, Herbert Freiherr von, *Trauerrede für Friedrich Herbordt gehalten am 12. Mai 1958* (Kassel, 1958).

Büttner, Ursula, 'Gomorrha': Hamburg im Bombenkrieg. Die Wirkung der Luftangriffe auf Bevölkerung und Wirtschaft* (Hamburg: Landeszentrale für Politische Bildung, 1993).

Cassel und Wilhelmshöhe in alten Stichen und Lithographien (Kassel: Friedrich Lometsch, 1955).

Chickering, Roger, 'Ein Begräbnis in Freiburg 1917. Stadtgeschichte und Militärgeschichte im Zeitalter des "Totalen Krieges"', *Schau-ins-Land* 119 (2000), 113–26.

Chickering, Roger and Stig Förster (eds.), *Great War, Total War: Combat and Mobilization on the Western Front, 1914–1918* (Cambridge University Press, 2000).

Childers, Thomas, '"Facilis decensus averni est": the Allied Bombing of Germany and the Issue of German Suffering', *CEH* 38/1 (2005), 75–105.

Confino, Alon, *Germany as a Culture of Remembrance: Promises and Limits of Writing History* (Chapel Hill: University of North Carolina Press, 2006).

'Introduction: Histories and Memories of Twentieth-Century Germany', *History and Memory*, special issue 17/1–2 (2005), 5–11.

'The Nation as Local Metaphor: *Heimat*, National Memory and the German Empire, 1871–1918', *History and Memory* 5/1 (1993), 42–88.

The Nation as Local Metaphor: Württemberg, Imperial Germany, and National Memory, 1871–1918 (Durham, NC: University of North Carolina Press, 1997).

'Telling about Germany: Narratives of Memory and Culture', in: Confino (ed.), *Germany as a Culture of Remembrance*, pp. 188–213.

'"This Lovely Country You Will Never Forget": Kriegserinnerungen und Heimatkonzepte in der westdeutschen Nachkriegszeit', in: Habbo Knoch (ed.), *Das Erbe der Provinz. Heimatkultur und Geschichtspolitik nach 1945* (Göttingen: Wallstein, 2004), pp. 235–51.

Confino, Alon and Peter Fritzsche (eds.), *The Work of Memory: New Directions in the Study of German Society and Culture* (Urbana: University of Illinois Press, 2002).

Confino, Alon, Paul Betts and Dirk Schumann (eds.), *Between Mass Death and Individual Loss: the Place of the Dead in Twentieth-Century Germany* (New York: Berghahn, 2008).

Connelly, Mark, *Reaching for the Stars: a New History of Bomber Command in World War II* (London and New York: I.B. Tauris, 2001).

Conrad, Christoph (ed.), *Mental Maps*, special issue of *GG* 3/28 (2002).

Conrad, Sebastian, *Auf der Suche nach der verlorenen Nation. Geschichtsschreibung in Westdeutschland und Japan 1945–1960* (Göttingen: Vandenhoeck & Ruprecht, 1999).

Conze, Eckart, 'Sicherheit als Kultur. Überlegungen zu einer "modernen Politikgeschichte" der Bundesrepublik Deutschland', *VfZ* 3 (2005), 357–80.

Die Suche nach Sicherheit: Eine Geschichte der Bundesrepublik Deutschland von 1949 bis in die Gegenwart (Munich: Siedler, 2009).

Cornelißen, Christoph, 'Was heißt Erinnerungskultur? Begriff – Methoden – Perspektiven', *GWU* 10/54 (October 2003), 548–63.

Corum, James S., 'Die Luftwaffe, ihre Führung und Doktrin und die Frage der Kriegsverbrechen', in: Wolfram Wette and Gerd R. Ueberschär (eds.), *Kriegsverbrechen im 20. Jahrhundert* (Darmstadt: Wissenschaftliche Buchgesellschaft, 2001), pp. 288–302.

Cox, Sebastian, 'The Dresden Raids: Why and How', in: Addison and Crang (eds.), *Firestorm*, pp. 18–61.

Cramer, Kevin, *The Thirty Years' War and German Memory in the Nineteenth Century* (Lincoln, NE: University of Nebraska Press, 2007).

Crane, Susan A., 'Writing the Individual Back into Collective Memory', *AHR* 102/5 (1997), 1372–85.

Czesany, Maximilian, *Nie wieder Krieg gegen die Zivilbevölkerung. Eine völkerrechtliche Untersuchung des Luftkrieges 1939–1945* (Graz: Selbstverlag, 1961).

Czubatynski, Ralf, 'Domprediger Ernst Martin (1885–1974) im Spannungsfeld von Politik und Kirchenpolitik in der Zeit der Weimarer Republik und des Nationalsozialismus', *Sachsen-Anhalt. Beiträge zur Landesgeschichte* 15 (1999), 101–24.

Dähn, Horst, 'Die Kirchen in der SBZ/DDR (1945–1989)', in: Rainer Eppelmann, Bernd Faulenbach and Ulrich Mählert (eds.), *Bilanz und Perspektiven der DDR-Forschung. Festschrift in honour of Hermann Weber* (Paderborn and Munich: Schöningh, 2003), pp. 205–16.

'Dann färbte sich der Himmel blutrot . . . ' Die Zerstörung Magdeburgs am 16. Januar 1945. Exhibition in the Kulturhistorisches Museum Magdeburg, 15 January to 14 May 1995. Ed. Matthias Puhle (Calbe: Grafisches Centrum, 1995).

Danyel, Jürgen, 'Die Opfer- und Verfolgtenperspektive als Gründungskonsens? Zum Umgang mit Widerstand und Schuldfrage in der DDR', in: Danyel (ed.), *Die geteilte Vergangenheit*, pp. 31–46.

'Politische Rituale als Sowjetimporte', in: Konrad Jarausch and Hannes Siegrist (eds.), *Amerikanisierung und Sowjetisierung in Deutschland 1945–1970* (Frankfurt and New York: Campus, 1997), pp. 67–86.

Danyel, Jürgen (ed.), *Die geteilte Vergangenheit: Zum Umgang mit Nationalsozialismus und Widerstand in beiden deutschen Staaten* (Berlin: Akademie Verlag, 1995).

Dennis, David, *Beethoven in German Politics, 1870–1989* (New Haven, CT: Yale University Press, 1996).

Derenthal, Ludger. *Bilder der Trümmer- und Aufbaujahre. Fotografie im sich teilenden Deutschland* (Marburg: Jonas Verlag, 1999).

Deres, Thomas and Martin Rüther (eds.), *Fotografieren verboten! Heimliche Aufnahmen von der Zerstörung Kölns* (Cologne: Emons, 1995).

Dettmar, Werner, 'Kassel im Luftkrieg', in: *Leben in Ruinen. Kassel 1943–1948*, pp. 11–32.

Die Zerstörung Kassels im Oktober 1943. Eine Dokumentation (Fuldabrück: Hesse, 1983).

Deutsche Fotografie. Macht eines Mediums 1870–1970. Exhibition catalogue. Kunst- und Ausstellungshalle der Bundesrepublik Deutschland (Cologne: DuMont, 1997).

Deutsche Gedichte. Eine Anthologie, ed. Dietrich Bode (Stuttgart: Reclam, 1988).

Das Deutsche Reich und der Zweite Weltkrieg (DRZW), ed. Militärgeschichtliches Forschungsamt, 10 vols. (Stuttgart: DVA, 1979–2008).

Deutsches Wörterbuch. Von Jacob und Wilhelm Grimm, 33 vols. Facsimile reprint of the 1st edn, 1854–1971 (Munich: dtv, 1984).

Diefendorf, Jeffry M., *In the Wake of War: the Reconstruction of German Cities after World War II* (Oxford University Press, 1993).

Diner, Dan, *Verkehrte Welten. Antiamerikanismus in Deutschland. Ein historischer Essay* (Frankfurt am Main: Eichborn, 1993).

Diner, Dan (ed.), *Zivilisationsbruch. Denken nach Auschwitz* (Frankfurt am Main: Fischer, 1988).

Döblin, Alfred, 'Schicksalsreise', in: Enzensberger (ed.), *Europa in Ruinen*, pp. 188–91.

Doerry, Martin, *'Mein verwundetes Herz'. Das Leben der Lilli Jahn, 1900–1944* (Munich: DVA, 2002).

Dokumente deutscher Kriegsschäden. Evakuierte, Kriegssachgeschädigte, Währungsgeschädigte. Die geschichtliche und rechtliche Entwicklung, ed. Bundesminister für Vertriebene, Flüchtlinge und Kriegsgeschädigte, 5 vols. (Bonn: Zentraldruckerei, 1958–62).

Domansky, Elisabeth, 'A Lost War: World War II in Postwar German Memory', in: Alvin Rosenfeld (ed.), *Thinking about the Holocaust* (Bloomington: Indiana University Press, 1997), pp. 233–72.

'"Kristallnacht", the Holocaust and German Unity: the Meaning of November 9 as an Anniversary in Germany', *History and Memory* 4/1 (1992), 60–94.

Druve, Freimut (ed.), *Die Nachrüstungsdebatte im deutschen Bundestag: Protokoll einer historischen Entscheidung* (Reinbeck bei Hamburg: Rowolth, 1984).

Dubiel, Helmut, *Niemand ist frei von der Geschichte. Die nationalsozialistische Herrschaft in den Debatten des Deutschen Bundestages* (Munich and Vienna: Hanser, 1999).

Duden. Das Herkunftswörterbuch. Etymologie der deutschen Sprache, 3rd edn (Mannheim, Leipzig, Vienna and Zurich: Dudenverlag, 2001).

Durth, Werner and Niels Gutschow, *Träume in Trümmern. Planungen zum Wiederaufbau zerstörter Städte im Westen Deutschlands 1940 bis 1950*, 2 vols. (Braunschweig and Wiesbaden: Vieweg, 1988).

Ebbinghaus, Angelika, 'Deutschland im Bombenkrieg – Ein missglücktes Buch über ein wichtiges Thema', *Sozial Geschichte* 18/2 (2003), 101–22.

Echternkamp, Jörg, 'Im Kampf an der inneren und äußeren Front. Grundzüge der deutschen Gesellschaft im Zweiten Weltkrieg', in: Echternkamp (ed.), *DRZW*, vol. IX/1, *Die deutsche Kriegsgesellschaft: 1939 bis 1945. Politisierung, Vernichtung, Überleben* (Stuttgart: Dt. Verlag-Anst, 2004), pp. 1–98.

Echternkamp, Jörg and Stefan Martens (eds.), *Der Zweite Weltkrieg in Europa: Erfahrung und Erinnerung* (Paderborn: Schöningh, 2007).

Eckardt, Götz (ed.), *Schicksale deutscher Baudenkmale im zweiten Weltkrieg. Eine Dokumentation der Schäden und Totalverluste auf dem Gebiet der Deutschen Demokratischen Republik*, vol. I (Berlin: Henschelverlag, 1978).

Eghigian, Greg and Matthew Paul Berg (eds.), *Sacrifice and National Belonging in Twentieth-Century Germany* (College Station: Texas A&M University Press, 2003).

Enzensberger, Hans Magnus (ed.), *Europa in Ruinen: Augenzeugenberichte aus den Jahren 1944 bis 1948* (Frankfurt am Main: Eichborn, 1990).

Erll, Astrid, *Kollektives Gedächtnis und Erinnerungskulturen. Eine Einführung* (Stuttgart and Weimar: J.B. Metzler, 2005).

Erwägen, Wissen, Ethik – Deliberation, Knowledge, Ethics 13/2 (2002).

Eschebach, Insa, *Öffentliches Gedenken. Deutsche Erinnerungskulturen seit der Weimarer Republik* (Frankfurt and New York: Campus, 2005).

Essbach, Wolfgang, 'Gedenken oder Erforschen. Zur sozialen Funktion von Vergangenheitsrepräsentation', in: Nicolas Berg, Jess Jochimsen and Bernd Stiegler (eds.), *SHOAH. Formen der Erinnerung. Geschichte, Philosophie, Literatur, Kunst* (Munich: Wilhelm Fink, 1996), pp. 131–44.

Evangelische Kirche in Deutschland, *Die Denkschriften der EKD*, 1/1–4: Frieden / Versöhnung / Menschenrechte (Gütersloh: Gerd Mohn, 1978–93).

Evangelisches Gemeindebuch der Kirchengemeinden Kassel, ed. Dekanat (Suttgart: Ev. Verlagswerk, 1953).

Evangelisches Kirchengesangbuch der Evangelischen Kirche von Kurhessen-Waldeck (EKG) (Kassel: Bärenreiter, 1976).

Fache, Thomas, 'Gegenwartsbewältigungen. Dresdens Gedenken an die alliierten Luftangriffe vor und nach 1989', in: Arnold, Süß and Thießen (eds.), *Luftkrieg*, pp. 221–38.

'Faltblatt zur künstlerischen Neugestaltung der Gedenkstätte für die Opfer des Luftangriffs vom 16. Januar 1945' (Magdeburg: Landeshauptstadt Magdeburg, 1995).

FDP-Kreisvorstand Kassel (ed.), *Freie Demokratische Partei. Landesparteitag Hessen. Kassel 10.-12. März 1950* (Kassel: FDP-Kreisvorstand Kassel, 1950).

Feller, Hans. '"Gedenket aber der früheren Tage …" Stadtgeschichte und Gedenken am Beispiel der Martinskirche zu Kassel', in: Hans Werner Dannowski (ed.), *Erinnern und Gedenken* (Hamburg: Steinmann, 1991), pp. 45–61.

Feuchter, Georg W., 'Der Luftkrieg über Deutschland', in: *Dokumente deutscher Kriegsschäden*, vol. I, pp. 5–66.

Fischer, Jörg, 'Zivilisation, Kultur', in: *Geschichtliche Grundbegriffe*, vol. VII, pp. 679–774.

Fischer, Norbert, *Geschichte des Todes in der Neuzeit* (Erfurt: Sutton, 2001).

Flex, Walter, *Der Wanderer zwischen beiden Welten. Ein Kriegserlebnis* (Munich: Beck, 1917).

Förster, Alice and Birgit Beck, 'Post-Traumatic Stress Disorder and World War II: Can a Psychiatric Concept Help Us to Understand World War II?' in: Bessel and Schumann (eds.), *Life after Death*, pp. 15–35.

Förster, Stig, 'Introduction', in: Chickering and Förster (eds.), *Great War, Total War*, pp. 1–15.

Frei, Norbert, *1945 und wir. Das Dritte Reich im Bewusstsein der Deutschen* (Munich: Beck, 2005).

'1945 und wir. Die Gegenwart der Vergangenheit', in: Frei, *1945 und wir*, pp. 7–22.

'Auschwitz und Holocaust. Begriff und Historiographie', in: Hanno Loewy (ed.), *Holocaust: Die Grenzen des Verstehens. Eine Debatte über die Besetzung der Geschichte* (Reinbek bei Hamburg: Rowohlt, 1992), pp. 101–9.

'Deutsche Lernprozesse: NS Vergangenheit und Generationenfolge seit 1945',
in: Frei, *1945 und wir*, pp. 23–40.

Vergangenheitspolitik. Die Anfänge der Bundesrepublik und die NS-Vergangenheit
(Munich: Beck, 1996).

Frei, Norbert and Johannes Schmitz, *Journalismus im Dritten Reich*, 3rd edn
(Munich: Beck, 1999).

Frenz, Wilhelm, 'NS-Wirtschaftpolitik und die soziale Lage der arbeitenden
Bevölkerung', in: Frenz, Kammler and Krause-Vilmar (eds.), *Volksgemeinschaft und Volksfeinde. Kassel 1933–1945*, vol. II, pp. 255–90.

'Organisation, Mitglieder und Wähler der NSDAP in Kassel', in: Frenz,
Kammler and Krause-Vilmar (eds.), *Volksgemeinschaft und Volksfeinde*, vol.
II, pp. 47–57.

*Die politische Entwicklung in Kassel von 1945 – 1969. Eine wahlsoziologische Unter-
suchung* (Meisenheim am Glan: Verlag Anton Hain, 1974).

Frenz, Wilhelm, Jörg Kammler and Dietfrid Krause-Vilmar (eds.), *Volksgemeinschaft und Volksfeinde. Kassel 1933–1945*, vol. I: documentation; vol. II: essays
(Fuldabrück: Hesse, 1984 and 1987).

Freud, Sigmund, *Studienausgabe*, ed Alexander Mischerlich (Frankfurt am Main:
Fischer, 1969–75).

Frevert, Ute, 'Geschichte als Erlebnis: Wege aus der Geschichtsmüdigkeit',
in: Assmann and Frevert, *Geschichtsvergessenheit. Geschichtsversessenheit*,
pp. 250–4.

Friedrich, H. *Magdeburg. Bildmappe 1 & 2* (Magdeburg: Otto Lindner, 1946).

Friedrich, Jörg, *Brandstätten: der Anblick des Bombenkrieges* (Berlin: Propyläen,
2003).

The Fire: the bombing of Germany, 1940–1945, trans. Allison Brown (New
York: Columbia University Press, 2006) (originally published as *Der Brand.
Deutschland im Bombenkrieg 1940–1945* (Munich: Propyläen, 2002)).

Friedrich, Willi, *Kassel. Zerstörung und Wiederaufbau* (Kassel-Bettenhausen: Selbstverlag, 1980).

Fritzsche, Peter, *Life and Death in the Third Reich* (Cambridge, MA: The Belknap
Press of Harvard University Press, 2008).

'Machine Dreams: Airmindedness and the Reinvention of Germany', *AHR*
98/3 (June 1993), 685–709.

A Nation of Fliers: German Aviation and the Popular Imagination (Cambridge,
MA: Harvard University Press, 1992).

'Volkstümliche Erinnerung und deutsche Identität nach dem Zweiten
Weltkrieg', in: Jarausch and Sabrow (eds.), *Verletztes Gedächtnis*, pp. 75–
97.

Führer durch Kassel und Wilhelmshöhe. Ein Wegweiser für Einheimische und Fremde
(Kassel: Basch, 4th edn, 1956; 5th edn, 1957; 6th edn, 1958; 7th edn,
1959).

Führer durch Kassel und Wilhelmshöhe. Ein Wegweiser für Fremde und Einheimische
(Kassel: Basch, 8th edn, 1960; 9th edn, 1961; 10th edn, 1962).

Führer durch Magdeburg. Die Stadt des Schwermaschinenbaus, ed. Rat der Stadt
Magdeburg, Abt. Kultur (Magdeburg: Druckerei Volksstimme, [1961]).

Fulbrook, Mary, *Anatomy of a Dictatorship: Inside the GDR 1949–1989* (Oxford University Press, 1995).

German National Identity after the Holocaust (Cambridge, Oxford and Malden: Polity Press, 1999).

The People's State: East German Society from Hitler to Honecker (New Haven, CT: Yale University Press, 2005).

Funck, Marcus, 'Stadt und Krieg im 20. Jahrhundert', *IMS* 2 (2004), 5–9.

Funck, Marcus and Roger Chickering (eds.), *Endangered Cities: Military Power and Urban Societies in the Era of the World Wars* (Boston and Leiden: Brill, 2004).

Galland, Adolf, *Die Ersten und die Letzten. Die Jagdflieger im Zweiten Weltkrieg* (Munich: Franz Schneekluth, 1953).

Ganßauge, Gottfried, 'Was blieb vom alten Kassel erhalten?' *Hessische Heimat*, n.s., 11/2–3 (1961), 28–32.

Garrett, Stephen A., *Ethics and Airpower in World War II: the British Bombing of German Cities*, 2nd edn (New York: St Martin's Press, 1997).

Gedi, Noa and Yigal Elam, 'Collective Memory – What Is It?' *History and Memory* 8/1 (1996), 30–50.

Geinitz, Christian, 'The First Air War against Noncombatants. Strategic Bombing of German Cities in World War I', in: Chickering and Förster (eds.), *Great War, Total War*, pp. 207–25.

Gerling, Heinz, *Denkmale der Stadt Magdeburg* (Magdeburg: Helmuth Block, 1991).

Geschichtliche Grundbegriffe. Historisches Lexikon zur politisch-sozialen Sprache in Deutschland, ed. Otto Brunner *et al.*, 8 vols. (Stuttgart: Klett-Cotta, 1972–97).

Geyer, Michael, 'Endkampf 1918 and 1945: German Nationalism, Annihilation, and Self-Destruction', in: Lüdtke and Weisbrod (eds.), *No Man's Land of Violence*, pp. 36–67.

'Der Kalte Krieg, die Deutschen und die Angst. Die westdeutsche Opposition gegen Wiederbewaffnung und Kernwaffen', in: Naumann (ed.), *Nachkrieg in Deutschland*, pp. 267–318.

'Eine Kriegsgeschichte, die vom Tod spricht', in: Thomas Lindenberger and Alf Lüdtke (eds.), *Physische Gewalt. Studien zur Geschichte der Neuzeit* (Frankfurt am Main: Suhrkamp, 1995), pp. 136–61.

'"There is a Land Where Everything is Pure: Its Name is Land of Death": Some Observations on Catastrophic Nationalism', in: Eghigian and Berg (eds.), *Sacrifice and National Belonging*, pp. 118–47.

Gibas, M. and R. Gries, '"Vorschlag für den ersten Mai: die Führung zieht am Volk vorbei!" Überlegungen zur Geschichte der Tribüne in der DDR', *Deutschlandarchiv* 5 (1995), 481–94.

Glade, Heinz, *Magdeburger Tagebuch* (Berlin: Kongress-Verlag, 1957).

Glasenapp, Jörn, *Die deutsche Nachkriegsfotografie. Eine Mentalitätsgeschichte in Bildern* (Paderborn: Schöningh, 2008).

'Nach dem Brand. Überlegungen zur deutschen Trümmerfotografie', *Fotogeschichte* 91 (2004), 47–64.

Goebel, Stefan, *The Great War and Medieval Memory: War, Remembrance and Medievalism in Britain and Germany, 1914–1940* (Cambridge University Press, 2007).

Goebbels, Joseph, 'Appell der Kasseler Amtswalter', in: *Goebbels-Reden*, ed. Heiber, vol. II, pp. 259–85.

   Das eherne Herz. Reden und Aufsätze aus den Jahren 1941/42 (Munich: Eher, 1943).

   Goebbels-Reden, ed. Helmut Heiber, 2 vols. (Düsseldorf: Droste, 1971–2).

   'Der Luft- und Nervenkrieg', in: Goebbels, *Das eherne Herz*, pp. 344–50.

   Die Tagebücher von Joseph Goebbels: sämtl. Fragmente. Part I: Aufzeichnungen 1924–1941; part II: Diktate 1941–1945, ed. Elke Fröhlich (Munich: Saur, 1987–95).

Goffmann, Erving, 'Frame Analysis: an Essay on the Organization of Experience', in: Charles Lemert and Ann Branaman (eds.), *The Goffmann Reader* (Malden, MA: Blackwell, 1997), pp. 149–66.

Goltermann, Svenja, *Gesellschaft der Überlebenden: Deutsche Kriegsheimkehrer und ihre Gewalterfahrungen im Zweiten Weltkrieg* (Munich: DVA, 2009).

Göpner, W. 'Die zerstörte Stadt im Kartenbild. Darstellungsformen in Schadensplänen', *Berichte zur deutschen Landeskunde* 6 (1949), 95–117.

Gray, Peter and Kendrick Oliver (eds.), *The Memory of Catastrophe* (Manchester University Press, 2004).

Grayling, A. C., *Among the Dead Cities: Was the Bombing of Civilians in WWII a Necessity or a Crime?* (London: Bloomsbury, 2006).

Gregor, Neil, *Haunted City: Nuremberg and the Nazi Past* (New Haven: Yale University Press, 2008).

   '"The Illusion of Remembrance": the Karl Diehl Affair and the Memory of National Socialism in Nuremberg, 1945–1999', *The Journal of Modern History* 75 (September 2003), 590–633.

   '"Is He Still Alive, or Long Since Dead?" Loss, Absence and Remembrance in Nuremberg, 1945–1956', *German History* 21/2 (2003), 183–203.

   'Nazism – a Political Religion? Rethinking the Voluntarist Turn', in: Gregor (ed.), *Nazism, War and Genocide: Essays in Honour of Jeremy Noakes* (University of Exeter Press, 2005), pp. 1–21.

   'A *Schicksalsgemeinschaft*? Allied Bombing, Civilian Morale, and Social Dissolution in Nuremberg, 1942–1945', *The Historical Journal*, 43/4 (2000), 1051–70.

   'Trauer und städtische Identitätspolitik. Erinnerungen an die Bombardierung Nürnbergs', in: Arnold, Süß and Thießen (eds.), *Luftkrieg*, pp. 131–45.

Gregor, Neil (ed.), *Nazism* (Oxford University Press, 2000).

Grenzendörfer, Helene, *Wie ich die Zerstörung der Stadt Magdeburg am 16. Januar 1945 erlebt habe* (Munich: UNI-Druck, 1979).

Groehler, Olaf, 'Antifaschismus – Vom Umgang mit einem Begriff', in: Herbert and Groehler, *Zweierlei Bewältigung*, pp. 29–40.

   Bombenkrieg gegen Deutschland (Berlin: Akademie Verlag, 1990).

   'Dresden: Kleine Geschichte der Aufrechnung', *Blätter für deutsche und internationale Politik* 2 (1995), 137–41.

Geschichte des Luftkrieges 1910 bis 1970 (Berlin (Ost): Militärverlag der DDR, 1975; 2nd edn 1977).

'Der Holocaust in der Geschichtsschreibung der DDR', in: Herbert and Groehler, *Zweierlei Bewältigung*, pp. 41–66.

'The Strategic Air War and its Impact on the German Civilian Population', in Boog (ed.), *Conduct of the Air War*, pp. 279–97.

Groh, Christian, '"Was Pforzheim angetan wurde!" Erinnerungsorte und Denkmäler zum Luftkrieg', in: Arnold, Süß and Thießen (eds.), *Luftkrieg*, pp. 183–99.

Großbölting, Thomas, 'Das Bürgertum auf dem Rückzug', in: *Magdeburg. Geschichte der Stadt*, pp. 867–87.

SED-Diktatur und Gesellschaft. Bürgertum, Bürgerlichkeit und Entbürgerlichung in Magdeburg und Halle (Halle: mdv, 2001).

Großdeutscher Reichskriegertag 1939, ed. Propagandaabteilung des NS-Reichskriegerbundes (Berlin: Kyffhäuser, 1939).

Großdeutscher Reichskriegertag 1939 in Kassel vom 2.–5. Juni, ed. NS-Reichskriegerbund (Kyffhäuserbund) (Kassel: Reichskriegertag Kassel, 1939).

Große Brockhaus, Der, 15th rev. edn (Leipzig, 1931; 16th edn, 1955).

Große Kracht, Klaus, 'Gedächtnis und Geschichte: Maurice Halbwachs – Pierre Nora', *GWU* 47/1 (1996), 21–31.

Grünflächenamt (ed.), *100 Jahre Westfriedhof Magdeburg* (Magdeburg, no year).

Gutschow, Niels, 'Stadtzerstörung und Gedenken: Hamburg – Dresden – Berlin – New York', in: Assmann, Maciejewski and Michaelis (eds.), *Der Abschied von den Toten*, pp. 267–93.

Hagelstange, Rudolf, 'Das Beispiel', *Merian* 4/10: Kassel, 49–52.

Halbwachs, Maurice, *The Collective Memory*, trans. Francis J. Ditter, Jr. and Vida Yazdi Ditter (New York: Harper & Row, 1980).

Das Gedächtnis und seine sozialen Bedingungen (Frankfurt am Main: Suhrkamp, 1985).

Das kollektive Gedächtnis (Stuttgart: Ferdinand Enke, 1967).

Stätten der Verkündigung im Heiligen Land. Eine Studie zum kollektiven Gedächtnis (Konstanz: Universitätsverlag, 2003).

Hamecher, Horst (ed.), *Kassel in alten Ansichtskarten. Neue Folge* (Frankfurt am Main: Flechsig, 1980).

Hartwig, Rudi, 'Bomben auf Frauen und Kinder. Zu den anglo-amerikanischen Luftangriffen im zweiten Weltkrieg auf Städte im Territorium des heutigen Bezirks Magdeburg', *Magdeburger Blätter. Jahresschrift für Heimat- und Kulturgeschichte im Bezirk Magdeburg* (1985), 4–13.

Hartwig, Rudi and Manfred Wille, *Magdeburg im Feuersturm. Ein Dokumentarbericht. Zur Geschichte der Zerstörung der Stadt durch anglo-amerikanische Bombenangriffe im 2. Weltkrieg* (Magdeburg: Druckerei Volksstimme, 1985).

Hattenhorst, Maik, 'Stadt der Mitte: Zentrum der Aufrüstung und zweite Zerstörung', in: *Magdeburg. Geschichte der Stadt*, pp. 779–810.

'Städtische Identität im Wandel: Magdeburger Leit-Bilder im 20. Jahrhundert', in: Ramona Myrrhe (ed.), *Geschichte als Beruf. Demokratie und*

Diktatur, Protestantismus und politische Kultur. Festschrift in honour of Klaus Erich Pollmann (Halle, Saale: Stekovics 2005), pp. 407–20.

Hausen, Karin, 'The "Day of National Mourning" in Germany', in: Gerald Sider and Gavin Smith (eds.), *Between History and Histories: the Making of Silences and Commemorations* (University of Toronto Press, 1997), pp. 127–46.

Hausmann, Clemens, *Handbuch Notfallpsychologie und Traumabewältigung*, 3rd edn (Vienna: Facultas, 2009).

Hausmann, Manfred, 'Das alte Cassel. In Jahrhunderten gewachsen – in Stunden vernichtet', *Merian* 30/3: 'Kassel', 24–29.

Kassel – Portrait einer Stadt (Hanover: Fackelträger, 1964).

Hays Parks, W., 'Air War and the Laws of War', in: Boog (ed.), *Conduct of the Air War*, pp. 310–72

Hebbel, Friedrich, 'Requiem', in: *Deutsche Gedichte. Eine Anthologie*, pp. 214–15.

Hehl, Ulrich von, 'Die Kirchen in der NS-Diktatur. Zwischen Anpassung, Selbstbehauptung und Widerstand', in: Karl Dietrich Bracher, Manfred Funke and Hans-Adolf Jacobsen (eds.), *Deutschland 1933–1945. Neue Studien zur nationalsozialistischen Herrschaft*, 2nd edn (Bonn: bpb, 1993), pp. 153–81.

Heidelbach, Paul, *Casseler Spaziergänge* (Kassel: Schneider & Weber, 1969).

Kassel. Ein Jahrtausend Hessischer Stadtkultur, ed. Karl Kaltwasser (Kassel and Basel: Bärenreiter, 1957).

Heidelmayer, Alfred, 'Magdeburg 1945. Zwischen Zerstörung und Kriegsende – Ein Bericht', in: *'Dann färbte sich der Himmel blutrot . . . '*, pp. 112–44.

Heinemann, Elizabeth, 'The hour of the Woman: Memories of Germany's Crisis Years and West German National Identity', *AHR* 101/2 (1996), 354–95.

Heinicke, Erich. 'Kassel – einst – jetzt – später', *Baurundschau* 37/17–18 (1947), 98–112.

Hellweg, Uli, 'Wiedergründung der Unterneustadt – Eine große Chance für Kassel', in: *Wege zur Unterneustadt*, pp. 5–6.

Helm, Rudolf (ed.), *Kassel vor dem Feuersturm* (Kassel: Schneider & Weber, 1950; 2nd edn 1953).

Herbert, Ulrich, 'Drei politische Generationen im 20. Jahrhundert', in: Jürgen Reulecke (ed.), *Generationalität und Lebensgeschichte im 20. Jahrhundert* (Munich: Oldenbourg, 2003), pp. 95–114.

Fremdarbeiter. Politik und Praxis des 'Ausländer-Einsatzes' in der Kriegswirtschaft des Dritten Reiches (Bonn and Berlin: Dietz, 1985; 3rd edn 1999).

'Der Historikerstreit. Politische, wissenschaftliche, biographische Aspekte', in: Sabrow, Jessen and Große Kracht (eds.), *Zeitgeschichte als Streitgeschichte*, pp. 94–113.

'Vernichtungspolitik. Neue Antworten und Fragen zur Geschichte des "Holocaust"', in: Herbert (ed.), *Nationalsozialistische Vernichtungspolitik 1939–1945. Neue Forschungen und Kontroversen*, 4th edn (Frankfurt am Main: Fischer, 2001 [1st edn 1998]), pp. 9–66.

Herbert, Ulrich (ed.), *Wandlungsprozesse in Westdeutschland. Belastung, Integration, Liberalisierung 1945–1980*, 2nd edn (Göttingen: Wallstein, 2003).

Herbert, Ulrich and Olaf Groehler, *Zweierlei Bewältigung. Vier Beiträge über den Umgang mit der NS-Vergangenheit in den beiden deutschen Staaten* (Hamburg: Ergebnisse Verlag, 1992).

Herbordt, Friedrich, *Bilder aus dem alten Kassel* (Kassel: Druck und Verlag GmbH Kassel, 1968).

Herf, Jeffrey, *Divided Memory: the Nazi Past in the Two Germanys* (Cambridge, MA: Harvard University Press, 1997).

The Jewish Enemy: Nazi Propaganda during World War II and the Holocaust (Cambridge, MA: The Belknap Press of Harvard University Press, 2006).

'"Der Krieg und die Juden". Nationalsozialistische Propaganda im Zweiten Weltkrieg', in: *DRZW* IX/2, pp. 159–202.

Hermsdorff, Wolfgang, *Kassel 1900 bis heute: eine Dokumentation / mit 170 Fotos von Carl Eberth*, 3rd edn (Kassel: Stauda, 1981).

Ein Blick zurück aufs alte Kassel. 50 ausgewählte Themen der HNA-Serie (Kassel: Dierichs & Co., 1978).

Hermsdorff, Wolfgang and Carl Eberth, *Es geschah in Kassel von 1900 bis heute* (Kassel: Verlag Schneider und Weber, 1964).

Hessisches Land, with a foreword by G. M. Vonau (Kassel: Karl Winter, 1948).

Heuss, Alfred, *Verlust der Geschichte* (Göttingen: V & R, 1959).

Hinz, Berthold and Anreas Tacke (eds.), *Architekturführer / Architectural Guide Kassel*, intro. by Sascha Winter and Stefan Schweizer (Berlin: Ditrich Reimer Verlag, 2002).

Hitler, Adolf, *Mein Kampf*, 71st edn (Munich: Franz Eher Nachfolger, 1933).

Ho Tai, Hue-Tam, 'Review Essay: Remembered Realms: Pierre Nora and French National Memory', *AHR* 106/3 (2001), 906–22.

Hoch, Anton, 'Der Luftangriff auf Freiburg am 10. Mai 1940', *VfZ* 4/2 (1956), 115–44.

Hockerts, Hans Günter, 'Zugänge zur Zeitgeschichte: Primärerfahrung, Erinnerungskultur, Geschichtswissenschaft' in: Jarausch and Sabrow (eds.), *Verletztes Gedächtnis*, pp. 39–73.

Hoffmann-Axthelm, Dieter, 'Die Idee der kritischen Rekonstruktion', in: *Wege zur Unterneustadt*, pp. 20–1.

Die verpasste Stadt. Innenstadt Kassel, Zustandsanalyse und Methodik der Wiedergewinnung (Kassel: Gesamthochschule, 1989; 2nd edn 1994).

Hohn, Uta, *Die Zerstörung deutscher Städte im Zweiten Weltkrieg. Regionale Unterschiede in der Bilanz der Wohnungstotalschäden und Folgen des Luftkrieges unter bevölkerungsgeographischem Aspekt* (Dortmund: Vertrieb für Bau- und Planungsliteratur, 1991).

Holl, Karl, *Pazifismus in Deutschland* (Frankfurt am Main: Suhrkamp, 1988).

Holtmeyer, Alois, *Alt Cassel* (Marburg: Elwert, 1913).

Die Bau- und Kunstdenkmäler im Regierungsbezirk Kassel, vol. IV (Marburg: Elwert, 1923).

Homburg, Herfried, *Kassel – das geistige Profil einer tausendjährigen Stadt* (Kassel: Schneider & Weber, 1969; 2nd edn 1977; 3rd edn 1993).

Homburg, Herfried (ed.), *Kassel in alten Ansichtskarten* (Frankfurt am Main: Flechsig, 1978).

Huber, Wolfgang, 'Frieden V', in: *TRE* XI, pp. 618–44.

Huyssen, Andreas, 'Air War Legacies: From Dresden to Baghdad', *New German Critique* 90 (Autumn 2003), 163–76.

Iggers, Georg G., Konrad H. Jarausch, Matthias Middell and Martin Sabrow (eds.), *Die DDR-Geschichtswissenschaft als Forschungsproblem* (Munich: Oldenbourg, 1998).

Ihme-Tuchel, Beate, *Die DDR*, 2nd edn (Darmstadt: Wiss. Buchgesellschaft, 2007).

Institut für angewandte Sozialwissenschaften (IFAS), *IFAS report Sonderheft Kassel* (Bad Godesberg: IFAS, 1964).

Irving, David J., *Und Deutschlands Städte starben nicht. Ein Dokumentarbericht* (Zurich: Schweizer Druck- und Verlagshaus, 1963).

Von Guernica nach Vietnam (Munich: Heyne, 1982).

Irwin-Zarecka, Iwona, *Frames of Remembrance: the Dynamics of Collective Memory* (New Brunswick and London: Transaction Publishers, 1994).

Jäger, Jens, *Bilder der Neuzeit. Einführung in die Historische Bildforschung* (Tübingen: Edition Diskord, 2000).

'Fotografie – Erinnerung – Identität. Die Trümmeraufnahmen aus deutschen Städten 1945', in: Jörg Hillmann and John Zimmermann (eds.), *Kriegsende 1945 in Deutschland* (Munich: Oldenbourg, 2002), pp. 287–300.

Ein Jahr Aufbauarbeit in Magdeburg, ed. Magistrat der Stadt Magdeburg (Magdeburg, 1946).

Jakobs, Friedrich, 'Wie Phönix aus der Asche', in: *'Dann färbte sich der Himmel blutrot . . . '*, pp. 165–77.

Jarausch, Konrad H., 'Der nationale Tabubruch. Wissenschaft, Öffentlichkeit und Politik in der Fischerkontroverse'; in: Sabrow, Jessen and Große Kracht (eds.), *Zeitgeschichte als Streitgeschichte*, pp. 20–40.

Die Umkehr: Deutsche Wandlungen 1945–1995 (Munich: Deutsche Verlags-Anstalt, 2004).

'Zeitgeschichte und Erinnerung. Deutungskonkurrenz oder Interdependenz', in: Jarausch and Sabrow (eds.), *Verletztes Gedächtnis*, pp. 9–39.

Jarausch, Konrad H. and Michael Geyer, *Shattered Past: Reconstructing German Histories* (Princeton University Press, 2003).

Jarausch, Konrad H. and Martin Sabrow (eds.), *Verletztes Gedächtnis. Erinnerungskultur und Zeitgeschichte im Konflikt* (Frankfurt am Main: Campus, 2002), pp. 9–39.

Jordan, Rudolf, *Erlebt und erlitten. Weg eines Gauleiters von München bis Moskau* (Leoni am Starnberger See: Druffel, 1971).

Wir und der Krieg. Gedanken aus Reden in diesem Krieg (Dessau: Trommler, 1941).

Jung, Hans-Gernot, *Rechenschaft der Hoffnung. Gesammelte Beiträge zur öffentlichen Verantwortung der Kirche*, ed. Martin Hein (Marburg: Elwert, 1993).

'Unter dem Evangelium', in: Jung, *Rechenschaft der Hoffnung*, pp. 158–74.

Jureit, Ulrike and Michael Wildt (eds.), *Generationen. Zur Relevanz eines wissenschaftlichen Grundbegriffs* (Hamburger Edition, 2005).

Kaiser, Alexandra, 'The *Volkstrauertag* (People's Day of Mourning) from 1922 to the Present', in: Niven and Paver (eds.), *Memorialization in Germany*, pp. 15–25.

Kantsteiner, Wulf, 'Finding Meaning in Memory: a Methodological Critique of Collective Memory Studies', *History and Theory* 41/2 (2002), 179–97.

Kassel 1955, ed. Press Office of the City of Kassel (Kassel: Weber & Weidemeyer, 1955).

Kassel 1955. Die Stadt im Jahr der ersten documenta. Exhibition catalogue. Ed. Karl-Hermann Wegner, Christian Bromig and Alexander Link (Marburg: Jonas, 1992).

Kassel 1956, ed. Press Office of the City of Kassel (Kassel, [1956]).

Kassel. Bauwerke einer alten Stadt; Cassel und Wilhelmshöhe in alten Stichen und Lithographien (Kassel: Friedrich Lometsch, 1955).

Kassel. Informationen für Gäste und Bürger (Kassel: Schneider & Weber, 1971–2).

Kassel. Moderne Stadt mit Tradition, with contributions by Christine Brückner, Manfred Hausmann, Hans Werner Kalbfuß and Karl-Hermann Wegner, 2nd edn (Kassel: Lometsch, 1985).

Kassel baut auf 1952–1953 (Kassel, 1952).

Kassel einst und jetzt, dir. Kurt Lange (1938/45).

Kassel einst und jetzt, with contributions by Rudolf Helm, Karl Kaltwasser and Kurt Mitte; drawings by Christian Beyer (Kassel: Schneider & Weber, 1960; 4th rev. edn 1966; 7th rev. edn 1981).

Kassel vor dem Feuersturm, ed. Rudolf Helm, with an afterword by G. M. Vonau, 2nd edn (Kassel: Schneider & Weber, 1953).

Kassel lebt . . . trotz alledem! ed. Willi Seidel (Kassel: Kasseler Druck- und Verlagshaus, 1948).

Kassel – die Stadt der documenta, ed. Magistrat der Stadt Kassel, press office, Richard Litterscheid (Kassel, 1959).

Kassel-Wilhelmshöhe, die schöne deutsche Kunst- und Parkstadt (Berlin: Universum, [1935]).

Kasseler Altstadt vor ihrer Zerstörung 1943, Die: ein Bildspaziergang mit Hans Germandi (VHS) (Kassel: Out Take Films, 2000).

Kästner, Friedrich, 'Kriegsschäden', in: *Statistisches Jahrbuch Deutscher Gemeinden* 37 (1949), 361–91.

Kelly, Petra, 'In der Tradition der Gewaltfreiheit (1983)', in: Rathgeb (ed.), *Deutschland kontrovers*, pp. 311–14.

Kemp, Wolfgang and Floris Neusüß (eds.), *Kassel 1850 bis heute. Fotografie in Kassel – Kassel in Fotografien* (Munich: Schirmer-Mosel, 1981).

Kempowski, Walter, *Das Echolot. Fuga furiosa. Ein kollektives Tagebuch Winter 1945*, vols. I–III (Munich: Knaus, 1999).

Kershaw, Ian, *The 'Hitler Myth': Image and Reality in the Third Reich* (Oxford: Clarendon Press, 1987).

Popular Opinion and Political Dissent in the Third Reich: Bavaria 1933–45 (Oxford: Clarendon Press, 1983).

Kessler, Ludwig. '*Kassel baut auf . . . !*' (Berlin: Verlag für Technik und Kultur, [1946]).

Kettenacker, Lothar (ed.), *Ein Volk von Opfern? Die neue Debatte um den Bombenkrieg 1940–45* (Berlin: Rowolth, 2003).

Kimpel, Harald, *Documenta. Mythos und Wirklichkeit* (Cologne: Du Mont, 1997).

Kirche als Lerngemeinschaft. Dokumente aus der Arbeit des Bundes der Evangelischen Kirchen in der DDR (Berlin: Ev. Verlagsgemeinschaft, 1981).

Kirwin, Gerald, 'Waiting for Retaliation: a Study in Nazi Propaganda Behaviour and German Civilian Morale', *JCH* 16 (1981), 565–83.

Klaube, Frank-Roland, *Alt-Kassel. Ein verlorenes Stadtbild. Historische Photographien* (Gudensberg-Gleichen: Wartberg, 1988).

Chronik der Stadt Kassel. 2500 Ereignisse in Wort und Bild (Gudensberg-Gleichen: Wartberg, 2002).

'*Kassel lebt!*' *Neubeginn aus Trümmern* (Gudensberg-Gleichen: Wartberg, 1990).

Klee, Katja, *Im 'Luftschutzkeller des Reiches'. Evakuierte in Bayern 1939–1953: Politik, soziale Lage, Erfahrungen* (Munich: Oldenbourg, 1999).

Klein, Thomas (ed.), *Die Lageberichte der Justiz aus Hessen 1940 – 1945* (Darmstadt: Hessische Historische Kommission, 1999).

Klemperer, Victor, *Ich will Zeugnis ablegen bis zum letzten. Tagbücher 1933–1945*, 10th edn (Berlin: Aufbau, 1998).

LTI. Notizbuch eines Philologen, 15th edn (Leipzig: Reclam, 1996).

Kleßmann, Christoph, *Die doppelte Staatsgründung. Deutsche Geschichte 1945–1955*, 5th edn (Bonn: bpb, 1991).

'Kontinuitäten und Veränderungen im protestantischen Milieu', in: Schildt and Sywottek (eds.), *Modernisierung im Wiederaufbau*, pp. 403–17.

'Verflechtung und Abgrenzung. Aspekte der geteilten und zusammengehörigen deutschen Nachkriegsgeschichte', *APuZ* B 29–30 (1993), 30–41.

Knabe, Hubertus, *Die unterwanderte Republik. Stasi im Westen*, 3rd edn (Berlin: Propyläen, 2000).

Knigge, Volkhard and Norbert Frei (eds.), *Verbrechen erinnern. Die Auseinandersetzung mit Holocaust und Völkermord* (Munich: Beck, 2002).

Knoch, Habbo, *Die Tat als Bild. Fotografien des Holocaust in der deutschen Erinnerungskultur* (Hamburger Edition, 2001).

Kocka, Jürgen, *Vereinigungskrise. Zur Geschichte der Gegenwart* (Göttingen: V & R, 1995).

Köhler, Georg, 'Bevölkerungsstruktur von Magdeburg', in: Ingrid Hölzler and Eckhard Dittrich (eds.), *Sozialstrukturanalyse der Städte Magdeburg und Lodz* (Magdeburg: Universität Magdeburg, 1997), pp. 32–43.

Könczöl, Barbara, *Märtyrer des Sozialismus: die SED und das Gedenken an Rosa Luxemburg und Karl Liebknecht* (Frankfurt am Main: Campus, 2008).

König, Thomas, 'Der Konflikt um die Erhaltung historischer Bausubstanz', in: *Leben in Ruinen*, pp. 97–102.

Koonz, Claudia, *The Nazi Conscience* (Cambridge, MA: Harvard University Press, 2003).

Koselleck, Reinhart, 'Einleitung', in: Koselleck and Jeismann (eds.), *Totenkult*, pp. 9–20.

'"Erfahrungsraum" und "Erwartungshorizont" – zwei historische Kategorien', in: Koselleck, *Vergangene Zukunft. Zur Semantik geschichtlicher Zeiten* (Frankfurt am Main: Suhrkamp, 1989), pp. 349–75.

'Erinnerungsschleusen und Erfahrungsschichten. Der Einfluss der beiden Weltkriege auf das soziale Bewusstsein', in: Koselleck, *Zeitschichten. Studien zur Historik* (Frankfurt am Main: Suhrkamp, 2000), pp. 265–84.

'Formen und Traditionen des negativen Gedächtnisses', in: Knigge and Frei (eds.), *Verbrechen erinnern*, pp. 21–32.

'Gebrochene Erinnerung? Deutsche und polnische Vergangenheiten', in: *Deutsche Akademie für Sprache und Dichtung Jahrbuch 2000* (Göttingen: Wallstein, 2000), pp. 19–32.

'Kriegerdenkmale als Identitätsstiftungen der Überlebenden', in: Odo Marquard and Karlheinz Stierle (eds.), *Identität* (Munich: Wilhelm Fink, 1979), pp. 255–76.

Koselleck, Reinhart and Michael Jeismann (eds.), *Der politische Totenkult. Kriegerdenkmäler in der Moderne* (Munich: Wilhelm Fink, 1994).

Koshar, Rudy, *Germany's Transient Pasts: Preservation and National Memory in the Twentieth Century* (Durham, NC: University of North Carolina Press, 1998).

From Monuments to Traces: Artifacts of German Memory 1870–1990 (Berkeley: University of California Press, 2000).

Kösters, Christoph, 'Christliche Kirchen und nationalsozialistische Diktatur', in: Dietmar Süß and Winfried Süß (eds.), *Das 'Dritte Reich'. Eine Einführung* (Munich: Pantheon, 2008), pp. 121–41.

Kramer, Nicole, 'Mobilisierung für die "Heimatfront". Frauen im zivilen Luftschutz', in: Sybille Steinbacher (ed.), *Volksgenossinnen. Frauen in der NS-Volksgemeinschaft*, 2nd edn (Göttingen: Wallstein, 2007), pp. 69–92.

Kramm, Walter. *Kassel. Wilhelmshöhe Wilhelmstal* (Berlin: Dt. Kunstverlag, 1933; 2nd edn 1951).

Krause, Michael, *Flucht vor dem Bombenkrieg. 'Umquartierungen' im Zweiten Weltkrieg und die Wiedereingliederung der Evakuierten in Deutschland 1943–1963* (Düsseldorf: Droste Verlag, 1997).

Krause-Vilmar, Dietfrid, 'Ausländische Zwangsarbeiter in der Kasseler Rüstungsindustrie (1940–1945)', in: *Volksgemeinschaft und Volksfeinde*, vol. II, pp. 388–414.

'Ausländische Zwangsarbeiter in der Kasseler Rüstungsindustrie (1940–1945)', in: *Leben in Ruinen*, pp. 57–72 and 73–88.

'Hitlers Machtergreifung in der Stadt Kassel', in: *Volksgemeinschaft und Volksfeinde*, vol. II, pp. 13–36.

Krenzke, Hans-Joachim and Jürgen Goldammer, *Magdeburg. Bewegte Zeiten – Die 50er und 60er Jahre* (Gudensberg-Gleichen: Wartberg, 1997).

Kriewald, Heike, 'Gerling, Heinz', in: *Magdeburger Biographisches Lexikon*, pp. 208f.

Kritzman, Lawrence D., 'In Remembrance of Things French', in: *Realms of Memory: Rethinking the French Past*, vol. I: Conflicts and Divisions (New York: Columbia University Press, 1992), pp. ix–xiv.

Kropat, Wolf-Arno, *'Reichskristallnacht'. Der Judenpogrom vom 7. bis 10. November 1938 – Urheber, Täter, Hintergründe* (Wiesbaden: Kommission für die Geschichte der Juden in Hessen, 1997).

Kuckei, Max, 'Wo de Nordseewellen', *Niederdeutsche Welt* 15/6 (1940), 94f.

Kühne, Thomas, *Kameradschaft. Die Soldaten des nationalsozialistischen Krieges und das 20. Jahrhundert* (Göttingen: V & R, 2006).

'Männergeschichte als Geschlechtergeschichte', in: Kühne (ed.), *Männergeschichte – Geschlechtergeschichte: Männlichkeit im Wandel der Moderne* (Frankfurt and New York: Campus, 1996), pp. 7–30.

'Der nationalsozialistische Vernichtungskrieg im kulturellen Kontinuum des Zwanzigsten Jahrhunderts', Forschungsprobleme und Forschungstendenzen der Gesellschaftsgeschichte des Zweiten Weltkrieges, vol. II, *AfS* 40 (2000), 440–86.

Kulka, Otto Dov and Eberhard Jäckel (eds.), *Die Juden in den geheimen NS-Stimmungsberichten 1933–1945* (Düsseldorf: Droste, 2004).

Kulturamt Kassel (ed.), *50. Jahrestag der Zerstörung Kassels am 22. Oktober 1943*. Programme of events [Kassel, 1993].

Kulturhistorisches Museum Magdeburger (ed.), *Das Magdeburger Stadtbild im sechs Jahrhunderten* (Zeichnung: Reinhard/Rautengarten, 1959).

Kuratorium für den Wiederaufbau der Johanniskirche zu Magdeburg (ed.), *Die Johanniskirche – älteste Stadtkirche Magdeburgs in Wort und Bild* (Magdeburg, [1992]).

Laeger, Alfred, *Vereinigtes Dom- und Klostergymnasium Magdeburg 1675–1950. Gedenkschrift* (Frankfurt am Main: Wolfgang Weidlich, 1967).

Lagrou, Pieter, 'The Nationalisation of Victimhood: Selective Violence and National Grief in Western Europe, 1940–1960', in: Bessel and Schumann (eds.), *Life after Death*, pp. 243–57.

Landeshauptstadt Magdeburg (ed.), *Magdeburg 16. Jan. 1945–16. Jan. 1995*. Programme of events [Magdeburg, 1995].

Landeshauptstadt Magdeburg and Stadtplanungsamt (eds.), *Magdeburg. Architektur und Städtebau* (Halle: Janos Stekovics, 2001).

Landeshauptstadt Magdeburg and Stadtplanungsamt Magdeburg, *Städtebau in Magdeburg 1945–1990*, 2 vols. (Magdeburg: Landeshauptstadt Magdeburg, 1998).

Langenbacher, Eric, 'Changing Memory Regimes in Contemporary Germany?' *German Politics and Society* 67, 21/2 (Summer 2003), 46–68.

'The Allies in World War II: the Anglo-American Bombardment of German Cities', in: Adam Jones (ed.), *Genocide, War Crimes and the West: History and Complicity* (London & New York: Zed Books, 2004), pp. 116–33.

Large, David Clay, *Germans to the Front: West German Rearmament in the Adenauer Era* (Durham, NC: University of North Carolina Press, 1996).

Latzel, Klaus, *Deutsche Soldaten – nationalsozialistischer Krieg? Kriegserlebnis – Kriegserfahrung 1939–1945* (Paderborn: Schöningh, 1998).

'Die Soldaten des industrialisierten Krieges – "Fabrikarbeiter der Zerstörung"? Eine Zeugenbefragung zu Gewalt, Arbeit und Gewöhnung', in: Rolf Spilker and Bernd Ulrich, *Der Tod als Maschinist: Der industrialisierte Krieg 1914– 1918*, exhibition catalogue (Bramsche: Rasch, 1998), pp. 125–41.

Leben in Ruinen. Kassel 1943–1948. Exhibiton catalogue. Im Gedenkjahr der Stadt Kassel zur Erinnerung an ihre Zerstörung am 22. Oktober 1943. Ed. Magistrat der Stadt Kassel, Christina Coers-Dittmar and Alexander Link (Marburg: Jonas, 1993).

Lemke, Bernd, *Luftschutz in Großbritannien und Deutschland 1923 bis 1939* (Munich: Oldenbourg, 2005).

Lemke, Michael, 'Instrumentalisierter Antifaschismus und SED-Kampagnepolitik im deutschen Sonderkonflikt 1960–1968', in: Danyel (ed.), *Die geteilte Vergangenheit*, pp. 61–86.

Lepp, Claudia and Kurt Nowak (eds.), *Evangelische Kirche im geteilten Deutschland (1945–1989/90)* (Goettingen: V & R, 2001).

Lexikon Geschichtswissenschaft. Hundert Grundbegriffe, ed. Stefan Jordan (Stuttgart: Reclam, 2002).

Lindenberger, Thomas, '"Alltagsgeschichte" oder: Als um die zünftigen Grenzen der Geschichtswissenschaft noch gestritten wurde', in: Sabrow, Jessen and Große Kracht (eds.), *Zeitgeschichte als Streitgeschichte*, pp. 74–91.

Lometsch, Fritz, *Bauten aus dem alten Kassel* (Kassel: Lometsch, 1981).

Cassel in alten Bildern (Kassel: Lometsch, 1966).

Lübbe, Hermann, 'Der Nationalsozialismus im deutschen Nachkriegsbewusst-sein', *HZ* 236 (1983), 579–99.

Lüdtke, Alf, 'Histories of Mourning: Flowers and Stones for the War Dead, Confusion for the Living – Vignettes from East and West Germany', in: Sider and Smith (eds.), *Between History and Histories*, pp. 149–79.

Lüdtke, Alf and Bernd Weisbrod (eds.), *No Man's Land of Violence: Extreme Wars in the 20th Century* (Göttingen: Wallstein, 2006).

Lüken-Isberner, Folckert. 'Kassel: Neue Stadt auf altem Grund', in: Beyme *et al.* (eds.), *Neue Städte aus Ruinen*, pp. 251–98.

'Von der Gauhauptstadtplanung zur Gigantomie in Trümmern', in: *Leben in Ruinen*, pp. 173–80.

Lurz, Meinhold, *Kriegerdenkmäler in Deutschland*, 6 vols. (Heidelberg: Esprint, 1985–7).

Lütgemeier-Davin, Reinhold, 'Basismobilisierung gegen den Krieg: Die Nie-wieder-Krieg-Bewegung in der Weimarer Republik', in: Karl Holl and Wolfram Wette (eds.), *Pazifismus in der Weimarer Republik* (Paderborn: Schöningh, 1981), pp. 47–76.

Magdeburg, ed. Magistrat der Stadt Magdeburg (Berlin-Halensee: Dari, 1927).

Magdeburg, ed. Gemeinsame Kommission der Stadt Magdeburg zur Vorbereitung des 10. Jahrestages der DDR (Magdeburg, [1959]).

Magdeburg, ed. Rat der Stadt Magdeburg (Magdeburg: Druckerei Volksstimme, [1964]).

Magdeburg: the City in the Heart of Germany, ed. Magdeburger Verkehrsverein und Verkehrsamt (Magdeburg: Richter, [1939]).

Magdeburg. Die Geschichte der Stadt 805–2005, ed. Matthias Puhle and Peter Petsch (Dössel (Saalkreis): Janos Stekovics, 2005).

Magdeburg: Portrait einer Stadt, ed. Landeshauptstadt Magdeburg, Landesheimatbund Sachsen-Anhalt e.V. and Janos Stekovics (Halle an der Saale: Stekovics, 2004).

Magdeburg, Sechs Jahre Demokratischer Aufbau für den Frieden 1945/1951 (Magdeburg, [1951]).

Magdeburger Biographisches Lexikon (Magdeburg: Scriptum, 2005).

Magdeburgische Gesellschaft von 1990 zur Förderung der Künste, Wissenschaften und Gewerbe e.V., *Festreden zur Eröffnung der Johanniskirche am 2.10.1999* (Magdeburg: Werbung und Marketing Gudrun Seffers, 1999).

Magdeburgische Philharmonie (ed.), *100 Jahre städtisches Orchester Magdeburg* (Magdeburg, 1997).

Magistrat der Stadt Kassel, press office (ed.), Sonderbeilage 'Unsere Stadt 1943 bis 1968', *Unsere Stadt Kassel* (Kassel: Magistrat der Stadt Kassel, [1968]).

Maier, Charles S., 'Targeting the City: Debates and Silences about the Aerial Bombing of World War II', *International Review of the Red Cross* 87/859 (September 2005), 429–44.

Maier, Hans and Michael Schäffer (eds.), *'Totalitarismus' und 'Politische Religionen'. Konzepte des Diktaturvergleichs*, 3 vols. (Paderborn: Schöningh, 1996–2003).

Manz, Hermann, *Der Wiederaufbau der Zentren der beiden Städte Magdeburg und Hannover nach dem Zweiten Weltkrieg* (Cologne: Geograph. Inst., 1995).

Marchand, Bernard, 'Nationalsozialismus und Großstadtfeindschaft', *Die alte Stadt* 1 (1999), 39–50.

Margalit, Gilad, 'Dresden and Hamburg: Official Memory and Commemoration of the Victims of the Allied Air Raids in the Two Germanies', in: Helmut Schmitz (ed.), *A Nation of Victims? Representations of German Wartime Suffering from 1945 to the Present* (Amsterdam: Rodopi, 2007), pp. 125–40.

Guilt, Suffering and Memory: Germany Remembers Its Dead of World War II (Bloomington and Indianapolis: Indiana University Press, 2010).

'Der Luftangriff auf Dresden. Seine Bedeutung für die Erinnerungspolitik der DDR und für die Herauskristallisierung einer historischen Kriegserinnerung im Westen', in: Susanne Düwell and Matthias Schmidt (eds.), *Narrative der Shoah. Repräsentationen der Vergangenheit in Historiographie, Kunst und Politik* (Paderborn: Schöningh, 2002), pp. 189–207.

Markowitsch, Hans J., 'Die Erinnerung von Zeitzeugen aus Sicht der Gedächtnisforschung', *BIOS* 13/1 (2000), 30–47.

Marsen, Holger, Ulrike Kulbarsch and Peter Soltau, *Stadtteilgeschichte als Stadtgeschichte. Kassel* (Kassel: Kulbarsch, 1978).

Märtesheimer, Peter and Ivo Frenzel (eds.), *Im Kreuzfeuer: Der Fernsehfilm 'Holocaust': Eine Nation ist betroffen* (Frankfurt am Main: Fischer, 1979).

Martin, Ernst, 'Memento', in: Herbert Martin (ed.), 'Ernst Martin: Aus seinem Leben', unpublished manuscript (Bad Harzburg, 1979), pp. 57–61.

Marx, Karl, *The Eighteenth Brumaire of Louis Bonaparte* (1852) (New York: International Publishers, 1963).

Mason, Timothy W., 'Die Erbschaft der Novemberrevolution für den Nationalsozialismus', in: Mason, *Arbeiterklasse und Volksgemeinschaft. Dokumente und*

Material zur deutschen Arbeiterpolitik 1936–1939 (Opladen: Westdt. Verlag, 1975), pp. 1–17.

Meier, Helmut and Walter Schmidt, *Erbe und Tradition. Geschichtsdebatte in der DDR* (Cologne: Pahl-Rugenstein, 1988).

Meinhardt, Matthias, 'Der Mythos vom "Alten Dresden" als Bauplan. Entwicklung, Ursachen und Folgen einer retrospektiv-eklektizistischen Stadtvorstellung', in: Ranft and Selzer (eds.), *Städte aus Trümmern*, pp. 172–200.

Meldungen aus dem Reich. Die geheimen Lageberichte des Sicherheitsdienstes der SS 1938–1945, ed. Heinz Boberach, 17 vols. (Herrsching: Pawlak, 1984).

Merian 4/10, 'Kassel' (Hamburg: Hoffmann & Campe, 1952).

Merian 30/3, 'Kassel' (Hamburg: Hoffmann & Campe, 1977).

Messerschmidt, Manfred, 'Strategic Air War and International Law', in: Boog (ed.), *Conduct of the Air War*, pp. 298–309.

Metz, Ernst, *Hochfürstlich Hessische Residenzstadt Cassel*, intro. Leopold Biermer (Kassel: Lometsch, 1961; 2nd edn 1961).

Residenzstadt Cassel, intro. Gerhard Seib and Angelika Nold (Kassel: Lometsch, 1980).

Meyer-Eberhard, Gerda, *Ein sozialdemokratischer Oberbürgermeister in der Diktatur* (Wiesbaden: Selbstverlag, 2000).

Michaelis, Herbert and Ernst Schraepler (eds.), *Ursachen und Folgen: Vom deutschen Zusammenbruch 1918 und 1945 bis zur staatlichen Neuordnung Deutschlands in der Gegenwart*, vol. XXIV: *Deutschland unter dem Besatzungsregime* (Berlin: Dokumentenverlag, [1977]).

Mitscherlich, Alexander, *Die Unwirtlichkeit unserer Städte* (Frankfurt am Main: Suhrkamp, 1965).

Mitscherlich, Alexander and Margarete Mitscherlich, *Die Unfähigkeit zu trauern. Grundlagen kollektiven Verhaltens* (Munich: R. Piper, 1967).

Moeller, Robert G., 'Germans as Victims? Thoughts on a Post-Cold War History of World War II's Legacies', *History and Memory* 17/1–2 (2005), 147–94.

'On the History of Man-made Destruction: Loss, Death, Memory and Germany in the Bombing War', *History Workshop Journal* 1/61 (2006), 103–34.

War Stories: the Search for a Usable Past in the Federal Republic of Germany (Berkeley: University of California Press, 2001).

Mohr, Kurt, 'Bombenkrieg und Kassels Zerstörung 1943 (I)–(III)', *Feldgrau. Mitteilungen einer Arbeitsgemeinschaft* 14 (1966), 2: 33–40; 3: 64–74; 4: 93–100.

Moller, Sabine, *Die Entkonkretisierung der NS-Herrschaft in der Ära Kohl* (Hanover: Offizin, 1998).

Mommsen, Hans, 'Wie die Bomber Hitler halfen', in: Stephan Burgdorff and Christian Habbe (eds.), *Als Feuer vom Himmel fiel. Der Bombenkrieg in Deutschland* (Munich: DVA, 2003), pp. 115–21.

Mönch, Winfried, 'Städte zwischen Zerstörung und Wiederaufbau. Deutsche Ortsliteratur zum Bombenkrieg seit dem Zweiten Weltkrieg', *Die alte Stadt* 3 (2003), 265–89.

Moosmann, Elisabeth (ed.), *Heimat: Sehnsucht nach Identität* (Berlin: Ästhetik u. Kommunikation Verlag, 1980).

Moses, Dirk, 'Die 45er. Eine Generation zwischen Faschismus und Demokratie', *Die Sammlung* 40 (2000), 233–64.

Mosse, George L., *Fallen Soldiers: Reshaping the Memory of the World Wars* (Oxford University Press, 1990).

Müller, Rolf-Dieter, *Der Bombenkrieg 1939–1945* (Berlin: Christian Links Verlag, 2004).

Müller, Rolf-Dieter and Hans-Erich Volkmann (eds.), *Die Wehrmacht. Mythos und Realität* (Munich: Oldenbourg, 1999).

Murray, Williamson, 'The Combined Bomber Offensive', *Militärgeschichtliche Mitteilungen* 51 (1992), 73–94.

Mußner, Franz, 'Epheserbrief', in: *TRE* IX, pp. 743–52.

Naumann, Klaus, 'Bombenkrieg – Totaler Krieg – Massaker. Jörg Friedrichs Buch *Der Brand* in der Diskussion', *Mittelweg 36* 4 (2003), 49–60.

  'Einleitung', in: Naumann (ed.), *Nachkrieg*, pp. 9–26.

  'Die Frage nach dem Ende. Von der unbestimmten Dauer der Nachkriegszeit', *Mittelweg 36* 1 (1999), 21–32.

  Der Krieg als Text. Das Jahr 1945 im kulturellen Gedächtnis der Presse (Hamburger Edition, 1998).

  'Leerstelle Luftkrieg. Einwurf zu einer verqueren Debatte', *Mittelweg 36* 2 (1998), 12–15.

Naumann, Klaus (ed.), *Nachkrieg in Deutschland* (Hamburger Edition, 2001).

Neubert, Erhard, *Geschichte der Opposition in der DDR 1949–1989*, 2nd edn (Bonn: bpb, 2000).

Neumann, Klaus, 'Lange Wege der Trauer: Erinnerungen an die Zerstörung Halberstadts am 8. April 1945', in: Arnold, Süß and Thießen (eds.), *Luftkrieg*, pp. 203–20.

Neumann, Thomas W., 'Der Bombenkrieg. Zur ungeschriebenen Geschichte einer kollektiven Verletzung', in: Naumann (ed.), *Nachkrieg*, pp. 319–42.

Neutzner, Matthias, 'Vom Alltäglichen zum Exemplarischen. Dresden als Chiffre für den Luftkrieg der Alliierten', in: Reinhard, Neutzner and Hesse (eds.), *Das rote Leuchten*, pp. 110–27.

  'Vom Anklagen zum Erinnern', in: Reinhard, Neutzner and Hesse (eds.), *Das rote Leuchten*, pp. 128–63.

Niebelschütz, Ernst von, *Magdeburg: Deutsche Lande/Deutsche Kunst*, ed. Burkhard Meier (Berlin: Deutscher Kunstverlag, [1929]).

Niedhart, Gottfried, '"So viel Anfang war nie" oder: "Das Leben und nichts anderes" – deutsche Nachkriegszeiten im Vergleich', in: Niedhart and Riesenberger (eds.), *Lernen aus den Krieg?*, pp. 11–38.

Niedhart, Gottfried and Dieter Riesenberger (eds.), *Lernen aus dem Krieg? Deutsche Nachkriegszeiten 1918 und 1945* (Munich: Beck, 1992).

Niethammer, Lutz, 'Diesseits des "Floating Gap". Das kollektive Gedächtnis und die Konstruktion von Identität im wissenschaftlichen Diskurs', in: Platt and Dabag, *Generation und Gedächtnis*, pp. 25–50.

Nietzsche, Friedrich, *Kritische Studienausgabe*, ed. Giorgio Colli and Mazzino Montinari, 15 vols., new edn (Munich: dtv, 2003).

  Vom Nutzen und Nachteil der Historie für das Leben, in: Nietzsche, *Kritische Studienausgabe*, vol. I, pp. 243–334.

Niven, Bill, *Facing the Past. United Germany and the Legacy of the Third Reich* (London and New York: Routledge, 2002).

'Introduction: German Victimhood at the Turn of the Millennium', in: Niven (ed.), *Germans as Victims: Remembering the Past in Contemporary Germany* (Basingstoke: Palgrave Macmillan, 2006), pp. 1–25.

Niven, Bill and Chloe Paver (eds.), *Memorialization in Germany since 1945* (Basingstoke: Palgrave Macmillan, 2010).

Noakes, Jeremy (ed.), *Nazism 1919–1945*, vol. IV: *The German Home Front in World War II* (Exeter University Press, 1998).

Nolan, Mary, 'Air Wars, Memory Wars', *CEH* 38/1 special issue: Germans as Victims during the Second World War (2005), 7–40.

Nolte, Paul, 'Einführung: Die Bundesrepublik in der deutschen Geschichte des 20. Jahrhunderts', *GG* 28 (2002), 175–82.

Nora, Pierre, 'Das Abenteuer der *Lieux de mémoire*', in: Etienne François, Hannes Siegrist and Jakob Vogel (eds.), *Nation und Emotion. Deutschland und Frankreich im Vergleich 19. und 20. Jahrhundert* (Goettingen: V & R, 1995), pp. 83–92.

'Between Memory and History: *les Lieux de Mémoire*', *Representations* 26 (Spring 1989), 7–25.

Zwischen Geschichte und Gedächtnis (Frankfurt am Main: Fischer, 1998 [1st edn 1990]).

Oberkrome, Willi, *'Deutsche Heimat'. Nationale Konzeption und regionale Praxis von Naturschutz, Landschaftsgestaltung und Kulturpolitik in Westfalen-Lippe und Thüringen (1900–1960)* (Paderborn: Schöningh, 2004).

The Old Testament. The Authorized or King James Version of 1611, intro. George Steiner. Everyman's Library 175 (Cambridge University Press, 1996).

Osuch, Bruno, 'Die Bewegung gegen die Remilitarisierung in Kassel (1949–1956)', unpublished thesis, University of Kassel, 1977.

'Neubeginn im Rüstungszentrum Kassel', in: Ulrich Schneider *et al.* (eds.), *Als der Krieg zu Ende war. Hessen 1945: Berichte und Bilder vom demokratischen Neubeginn* (Frankfurt am Main: Röderberg, 1980).

Overmans, Rüdiger, *Deutsche militärische Verluste im Zweiten Weltkrieg* (Munich: Oldenbourg, 1999).

Overy, Richard J., *The Air War 1939–1945* (London: Europa, 1980).

Why the Allies Won (London: Jonathan Cape, 1995).

Die Wurzeln des Sieges. Warum die Alliierten den Zweiten Weltkrieg gewannen, 2nd edn (Stuttgart and Munich: DVA, 2001).

The Oxford Dictionary of Music, rev. edn (Oxford University Press, 1997).

Panse, Friedrich, *Angst und Schreck in klinisch-psychologischer und sozialmedizinischer Sicht. Dargestellt an Hand von Erlebnisberichten aus dem Luftkrieg* (Stuttgart: Georg Thieme, 1952).

Parks, W. Hays, 'Air War and the Laws of War', in: Boog (ed.), *The Conduct of the Air War*, pp. 310–72.

Pasche, Hans Günter, Joachim Diefenbach and Karl Hermann Wegner, *Todtenhof und Nordstadtpark. 150 Jahre Kasseler Hauptfriedhof* (Kassel: Verlag Evangelischer Medienverband, 1993).

Paul, Jürgen, 'Der Wiederaufbau der historischen Städte in Deutschland nach dem zweiten Weltkrieg', in: Cord Meckseper and Harald Siebenmorgen (eds.), *Die alte Stadt: Denkmal oder Lebensraum? Die Sicht der mittelalterlichen*

Stadtarchitektur im 19. und 20. Jahrhundert (Göttingen: V & R, 1985), pp. 114–56.

Paulus, Günter, 'Zur Verfälschung der Geschichte des Zweiten Weltkrieges in der westdeutschen Geschichtsschreibung', *ZfG* 1/3 (1953), 445–65.

Pethes, Nicolas and Jens Ruchatz (eds.), *Gedächtnis und Erinnerung. Ein interdisziplinäres Lexikon* (Hamburg: Reinbeck, 2001).

Peukert, Detlev J. K., 'Das "Dritte Reich" aus der "Alltags"-Perspektive', *AfS* (1986), 533–56.

Volksgenossen und Gemeinschaftsfremde: Anpassung, Ausmerze und Aufbegehren unter dem Nationalsozialismus (Cologne: Bund-Verlag, 1982).

Platt, Kristin and Mihran Dabag, *Generation und Gedächtnis. Erinnerungen und kollektive Identitäten* (Opladen: Leske & Budrich, 1995).

Preger, Franz, 'Aus meiner Kasseler Amtszeit 1908–1945', in: Hans-Dieter Stolze, 'Lutherkirche in der 1. Hälfte des 20. Jahrhunderts: Zwei Pfarrer berichten', unpublished manuscript (Kassel, 2005).

Prinz, Wolfgang, 'Die Judenverfolgung in Kassel'; in: *Volksgemeinschaft und Volksfeinde*, vol. II, pp. 144–222.

Rader, Olaf B., 'Dresden', in: Etienne François and Hagen Schulze (eds.), *Deutsche Erinnerungsorte*, vol. III (Munich: Beck, 2001), pp. 451–70.

Raim, Edith, 'Coping with the Nazi Past: Germany and the Legacy of the Third Reich', *CEH* 12/4 (2003), 547–60.

Ranft, Andreas and Stephan Selzer (eds.), *Städte aus Trümmern. Katastrophenbewältigung zwischen Antike und Moderne* (Göttingen: V & R, 2004).

Ranke, Winfried, 'Linke Unschuld? – Unbefangener oder unbedachter Umgang mit fragwürdig gewordener Vergangenheit', in: Dieter Vorsteher (ed.), *Parteiauftrag: Ein Neues Deutschland. Bilder, Rituale und Symbole der frühen DDR*. Exhibition catalogue (Berlin: Deutsches Historisches Museum, 1997), pp. 94–112.

Ranson, Lucien, *Vom Zwangsarbeiter zum Freund* (Magdeburg: Scriptum, 1994).

Rathgeb, Eberhard (ed.), *Deutschland kontrovers. Debatten 1945 bis 2005* (Munich and Vienna: Carl Hanser, 2005).

Reichel, Peter, 'Das Gedächtnis der Stadt. Hamburg im Umgang mit seiner nationalsozialistischen Vergangenheit', in Reichel (ed.), *Das Gedächtnis der Stadt*, pp. 7–28.

Politik mit der Erinnerung. Gedächtnisorte im Streit um die nationalsozialistische Vergangenheit, rev. edn (Frankfurt am Main: Fischer Taschenbuch, 1999).

Vergangenheitsbewältigung in Deutschland. Die Auseinandersetzung mit der NS-Diktatur von 1945 bis heute (Munich: Beck, 2001).

Reichel, Peter (ed.), *Das Gedächtnis der Stadt. Hamburg im Umgang mit seiner nationalsozialistischen Vergangenheit* (Hamburg: Dölling and Galitz, 1997).

Reichel, Peter, Harald Schmid and Peter Steinbach (eds.), *Der Nationalsozialismus – Die zweite Geschichte: Überwindung – Deutung – Erinnerung* (Munich: Beck, 2009).

Reinhard, Oliver, Matthias Neutzner and Wolfgang Hesse (eds.), *Das rote Leuchten. Dresden und der Bombenkrieg* (Dresden: Druckhaus Dresden, 2005).

Reinhardt, Helmut, *Magdeburg einst und jetzt* (Hanover: Fackelträger, 1964).

Reulecke, Jürgen (ed.), *Generationalität und Lebensgeschichte im 20. Jahrhundert* (Munich: Oldenbourg, 2003).

Reuther, Iris and Monika Schulte, 'Städtebau 1945–1990', in: *Magdeburg. Geschichte der Stadt*, pp. 915–32.

Richter, Michael, *Die Ost-CDU 1948–1952. Zwischen Widerstand und Gleichschaltung* (Düsseldorf: Droste, 1990).

Rödder, Andreas. *Die Bundesrepublik Deutschland 1969–1990* (Munich: Oldenbourg, 2004).

Rosenfeld, Gavriel D., *Munich and Memory: Architecture, Monuments, and the Legacy of the Third Reich* (Berkeley: University of California Press, 2000).

Rothfels, Hans, 'Zeitgeschichte als Aufgabe', *VfZ* 1/1 (1953), 1–8.

Rumpf, Hans, *Der hochrote Hahn* (Darmstadt: E.S. Mittler & Sohn, [1952]).

'Luftkrieg über Deutschland', in: *Bilanz des Zweiten Weltkrieges. Erkenntnisse & Verpflichtungen für die Zukunft* (Oldenburg and Hamburg: Gerhard Stalling, [1953]), pp. 159–75.

Das war der Bombenkrieg. Deutsche Städte im Feuersturm. Ein Dokumentarbericht (Oldenburg and Hamburg: Gerhard Stalling, 1961).

Rusinek, B.-A., 'Von der Entdeckung der NS-Vergangenheit zum generellen Faschismusverdacht – akademische Diskurse in der Bundesrepublik der 60er Jahre', in: Schildt, Siegfried and Lammers (eds.), *Dynamische Zeiten*, pp. 114–47.

Rytlewski, Ralf and Detlev Kraa, 'Politische Rituale in der Sowjetunion und der DDR', *APuZ* B3 (1987), 33–48.

Sabrow, Martin, 'Einleitung: Geschichtsdiskurs und Doktringesellschaft', in: Sabrow (ed.), *Geschichte als Herrschaftsdiskurs*, pp. 9–35.

'Kollektive Erinnerung und kollektiviertes Gedächtnis. Die Liebknecht-Luxemburg-Demonstration in der Gedenkkultur der DDR', in: Alexandre Escudier (ed.), *Gedenken im Zwiespalt. Konfliktlinien europäischen Erinnerns* (Göttingen: Wallstein, 2001), pp. 117–38.

Sabrow, Martin (ed.), *Geschichte als Herrschaftsdiskurs. Der Umgang mit der Vergangenheit in der DDR* (Cologne: Böhlau, 2000), pp. 9–35.

Sabrow, Martin, Ralph Jessen and Klaus Große Kracht (eds.), *Zeitgeschichte als Streitgeschichte. Große Kontroversen seit 1945* (Munich: Beck, 2003).

Sachsse, Rolf, *Die Erziehung zum Wegsehen. Fotografie im NS-Staat* (Bielsko-Biała: Philo Fine Arts, 2003).

Saint-Amour, Paul K., 'Air War Prophecy and Interwar Modernism', *Comparative Literature Studies* 42/2 (2005), 130–61.

Saldern, Adelheid von, 'Stand und Perspektiven der Stadtgeschichts- und Urbanisierungsforschung', *IMS* (2002), 54–62.

Sattler-Iffert, Juliane, *Die innere Heimat. Portraits von Kasseler Leuten* (Habichtswald-Ehlen: George Verlag, 1994).

Schaffer, Roland S., 'American Military Ethics in World War II: the Bombing of German Civilians', *Journal of American History* 67 (1980), 318–34.

Wings of Judgement: American Bombing in World War II, 2nd edn (Oxford University Press, 1988).

Schelsky, Helmut, *Die skeptische Generation. Eine Soziologie der deutschen Jugend* (Düsseldorf and Cologne: Diederichs, 1963 [first edn 1957]).

Schildt, Axel, '"German Angst". Überlegungen zu einer Mentalitätsgeschichte der Bundesrepublik', in: Daniela Münkel and Jutta Schwarzkopf (eds.), *Geschichte als Experiment: Studien zu Politik, Kultur und Alltag im 19. und 20. Jahrhundert. Festschrift in honour of Adelheid von Saldern* (Frankfurt and New York: Campus 2001), pp. 87–97.

'Das Jahrhundert der Massenmedien. Ansichten zu einer künftigen Geschichte der Öffentlichkeit', *GG* 27 (2001), 177–206.

'Materieller Wohlstand – pragmatische Politik – kulturelle Umbrüche. Die 60er Jahre in der Bundesrepublik', in: Schildt, Siegfried and Lammers (eds.), *Dynamische Zeiten*, pp. 21–53.

'Nachkriegszeit. Möglichkeiten und Probleme einer Periodisierung der westdeutschen Geschichte nach dem Zweiten Weltkrieg und ihre Einordnung in die deutsche Geschichte des 20. Jahrhunderts', *GWU* 44 (1993), 567–84.

Schildt, Axel and Arnold Sywottek (eds.), *Modernisierung im Wiederaufbau. Die westdeutsche Gesellschaft der 50er Jahre* (Bonn: Dietz, 1993).

Schildt, Axel, Detlef Siegfried and Karl Christian Lammers (eds.), *Dynamische Zeiten. Die 60er Jahre in den beiden deutschen Gesellschaften* (Hamburg: Christians, 2000).

Schleuning, Peter, '3. Symphonie Es-Dur Eroica op. 55', in: Albrecht Riethmüller, Carl Dahlhaus and Alexander L. Ringer (eds.), *Beethoven. Interpretation seiner Werke*, vol. I, 2nd edn (Darmstadt: Wiss. Buchges., 1996), pp. 386–400.

Schlögel, Karl, *Im Raume lesen wir die Zeit: Über Zivilisationsgeschichte und Geopolitik*, 2nd edn (Frankfurt am Main: Fischer, 2005).

Schmid, Harald, *Antifaschismus und Judenverfolgung: Die 'Reichskristallnacht' als politischer Gedenktag in der DDR* (Göttingen: V&R, 2004).

Erinnern an den Tag der Schuld: das Novemberpogrom von 1938 in der deutschen Geschichtspolitik (Hamburg: Ergebnisse-Verlag, 2001).

Schmidt, Wolfgang, 'Luftkrieg', in: Gerhard Hirschfeld, Gerd Krumeich and Irina Renz (eds.), *Enzyklopädie Erster Weltkrieg*, new edn (Paderborn: Schöningh, 2009), pp. 687–9.

Schmiechen-Ackermann, Detlef, 'Magdeburg als Stadt des Schwermaschinenbaus 1945–1990: Politische Geschichte und Gesellschaft unter der SED-Diktatur', in *Magdeburg. Geschichte der Stadt*, pp. 811–52.

Schnatz, Helmut, *Tiefflieger über Dresden?* (Cologne: Böhlau, 2000).

Schneider, Dieter Marc, 'Kommunalverwaltung und Verfassung', in: Martin Broszat and Hermann Weber (eds.), *SBZ-Handbuch* (Munich: Oldenbourg, 1990), pp. 297–319.

Schoch, Gunar, 'Economic Development and Labour Market Situation of the State Capital of Magdeburg from 1990 until 1996', in: Ingrid Hölzler and Eckhard Dittrich (eds.), *Sozialstrukturanalyse der Städte Magdeburg und Lodz* (Magdeburg: Universität Magdeburg, 1997), pp. 44–53.

Schörken, Rolf, *Luftwaffenhelfer und Drittes Reich. Die Entstehung eines politischen Bewusstseins* (Stuttgart: Klett-Cotta, 1984).

Schrader, Walter, 'Die wiedererstehende Großstadt Kassel', unpublished PhD thesis, Philipps-Universität Marburg, 1956.

Schultze, Harald (ed.), *Berichte der Magdeburger Kirchenleitung zu den Tagungen der Provinzialsynode 1946–1989* (Göttingen: V & R, 2005).

Schütte, Joachim (ed.), *Magdeburg in alten Ansichtskarten* (Würzburg: Weidlich Flechsig, 1988; 2nd edn, 1990; third edn, 2002).

Schwab, August (ed.), *Kreuz und Krone. Gedenkschrift zur Einweihung der wiederaufgebauten Martinskirche in Kassel* (Kassel: Hessische Druck- und Verlagsanstalt, 1958).

Schwarz, Hans-Peter, 'Die ausgebliebene Katastrophe. Eine Problemskizze zur Geschichte der Bundesrepublik', in: Hermann Rudolph (ed.), *Den Staat denken. Theodor Eschenburg zum Fünfundachtzigsten* (Berlin: Siedler, 1990), pp. 151–74.

Schweizer, Stefan, *Geschichtsdeutung und Geschichtsbilder. Visuelle Erinnerungs- und Geschichtskultur in Kassel 1866–1914* (Göttingen: Wallstein, 2004).

Schwendter, Rolf, 'Thesen zur radikalen Lösung der Innenstadtmisere', in: *Kasseler Jahrbuch zur Stadtentwicklung 1987*, ed. Fördergemeinschaft Kassel (Kassel: alp-druck, 1987), pp. 51–60.

Sebald, W. G., *Luftkrieg und Literatur,* with an essay by Alfred Andersch, 3rd edn (Frankfurt am Main: Fischer, 2002).

On the Natural History of Destruction, trans. Anthea Bell (New York: Random House, 2003).

Seegers, Lu, 'Kulturelles Leben in Magdeburg nach 1945', in: *Magdeburg. Portrait einer Stadt*, pp. 879–906.

'"Schaufenster zum Westen". Das Elbfest und die Magdeburger Kulturfesttage in den 1950er und 1960er Jahren', in: Adelheid von Saldern (ed.), *Inszenierte Einigkeit. Herrschaftsrepräsentationen in DDR-Städten* (Stuttgart: Steiner, 2003), pp. 107–44.

Seehase, Hans, 'Religion, Konfession und Dissidententum zwischen 16. und 20. Jahrhundert', in: *Magdeburg. Geschichte der Stadt*, pp. 687–712.

Seiderer, Georg, 'Der Luftkrieg im öffentlichen Gedenken. Wandlungen der Erinnerungskultur in Nürnberg und Würzburg nach 1945', *Jahrbuch für fränkische Landesforschung* 67 (2007), 333–55.

'Würzburg, 16 März 1945 Vom "kollektiven Trauma" zur lokalen Simmstiftung', in: Arnold, Süß and Thießen (eds.), *Luftkrieg*, pp. 146–61.

Sekula, Allan, 'On the Invention of Photographic Meaning', in: Victor Burgin (ed.), *Thinking Photography* (London and Basingstoke: Macmillan, 1982), pp. 84–109.

Sider, Gerald and Gavin Smith (eds.), *Between History and Histories: the Making of Silences and Commemorations* (University of Toronto Press, 1997).

Siebs, Benno-Eide, *Die Außenpolitik der DDR 1976–1989. Strategien und Grenzen* (Paderborn: Schöningh, 1999).

Siedler, Wolf Jobst, Elisbeth Niggemeyer and Gina Angress, *Die gemordete Stadt. Abgesang auf Putte und Straße, Platz und Baum* (Berlin: Herbig, 1964).

Siegfried, Detlef, 'Zwischen Aufarbeitung und Schlussstrich. Der Umgang mit der NS-Vergangenheit in den beiden deutschen Staaten 1958 bis 1968', in: Schildt, Siegfried and Lammers (eds.), *Dynamische Zeiten*, pp. 78–113.

Siemon, Thomas and Werner Dettmar, *Der Horizont in hellen Flammen. Die Bombardierung Kassels am 22. Oktober 1943*, 2nd edn (Gudensberg-Gleichen: Wartberg, 2003).

Silomon, Anke, 'Verantwortung für den Frieden', in: Lepp and Nowak (eds.), *Evangelische Kirche im geteilten Deutschland*, pp. 135–60.

Slenczka, Hans, *Die evangelische Kirche von Kurhessen-Waldeck in den Jahren von 1933 bis 1945* (Göttingen: V & H, 1977).

Sontag, Susan. *On Photography* (New York: Farrar, Straus and Giroux, 1977).

Speer, Albert, *Inside the Third Reich*, trans. Richard and Clara Winston (New York: Avon, 1971).

Spetzler, Eberhard, *Luftkrieg und Menschlichkeit. Die völkerrechtliche Stellung der Zivilpersonen im Luftkrieg* (Göttingen: Messerschmidt Verlag, 1956).

Staatliche Kunstsammlungen in Kassel, *Alt-Kassel. Aus Kunst und Geschichte einer schönen Stadt*. Exhibition in the Hessische Landesmuseum, April–June 1947 (Kassel: Karl Winter, 1947).

Stadt Kassel – Der Magistrat. Amt für Stadtplanung und Stadterneuerung (ed.), *Zur Diskussion: Innenstadt Kassel* (August, 1986).

Stadtarchiv Magdeburg, *Magdeburg. Ein verlorenes Stadtbild*, 2nd edn (Gudensberg-Gleichen: Wartberg, 1993).

Stargardt, Nicholas, 'Opfer der Bomben und Opfer der Vergeltung', in: Kettenacker (ed.), *Ein Volk von Opfern?*, pp. 56–71.

Witnesses of War: Children's Lives under the Nazis (London: Cape, 2005).

Staritz, Dietrich, *Geschichte der DDR*, 2nd edn (Frankfurt am Main: Suhrkamp, 1996).

Statistischer Bericht der Stadt Kassel, 1947–1954; 1956, ed. Statistisches Amt und Wahlamt der Stadt Kassel (Kassel: Statist. Amt u. Wahlamt, 1947–56).

Statistischer Bericht der Stadt Kassel, *1. Halbjahr 1952*, ed. Statistisches Amt und Wahlamt der Stadt Kassel (Kassel: Statist. Amt u. Wahlamt, 1952).

Statistisches Jahrbuch für Hessen, ed. Hess. Statistisches Landesamt (Offenbach: Statistisches Landesamt, 1948).

Statistisches Jahrbuch der Stadt Magdeburg für die Jahre 1945 und 1946 (Magdeburg: Stadt Magdeburg, 1947).

Stein, Hans-Peter, *Symbole und Zeremoniell in deutschen Streitkräften vom 18. bis zum 20. Jahrhundert* (Herford and Bonn: Mittler, 1984).

Steinert, Marlis G., *Hitlers Krieg und die Deutschen. Stimmung und Haltung der deutschen Bevölkerung im Zweiten Weltkrieg* (Düsseldorf and Vienna: Econ, 1970).

Steinweg, Johannes D., 'Die evangelische Kirche Kassels in den letzten zwei Jahrzehnten', in: *Evangelisches Gemeindebuch Kassel*, ed. Dekanat, pp. 12–21.

Stern, Frank, *Im Anfang war Auschwitz. Antisemitismus und Philosemitismus im deutschen Nachkrieg* (Gerlingen: Bleicher, 1991).

Stolze, Hans-Dieter, '. . . es soll uns doch gelingen' *Lutherkirche Kassel 1897–1997. Festschrift* (Kassel: Ev. Informationszentrum, 1997).

'Lutherkirche in der 1. Hälfte des 20. Jahrhunderts: Zwei Pfarrer berichten', unpublished manuscript (Kassel, 2005).

Stöver, Bernd, *Volksgemeinschaft im Dritten Reich: die Konsensbereitschaft der Deutschen aus der Sicht sozialistischer Exilberichte* (Düsseldorf: Droste, 1993).

Straub, Jürgen, 'Personale und kollektive Identität. Zur Analyse eines theoretischen Begriffs', in: Aleida Assmann and Heidrun Freese (eds.), *Identitäten* (Frankfurt am Main: Suhrkamp, 1998), pp. 73–104.

Stubbe, Hannes, *Formen der Trauer. Eine kulturanthropologische Untersuchung* (Berlin: Reimer, 1985).

Süß, Dietmar, 'Erinnerungen an den Luftkrieg in Deutschland und Großbritannien', *APuZ* 18–19 (2005), 19–26.

''Massaker und Mongolensturm''. Anmerkungen zu Jörg Friedrichs umstrittenem Buch ''Der Brand. Deutschland im Bombenkrieg''', *Hist. Jahrbuch* 124 (2004), 521–43.

'Nationalsozialistische Deutungen des Luftkrieges', in: Süß (ed.), *Deutschland im Luftkrieg*, pp. 99–110.

'Review Article: Memories of the Air War', *JCH* 43/3 (2008), 333–42.

'Tod aus der Luft: Deutschland, Großbritannien und der Bombenkrieg', unpublished habilitation dissertation, University of Jena, 2009.

Süß, Dietmar (ed.), *Deutschland im Luftkrieg. Geschichte und Erinnerung* (Munich: Oldenbourg, 2007).

Sywottek, Arnold, 'Wege in die 50er Jahre', in: Schildt and Sywottek (eds.), *Modernisierung im Wiederaufbau*, pp. 13–39.

Theologische Real-Enzyklopädie (TRE), ed. Horst Robert Balz, Gerhard Krause and Gerhard Müller, 36 vols. (Berlin: de Gruyter: 1977–2004).

Thießen, Malte, *Eingebrannt ins Gedächtnis: Hamburgs Gedenken an Luftkrieg und Kriegsende 1943 bis 2005* (Hamburg: Dölling und Galitz, 2007).

'Der ''Feuersturm'' im kommunikativen Gedächtnis. Tradierung und Transformation des Luftkrieges als Lebens- und Familiengeschichte', in: Arnold, Süß and Thießen (eds.), *Luftkrieg*, pp. 312–31.

'Gedenken an ''Operation Gomorrha''. Zur Erinnerungskultur des Bombenkrieges von 1945 bis heute', *ZfG* 1 (2005), 46–61.

'Gemeinsame Erinnerungen im geteilten Deutschland. Der Luftkrieg im ''kommunalen Gedächtnis'' der Bundesrepublik und DDR', *Deutschland Archiv* 2 (2008), 226–32.

'Die ''Katastrophe'' als symbolischer Bezugspunkt. Städtisches Gedenken an den Luftkrieg in der BRD und der DDR', in Natali Stegmann (ed.), *Die Weltkriege als symbolische Bezugspunkte. Polen, die Tschechoslowakei und Deutschland nach dem Ersten und Zweiten Weltkrieg* (Prague: Masarykuv, 2009), pp. 91–108.

'Lübeck's ''Palmarum'' and Hamburg's ''Gomorrha''. Erinnerungen an den Luftkrieg im Städtevergleich', in: Janina Fuge, Rainer Hering and Harald Schmid (eds.), *Das Gedächtnis von Stadt und Region: Geschichtsbilder in Norddeutschland* (Hamburg: Dölling und Galitz, 2010), pp. 61–89.

Trübners Deutsches Wörterbuch, 8 vols., vols. I–IV ed. Alfred Götze; vols. V–VII ed. Walther Mitzka (Berlin: De Gruyter, 1939–57).

Tullner, Mathias. 'Modernisierung und mitteldeutsche Hauptstadtpolitik – Das ''neue Magdeburg'' 1918–1933', in: *Magdeburg. Geschichte der Stadt*, pp. 729–64.

'Modernisierung und Scheinblüte – Magdeburg zwischen den Weltkriegen', in: *'Dann färbte sich der Himmel blutrot . . . '*, pp. 9–32.

Überlebensberichte. Der 22. Oktober 1943 in Protokollen der Vermisstensuchstelle des Oberbürgermeisters der Stadt Kassel, eds. Magistrat der Stadt Kassel, Kulturamt, and Frank-Roland Klaube. A publication on the fiftieth anniversary of the destruction of Kassel. (Marburg: Jonas, 1993).

Ueberschär, Gerd R., 'Dresden 1945 – Symbol für Luftkriegsverbrechen', in: Wette and Ueberschär (eds.), *Kriegsverbrechen im 20. Jahrhundert*, pp. 382–96.

Unerwünscht – Verfolgt – Ermordet: Ausgrenzung und Terror während der nationalsozialistischen Diktatur in Magdeburg 1933–1945, exhibition catalogue, ed. Matthias Puhle (Magdeburg: Grafisches Centrum Cuno, 2008).

United States Strategic Bombing Survey (USSBS), Morale Division, *The Effects of Strategic Bombing on German Morale*, 2 vols. (Washington, DC: United States Government Printing Office, 1947).

  Physical Damage Division, report no. 61: *Fire Raids on German Cities* (Washington, DC: United States Government Printing Office, 1945).

  Summary Report (European war) (Washington, DC: United States Government Printing Office, 1945).

US Department of State, *The Treaty of Versailles and After: Annotations of the Text of the Treaty* (Washington, DC: US Department of State, 1947).

Verbrechen der Wehrmacht. Dimensionen des Vernichtungskrieges 1941–1944, exhibition catalogue, ed. Hamburger Institut für Sozialforschung (Hamburger Edition, 1995).

Virchow, Fabian, 'Provocation, Mimicry, Authenticity: Symbolic Patterns of Speech and Protest in Neo-Nazi "Peace Propaganda" in the Federal Republic of Germany since the 1990s', in: Ziemann (ed.), *Peace Movements*, pp. 251–64.

Voegelin, Eric, *Die politischen Religionen*, ed. Peter J. Opitz, 3rd edn (Munich and Paderborn: Fink, 2007 [first edn 1938]).

Vogel, Hans, *Die Ruine in der Darstellung der abendländischen Kunst* (Kassel: Winter, 1948).

Vokabular der Psychoanalyse, Das (Frankfurt am Main: Suhrkamp, 1972).

Vollnhals, Clemens, 'Der deutsche Protestantismus: Spiegelbild der bürgerlichen Gesellschaft', in: Niedhart and Riesenberger (eds.), *Lernen aus dem Krieg?*, pp. 158–77.

  Evangelische Kirche und Entnazifizierung 1945–1949: Die Last der nationalsozialistischen Vergangenheit (Munich: Oldenbourg, 1989).

Vonau, German M., *Kassel. Bauwerke einer alten Stadt* (Kassel: Friedrich Lometsch, 1950).

  'Zehn Jahre danach', in: Helm (ed.), *Kassel vor dem Feuersturm*, 2nd edn (1953).

Vonau, German M. (ed.), *Führer durch Kassel und Wilhelmshöhe. Ein Wegweiser für Einheimische und Fremde*, 4th edn (Kassel: Karl Basch, 1956 [1st edn 1953]).

Vries, Wim de, *Zurück nach Kassel. Die Ballade vom Wahnsinn* ('s-Gravendeel: JMR, Verl. Robbemond, 1990).

Wanke, Gunther, 'Klagelieder', in: *TRE* XIX, pp. 227–30.

Was da in Schutt und Asche fiel. Magdeburg vor dem 16. Januar 1945, ed. MZ am Wochenende (Magdeburg: Magdeburger Druck, 1990).

Waßmann, Dieter, *Evangelische Pfarrer in Kurhessen und Waldeck von 1933 bis 1945* (Kassel: Ev. Medienverband Kassel, 2001).

Weber, Hermann, *Geschichte der DDR*, 2nd edn (Munich: dtv, 1999).

Webster, Charles and Noble Frankland, *The Strategic Air Offensive against Germany 1939–1945*, 4 vols. (London: Her Majesty's Stationery Office, 1961).

Wege zur Unterneustadt. So baut man eine Stadt, ed. Magistrat der Stadt Kassel (Kassel: Magistrat der Stadt Kassel, 1996).

Wege zur Unterneustadt. Wie baut man eine Stadt? Ed. Magistrat der Stadt Kassel (Kassel: Magistrat der Stadt Kassel, 1994).

Wegner, Bernd, 'Hitler, der Zweite Weltkrieg und die Choreographie des Untergangs', *GG* 26 (2000), 493–518.

Wegner, Karl-Hermann, *Bilder aus dem alten Kassel. Gemälde und Graphiken 1870 – 1940* (Kassel: Verein Freunde des Stadtmuseums e.V., 1995).

Kassel. Ein Stadtführer (Kassel: Stauda, 1981).

Weidenfeld, Werner and Karl-Rudolf Korte (ed.), *Handbuch zur deutschen Einheit 1949 – 1989 – 1999* (Bonn: bpb, 1999).

Welzer, Harald, 'Die Bilder der Macht und die Ohnmacht der Bilder. Über Besetzung und Auslöschung von Erinnerung', in: Welzer (ed.), *Das Gedächtnis der Bilder. Ästhetik und Nationalsozialismus* (Tübingen: Edition Diskord, 1995), pp. 64–84.

Wette, Wolfram and Gerd R. Ueberschär (eds.), *Kriegsverbrechen im 20. Jahrhundert* (Darmstadt: Wissenschaftliche Buchgesellschaft, 2001).

Wierling, Dorothee, 'Krieg im Nachkrieg: Zur öffentlichen und privaten Präsenz des Krieges in der SBZ und frühen DDR', in: Echternkamp and Martens (eds.), *Der Zweite Weltkrieg in Europa*, pp. 237–51.

Wilke, Jürgen (ed.), *Mediengeschichte der Bundesrepublik Deutschland* (Bonn: bpb, 1999).

Wille, Manfred, *Der Himmel brennt über Magdeburg. Die Zerstörung der Stadt im Zweiten Weltkrieg* (Magdeburg: Druckerei Volksstimme, 1990).

'Tod und Zerstörung durch Luftbombardements im zweiten Weltkrieg', in: '*Dann färbte sich der Himmel blutrot . . .* ', pp. 38–73.

Winkelnkemper, Toni, *Der Großangriff auf Köln. Englands Luftkrieg gegen die Zivilbevölkerung. Ein Beispiel* (Berlin: Frz. Eher NF., 1942).

Winkler, Heinrich August, *Der lange Weg nach Westen II. Deutsche Geschichte 1933–1990* (Munich: C. H. Beck, 2000).

Winter, Jay, *Sites of Memory, Sites of Mourning: the Great War in European Cultural History* (Cambridge University Press, 1995).

Winter, Jay and Emmanuel Sivan, *War and Remembrance in the Twentieth Century* (Cambridge University Press, 1999).

Winter-Heider, Christine E., *Festschrift für Rolf Schwendter. Fragmente einer Begegnung – Elemente einer Entgegnung* (Kassel University Press, 2005).

Wirsching, Andreas, *Abschied vom Provisorium: Die Geschichte der Bundesrepublik 1982–1990* (Munich: DVA, 2006).

Wisotzki, Peter and Karl-Hermann Wegner, *Auf der Suche nach der verlorenen Stadt. Chancen für die Stadtarchäologie in Kassel* (Baunatal: Ahrend, 1991).

Wolff, J., 'Kassel baut auf! Eine städtebauliche Betrachtung', *Baumeister* 2/3 (1947), 80ff.

Wolfrum, Edgar, *Die geglückte Demokratie. Geschichte der Bundesrepublik Deutsch-land von ihren Anfängen bis zur Gegenwart* (Stuttgart: Klett-Cotta, 2006).

Wolle, Stefan, *Aufbruch in die Stagnation. Die DDR in den Sechzigerjahren* (Bonn: bpb, 2006).

Wood, Nancy, *Vectors of Memory: Legacies of Trauma in Postwar Europe* (Oxford and New York: Berg, 1999).

Zerstörte Kirchen – lebende Gemeinde. Tatsachen und Zeugnisse zum Luftkrieg, ed. Evangelischer Bund (Berlin: Heliand, 1944).

Ziemann, Benjamin, 'The Code of Protest: Images of Peace in the West German Peace Movements, 1945–1990', *CEH* 17,2 (2008), 237–261.

'Republikanische Kriegserinnerung in einer polarisierten Öffentlichkeit: Das Reichsbanner Schwarz-Rot-Gold als Veteranenverband der sozialistischen Arbeiterschaft', *HZ* 267 (1998), 357–98.

'Situating Peace Movements in the Political Culture of the Cold War', in Ziemann (ed.), *Peace Movements*, pp. 11–38.

Ziemann, Benjamin (ed.), *Peace Movements in Western Europe, Japan and the USA during the Cold War* (Essen: Klartext, 2008).

Zboralski, Dietrich, 'Zum Luftangriff auf Freiburg am 10. Mai 1940', *Zeitschrift für Geschichtswissenschaft* 4/4 (1956), 755–7.

www.gedenkmarsch.de/magdeburg [6 July 2010].

www.peg.kassel.de [23 September 2009].

www.stadt.kassel.de [18 December 2009].

Index